THE WORLD ENCYCLOPEDIA OF

CARS

THE WORLD ENCYCLOPEDIA OF

CARS

The definitive guide to classic and contemporary cars

from 1945 to the present day

Martin Buckley & Chris Rees

LORENZ BOOKS

This edition published by Lorenz Books
an imprint of
Anness Publishing Limited
Hermes House
88-89 Blackfriars Road
London SE1 8HA

A CIP catalogue record for this book is available from the British Library

ISBN 0 7548 0170 5

Publisher: Joanna Lorenz
Editorial Manager: Helen Sudell
Project Editor: Joanne Rippin
Assistant Editor: Emma Gray
Designer: Alan Marshall
Additional text supplied by Paul Hardiman

Previously published as two separate volumes,
The Encyclopedia of Classic Cars and The Encyclopedia of Dream Cars

Printed and bound in Germany

© Anness Publishing Limited 1998
Updated © 1999
3 5 7 9 10 8 6 4 2

CONTENTS

PART ONE

The History of the
CLASSIC CAR

THE EVOLUTION OF THE MOTORCAR

Martin Buckley

INTRODUCTION

As government regulations threaten to engineer much of the character out of modern cars, as our roads become more congested and dangerous and the air we breathe gets more contaminated, we can look back to the "classic" era of the 1950s and 1960s as the romantic Golden Age of the motorcar. In Europe, more and better mass-produced cars were seen as a liberating force for families previously restricted to public transport. In North America, cars simply got bigger, reflecting the wealth and confidence of the most powerful nation on earth. Traffic was yet to reach its often gridlocked state of today, petrol was much cheaper and, in Britain at least, there were no speed restrictions on the newly-opened motorways.

Before the mergers and close-downs of the 1970s, buyers could choose from a far wider range of makes reflecting national identities. The Japanese motor industry, later so dominant, was not even a speck on the horizon in the 1950s and 1960s. In engineering and styling, too, cars tended to be more varied and individual – you could tell an Austin from a Morris, a Vauxhall from a Volvo without having to look at the badge. Safety was optional: it was speed, glamour and style that sold cars, and in the 50s and early 60s nobody had even begun to think of the exhaust-emission regulations that would strangle power outputs in the 70s. Back then, the motorcar was our servant. Now, through its very proliferation, it has become our master. In this part of the book we celebrate the glory days and beyond, and the marvellous machines which rode through them, fixing in our cultural consciousness a picture of the ideal motor – the classic car.

The Classic Era

Today we're hooked on nostalgia. As hopeless escapists, nothing feeds our need better than an old car – a classic car. After the Second World War, the motorcar came of age. As more and more people around the world took to the road, manufacturers began to stretch the boundaries. The makers set styling, engineering and safety trends in an increasingly competitive market: speeds increased; styling and engineering became more adventurous; and many devices we take for granted today, like disc brakes, four-wheel drive (4-WD) and automatic transmission, became widely used. The 1950s, 1960s and to an extent the 1970s were the most fertile period for the motorcar, a classic era and a perfect breeding ground for the classic car we cherish today, be it limousine or economy runabout, sportscar or apparently humdrum saloon.

EVOLUTION OF THE MOVEMENT

As the 20th century draws to a close, we seem to look back as much as forward, pining for what were, as we see it, better times. We can't revisit our Golden Age, but at least we can own and experience the material objects that evoke it: clothes, music, films and cars – classic cars. Glamorous, kitsch, humble or high bred, these mobile time warps powerfully conjure up a particular period.

New Vintage

The hobby of preserving and collecting cars built after the Second World War began to take shape in the early 1970s. Veteran (pre-1905), Edwardian (pre-1919) and Vintage (pre-1931) cars – as defined by Britain's Vintage Sports Car Club – have always been easy enough to categorize but, by the end of the 1960s, post-war motorcars of the better kind were coming of age. To call them simply "old cars" no longer seemed appropriate: whether beautiful, fast or technically pre-eminent, the post-1945 car had at its best all the gravitas of the pre-war machinery. Slowly, quietly, the "new Vintage" had arrived, filling the gap between Vintage and

■ ABOVE *Classics so evocative of their period as these – the AC Ace, Ferrari 166 and C-Type Jaguar – have always been in strong demand and are priced at a premium.*

■ BELOW *Racing cars with some historic significance are eagerly sought by collectors and achieve astonishing prices at auction.*

modern for a new generation of enthusiasts.

One-marque clubs for well-bred sporting marques such as Aston and Bentley had been around for years, but as enthusiasts for the less exalted makes felt the need to huddle together around a common banner, many new guilds and registers sprouted. Traditionalists had long complained that modern cars all "looked the same", but in the 70s there was a gut feeling that the motorcar had seen its best years as safety and pollution regulations made inroads into designers' freedom. Styling, particularly in Britain, seemed to be losing its way.

No wonder older cars began to look increasingly attractive. They were plentiful, cheap, easy to work on and still very usable on increasingly busy roads. Drive an old car and you made a statement about your individualism: you weren't prepared to become just another faceless, sterile tin can on the bypass to oblivion or obsessed with keeping up with the Joneses in the yearly new-model scrum. It all came together in 1973 when a UK magazine, *Classic Cars*, was launched.

The name "classic" stuck, a useful catch-all term for a sprawling, ill-defined genre that in

■ ABOVE *High prices obtained by auction houses for high-grade classics had a knock-on effect on the rest of the industry.*

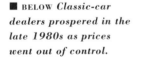

■ BELOW *Classic-car dealers prospered in the late 1980s as prices went out of control.*

just 20 years or so has blossomed from an eccentric pastime in to a multimillion-pound industry. Not much happened for about ten years, until about 1982-83 when the nature of the hobby began to change dramatically. Slowly, under the noses of true enthusiasts, market forces took hold as it dawned on investors that really prime machinery could prove a fine hedge against inflation or an appreciating asset. Suddenly, the market hardened as Americans came to Europe seeking prime collectables.

At first, gilt-edged pre-war hardware – Bentley, Bugatti, etc. – set the pace in auction rooms but, by mid-decade, supercars of the 50s, 60s and 70s were hyped on their coat tails. Once affordable Ferraris, Astons and Jaguar XKs and E-Types became "investor" cars,

commodities too expensive and precious to be driven (which was rather missing the point).

As the auction houses pulled even bigger numbers, hype went into overdrive. Banks and finance companies offered loans to buy classics. The increasing ranks of classic-car magazines bulged with advertizing. Enthusiasts' gentle hobby was turned into an ugly brawl driven by greed. Many found themselves with cars that were worth more than their houses, machinery they were now too nervous to use. The boom couldn't last, fortunately. The recession hit in 1989 and demand quickly fell.

A hobby again

Today, the investors are long gone, the market is stable and the cars are where they should be – with enthusiasts. Though we are unlikely to see such madness again, rare and high-calibre thoroughbred cars – especially those with a racing pedigree or an interesting provenance – will always be in strong demand. Fashion still has its part to play in the lower echelons of the market, but those who bought Citroëns and Jaguars have learnt about the dedication required to run an old car. Some went back to their moderns, others caught a lifelong bug.

TECHNICAL DEVELOPMENTS

In the beginning, cars were motorized horse carriages or, in the case of the three-wheeled Benz of 1889, relied heavily on cycle technology. Most cars were braked only by the rear wheel; steering, often by tiller, was slow and ponderous. A shoulder-high centre of gravity threatened to tip the car over. All this was containable at the 4mph (6.4kph) first allowed in Britain for motor vehicles and not too scary at the 14mph (22.5kph) allowed by 1896, but as speeds rose, something had to be done. Makers who introduced each refinement created classics along the way.

Technology filters down

Excellence began with high-class cars such as the Rolls-Royce and Bentley. Steadily, the technology filtered down to such humble transport as the Austin Seven. By the start of

■ LEFT *Cord's 810 used a supercharged V-eight Lycoming engine with revolutionary front-wheel drive.*

■ BELOW *The Chrysler Airflow was one of the first cars designed with an eye to aerodynamics.*

■ LEFT AND BELOW *The Lancia Aprillia was a groundbreaking saloon of the mid-1930s.*

the Second World War, bodies were generally made of steel, sat on a separate chassis, and there were brakes all round. Jaguar brought disc brakes to the world's notice at Le Mans in 1953; five years later they appeared on Jaguar's road cars and soon every maker used them.

Refinement follows

Four-wheel drive, with antilock brakes, was pioneered by Ferguson Formula. It first appeared in a passenger car on the Jensen FF of 1966, along with Dunlop Maxaret anti-lock brakes derived from aircraft technology. It was expensive and complex – only 320 were built.

Overhead camshafts allow more direct

operation of valves and a better combustion-chamber shape. They were used on specialist racing cars such as the Alfa Romeo and Bugatti from the 20s onwards and were introduced to the mainstream in the straight-six XK engine in the 120 of 1948. Soon, makers realized they could run double overhead camshafts and multivalve layouts.

Self-levelling was a standard feature of the futuristic DS launched in 1955 by Citroën. Even the cheaper 2CV had a modicum of levelling, because front and rear suspension were interconnected by springs. The British Motor Corporation (BMC) 1100 and 1800 of the 60s – and Minis of the period – are interconnected hydraulically. Self-levelling was used at the tail end of the Range Rover from its launch in 1970.

Front-wheel drive, used by BSA, Cord and Citroën since the 30s, did not hit the mainstream until the Mini appeared in 1959. While scorned by purists, this layout makes for

■ ABOVE *A 1956 Chevy: crude - but comfortable and well equipped.*

■ RIGHT *The Citroën 2CV: quirky, uncomfortable and poorly equipped. So who cares!*

■ BELOW RIGHT *The revolutionary Mini, a masterpiece of packaging.*

■ BELOW *The boxy body design of Lancia's Flavia an expensively-engineered, superb-handling car.*

safe, predictable handling and better packaging – more interior room for a given size – than rear-driven counterparts.

All the while, chassis improvements and tyre technology shadowed each other: Citroën's *Traction-avant* was the first car to use radial tyres, the narrow and distinctively treaded Michelin X.

America thinks big

In America, spacious cars with powerful, six- and eight-cylinder engines were common, even before the war. Makers loaded cars with every device to take the work out of driving: automatic transmission, power steering, power brakes, air conditioning, self-dipping headlamps. Engines, generally understressed by large capacity, showcased maintenance-free features such as hydraulic tappets (initially used for quietness).

MILESTONE MODELS

The following are technically important cars that made history from the 1930s to the 1970s, and had a lasting impact on the industry.

Citroën *Traction Avant*

Front-wheel drive and monocoque construction – in 1934! All this and unrivalled ride and handling from low centre of gravity and all-independent-torsion bar suspension came from the fertile mind of André Citroën.

Fiat 500

Dante Giacosa's master-stroke, the Italian car for the masses, was the Topolino. It was a full-sized car scaled down, with a tiny four-cylinder engine but all-steel unitary construction and independent suspension. (John Cooper plundered this for rear-engined racers.)

■ LEFT *The Citroën Traction Avant was a brave move but teething troubles nearly broke the company.*

■ BELOW *Spaceship: just imagine the effect of the Citroën DS's shape on the public in 1955.*

Citroën DS/SM

When launched to a stunned public in 1955, the DS looked like a spaceship. Its incredible other-worldly body style by Flaminio Bertoni used easily-removable outer panels; it had a glass-fibre roof and tail-lamps like rockets. A pressurised, self-levelling gas and oil system replaced suspension springs, and also pwered the brakes, steering, clutch and even gear change. Its complexity scared off many buyers.

■ BELOW *Fiat 500: poor man's transport, now the darling of the trendy.*

Mini

Alec Issigonis's revolutionary Mini of 1959 set the convention for every small car since and is a strong candidate for the most significant car of the 20th century. By mounting the engine transversely and making it drive the front wheels (not a first: Alvis, sundry American companies and Fiat had tried it before), Issigonis fitted space for four adults into a package 10ft (3m) long.

To keep the driveline package very short, the gearbox sat under the engine, in the sump. The use of a 10 in (25.5cm) wheel at each corner not only minimized the encroachment of

■ LEFT *Lotus Seven, the
greatest-handling road
classic, designed in
1956 and still in
production today.*

Jaguar E-type

With its gorgeous, curvy, phallic shape derived
from Malcolm Sayers's Le Mans-winning D-
Type racer, combined with a 3.8-litre version of
the classic XK engine, this is the car that
epitomized the racy end of the Swinging 60s. It
was fantastic value at its 1961 launch price
equivalent of only four Minis – and early
versions really would come near the alleged top
speed of 150mph (241kph). Forget the crunchy
gearbox and unpredictable brakes, this is one of
the world's most desirable cars.

Datsun 240Z

The Japanese had really arrived in 1969 with
this "Big Healey" beater. Its classic fastback
shape has never been bettered by Japan, and
the strong, 2.4-litre straight-six engine made all
the right noises. Good handling came from its
all-independent strut suspension and super
performance from its relatively light weight.
Later cars – the 260 and 280Z – became
heavier and softer. As is so often the case, first
is purest. This is Japan's first classic and the
world's best-selling sportscar.

wheel-arch space into the passenger
compartment but, together with the direct rack-
and-pinion steering and firm, rubber
suspension, took handling to new standards of
"chuckability". The Mini is still made to the
same familiar specifications, although big
changes are predicted for the model in the new
millenium.

The Mini has competed since it first
appeared; most notable performances were ace
Paddy Hopkirk's wins in Alpine rallies in the
60s, his finest moment being victory in the
1965 Monte Carlo Rally. Minis still hold their
own in historic rallying in the 90s.

■ ABOVE *The 246 Dino,
one of the most
gorgeous shapes ever,
although it never
badged Ferrari.*

■ RIGHT *Datsun's 240Z
took on the mantle of
the "Big Healey" - a
lusty six banger for the
1970s.*

LEADING ENGINEERS

These are some of the most innovative and imaginative engineers from the world motor industry.

André Citroën

A true innovator, Citroën followed his own direction to produce cars that led the world for refinement and technical innovation. His engineeering tour de force, the *Traction-avant* of 1934, was followed up by his utilitarian masterstroke, the 2CV of 1948.

Ferdinand Porsche

Porsche designed the world's best-selling car, the VW Beetle which became the basis for the Porsche 356 designed by his son Ferry, forerunner of the immortal 911.

Alec Issigonis

Issigonis's masterstroke was the Mini, a brilliant piece of packaging whose layout – transverse engine, front-wheel drive and an

■ ABOVE *André Citroën carried a torch for innovation; much of the detailed design work was done by others.*

■ ABOVE RIGHT *Ferry Porsche, son of the man responsible for the world's best-selling car, himself made a vital contribution – the 356.*

■ LEFT *Alec Issigonis left his legacy in the shape of two brilliant small cars, the Morris Minor and the immortal Mini.*

independently-sprung wheel at each corner – has been copied for every other small car in the world. But people forget he was also reponsible for the Morris Minor, the best-handling and most modern car of its generation.

Antonio Fessia

Engineering supremo behind the classic Lancia Fulvia – and its bigger siblings the Flavia and Flaminia – Professor Antonio Fessia joined Fiat in 1925. By 1936, at only 35, he was director of the central technical office. Under him, Dante Giacosa designed the Topolino. A demanding, sometimes difficult boss, Fessia approached design scientifically. His 1960 Lancia Flavia, harking back to the 47 Cemsa Caproni, was the first Italian car with front-wheel drive. He followed up with the smaller V-four Fulvia which shared many components. He stayed with Lancia until his death in 1968.

William Lyons

Lyons was responsible for the beautiful styling of his Jaguars, from SS through MkII to XJ6 –

LEFT *Dante Giacosa was responsible for the tiny Fiat Topolino, one of the world's great cars, and went on to design the 500.*

all classics. Another achievement was to keep prices low without sacrificing quality – Lyons's Jaguars were always superb value. An autocratic boss, he started Swallow Sidecars in the mid-1920s, at first building sidecars, then fitting more luxurious bodywork to Austin Sevens. The first SS Jaguars, brilliantly styled saloons and a beautiful SS100 sportscar appeared in the mid-1930s, all-time styling greats from Lyon's fertile pen. After the Second World War, his company became Jaguar.

■ ABOVE LEFT *WO Bentley was a gifted engineer, but he soon left the company that bore his name and went to Lagonda.*

■ ABOVE RIGHT *Colin Chapman, a brilliant and innovative designer, produced some of the best-handling cars ever.*

■ LEFT *Sir William Lyons, a great designer and an intuitive stylist: his cars always looked like a million dollars but represented superb value for money.*

Colin Chapman

A truly gifted structural engineer whose radical designs changed the face of racing – the road-car operation was intended only to shore up the racing effort. His first self-built car and the legendary Lotus Seven hit the road in 1953 and 1957 respectively. Chapman's weight-paring efforts, all for agility and speed, sometimes earned criticism for risking driver safety. He was devastated by the death of his star driver and friend Jim Clark in 1968.

Dante Giacosa

Dante Giacosa studied mechanical engineering at Turin Polytechnic and joined Fiat in 1928. From 1933 he was involved in the design of a small car. He put his watercooled Topolino against an aircooled design and won. More than four million Topolino's were made, taking their rightful place as one of the world's great small cars beside the Austin 7, the VW Beetle and the Mini.

Giacosa then created most archetypal small Italian cars, including the Fiat Nuova 500, 600, 127 and 128, and the masterpieces 8V and Cisitalia racer. He died in 1996.

MASS PRODUCTION

Henry Ford started it all with his Model T Ford. Production began in America in 1908 and later began in Britain. By 1913, Ford's plant at Old Trafford, Manchester, was making 8,000 cars a year by mass production whilst traditionalist Wolseley could manage only 3,000.

Where English cars were largely produced by hand, with chassis parts being individually made, drilled, reamed and assembled, Ford invested in huge machine tools that would

■ **BELOW LEFT AND RIGHT** *Henry Ford's automated production lines speeded car making, here a row of Model T's, beyond belief. He took his new methods to England, setting up a factory in Old Trafford, Manchester. In 1913 it could make 8,000 cars a year.*

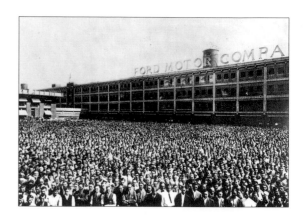

stamp out parts by the hundred, exactly the same every time, which did not need skilled labour to assemble.

The cost of these tools was huge, so selling the resulting cars cheaply in huge numbers was the answer. Where car bodies had traditionally been made by hand, all to slightly different specifications, Ford's T's were, with a few variations on the theme, all the same and had pressed and welded bodies, like today's cars. Spray painting saved hours over the traditional multicoat process with its laborious rubbing down by hand between coats.

■ **LEFT** *A test track was built on the roof of Fiat's factory at Lingotto, Turin.*

Conveyor-belt cars

To achieve this huge production, Ford installed its first moving-track assembly operations in Detroit, Michigan, the world's largest car-manufacturing centre, and in Trafford Park, Manchester, England. Instead of men moving to the cars to complete their specialist operation, or pushing cars by hand from one assembly station to another, the cars came to the men for each additional operation to be completed, with components fed in from overhead conveyors. Each man would walk beside the chassis until his task was completed and repeat the exercise on the next chassis. By the end of the line, the car was complete. Ford's basic T two-seater, the runabout, was produced in 1913. A classic was born.

Gradually, all other makers followed, although luxury cars were still largely hand built, just as prestige classics always have been. Morgan still hand builds cars in the same way it has since the 1920s, rolling partially-completed cars from one station to another. Yet by 1927, Citroën was producing a car every 10 minutes.

■ ABOVE *Fiat 850 coupés on production lines at Turin.*

■ BELOW *Ford Anglias being sprayed on a moving line at Dagenham, Essex. In time, robots replaced people.*

Robots lend a hand

Even greater speed and productivity were achieved by the use of power tools, suspended from the ceiling so they could be manhandled more easily. The next step was to cut manpower. First, spray painting was robotized, then the welding of bodyshells. To show how production methods continue to progress, of cars made today the one needing the most labour-intensive welding on its bodyshell is the Mini, first seen in 1959.

It was through mass production that cars such as the MG were born. The first MG Midget of 1929 used simple components borrowed from the Morris saloon cars in a more sporty body, just as all MGs since have done, right up to the F of 1995. Thanks to mass production, classic sportscars were made available to the general buying public.

The Growth of an Industry

Today the motor industry is essential to the commercial prosperity of almost all the world's industrialized nations, with production dominated by a handful of massive multi-nationals. Hundreds of individual marques have fallen by the wayside since the first motorcars were hand built at the turn of the century and the post-war classic period of mergers and take-overs saw the eclipse of many once famous names. It was in 1908 that this process began, when Henry Ford pioneered mass-production with his Model T, while over in Europe, a few years later, cars like the Austin Seven and Bullnose Morris began to be produced in sufficient numbers to bring motoring within the reach of the middle classes. Since the late 1970s robots have replaced some of the manual jobs on the production lines, but there will always be a place for hand crafted supercars and luxury cars from companies such as Aston Martin and Rolls Royce.

WHAT MAKES A CLASSIC?

"Without a certain amount of snobbery, efforts would be hopeless ... A motorcar must be designed and built that is a little different from and a little better than the product of the big quantity manufacturer."

Cecil Kimber, founder of MG, had it right. He sensed a need and virtually invented the concept of the classic – but MGs have never been particularly special or mechanically innovative. What they do have, however, is that little extra desirability, so that owners and onlookers alike *see* them as classic cars. MGs are instantly recognizable, even to many non-enthusiasts, in much the same way that Jaguars, Ferraris and Bentleys are – all of them true classics.

Most enthusiasts would categorize a classic car as one whose design is inalienably right: it must look good, handle well, probably be possessed of higher performance or equipment

■ ABOVE *Performance, grace - and a competition classic. NUB 120 is the most famous Jaguar XK120 ever.*

■ BELOW LEFT *BMW 328: a timeless classic, lithe, lean and light.*

■ ABOVE *The basic shape of the Porsche 911 endured for nearly 35 years from launch in 1964.*

levels than were normal for its day – but overall it must be desirable.

Age alone cannot make a classic, even though a common definition given today is "any car more than 20 years old". Those who use that definition would say that Avengers and Marinas are classics; most enthusiasts with other criterior would not.

Beauty is in the eye of the beholder but there is no disputing the beauty of a real classic. Who cannot be moved by the shape and form of a Bugatti Type 35, Alfa Monza,

■ LEFT *Bugatti Type 35,
a GP racer for the road
- a model of sparse
functional character.*

Duesenberg, Jaguar XK120 or early E-Type,
Ferrari 250 GT, AC Ace, Citroën DS and
Mercedes Gullwing, by the stark efficiency of
an early Porsche 911 or the simplicity of the
Austin Seven or Mini?

Then there were the "firsts", each with its
claim to classicdom: Colin Chapman's Lotus
Seven, a racer for the road; the Mini Cooper 'S'
which further defined the small car and was
the first "pocket rocket"; the Hispano-Suiza
and Pegaso, Spain's only, exquisitely made
supercars from the 20s and 50s respectively;
the Reliant Scimitar GTE which introduced a
new concept – the sporting estate car; the Golf
GTi, which spawned a whole new breed of
enthusiasts' car. Each of these counts as a
classic for defining a new niche in car-lovers'
hearts. That each one of these cars – and many
more like them – is notable in its own field
helps reinforce its claim to be a true classic.

■ ABOVE *Duesenberg:
coachbuilt elegance,
American style. It could
achieve more than
100mph (160kph).*

■ RIGHT *The straight
eight engined Alfa
Monza: epitome of the
classic vintage racer.*

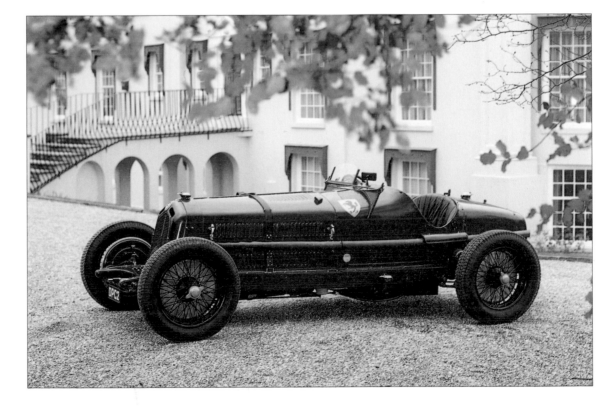

CLASSIC ENGINES

Once a classic is in motion, the engine does more than any other feature to give it character. The 1945–75 period started with almost universal use of sidevalve power, except on the most costly and exotic cars, and ended with multiple camshafts and valves, fuel injection and unusual materials becoming the norm. Most of these advances were first developed for racing, then refined for road use as they showed the way to efficiency.

Progress had meant more performance. Where 1940s power outputs were small, by the 70s, engines in better sportscars were up to 80bhp per litre. Efficiency came from ideally-shaped combustion chambers, usually hemispherical, for which a more complex valve arrangement is usually needed. The simplest way to operate these is by overhead cams, first seen on a Clément of 1902 and used by Alfa Romeo, Bentley and Bugatti in the 20s, MG in the 30s and Jaguar since the 50s, but not used on non-classics until the 80s. It's costly to develop but usually leads to better breathing.

Further advances included fuel injection,

■ ABOVE *The 16-cylinder powerplant used in the racing BRM: fantastically powerful, but too complicated to live.*

■ LEFT *The fearsome V-twelve of the racing Sunbeam Tiger. Aero engines were a convenient route to high power.*

■ BELOW LEFT *The light-alloy 3.5-litre Rover V-eight, beloved of specialist sportscar makers, is derived from an unwanted Buick unit of the 1960s.*

which did away with compromises forced by carburettors. It was first used on production cars, in rather basic form, by Chevrolet on its Corvette in 1954 and by Mercedes-Benz on its technical tour de force 300SL in 1955. In the early 70s, Bosch's Jetronic systems began to appear on performance classics such as the Porsche 911. Since 1993, with universal fitment of catalytic convertors, fuel injection has become a necessity, along with electronic ignition, which began to appear at the end of the 60s. For convenience, the hydraulic tappet was designed by Bollée in 1910. General Motors began to fit them in the 30s, leading to extra mechanical refinement and less servicing.

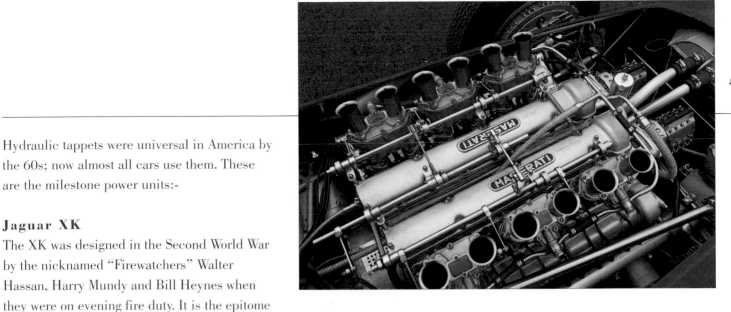

Hydraulic tappets were universal in America by the 60s; now almost all cars use them. These are the milestone power units:-

Jaguar XK

The XK was designed in the Second World War by the nicknamed "Firewatchers" Walter Hassan, Harry Mundy and Bill Heynes when they were on evening fire duty. It is the epitome of the classic in-line twin-cam engine and was sorely needed as an alternative to the pedestrian Standard engines Jaguar was forced

to use before and immediately after the war. Launched in the XK120 of 1948, displacing 3.4 litres and producing 160bhp, it enjoyed its finest moment in a road car as the 265bhp 3.8 which propelled the 1962 E-Type coupé to 150mph (241kph). In 3.0- and 3.4-litre dry-sumped form it took D-Types to Le Mans wins and powered Jaguar saloons right up to 1987.

Rover V-eight

A cast-off from Buick (the Americans had found themselves good at thin-wall iron casting so there was no need for fancy light-alloy stuff), this 3528cc engine was discovered by Maurice Wilks on a visit to America in 1966. Realizing

■ ABOVE *Classic Italian – the Maserati 250F V-twelve racing engine with twin camshafts and a separate carburettor choke for each cylinder.*

■ LEFT *Alfa Romeo's 2.9-litre engine of the 1930s used a twin double-overhead-camshaft, straight-eight layout.*

■ LEFT *For the Mini, the engine was cleverly turned sideways and integrated with the gearbox to produce a compact powerplant.*

■ ABOVE *Here's the same A-series engine, which first appeared in 1952, as it started out, mounted longitudinally.*

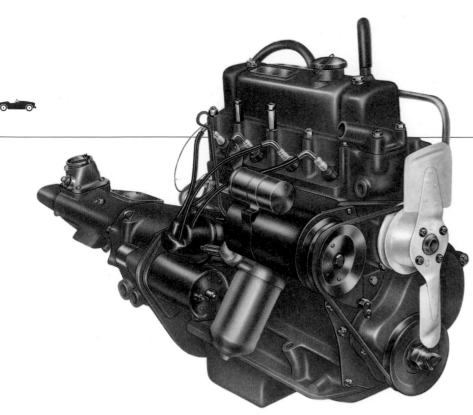

■ ABOVE *The B-series –
bigger brother to the
Mini engine – as used in
the Wolseley 1500. It
grew up to be a 1798cc
unit powering the MGB.*

Ferrari V-twelve

Complex, beautifully made and exquisitely
finished, Ferrari's engines are expensively
engineered for big power at huge revs. The V-
twelve was first seen in 1946 as the tiny
Colombo-designed two-litre V-twelve 166. The
larger Lampredi-designed engine appeared in
1951, in the 340 America. In front-engined
Ferrari V-twelve parlance, the model number
gives the displacement of one cylinder;
multiply by 12 and you have the engine size.
The four-camshaft layout arrived with the
275GTB/4 of 1966. This classic sports-car
power unit looks as good as it goes: almost
always with twin oil filters nestling together at
the front of the vee and black crackle-finish
cam covers cast with the legend "Ferrari".

this compact unit would be perfect for powering
Rover's big P5 saloon, he quickly acquired the
rights. It was a good move: the staid, heavy
saloon was transformed into one with a top
speed of 110mph (177kph) and 0–60 (96) in
10 seconds. The engine did sterling service in
the Rover 3500 before proving itself ideal for
the Range Rover of 1970. Light and tunable,
this engine has also found favour with MG,
TVR, Marcos – and survives in 4.6-litre form in
the Range Rover of 1996.

Porsche flat-six

One of the longest-lived engines ever, this air-
and oil-cooled flat six was derived from the flat
four first seen pre-war in the VW Beetle. It
grew from the 120bhp two-litre of 1963 to a
turbocharged 3.3-litre, punching out a seamless

■ LEFT *The Cosworth
DFV. Funded by Ford,
this engine won over
100 Grands Prix.*

■ RIGHT *Lessons learned
with the DFV spawned a
whole series of Cosworth
race engines. This is a
four-cylinder BDA,
showing the cogged belt
which drives the twin
camshafts.*

■ ABOVE *The rotary engine, used by Mazda and NSU, is so compact that it is almost hidden by its ancillaries.*

■ RIGHT *The mighty Cobras were all powered by the Ford V-eight of 4.2, 4.7 or 7 litres, producing up to 400bhp.*

output with the low engine weight he needed for his small sportscars, it made sense to base this hitherto prohibitively expensive arrangement on existing engine technology. Ford's simple, light and tough 1340cc Kent engine from the short-lived Capri was the ideal candidate. For it, *Autocar's* then technical editor Harry Mundy designed a light-alloy twin-cam head with hemispherical combustion chambers and near-perfect valve angles. When Ford announced that the base pushrod engine would be enlarged to 1600cc form Chapman's new engine displaced 1558cc and produced 105bhp on twin carburettors. It has appeared in the Elan, the Europa, Lotus Cortinas and even early Escorts and inspired many followers.

300bhp with so much torque that only a four-speed gearbox was needed. Pioneering the Nikasil cylinder lining that did away with iron liners, and always with a single camshaft per cylinder bank, these exactingly engineered powerplants have a Germanic reputation for reliability and longevity. In the most classic 911 of all, the RS Carrera of 1973, it produces 210bhp at 7000rpm on mechanical fuel injection – accompanied by raw exhaust snarl that tingles the spine. A derivative still powers the current 911.

■ ABOVE *The two-litre four-cylinder Standard engine used in the Triumph TR3 also powered Vanguards, Morgans and, in modified form, the Ferguson tractor.*

■ RIGHT *The other side of the B series, as used in twin-carburettor 68bhp form in the Riley 1.5. The carburettor and exhaust are on the same side as the engine.*

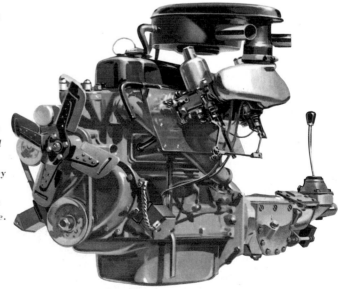

Lotus/Ford twin-cam

When Colin Chapman realized in the 60s that twin camshafts were the way to achieve higher

SUSPENSION

The first suspension for cars – the most classically simple arrangement of all – was copied from horse-drawn carts. The beam axle, held to the chassis by leaf springs, is the simplest form of springing. It's still used, in little-modified form, on many of today's trucks. The system was used on the most basic cars until the 50s, and at the rear end of many cheaper cars until the 80s.

Soon, however, with increasing engine sophistication and speed, cart springs put limits on a car's ability to ride well and handle safely. By 1924, makers like Frazer Nash were trying extra links to control the axle's movement better while still springing it by leaf. The next big move was to independent suspension – where the movement of one wheel does not affect the other. Most of the world's favourite classic cars have this in some form but the way suspension is arranged seems to be national preference.

Americans were keen on independent front suspension by wishbones from the 1930s. An American invented the now universal MacPherson strut, although it was first used on a British car, the Ford Consul, in 1950.

Germans pioneered independent suspension

■ LEFT *The front suspension of the MG Magnette uses coil springs and double wishbones and is steered by rack and pinion.*

■ LEFT *Rover used a similar but larger system for its P4, this time with an anti-roll bar and separate, telescopic shock absorbers.*

■ LEFT *Mercedes used air suspension to provide a supple ride on its big 600 and 300SEL 6.3 saloons. A compressor inflates rubber bags incorporated between suspension members.*

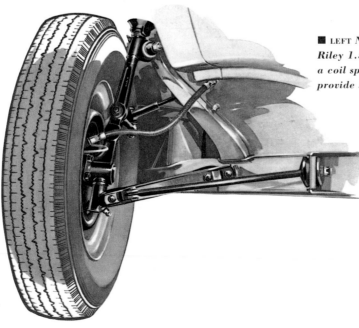

■ LEFT *No springs! In fact the Riley 1.5 uses torsion bars – like a coil spring straightened out – to provide suspension.*

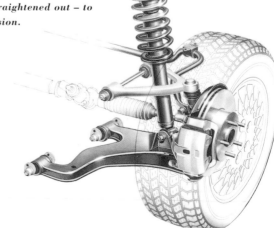

■ LEFT *Mounting the coil spring and damper concentrically solves a space problem but makes removal more complicated.*

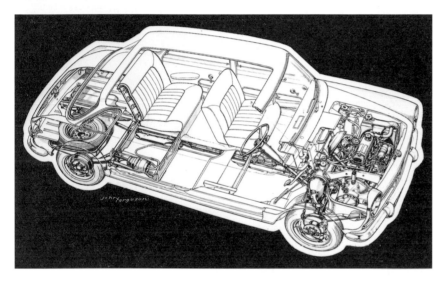

■ ABOVE AND LEFT *Struts can be used to provide independent suspension at the front or rear.*

■ ABOVE *The Austin/Morris 1800 used Hydrolastic (fluid/air) suspension. One Hydrolastic unit can be seen under the cut-away rear seat.*

■ OPPOSITE *The modern solution is to suspend the car on struts, which incorporate both spring and damper. A MacPherson strut also locates and steers the wheel.*

by swing axles with the Mercedes, which lasted into the 60s. VW used a pair of trailing links, in parallel on each side of the car, for independent front suspension for the Beetle, which had a semiswing axle rear suspension. The typical set-up to be found on a performance saloon of the 60s and 70s consisted of MacPherson struts at the front and semitrailing arms at the rear. With liftoff or extreme power oversteer (tail slides) easily available, this produced what most enthusiasts would count as "classic" handling. The tail-heavy Porsche 911 and all BMWs of the 60s and 70s that were equipped with semitrailing arms tended to oversteer.

The Italian Fiat Topolino was ingeniously sprung by lower wishbones, transverse leaf springs, forming the upper links. Lancia used the same set-up in the 60s at the front of its

Fulvia and Flavia models and it could be found under Fiat-drive Seats of the 80s.

The purest and most classic suspension system of all, however, is the double wishbone set-up, used by practically all single-seat racing cars since the 50s and on most supercars thereafter. It's costly to make and can be tricky to set up correctly but offers the best fully-independent wheel control thanks to its ideal geometry and acceptable unsprung weight.

MacPherson struts

Ford's slab-sided new Consul of 1950 broke new ground with its full-width body hiding a new suspension system that revolutionized the way cars were built. An American Ford engineer, Earle S. MacPherson, came up with a new design for independent suspension whose beauty lay in its simplicity. MacPherson struts were used on every new small Ford – including the Classic of 1961 – and are the most common front suspension system used today.

Air suspension

Air suspension was tried by Cadillac on the 1958 Brougham and by Mercedes on its 300 and 600 saloons of the 60s. Air suspension provides a truly supple ride but air-bag durability, a fall in handling precision and the fact that modern, computer-controlled suspension is better made it a blind alley.

BRAKES AND TYRES

The first brakes were blocks of wood made to rub against wheel rims by a system of levers. This is how Trevithick's steamer of 1804 was slowed. As a method of stopping, it was woefully inadequate even for horse-drawn transport.

The 1886 Daimler used a wire hawser wrapped around a wooden ring mounted to the wheel hub. Pulling a lever tightened the wire, which slowed the rotating drum. A refinement of this was the use of a flexible steel band lined with wooden blocks or a strip of leather. This increased the brake's efficiency by extending its friction area.

In 1901, Maybach introduced the internally-expanding drum brake. It used a ring of friction material pressed against the inside of a brake drum by rollers. This was used on the 1903 Mercedes 40hp. Meanwhile, in 1902, Louis Renault designed the definitive drum brake still used today.

Renault's brake used two curved shoes fixed to a backplate, each pivoted at one end. The other ends rested on a cam. When the brake pedal was pressed, the cam forced the shoes

■ ABOVE LEFT *A very early Girling disc brake, as fitted to the TR3 from 1956. The pads were bolted in place.*

■ ABOVE *Power brakes were something to shout about in the 1940s; now nearly all cars have servo assistance.*

■ ABOVE *Disc brakes work by squeezing the rotor (the round bit) between a pair of friction pads which are fixed into the caliper (the lumpy bit).*

■ ABOVE *The next development was easier replacement of brake pads. On this 1959 Lockheed caliper, the pads are retained by pins.*

■ ABOVE *Drum brakes work by forcing the curved shoes against the inside of a drum, which rotates with the road wheel. They do not stand up to repeated stops as well as disc brakes.*

apart and against the inside of the drum.

Drum brakes served for 50 years. Initially, they were used on rear wheels only, for it was feared front brakes could cause skids. Mercedes was the first maker to fit four-wheel brakes, but only as an option, in 1903. All-wheel braking did not become a universal fitting until the 20s. Ever-increasing power and speed demanded more powerful drum brakes, which meant larger and wider. The ultimate form was the huge twin-leading shoe drums used by the Auto-Union and Mercedes "silver arrows" racing cars just before the Second World War. These incorporated scoops and fins

■ LEFT *A Rover SD1
showing off its Dunlop
Denovo tyres, which
were self-sealing and
could run flat for
moderate distances.*

for maximum ventilation to keep temperatures moderate and reduce brake fade. When friction material becomes too hot, it stops working.

Discs take over

Nothing bettered these until Jaguar turned the brake world on its head with the disc brakes it pioneered on its C-Types at Le Mans in 1953. Crosley in America had tried discs in 1949 but soon stopped production. Jaguar gave discs worldwide acceptance. These brakes, borrowed from the aircraft industry, use a pair of friction pads to grip and slow a disc mounted to and spinning with the wheel hub. Because they dissipate heat better and are far more resistant to fade, they give much more powerful stopping for longer than drum brakes. Jaguar won the race that year. There was no going back. By 1956, Girling disc brakes were a standard fitment to Triumph's new sportscar, the TR3,

■ ABOVE *The Dunlop
Road Speed RS5 – a
crossply that was the
performance choice if
you had a big, powerful
car in the 1950s.*

■ ABOVE *The Michelin
XM+S – a "mud and
snow" radial designed
for severe winter
conditions. It was fitted
as standard to early
Range Rovers.*

■ ABOVE *The Pirelli P600, an update of the legendary
P6, was the performance tyre of the 1980s – here it's
on a Golf GTi wheel. As well as having superb grip, its
classic tread pattern also looked good.*

and the Jensen 541 had Dunlops. Jaguar offered Dunlop disc brakes as an option that year on its XK140. Every model since has had all-round discs as standard.

By the time four-wheel drum brakes were standardized at the end of the 20s, they operated by cables, rods and levers, or hydraulics, or a combination of both. Austin's Hydro-mechanical system, used on its small cars of the 40s and 50s, operated front brakes by hydraulics and rear by a system of rods. The MG Magna sportscar of the 30s had brakes operated by a system of cross-linkages and cables which needed frequent adjustment. The Americans had been using hydraulics since the Chrysler 58 of 1926. Citroën had its own ideas. Since the revolutionary DS of 1955, its cars have had fully-powered disc brakes all round. This gives powerful braking with light pedal pressure. Rolls-Royce used Citroën's high-pressure braking system for its Silver Shadow first seen in 1965.

The classic supercar brake setup, of servo-assisted, multipiston calipers gripping a ventilated disc brake at each wheel, has not been bettered. Antilock brakes – derived from aircraft technology – were pioneered in production on the four-wheel drive Jensen FF in 1966. They were not generally available until the 80s.

Tyres

The classic tyre always seems to be a bit wider and fatter than those on a modern car. Since cars began, the trend has been for fatter and stickier tyres. But it's the high-performance, most costly cars – the classics – that get them first. Crossply tyres, tall, unstylish, inflexible and short on grip, hung on into the 60s, but the classic tyres have all been radials.

CLASSIC STYLE

Body styling, the car's skin, is the emotional
trigger that attracts most of us to a motorcar:
driving it comes later, to seal the love affair – or
end it. A pretty but underachieving car will
always have more followers than one that drives
like a dream but doesn't look like one.

1945–55

Many mass-produced cars were still tall and
spindly. They had separate headlights and
mudguards and narrow, letter-box screens.

In Italy, however, coachbuilder Battista
"Pinin" Farina (later Pininfarina) had not been
idle. His pre-war aerodynamic bodywork on the
Lancia Aprillia chassis hinted at the
disappearance of the separate wing profile
within fully enveloping sides. With the Cisitalia
202 and Maserati 1500 Berlinetta, the theme
found full expression. Simple and slender, these
cars inspired a generation to come, including
the beautiful Lancia Aurelia B20 of 1950, the
first of the modern Gran Turismo coupés and a
masterpiece of its period. Pininfarina styled
many of the great Ferraris too, but it was
Touring's classic 166 Barchetta, a model of
elegant simplicity, that got the ball rolling in
1948. It directly influenced the AC Ace of

■ ABOVE *The 1951
Hudson, nicknamed
"Step-down" for its low-
slung construction.*

■ RIGHT *The classic
Pininfarina-styled
Cisitalia 202 coupé, a
landmark.*

■ BELOW *The BMW 503
had clean, well-
balanced lines that
influenced BMW coupés
of the 1960s and
1970s.*

1954, another stunningly pretty shape later
tarnished by the bulging arches of the hybrid
Cobra in the early 60s. There was nothing so
radical going on in Britain, though few could
argue with the perfect poise and elegant purity
of Jaguar's XK120, inspired by the pre-war
BMW 328s.

It was in America that some of the most
influential, if not the best, styling would be
created over the next decade or so. By 1948,
the Americans were starting to shake off the
pre-war left-overs and were shaping some
radical cars: Ford's Custom series brought with
it the new all-enveloping styling – later imitated
on the British MkI Ford Consul/Zephyr series –
while the "step-down" Hudson Super Six
looked rakishly low and modern. The first tiny
rear fins were beginning to appear on the Series

■ BELOW *A Studebaker by industrial designer Raymond Loewy.*

■ BELOW *An Austin A40, one of the Farina-styled British cars of the 1950s and 1960s.*

■ BELOW *Big American cars of the 1950s could retain elegance, as with this Cadillac.*

62 Cadillacs, a taster of what was to come.

It was Europe's sportscars that Americans were developing a real taste for by the early 50s: the 1953 Healey 100/4 was undeniably attractive, with a simple, perfectly balanced shape that was to survive 15 years. The TR2 was bug-eyed and awkward by contrast, yet enormously successful.

1955–65

The American influence was still strong during this period as the seperate mudguard all but disappeared in the name of full-bodied, all-enveloping modernity. The trend was towards lower, wider cars. Chrome was still used in abundance but glass areas increased, hand in hand with half-framed doors and dog-leg wraparound screens. In Britain, coach-building was

■ ABOVE *Bertone's Alfa Guilia, an early GT car.*

■ BELOW *Pininfarina was also responsible for the clean, elegant styling of the Lancia Flaminia coupé.*

still a lively trade as big luxury cars – mostly those of Rolls-Royce and Bentley – still had separate chassis construction, but this decade was to see many famous old names – even Rolls-Royce – switch to unitary construction which didn't really allow for coachbuilt bodywork.

Pininfarina took the styling initiative in the second half of the 50s with the Lancia Florida show car. Like the Cisitalia nine years earlier, here was a true turning point in design. The Florida's taut, chisel-edged architecture was set to influence big-car styling for decades (the 1957 Lancia Flaminia saloon came closest to original expression). An even more radical big saloon was Citroën's DS of 1955, a car that was as futuristic in looks as it was in technical detail. Another frontrunner in the beauty stakes was the 507 of 1955 from BMW, styled by Albrecht Goertz. Created to capture American sales and to challenge the 300SL Mercedes, it was always too expensive, but its slender,

pinched-waist design remains one of the greats.

The Americans were on the verge of the tail-fin craze at this point, particularly General Motors designs. Under styling supremo Harley Earl, everything from the humble Chevrolet Bel Air upwards had rocket-inspired fins by 1957.

In Britain the second half of the 50s brought MG's pretty A roadster, the best-looking car they ever built, while Lotus was about to break into the mainstream with the delicate Elite, a timelessly elegant little coupé. Meanwhile, Bertone of Italy built the first of its memorable, long-lived Guiletta Sprint Coupés in 1955, offered with a Pininfarina Spider version.

Form came second to function with the revolutionary Mini Minor of 1959, so the car

■ ABOVE *One of the most mouthwatering Ferraris ever, the 250 Lusso.*

■ RIGHT *The Facel Vega combining Italiante good looks with V-eight power was French.*

■ BELOW *Lancia Stratos, brutal but beautiful, derived from a Bertone show car. Fewer than 1,000 were built.*

was never designed to win catwalk prizes. Yet the boxy shape was so right and so eternally fashionable (and has changed so little) that it surely deserves a styling accolade.

Pininfarina – a big fan of the Mini – was virtually Ferrari's official stylist by the end of the 50s, shaping such classics as the Spider California, the 250 GT and countless show-stopping one-offs. He never got it more right

than with the 250 Berlinetta Lusso: here was a compact two-seater with perfect proportions.

Much the same could be said of Jaguar's sensational E-Type roadster and coupé launched at Geneva in 1961. Malcolm Sayers's slim and sensual design was a lesson in motorcar archi-tecture, derived from his D-Type racer of the mid-50s. American styling was finding its way again in the early 60s with clean, well-propor-tioned cars like the Corvair, the Studebaker Avanti and the Buick Riviera coupé. The 1961 Lincoln "Clap door" Continental was Detroit styling at its most elegant.

1965–75
The tailfin had all but disappeared by 1965 and even the Americans were cleaning up their act with handsome, clean-lined, if still huge, cars. The fuss and clutter of 50s saloon cars was being swept away by cleaner, classier styling,

■ RIGHT *The Lotus Europa combined a svelte glass-fibre body with super-sharp handling. This is a later, twin-cam car with a more pleasing, lower rear roof line.*

boxy at worst (e.g. the Fiat 124), elegant at best.

In Europe, Bertone was a force in the mid-60s, its crowning glory the magnificent mid-engined Miura. Bertone made waves with the Lamborghini Espada, too, although it was cleverly conceived rather than beautiful in the conventional sense, a big four-seater coupé with a bold, uncompromising profile. With the introduction of the Ghia-styled Ghibli in 1965, Maserati finally had a supercar to challenge Ferrari. Conventionally front-engined, it was every bit as beautiful as the Miura, cleaving the air with a sharply-profiled snout.

The Ferrari Dino 206 of 1967 was the finest-looking car Pininfarina had launched for some time, a jewel-like mid-engined coupé that survived well into the 70s. The 1967 NSU Ro80 was certainly the most futuristic production saloon of the decade, its rising waistline, tall glasshouse and low prow prophetic of aerodynamic saloons yet to come.

Jaguar proved they could still build a good-looking car with the wide, curvy XJ6 of 1968, a classic shape that was to prove very durable: it was still being made in 1990. The trendsetter of 1968, however, came from Staffordshire, in the English Midlands, in the shape of the Reliant Scimitar GTE, the first sporting estate car.

Citroën made a dramatic start to the 70s with a swoopy glass-nosed coupé called the SM.

Here was a real piece of automotive sculpture with presence and enormous class. Fiat's classic 130 coupé was more chisel-edged, its glass-to-steel areas perfectly balanced with wonderful detailing and fine, sharp lines.

Though many beautiful cars have been made since the mid-70s, it is only when the passage of years has allowed us to see them in the context of their time and ours that the truly classic shapes will emerge.

■ ABOVE LEFT *Alfa Romeo Montreal - a front-engined supercar with mid-engined looks.*

■ ABOVE RIGHT *Spen King's Range Rover was the first luxury offroader in 1970. Its classic lines remained in production for 25 years.*

■ LEFT *Alfa's 2000 coupé was an enduring design by Bertone.*

BODYWORK CONSTRUCTION

Car bodywork followed horse-carriage procedure until the 1920s – in style and construction. With the first cars and until the start of the 50s on prestige cars like Rolls-Royce and Bentley, the customer chose throughout – buying first the rolling chassis from the maker, then having it bodied in a selected style by a chosen coachbuilder.

A typical light or sporting car of the 20s would have had fabric body panels stretched over a wooden frame – with aluminium used to form the bonnet and wings. Notable examples were Weymann bodies and classic Vanden Plas

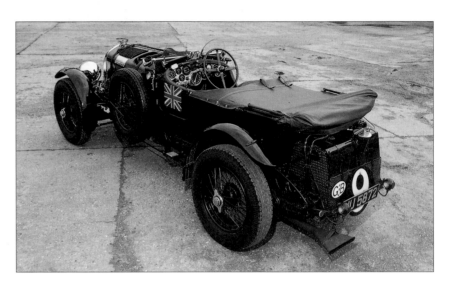

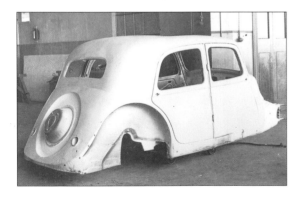

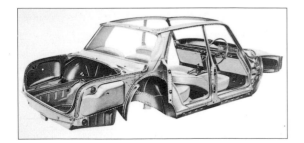

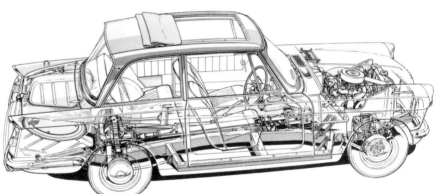

■ LEFT *Fiat's Topolino featured an all-steel one-piece body. It was one of the first small cars so built.*

■ ABOVE *Le Mans Bentley: ash frame, fabric covering and an aluminium bonnet.*

■ ABOVE *A cutaway of the Triumph Herald showing its separate chassis.*

■ LEFT *The Citroën Traction Avant's monocoque (one-piece) body exposed. Front outriggers supported the powertrain.*

■ BELOW LEFT *"Skeleton" of a unitary-construction steel body. Outer panels will be welded or bolted in place.*

open-tourer bodies used on Bentleys. Even when aluminium was later used for all the outer panels, the traditional ash frame remained underneath until the advance of machine-pressed steel panels which could be welded together. The BSA of 1912 was one of the first cars to use this construction. Soon, it was adopted for all small cars, leading to a standardization of body styles. But bodies were still built separately and then mounted on to a chassis which held all the mechanicals. Surely, it would be simpler and more efficient to build the body and chassis as one? Vincenzo Lancia thought so and his beautiful Lancia Lambda of

■ RIGHT *Superleggera (superlight) bodies are made by clothing a lightweight tubular frame in steel or aluminium panels.*

■ FAR RIGHT *The Lotus Elan's backbone chassis holds all major mechanical components. The glass-fibre body slips over the top.*

■ BELOW *The Lotus Elite was the first glass-fibre monocoque body. It had steel strengthening bonded in at all key points to mount the suspension.*

1923 was the world's first monocoque passenger car. Monocoque means all or most of the loads are taken by the car body's skin. It took a while, however, for other makers to catch up. The VW Beetle of 1938 was a half-way house, relying on the body being bolted on top to provide full rigidity. It was Citroën's revolutionary front-wheel-drive *Traction-avant* of 1934 which popularized the monocoque. Full unitary construction, where the chassis and body are made in one shell with openings for doors and windows, came along with the Ford Consul in 1950. This is the way nearly all cars have been built since.

Superleggera

In this construction, thin steel tubes are built up from the floorpan or chassis, into the shape of the finished body. Aluminium panels are then painstakingly formed by hand (rolled between shaped wheels, or beaten over a suitable wooden former, often a section of tree stump) until they fit the shape. They are then

welded together over the frame. Most Ferraris and Maseratis were built this way until the end of the 1950s; the Aston Martin DB4, 5 and 6 were Superleggera cars, too.

Glass fibre (Lotus and Corvette)

Glassfibre is light and easy to work with but usually needs a separate chassis underneath to carry all heavy mechanicals. The Lotus Elan of 1962 is a good example: the one-piece glass-fibre body of this classic small sportscar sits over a simple Y-shaped pressed- and welded-steel backbone. Originally, the Elan was intended to have a much more complicated chassis, but designer Ron Hickman drew up the simple steel chassis as a temporary measure so development on the rest of the car could continue. It stayed. The first glass-fibre-bodied car was the classic Chevrolet Corvette of 1953.

Lotus Elite (glass fibre monocoque)

This car has no steel in the body and chassis, except for localized strengthening. All the stresses are taken through the one-piece (monocoque) body and floorpan unit. Production and budget troubles almost caused Lotus to go under, and Chapman's next car was the more conventional Elan.

THE INDUSTRY, 1945–55

After the Second World War, factories that had been used to make aircraft, aero engines and munitions were turned back to car making. Such had been the industry's preoccupation with war work, however, that there were no new car designs. If you could afford a new car, a pre-war design was what you got, such as Ford's Prefect, which started production in 1938. Even these were in short supply on the home market, for the Government's message to put the economy on its feet was "export or die".

In Germany, production of the KdF Wagen, or "Strength through Joy" car, which became known as the VW Beetle, had got under way again after a faltering pre-war start. Hitler's pre-war dream was for Germany to make a car that every family could afford; in a shattered post-war country, it took the British Army's Royal Electrical and Mechanical Engineers, under Major Ivan Hurst, to get Ferry Porsche's inspired design back into production in post-war Germany.

Later in the 1950s, former aircraft producer Messerschmitt made its own idea of cheap transport for the masses, an alternative to the motorcycle, in its KR200, a tandem two-seater with an aircraft-style canopy and a tiny two-stroke engine in the rear. Today, these cars,

which look like fighter planes on three wheels, are much prized. BMW, trying to keep its head above water now that few of its aircraft engines were needed, tried a different but equally humble route: the Isetta "bubblecar".

Britain thought it needed to earn money after the war with a "world car" for export. A first all-new British design was the Standard Vanguard of 1947, intended to take on the Americans and Australians in their markets. But the most successful export was the Land-Rover of 1948, designed by Rover's Maurice Wilks as a farm runabout and based on a Jeep

■ ABOVE *Typical British cars of the 1950s were small and austere, such as Ford's Popular and Anglia.*

■ LEFT *This 1953 Buick typifies America and the cars it made in the 50s - big and brash.*

■ RIGHT *The Standard Vanguard was Britain's idea of a "world car".*

■ LEFT *The Wilks brothers' Land-Rover brought utility vehicles to the masses, courtesy of the Jeep.*

■ ABOVE *The "people's car", the VW Beetle, still in production - in Mexico - in 1997.*

chassis, after the Jeep he used on his farm wore out. The Morris Minor of the same year could have been a true world car if it had been marketed as aggressively as the Beetle. Its excellent handling and spritely performance guaranteed it true classic status – and it was Britain's first million-selling car. Ford remained true to its cheap, simple, slightly American-influenced but refined formula first

used for the monocoque-shelled, MacPherson-strutted Consul and continued with its successors through the 1950s.

Rolls-Royce, having taken over Bentley in 1931, continued its line of separate-chassis large saloons, its modern new Silver Cloud and sister Bentley S-Type with classical lines by in-house stylist John Blatchley that still have commanding presence.

In America, less badly affected by the war, car output continued unabated. Exciting, plush new models appeared every year. Even ordinary American passenger-cars offered labour-saving convenience items that would only be seen on luxury cars elsewhere. Citroën stunned the world with its futuristic and technically-advanced DS of 1955, but real innovations were still around the corner, and yet no one took Japan's increasing interest in car production seriously.

■ RIGHT *Messerschmidt 500 - the hot version. Most of these tandem two-seaters were 175 or 200cc.*

■ LEFT *An early advertisement for Maxis, and its Minor, Cowley, Oxford and Isis models.*

■ FAR LEFT *The German DKW had a two-stroke engine and front-wheel drive.*

THE INDUSTRY, 1956–60

A new wave of post-Second World War optimism made the mid-50s an era of exciting new sportscars and saloons.

The "Big Healey" – the Austin-Healey 100, later the 3000 – had been with us since 1952 and the Chevrolet Corvette had appeared the next year. MG slotted its curvy new A in at sub-Healey level in 1955. Aston Martin's fast DB2/4 had metamorphosed into the three-litre DB MkIII by this period but was about to be superseded by 1958's DB4. That year along came a cheeky baby, the Austin-Healey Sprite. At first made with no boot lid and the raised headlamps that gave it the "Frogeye" nickname ("Bugeye" in America), this little car was mechanically an Austin A35.

The AC Ace had been in production from 1953 and a decade later formed the basis for one of the most infamous classics of all – the Cobra which appeared in 1962–63.

The Morgan 4/4 reappeared in 1956. In company nomenclature, this stood for four wheels and four cylinders, using Ford's 1172cc sidevalve engine. Other Morgans were powered by the two-litre TR3 unit. The only significant change was use of a cowled nose, rather than

the "flat radiator" style, from 1954.

The big Jaguar news was that the Coventry company complemented its big MkVII saloon with an exciting new compact. Sold initially with 2.4-litre power, it gained its claws as the

■ LEFT *The "fintail" saloons of the 1960s continued to build on Mercedes' reputation for longevity and excellence – the larger 220S in the background first appeared in 1959.*

■ BELOW LEFT *The oddly styled, air-suspended Borgward 2.3 is hardly remembered now, but in its day was a serious rival to Mercedes.*

■ BOTTOM LEFT *Ford's stylish Zodiac MkII was an update of the MkI and helped move technology forward with MacPherson struts and higher-revving engines.*

■ BOTTOM RIGHT *The "Auntie" Rover P4 stuck to traditional wood-and-leather values; later models like this 80 from 1960 were more conservatively styled than the first "Cyclops" 75 of 1950.*

MkII in 1959, with disc brakes and the 3.8-litre version of the XK straight six.

Ford's MkII Consul and Zephyr saloon arrived in 1956, essentially a slightly larger, restyled version of the MkI. Porsche's 356 continued to be improved with better engines. By 1960, 125mph (201kph) was available from the exotic, four-cam 356A Carrera.

In 1959 as American cars were getting bigger and flashier, Alec Issigonis stunned the world with his revolutionary new Mini. Fitting four adults into a 10-ft bodyshell is not easy, but he did it by exemplary packaging – putting in the engine sideways and mounting the gearbox underneath it so the powertrain used the shortest possible space, and fitting a small, 10-in wheel at each corner.

In 1958 the first two-box design and precursor of the hatchback, the Pininfarina-styled A40, appeared. Italian stylists were in vogue: 1959 saw the Michelotti-styled Triumph Herald, which was to give birth to the MG

■ ABOVE *The Austin Healey Sprite lost its "frog eyes" by 1961, and was joined by the identical, badge-engineered MG Midget. This is a 1275cc MkIV Sprite from 1968.*

■ ABOVE RIGHT *Like all proper (pre-Fiat take-over) Lancias, the Flaminia GT was gorgeous, superbly engineered – and expensive.*

■ BELOW LEFT *The Armstrong Siddeley Star Sapphire harked back to a golden age of British luxury saloons, but it was the last car the company made. Production finished in 1960.*

■ BELOW *Even the sporty MG Magnette saloon had its virtues extolled by exaggerated artwork.*

Midget competitor, the Spitfire, in 1962.

In Italy, Alfa Romeo was gearing up for true mass production with its boxy but highly competent Giulietta Berlina. Even more exciting was the Giulietta Sprint, styled by Bertone, a proper little GT that could run rings around many bigger sportscars. The mainstay of Fiat production was still the little rear-engined 500 and 600 models with a wide range of ultra-conventional rear-wheel-drive three-box saloons, from the little 1100 through to the sharp-edged 2100 six-cylinder cars. Lancia, though still losing money because of their obsession with tool-room standards of engineering, produced the most significant car of 1960 – the Flavia. Here was the first Italian car with front-wheel drive, a modern roomy body and superbly insulated suspension.

MAGNETTE MG SALOON

safety fast in airsmoothed style

THE INDUSTRY, 1961–75

For the British industry, the 1960s began successfully, but a series of mergers and takeovers and closure of several established British car-makers left it faltering by the decade's end.

The years of triumph had really begun in 1959 when the Mini appeared and, after the E-Type stunned the world at the Geneva Motor Show, other future classics emerged. There was Chapman's new Elan for 1962, closely following the Mini Cooper – a whole new breed of "pocket rocket", or hot small car. By this time, Ford's Cortina had also appeared; larger than

■ ABOVE *Cadillac was still making huge landcruisers in the 1960s but at least the fins were shrinking.*

■ LEFT *The 250 GTO was the last of Ferrari's front-engined racers.*

to improve handling. The Lotus Cortina quickly became the darling of competition drivers. The cars were used successfully for racing and rallying and still compete in historic events.

The 60s were the golden era for muscle cars in the USA. Cheap petrol meant there was no restraint on makers shovelling more and more horsepower into medium-sized saloons, a trend started with the Chrysler 300 series in 1955.

In Germany, NSU pioneered its futuristic new Ro80. Problems with its rotary power unit made it an engineering blind alley but the cars, when running, were amazingly good. Look how

■ RIGHT *NSU's Ro80 was far ahead of its time but engine-reliability problems killed it.*

the Austin 1100, the best-selling car for much of the 60s, it was simple, cheap and light and returned adequate performance from its modest 1200 and 1500cc engines. This car gave birth to a true classic when Colin Chapman got his hands on it, slotting in the twin-cam engine used in the Elan and sorting out the suspension

■ RIGHT *Germanic excellence is epitomized by the 928, a heavyweight grand tourer launched in 1970.*

■ ABOVE *Ford's Cortina 1600E opened up a new class of car, the sporty "executive saloon".*

■ ABOVE *Early 1970s muscle. This Chevrolet Camaro represents the peak years of the American "pony car".*

similar modern Audis are to that car now.

In 1962, the world saw one of the most sensual classics of all: the Ferrari GTO. Lightweight homologation specials and the last of Ferrari's front-engined racers, these cars are possibly the most desirable anywhere in the world today. Despite once being valued at up to £6 million each, many are still racing. Slightly more affordable was the 275GTB/4 of 1966, considered by some to be the best all-round Ferrari. Then in 1968, two of the most important and memorable of Ferrari's cars appeared – the heavyweight 365GTB/4 Daytona and the delicate mid-engined 246 Dino.

When the 1970s began, the British motor industry, was down to three major players: Leyland, Rootes and Ford. By now BMC was

under the control of Leyland. Alvis had become part of Rover, which itself had been swallowed up by Leyland and thus found itself in the same group as its old rival, Jaguar, which had gone under the protective arm of BMC.

Elsewhere, news was brighter. The beautiful, shark-like Ferrari 308 GTB (a Dino replacement) appeared in 1975. In Germany, BMW had taken a lead in aerodynamics to produce one of the the most classic saloon racers of all time, the CSL. Porsche was just putting the final touches to turbocharging its 911. But for Britain, whose industry was by now on a three-day week and would never be the same again, all that emerged at the end of this period was Jaguar's disappointing XJS. 1975 was the dim end of a classic era.

■ ABOVE *The 1970s Wedge Princess showed how styling had lost its way. Such lame ducks helped nearly finish Britain's motor industry.*

■ BELOW LEFT *De Tomaso Panterra, an Italian supercar powered by Ford V-eight muscle.*

■ BELOW RIGHT *MGB - the classic roadster, launched in 1962. Everyone seems to have owned one...*

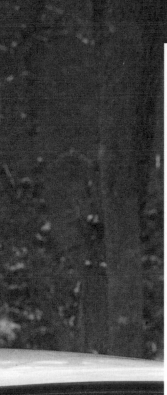

Building the Pedigree

Motor racing in all forms has been a consuming passion of each successive generation of car enthusiasts since the first organized competition. The pioneers, by pitching car against car and driver against driver, learned not only about their own skills and how well their vehicles performed at the limit, but also about the durability of components. In those days, racing really did improve the breed. In the years after the Second World War, technological discoveries made in competition, including better tyres, oil and fuel, filtered down gradually to the ordinary family saloon. In the following pages we will guide you through the classic years of Formula One and the top class of professional motor racing. We also take a look at the romance of long-distance rallying and examine lesser-known activities like saloon-car racing, when cars just like the one dad drove battled it out on the track every weekend.

GRAND PRIX

As soon as two cars met, motor racing was invented. The first organized competition was the Paris–Bordeaux–Paris road race of 1895, won by Emile Levassor in a car of his own make. The average speed was 15mph (24kph), but by 1900, in a similar race from Paris to Lyons (Lyon), this rose to nearly 40mph (64kph). With little in the way of progress except lack of tyre technology, monster racing cars were soon thundering down dusty, unmade

■ ABOVE *Colin Chapman's revolutionary Grand Prix cars put the driver in a monocoque "tub" with the* *engine behind him. Here a 25 heads up a Type 23 sports racer.*

roads at up to 100mph (160kph).

Racing on public roads did not last long. Fatalities in the 1903 Paris–Madrid and Gordon Bennett Trophy races created the need for dedicated circuits. The world's first, Brooklands, opened in 1907; in the 1920s and 30s heroes such as Birkin and the Bentley boys thundered around here and Le Mans. On these closed circuits, the need for riding mechanics was gone. Single-seater racing was born.

The golden age of racing

Think classic Grand Prix racer and you think 1930s Bugatti. But the greatest era of single-seater racing was the 50s. This was the golden age: with little to separate the crowds from the track apart from rows of straw bales, the racing

enthusiast could actually see his heroes at work, unfettered by high cockpit sides, full-faced helmets or the drivers' need to dress up as mobile billboards. While Fangio was still king of the hill on a good day and a quiet American called Phil Hill took his first drives with Ferrari, greats such as Stirling Moss, Peter

■ ABOVE LEFT *Heroic drivers set off at the start of the 1933 500 miles race at Brooklands, the first purpose-built racing track. The curved banking can clearly be seen in the distance.*

■ ABOVE *Stirling Moss, one of the world's greatest drivers, handles his Cooper 500 around a wet Silverstone in 1954.*

■ LEFT *Mike Hawthorn, one of the most charismatic drivers and Britain's first world champion, in 1958. He retired from racing in 1959.*

■ LEFT *Porsche 917s (20, 21, 22) get a strong start at the beginning of Le Mans, 1970. These cars took over from the Ford GT40s to dominate the 24-hour endurance race for much of the following decade.*

Collins and Mike Hawthorn were at the peaks of their careers – and remained great mates, too. Grand Prix racing had become so popular by the early 50s that crowds of 100,000 flooded to the two big races of the year at Silverstone. This ex-airfield circuit was the home of British motor racing and hosted the British Grand Prix and the British Empire Trophy. Even in those days, you had to be through Buckingham or Bicester by 7.30am to make the start – and little has changed.

This decade and the one after also saw the quickest evolution of racing machinery. At the

■ ABOVE *Mercedes' W154 "Silver Arrow" GP racer. Thorough engineering made these cars nigh-on invincible in the 1930s.*

■ RIGHT *Ford GT40. After Ford had failed to buy Ferrari it built its own cars to win Le Mans. They were successful in four consecutive years from 1966.*

■ BELOW RIGHT *The Lotus 78 Formula 1 car was one of the last of Colin Chapman's innovative designs.*

■ LEFT *One-off V12 version of the Maserati 250F, in six-cylinder form perhaps the greatest front-engined Grand Prix car the world has ever known.*

start, Alfa Romeo dominated the scene with the glorious Tipo 158 and 159, but Ferrari, BRM and Mercedes continued to push the tried and tested rear-engined formula, and Maserati's 250F – the classic racing car – won the hearts of drivers and spectators alike. Mercedes used its revolutionary W196 streamliners to steamroller the French Grand Prix at Reims (Rheims) in 1954. But it was Cooper which turned the racing world on its head by the end of the 50s with light, home-built rear-engined single-seaters.

The Chapman revolution

The man who had the greatest influence on Grand Prix cars and took racing-car design into the 60s, having started building his own cars in the 50s, was Colin Chapman. This structural engineer started racing with his Lotus Six and Seven (still with us as the Caterham Seven).

RALLYING FROM THE 50S TO THE 70S

Rallying in the 50s usually meant long-distance time trials where navigational accuracy and not necessarily outright speed was the criterion. Crews of two or three would battle through adverse conditions against an exhausting time schedule, armed with little more than standard cars upgraded only by extra lights and knobbly tyres. The most famous endurance events are the winter Monte Carlo and Alpine rallies where machinery as diverse as Sunbeam Rapiers, big and small saloons and sportscars, contemporary and vintage, competed against each other. Many entries would be "works" ones, from car makers anxious to prove their model's reliability. Later, in the 1960s, the Porsche 91 made its name as a durable car that withstood all that long-distance rallying could throw at it – and the 911 remains the car to beat in historic rallying in the 90s.

There were rallies at a local level, accessible to anyone who had a car and joined a motor club. These again were tests of navigational and timing accuracy, not speed, often at night.

■ LEFT *Tough hardtop saloons like the Ford Escort dominated rallying from the late 1960s.*

■ LEFT *Alpine rallies were tests of reliability, not outright speed.*

■ BOTTOM LEFT *The light, nimble Austin-Healey Sprite made a capable rally car.*

No helmets or elaborate safety procedures would be needed in those days when even such ungainly machinery as Austin A90 Atlantics would have had a chance.

Stage rallying

By the 70s, rallying to most people had come to mean "stage rallies". These are essentially a series of rough-road sprints. Cars blast sideways in crowd-pleasing power-slides, often on slippery shale or in treacherous ice conditions, through a narrow, twisty course accessible to spectators. The timed sections, or stages, range from a couple of miles to more than 30 (48km), and the object is to get down them as fast as

■ LEFT *The Austin-Healey 3000 in its element. This was one of the rally cars to have in the 1960s.*

■ LEFT *The Mini has been one of the most successful rally cars ever.*

■ ABOVE *A highly-modified Ford Escort being serviced on the 1970 London-Mexico rally.*

■ BELOW *Lancia Stratos, the Ferrari-powered purpose-built rally car, on a special stage.*

possible. The navigator's job is to get driver and car to the start of each stage at the right time, but in the frantic activity of negotiating the stage he is more than mere ballast. Using maps or "tulip" diagrams, he warns the driver of the severity of approaching corners, for advance reconnaissance has often been banned. Shrewd navigation is needed on the road sections between stages: these are subject to strict timing, too, and point loss is possible.

The premier event in Britain has always been the RAC Rally. By the end of the 60s the Ford Escort was king, driven by such stars as Roger Clark and the "Flying Finns", Timo Makinen and Ari Vatanen.

Classic 50s rally car – Austin-Healey

The durability of the powerful, separate-chassis two-seater Austin-Healey, launched in 1954, made it the favourite for long-distance rallies over the Alps. Its first successes were with the Morley brothers. Rally legend Timo Makinen first came to fame driving a "Big Healey". But there was tremendous noise from the bellowing, three-litre straight-six engine,

and lack of suspension movement made for poor ground clearance and a boneshaking ride.

First of the evolution specials – Stratos

With its show-car derived styling and Ferrari V-six engine, the Stratos was conceived with the sole purpose of winning rallies once Lancia's mainstay, the front-wheel-drive Fulvia, had aged. This twitchy, short-wheelbase homologation special (legend has it not even the requisite 500 were built) won the World Rally Championship three times, from 1974–76, and was forerunner of the short-lived, rally-specific Group B cars banned in 1986 for being too dangerous. The Stratos's last win was in the 1979 Monte Carlo Rally.

SALOON CAR RACING

Saloon racing has always been used by car makers – officially or not – to prove the excellence of their products. "Win on Sunday, sell on Monday" is the slogan. If Joe Public saw a car winning that he perceived as being like his own, then brand loyalty was strengthened and could even lead to new sales.

Saloon-car racing began soon after the Second World War, but, even well into the 50s, racing saloon cars were terrifyingly similar to their standard counterparts. Perhaps the tyres would be inflated, the hubcaps removed and a helmet worn, but there would be little safety gear until the 60s.

Professionals such as Graham Hill, who started in saloon cars and continued to race Jaguar MkIIs and Lotus Cortinas into the 60s, might wear overalls or at least matching polo shirt and trousers, but for the rest it would be everyday wear – taking a cue from 50s Grand Prix ace Mike Hawthorn who always raced in a sports jacket and bow-tie.

As new models came on stream, so they would be pressed into service on the tracks, becoming faster as more was learned about their tuning potential. The powerful MkI and MkII Jaguars, first seen in 1957, were naturals, as were to a lesser extent the six-cylinder Ford

■ ABOVE *Modern suspension and a light, stiff unitary body gave 50's Mk1 Ford Zephyrs a chance of success.*

■ BELOW LEFT *The humble Austin Westminster was surprisingly successful in 1950s saloon-car racing.*

■ BELOW RIGHT *Cars were surprisingly standard, hence alarming roll angles.*

Zephyr and Zodiac, but by the early 60s the Mini had started to creep on to the grid, aided by John Cooper of Formula 1 fame. The Mini was a landmark car in this respect; racing people who started their careers in Minis include Ken Tyrrell, James Hunt and the great John Rhodes whose tyre-smoking sideways cornering antics are legend. Others who enjoyed rattling around in unsuitable old cars included Stirling Moss and Jim Clark.

By the 60s, proper championships for touring and modified saloons had become

■ BELOW *Big, heavy Jaguar MkVII saloons were more nimble than they looked.*

■ BELOW *The BMW CSL dominated Group 2 in the 1970s.*

established, leading to exciting racing among Formula 2-engined Escorts, for example, and to the birth of the extensively modified saloons with the Group 2 and 4 BMW "Batmobiles" – and fearsome devices such as the series of Blydenstein Vauxhalls fielded in 70s "Supersaloon" racing by the larger-than-life Gerry Marshall.

America had evolved its own racing for "stock", or standard, saloons. This had started as a 200-mile (322km) sand/Tarmac race at Daytona Beach, Florida, in 1936. By 1959, the course had been transformed into a purpose-built two-mile (3.2km) banked oval track in the same location, and similar tracks sprang up all over the country under the auspices of NASCAR, the National Association for Stock Car Auto Racing. By the end of the 60s, "stock" cars were circulating at up to 200mph (322kph), aided by careful attention to aerodynamics and the rule book.

In Sports Car Club of America racing, where cars had to turn right as well as left, the AC Cobra/Corvette wars of the mid-60s gave way to multiround contests between modified Mustangs and Camaros, making heroes of men like Mark Donohue and Peter Revson.

Farther south, Mexico hosted the maddest road race ever, the 1,864 miles (3,000km) Carrerra Panamericana. This flat-out spectacle, which included a class for saloons among the diverse machinery taking part, was run annually from 1950 until 1954, when the growing number of fatalities forced closure. Since 1991, it has been run again as a retrospective road event.

■ BELOW *"Big Bertha", the V-eight-powered Vauxhall Ventura supersaloon built in the 1970s by Bill Blydenstein for the race ace Gerry Marshall to drive.*

CLASSICS IN COMPETITION TODAY

Classic motor sport has never been more popular. Purists think it's a shame to use up venerable old machinery, but the pragmatic say racing cars were built to race.

Historic motor sport doesn't have to mean big bucks or major track extravaganzas; there are plenty of gentler sprints, hill climbs or rallies populated by more modest machinery. Whatever the car, there's an extra-curricular activity you can do with it. Here are some of the activities that enthusiasts get up to with their classics.

Road runs

Not competition but open to anyone with a suitable classic (usually at least 20 years old) and a road licence, these are run by many clubs as a way of providing their major events with a focal point and also by large organizations such as the RAC MSA which runs the UK's largest annual road run.

Trials

You can enter a production-car trial in pretty much anything with four wheels – but the most stylish trials for classics are the ones operated by the Vintage Sports Car Club (VSCC), for

cars made before 1930. The point of a trial is to arrive at the right place at the right time and to clear certain muddy hill climb sections without stopping. The winner is the driver with fewest errors.

Sprints and hill climbs

Within reason, you can sprint or hill climb any classic, vintage or veteran car you want. Only the most basic safety gear and the cheapest competition licence are needed. Each competitor embarks on two practice and two timed runs on a short, usually twisty course.

■ ABOVE *Historic endurance rallies, following the routes of the classic Alpine rallies of the '50s, are usually for cars made before 1962 and can easily be won in cars like this Jowett Jupiter: accuracy is the key, in both navigation and timing.*

■ ABOVE *Special-built post-war vintage racing combines Napier aero engine and Bentley chassis.*

■ ABOVE *Fast roads tours are available for more rarefied machinery on an invite-only level. Here an Alfa chases an HWM.*

■ ABOVE *Historic sports car racing has never gone away. Here a Cooper Monaco leads at Brands Hatch.*

■ BELOW *The famous paddock shelters at Shelsley Walsh near Worcester, where hillclimbs have been held since 1905.*

■ RIGHT *Historic Grand Prix cars, such as this Lotus, have a strong following, and more are being brought back to the race tracks all the time.*

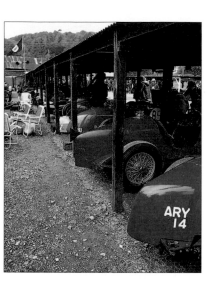

Navigational rallies

Usually run at night, navigational rallies are tests of map-reading, navigation and time-keeping. Although they aren't speed events as such, an accurate average must be kept.

Stage rallies

There's some navigation in these events, but only to get the car to the beginning of each special stage in good time – and then all hell breaks loose. The stage, often on narrow forest gravel tracks, is closed to traffic, and the object is to get to the other end as fast as possible.

■ ABOVE *A supercharged MG tackles Shelsley, where competitors ascend the hill in less than a minute.*

■ BELOW *Like Lincoln's axe, many historic cars have had parts replaced, but have never stopped racing. Some are going faster than ever.*

Endurance rallies

From the three-day Monte Carlo Challenge over the snowy Alps to the 10-week London-Mexico, run in 1995 as a 25th anniversary of the first event, these gruelling runs demand meticulous car preparation and tremendous self discipline – but generate fantastic camaraderie between entrants.

Saloon car racing

Back to the glory days, pure and simple, with Anglias, BMW 2000s, Alfa GTAs and Minis scrabbling round on Dunlop racing tyres in scenes straight from the 60s.

Historic single-seater and sportscar racing

From ERA through Maserati 4CM and Alfa Monzas, including Blower Bentleys and Mercedes SSKs, right up to fairly recent Formula 1 material, this evocative, heady mix stirs up memories for everyone. In the sportscar class, glorious packs of Lotus Elevens battle it out with Jaguar D-types, Maseratis, Birdcages and Coopers too. But you have to be rich.

Classic Culture

The first flickerings of interest in classic motorcars made after the Second World War began nearly three decades ago. Now, that interest has grown into an all-consuming passion for millions of men and women all over the world. Some use their classics daily, others just on high days. Some preen them like beauty queens in the concours d'élegance, parades of vehicles to the most elegant, best designed or best turned-out of which prizes are awarded. Many owners are driven by nostalgia, a need to own or recreate a piece of their past; others by simple love of old machinery. As modern cars become ever more amorphous and as image-conscious individuals wear their classics like designer suits, as a statement, the classic is no longer the preserve of bearded, middle-aged men. To own an old car has become trendy. For some, the word classic has become debased down the years, seeming to embrace any number of awful machines. To them, classics, derided by many in their prime, are now dignified merely by rarity. In the early 1970s, however, could the pioneers of the classic-car movement have guessed that the then-new Austin Allegro would one day inspire an enthusiastic owners' club?

WORKING CLASSICS

The attributes that make a vehicle a classic also bring the best cars to the top in the tough world of work. This applies whether services need them to be out in all weathers rescuing stranded motorists, attending a breakdown or accident, pursuing villains and keeping traffic flowing or simply carting goods around reliably.

Each service has its favourites, each vehicle's special abilities suiting it to its chosen job. The Automobile Association (AA) (1905), finding its motorcycle-and-sidecar outfits no longer efficient, bought Land-Rovers almost from inception in 1948 to aid motorists.

■ RIGHT *The "woody" estate, a popular variation on a saloon car which could carry more.*

■ RIGHT *The emergency services found Land-Rovers ideal for rescuing motorists in remote spots. This is one of the AA's first Landoes now restored.*

■ ABOVE *Rare Aston Martin shooting brakes (estate cars) based on the DB5.*

■ RIGHT *The Ford Thames was available in van and pick-up forms. Designed to drive in a similar way to a car, it was ancestor to the ubiquitous Transit.*

Likewise, the Royal Automobile Club (RAC) (1897) used a selection of cars and car-derived vans: Austin Sevens, Morris Minors and then Mini-vans for lighter-duty breakdowns and Bedford CA vans and trucks at the heavier end before they universally adopted the Ford Transit in the 1970s. In the 50s, the RAC ran six Isetta bubblecars in London to reach motorists through the clogged traffic. These tiny two-strokes' towing ability is not recorded!

Policemen and postmen

The police have long used big, powerful and reliable saloons, from the classic, fast, bell-equipped and evil-handling Wolseleys of the 50s to the Rovers and Jaguars of the 70s. Various forces have at times tried to beat the villains at their own game by adopting the same wheels – Jaguar MkIIs in the 50s and Lotus Cortinas in the 60s. The police have also tried out new types of vehicle. In the 60s, forces ran an experimental four-wheel-drive

(by Ferguson Formula) Ford Zodiac Mk4, which may have paved the way for the near-universal adoption of the classic, big-hearted Range Rover for motorway patrols.

In the 50s, a Morris Minor van with ugly rubber wings was a familiar sight. Britain's General Post Office (GPO) thought the wings were unbreakable and immune to minor knocks. Alas, they meant the headlamps sat up in separate pods and setting alignment was nigh-on impossible. The GPO then turned to another car-derived van, the Bedford version of the first Vauxhall Viva, the HA of 1963. In France, the entire postal service was served by a pair of rugged, front-wheel-drive hold-alls, the Citroën 2CV and Renault 4 vans.

Civilian workers

For "civilian" use, car-derived vans have long been another way for makers to sell to motorists unfamiliar with the size and vision difficulties of the large-panel vans like them. Since the 1920s, panelled-in versions of most popular cars have been available. They are often

simply an estate version with the windows filled in and the back seat missing. Before Purchase Tax applied to commercial vehicles, this was the cheapest way to own an estate car – buy a van and fit side windows!

Ford's Transit of 1968 was the trendsetter whose name became generic for one-tonne (1,016kg) vans. This much-loved, tough and surprisingly fast hauler was a natural to carry everything from parcels to builders' gear. It was a big hit with criminals, too: they could hide in it until the coast was clear and carry a lot of booty. Where there's work to be done, the chances are you'll find there will be a classic that has completed it.

■ ABOVE *The Ford V-eight Pilot, an attractive and powerful chase car in its day.*

■ BELOW LEFT *Some Dutch police forces used the Porsche 911.*

■ BELOW RIGHT *Many forces in Britain used unusual machines – such as this MU2 Lotus Cortina.*

CLASSICS ON FILM AND TV

Nothing does more for a classic car's kudos than appearing in a classic film or television series. Who could forget the Volvo P1800 in Britain's *The Saint* series of the 60s or the Alfa Spider in *The Graduate* (1967) with Dustin Hoffman? Both made these cars world-famous and boosted sales. As dynamic and often beautiful objects, motorcars have always looked good on screen as set decoration or the focus of the action. The catalogue of classic-car screen moments is huge.

The Americans have long been masters of putting the motorcar on screen, in everything from Herbie *The Love Bug* (1969) to cult films like *Vanishing Point* (1971), *Two-Lane Blacktop* (1971) or *Duel* (1971). For many connoisseurs it is the 1968 film *Bullitt* starring Steve McQueen that features perhaps the best car chase ever filmed: his Mustang pursues a sinister Dodge Charger at speed through the hilly streets of San Francisco to a superb V-eight soundtrack. The scene lasts 12 minutes,

■ LEFT *MkII Jaguars featured as heavily as getaway cars on film as in real life.*

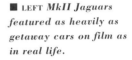

■ BELOW *An S-Type Jaguar appeared in the 1967 film Robbery.*

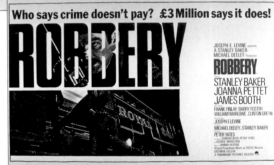

■ BELOW *A white Volvo P1800 became a trademark for The Saint played by Roger Moore.*

■ LEFT *Big saloons featured in many British crime films: Richard Burton, Jaguar S-Type in Villain (1971).*

with McQueen, a good driver, doing much of the stunt work himself. In his 1971 film *Le Mans*, McQueen did more driving than acting and added to the list of motor-racing films such as *The Green Helmet* and *Grand Prix* (1966) and *Winning* with Paul Newman (1969) that were neither critical nor box-office successes.

■ RIGHT *What the public did not see – Michael Caine providing extra damage to the red E-Type in The Italian Job (1969).*

Cops, robbers and spies

In British films, the crime genre has long been a fertile hunting ground for classic-spotters. *Robbery* (1967, based on the Great Train Robbery) has a hair-raising pursuit with a police S-Type Jaguar and felons in a silver Jaguar MkII. In *The Italian Job* (1969), a tongue-in-cheek take of an audacious gold robbery starring Michael Caine and Noël Coward, cars outshone actors. The getaway cars are three Mini Coopers that make a cheeky escape along Turin rooftops and drains. Other motorized stars include a Lamborghini Miura, a pair of E-Types and an Aston Martin DB4 convertible. Jaguars provide aura in gangland classics like *Performance* and *Get Carter* (both 1971), while *Villain* (1971), starring Richard Burton, features a payroll heist: look out for the Jaguar S-Type, Ford Zodiac and Vanden Plas three-litre, all wrecked. And look out for the Lamborghini Islero and the Rover 3.5 *The Man Who Haunted Himself*, also of 1970.

James Bond films feature cars heavily as part of 007's equipment. The gadget-laden Aston DB5 caused a sensation when it appeared in *Goldfinger* in 1964 with its ejector seat,

machine guns and radar. Toyota built a special convertible 2000GT for *You Only Live Twice* (1967) but it had no real gadgets. In *On Her Majesty's Secret Service* (1969) new Bond George Lazenby drove a stock Aston DBS and a Mercury Cougar in an ice-racing sequence.

■ ABOVE *A Lotus Elan starred alongside Emma Peel and John Steed in The Avengers.*

■ LEFT *The British TV series, The Sweeney featured Jaguars weekly.*

■ LEFT *Goldfinger: 007's Aston Martin DB5 featured overrider hooks, machine guns behind sidelights and revolving number plates. Three more were built for Goldeneye (1995).*

CHOOSING & OWNING A CLASSIC

Saloon or estate, two doors or four, open or closed – only you know which type of classic will suit your needs and pocket but, generally speaking, options like power steering, overdrive and air conditioning are always worth searching out if you want the most usable classic in modern conditions. Be prepared in most cases for higher maintenance costs or a lot more unreliability than with a modern car.

Bodywork bother

Rust is the biggest enemy of the older car. Before the 1980s most ordinary – and indeed many expensive – motorcars were only given token rust-proofing, so if you live in a damp climate corrosion will be much more of a problem. Unitary or monocoque construction was coming in across the board by the 60s on mass-produced cars, and any rust in the sills, floor or inner wing areas with this type of bodywork will seriously compromise the car's strength and rigidity.

Cars with separate chassis are generally less of a worry because the bodywork is not self-supporting. That doesn't mean the chassis won't rust eventually, and removing bodywork for restoration is not for the faint-hearted. Aluminium panels – as found on high-calibre

classics like Aston Martins – don't rust in the same way but do suffer from electrolytic action between the aluminium and the steel frame of the car. Aluminium is also more susceptible to damage. Glass-fibre bodywork doesn't rust, of course, and in most cases – apart from the Lotus Elite – features a separate steel chassis, too. However, the passage of time can cause the gel coat to craze, which is a specialist job to rectify. Taking paintwork more generally, look for signs of over-spray on door rubbers and window surrounds, indicating a hasty respray. Brightwork – badges, bumpers, grilles, etc – is

■ ABOVE *The Triumph Spitfire is a relatively easy car to restore because of its separate chassis.*

■ BELOW *A bubblecar could be an ideal project for those with limited space.*

■ LEFT *There are still plenty of unrestored "popular" classics to choose from.*

notoriously costly to refurbish and many pieces
are difficult to find for more unusual models.

Mechanical matters

Mechanically, older cars tend to be simpler,
although by the end of the 60s fuel injection
and complex air suspension was putting many
of the more expensive cars beyond the abilities
of the home mechanic. Generally, with the
engine, you should be looking for signs of
excessive smoke from the exhaust and of
overheating with watercooled engines,
particularly if they are of exotic aluminium
construction as with many Alfa Romeo and
Lancia models. Gearboxes should be
reasonably quiet, though many 50s and even
60s cars featured "crash" bottom gears which
give a rather evocative whine. Automatic gear
changes won't be as smooth as on a modern
luxury car but, even so, changes shouldn't be
rough, either. Woolly steering and soggy brakes
characterize many big saloons of the classic
era, but many sportscars of the 50s and 60s
have handling that is rewarding.

Looking inside

Although scruffy interior trim won't stop you
driving a classic, a car's interior condition is
vital to its feel and ambience. A Jaguar, for
instance, with damp carpets, peeling wood

■ ABOVE LEFT *The
interior of this "woody"
station wagon would be
complex and expensive
to put right.*

■ ABOVE *Welding is a
useful skill if you intend
to tackle restoration
yourself.*

■ ABOVE RIGHT *It is
essential that leather and
wood are in good
condition. Refurbishment
is expensive.*

■ BELOW *Rust curses cars
of the 1950s and 1960s
such as this Jaguar.*

veneer and cracked or split leather seats loses
much of its appeal. Retrims are expensive and
obscure interior parts difficult to source. The
generally far more basic interiors of sportscars
are easier to refurbish and, again, for the
popular British marques everything is usually
available. Hoods are expensive to replace on
sportscars – look out for tears – while a hard
top is definitely worth paying extra for if you
intend using an open classic all year. If you are
determined to buy a classic car, do your
homework. Join the relevant club, get to know
the pitfalls of the model you are after, then go
out and look at as many as you can before
making a decision.

FUTURE CLASSICS

New "classics" appear all the time. These are cars that, because of sheer appeal, excellence or exclusivity, are instantly memorable and desirable from first sightings at a motor show. Others, cult darlings such as the Golf GTI, have become the definitive cars of their era and have never truly fallen out of fashion with enthusiasts. Others again, such as the Mini, VW Beetle or 2CV, still in or recently out of production, are simply the modern versions of

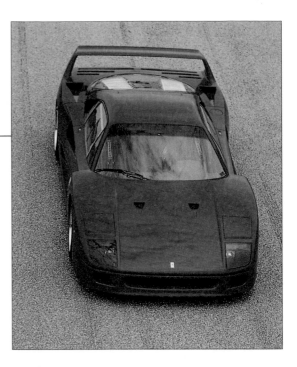

■ RIGHT *All Ferraris will be classics, especially the stunning, 200mph (321kph)-topping supercar F40 of which 1500 were made.*

■ FAR LEFT *Mazda's MX5 aped the Lotus Elan of 20 years earlier – but bits did not fall off.*

■ LEFT *BMW's M3 was a fine-handling supersaloon. Later versions could not quite match its raw appeal.*

acknowledged classic designs. They don't have to be supercars to qualify, although some of the most obvious contenders clearly are: any new Ferrari or Lamborghini is so eagerly awaited that its status upon arrival is guaranteed. In these cases, simply belonging to the right marque is enough to confer immortal desirability.

Porsche 911s all qualify as future classics because of their unique blend of robustnesss and driveability, even if the dashboard design is as confusing as ever. The wide-bottomed 928 will forever hover on the fringes of true classicdom, although some of the early 944 Turbos will be allowed into the hallowed club, and the Speedster-inspired Boxster is clearly on the VIP list from the word go. It's all a question of attitude.

Dodge's awesome eight-litre V-ten Viper has

■ RIGHT *First of the breed – the VW Golf^ GTi. Purists say the first, lightest cars were the best. This is an 1800cc MkI.*

■ RIGHT *The Delta Integrale was a homologation special built so that Lancia could win rallies. It made a scorching road car, too.*

■ RIGHT *Classic coupé, German style.*
BMW 635 coupés were fine-handling
cruisers.

■ ABOVE *US brutality.*
The Dodge Viper with
its eight-litre V-ten
engine is a "Cobra for
the 90s".

■ BELOW *The Peugeot*
205GTI, the classic hot
hatch, once described
as a Mini Cooper for the
1980s. High insurance
premiums killed off this
breed of car.

already made a name for itself as the AC Cobra of the 1990s, but its compatriot the Corvette has never been the same since it was emasculated after 1970. Nearly all TVRs occupy the same specialist slot – they are beefy, brutal, British and rear-drive, with that gorgeous V-eight woofle. The Ford Escort RS Cosworth and Sierra Cosworth, both astonishingly fine road cars, have won themselves a place in the hearts of the sort of people who worshipped anything that followed the rally-winning RS Escorts out of Ford's Advanced Vehicle Operation at Boreham, Hertfordshire, in the 1970s. Buying yourself a Lancia Delta Integrale gives the same full-on

driving appeal with even more exclusivity. The first-shape BMW M3 of the late 80s falls into much the same bracket – a rock-hard driving machine – and effectively upgrades the reputation carved out by the 2002 Turbo in 1973, but those in the know say the later cars lack the raw appeal. As ever, the first versions are the purest.

Today's little classics

With cheeky good looks and world's-best handling, Lotus's new Elise, which sadly may not survive a difficult birth, is obviously the Elan of modern times. But for the nearest thing to a real Elan, look no further than Mazda's MX-5, or Miata. Like the original, it's a 1600cc twin-cam rear-driver with sublime handling – it even looks similar – yet nothing falls off it. MGF's, while uninspiring in looks, handles so well that people will always want them; it's also descended from the very first classic sportscar of all.

All Minis will be classics, however feebly powered; its trademark shape, unchanged since it shot to fame in the 60s by winning Monte Carlo rallies, will see to that. And so will that "Mini Cooper for the 90s" – the Peugeot 205 GTI, the best example of that 80s phenomenon, the hot hatch. The choice is huge.

PART TWO

The A–Z Guide to CLASSIC AND DREAM CARS

A GUIDE TO CLASSIC, CONTEMPORARY AND FANTASY CARS

Martin Buckley and Chris Rees

Continental R

INTRODUCTION

Everyone knows a classic car when they see one, even if they can't actually tell you what makes a car a "classic". Most people associate advancing age with classic credentials, but that ignores the existence of "living classics" and future classics.

The first A-Z section starts after the second world war and finishes in 1975. During this time the first flickerings of interest were shown in classic motorcars. A variety of models are covered, from those that many will have heard of, and the more unusual classic makes.

The second section begins with models from 1976 and ends with the cars of the future. The 1970s was a difficult time for motoring, with oil crises, escalating congestion, pollution issues and industrial troubles. Yet a true golden age of cars began at this time, reaching full bloom in the late 1980s and 90s, as cars became more rewarding to drive, leapt ahead in technical terms and grew in design appeal.

There are few, if any, pieces of hardware as emotive as the car. The third section aims to chart the evolution in dream-car design over 60 years. With the birth of car *designers* rather than pure engineers, the door was open for them to express their visions of the future. These cars are celebrated here as we look back at what fired the imaginations of yesterday's creative minds and look to future creations, which will address the current issues of congestion, energy consumption and pollution.

The story of classic and dream cars charts the progress of our own history and experience. This part of the book is a celebration of that progression and a recognition of the value and importance of these cars in our lives.

A–Z of Classic Cars from 1945–1975

This section is a guide to the manufacturers making the world's best-loved and most famous classic cars from 1945–1975. It spotlights the models like the XK120 and Morris Minor that many will have heard of, while giving more esoteric classics like the Iso Grifo and Fiat 130 Coupé a fair crack of the whip. Some cars were classics from birth. Others earned the title. Some earned it with outstanding dynamic qualities and advanced engineering; some by sheer commercial success or conspicuous lack of it. Failures like the Edsel or Austin Atlantic add colour to the motorcar's history. Their stories show how even the top companies can get it wrong – and they make great reading.

AC

■ AC ACE

AC Cars of Thames Ditton, England, came back to the market after the Second World War with the staid two-litre range in 1947, but it was with the Ace sportscar of 1953 that the company really made its reputation in the post-war years. Casting around for a replacement for the aging two-litre cars, they took up a design by John Tojeiro that used a ladder-type tubular frame, all-independent transverse leaf-spring suspension and an outstandingly pretty, open two-seater alloy body, clearly inspired by the Ferrari Barchetta of the day.

Early cars used AC's elderly two-litre overhead-cam straight-six engine (first seen soon after the end of the First World War) to give a top speed of 102mph (164kph) and 0–60 (96kph) in 13 seconds. It was hardly a sporting engine, however, and it was felt that

■ LEFT *The classic lines of the Ace were penned by 1950s specials builder John Tojeiro, inspired by Ferrari Barchetta.*

■ LEFT *All Aces had a hand-crafted aluminium body. This is the rare Ford Zepyhr-engined model.*

■ BELOW *Production of the Ace ran from 1953 to the early 60s. Note the minimal parking protection.*

■ BELOW *The AC six-cylinder engine was the least powerful of the trio used in the Ace. The ultimate version has a triple-carb set-up.*

■ LEFT *The Ace always looked its best with the hood down. It folded right out of sight to give a clean profile.*

■ BELOW LEFT *With its stiff leaf-spring suspension, the Ace's handling was taut, its ride hard.*

■ BELOW RIGHT *The Aceca was a sleek coupe version of the Ace, inspired by the Aston Martin DB2.*

something more modern and powerful was required to put the modern chassis to good use. Thus, from 1956, there was the option of Bristol's superb two-litre 120bhp straight-six engine and slick four-speed gearbox. Top speed leapt to 116mph (186kph) with 0–60 (96kph) in the nine-second bracket, and response was much sweeter and more modern. Overdrive was available from 1956, and front disc brakes were an option from 1957, although they were later standardized. With the engine well back in the chassis, the Ace handled well and was successful in competition.

Joining the Ace in 1954 was the Aceca hard top coupé, which had an early form of hatchback rear door but used the same basic timber-framed alloy body. Like the Ace, it came with AC or Bristol power and, with a better drag factor, was slightly quicker in a straight line, although extra weight affected acceleration a little.

From 1961 to 1963 a few Aces were built with Ford's 2.6-litre straight-six to replace the Bristol unit, these new Ken Rudd-modified units; gave up to 170bhp. By then, Thames Ditton were gearing up for the Cobra, an altogether different kind of AC.

Today the pretty AC Ace is much sought after, particularly in its Bristol-engined form.

AC ACE	(1953-63)		
Engine	Straight six (AC, Bristol and Ford)		
Capacity	1991/1971/2553cc		
Power	102/125/up to 170bhp		
Transmission	4-speed optional overdrive		
Top speed	117mph (187kph) (Aceca Bristol)		
No. built	Ace	266	
	Ace Bristol	466	
	Ace 2.6	47	
	Aceca	320	
	Total:	1,099	

AC

■ AC COBRA 289 & 427

In the autumn of 1961, Texan racer Carroll Shelby approached AC Cars with the idea of fitting a 4.2-litre Ford V-eight engine into their lithe and handsome light alloy Ace sportscar. By early 1962, AC had built the first prototypes and by the autumn had dispatched 100 cars to America for completion. Enter the legendary Cobra, perhaps the most famous muscle-car of them all and certainly one of the fastest.

Using essentially the same tubular steel chassis layout as the six-cylinder Ace, with transverse-leaf springing for the front and rear suspension, this spare

■ LEFT *The seven-litre cars had a stiffer chassis and coil-sprung suspension to handle the power.*

■ BELOW LEFT *With so much power – up to 480bhp and 180mph (290kph) – driving a Cobra at speed is for experts only.*

and handsome two-seater sportscar had electrifying performance thanks to the relatively light weight of the body and the high torque of the pushrod V-eight engines. The first cars used a 4.2-litre unit with the famous top-loader gearbox, but it wasn't long before a bigger 4727cc engine was slotted in by Shelby, boosting power from 164 to 195bhp. Top speed of the 289 car was 138mph (222kph), but even more impressive was the acceleration: 60mph (96kph) came up in 5.5 seconds, the standing quarter-mile in 13.9. It was in this form that the car first became available in Britain in 1964. Naturally, four-wheel discs were

■ LOWER RIGHT *Early 260/289 cars were much prettier and still stunningly quick – 0-60mph (90kph) in 5.5 seconds.*

■ FAR RIGHT *Its arches house massive Goodyear tyres but make the seven-litre Cobra into something of a caricature.*

■ LEFT *In North America, the Cobra was marketed as a Shelby Cobra or a Ford Cobra rather than an AC, who supplied the bodyshells.*

■ BELOW *289 and 427 Cobras shoulder to shoulder. The bigger-engined cars had alloys, the 289 wires.*

AC COBRA (1962–68)	
Engine	V-eight
Capacity	4261/4727/6997
Power	164/195/345/490bhp
Transmission	4-speed manual
Top speed	136–180mph (218–290kph)
No. built	979

specified and, when the 289 engine replaced the 260, rack-and-pinion steering (rather than Ace-derived cam-and-peg). Even then the Cobra was no car for the novice.

This wasn't enough for Shelby. In 1965 he slotted in the 6989cc engine to produce the seven-litre Cobra. It had claimed 345bhp in its standard form – tuned SC cars gave 480bhp or more – and acceleration that put the Cobra in the record books in 1967 as the world's fastest-accelerating production car: 0–60mph (96kph) in 4.2 seconds. There was a milder Cobra 428 version with the 390bhp 6997cc V-eight from the Ford Thunderbird. In reality the seven-litre was virtually an all-new Cobra and no longer a slim and sylphlike beauty with fat arches front and rear housing huge Goodyear tyres. It shared only the doors and bonnet with the 289. More importantly, the chassis was totally redesigned and much stiffer, while the suspension now used coil springs rather than antiquated leaf springs.

The production of Cobras stopped in 1968 when 4.7 and 7-litre cars were running concurrently. Since 1965 the "baby" Cobra had been known in Britain as the AC 289 Sports and used the same flared-arch body as the seven-litre. In America, the cars went under the names Shelby Cobra and Ford Cobra and were homologated as Shelby American Cobras.

There are a couple of footnotes to the Cobra story. The chassis lived on under an elegant Italian coupé body designed by Frua and was known as the AC 428, launched in 1966. As recently as 1983 Brian Angliss revived the car as the MkIV Cobra – but that's another story.

ALFA ROMEO

■ BELOW *A 1970s two-litre Alfa Romeo Spider in its natural hunting-ground– the open road. This version had the most torque, but the 1750 was sweeter.*

■ ALFA ROMEO SPIDER

Launched at the 1966 Geneva Motor Show, the Alfa Romeo Duetto Spider was the last complete design by Battista Pininfarina, founder of the Turin-based design house. With sales initially disappointing (the previous Giulietta Spider's best figure of 5,096 in 1960 was not exceeded until after the arrival of the Spider 2000 in 1972), who could have believed that the basic model would remain in production for 27 years? The shape wasn't much admired at first, but the lines matured gracefully over the years through a couple of restyles culminating in the square-tailed cars of the late 80s that ceased production in 1993.

The classic Alfa twin-cam engine grew from 1600 through 1750 and even 1300cc variations to become a fully fledged two-litre in 1971. Experts rate the 1750 highest for its combination of sweetness and refinement, while even the 1600 offers lusty acceleration, and the two-litre offers the most torque. The cars were always highly priced – the 1750 Spider's British price tag in 1969 was not much less than a much faster E-Type – but, with smooth steering, slick gearchange and fine disc brakes, offered

■ ABOVE *In the mid-1980s the Spider gained big bumpers and an unhappy-looking tail spoiler in an attempt to prolong its showroom life.*

■ LEFT *The cars of the 1980s had a chin spoiler and bigger wing mirrors but did without plastic headlamp covers.*

driver involvement and satisfaction that few cars could equal. It was a civilized car too, with a good ride and a watertight hood that could be raised with one hand.

The first-generation Spider's name, Duetto, was chosen after a contest drew 140,501 suggestions. One Guidobaldi

Trionfi of Brescia won a new Duetto for his, which was intended to symbolize the twin-cam engine and two-seater configuration. Rejected names included Pizza, Sputnik, Panther and Al Capone. These early "boat-tail" models gained fame in the 1967 film *The Graduate*.

ALFA ROMEO SPIDER 2000 (1966-93)	
Engine	4-cylinder DOHC
Capacity	1962cc
Power	131bhp @ 5500rpm
Transmission	5-speed manual
Top speed	124mph (199kph)
No. built	82,500

■ LEFT *The rounded lines of the boat-tail or Duetto Spider (nearest camera) alongside the square-tail look of the 1750 of 1970.*

ALLARD

■ ALLARD J2/J2X

South London motor trader Sydney Allard based his famous rugged sportscar on a reliable Ford V-eight engine. His pre-war Special cut its teeth in mud-lugging trails, but it wasn't until after the Second World War that Allard decided to go into production. The K1 and J1 of 1946–48 were spare and primitive but very fast, especially when fitted with the bigger 3.9 Mercury version of the well-tried flat-head Ford V-eight. Production blossomed with the more civilized versions such as the four-seater L Type and M1, with their hallmark waterfall grilles and the best-selling P1 saloon, with up to 4.4 litres, which won the Monte Carlo rally.

Best and most coveted of the breed, however, was the J2/J2X of 1949, a stark, four-wheeled motorbike of a car that, with the more modern type of overhead-valve Cadillac V-eight, could accelerate quicker than the Jaguar

XK120. Nevertheless, it was the Jaguar that spelled the beginning of the end for Allard and many of its ilk. The cars were produced in tiny numbers and could not compete with the mass-market Jaguar on a value-for-money basis. Sales fell sharply after 1953 and the company produced its last car, the Palm Beach, in 1958, in a belated bid for the Austin Healey market.

ALLARD J2/J2X (1946-59)	
Engine	V-eight
Capacity	5420cc
Power	180bhp
Transmission	4-speed manual
Top speed	130mph (209kph)
No. built	173

■ ABOVE *A cross-section of classic Allards: early special, K1, J1 and – furthest from the camera – P1.*

■ FAR LEFT *The evergreen Ford flat-head V-eight engine was at the heart of all classic Allards, giving up to 180bhp in the J2/J2X.*

■ LEFT *Dashboards were Spartan, with parts-bin instruments and a huge steering wheel.*

■ NEAR RIGHT *The J was a short-chassis two-seater with cut-away doors, capable of over 100mph (160kph).*

■ FAR RIGHT *The J2 and J2X, ultimate Allards with minimal creature comforts and stunning performance: 0-60mph (90kph) in 5.9 seconds was sensational in 1949.*

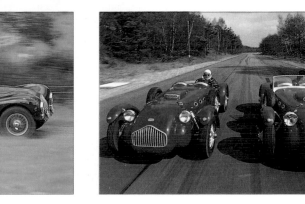

ALVIS

■ **LEFT** *Alvis of Coventry forged its reputation with cars like this 12/50 tourer in the 1920s.*

■ ALVIS TD/TE/TF

By the time the Graber-styled cars came out in the late 1950s, Alvis of Coventry had seen its best days with pre-war classics such as the fast and beautiful Speed 20 and 4.3. Post-war car production became something of a sideline to the company's armoured vehicle interests, nevertheless, the TD, TE and TF were fine cars. Developed from the "Greylady" TC21, they were mature motorcars for discerning enthusiasts: luxurious, well built and well mannered yet with a surprising turn of speed.

The TD's shape was the work of Graber, who had licensed Willowbrooks of Loughborough to build the bodies in Britain. These cars, dating from 1956, were known as the TC108G. Quality was

■ **BELOW LEFT** *This Speed 25 of the mid-30s was a supercar in its day with a top speed of more than 100mph (160kph).*

■ **BELOW RIGHT** *Today the Alvis badge is only to be found on armoured vehicles: car production finished in 1967.*

■ **LEFT** *The TF was the ultimate Graber-styled car with 150bhp triple-carb engine and five-speed ZF transmission.*

■ **OPPOSITE LEFT** *Interiors were traditional with large leather seats and walnut veneer. Only Bentley and Rolls-Royce were better.*

■ **OPPOSITE RIGHT** *Graber-inspired lines were slim and well balanced with a large glass area. Bodywork was coach built at Parkward.*

■ BELOW *Earlier TD models had single front light treatment and slightly less power.*

■ BELOW *Today these cars are highly sought after and have an enthusiastic owners club.*

not all that it should have been, and for the TD of 1958 Alvis commissioned Parkward of London to build its bodywork, while at the same time tidying up the rear of the roof line. Powered by a 120bhp version of the familiar Alvis three-litre straight six, the TD could achieve 100mph (160kph) with ease and looked particularly elegant in drophead form. Series II TDs had disc brakes, and, from October 1962, a desirable ZF five-speed gearbox

of the type used in the contemporary Aston Martin. The four-headlamp 1963 TE had 130bhp and could be bought with automatic transmission or power steering. Best, and last, of the breed was the TF of 1965, which had a triple-carburettor 150bhp engine and a top speed of 120mph (193kph) with the five-speed box. By then the writing was on the wall for Alvis as a passenger-car maker. Rover took a controlling interest and stopped TF production in 1967.

ALVIS TD/TE/TF 21 (1958–67)	
Engine	Straight six
Capacity	2993cc
Power	120–150bhp
Transmission	4/5-speed manual 3-speed auto
Top speed	110–120mph (177–193kph)
No. built	Total: 1528

ASTON MARTIN

■ ASTON MARTIN DB2/ DB2/4 & DB MKIII

Tractor tycoon David Brown, who had bought Aston Martin in 1947, made something of a false start with the underpowered four-cylinder Aston Martin DB1 of 1948. He more than redeemed himself, however, with the DB2 of 1950, a car that set the pace for all subsequent Astons. Here was a luxurious upper-crust coupé with modern performance and old-world charm packing a smooth, powerful six-cylinder twin-cam 116bhp engine from the Lagonda 2.6 saloon (Brown had bought Lagonda too, in 1947). "DB"

ASTON MARTIN DB2, DB2/4, DB2/4 MK II & DB MKIII (1950–59)	
Engine	DOHC straight six
Capacity	2580–2922cc
Power	107–196bhp
Transmission	4-speed manual
Top speed	115–130mph (185–209kph)
No. built	1,728

had his sights held high: there would be no more four-cylinder Astons.

Clothed in handsome open or closed alloy bodywork by Frank Freeley, these cars would top 115mph (185kph) with the standard engine, and more than 120mph (193kph) in high-compression Vantage form, which by early 50s standards represented supercar performance. Underneath, the classic cruciform chassis, with its pre-war belt-and-braces rectangular section tubing, produced thoroughbred handling of the highest order. Coil sprung, the live rear axle was located by trailing links – with

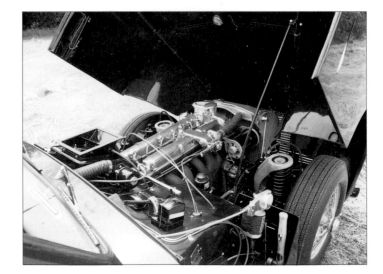

■ TOP *Drophead treatment lent itself well to Frank Freeley's smooth shape.*

■ CENTRE *MkIII models had the most power and could achieve up to 130mph (209kph).*

■ LEFT *The engine was designed by WO Bentley and was originally intended for a big Lagonda saloon.*

■ LEFT *The DB2/4 had an early form of rear hatch and two extra seats in the back. The body was aluminium.*

■ BELOW LEFT *A functional interior featured a full set of instruments, a big wheel and full leather trim. The build quality was superb.*

a Panhard rod for the high side-loads the car was capable of generating – and damped by Armstrong lever-arms. Front suspension was unusual, a trailing-link design with the main lower locating member running across the front of the car, its shaft turning in widely-spaced bearing with continuous oil-bath lubrication. It had big wire wheels: 15-in (38cm) centre-lockers shod with the best contemporary high-speed Dunlop crossplys.

For the DB2/4 of 1953, Freeley's smoothly contoured fastback shape was made more practical, if not so pretty, by the addition of rear seats and a side-hinged rear hatch which meant stretching the tail by four inches. By the time the MkIII arrived, the tall DB2 grille had evolved into a broad mouth (derived from the DB3S racer) and small fins had sprouted on the rear wings with slim tail lights.

The WO Bentley-designed twin-cam six, in three-litre form since 1954, was upgraded for the MkIII with a stiffer block, beefier crank, and much improved timing chain and intake manifolds. It breathed better, too, thanks to the larger valves and higher-lift camshafts, technology lifted from the latest DB3-S racers. Twin SU carburettors remained, but the "DBA" engine produced 162bhp at 5500rpm.

Mildly tweaked three-litre engines were fitted to a handful of MkIIIs in 1958, of which 10 had a Weber-carbed, twin-exhausted engine giving 195bhp (known as DBB), while a further 47 had a 178bhp running SUs but the hotter cams and twin exhaust of the DBB.

David Brown supplied the gearbox on all models. It had a crash first gear and the option of overdrive on top gear on the MkIII, giving 28.4 per 1000rpm. Girling front discs were another innovation on the MkIII.

The DB MkIII was replaced by the DB4, although production overlapped for some months. The last MkIII was built in July 1959.

■ ABOVE *The MkIII had a bigger, wider grille, a three-litre engine and disc brakes, plus the option of overdrive.*

■ BELOW *All cars featured a separate chassis and unusual trailing-link front suspension.*

ASTON MARTIN

■ ASTON MARTIN DB5

The Aston Martin DB5 was an aristocrat among 1960s sportscars, as exclusive as a Savile Row suit and in Britain on its introduction in 1963, priced accordingly. The same amount of money would have bought you a nice little place in the Surrey stockbroker belt, while Jaguar's faster E-Type was just half the cost. The model's appearance in the James Bond film *Goldfinger* in 1964 put the name of Aston Martin on the lips of the world. Even today Ian Fleming's hero is still synonymous with the marque.

The DB5 was the fifth Aston built

■ LEFT *The lines of the DB5 evolved from the Touring-designed DB4 of 1958, with flared-in lights and a different roof line.*

■ BELOW *The short-chassis DB4 GT was a two-seater intended for competition work. It had a twin-plug engine and always had cowled lights like the DB5.*

under the regime of David Brown. It wasn't a new car, but a development of the sometimes troublesome Touring-styled 3.7-litre DB4 that had been around in one form or another since 1958. By fitting a bigger four-litre version of the twin-camshaft six-cylinder engine – with 240bhp – and a five-speed ZF gearbox, Aston claimed more punch with longer legs. Top speed was 140mph (225kph) – nearer 150mph (241kph) with the optional tuned Vantage engine – with meaty acceleration to match.

■ ABOVE *Made famous in the 1964 James Bond film Goldfinger, this beautiful shape has a timeless appeal.*

■ RIGHT *The standard DB5 was capable of 140mph (225kph), the Vantage version near 150mph (241kph).*

■ LEFT *In its handling the DB5 was well-bred if not quite in the same class as the E-Type*

■ BELOW *Aston Martin boss David Brown had 12 of these shooting-brake DB5s built.*

■ FAR LEFT *The alloy body was beautifully hand-built at Aston's Newport Pagnell factory.*

■ NEAR LEFT *The Volante was the convertible version – one of the fastest open cars of its day.*

■ BELOW LEFT *Early DB5s had three circular lights, later cars had single oblong units.*

Strange to think that in the carefree early 1960s Aston could test its cars on the still new and unrestricted M1 motorway, a spark plug's throw from the Newport Pagnell factory.

Like all Astons before it, the DB5 broke no new technical ground but kept pace with developments. Disc brakes, fitted all round, were becoming the norm on fast cars like the DB5, but Aston were still suspicious of newfangled independent rear suspension and felt they could make their solid axle work just as well. For the most part they were right, although the DB5 was always happier on fast main roads than being chucked about on country lanes. Flared-in lights for Touring's fashionable Italian bodywork, consisting of alloy panels draped over a labyrinth of small tubes, were a nod towards modern aerodynamic

ASTON MARTIN DB5 (1963–65)	
Engine	Straight six
Capacity	3955cc
Power	282bhp @ 5500rpm
Transmission	4/5-speed manual 3-speed auto
Top speed	140mph (225kph)
No. built	1,018

thought, but inside the DB5 retains its club-land feel with rich leather everywhere, electric windows (still rare in 1963) and a push-button radio: switch on and the words "Aston Martin" glowed in red from the tuner. As well as the fastback saloon, Aston built the swish Volante convertible, and David Brown even sanctioned 12 shooting-brake DB5s to sell to his uppercrust country house-owning pals. These were surely the most beautiful estate cars ever built.

With sales of more than 1,000 in a little over two years, the DB5 has to be counted as one of the most successful Astons. It is certainly one of the most memorably beautiful, a slender, sensual machine highlighting how the later, more macho cars from Newport Pagnell lost their way.

ASTON MARTIN

■ ASTON MARTIN V8

The Aston Martin V8 was built in many guises over its 21-year career. The shape, styled by William Towns and fashioned in alloy, was first seen in 1967 as the DBS, but with the old four-litre six-cylinder engine because the V8 was still not ready for production. With its new DeDion rear suspension, the wide, wedge-shaped four-seater DBS handled well but was really a little heavy for its engine, especially when fitted with the power-sapping automatic gearbox. To be fair, a Weber-carbed Vantage version restored the status quo to some extent, but the six-cylinder cars have never been much fancied.

The quad-cam all-alloy 375bhp V8 was thus much welcomed when it arrived in 1969, catapulting the top

■ RIGHT *The Vantage version of the V-eight had a deep chin spoiler and a blanked-out grille. It was good for 170mph (273kph).*

■ BELOW *Like all Astons, the V-eight's body was crafted in alloy. The shape was by English designer William Towns.*

speed up to a Ferrari-challenging 160mph (257kph), although early misgivings about the reliability – and thirst – of the Lucas fuel injection caused Aston to change to Webers in 1973. By then, the shape had already had its first make-over with a new grille and single lamps on either side. Five-speed manual was the standard transmission, but many cars came with the Chrysler automatic gearbox.

A Vantage version of the V8 gave Aston a challenger in the supercar stakes with its 170mph (273kph) top speed and shattering acceleration, while the elegant Volante convertible proved to be a top

seller for this British company. The dramatic Lagonda four-door of 1976 was pure Aston V8 under the skin and appealed to Arab oil sheiks.

The last V8 was made in 1990. By then, the engine had reverted to injection. Large, thirsty, very expensive and fast, the V8 was viewed as a dinosaur yet it had enormous appeal as a traditionally-built high-speed express. Its spirit survives in today's Virage.

■ FAR LEFT *The cabin featured acres of the finest leather, electric windows and air-conditioning.*

■ NEAR LEFT *The standard "saloon" V-eight in Oscar India specification of the late 1970s. By this time many Astons were being built with automatic transmission.*

ASTON MARTIN (1969–90)	
Engine	V-eight
Capacity	5340cc
Power	340–436bhp
Transmission	5-speed manual 3-speed auto
Top speed	160mph (257kph)
No. built	About 1,600

AUSTIN

■ **ABOVE** *The dramatic Atlantic dates from the austere late 1940s and was built to woo the Americans.*

■ AUSTIN A90 ATLANTIC

Austin was first off the mark into post-war production in 1945, and the A90 Atlantic was Britain's first car designed specifically for the American market. It had a promising start. Launched at the Earls Court Motor Show in 1948, it was a sensation.

While other makers continued with warmed-up pre-war leftovers, here was an all-new 95mph (152kph) British convertible with modern full-width styling: the front wings were bulbous and full, sweeping down across the deep, thick doors to blend gently into the big one-piece rear wings and cowled-in wheel arches, forming a rakish, bold profile. Incredibly for 1948, the Atlantic could be had with a power top and door glasses, unheard-of in Britain: a switch had the top up and latched down in 22 seconds. Other Atlantic luxuries included such rare

AUSTIN A90 ATLANTIC (1948–52)	
Engine	OHV in-line four
Capacity	2660cc
Power	88bhp @ 4000rpm
Transmission	4-speed manual
Top speed	90mph (145kph)
No. built	7,981

refinements as an Ecko radio, adjustable wheel and a heater.

The rugged internals were warmed-up A70 saloon, a long-stroke, overhead-valve 2199cc four-cylinder engine bored out to 2660cc and giving 88bhp on twin SUs: Longbridge rounded the output up to 90 to give the new flagship its name. More telling was the 140lb/ft (190.5 newton metres [N m]) of torque that peaked at 2500rpm. There were four speeds on a very American steering-column shift.

It was the Atlantic's pace, above all, that impressed the pundits. It was one of a handful of cars since the war that could top 90mph (145kph), and of those, the Atlantic was easily the cheapest. 0–60mph (96kph) in 16.6 seconds wasn't hanging about in 1948 either and, with petrol still rationed, up to 25mpg could be obtained. In America, where buyers expected six or eight cylinders, not four, sales never took off. In 1949 an Atlantic broke 63 American stock-car records at Indianapolis over seven days.

The Atlantic was short-lived. Austin tried to sustain interest in it with a $1,000 price-cut in 1949 and then, in 1951, a fixed-head saloon version with hydraulic brakes and a lower axle ratio but the convertible ceased production in January 1951. The saloon struggled on until September 1952, ousted by the BMC merger that year. The final tally was 7,981 cars and of the 3,597 exported, only 350 made it to America.

■ **ABOVE** *The interior featured white steering wheels and the column gearchange.*

■ **ABOVE RIGHT** *Twin Austin of England badges and Pontiac bonnet strakes were unusually flash for a British car.*

■ **RIGHT** *The A90 Atlantic was impressively swift with a top speed of 90mph (145kph). It also featured an advanced power-operated hood.*

AUSTIN HEALEY

■ BELOW *The MkII 3000 has shapely lines. The body was built by Jensens of West Bromwich in central England.*

■ AUSTIN HEALEY 3000

The original "big" Healey was the Healey 100, first shown at the Earls Court show in 1952 and hastily adopted by BMC as the Austin Healey 100 with the 2.6-litre four-cylinder engine from the Austin Atlantic. Bodies were built by Jensen of West Bromwich, central England, with final assembly at the MG factory at Abingdon, Oxfordshire. In no way was the Healey a sophisticated motorcar: it had a separate chassis, cam-and-peg steering and a solid rear axle sprung and located by half elliptic leaf springs.

In 1956 the six-cylinder BMC series C engine from the Austin Westminster was shoehorned into a stretched version

AUSTIN HEALEY 3000 (1959–67)	
Engine	6-cylinder
Capacity	2912cc
Power	124–150bhp
Transmission	4-speed, optional overdrive
Top speed	114–120mph (183–193kph)
No. built	42,926 all types

■ LEFT *The Healey 100 had the four-cylinder engine from the Austin Atlantic.*

■ BELOW *The last-of-the-line MkIII had opening quarter windows and 120mph (193kph) potential.*

of the car to make the 100/6. However, this wasn't entirely successful: performance was down compared with the torquey old four.

Redemption arrived in the form of the three-litre 3000 MkI in 1959: outwardly the same pretty, shapely, low-slung two-seater but with a 2912cc 124bhp engine. Performance went up to 114mph (183kph), while new front disc brakes improved the stopping power. Overdrive, wire wheels and nominal two-plus-two seating were optional as before. For

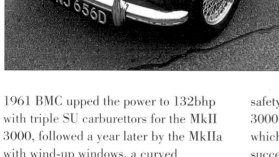

■ LEFT *The Austin Healey 100 was originally to be just a Healey.*

■ BELOW LEFT *The MkIII was probably the least pretty but most comfortable of the breed and featured small rear seats.*

■ BELOW *The Healey looks wonderful from the rear. The four-cylinder cars had the best handling.*

■ LEFT *The early cars had a functional dashboard: the MkIII had wood veneer.*

1961 BMC upped the power to 132bhp with triple SU carburettors for the MkII 3000, followed a year later by the MkIIa with wind-up windows, a curved windscreen and a proper, fully convertible hood. From this point the cars were two-plus-two only and can be recognized by a vertical-slat front grille.

Last, and best, of the line was the 1964 MkIII with improved breathing for 148bhp, pushing the top speed to over 120mph (193kph). Brakes were improved by a servo and, inside, the car had a rather opulent wooden dashboard, somewhat at odds with its macho reputation as a rugged driver's car.

North America was always the car's biggest market and it was American

safety legislation that finally ousted the 3000 from production in 1967, after which BMC replaced it with the far less successful MGC. Despite its low ground clearance the Healey was a formidable

works rally car in three-litre form and was never quite the crude and rugged car of legend, certainly in later form. It remains one of the most sought-after British sportscars of the 1960s.

■ ABOVE *The Healey lasted until 1967, when it was ousted by American safety regulations.*

■ ABOVE *The 2.6-litre four-cylinder engine, also found in the Austin Atlantic, had excellent torque.*

AUSTIN HEALEY

■ AUSTIN HEALEY SPRITE

There may have been faster, smaller
sportscars than the 1958 Austin Healey
Sprite, but few have been more
endearing. With its gaping grin and the
pop-eyed headlights that gave it its
"Frogeye" nickname, this little brother
to the big 3000 Healey captured the
hearts of enthusiasts the world over. In
fact, the trademark protruding lights
were an afterthought when the extra cost
ruled out Donald Healey's idea for
retracting headlights. Taking its
mechanics from the well-filled BMC
parts-bin (mostly Morris Minor and
Austin A35), the 11ft 5in (3.5m) Sprite
had a chirpy character on the road, too,
with a respectable top speed of 84mph

AUSTIN HEALEY SPRITE (1958–61)	
Engine	In-line four
Capacity	948cc
Power	43bhp
Transmission	4-speed manual
Top speed	84mph (135kph)
No. built	38,999

■ ABOVE *The Austin
Healey Sprite got
its "Frogeye"
nickname because
of its pop-eyed
headlights.*

■ LEFT *Little
brother to the
Healey 3000, the
Sprite could attain
84mph (135kph).*

■ LEFT *The whole nose section tipped
forward to give access to the engine.*

■ BELOW *Donald Healey's original idea was
to give the Sprite pop-up headlights, but
this proved too expensive.*

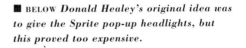

(135kph) and up to 45mpg attainable. Its one-piece front-end lifted up to give excellent access to the 948cc A Series engine, which gave all of 43bhp.

It spawned many variants with increasing levels of ugliness and luxury, though the performance of the last Austin Sprite of the early 70s was way above the original Frogeye. There was a badge-engineered MG variant, too, reviving the old Midget name, that lasted until the late 70s in hideous rubber-bumpered form. The less said about that the better.

■ ABOVE *The Frogeye was unmistakable from the rear too, with its tiny lights and minimal bumpers.*

OTHER MAKES

■ ABARTH
Italian Carlo Abarth launched his firm in 1950 as a tuning concern specializing in the Fiat marque. His first car was the Tipo 207/A Spider of 1955, using Fiat 1100 parts, followed rapidly by the first of the 600-based machines. Through the 1960s, Abarth continued to build cars based on the Fiat 500/600 and latterly the 850, as well as branching out into production of stunning little Simca-Abarth coupés, sports-racers and prototypes with twin-cam engines of entirely his own design. Racing activities pushed the company into liquidation in 1971. Fiat took over the Abarth for its own competition activities.

■ AMPHICAR
Originally the A35-powered Eurocar, this quirky German amphibian was the brainchild of Hans Trippel, creator of the wartime VW Schwimmwagen and various subsequent amphibious cars. An annual production of 20,000 Amphicars was projected, a farcical overestimate which led to formal production ceasing in 1963, with cars then being assembled from the vast stock of parts at the works.

■ ARMSTRONG SIDDELEY
The firm came into being through the fusion of Armstrong-Whitworth's car-making activities with Siddeley-Deasy of Coventry in 1919. The last products from the firm were distinctly luxurious but were always too expensive compared with the main competition from Jaguar. Car manufacture ceased in 1960 with the big Star Sapphire, and the company concentrated on its core business of aero engines.

■ AUDI
The first cars from the German firm Audi were four-cylinder and were successful in sport, but after the First World War came "sixes" and then the first as a manufacturer of mainly-front-wheel-drive Wanderer-based cars under the umbrella of the Auto-War. The marque remained dormant within the latterly Mercedes-controlled Auto-Union until 1965, when ownership of the combine passed to Volkswagen. Today, Audi is best known for its Quattro four-wheel-drive system, first seen on the groundbreaking Quattro Turbo Coupé of 1979.

■ AUSTIN
The Longbridge-based company was founded in 1905 by Herbert Austin (later Sir Herbert), whose earliest designs were conventional and reliable, if uninspiring. The Seven of 1922 was a revolution and on this design the firm's fortunes were made. Most products through the inter-war period were dull but worthy, and the trend continued after 1945. The British Motor Corporation (BMC) was formed in 1952 by uniting Austin and Morris, with the former firm emerging dominant.

The most significant post-war BMC was the Mini, and this led to a family of front-wheel-drive models; however, the last of the old line, the Cambridge, survived until 1969. Austin no longer exists as a marque, but its Longridge works is the Rover Group's principal plant.

BENTLEY

■ BENTLEY CONTINENTAL

The Bentley Continental was one of motoring's ultimates in the 1950s. It was not only the fastest genuine four-seater car in the world – it could top 120mph (193kph) with ease – but also one of the most beautiful: big, swoopy and as stunningly elegant as anything from the fashionable design houses of Italy.

Shaped in Rolls-Royce's Hucknall wind tunnel under the direction of styling supremo John Blatchley, this was Crewe's flagship owner-driver super-coupé, its bold, distinctive fastback profile influenced, though no one would admit it, by the Cadillac 62 Series coupé of 1948. The Bentley grille still stood tall and proud, as on the R-Type saloon, but at the rear those hallmark embryonic tail fins kept the Continental tracking straight at high speed. The Continental's alloy bodywork was built in London by HJ Mulliner on a special high-performance chassis.

The gearing was higher than on the saloon, and the 4566cc engine breathed more freely thanks to a higher compression ratio and a big-bore exhaust system. There was a weight-loss regime for this, the first sporting Bentley since the 1930s: bumpers were made of aluminium, not steel, and, inside, the armchair seats of the R-Type saloon had given way to smaller sports buckets with alloy frames.

Even so, the Continental was no Spartan lightweight: four people and all

BENTLEY CONTINENTAL R (1952–55)	
Engine	Straight six
Capacity	4566cc (later 4887cc)
Power	Not quoted
Transmission	4-speed manual
Top speed	124mph (199kph)
No. built	208

■ ABOVE *The distinctive Bentley grille was retained for the Continental.*

■ ABOVE *Its sweeping lines were among the most beautiful of their time and belied the car's bulk.*

■ LEFT *Despite its weight the Continental handled well, especially on fast roads with wide sweeping corners.*

■ LEFT *The Continental shape continued with minor alterations on the new Silver Cloud/S1 chassis.*

■ BELOW *From the rear the sweeping roof line was especially elegant. The shape was evolved in an aircraft wind tunnel.*

their luggage could travel in magnificent comfort in familiar drawing-room surroundings, the driver enjoying a full set of instruments that included a rev counter and an oil temperature gauge, items not normally deemed necessary on the saloon. Out on the road that tall gearing gave the Continental a fantastically long stride with 80mph (128kph) on tap in second, 100mph (160kph) in third and 124mph (199kph) in top, all achieved in fuss-free refinement. For the seriously rich, there was no faster or more stylish way to escape austere, post-war Britain.

Later, the original lightweight R-Type Continental concept was watered down. Tycoons wanted fatter seats, drivers wanted automatic gearboxes, steel bumpers replaced aluminium and before long the Continental was just another heavy coachbuilt Bentley, albeit superbly handsome. The Continental look survived on the "S" Series chassis of 1955, but by then the Continental appellation applied to all coachbuilt Bentleys. Most were desirable, but only that original R-Type will go down as one of the greats, in its time perhaps the finest car in the world.

■ ABOVE *The interior featured a full-width wooden dash with more complete instrumentation. The Continental was at its best as a right-handed manual.*

■ LEFT *The Continental was a genuine four-seater with unbeatable long-distance touring ability. Powered by a six-cylinder engine, it could do 80mph (128kph).*

■ ABOVE *The Continental was for the super-rich only and gradually got heavier and less sporting as it evolved. The body was built by HJ Mulliner in London.*

BMW

■ BMW 507

In search of a flagship glamour car to
boost American market sales, as well as
their flagging post-war image, in the
mid-1950s BMW asked Albrecht
Goertz, a German aristocrat with an
American-based industrial design
agency, to style a new super sportscar.

Using a drastically shortened version

■ ABOVE *The BMW 507 was
one of the most beautiful cars
of the 1950s. This one has*
*knock-on wheels. The styling
was by Albrecht Goertz, later to
style the 240Z Datsun.*

■ ABOVE LEFT *From the rear the track looks
wide. Vision was poor with the hood up.*

■ ABOVE RIGHT *The 507 even looked good
with the hood up. Its lines had near perfect
balance.*

BMW 507 (1955–59)	
Engine	V-eight
Capacity	3168cc
Power	150–160bhp
Transmission	4-speed manual
Top speed	125–140mph (201–225kph)
No. built	253

of the big V-eight saloon's box-section
chassis as his base, Goertz – later to
design the best-selling Datsun 240Z –
sketched a slim, pinched-waist roadster
that was an object lesson in elegant
purity. With its long bonnet, pert tail and
impeccable detailing it was an instant
classic. Producing 150bhp from a high-
compression version of BMW's fine all-
alloy V-eight engine (with a four-speed
manual gearbox), it went as well as it
looked: with the longest of the axle
ratios offered, it was capable of 140mph
(225kph) and 0–60 (96) in the order of
nine seconds. Its exhaust note, a creamy
full-blooded wuffle from twin rear pipes,

was almost as memorable as its profile.
Torsion-bar suspension front and rear
gave a supple ride with confident
handling, perfect for its role as a suave
high-speed express for the Monte Carlo
set. A handsome factory hardtop quickly
converted the 507 into a snug, roomy
two-seater coupé.

Beautifully crafted in alloy, the 507 of
1955 was aimed squarely at the
Mercedes 300SL's market, but somehow
it was more of a soft tourer than the
complex, difficult-to-handle SL: serious
drivers never really took it to their
hearts. Its saloon-derived steering was
never its best feature, which is probably

■ BELOW LEFT *The 507 was a superb long-legged tourer rather than a sportscar. The longest axle ratio gave up to 140mph (225kph) with the four-speed manual box.*

■ BELOW RIGHT *The stylish vents on the wings were for extracting heat from the engine bay.*

■ RIGHT *The front end was a stylized version of the traditional BMW "kidneys".*

■ BELOW *The alloy V-eight engine came from the 502 saloon but had high compression and up to 160bhp. It was smooth and flexible.*

why its competition pedigree makes short and unimpressive reading. Like the SL, though, it was viciously expensive and each one took a long time to put together, mostly by hand.

There were few uplifting developments in its short four-year career, the most notable being more power – 160bhp – and latterly front disc brakes. Production ceased in 1959, just 253 cars down the line. If anything, it added to BMW's financial problems.

Nonetheless, almost 40 years on, it rates as perhaps the most collectable of all post-war BMWs.

■ BELOW *The typically 50s interior was comfortable and roomy for two people. It featured an excellent hood, and there was the option of a factory hardtop.*

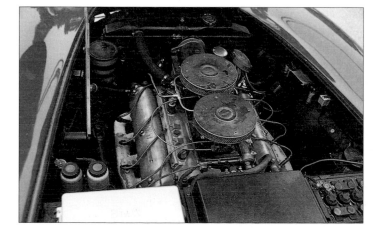

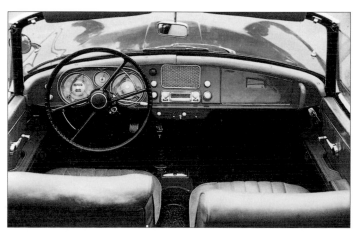

BMW

■ BMW 2002 TURBO

Marketed to bolster the ebbing
reputation of BMW's entry-level saloon
in its run-out twilight years, the BMW
2002 Turbo lasted only 10 months into
1973. When petrol prices almost
doubled overnight, shocked car buyers
became acutely aware of the delicacy of
oil supply from an Arab monopoly:
suddenly this 17-mpg tearaway looked
like an anachronism. The first sign of
BMW's loss of nerve was the
disappearance of the aggressive
reversed Turbo lettering on the front
spoiler, but by then the Turbo's days
were already numbered: it was
discontinued by a nervous Munich after
only 1,672 had been produced.

BMW 2002 TURBO (1972–73)	
Engine	4-cylinder
Capacity	1990cc
Power	170bhp @ 5800rpm
Transmission	5-speed
Top speed	130mph (209kph)
No. built	1,672

■ LEFT *The 2002 Turbo was based on the
bodyshell of the 2002 Tii, itself a quick,
yet much more usable and practical car,
good for almost 120mph (193kph).*

The Turbo, all left-hand drive because
the blower occupies the space normally
reserved for the steering column in the
right-hand drive car, used the injected
two-litre slant-four engine fitted with a
KKK turbocharger and made an
impressive 170bhp. It did without a
wastegate, intercooler or complex
electronics and felt much the same as
the standard 2002 at low to medium
revs, though the turbo boost – from 4500
rpm – tended to cut in rather suddenly

and could make the car a handful.
Geared for 20mph (32kph) per 1000rpm
in the fifth gear of its special ZF five-
speed box, the Turbo ran out of breath at
130mph (209kph). Turbos ran a 3.36:1
ratio in their 40 per cent limited slip
back ends.

The Turbo had stronger driveshafts
and bearings all round, but still used the
usual BMW configuration of
MacPherson struts at the front and semi-
trailing arms at the rear. Spring rates

■ ABOVE *Fat wheel-arch extensions hid
bigger wheels. "Turbo" logos raised the
hackles of safety campaigners in the 1970s.*

■ OPPOSITE *The tearaway BMW Turbo was a short-lived and unlucky model, launched at the dawn of the fuel crisis.*

■ BELOW *The 2002 shell dates back to the mid-1960s and the 1600-2, an entry-level four-cylinder BMW that survived well into the 70s.*

were increased all round, and there were anti-roll bars at both ends and Bilstein dampers on the back. The tyres – on special 6in x 13in (15cm x 33cm) Mahle alloy wheels – were 185/70x13s Michelin XWXs. The brakes, which were vented discs gripped by four-pot callipers up front, large drums at the rear, had only one servo to the standard 2002's two. Inside, the Turbo featured rake-adjustable buckets. The only other changes were the addition of a boost gauge in a pod tacked on to the centre of the dash and a three-spoke sports steering wheel, while the face of the instrument binnacle became red.

The rare and exciting 2002 is now one of the most collectable 70s BMWs.

■ LEFT *The Turbo, inspired by a factory racer, was a 130mph (209kph) hot-shot with 170bhp.*

■ BELOW *From the front the Turbo was easy to spot – bereft of front bumper and wearing a deep chin spoiler with flashy decals.*

■ ABOVE *The Turbo's cabin featured a thick-rimmed sports wheel, hip-hugging seats and a special instrument pack. All were left-hand drive.*

■ RIGHT *The slant-four engine produced 170bhp with the KKK turbocharger but had somewhat on-off delivery.*

B M W

■ BMW 3.0 CSL

The CSL was a lightweight version of BMW's flagship six-cylinder coupé, built to homologate the car for European Touring Car Group 2 racing. The first CSLs, announced in May 1971, were real stripped-for-action 135mph (217kph) road racers with thinner body panels, no front bumper, fibreglass rear bumper, racing latches on the bonnet, manual winding side windows made from Plexiglas, and of course the alloy-skinned opening panels, all in the name of weight reduction. BMW even skimped on underbody rust protection and sound deadening, along with some drastically cheaper interior trim (400lb [181kg] was pared off the coupé). Top speed wasn't much affected but acceleration was decisively quicker. Suspension was stiffened by Bilstein gas shock absorbers with advanced progressive-rate springs. Wheels were fat Alpina 7-in (17.8-cm) alloys with chrome wheel-arch extensions to keep them legal. Black accent stripes distinguished the *Leichtgemetal* from the standard CS/CSi. 169 were built, all left-hand drive.

Although the CSL was originally fitted with the 2958cc carburettor version of the in-line six (giving 180bhp), a slight bore increase in August 1972 gave 3003cc which allowed it to slip into three-litre Group 2 competition. At the same time Bosch electronic injection replaced the twin Zenith carburettors and power rose to 200bhp, although brochures of the time quote a carburettor-fed 3003cc engine too. 539 were built.

The British specification RHD car was introduced in the UK in October 1972 and came with the "RHD City package" to appease drivers who wanted the lightweight racer cachet without the discomfort. Most of the excess weight previously stripped off the car was put

BMW 3.0CSL (1971–75)	
Engine	In-line six
Capacity	2985/3003/3153cc
Power	180–206bhp
Transmission	3/5-speed manual
Top speed	133–140mph (213–225kph)
No. built	1,095

back. British importers took 500 CSLs but prices were high – more than an Aston or Jensen – and not everybody liked the Scheel bucket seats, awkward to get into, or wanted easily-damaged alloy panels.

The 3.2-litre CSL – nicknamed Batmobile – was announced in August 1973. It was left-hand drive only and had a bigger 3.2-litre (actually 3153cc) 206bhp engine to homologate the 84mm

stroke used on the 3.5-litre works racing coupé. It was still badged three-litre. The same lightweight shell (initially available only in Polaris silver or Chamonix white with optional motorsport stripes) was used with alloy doors and bonnet, but, to take the weight and downforce of the rear wing, the bootlid was steel with a fitting for the spoiler. The spoiler (racing kit) was packed in the boot on cars sold in West

■ RIGHT *The interior featured special Scheel bucket seats, black trim and a sports steering wheel.*

■ FAR RIGHT *With firmer springs and dampers, the CSL had sure-footed, almost roll-free handling, though oversteer could be a problem in the wet.*

Germany, where such appendages were illegal. Daft as it looked, the wing was intrinsic to the coupés' success in the European Touring Car (ETC) series, clamping tail to road with massive aerodynamic downforce. It was created in a panic session in a Stuttgart wind tunnel after Jochen Neerspach and Martin Braungart of BMW Motorsport found a loophole in FIA rules that allowed "evolutionary improvements" for existing models. With the works CSL about to return to the ETC, they were looking for a way to eliminate aerodynamic lift at speeds over 124mph (199kph).

It worked. Works CSL coupés easily outpaced Capris first time out at the Nürburgring, cutting lap times by 15 seconds. To use the wing on the track it had be homologated on a production car, hence the Batmobile bits. These also

■ LEFT *The standard CSL lines up with the more radical "Batmobile". Note the spoilers, plastic bumpers and slightly lower stance of the later car.*

included a deep front spoiler, a roof hoop spoiler just above the rear window, a small lip spoiler on the edge of the bootlid and rubber "spitters" on the front wings. Manual steering and Bilstein gas-pressure shock absorbers

with three alternative levels of hardness meant the 3.2-litre CSL didn't need an anti-roll bar. The last CSLs, built in 1974-75, had minor differences such as a three-fin rear batwing and a driver's seat with an adjustable backrest.

■ OPPOSITE *Some CSLs had a deep chin spoiler but panels identical to all-steel CS coupes. "L" stood for lightweight.*

■ RIGHT *The road-going CSL was built to homologate racing coupés like this one for Group 2 Touring Car racing in the 1970s. It remained competitive long after the old-type coupés had gone out of production.*

BRISTOL

■ BRISTOL 401

The Bristol 401, announced in 1949, was only the second model built by the fledgling car builder whose 1946 400 looked much like the pre-war BMW on which it was based. It being a car built by a planemaker, where quality is a matter of life or death, there was no room for penny-pinching compromise in design or construction.

The 401's alloy body was but one example of high-minded extravagance permeating the car's design. Alloy panels, wrapped around small diameter tubes, were graded in thickness according to function, heavier on top of the wings, for instance, where mechanics would lean during servicing. Under the skin was a separate chassis, derived from the first Bristol, which continues in its essentials to this day.

The engine, a throaty straight six appropriated from BMW after the war as reparations, was a gem. Almost 100mph (160kph) from an 85bhp two-litre engine (pulling an opulently trimmed full four-seater) *was* something to write home about in the late 1940s – the likes of Bentley and Jaguar needed double the capacity to do the same job – and to row

■ BELOW LEFT *The steering-wheel was similar to the one used in Bristol aircraft.*

BRISTOL 401 (1949-1953)	
Engine	Straight six
Capacity	1971cc
Power	85-100bhp
Transmission	4-speed manual
Top speed	97mph (155kph)
No. built	650

it along with that beautifully slick four-speed gearbox was a constant delight.

Outright speed, however, was not what this car was all about. Fine handling, especially in the days before motorways, was even more important, and the 401 was well blessed with light precision steering and a general feeling of poised good manners that made the marque many lifelong friends.

The memorable "Aerodyne" body shape, inspired by Touring with its elegant teardrop tail and smooth

contours, was honed on Bristol's two-mile-long Filton runway and was truly aerodynamic for the time. In tests carried out at the MIRAS wind tunnel 20 years after the 401's demise, only four modern cars were found to be more aerodynamic. Low levels of wind noise even at high speed were one side benefit from this attention to aerodynamic detail; another was fuel economy: up to 25 miles (40km) to every gallon of the filthy poor petrol that was still all you could get in 1949.

■ FAR LEFT *The shape of the 401/403 was evolved in streamlining experiments and allowed this heavy car a top speed of 100mph (160kph).*

■ NEAR LEFT *The 404 was a special short-chassis model with just two seats. Although few were made, it is among the most sought-after of the Bristols today.*

■ RIGHT *A Bristol 407 with a 411 Series II. The size of the V-eight engine, always from Chrysler, went up from 5.4 to 6.2 litres.*

■ BELOW *From the Series SIII onwards, the 411 had this better-looking full-width grille. Performance was up to 140mph (225kph), with automatic transmission.*

■ BRISTOL V8s 407–411

The 1961 407, with its Canadian-built Chrysler 5.2-litre engine, was the first V8 Bristol, instantly catapulting the big four-seater into the 130mph (209kph) class with standing quarter-mile times equal to the contemporary two-plus-two Ferrari. Gone was the delicate two-litre six, and the four-speed Bristol gearbox was replaced by a Chrysler Torqueflite

■ LEFT *The 410 shown here was an intermediate model with recessed headlamps and chrome strips on its flanks.*

■ BELOW *The interiors were always finished to a high standard.*

automatic with flashy push-button selection and seamless gearchanges. Though the classic Bristol chassis remained, the front suspension was new, coils supplanting the transverse leaf. Gone too was that lovely rack-and-pinion steering, replaced by a Marles worm-type unit which, together with the sheer weight of the engine, conspired to make the 407 less nimble than its thoroughbred predecessors.

The cars were improved through the 1960s. The 408 had the same 5.2 Chrysler engine but new front-end styling and select-a-ride dampers. The 409, from 1965 on, had rounded corners on the grille, power steering and better brakes. The 410 of 1968 had smaller wheels, floor-shift for automatic gearbox and twin-circuit brakes.

The 1969 411 had lower ride-height with clipped fins, less brightwork and a 6.2-litre engine. Series 2 (1970) had

auto self-levelling, Series 3 (1972) entirely new front-end styling with twin 7-in (17.8cm) lights. Series 4 (1973) had a 6.6-litre engine, giving 330bhp. Series 5 411 (1975) had a black grille, stiffer chassis and improved cooling. 411s could pull 140mph (225kph).

All offered drawing-room luxury with muscular performance. Later versions' superb power steering made them remarkably agile for size. The ride was excellent, build quality superb. The

BRISTOL 411 (1970–76)	
Engine	V-eight
Capacity	6277cc
Power	335bhp @ 5200rpm
Transmission	3-speed auto
Top speed	140mph (225kph)
No. built	600

relatively narrow build meant that, in town, drivers could thread through gaps that would stop most luxury cars and all from a commanding driving position in big, armchair seats.

That the little-known Bristol marque survived into the 90s is an achievement itself. Rivals such as Aston and Jensen faced liquidation and disaster in the 70s and 80s as Bristol plodded on by staying small (boss Tony Crook has never planned to make more than 150 cars a year) and satisfying a small, loyal clientele.

BUICK

■ **BUICK RIVIERA**

The Riviera was a kind of American Bentley Continental. Conceived as Buick's answer to the best-selling Ford Thunderbird, but eschewing the chrome and glitz of its contemporaries, the Riviera was blessed with some of the finest styling to come out of Detroit in

■ ABOVE *The Riviera was the most beautiful Buick of the 1960s, an all-American Grand Tourer.*

■ LEFT *Early cars had a 6.5-litre engine, but this later went up to seven litres, giving a top speed of 130mph (209kph).*

BUICK RIVIERA (1963–65)	
Engine	V-eight
Capacity	6572cc
Power	325bhp
Transmission	2-speed automatic
Top speed	130mph (209kph)
No. built	112,244

the 60s. It was swoopy yet restrained and had presence and gravitas where Cadillacs and Chrysler Imperials were merely big. In a word, it had class.

Under the bonnet was the inevitable V-eight engine, initially a 6.5-litre, later

with 7.0 litres and anything up to 365bhp. Even with the obligatory two-speed automatic gearbox, this huge five-seater was good for 130mph (209kph), although handling was strictly conventional on the separate chassis

and the brakes were never really up to the job, quickly succumbing to the dreaded fade at high speed. Inside, the Riviera driver wanted for nothing, with electric windows and power steering as part of the package and a dashboard that

■ LEFT *In the 1950s Buick was known for its solid, family cars: this is a 1956 Roadmaster.*

■ ABOVE *The Riviera's clean profile was a breath of fresh air after the fins and chrome of its contemporaries.*

■ RIGHT *Later cars had clamshell headlights but, as ever, the original was best.*

looked distinctly tasteful by Detroit standards.

Inevitably, in a land of built-in obsolescence, Buick fiddled with the Riviera's classic styling – most memorably the clamshell-covered lights – and after 1965 the car lost something of its unique personality, sharing its underpinnings and structure with the Cadillac Eldorado. The model redeemed itself in the early 70s with the "boat-tail" version but lost all credibility from 1973 onwards as Detroit's big cars began to lose their way.

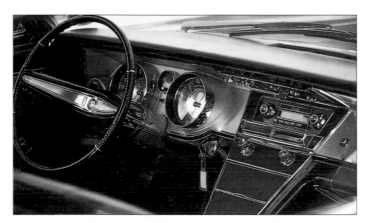

■ ABOVE *Under the skin the Riviera was conventional, with a live rear axle and hardly adequate drum brakes.*

■ LEFT *Inside the Riviera had a European flavour with circular dials and a floor-mounted gear-shift.*

OTHER MAKES

■ BERKELEY

The Berkeley was built between 1956 and 1961 by Charles Panter's firm of caravan manufacturers in Biggleswade, Bedfordshire. It was designed by Laurie Bond, who had a particular affection for front-wheel-drive microcars. Technically clever, the cars never really caught on, unsurprisingly, perhaps, given the 1958 advent of the Austin-Healey Sprite. A Ford-based car, the Bandit, never made it to production.

■ BOND

Sharp's Commercials Ltd of Preston, Lancashire, produced Laurie Bond's eccentric three-wheeler Minicar from 1948 to as late as 1966. In 1966, the company diversified into four-wheeler GT coupés based on the Triumph Herald range. In 1969, it was bought out by Reliant, who closed the Preston works and transferred production to its Tamworth factory, Staffordshire, where the only Bond car made was the Bug, an odd sporting three-wheeler.

CADILLAC

■ CADILLAC ELDORADO BROUGHAM

The 1957 Cadillac Eldorado Brougham was a General Motors dream car brought to life. The most prestigious Cadillac out of Detroit since the V-16 17 years earlier, it started life at the 1954 Motorama as the Park Avenue, a four-door town sedan which looked like, but wasn't, a hardtop. It was a minor hit, and in May 1954 Harley Earl, all-powerful GM design supremo, began holding discreet meetings about a super Eldorado, a production version of the Park Avenue for 1956.

The 1955 Motorama Cadillac was the prototype Eldorado Brougham. Curvacious, almost tasteful for this gaudy period, it had pillarless clap-hands doors, restrained knife-edged fins

CADILLAC ELDORADO BROUGHAM (1957–58)	
Engine	V-eight
Capacity	6384cc
Power	325bhp
Transmission	3-speed automatic
Top speed	118mph (189kph)
No. built	704

■ RIGHT *From the rear the fins were reasonably restrained. When it appeared in 1957, the Eldorado Brougham was the most expensive and exclusive Cadillac yet built.*

and a 90-degree wraparound on the front screen. Its stainless-steel roof, narrow white sidewalls and twin headlights were industry firsts. It sat on a new X-frame chassis with air suspension. Steel domes were pressurised by a small compressor regulated by levelling valves. A 6.3-litre 325bhp V-eight engine was hitched to GM's Hydramatic transmission as standard.

The Brougham had power steering, brakes, seats and windows and dripped with electric baubles: automatic headlamp dipper, cruise control, signal-seeking radio, electric aerial and door locks, a drum-type electric clock and an automatic bootlid opener. Other ultra-luxuries included polarized sun visors, magnetized drinks tumblers in the glove box, cigarette and tissue dispensers, special lipstick and cologne, ladies' compact and powder puff, mirror and matching notebook and comb and an Arpege atomizer with Lanvin perfume. The buyer could choose from 44 trim combinations and between karakul and lambskin carpeting.

The Broughton sold for a fraction of building cost and soon the accountants pulled the plug. It survived two years.

■ FAR LEFT *The Brougham's luxury touches ranged from polarized sun visors to electric seat adjustment – with memory.*

■ LEFT *Twin headlights were still a novelty in the mid-1950s – another industry first on the Brougham.*

■ OPPOSITE *The Brougham had restrained styling for its period, with its clap-hands doors and pillarless roof of brushed aluminium.*

■ LEFT *The rocket-inspired fins on the 1959 Cadillacs were the biggest in the industry and were never surpassed. Cadillac had begun the craze for fins in the late 1940s.*

■ BELOW *The tail lights were shaped like after-burners. The grille across the rear was purely decorative.*

■ CADILLAC ELDORADO BIARRITZ

The American obsession with the tail fin reached its zenith in 1959 and nobody did it bigger, or better, than Cadillac, makers of Detroit's premier luxury motorcar. The 1959 Cadillacs had the biggest fins in the industry, an outrageous 42 inches in height. Their jet-age imagery was accentuated by a pair of bullet-shaped turn and stop lights. Front-end styling was equally distinctive, with twin headlights and double-decker grilles across the board. 20ft long, 6ft wide and scaling two tons in weight the 1959 car came as a two-door coupé de ville, a pillarless four-door hardtop or as an even bigger Fleetwood 75 formal limousine. There was also a high-spec Fleetwood version of the stock four-door saloon. All were based on a simple perimeter frame chassis with drum brakes all round. Best remembered is the Eldorado Biarritz convertible, which had a more powerful 345bhp version of Cadillac's famous 6.3-litre V-eight engine.

All these six-seater land yachts, the ultimate in four-wheeled glamour, came

CADILLAC ELDORADO BIARRITZ (1959)	
Engine	V-eight
Capacity	6384cc
Power	345bhp
Transmission	3-speed auto
Top speed	115mph (185kph)
No. built	11,130

fully equipped with power-operated seat adjustment, electric boot opening and even automatic headlamp dipping over and above the obligatory power steering,

automatic transmission, power hood in the case of the Biarritz, and electric windows. Air-bag suspension was one of the few optional extras on the Biarritz, which cost three times the cheapest Chevrolet that year. It was fast in a straight line at 115mph (185kph) but sheer weight and soggy springs gave it handling qualities comparable with a boat. Fuel consumption was in the 8mpg range, but economy was not then an issue in a country where this resource was still cheap.

Nearly four decades on, none of that matters. The 1959 Cadillac has passed into legend, symbolizing an era when the world's most powerful nation was at its most confident.

■ LEFT *The Sedan version of 1959 was not as well balanced as the two-door car, and the handling was awful.*

■ ABOVE *The wild styling of the 1959 Cadillacs was always irresistible to customizers.*

CHEVROLET

■ CHEVROLET STINGRAY

Although the first of the Chevrolet Corvette sportscars were produced in 1953, the marque didn't reach maturity until 1962 and the introduction of the Stingray. Like its ancestors, the new car had a fibreglass body, but the styling, was all new, a mixture of muscular haunches and chisel-edged tension that gave it a unique appeal. The coupé version lost its split rear window after the first year owing to customer resistance: ironically these 1963 cars are now the most collectable Corvettes of all. The convertible looked good with its hood either up or down, the top stowing neatly under a lid. Underneath, the separate chassis remained, but the Corvette was unusual for an American car in having independent rear suspension. Its cheap but effective system used the drive shaft as the upper link, with a simple steel rod as the lower link and a transverse leaf spring.

A range of small-block 5.4 V-eight

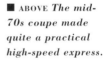

■ ABOVE *The mid-70s coupe made quite a practical high-speed express.*

■ LEFT *The Stingray's shape was launched in 1967 and ran through until 1984. It was inspired by the Mako-shark dream car.*

■ RIGHT *1956-62 Corvettes only came with V-eight engines, giving up to 360bhp in fuel-injected form. Manual or automatic transmissions were available, the body was glassfibre.*

engines were offered, from a base model giving 250bhp to a 300bhp unit with a bigger carburettor and the 340bhp L76 with solid tappets and a higher 11.25:1 compression ratio. The latter was available with the famous Rochester fuel injection, unleashing a further 20bhp. The performance of the relatively light

■ ABOVE *The 1963–67 Stingray, seen here as a big-block convertible, was perhaps the best-looking of the Corvettes.*

■ LEFT *The engine was Chevrolet's famous small block of 5359cc. It was strong, torquey and very tunable.*

■ RIGHT *The rare T-top Targa roof model that replaced the full convertible. It was outlawed in America by federal crash protection regulations.*

■ BELOW *The mid-60s Stingray interior shows very complete instrumentation. The twin-cowled effect of the dashboard was inspired by jet-fighter planes.*

Corvette was electrifying, with 0–60 (96) in 5.6 seconds. Transmissions were either three-speed manual (rarely specified), two-speed auto or, more usually, four-speed manual.

Each year of production brought minor cosmetic and technical changes, but the big news for the 1965 model was the big-block 396cu in V-eight engine, packing a colossal 425bhp and 415lb/ft (565.5 N m) of torque at 4000rpm. Now sporting four-wheel disc brakes to keep the huge performance in check, the engine went up to a full seven litres (427cu in) and in 1966 could be had with hydraulic tappets (lifters in American parlance), lower-compression L36 form with a "soft" 390bhp or a solid-lifter, high-compression L72 with 425bhp. The small-block cars, slower but better balanced than the seven-litre machines, remained in production though the fuel-injection version faded away as demand for the big-block took over.

The last year for Stingray was 1967. It was offered with 300 and 350bhp small blocks and big blocks ranging in output from 390 to 435bhp depending on carburation and compression ratio.

For racers, there was the L88 engine, giving 560bhp on 103 octane petrol. With its sky-high 12.5:1 compression ratio, alloy heads and fancy forged

CHEVROLET CORVETTE STINGRAY (1963–67)	
Engine	V-eight
Capacity	5356–7000cc
Power	250–560bhp
Transmission	3/4-speed manual 2-speed auto
Top speed	118–145mph (189–233kph)
No. built	45,456 small block 72,418 big block

crank, this car was virtually unusable on the road anyway. The catalogues rated it at "only" 430bhp to keep GM bosses, safety legislators and unworthy owners at bay. For the 1968 model year the new "Coke bottle" Stingray was announced, a worthy successor that, somehow, never recaptured the sporting spirit of the 1963–67 Stingrays.

■ ABOVE *This is how the Corvette looked from 1984, although many of the mechanical items were carried over. The new body was still glassfibre: this was the only American production car apart from the Studebaker Avanti to use it.*

■ BELOW *Stiff suspension meant that the handling of later Corvettes was roll-free but the ride was harsh. Many had power steering and automatic transmission.*

CHEVROLET

■ LEFT *The original Corvair with its clean styling influenced the Hillman Imp and NSU Prinz.*

■ CHEVROLET CORVAIR

The Chevrolet Corvair, launched in 1959 as a 1960 model, was the response of General Motor (GM) to the influx of low-priced European economy cars into the North American market in the late 50s and early 60s. In style and engineering it was refreshingly different from the general run of technically very conservative American cars, which makes it doubly disappointing that it fell

■ RIGHT *The 1964 restyle made the car look more conventional.*

■ FAR RIGHT *The style was copied for the late 60s Vauxhall Victor.*

so disastrously foul of public opinion and safety hysteria. The controversy surrounding the handling of the early Corvairs inspired consumer rights and safety campaigner Ralph Nader to write a book called *Unsafe at Any Speed*. It was a best seller and began a new era of

government regulations and safety legislation that continues to this day.

With its rear-mounted, air-cooled, flat-six engine and fully independent suspension, the Corvair was far removed from the general run of American cars and its "compact" rivals from Ford and

Chrysler which were really just scaled-down large cars. By European standards, of course, it wasn't compact, with similar dimensions to cars like Ford of Britain's flagship Zephyr.

Enthusiasts loved the car's European flavour, but ordinary buyers weren't so

■ LEFT *The Monza was a sporty coupé with a more powerful version of the flat-six engine.*

■ ABOVE *Though the Corvair was marketed as a compact in Britain, it was actually the size of a Ford Zephyr.*

■ BELOW *The original Corvair saloon. The car earned bad publicity for its handling.*

■ ABOVE *The power output of the first Corvairs was just 80bhp for a top speed of 87mph (139kph).*

■ BELOW *The Monza Turbo was one of the first turbocharged production cars, capable of over 100mph (160kph).*

sure and the Corvair's more conventional rivals comfortably outsold it. It took the introduction of the little Monza coupé with its punchier engine for the Corvair to find its niche in the market as a compact sporty car. Its fortunes took another turn for the better when a convertible version was launched in 1962. There was even a turbocharged version, one of the first on a production car.

Sadly the honeymoon wasn't to last. Bad publicity from Nader's book had given the car a reputation for wayward handling it didn't altogether deserve, and when Ford introduced the Mustang in 1964 the Corvair didn't stand a chance. Buyers gravitated to the Mustang's more conventional, safer engineering and equally sporty image. The Pony car era had begun and the

Corvair was left behind. GM tried a rescue with a restyle for 1964, curing the supposedly oversteer-biased handling with improved rear suspension. But the damage was done. Sales never recovered, though Chevrolet kept the

Corvair in its line-up until 1969.

Although the Corvair is little known in Europe, it has a thriving owners' club in North America. For reasons Chevrolet would probably rather forget, it is an important car in US motoring history.

■ LEFT *Chevrolet ditched the Corvair in 1969. The main reasons for its demise were bad publicity and the arrival of the Mustang.*

CHEVROLET CORVAIR (1959–69)	
Engine	Aircooled flat six
Capacity	2377/2684cc
Power	80–180bhp
Transmission	3/4-speed manual 2-speed auto
Top speed	87–105mph (139–169kph)
No. built	1,271,089

CISITALIA

■ CISITALIA 202

Cisitalia was founded in 1946 by racing driver and businessman Piero Dusio. His first project, for which he called on the services of Fiat engineers Giacosa and Savonuzzi, was a single-seater racing car with Topolino front suspension and the four-cylinder engine from the Balilla. This was followed in 1948 by the 202 coupé using essentially the same ingredients but with a memorable full-width body on a round-tube frame by Pininfarina. This was a seminal moment in post-war

■ LEFT *The Cisitalia 202 Coupé was a landmark in styling, having no separate mudguards or free-standing lights.*

■ BELOW *One would never guess that this car was introduced in 1948. Only the split screen dates it.*

■ ABOVE *The interior was typically severe, with just the bare minimum of instruments.*

■ ABOVE *Flip-out door handles were a favourite Pininfarina touch.*

■ ABOVE *Pininfarina had begun his ideas on the Maserati AG chassis, and in many ways the Lancia Aurelia was a continuation of this theme.*

■ RIGHT *The clean lines of the Cisitalia were copied on cars as diverse as the Simca 8 and Ferrari 166 Inter.*

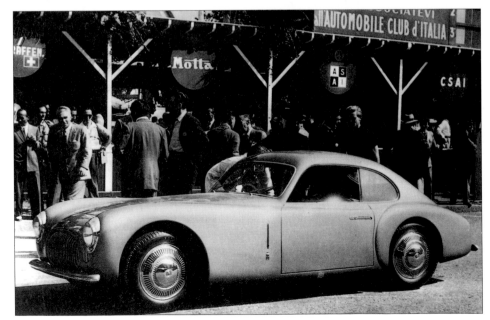

■ RIGHT *Touring made this open Barchetta version not unlike the Ferrari 166 Barchetta of the period.*

■ BELOW *The four-cylinder engine was based on a Fiat design and gave upwards of 50bhp.*

■ BELOW *On just 1100cc the Cisitalia could manage 105mph (168kph) with the most highly tuned road engine.*

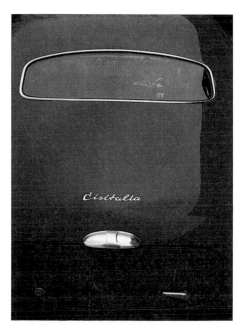

■ ABOVE *Just 485 Cisitalias were built, with bodies by Vignale and Frua as well as Pininfarina.*

styling, the coupé having its bonnet lower than the front wings, headlights blended into the wings (rather than free standing) and smoothly sweeping, simple lines. Farina explored these themes on other chassis but never again to such remarkable effect. The New York Museum of Modern Art has, since 1951, kept a Farina-bodied Cisitalia as an example of "sculpture in movement". Vignale, Frua and Stabilmenti Farina, as well as Pininfarina again, designed convertible variants. Thanks to slippery aerodynamics, the Cisitalia could achieve 102mph (164kph) on just 50bhp from a tweaked Fiat 1100 engine. Competition-tuned variants had up to 120mph (193kph) capability.

As early as 1949, Cisitalia was facing bankruptcy thanks to overambitious

plans for a Porsche-designed Grand Prix car. Dusio upped sticks to Argentina, but the 202 continued in production until 1952.

The marque survived until 1965 under the control of Dusio's creditors but was never to regain the eminence it achieved with the classic 202 coupé. Today these cars are highly sought after.

CISITALIA 202 COUPÉ (1948–52)	
Engine	In-line four
Capacity	1089cc
Power	50 bhp
Transmission	4-speed manual
Top speed	105mph (168kph)
No. built	485

CITROËN

■ LEFT *The Traction-avant in its rare long-wheelbase form. A few were built as "hatchbacks" and called Commerciale.*

■ BELOW *The pre-war cabriolet used a long- or short-wheelbase chassis and came with four- or six-cylinder power.*

■ CITROËN LIGHT 15

The Citroën Light 15, or *Traction-avant* to its many admirers, is a towering reference point in the history of the motorcar, pioneering front-wheel drive on a mass-produced family saloon. It had a three-speed gearbox mounted ahead of the engine in the nose of the car, and the drive went through CV-jointed drive shafts to torsion-bar-suspended front wheels; this was cutting-edge technology in those days. By the standards of 1934, the roadholding of the *Traction-avant* was almost unbelievably good, albeit at the expense of heavy steering.

Sadly, the high development costs sent a penniless André Citroën to an early grave and his company into the arms of

■ BELOW LEFT *The cabriolet had a windcreen that folded flat, and there is a dicky seat in that long, flowing tail.*

■ BELOW RIGHT *Tractions were built for some years in Britain. The British market model had a wooden facia and disc wheels.*

CITROËN LIGHT 15/BIG 15 & 6 (1934–55)	
Engine	In-line 4/6-cylinder
Capacity	1911/2866cc
Power	46–80bhp
Transmission	3-speed manual
Top speed	70–85mph (112–137kph)
No. built	759,123/47,670

■ BELOW *The shape of the Traction saloon is unmistakable. With its front-drive roadholding it was much favoured by the French police – and criminals.*

■ LEFT *Early Tractions had a three-bearing wet-liner engine and three-speed all-synchro gearbox. Not much urge on 32bhp.*

■ BELOW *With the 1.9-litre OHV engine the Traction would do around 75mph (120kph). All-round independent springing by torsion bars gave the car an excellent ride.*

■ ABOVE *The big six-cylinder Traction was fast in a straight line but suffered from heavy steering. A few had an early version of the hydraulic rear suspension later used on the DS.*

Michelin, but the Light 15 and its many derivatives went on to success, selling strongly for 23 years. Front-wheel drive wasn't the whole story. The Light 15's unitary construction was still a rarity in 1934 and the car was both roomy and comfortable to ride in, with torsion-bar independent suspension at the rear too. Top speed with the 45bhp 1911cc four-cylinder engine was 70mph (112kph).

There were many variations on this enduring theme. The Big 15 had an extra seven inches (17.8cm) added to its wheelbase. The *Commerciale* had an early form of rear hatchback. Big families could opt for the eight-seater *Familiale*. For sporty drivers there were rakish coupés and cabriolet models. Top of the range from 1938 was the six-cylinder, 2866cc 15CV, or Big 6, its 77bhp engine pushing the top speed to a

respectable 85mph (137kph). Citroën pioneered its hydropneumatic suspensions on the rare 6H version of this model which already featured their self-levelling system on rear wheels only. Styling changed little over the years, but the post-1953 *Traction* has a distinctive projecting boot. From 1938 to 1940 (and, after the Second World War, between 1948 and 1955) these Citroëns were built in significant quantities in the UK. A Slough-built car is recognizable by its wooden dash, leather trim and 12-volt electrics.

It was years before rivals began to catch up with standards set by the Light 15. Only when Citroën had another world-beater, the DS of 1955, did it finally feel obliged to let the *Traction* die. Many examples survive and this stylish, groundbreaking car has a cult following.

CITROËN

■ CITROËN DS

Never before has a single model embraced so many innovations as the Citroën DS, launched in Paris in 1955. Chief among these was the suspension: eschewing conventional springs, Citroën engineers suspended their new saloon on hydraulic self-levelling hydropneumatic struts, with a unique adjustable ride-height facility that meant the DS could raise itself to negotiate rough terrain. At rest, ignition off, it gradually sank until it sat squat to the floor. The same engine powered a high-pressure hydraulic central nervous system which controlled ultra-sharp

CITROËN DS (1955–75)	
Engine	4-cylinder
Capacity	1911/1985/2175/2347cc
Power	63/84/109/115/141bhp
Transmission	4/5-speed manual and semi-auto
Top speed	84–117mph (135–188kph)
No. built	1,455,746

■ ABOVE *The trend-setting DS was a commonly seen family car in France. This is the later version, with four headlights in its shark-nose front. The inner pair turned with the steering so that the car could "see" around corners.*

power steering, powerful four-wheel disc brakes (in board up-front) and the clutchless hydraulic gearchange.

Clothed in a beautiful and futuristic windcheating five-seater body (with detachable panels) that made its contemporaries look distinctly stale, the DS was a decade, maybe two, ahead of the game and a true show stopper. With front-wheel drive (as all Citroëns had been since the equally revolutionary Light 15), its handling and stability were almost as sensational as its magic-carpet ride. Only its elderly engine let it down, a clattery 1934 design from the old *Traction-avant* which was unworthy

■ ABOVE *The high-geared DS was perfect for relaxed long-distance cruising. Its suspension ironed out anything that France's poorly surfaced roads could throw at it.*

■ RIGHT *The body panels, bolted on, could be removed quickly, making accident damage easy to repair.*

DS 19 or 21 PRESTIGE

■ ABOVE *The interior of the DS had futuristic styling to match the exterior and plenty of room too. Cut-price ID models, without power steering, were much loved by French taxi drivers.*

■ LEFT *The main body styles were saloon, estate and flagship convertible, though various French coachbuilders like Chapron built coupes and amazing stretched limousines.*

■ BELOW *The gearchange – manual or semi-automatic – was on the steering column. The single-spoke wheel gave a better view of the instruments. Seats were soft and cosseting.*

of such an advanced machine. From the mid-1960s there was a more modern two-litre four-cylinder engine, which was better, but somehow the DS never quite got the kind of smooth, unstressed motor it deserved.

Early reliability problems associated with suspension were soon forgotten and the DS spawned a whole raft of derivatives during the 1950s and 60s. Downgraded models such as the ID19 and, later, the D super, with fewer power-assisted systems and less bhp, appealed to thousands of Paris cabbies; the cavernous Safari Estate cars were the ultimate in family haulers; while the beautiful DS *décapotable* convertibles were expensive and exclusive. High-spec prestige models and the last-of-the line 2.3-litre DS23 cars with five speeds and fuel injection further broadened the appeal in the face of younger rivals. For the true DS connoisseur, meanwhile, there were special coachbuilt coupés by the likes of Henri Chapron, not to mention impressive stretched presidential cars.

The shark-like shape of the basic DS saloon changed little in 20 years – the twin swivelling lights arrived in 1965 – and even when it was finally replaced by

the CX in 1975, the competition were only just beginning to catch up with its degree of refinement. Many have now raised the styling of the DS to the level of automotive art – how many other cars have inspired their own art gallery exhibition? Good examples untainted by rust are highly prized.

■ LEFT *With injection and the biggest 2.3-litre engine, the last-of-the-line DS was capable of almost 120mph (193kph). Ride comfort was its best quality.*

CITROËN

■ BELOW *It is hard to believe that the futuristic SM dates from 1970. This car wears rare Cabron fibre sports wheels.*

■ CITROËN SM

In the late 1960s, Citroën acquired a controlling interest in the Italian sportscar manufacturer Maserati. First fruit of this marriage was the big Citroën SM of 1970, a prestige GT car utilizing the best from both companies. Power came from a smaller V-six version of Maserati's long-lived quad-cam V-eight engine. At 2.7 litres, it stayed just the right side of the punitive French tax laws that came down heavily on engines over 2.8 litres. Like the DS, the SM had front-wheel drive, with the gearbox/transaxle unit slung out ahead of the compact engine. Its 170bhp through the front wheels was handled by Citroën's now well-tried

hydropneumatic self-levelling suspension, interconnected with the four-wheel disc brakes (in-board up front) and ultra-quick power steering.

Fast and refined, with excellent handling, once a sensitive touch with the steering and brakes had been learnt, the SM was a consummate long-distance GT, superbly stable at speed and with the magic-carpet ride familiar to DS owners.

It was the shape, though, that captured enthusiasts' hearts: crafted inside Citroën, it was dramatic and purposeful with a broad nose fully

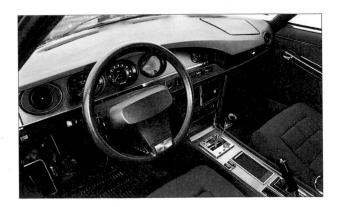

■ ABOVE *The SM was a four-seater with a practical hatchback. 12,920 were built before production stopped in 1974.*

■ LEFT *The big, sweeping dashboard was as futuristic as the body. Note the single-spoke wheel.*

CITROËN SM (1970–75)	
Engine	V-six
Capacity	2670cc/2965cc
Power	170–180bhp
Transmission	5-speed manual 3-speed auto
Top speed	140mph (225kph)
No. built	12,920

■ BELOW *The V-six engine was a Maserati unit shared with the Bora. The five-speed gearbox sits ahead of it.*

■ ABOVE *The SM's lights were faired in behind a glass cover on European models: in America they had to be open.*

■ ABOVE *The SM's profile is still stunning today and, like the DS, is very aerodynamic for a 70s car.*

■ LEFT *The five-speed manual SM could do 140mph (225kph), though its weight hampered hot-rod acceleration times. Unfussed high-speed cruising was the car's greatest strength.*

flared in glass and a tapering tail that was as slippery as it looked. It was a four-seater, just, with a futuristic cabin that matched the body.

Sales were initially strong as French enthusiasts flocked to buy their first high-class GT car since the death of the Facel Vega. The love affair was to be short-lived. The fuel crisis hit in 1973, making big 18mpg supercars somewhat unfashionable.

Citroën improved the car with injection, a bigger three-litre version and an automatic option, but it was to little avail. Production ground to a halt in 1975, just short of 13,000 cars down the line.

OTHER MAKES

■ CONNAUGHT
The brainchild of Rodney Clarke and Mike Oliver of Bugatti specialists Continental Cars, the British firm Connaught began as a manufacturer of road and racing sportscars. As racing became ever more important, the Lea-Francis-engined Type A F2 car evolved into the streamlined Type B. In 1955 an unstreamlined Type B became the first British car to win a Grand Prix since 1924; two years later Connaught withdrew from race-car manufacturing. Their only road car was the Lea-Francis-engined L2 of 1949–51.

■ COSTIN
Building his own car was a bold move by Frank Costin. The Amigo, with its wooden monocoque, was doomed to failure: it cost far too much money when it finally came on sale in Britain in 1972. The eight cars, using Vauxhall Victor engines, were built at Little Staughton, Bedfordshire, backed by Paul Pycroft. Claimed top speed was 134mph (214kph) on two litres.

DAIMLER

■ DAIMLER SP250 "DART"

The SP250 "Dart" was something completely new for Daimler, a company with no tradition of sportscars. The decision to build it came after a change of management in the late 1950s: Daimler was in trouble and the top brass thought a new sportscar would be a fine way to woo American buyers, just as

■ LEFT *The SP250 "Dart" was a complete departure for Daimler: previously its one and only sporty car had been the Conquest Roadster of the mid-50s, which had much less performance.*

■ BELOW LEFT *The body of the Dart was moulded in glassfibre and lacked rigidity: doors on early cars could fly open on bumpy corners.*

Jaguar, Triumph and MG had done before them. Using a chassis and suspension layout hastily copied from the Triumph TR3, Daimler took the then radical step of adding a glassfibre body, a gawky be-finned affair with a guppy-like grille and pop-eyed lights that found few friends.

Its major redeeming feature was its engine, a 2548cc V-eight producing a sweet 140bhp. Designed by Daimler's managing director Edward Turner – famed for his Triumph motorcycle engines – this smooth, torquey free-revving engine with its hemispherical combustion chambers and twin SU carburettors could power the unlovely

■ ABOVE *A rear shot of the SP250 Dart emphasises its then fashionable, but quickly dating, fins. The car's huge steering wheel is evident in this shot too.*

■ LEFT *Styling was done in-house by Daimler and was not deemed a success at the time, but almost 40 years later it seems full of period character.*

■ BELOW *The narrow interior featured a full set of gauges, an outsize steering wheel and a stubby four-speed gear-lever, but few creature comforts.*

but fairly light SP250 to 125mph (201kph). It's acceleration, 0–60 (96) in 9.5 seconds, was not to be sniffed at either, yet the excellence of the performance and the fine, throaty V-eight seemed somehow at odds with the amateurish, hastily designed body and chassis. The critics said as much, but as a niche filler between the cheaper TR and MGs and Jaguar's big XK150, the Daimler SP250 did make a certain amount of sense, especially as it would do a regular 25mpg. Four-wheel Dunlop disc brakes meant that it stopped well too, but its handling never earned top ranking as the steering was heavy, the chassis somewhat whippy: early examples (up to 1961) would pop their doors open alarmingly on rough roads. "B" specification SP250s – the Dart name had to be dropped because Dodge held the patent – had a stiffer chassis

and bumpers as standard, while "C" cars had a few extra luxury touches.

The fate of the SP250 was sealed as early as 1960 when Jaguar took over the ailing Daimler concern to boost its production capacity. Sir William Lyons never liked the Dart, because the styling offended him, but also because it would have been seen as low-level competition for the E-Type. Jaguar made a half-hearted attempt to restyle the car, but it was never really on and Lyons pulled the plug with no regrets in 1964. He was bright enough to see the potential in the SP250's excellent engine, however, and since 1962 had been offering it in a highly successful Daimlerized version of the MkII called the 2½-litre V-eight.

Today the many flaws of the unhappy Daimler SP250 are seen as endearing and characterful, and survivors are highly prized.

■ ABOVE *Priced between the MGA and Jaguar XKs, the Daimler filled a niche in the market but sales were slow – just 2,644 cars between 1959 and 1964.*

DAIMLER SP250 "DART" (1959–64)	
Engine	V-eight
Capacity	2548cc
Power	140bhp
Transmission	4-speed manual 3-speed auto
Top speed	125mph (201kph)
No. built	2644

■ BELOW LEFT *The Daimler's greatest asset was its smooth and flexible V-eight engine designed by Edward Turner.*

■ BELOW RIGHT *Jaguar boss Sir William Lyons had no time for the awkwardly styled SP250 and pulled the plug on it in 1964.*

DAIMLER

■ DAIMLER MAJESTIC MAJOR

The Daimler Majestic Major was one of the most intriguing – and unlikely – high -performance saloons of the early 60s. By fitting a brand-new hemi-head 4.7 litre V-eight (an enlarged version of the unit found in the 2.5 litre Dart) into its biggest executive saloon, Daimler created a 120mph (193kph) hot-rod limousine that was quicker than the contemporary Jaguars – an embarrassing situation given the Jaguar takeover of Daimler in 1960 – and had astonishing acceleration: 0-60 took just 9.7 seconds.

Despite its traditional separate chassis and tall, dignified body, the Majestic Major had good manners to match its performance and was well reviewed in the press.

The Majestic Major was good value too, with automatic transmission, power steering and disc brakes as standard. Busy managing directors could lounge in leather-lined comfort as they were driven around in the Majestic Major, which had an appropriately huge boot too.

For its carriage trade customers there was a limousine version of the Majestic

■ ABOVE *From the front this is unmistakably a Daimler. In its stretched, long-wheelbase form the car was a favourite with funeral directors.*

■ ABOVE *The styling of the Majestic was by the same man who gave the English the FX4 taxi-cab. Spot the resemblance?*

■ FAR LEFT *The Majestic limousine was replaced by the Jaguar MkX-based DS420 Daimler limousine, here in very rare landaulette form.*

■ NEAR LEFT *The Majestic Major's fine, high-revving 4.5-litre 220bhp V-eight engine.*

Major called DR450, with a stretched chassis to accommodate extra occasional seats. It was a little heavier but had scarcely less performance – it was one of the quickest ways of getting to the cemetery.

So impressive was the Daimler's engine that Jaguar briefly toyed with the idea of fitting it to a Daimlerized version of the big MkX. The resulting V-eight prototype was canned when it proved embarrassingly faster than the Jaguar production model.

Production of the Majestic Major was always small scale, so sales were low. Production finished, after 1,180 cars and 864 limousines were built, in 1968. From then on, all Daimlers were destined to be badge-engineered Jaguars.

DAIMLER MAJESTIC MAJOR	
Engine	V-eight
Capacity	4561cc
Power	220bhp
Transmission	3 speed auto
Top speed	122mph (194kph)
0-60	9.7 secs
No. built	1180 (plus 864 DR450 limousines)

■ LEFT *Just 1,180 Majestic Majors were built in a 10-year production run. The car's performance embarrassed the Jaguar MkX.*

■ BELOW *The DS420 again, here in early standard-bodied limousine form. They were the last cars to use the famous Jaguar XK engine.*

■ FAR LEFT *The Majestic Major had a traditional dashboard with all the instruments grouped in the centre. Power steering was standard.*

■ LEFT *There was room for the tired executive to stretch out in the back on generous leather seats.*

DATSUN

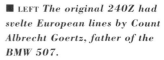

■ LEFT *The original 240Z had svelte European lines by Count Albrecht Goertz, father of the BMW 507.*

■ DATSUN 240Z

In the 1960s, Japan built its credibility as a sportscar maker with cars like the Honda S800 and the Toyota 2000GT. What it lacked was a high-volume market-leader to sell to the Americans, a car that could step into the shoes of the Austin Healey 3000 whose days were numbered and challenge the aging E-Type Jaguar and Triumph TR in this big, profitable market.

Into the fray, in 1969, stepped the Datsun 240Z, the best-selling sportscar of the 1970s. What the badge lacked in

■ ABOVE RIGHT *The Datsun badge had little credibility with sportscar drivers before the able and low-priced 240Z.*

DATSUN 240Z (1969–75)	
Engine	Straight six
Capacity	2392cc
Power	151bhp
Transmission	4/5-speed manual
Top speed	125mph (201kph)
No. built	156,076

romance and cachet, the 240Z more than made up for with its well-balanced muscular lines, designed by Albrecht Goertz, father of the beautiful BMW 507. With its long bonnet, recessed lights and flowing, tense rear haunches, the Z clearly took styling cues from the fixed-head E-Type Jaguar; yet it was pure and elegant enough, apart from unattractive wheel trims – a typical weakness of Japanese cars – to have its own appeal. A well-equipped two-seater with a rear hatchback, the 240Z held few surprises under the skin, yet lacked for nothing: the engine was a smooth and punchy straight six, making 151bhp from

■ ABOVE *Its rear hatchback made the Z extremely versatile. These Wolf race wheels are non-standard but look better than the gruesome original trims.*

■ BELOW *It was hard to believe the 240Z was a Japanese car, so pure and elegant was its profile.*

■ BELOW *With all-independent suspension the 240Z had thoroughbred cornering abilities.*

■ RIGHT *The classic appeal of the 240Z was quickly recognized, and there are owners clubs for the cars all over the world.*

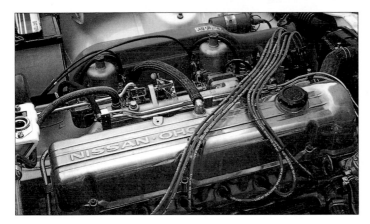

■ ABOVE *The engine was a lusty straight six from the big Cedric saloon. It was smooth and flexible and sounded great.*

■ RIGHT *The Z cars suffered from the cheap-looking finish of the day, but equipment levels were high.*

2393cc. Power went via a five-speed gearbox to a well-sorted strut-and-wishbone rear end. There were struts at the front, too. Precise rack-and-pinion took care of the steering. Butch and meaty in character – not unlike the big Healey – the 240Z was a far superior car even if never offered as a drophead. For the same price, in America, as Triumph's abysmal GT6, the customer received a car that handled superbly, if traditionally, and topped 125mph (201kph) with ease. It even sounded the part, with a gruff straight-six growl that was pure machismo.

Datsun sold 150,076 before the 260Z

■ ABOVE *There was more than a hint of Ferrari about the front end of the 240Z. The spoiler is a period after-market extra.*

took over in 1975. Seeking more refinement, Datsun made the 260 a softer, less aggressive car and, inevitably, a heavier, slower one. Nevertheless, it was what the public, certainly the American public, wanted. Sales continued to climb. Automatics and a two-plus-two, longer-wheelbase version broadened the Z's appeal, though today's purist enthusiasts turn their noses up at this uglier variant.

With the 280ZX, Datsun finally lost the plot altogether. This unattractive parody of the purebred original was unworthy of the name. A good 240Z is a rare find today. Rust got many.

DODGE

■ DODGE CHARGER

If one car encapsulates the "muscle" era of the 1960s, it has to the Dodge Charger. Made famous by the classic chase sequence in the 1968 Steve McQueen film *Bullitt*, in which it was driven by the villains, the Charger was a full-sized fastback coupé, huge for a two-door four-seater yet gracefully styled by Detroit standards. With its buttressed rear pillars and tastefully simple front end, yet with a hint of menace about its blanked-out grille (twin-headlights were mounted behind electric flaps), it was a far cry from the chintzy, gin-palace American cars of the 1950s.

The first car to bear the Charger name, a bold but somehow bland fastback, had lasted just a season. The 1968 shell was to last, with minimal changes, until 1970, unless you count the rare hoop-tailed Charger Daytona, built for the 1970 model year as a homologation special. Myriad options meant that the Charger could be tailored to customer requirements – some had quite mild 5.2-litre V-eight engines – but for the cognoscenti the 1968 R/T (Road and Track) model was the only one to have.

Under the bonnet was a 7.2-litre engine giving 375bhp and fairly throbbing with tyre-smoking torque: off

■ LEFT *Buttresses beside the rear window were probably inspired by Italian design, but the Charger has an all-American muscle-car look of its own.*

the line, the Charger could outpace most Italian exotica with a 0–60 (96) time of six seconds, steaming up to 100 (160) in 13 seconds with wheel spin in every gear; foot to the floor, it would eventually wind up to 150mph (241kph). By the simple expedient of bolting the heavy-duty suspension down rock hard and fitting scaffolding-sized anti-roll bars, Dodge actually made the Charger R/T handle. With the optional front discs you had half a chance of

DODGE CHARGER R/T (1967–70)	
Engine	V-eight
Capacity	7206cc
Power	375bhp
Transmission	3-speed auto 4-speed manual
Top speed	150mph (241kph)
No. built	96,100

■ FAR LEFT *Rear wheel drive and the massive power of the R/T version meant wild handling, especially on loose surfaces.*

■ NEAR LEFT *The fastest versions of the Charger could manage up to 150mph (241kph).*

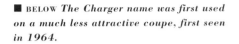

stopping it, too. Like most American cars the Charger came as a 3-speed automatic, but for serious drivers there was a heavy-duty Hurst manual box.

The Charger model line continued until 1978, but its credibility as a performance car was progressively whittled away as the American automotive industry moved its emphasis away from performance towards luxury, safety and economy.

OTHER MAKES

■ DAF

Dafs first appeared in 1958, from a Dutch firm which had been making commercial trailers since 1928 and HGVs since 1950. A unique "easy driving" transmission was their main distinguishing feature. In the 1960s, this belt-drive transmission was adapted to both military and racing (Formula 3) uses. In 1975, a majority share in the car side of the firm was acquired by Volvo, which has ousted Daf models from its inventory.

■ DELAGE

Louis Delage was a real maverick of the French motor industry, a perfectionist who would build only the finest vehicles. He started modestly enough in 1905 with a conventional shaft-drive-single-cylinder 6.5hp car, and this was followed by equally conventional touring machines, early examples having De Dion engines. It was in racing that the firm made its mark, and after the First World War it made superb touring cars and several vastly expensive forays into Grand Prix racing and record-breaking. It was acquired by Delahaye

in 1935 and thereafter the cars evolved into derivatives of that make. Along with Delahaye, it died in the Hotchkiss merger.

■ DELAHAYE

This French firm is best known for its stunning sportscars built in the 1930s, but its history dates back to the dawn of motoring when Emile Delahaye branched out into car production in 1894. Before the First World War, the range was diverse, but this changed in the 1920s when the firm only offered lacklustre "cooking" vehicles. After 1935, it made conventional but soundly-executed sporting cars as well as venturing into Grand Prix racing. This was its heyday. After the Second World War, the French Government's penal taxation killed off luxury-car manufacture. The firm merged with Hotchkiss in 1953 and from shortly afterwards made only trucks and Jeeps.

■ DELLOW

A rugged British mud-lugging trials car, the Dellow originally used a Ford Ten engine in an Austin Seven chassis, with a tubular-framed alloy body. In production, the Seven chassis was replaced by one made of chrome-moly

rocket tubes. A part-time project, manufacture fell away by the early 50s and in 1955 a new company took over the enterprise. The uncompetitive MkVI followed and in 1959 Dellow Engineering was wound up.

■ DE TOMASO

The Italy-based Argentine Alejandro de Tomaso made racing cars, but in 1967 he entered passenger-car production in earnest with the mid-engined Mangusta supercar. His 1970s products include the Pantera, still made in small numbers today. In 1976 he acquired Maserati and in the 80s the De Tomaso marque faded away.

■ DKW

The German firm DKW initially made motorcycles, starting car manufacture in 1928. In 1931 it introduced the pioneering front-wheel-drive F1 model, retaining two-stroke power and a year later became part of the Auto Union combine. This was re-established in the then Federal Republic of Germany in 1949 and resumed building cars in 1950. The firm came under Daimler-Benz control in 1958 and was bought by Volkswagen in 1965.

EDSEL

EDSEL

The 1957 Edsel has become a byword for the marketing man's blunder.

Ford pitched their new car at the lower medium market sector, between the bigger Fords and the budget Mercury models. Sadly for Ford, by the time it was launched the market was in a slump: buyers were looking for smaller cars, and the Edsel, the wrong car at the wrong time, became an unfortunate victim of its own massive hype. Forecasting 200,000 sales in the first year, Ford claimed that the new car – named after the dead son of Henry Ford – had cost $250,000,000 to develop.

When only 62,000 buyers were tempted in the first season, the critics blamed the styling with its unusual vertical grille, described by one wag as an Oldsmobile sucking a lemon. In fact, the Edsel was reasonably restrained by the extreme standards of the period, with fins well clipped and with a clean profile.

Spanning 15 different models, the Edsel was actually a separate Ford division with saloon, convertible and station-wagon bodies on the same ultra-conventional basic floorpan. As usual, there were six-cylinder and V-eight engine options (ranging in output from 145 to 345bhp) with three-speed

■ ABOVE *The Edsel missed the mark by a mile and cost Ford millions.*

■ ABOVE *The car's unusual grille – one of its trade marks – was not liked by customers.*

■ ABOVE *Ford marketed the Edsel as a marque on its own in a range spanning 15* *different models. This is the top-of-the-line Citation of 1958.*

EDSEL (1957–59)	
Engine	Straight six and V-eight
Capacity	3655–6719cc
Power	147–350bhp
Transmission	3-speed manual 3-speed auto
Top speed	90–108mph (145–174kph)
No. built	110,847

■ RIGHT *The styling was toned down for 1959 but the controversial grille remained. The car came as an estate (Villager), a two- or four-door saloon or a convertible.*

■ RIGHT *Today the relatively rare Edsel is a coveted collectors' piece, particularly the early cars as shown here.*

■ BELOW *Ford claimed that the Edsel had cost $250,000,000 to develop and predicted sales of 200,000 in the first year.*

manual and automatic transmission options. There was a mild restyle for 1959, as Ford tried to arrest a dramatic fall in sales, and in 1959 a totally new shell appeared in a much-reduced line-up for the 1960 model year. In the event, the Edsel line was dead by the turn of the new decade, cancelled owing to lack of interest.

Today, ironically, the once-shunned Edsel is a prized collectors' piece, a prince among lemons.

OTHER MAKES

■ ELVA

The name of this British car is derived from the French for "she goes" ("*Elle va*"), and the original 1955 Frank Nichols design was a low-cost sports/racing car with various power units. The most successful model was the Courier road-going sportscar. Manufacture was taken over by Trojan Ltd in 1962 and the company later bought Elva. Production passed in 1964 to Ken Sheppard Customised Sports Cars Ltd, of Hertfordshire.

■ ABOVE *The interiors featured all the usual glitz expected of a mid-range American car.*

■ RIGHT *The Edsel came with six-cylinder or V-eight engines giving as much as 350bhp.*

FACEL VEGA

■ RIGHT *With this vast array of dials and switch gear, Facel tried to give its V-eight models the feel of a small aircraft.*

■ FACEL VEGA FACEL II

Rolls-Royce comforts; super sports-car urge; American reliability and driving ease. The Facel Vega Facel II offered a combination of qualities you couldn't buy anywhere else in the early 1960s, though there were plenty of imitators on the scene by the time Facel – Forges et Ateliers de Construction d'Eure et Loire, of Paris – closed its doors in 1964. This, perhaps, was at the core of the Facel Vega's unique appeal. To drive a Facel, unlike an Aston Martin or a Ferrari, you didn't need racing-driver skill or a mechanic in the boot.

You would, nevertheless, have to put uniquely French elegance at the top of its list of attributes. As a pure piece of automotive artistry in the Pininfarina mould, the Facel II might never make the Museum of Modern Art; but as a stylishly charismatic period piece, there is nothing to touch it. This was a car with glamour by the truckload, true gravitas of a calibre that no mere hybrid – for the big Facels were unashamed mongrels with their Chrysler V-eight engines – has since achieved. Celebrities lined up to buy them in the early 60s, while race-owners like

■ BELOW *The Facel marque died in 1964, when the firm was made bankrupt by warranty claims on its unreliable smaller car, the Facelia.*

■ LEFT *Facel Vega was easily France's most stylish and expensive marque in the 1950s and 60s, favoured by celebrities, royalty and racing drivers.*

■ BELOW *Top of the range was the four-door Excellence, built to compete with Rolls-Royce and Mercedes. Its structure was too flexible, giving problems with doors.*

FACEL VEGA FACEL II (1962–64)	
Engine	90-degree V-eight
Capacity	6286cc
Power	355–390bhp
Transmission	4-speed manual
	3-speed auto
Top speed	140mph (225kph)
No. built	184

■ RIGHT *The HK500's styling was inspired by American models – hence the wrap-around screen – but had a brutish look all of its own.*

Stirling Moss and Rob Walker gave the marque the stamp of approval. As you would expect, it was an expensive car, costing the equivalent of two E-Type Jaguars and a Lotus Elan.

The shape suggested weight and strength. The bold, sculptured rear flanks – forming clipped, tense tail fins – looked hewn from solid rock; the squat, square roof was taut and spare. Cast in the mould of France's pre-Second World War *Grand Routiers*, the Facel II, like the HK500 before it, was as stormingly quick as these rocket ship looks promised. The automatic version could top 130mph (209kph). The rare manual was good for 140mph (225kph). This four-speed manual Pont a' Mousson box, with a twin-carburettor 390bhp V-eight from the Chrysler 300, was a no-cost option. With the Torqueflite came the slightly less powerful 355bhp (gross) single-carburettor version of the 6.3-litre Chrysler engine. The simplistic suspension was unchanged from the HK: coils and wishbones at the front – with anti-roll bar – and beefy half-elliptics on the live rear axle. To soften the car's thumpy ride, importers HWM would fit Armstrong selecta-ride rear dampers as an option. Dunlop discs were used all round. Power steering,

■ LEFT *The fastest of the HK500 and Facel II models could top 140mph (225kph) and came with manual or automatic transmission. The V-eight engines were American Chrysler units.*

leather seats and electric windows were standard.

Like the HK500, the Facel II did not escape the tyranny of excess weight. Even among contemporary big GTs it

was a heavy car at 37-cwt (1880kg) dry, actually nearer two tons with four passengers and its 22-gallon (100-litre) fuel tank topped-up. A total 182 Facel IIs were built. The Facel Register shows the survival rate in Britain is good: 15 or 16 survive out of 23 right-hand-drive cars sold.

■ LEFT *The last of the V-eight cars was the Facel II, with cleaned-up styling but almost identical running gear.*

FERRARI

■ FERRARI 275 GTB

With the 275 GTB of 1964 the Ferrari road car really came of age. For the first time, here was a Ferrari with sophisticated suspension, answering demands for a car that could be driven quickly in comfort.

For good weight distribution and traction the five-speed transmission was separated from the engine, in unit with the final drive casing, connected on early cars by a slim prop shaft, later replaced by a torque tube for better rigidity. Double wishbone rear suspension replaced the usual solid axle with leaf spring found on the 250 GT Series, and there were obligatory four-wheel Dunlop-type disc brakes all round. Up front was Ferrari's famous all-alloy 3.3-litre 60-degree V-twelve engine, producing 280bhp in this single overhead-cam form. The 275 nomenclature was taken from the capacity, expressed in cubic centimetres, of each of the engine's cylinders.

Clothing all this was a two-seater coupé body, styled by Ferrari's favoured couturier Pininfarina, on a short 94.5-in

■ ABOVE *The nose styling was influenced by the 250GTO.*

■ ABOVE *For lightness and strength, Ferrari used Borrani alloy wheels with knock-on centre hubs.*

■ ABOVE *The exquisite cabin featured the traditional Nardi steering-wheel and open transmission gate.*

■ LEFT *The long-nose four-cam 275 GTB/4 did a claimed 165mph (265kph).*

■ BELOW *There was more than
a hint of the 250 short
wheelbase in the rear pillar.*

■ LEFT *The sensual
and curvaceous
275 was as
delicate as the
Daytona that
replaced it was
brutal.*

(240-cm) wheelbase. The hunched and
organically muscular steel body was
built by Scaglietti, just up the road from
Ferrari's Modena factory. The frame was
of the traditional multi-tube type, and
the car sat on handsome Campagnolo
alloy wheels.

From 1965, there was a Series Two car
with a longer nose and a smaller air
intake and, from 1966, the four-cam 275
GTB/4 with six carburettors and dry-
sump lubrication. Top speed soared from
about 150mph (241kph) to 165
(265kph), with 0-60 (96) in under seven
seconds.

As well as the 275 GTB there was the
GTS, an open version developed
specifically for the American market. It
looked completely different from the
GTB and its heavier body was actually

built in the Pininfarina factory. Much
rarer were the nine NART Spider
versions of the GTB and the 12
lightweight aluminium GTB/C cars built
for competition drivers.

The 275 was replaced in 1968 by the
365 GTB/4 Daytona, which was faster
but perhaps not as well balanced.

■ ABOVE *There was
a lightweight GTC
version of the 275
with all-aluminium
bodywork.*

■ LEFT *With its
rear-mounted
transaxle, the 275
had superbly
balanced handling.*

FERRARI 275 GTB AND GTB/4 (1964–68)	
Engine	V-twelve
Capacity	3286cc
Power	280-300bhp
Transmission	5 speed
Top speed	150-165mph (241-265kph)
No. built	200/280

■ RIGHT *For those
addicted to open-
topped motoring,
Pininfarina also
built the 275GTS.*

FERRARI

■ FERRARI DINO 206/246

Although the 206/246 Dino was never to
wear a Ferrari badge (Enzo tried to
market it as a separate marque) it was,
in every respect other than the number
of cylinders, a "proper" Ferrari. A
140mph (225kph) car with superb
handling and a stunningly beautiful
shape – one of Pininfarina's finest
moments – it was for many the first step
on the ladder of Ferrari ownership.

To understand the 206/246 Dino you
have to understand the Fiat Dinos, the
first fruit of Ferrari's liaison with Fiat
and the first road car to bear the name of
Enzo Ferrari's much-missed son and
heir. A conventional front-engined, rear-
wheel-drive monocoque design – made
as a Pininfarina Spider and a low-key
Bertone coupé – it had its genesis in the
1967 1.6-litre Formula 2 racing
regulations. Ferrari's Dino V-six engine
dating from the mid-1950s was ideal for
the job, but the rules stipulated a 500-
off, production-based block. Ferrari
didn't have the capacity, whereas
producing 500 cars was a mere sneeze

FERRARI DINO 206/246 GT (1968–73)	
Engine	V-six
Capacity	1987/2418cc
Power	180–190bhp
Transmission	5-speed manual
Top speed	140–148mph (225–238kph)
No. built	152 206GTs 2,487/1,274 GT/GTS

■ ABOVE *The Dino GTS was popular in
sunny North American climes because of its
removable "Targa" roof panel.*

■ ABOVE *From any angle, Pininfarina's
Dino was stunningly beautiful.*

■ LEFT *Early Dino 206 models had more
fragile two-litre engines, alloy bodywork
and knock-on alloy wheels*

■ BELOW *The styling of the 206/246 Dino
evolved gradually from a series of mid-60s
Pininfarina dream cars. Mid engine
location was inspired by racing practice.*

■ RIGHT *The Dino name is shared by a family of racers – this is the 246S of 1959. "Dino" correctly refers to the racing V-sixes and V-eights on which Ferrari's son Alfredino was working when he died in 1956.*

■ BELOW *The featured Alacantra covered dash, sports wheel and plastic seats.*

■ LEFT *The 246 was replaced in 1974 by the uglier 308GT4, with a V-eight engine and two tiny extra rear seats.*

■ BELOW *The Ferrari badge on the rear of this car is an extra added by the owner: the 246 wore only Dino badges and was marketed at first as a separate marque.*

to Fiat. Enter the Fiat Dino, powered by a production version of Ferrari's quad-cam V-six, first as an all-alloy two-litre, later a 2.4-litre with an iron block. The ruse allowed Ferrari to qualify its engine for F2 racing, and for Fiat this was something of a prenuptial courtship before the eventual marriage of the two companies in 1969. The alloy-bodied two-litre Dino 206 arrived in 1968 with 180bhp and was powered by the same 65-degree V-six engine as in the Fiat Dino. The big difference was that this was turned through 90 degrees and mounted transversely behind the two-seat passenger cell, with five-speed gearbox and transaxle. Clothed in alloy by Pininfarina, it handled as well as it looked, but it soon became apparent that, in the face of faster opposition from Porsche, the 206 was underpowered. The 246 was Ferrari's answer, with 195bhp from a 2418cc iron-blocked version of the V-six with more torque produced lower down. Made as a fixed-head GT and GTS open targa (from 1971), it now had a steel body. Bolt-on alloys, rather than the more attractive centre-locking hubs found on the 206, were another recognition point. Just over 4,000 of the 206/246 were made between 1968 and 1973 before the introduction of the much less attractive two-plus-two Dino 308GT4.

FERRARI

■ LEFT *The ultimate Daytona was the 365 lightweight competition model with alloy body and Spartan trim.*

■ FERRARI DAYTONA

The Daytona 365GTB/4 was a proud, last-gasp statement by Ferrari in the superfast front-engined Grand Tourer stakes. It was named Daytona in honour of Ferrari's success in the American 24-hour race of the same name; 365 denoted the capacity of each cylinder; four stood for the number of camshafts.

It is odd to think that when this sensational V-twelve supercar appeared, replacing the 275GTB/4, it was greeted with a sense of disappointment. The world had been waiting for a mid-engined Ferrari to challenge the Lamborghini Miura, but what was shown at the 1968 launch was a conventional, front-engined Grand Tourer clothed in a boldly elegant, muscularly handsome coupé steel shell – with a classic multitube chassis frame – from the pen of Pininfarina.

Early cars had Plexiglas covered lights, but most used retractable units that gave the Daytona a menacing squint from the front. At 3,530lb (1,601kg)

unladen it was a heavyweight, but it packed a punch to match: against the clock it would wind out to 174mph (280kph), out of the reach of the more radical Miura, soaring to 60 (96) in a neck-straining 5.4 seconds. It would even do 70mph (112kph) in reverse, if you felt the need.

If the Daytona wasn't exactly cutting-edge under the skin, neither was it technically backward. The engine was a magnificent 4.4-litre quad-cam V-twelve producing 352bhp at 7500rpm. For good weight distribution and traction, power went through a rear-mounted five-speed gearbox/transaxle unit while suspension was by classic wishbones and coils all round, stiffly set up to resist roll. Inside,

■ ABOVE *The standard Daytona had a well-equipped cabin with leather seats, electric windows and a superb Nardi steering-wheel.*

■ LEFT *Most sought-after of the road-going models is the Spider, of which only 165 were produced.*

■ RIGHT *Only five competition specification Daytonas were built: with up to 450bhp it also made a sensational road car.*

FERRARI DAYTONA 365 GTB/4 (1968–73)	
Engine	V-twelve
Capacity	4390cc
Power	352 @ 7500rpm
Transmission	5-speed manual
Top speed	174mph (280kph)
No. built	1,426

it was comfortably functional rather than luxurious, though electric windows and leather for the hip-hugging seats was standard. A few buyers wisely opted for air-conditioning too, because the cabin could get pretty stuffy when you were heaving away at the heavy unassisted steering around town. It was on the open road, of course, that the 365GTB/4 – often accused of being truck-like by its detractors – really sparkled: the steering shed its weight, the clunky suspension seemed to smooth out and the car simply flew. For many years it was the world's fastest road car. As word got around about the Daytona, buyers began to knock on Ferrari's door and, far from being a failure, the Daytona turned out to be one of the best-selling big Ferraris. When production ended in 1973, sales had reached 1,426, of which 165 were of the much-fancied Spider. Its replacement, the Boxer, never recaptured Daytona's muscular appeal.

■ FAR LEFT *The production Daytona coupe was surprisingly successful, with 1,426 built in less than five years.*

■ NEAR LEFT *Early Daytonas had plexiglass headlight covers, but flip-up lights were a much more elegant solution.*

■ ABOVE *The dramatic profile of the Daytona-inspired Rover's 1976 SD1 saloon. It is now one of the most sought-after road Ferraris of all.*

■ RIGHT *The classic all-alloy Ferrari V-twelve had four overhead camshafts, 4.4 litres and 352bhp.*

FIAT

■ BELOW *Fiat built more than four million of the tiny 500s in a 20-year run, helping to put ordinary Italians on four wheels for the first time.*

■ FIAT 500

The tiny Fiat 500 is now something of a trendy cult car, its rounded egg-like body and diminutive size endearing it to millions. It was no joke when it was introduced in 1957: designed as utilitarian transportation for the masses, it put Italy on wheels during the 1960s and spawned several variants. More than four million were built in a 20-year production run.

A minimalist four-seater with kart-like handling, the original cars were powered by an aircooled 479cc flat-twin, mounted in the rear, later boosted

■ ABOVE *Early cars had rear-hinged "suicide" doors, but this is a post-1965 model with conventional arrangements.*

■ LEFT *The 500's tiny proportions still give it great appeal to modern drivers. All cars had sun-roofs.*

to 499cc that gave 18bhp. Hardly breath-taking – but the 500 could cruise at 55mph (88kph) and boasted Scrooge-like economy within over 52mpg with reach. Early, poorly built cars had rear-hinged "suicide" doors and a full-length sun-roof, post-1965 500F models had conventional front hinges, but the 500 kept its drum brakes and crude non-synchro "crash" gearbox to the end. The 1968 500L version gave buyers an alternative to the stark basic car, with reclining seats and carpets. The 500R was a last-of-the-line model using the engine and floorpan from the 126.

■ RIGHT *The Giardiniera was a useful estate version that outlived the standard saloon by two years.*

■ ABOVE *For the ultimate in 500 memorabilia, how about the wooden styling bucks for the 500? They are still retained by Fiat.*

From 1960, there was an estate version called the Giardiniera, with a surprisingly useful load area, and this model, latterly badged as an Autobianchi, outlived the standard model by a couple of years. Till the end, it retained rear-hinged doors. The pick of the crop, however, must be Carlo Abarth's SS models, which in 695 form were good for nearly 90mph (145kph).

You can recognize an Abarth by its flared arches, oil cooler and raised rear engine cover, which assist both cooling and stability.

■ BELOW *The Jolly was a special Vignale-built fun-car, now highly prized by collectors of 500s.*

■ ABOVE *The 500L of 1968 had plusher trim than the stark standard model, with carpets and reclining seats.*

FIAT 500 (1957–77)	
Engine	2-cylinder
Capacity	499cc
Power	18bhp
Transmission	4-speed manual
Top speed	60mph (96kph)
No. built	3,427,648 saloon 327,000 Giardiniera

FIAT

■ FIAT 850 COUPÉ

The sports versions of Fiat's bread-and-butter 850 arrived a year after the saloon version in 1965. Bertone styled a pretty two-seater spider variant while Fiat's own styling department produced a neat fastback four-seater coupé. The rear seats were near useless and the luggage space in the nose was modest, but this didn't stop people buying the little 850 in huge numbers.

■ ABOVE *With its sporty wooden steering-wheel and hooded instrument binnacle, the 850 had a real mini-Ferrari touch.*

■ ABOVE *The 850 coupé was styled in-house by Fiat rather than by an outside designer.*

■ ABOVE *The softer front-end treatment means this car is a Series 2 with the bigger 903cc engine.*

FIAT 850 COUPÉ	
Engine	4-cylinder
Capacity	843/903cc
Power	45-52bhp
Transmission	4-speed manual
Top speed	91mph (146kph)
No. built	380,000

With a little more power than the stock saloon, the coupé had a top speed of 90mph (145kph) and, despite the overhanging rear position of the willing little water-cooled pushrod engine, the handling was excellent, with light, positive steering, lots of grip and responsive brakes (discs at the front). 40mpg was another inducement.

The Geneva show of 1968 saw the introduction of a revised coupé with a bigger 903cc engine that pushed the top speed to about 95mph (152kph). There were minor styling revisions too, and the car carried on in this form until 1971, by which time the number of 850 coupés produced was 380,000. The Spider soldiered on until 1974 because of its popularity in America, although it was effectively replaced by the mid-engined X1/9.

■ NEAR RIGHT *The slats in the engine cover were the only give-away that the 850 was rear-engined.*

■ FAR RIGHT *Although 380,000 of the 850 coupes were built, rust has got the better of most.*

■ FIAT 124 SPIDER

With a production run of nearly 20 years, the Fiat 124 Spider must be the most successful Italian sportscar ever. It was deservedly successful and much more than just a pretty face. With a belt-drive twin-cam engine under the bonnet,

■ ABOVE *The 124 Spider in late form, with extra ride height and big Federal bumpers.*

■ FAR LEFT *The interiors had a high level of trim compared with rivals, as well as a superb hood that could be raised or lowered with one hand.*

■ NEAR LEFT *Abarth did a handful of specially tuned 124s to homologate the model for rallying.*

it was a spirited and sweet performer, while a well-located, coil-sprung rear suspension and four-wheel disc brakes gave it handling and refinement way beyond its British competitors. The handsome body was by none other than Pininfarina and had enduring appeal, even when ugly federal safety bumpers were hung on it in the mid-70s for North America, which was always the model's biggest market. Five gears were initially optional, later standard, and in later years there was even an automatic.

Engine size grew over the years, first

to 1608cc in 1969, then to 1756cc in 1972, with a new 1592cc 1600 base model. A two-litre engine was standard across the board from 1979 as Fiat tried to counter progressively power-strangling emission regulations. Injection was introduced in 1980. The ultimate version was the supercharged VX, with a 135bhp engine.

Production ceased in 1985, later variants being marketed as Pininfarina rather than Fiat Spiders. There would be no proper Fiat-badged sportscar for another 10 years.

FIAT 124 SPIDER (1966–85)	
Engine	In-line four
Capacity	1438/1608/1756/1995cc
Power	90–135bhp
Transmission	4/5-speed manual 3-speed auto
Top speed	102–120mph (164–193kph)
No. built	198,000

■ ABOVE *A specially tuned 124. Note the special alloys and hardtop.*

■ LEFT *The Spider Abarth was successful in international rallying. Its best results were second and third in the Monte Carlo Rally.*

FIAT

■ FIAT 130 COUPÉ

Fiat's unloved, unlovely 130 saloon of the late 60s was always a much better car than people gave it credit for, with some fine engineering under its square-rigged body. Ironically, it spawned one of the best-looking cars of the 70s, the Pininfarina-styled 130 coupé of 1971. Perfectly proportioned and superbly elegant from any angle, it stood apart from many luxury coupés of its day in having ample room inside for four. Few coupés were as sumptuous either, with rich velour on the seats, veneer door cappings and high equipment levels:

■ LEFT *Simplicity and lack of fuss are the keys to the success of the shape. Few big cars look this good even today.*

■ BELOW *The original prototype wearing 130 saloon-style alloy wheels. Production lasted from 1971 to 1977.*

FIAT 130 COUPÉ (1971–77)	
Engine	V-six
Capacity	3235cc
Power	165bhp
Transmission	3-speed auto 5-speed manual
Top speed	115–118mph (185–189kph)
No. built	4,491

electric windows, twin-tone "town and country" horns and an electric aerial were all standard.

Mechanically it was identical to the saloon, the smooth, free-revving V-six recently uprated from 2.8 to 3.2 litres to answer gripes about power performance. Power was a still modest 165bhp but torque went up dramatically, and these heavy 130s always felt quicker on the road than they were against the clock. Most were autos – by Borg Warner – though there was a five-speed manual option. These cars had the sophisticated independent suspension, shared at the rear with the Fiat Dino, and fine balance as well as a supple ride worthy of a

■ OPPOSITE *Pininfarina still rates the 130 coupé as one of the best designs it has ever put its name to.*

■ BELOW *More than anything, it was the unprestigious Fiat badge that led to the cars' poor sales.*

■ ABOVE *The style of the 130 influenced the Lancia Gamma coupé and the Rolls-Royce Camargue.*

■ LEFT *The interior was sumptuous with velour seats, electric windows and plenty of room in the back.*

world-class luxury car. Power steering was standard.

In the end, it was the Fiat name that killed off the 130 coupé before its time: its prestige pulling power, in a class dominated by BMW and Mercedes, was always going to be limited. Production ceased in 1977, the coupé holding on a year longer than the saloon.

Today, rust has savaged many of the 130 coupés and good ones are highly sought-after.

■ ABOVE *The 130 competed head-on with the likes of BMW's 3.0 CS coupé and the Citroen SM.*

■ RIGHT *The 130 was the biggest and most expensive car in Fiat's range. The company has not made anything like it since.*

FORD

■ FORD CONSUL/ ZEPHYR/ZODIAC MK I/II

The 1950 Consul was the first of the modern post-war cars from Dagenham, with a whole raft of new technology that brought the big Ford bang up to date.

Out went the separate chassis frame, in came unitary construction for the first time, making for a lighter, stiffer structure. Front suspension was by Macpherson struts – the old Pilot had to make do with a beam axle – while brakes were fully hydraulic at last. Overhead valves for the 1508cc four-cylinder engine meant more power, though it wasn't until 1951 that the big Ford got much-needed performance in the 2262cc six-cylinder Zephyr. There was a power-top convertible version by

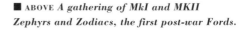

■ ABOVE *A gathering of MkI and MKII Zephyrs and Zodiacs, the first post-war Fords.*

■ LEFT *The 90mph (145kph) Zephyr MkII, built by Carbodies, is one of the most sought-after models.*

FORD CONSUL/ZEPHYR/ZODIAC (1950–62)	
Engine	In-line 4 and 6-cylinder
Capacity	1508, 1703, 2262, 2553cc
Power	48–87bhp
Transmission	3/4-speed manual 3-speed auto
Top speed	75–90 mph (120–145kph)
No. built	406,792/682,400

■ FAR LEFT *The MkI Zephyr was the top-of-the-range six-cylinder car, here in typical two-tone livery with whitewall tyres.*

■ NEAR LEFT *Press advertizement for the new MkII models of 1956.*

Carbodies, an Abbott-bodied estate and, from 1954, a top-of-the-range Zodiac with fashionable two-tone paint, whitewall tyres and fog lamps.

The cars were well received and sold well, but Ford did not rest on their laurels: the MkII Consul, Zephyr and Zodiac range arrived in 1956 with new, bigger styling and bigger four and six-cylinder engines of 1703 and 2553cc. The Zephyr/Zodiac could now top 90mph (145kph), the Consul about 80

(128). Again there was a Carbodies convertible – flash and now much sought-after – and a rare Abbott estate. From 1959, a sleeker MKII version had a lower roof line. Options included disc front brakes (from 1960), overdrive and Borg Warner automatic transmission.

Introduction of the MkIII in 1962 marked the end of the classic 50s-style Consuls, Zephyrs and Zodiacs. They had been among the best-loved British family saloons of their era.

■ ABOVE *The Zepyhr MkIII was made famous by the TV series Z Cars.*

■ RIGHT *All early Lotus Cortinas were finished in white with a green side flash.*

■ FORD LOTUS CORTINA

The 1963 Lotus Cortina was the product of a deal between Colin Chapman and Ford to produce a race and rally winner: Ford wanted to reflect a more sporting image on to its run-of-the-mill family saloon, while Lotus needed an entry into the mass production mainstream and another outlet for their twin-cam Ford-based engine. Ford supplied the basic two-door Cortina shell – with front suspension – to the Lotus factory at Cheshunt, Hertfordshire. Lotus installed their own 105bhp twin-cam engine, close-ratio four-speed gearbox and special rear suspension comprising coil springs, radius arms and an A bracket. Sitting lower on wider wheels and fitted with disc front brakes, all the MkI Lotus

Cortinas were painted cream, with a green flash on their flanks and featured split front bumpers and a matt black front grille. The light, powerful Lotus Cortina was an instant winner in saloon car racing and particularly memorable in the hands of Grand Prix ace Jim Clark. Its rallying prowess was initially held back by its unreliable A-frame rear suspension, but this reverted to semi-elliptics in 1966. Just 3,301 were built.

LOTUS CORTINA (1963–70)	
Engine	In-line four
Capacity	1558cc
Power	105–109bhp
Transmission	4-speed manual
Top speed	105–107mph (168–172kph)
No. built	3,301/4,032

■ RIGHT *The MkII version looked much more ordinary but had more power and was slightly quicker.*

■ FAR RIGHT *The MkII twin-cam engine gave 109bhp, pushing the car up to 107mph (171kph).*

■ RIGHT *MkII models were closer to stock production models inside and a bit plusher than the MkI.*

■ LEFT *The twin-cam engine was essentially as found in the Lotus Elan sportscar.*

The MkII of 1967 had all new bodywork but underpinnings basically similar to the MkI. Power rose to 109bhp. A limited slip diff and an oil cooler became options. The cream-green livery was no longer obligatory. The MkII was slightly quicker than the MkI but has not proved as sought-after. Connoisseurs see it perhaps as less authentic because it was built among ordinary Cortinas on Dagenham production lines. Ford removed the Lotus badges after seven months and called the car Cortina Twin Cam. Production ended in 1970.

FORD

■ FORD ESCORT RS

In Britain in the 1970s a young man's four-wheeled fantasy was a quick Escort, the hot-shot saloon based on the best-selling Ford family runabout.

Leaving the exotic Lotus and Twin-Cam cars on one side, the mass-market hot Escort generation really began with the Mexico (named in honour of Ford's victory in the London to Mexico Rally) and RS2000 models of 1970 and 1973. These were punchy, raucous cars with knockabout rear-wheel-drive handling

■ ABOVE *MkI and MKII Escorts were formidable rally contenders throughout the 1970s.*

■ ABOVE *RS Escorts got more instruments on the dashboard, special bucket seats and a sports wheel.*

■ ABOVE *Many RS Escort owners removed the bumpers to make their cars look even more aggressive.*

and distinctive trim, including laddish quarter bumpers and broad body striping. They were capable of more than 100mph (160kph) in their day, and their enormous appeal was bolstered by Ford's endless rallying success with the model.

Technically the cars were straightforward and they performed all the better for it, with MacPherson strut suspension and disc brakes at the front and a live rear axle suspended on leaf springs at the rear. The steel shell was a monocoque which was stiffened on some

FORD ESCORT RS (1968–80)	
Engine	In-line four
Capacity	1993cc
Power	86–110bhp
Transmission	4-speed manual
Top speed	103–112mph (165–180kph)
No. built	N/A

versions to take the extra power.

The MkII Escort-based RS2000 of 1975 took the concept a stage further, its shovel-nosed styling (the "droopsnoot" was a tacked-on piece of polyurethane

■ ABOVE *A shovel-nosed RS2000 MkII lines up with a MkI RS model and a Mexico.*

■ ABOVE *Relatively light bodywork, lots of power and agile rear drive handling gave the Escort its competition prowess.*

said to reduce drag by 16 per cent) and up-market interior setting it apart from both the lesser family car Escorts and the enthusiast types who bought the original MkI RS cars.

Not that the Escort had gone soft: with 100bhp the RS2000 was quicker than ever and just as much fun to drive on a twisty road. Order books were soon

■ ABOVE *The RS 1800 in action. This model was a low volume homologation special with a twin-cam engine and four wheel disc brakes: many were rallied by their owners.*

■ LEFT *The rounded MkI shell with its dog-bone shaped grille has more appeal for collectors...*

■ BELOW...*than the squared-up MKII which appeared in 1975. This is an RS1600 MkII.*

bulging, its profile undoubtedly raised by regular rubber-burning television appearances in a British TV show called *The Professionals*.

Ford boosted its profit margins even more with X-Pack options for boy racers who wanted to go that bit faster.

The MkII Escorts were replaced by front-wheel-drive cars in 1980, the sporty flagship role taken over by the XR3. Totally different in style and engineering it might have been, but in many ways the appeal – purebred boy-racer – was identical.

FORD

■ FORD MUSTANG

The Ford Mustang is one of the great American success stories, a sporty compact with youthful appeal that captured the spirit of the times perfectly when it was launched in 1964 and entered the history books as one of the fastest-selling cars of all time: 418,000 in the first year, over a million by 1966.

Such was the hype surrounding the Mustang when it appeared at the New York World Fair in 1964 that the first cars were auctioned off to the highest bidders: one buyer slept in his car overnight while the cheque cleared, to ensure he wasn't out bid. Brainchild of young hotshot Ford executive Lee Iacocca, the Mustang was based on the floorpan of the Budget Falcon range, with coil-spring and wishbone suspension at the front and a beam axle on leaf springs at the rear. Its crisp, pseudo-European styling came in notchback, fastback and convertible

FORD MUSTANG (1964–73)	
Engine	Straight six and V-eight
Capacity	2788–6997cc
Power	101–390bhp
Transmission	3/4-speed manual 3-speed auto
Top speed	90–130mph (145–209kph)
No. built	2,204,038

MUSTANG BOSS 302

■ ABOVE LEFT *From the late 1960s onwards, Mustangs started to get bigger and uglier, though top-of-the- range models like this Boss 351 were certainly rapid.*

■ ABOVE RIGHT *Worst of the bunch was the flabby Grande model with its ugly vinyl roof, an attempt to take the Mustang up-market.*

■ ABOVE *With Mustangs first is best: the original 1964 shape has nice details and isn't too big by American standards. It was a huge seller.*

■ RIGHT *The convertible Mustang.*

■ ABOVE *Sport models tried to emulate European sportscars with a dashboard packed with dials. This is a rare manual.*

■ RIGHT *Caroll Shelby built a tuned version of the fastback Mustang, badged GT350, the most collectable of them all.*

form and could be ordered with a vast range of options that allowed buyers to tailor the car to their own requirements: poseurs could opt for the weakling straight six, enthusiasts for a whole raft of V-eights escalating in power from 195 to 390bhp. There were lazy automatics, urgent "stick-shift" manuals, sports handling packages, disc front brakes (to counter fade on the more powerful models) and innumerable trim options.

For the ultimate in Mustang muscle, Carroll Shelby offered an officially sanctioned road racer based on the fastback called the GT350 that has passed into legend, a muscle car par excellence with up to 425bhp in later seven-litre GT500 form. In the film *Bullitt* (1968), it was a GT390 that Steve McQueen used to pursue the Dodge Charger.

The basic, pretty shape continued fairly unmolested into 1968 as rivals began to hurriedly prepare their own "Pony" cars.

Then longer, paunchier 1969 Mustangs marked the start of the rot (particularly the awful vinyl-roofed Grande) and by 1971 the once lithe 'stang had become a tubby nag, though high-performance models such as the Mach 1 and the Boss were at least still quick.

The Mustang reached its nadir with the 1973 model Mustang II, a meek and mild little economy car launched in the wake of the oil crisis that was intended to recapture a little of the spirit of the original.

Nobody was fooled but it sold well, notching up more than a million sales. Unlike the 1964 car, however, it will never be a classic.

■ LEFT *The fastback is the best-looking of the Mustangs. A GT350 like this one could top 130mph (209kph), while the meekest of the six-cylinder shopping models could hardly manage 90 (145).*

FORD

■ FORD THUNDERBIRD

Designed as a retort to the Chevrolet Corvette, the original 1955 Ford Thunderbird was a styling high-water mark in 1950s America. Standing aside from the hordes of wallowing barges that ruled the American roads, Ford created a two-seater sporty "personal car" with simple, elegant lines (modest fins, restrained bumpers) and minimal brightwork but with a classic long nose and sweeping rear deck proportions around a snug-two seater cockpit.

It wasn't a sportscar in the true European sense, more of a brisk luxury tourer, but the image was right and the car scored over the contemporary

■ LEFT *From 1957, the previously clean shape gained bigger fins. The "Continental" spare wheel kit was optional.*

■ BELOW *The dashboard was typical 1950s fare, with fussy details and poor ergonomics. Power steering and automatic transmission were standard.*

Corvette – which it outsold handsomely – in having a V-eight engine under the bonnet. With 200bhp from a Mercury-sourced 4.8-litre V-eight, the Thunderbird would steam up to 114mph (183kph) and whisk you up to 60 (96) in under 10 seconds: rather quicker, in other words, than an Aston Martin of the

day. Bigger 5.1-litre engines saw a power hike to 212bhp in 1957. Around corners it was a different story with its soft springs and low-geared steering, though compared to the average Detroit barge it was reasonably nimble.

There was an automatic model and a three-speed manual with optional

overdrive transmission available. There was a power soft-top and an optional hardtop (with that whimsical porthole in the pillar for 1956), while the 1956 Thunderbirds also had the "Continental" spare wheel.

It wasn't to last. The grille and fins grew more gawky for 1957, and for 1958

■ TOP *In America, the early Thunderbirds have a loyal following.*

■ ABOVE *The cigar-shaped styling of 1960s Thunderbirds was clean, but the cars had grown much bigger.*

■ ABOVE *Fins were restrained on the first cars, which were strictly two-seaters.*

■ LEFT *Although the Thunderbird was no sportscar, it was at least fast, capable of 120mph (193kph) with the biggest 212bhp 5.1-litre V-eight engine.*

■ BELOW *By the 1970s, the Thunderbird had become just another big American car, based closely on contemporary saloon models.*

FORD THUNDERBIRD (1955–57)

Engine	V-eight
Capacity	4785–5113cc
Power	193–212bhp
Transmission	3-speed manual 3-speed auto
Top speed	110–120mph (177–193kph)
No. built	53,166

Ford introduced a completely new Thunderbird, a bigger, flabbier device with ugly squared-up styling and a grille like a mouth organ. In the early 60s the "Bird" regained some of its youthful good looks, if not its sports-car pretensions. The 1955–57 cars, almost a legend, are highly collectable.

FORD

■ LEFT *MkI and MkIII Capris compared:*
the MkIII had a rear hatchback and
cleaner lines, but most of the mechanics
and general proportions were identical.

■ FORD CAPRI

The Ford Capri of 1969 was the
European version of the hugely
successful Mustang, a basic four-seater
GT sold in endless combinations of
engine and trim. Built in Britain and
West Germany, the range started with a
humble 1.3-litre in-line four as found in
the Escort. In Britain there were 1.6 and
2.0-litre V-four models going right up to
the three-litre V-six. In Germany there
were additional 1.7 and 2.3-litre
models. There were enough trim options
to send your head reeling: the L was the
poverty model, the XL the mid-ranger,
with the GT and luxury GXL models at
the top of the range. The basic shell and
struts with beam rear axle were the same
throughout. There were various types of
four-speed manual gearbox and, on the
bigger-engined versions, an automatic
option. All cars had front disc brakes,
with drums at the rear, and rack-and-
pinion steering power assisted on some
of the 3 litre models.

Everything from the 1.6 GT up could

do over 100mph (160kph), with 117mph
(189kph) on offer from the fastest 3.0-
litre model, quite a hairy car in its day.
Easily the most desirable of the MkI
Capris were the RS2600 and 3100 cars:
the German-built RS2600 with its Harry
Weslake-improved, fuel-injected V-six
was a hot homologation special with
150bhp. The 3100 followed it in 1973,

FORD CAPRI (1969–86)	
Engine	In-line four, V-four, V-six
Capacity	1297–2994cc
Power	61–160bhp
Transmission	4/5-speed manual 3-speed auto
Top speed	86–130mph (138–209kph)
No. built	1,172,900 MkI/403,612 MkII/ 324,045 MkIII

■ LEFT *The RS2600 and 3100 models were*
homologation specials with more power,
produced in small numbers.

■ ABOVE *The MkII Capri of*
1974, here in mid-range
XL trim. Mechanically the
cars shared much with the
Escort.

■ RIGHT *Early MkI Capris*
like this are now rare.
This is the top-of-the-
range 3.0 GT.

■ LEFT *The Capri made an ideal tin-top racer. Here a pair of MkIII models fight it out at Silverstone.*

■ RIGHT *Perhaps the best of all the Capris was the 280 Brooklands, a special last-of-the-line model with leather seats and special green paintwork.*

■ LEFT *The 2.8 Injection could manage 130mph (209kph) and had improved suspension and a five-speed gearbox.*

OTHER MAKES

■ FAIRTHORPE

The initial attempts by Air Vice-Marshal Donal "Pathfinder" Bennett to produce a British "people's car" (the bubble-like Atom) gave way to the manufacture of sportscars. The cars – the Electron, the Electrina, the Zeta and latterly the TX-S/TX-SS – were always on the fringes and in the late 70s the firm closed its doors.

■ FALCON

Falcon Shells was formed in Britain in 1957 to produce glassfibre shells for Ford-based specials. About 2,000 were made. The closest the company got to making a complete car was the 515, a pretty coupé with, as usual, a Ford engine on a tubular chassis. Only 25 were built.

■ FRAZER NASH

Frazer Nash Cars built in the 1920s and early 1930s were stark, chain-driven and fast, but after 1936 virtually the only cars coming through the Isleworth showrooms, Middlesex, were BMWs with Frazer Nash badging. After 1945, Frazer Nash sportscars were modern and well-engineered and used the Bristol engine and gearbox – the result of an ultimately aborted collaboration between the two British companies. Its most famous post-war car was the Le Mans, with Bristol power: just 34 were built.

again built to homologate Ford's race Capri of the day with its 400bhp quad-cam V-six. The British-built road car made do with a Weber carburettor and an over-bored version of the stock V-six, giving a still respectable 148bhp. These rare and highly desirable Capris are not difficult to spot with their fat alloy wheels, sporty quarter bumpers and – on the 3100 – duck-tail spoiler.

The MkII Capri of 1974 updated the model with a three-door hatchback body on the same floorpan. The MkIII Capri four years later smartened up the look with four-shot lights and detail improvements. It lived until 1986 when the final 280 Brooklands Limited edition rolled off the German production lines.

Today, early Capris are rare and all of the more interesting high-performance versions are much sought-after.

GORDON KEEBLE

■ GORDON KEEBLE

The Gordon Keeble sounded like and should have been an ideal recipe for commercial success: cheap American V-eight muscle combined with Italian styling and British chassis know-how.

First seen in 1960 as the prototype Gordon GT (and inspired by the Corvette-powered Peerless created by Jim Keeble and John Gordon), the Gordon Keeble didn't go into faltering production until 1964, renamed GK1. With a 300bhp engine from the Chevrolet Corvette, the Gordon Keeble, with its glassfibre body – the prototype

GORDON KEEBLE (1964–66)	
Engine	V-eight
Capacity	5395cc
Power	300bhp
Transmission	4-speed manual
Top speed	135mph (217kph)
No. built	99

■ BELOW *The original steel-bodied prototype at its Motorshow debut in 1960. It was nicknamed "The Growler".*

■ ABOVE *Styled by Bertone, the Gordon Keeble was produced at Eastleigh near Southampton. It was one of the fastest four-seaters of its day.*

■ BELOW *Gordon Keeble boss George Wansborough hands over a new GK to a happy customer. By this time the company was already in trouble.*

■ ABOVE *The dashboard looked like something from a jet flight-deck, with toggle switches for everything.*

■ LEFT *Just 99 Gordon Keebles were built, but because the glassfibre body does not suffer from rust, the survival rate is high. The styling had echoes of Bertone's Alfa 2600 Sprint of the same period.*

was steel bodied – was devastatingly quick, good for 70mph (112kph) in first and nearly 140 (225) in top. In fact, so lusty was the torque, the gearbox was nearly superfluous. Handling was good too, with a DeDion axle at the rear and a complex space-frame chassis of square section providing grip, balance and a good ride although the unassisted steering suffered from too much kickback. The simple, restrained four-seater coupé shape with its elegantly slanted twin lamps was the work of a 21-year-old Giugiaro, then chief stylist at Bertone, who later to moved on to Ghia before finally setting up his own studio in the late 60s.

By 1965 only 80 cars had been built as the fledgling company battled with component supply problems and under-capitalization. Had the factory – based at Eastleigh, Southampton, on the site of the local airport – been able to build the cars quickly enough, there was no doubt the Gordon Keeble would have been a success, if only because it was under-priced. A further 19 were built under new management in 1966, but to no avail, and the company closed its doors that year. Today, 90 Gordon Keebles are still on the road.

OTHER MAKES

■ GILBERN

The only car manufacturer based in Wales, Gilbern was started in 1959 by Giles Smith and Bernard Driese, and they marketed some fine sporting products until 1973. The firm successfully made the transition from kit cars to genuine complete cars. These included the Genie and the last-of-the-line Invader with Ford V-six power. Genie and Invader were also sold in component form to beat purchase tax.

■ GINETTA

Four enthusiastic British brothers, Bob, Ivor, Trevor and Douglas Walklett made their first production vehicle, the G2, in 1958. Before 1968, the cars were remarkably successful in club racing, and thereafter the firm's staple product was the G15 coupé, with the Hillman Imp power unit, until the imposition of VAT in 1973 killed the fiscal attraction of component cars.

■ GLAS

Hans Glas GmbH was an old-established German manufacturer of agricultural machinery when it started making the Goggo scooter in 1951, following up with the production of the Goggomobil in 1955. By 1965 the firm was offering a full range of cars, including a pretty 1700GT and a 2600 V-eight coupé, both with styling by Frua of Italy. In 1966 BMW acquired Glas, and the marque name disappeared in 1968, the last GT coupés using BMW engines. The Glas 1700 saloon stayed in production in South Africa for some years.

■ GSM

A successful club racer in its day, the GSM Delta was another Ford-based British sportscar. Its origins were in Capetown, where in 1958–59 Bob van Niekirk built the Ford-based Dart, styled out-of-hours in England by a Rootes stylist. A subsidiary venture saw the car also being made in Kent, in England. Undercapitalization led to collapse in 1961, just a year after the car came to England.

HONDA

■ BELOW *The
Honda started life
as the S500 but
wasn't exported
until it had become
the S800 in 1965.*

■ HONDA S800

After the Second World War, Honda made
its fortune building motorcycles. Only in
1962 did it make its first car, the tiny
S500 sportscar. Available in convertible
and coupé, it was heavily influenced by
motorcycle design, its double overhead
camshaft (DOHC), hemi-head 531cc
engine having a roller-bearing crank and
four carburettors. Maximum power –

■ ABOVE *The interior was cozy but well-
equipped by small sportscar standards.*

HONDA S800 (1965–79)	
Engine	In-line four
Capacity	791cc
Power	70bhp
Transmission	4-speed manual
Top speed	95mph (152kph)
No. built	11,400

44bhp – came at a screaming 8000rpm,
almost unheard-of in a road car you could
buy in a showroom. Interestingly, the car
had chain drive to independently-sprung
rear wheels, redolent of motorcycle
practice. Discs on front wheels hinted at
the S500's cost-no-object specification,
although the separate chassis was
backward even in the mid-1960s. In
1964 the S500 became the 606cc S600,
and finally in 1965 the S800, the best-
known variant.

When the S800 became available in
Britain in 1967 it had conventional
drive to the rear wheels and an ordinary
live axle located by trailing arms and a
Panhard rod. It was good value,
undercutting the Mini Cooper and
Triumph Spitfire, and was praised for
slick gearchange, excellent 30mpg
economy and remarkable acceleration
for engine size. Handling was
predictable, ride firm.

■ LEFT *The coupé version was
offered alongside the
convertible. With an amazing
70bhp from just 800cc, the
S800 could do 95mph (152kph).*

■ OPPOSITE *The S800 was Honda's answer to small British sportscars like the Triumph Spitfire and Austin Healey Sprite, although it tended to be more expensive.*

■ BELOW LEFT *The last S800s were built in 1970 and have since gained a dedicated following among sportscar enthusiasts.*

■ BELOW RIGHT *The tiny powerhouse of the S800. With its roller-bearing crankshaft – inspired by Honda's motorcycle experience – it would rev to 10,000rpm.*

OTHER MAKES

■ HEINKEL

This aircraft-manufacturing firm from Stuttgart was a robust player in the bubblecar boom of the mid-1950s, with its 174cc Cabin Cruiser models. With one wheel to the rear and two at the front, the cars featured entry through the front – the whole nose of the car was a hinged door. In 1958, the last year of German production, the design was sold to Dundalk Engineering in the Irish Republic, and from 1961 the machine was manufactured in England by Trojan. Approximately 2,000 were also made in Argentina.

■ HERON

Heron Plastics of Greenwich, London, manufactured its first Europa coupé in 1960, having earlier made special bodies for cars such as the Austin Seven. The car finally made limited production in 1962, and Peter Monteverdi used it as a basis for his two-off MBM coupé. Unfortunately, after only 12 cars had been sold, Heron was wound up.

■ HILLMAN

Hillmans were always fairly conventional British cars, a trend continued after the Second World War with the mainstay Minx model. One highlight was the rear-engined Imp, but the manufacturing facility at Linwood, near Glasgow, in Scotland, was to prove disastrous. In 1964 the Chrysler Corporation acquired a substantial stake in Rootes, leading to a full take-over in 1967. The Hillman name disappeared in 1976, before the company's purchase by Peugeot in 1979.

■ HOTCHKISS

Hotchkiss began making cars in France in 1903. Early products were medium-to-large tourers. In 1937 Hotchkiss acquired Amilcar but this did not much help the company, nor did its post-war manufacture of the front-wheel-drive Hotchkiss-Grégoire, though its post-war cars maintained a reputation for good performance and quality. In 1950 Peugeot bought controlling interest. Three years later amalgamation with Delahaye saw the end of car manufacture.

■ HRG

HRG of Tolworth, Surrey, was founded in 1936 by Ron Godfrey, Guy Robbins and EA Halford. After the Second World War the firm's 1100 and 1500 models were intended to carry on the Frazer Nash tradition and looked much the same as they had done pre-war, although the 1500 Aerodynamic was a brief experiment with a modern low-drag closed-body design. After 1956 the firm concentrated on general engineering. Either Meadows or Singer engines were employed and the drive was by propshaft.

■ HUMBER

Sister marque to Hillman, Humber was always at the upper end of the British market. Like many Midlands car firms in Britain, the classic Humber, the Super Snipe, came in the late 1940s and typified a range of luxurious saloons used as official cars and as chauffeur-driven bank managers' carriages, which continued until the late 60s. From 1967, when Rootes was taken over by Chrysler, the only Humber produced was an up-market version of the Hillman Hunter.

Iso

■ ISO GRIFO

Iso of Italy began its car manufacturing career in the mid-1950s producing the Isetta bubblecars (also built under licence by BMW), but in 1962 they decided to enter the high-class GT car market with the Rivolta. In many ways this cleanly styled four-seater coupé was an Italian Gordon Keeble featuring a similar box-section frame with Dedion rear suspension and a Bertone-built steel body. Like the Keeble, it had a Corvette V-eight engine under the bonnet, so performance was impressive:

■ ABOVE *The ISO Grifo of 1963 had styling by Bertone, with the panels pressed out in steel. The engine was not their own unit, but a Corvette V-eight.*

■ LEFT *In profile, the Grifo looked as exciting as any Ferrari and had better roadholding than many of its supercar contemporaries.*

■ BELOW *The four-seater Rivolta was the first ISO and used many of the same mechanicals as the Grifo in a more sober coupé body, also styled by Bertone.*

it had a top speed of 140mph (225kph) with the manual gearbox. Comfortable and agile, the Rivolta was well received – and enjoyed much more success than its Gordon Keeble alter ego. It was only with the début of the Grifo a year later, however, that the fledgling supercar builder really made its mark. By shortening the Rivolta chassis (schemed by the celebrated ex-Ferrari engineer Bizzarrini) and clothing it in a sensational coupé body – again by Bertone – Iso now had a car to challenge Ferrari, even if purists would always turn their noses up at the American V-eight engine.

The original 5.4-litre V-eight came in two states of tune – 300 and 365bhp –

■ RIGHT *The Grifo came first as a 5.4-litre, then as a 7-litre – each with a unit borrowed from the Chevrolet Corvette range. A few late cars had Ford engines.*

with a top speed of up to 160mph (257kph) in its most potent form. Buyers could opt for four- or five-speed gearboxes or even an automatic, a fitment unheard-of on the Grifo's pure-bred rivals. Naturally, four-wheel disc brakes were deemed necessary for a car of such weight and power and in the right hands these elegant, well-engineered cars were as quick as anything on the road. The ultimate version was the 390bhp seven-litre, manufactured from 1968 to challenge the Ferrari Daytona and Maserati Ghibli.

■ LEFT *From any angle the Grifo had stunning good looks.*

ISO GRIFO (1963-74)	
Engine	V-eight
Capacity	5359-6998cc
Power	300-390bhp
Transmission	4/5-speed manual 3 speed auto
Top speed	150-170 mph (241-273kph)
No. built	504

Iso claimed 170mph (273kph) for this flagship coupé and, although this figure was never confirmed independently, there was no doubting its formidable acceleration: 70 (112) was attainable in the first gear alone. A bonnet hump distinguished the seven-litre car from lesser Grifos.

Later Grifos had a redesigned, chisel-edged nose with pop-up lights and for the last two years of production employed Ford "Cleveland" V-eights rather than Corvette engines. By then Iso were on the rocks financially, and the company died in the midst of the fuel crisis in 1974.

■ ABOVE *Just 504 Grifos were built in a production run lasting ten years. Later cars* had a restyled nose with retractable headlights.

OTHER MAKES

■ INVICTA

The British marque Invicta lasted only four years after the Second World War. By 1950, AFN Ltd had taken over its assets after the failure of the mythical Black Prince model with its twin-cam straight six, semi-auto gearbox and built-in hydraulic jacks. Before the war, the firm, founded by Noel Macklin and Oliver Lyle (of Tate & Lyle) in 1925, had made some very fine cars with Henry Meadows and Blackburne power units, but they were always extremely expensive.

JAGUAR

■ JAGUAR XK 120/140/150

In a Britain battered by war and starved of motoring excitement, it is perhaps little wonder that the Jaguar XK120, launched at the Earls Court Motor Show in 1948, was such a sensation. Conceived as a low-volume dream car rather than a serious production machine, it was destined to become a great dollar-earner for Britain (most XKs went to America) and one of the most celebrated classics of all.

The package was unbeatable. Jaguar boss William Lyons shaped a flowing two-seater roadster body that was a model of elegant purity, taking for inspiration the pre-war BMW 328 roadster. On looks alone it would have sold handsomely, but there was more: under the long, tapering bonnet was a brand-new twin-cam straight-six engine, the classic 3.4-litre XK unit that was to survive well into the 90s and power everything from Le Mans winners to tanks and fire engines. Pumping out a smooth 160bhp on twin SU carburettors, it made sure the '120' tag was no idle boast: in fact the 120mph (193kph) XK was for a time the world's fastest

■ ABOVE *The XK in-line six in its original form. It made the 120 the world's fastest production car.*

■ ABOVE *The drophead coupé version of the XK140.*

standard production car. Later SE (Special Equipment) versions with high-lift cams and twin exhausts would hike power to 180bhp. Few sportscars were as civilized as the XK with its supple suspension, though the brakes (drums, of course, but poorly cooled because of the modern all-enveloping bodywork) were never much to write home about.

Jaguar were unprepared for the demand, and XK production remained tiny in 1949 as the company tooled-up for the big-volume steel-body version that came on stream in 1950.

From then on, there was no looking back. An elegant fixed-head version was announced in 1951 and a roomier drophead coupé in 1953. The XK140 of

■ ABOVE *NUB 120, the famous Alpine Rally-winning XK120.*

■ RIGHT *The interior of the XK120 coupé was more luxurious than that of the roadster, with wood veneer on the dash.*

■ OPPOSITE *The XK120 in coupé form, its bulbous roof-line inspired by Bugatti coupés of the 1930s.*

■ RIGHT *The XK140 – here in coupe form – had new bumpers and a different grille as well as improved steering.*

JAGUAR XK 120/140/150 (1948-61)	
Engine	Straight six
Capacity	3442-3781cc
Power	160-265bhp
Transmission	4-speed manual 3-speed auto
Top speed	120-135 mph (193-217kph)
No. built	12,055/9,051/9,398

■ BELOW LEFT *Last of the XK line was the 150 of 1957, now with disc brakes all round and an optional 3.8-litre engine.*

■ BELOW RIGHT *In S form with the triple-carb 3.8-litre engine, the XK150 was good for 130mph (209kph).*

1954 gained more power (190bhp as standard, 210 with SE pack), bigger bumpers and – best of all – rack-and-pinion steering while retaining all three body options. If the coupé's roof line didn't improve its looks, then at least it offered rear seats for the first time.

Last of the XK line was the 1957 150, basically on the same chassis but with all new body panels: there was a voguish wrap-around front screen, a higher scuttle and more width as Jaguar tried to string out the model's appeal until the E-Type arrived in 1961. The braking problem was met with four-wheel Dunlop discs, and in the car's triple-carburettor 3.8-litre 'S' form (from 1959) power soared to 265bhp with a top speed of 135mph (217kph). There were 210bhp and 250bhp 3.4 cars, twin-carburettor 3.8s, and the odd automatic, highlighting demands for more luxury, particularly from Americans. Like all XKs, the 150 was great value, half the price of the contemporary Aston DB4 and Mercedes 300SL. It was getting old, though, and Jaguar had something more exciting in the wings – the E-Type.

■ ABOVE *The 150 came as roadster, drophead or coupé and with a choice of manual or automatic transmission.*

JAGUAR

■ JAGUAR MKII

The sight of a Jaguar MkII inspires a misty-eyed emotional response like no other 60s saloon. For a decade from 1959, the year of Britain's first motorway, the compact Jaguar was the bread and butter of Browns Lane, Coventry. It was the last proper sports saloon the company ever made.

The MkII was nothing if not versatile. It was favoured not just by the criminal fraternity (it was no accident that the James Fox character drove a white MkII in Donald Cammell's superb 1970 film *Performance*, or Michael Caine's pursuers a red one in the classic *Get Carter* of 1971) but also by the law itself because it was so wickedly fast. At the same time the MkII was also a very respectable car: a quiet, comfortable and classy businessman's express for the stockbroker belt. It made a fine name for itself on the track as a saloon-car racer, and industry personalities such as

■ ABOVE *The classic lines of the Jaguar MkII, first seen in 1959, were derived from the MkI 2.4, announced in 1955.*

■ BELOW *The MkII featured leather seat trim and up-market wood veneer for the dash and door cappings.*

■ LEFT *Jaguar gave the MkII a bigger rear window and different semi-open wheel spats to help brake cooling.*

■ LEFT *With the 3.8 engine the MkII could reach 125mph (201kph).*

■ BELOW *This 1966 MkII is one of the last to have big bumpers: slimline bumpers were announced for the 240/340 models of 1967.*

Graham Hill and Colin Chapman gave the MkII the stamp of approval by using them off-duty too.

Technically the MkII wasn't vintage Jaguar (though the unitary shell had broken new ground for the company on its 2.4 'MkI' progenitor of 1955), but its beautifully-balanced shape had the classic William Lyons touch, as did the interior with its leather seats and wooden dash and door cappings, the facia packed with dials and switches like a wartime bomber's flight deck. The MkII owner could do a legal 125mph (201kph) if he owned the full-house 3.8

manual overdrive car – it was the fastest saloon on the road for a time in the early 60s – or 120 (193) in the 3.4. The leisurely 2.4, on the other hand, couldn't even manage 100 (160) – which was why Jaguar's press department never allowed one out to be tested.

More than 80,000 MkIIs were sold, and the model inspired a whole raft of more expensive variations on the same theme: the S-Type, the 420 and even a Daimler with its own special V-eight engine. It is the pure original MkII, however, that has won the hearts of the public.

JAGUAR MKII (1959-69)	
Engine	Straight six
Capacity	2483/3442/3781cc
Power	120-220bhp
Transmission	4-speed manual 3-speed auto
Top speed	(3.8) 125mph (201kph)
No. built	83,980

■ BELOW *The 3.8-litre engine gave a claimed 220bhp, making the MkII one of the fastest saloons on the road.*

■ ABOVE *The famous leaping Jaguar designed by motoring artist Gordon Crosby. Safety legislation outlawed its use on later Jaguars.*

■ RIGHT *The XK engine was a tight fit in the MkII, with not much room for maintenance.*

JAGUAR

■ JAGUAR E-TYPE

The Jaguar E-Type was an instant classic, an exercise in cool aerodynamic theory and unashamed showmanship producing probably the most beautiful sportscar of the 60s. It had the ability to live up to the looks, too. The 150mph

■ RIGHT *From the outside the 3.8 and 4.2 Series 1 E-Types are hard to tell apart, but the bucket seats are a giveaway: this is a 3.8.*

■ ABOVE *On the open road the E-Type was good for over 140mph (225kph). The car nearest the camera is an early Series 1 3.8 roadster, behind is a Series 2 coupe.*

(241kph) that Jaguar claimed for the E-Type was devastatingly quick in 1961 (in reality only the tweaked-up press cars could achieve it, and 140 [225] was nearer the truth), making the new Jaguar Britain's fastest production car. Better still, it was probably Britain's greatest bargain pricewise, undercutting its nearest rival, the Aston Martin DB4, by a third.

That curvy shell, inspired by the Le Mans-winning D-Type racer, was immensely stiff – all the better to take advantage of its new wishbone and coil-spring independent rear suspension. Combining near-limousine ride comfort with vice-like grip, even on the slender cross-ply tyres that looked like something off a bike to modern eyes, the new Jaguar handled superbly. Providing the power was the 3.8-litre XK engine, already 13 years old but still well worthy of the new chassis. The same couldn't be said of the elderly, slow-shifting Moss gearbox, a feature of all Jaguars since the 1930s or the disc brakes that were spoilt by an uncertain-feeling pedal.

■ LEFT *Series 1 and Series 2 compared. The later car has open headlights to comply with American safety regulations.*

JAGUAR E-TYPE (1961-75)	
Engine	Straight six/V-twelve
Capacity	3781/4235/5343cc
Power	265bhp
Transmission	4-speed manual 3-speed auto
Top speed	Up to 150mph (241kph)
No. built	All models: 72,507

■ LEFT *In 1971 the E-Type became a Series 3 with a brand new V-twelve engine. Performance was back up to levels achieved with the Series 1 cars. Note the bigger grille and flared arches.*

■ BELOW *The E-Type's classic shape was derived from the D-Type sports racing car.*

■ ABOVE *Early E-Types had rather shallow footwells, restricting legroom. These "flat-floor" models are now few and far between.*

Pop stars, racing drivers and royalty jostled for position in an ever-lengthening waiting list for the car. Lew Grade wanted to borrow one for his new British TV series, *The Saint*, but Jaguar turned him down – they could sell every car they could make.

Despite the demand, development continued. The bigger 4.2 engine from 1964 was torquier and came with a much better gearbox and brakes. Seats and trim improved, as did the electrics,

making the 4.2 Series 1Es the best of the bunch. Appeals for a roomier car were answered by a two-plus-two version in 1966 and there was even an automatic as Jaguar tried to reconcile the E's performance image with a need to increase sales in America.

The rot was beginning to set in, however, and from the launch of Series 2 in 1968, middle age seemed to creep up on the E unawares. North American safety demands tarnished the purity of its styling with fussy open lights and strangled its power with emission controls, so that by the turn of the decade the car was a shadow of its youthfully vigorous former self. The final V-twelve Series 3 cars completed the sanitation process. Smooth and fast but somehow less soulful, the sylphlike shape was ruined on the longer, fatter V-twelve by fashionable fat arches and a cheap chrome grille. The once legendary sex symbol was a flabby spent force, living on old glories, not to mention borrowed time. It is amazing to think that Jaguar, gearing up for the E's

■ ABOVE *The shape everyone recognizes. The bonnet hump was needed to make room for the tall XK power unit.*

successor, the XJS, had trouble getting rid of the last few in 1975.

The E-type's design found a place in the Museum of Modern Art and is sensual rather than sexy, for the car was designed from the heart and the world has been in love with it from the start.

JAGUAR

■ JAGUAR XJ6

When Jaguar launched the XJ6 in 1968 they brought together in one design the standards of ride comfort, quietness, handling and roadholding – qualities previously thought incompatible in a luxury car – that eclipsed the best in Europe and set the pace for the succeeding 20 years.

In one stroke, Jaguar's boss Sir William Lyons rewrote the luxury-car rule book, not with radical new concepts – the XJ was a conventional front-engine, rear-wheel-drive coil-sprung saloon – but by fine-tuning existing components. On its plump tyres,

■ LEFT *To get around European tax laws regarding engine capacity, Jaguar offered the XJ6 with a short-stroke 2.8-litre engine. The only outward difference was the badge on the back.*

JAGUAR XJ6 (1968–87)	
Engine	6-cylinder
Capacity	2791/4235/3442cc
Power	180-245bhp
Transmission	4/5-speed manual 3-speed auto
Top speed	(4.2) 124mph (199kph)
No. built	(Series 1) 79,000

specially designed for it by Dunlop, this new British world-beater would out-corner Jaguar's own E-Type but had a ride that was softer and quieter than a Rolls-Royce. This was the world's most beautiful saloon too, a car with a feline aggression and organic muscularity that proved amazingly enduring: the last XJ saloons, the V-twelves, were built in 1991 and looked embarrassingly more attractive than the new XJ40.

Initially using the well-proven six-

■ LEFT *By 1979 the XJ had become the Series 3, with new styling touches by Pininfarina.*

■ BELOW *There was a Daimler version from 1970. This is the V-twelve engined double-six Vanden Plas in rare Series 1 form.*

■ RIGHT *The two-door coupé was a short-lived variant with pillarless side windows and a vinyl roof.*

■ RIGHT *The Series 3 XJ suffered build quality problems in its early career but went on to break all sales records in the 1980s.*

■ BELOW *Panther built a few up-rated XJ Series 3s in the 1980s.*

cylinder XK engine – the V-twelve didn't arrive until 1972 – most XJs were automatics, all had power steering and Jaguar built a few with a short-stroke 2.8-litre engine to beat European tax laws. That proved unreliable and is rare today. Like all Jaguars before it, the XJ was a bargain, often undercutting the nearest comparable Mercedes by more than half. As production got up to speed during the early 70s, the four-door XJ began to spawn other variants: the

inevitable badge-engineered Daimler, the short-lived XJC coupé (complete with vinyl roof), long-wheelbase and V-twelve cars.

The XJ wasn't perfect, of course. Quality, never top-drawer stuff, was looking very shaky on the first of the face-lifted Series 3 models at a time when the future seemed bleak for the still publicly-owned, strike-torn Jaguar. Buyers lost confidence and sales began to nose-dive. Enter, in March 1980, John

Egan, the man given the job of making or breaking British-flagship Leyland's problem child. The rest, as they say, is history: as his drive to improve quality at Browns Lane began to take hold, the flagging sales were arrested. Jaguar went public with spectacular success in 1984 and in North America the Jaguar range, spearheaded by the now 15-year-old XJ6, was breaking all sales records and creating the profits that allowed Jaguar to develop and build its successor.

JAGUAR

■ JAGUAR MK X

Broad in the beam, sumptuously curvaceous, the MkX/420G still holds the title of widest British production saloon, with 6ft 4in (1.93m) across its bulbous hips. It had and still has a chunky, slick elegance all of its own. A huge advance on its separate-chassis forefathers, this all-independently suspended and power-steered saloon was, half the price of its nearest true competitors in the tycoon luxury class of 1961.

British buyers were always resistant to the sheer bulk of the car – 5½in longer than the big MkIX it replaced, and a squat 8½in lower – yet if the scale of the MkX was very Detroit, the line was unmistakably Lyons.

The MkX was originally equipped with the triple-carburettor 3.8-litre XK engine from the E-Type. The 4.2-litre unit of 1964 brought more torque

■ ABOVE *With its E-Type three-carb engine, the MkX had excellent performance for its size.*

■ ABOVE *Handling was good too, thanks to its independent rear suspension derived from the E-Type.*

(283lb/ft – 384.9 N m – at 4000rpm) but an identical power curve (peaking at 265bhp at 3000rpm), enough to push the 4300lb (1950kg) saloon along at 120mph (193kph) even in automatic transmission form. In fact, through the gears, the automatic car was consistently faster than the manual, beating 10 seconds to 60mph (96kph); a hard-

driven MkX wouldn't have been far behind the tearaway MkII 3.8 and is quicker than a 4.2 XJ all the way up to 100mph (160kph). All this from a truly lavish five-seater saloon with a boot you could rent out as a bijou flatlet.

Yet buyers never took to this gentle giant of a car in the way they had to the Mks VII, VIII and IX before it. Interest

■ LEFT *The MkX, still Britain's widest ever saloon, featured monocoque construction, all-independent suspension and power steering as standard. Early cars had 3.8-litre engines, later models – from 1964 – 4.2-litre.*

■ RIGHT *The MkX competed head-on with large Mercedes models and even the Bentley S3, but was much cheaper.*

NEW 4·2 LITRE MARK TEN SALOON

■ ABOVE *The 4.2-litre MkX had more torque for better acceleration. There was a manual option, but most MkXs had automatic transmission.*

■ BELOW *In 1966 the MkX became the 420G, with detail improvements.*

had fallen away dramatically even by the time the 4.2 was announced, and it took a mid-term name change to rejuvenate sales in its final years. Thus, at Earls Court in 1966, MkX became 420G, causing instant confusion with its slimmer sibling, the new S-Type-based 420, that continues to this day.

Nobody really knows what the G stood for – there was no official line – but the general consensus seems to be "Grand". The shape remained unchanged but an instant recognition point was a new bright metal beading which broke up the car's massive flanks. The front grille was

changed too – with a thick central strip – as were the wheel trims with their new black centre badges. Inside the G, the skull-threatening timber dash rail was now padded (and equipped with a transistorized clock), while its seats were reshaped slightly to give more lateral support – something that road testers had consistently griped about. The last 420Gs were built in 1970 as the standard-setting XJ got into its stride, but the model lived on, in a sense, as the big DS420 Daimler Limousine which used a stretched version of the same floorpan.

■ ABOVE *This shot shows the sheer width of the MkX – 6ft 4in. It was common to see MkXs with scratched doors and wings.*

JAGUAR MK X/420G (1961-70)	
Engine	Straight six
Capacity	3781/4235cc
Power	265bhp @ 5400rpm
Transmission	4-speed manual 3-speed auto
Top speed	120mph (193kph)
No. built	10,870

JENSEN

■ JENSEN INTERCEPTOR & FF

Of all the cars Jensen of West Bromwich ever made, the interceptor and FF were easily the most outstanding. Beautiful and fast, the Interceptor was based on the previous glassfibre-bodied CV8, but featured a new Touring-style body.

FF stood for Ferguson Formula, the four-wheel-drive system developed by Harry Ferguson that, not unlike systems found on off-road vehicles, split the torque unequally between the front and rear wheels – 67 per cent to the rear, 37 per cent to the front – to give the car unreal handling qualities for a big GT car of the mid-60s. This, combined with Dunlop Maxaret anti-lock braking – another first – is what led the pundits to call the FF the world's safest car. Not until the Audi Quattro appeared 15 years later was four-wheel drive again offered on a performance road car.

■ ABOVE *The Interceptor convertible was designed to appeal more to American buyers. Frank Sinatra owned one.*

■ BELOW *This is a late 7.2-litre SIII Interceptor on alloy wheels.*

■ LEFT *The Interceptor as it appeared in 1966. The styling was by Touring and early cars were built in Italy, sharing some bits with contemporary Maserati models.*

JENSEN FF (1966-71)	
Engine	V-eight
Capacity	6276cc
Power	330bhp
Transmission	3-speed auto
Top speed	130mph (209kph)
No. built	320

At first glance the FF, with its distinctive Vignale shape, looked identical to the much more conventional Interceptor, and indeed they had much in common. Under the bonnet was a 6.3-litre 325bhp V-eight engine driving through a three-speed Torqueflite automatic transmission to a live rear axle. A closer look revealed a 4-in (10cm) longer wheelbase and a slightly different nose, while the most obvious recognition point was the extra vent on either front wing. Underneath, the tubular chassis – welded to the steel body – was almost totally different, with the prop shaft passing along the left of the engine and box and, at the front, a chassis mounted differential taking the drive to the front wheels. Extra weight slightly blunted the performance of the car compared with the two-wheel-drive Interceptor, but not much: the FF was still good for 130mph (209kph) with 0-60 (96) in eight seconds.

Although the car was widely acclaimed, it suffered by comparison with the near identical-looking Interceptor, which was nowhere near as accomplished but a third less costly. A Series II version was introduced in 1969 with a tidied-up interior and front-end styling.

Sales were slow compared with the two-wheel-drive car. The FF was discontinued in 1971, the Interceptor in 1976.

■ OPPOSITE *With four-wheel drive and anti-lock brakes the Jensen FF was an outstanding road car. Extra vents in the wings distinguish the FF from the Interceptor.*

■ LEFT *The 541 had a low-drag aerodynamic shape for its day, designed by Jensen's own stylist Eric Neale.*

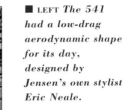

JENSEN 541R

When *Autocar* magazine's testers drove the 125mph (201kph) Jensen 541R in 1958 it was the fastest four-seater car they had ever tested. Its low-revving six-cylinder four-litre engine (from the Austin Sheerline) made light work of this high-quality, streamlined glass-fibre coupé. Low revs and ultra-long gearing gave the car a uniquely relaxed character.

Elegantly styled by Eric Neale, the 541's full-bodied, sweeping roof line blended into a clean, rounded tail. It was a low-drag shape, too: Jensen recorded a lowest-ever 0.39 candela (cd) at the Longbridge wind tunnel.

Work on the original 541 began in early-1953 and the car appeared at that year's Earls Court show. The show prototype was aluminium but production 541s were built in the newfangled glassfibre which was light and ideal for the new car's rounded form and subtle detail. It covered a new chassis consisting of 5-in (12.7-cm) tubes, braced by a blend of steel pressings and cross-members to make a platform. Suspension was modified Austin A70 with a live axle spring on half-elliptic at the back. For the steering a cam-and-roller system was used. There were big drum brakes all round.

JENSEN 541R (1957-60)	
Engine	OHV 6-cylinder
Capacity	3993cc
Power	150bhp @ 4100rpm
Transmission	4-speed with overdrive
Top speed	125mph (201kph)
No. built	193

■ BELOW *The 541R was for a time the fastest four-seater car you could buy, with a top speed of 120mph (193kph).*

The 541R of 1957 had the fittest DS7 version of the Sheerline four-litre engine, with twin carburettors on the right and a reworked cylinder-head In conjunction with higher 7.6:1 compression and a "long dwell" the power rose to 150bhp at 4100rpm with 210lb/ft (285.6 N m) of torque at 2500rpm.

Only 53 cars had the DS7 engine. Last of the 541 line was the S of 1961. This had a longer, wider body and standard Rolls-Royce automatic transmission. Styling never recaptured the earlier elegance and performance was down. Just 108 were built.

OTHER MAKES

■ JOWETT

Based in Bradford, Yorkshire, Jowett had its most exciting period after 1945. Both the Javelin and the Jupiter were technologically advanced flat-four engines, all torsion-bar springing and with a top speed of over 80mph (128kph). The R4 sports model was shown at Earls Court in 1953, but by then the firm was already in terminal financial trouble. It died the following year.

■ KIEFT

Cyril Kieft started making Formula 3 cars in 1950, progressing to produce a number of special sports-racing cars. These were succeeded by a pretty Climax-engined model in 1954, which was offered as a road car. In 1955 Kieft moved back into the steel industry from which he had come, selling out to Berwyn Baxter. He eventually sold the assets to Burman's, who showed a Formula Junior car in 1960.

■ RIGHT *The Jensen used many parts from the Austin range, including its big four-litre engine and some suspension components.*

LAGONDA

■ LAGONDA

A heroic last minute effort by freelance stylist William Towns, the Lagonda saloon that stole the 1976 Earls Court show looked as if it could have been beamed down from another planet: low and razor edged it was a show-stopper – and just the publicity – that back-from-the-dead Aston Martin needed.

170 deposits were taken at that show but prospective buyers weren't to know that their cars wouldn't be ready until 1979 because of problem with the high-tech electronics.

Towns' ambitious ideas for the interior with its digital dashboard and touch sensitive controls was somewhat in advance of the available technology as applied to motorcars, and in the interests of reliability, his concepts had to be watered down for production. Somewhere along the line the price had gone up by £10,000 – to £32,0000 – by the 1979 launch date but buyers willingly coughed-up. First to take delivery were Lord and Lady Tavistock.

Mechanically the Lagonda was well proven, essentially a stretched Aston Martin V-eight with meaty four-camshaft 5.3 litre V-eight engine. Suspension was same-again, too, but with the geometry and spring rates adjusted to cope with the extra weight, as well as self-levelling

■ ABOVE LEFT *The 1976 Lagonda, with its out of this world styling was the show stopper of the 1976 Earls Court show.*

■ ABOVE RIGHT *The engine was the familiar Aston 5.3-litre V-eight.*

LAGONDA	(1976–90)
Engine	V-eight
Capacity	5340cc
Power	340bhp
Transmission	3-speed auto
Top speed	140mph (225kph)
No. built	645

for the De Dion rear suspension. Scaling almost two tons, this was the biggest, heaviest and most opulently luxurious Lagonda since the war, nothing was left to chance in the labour-saving department, with air conditioning and electric seats all included in the price.

Pundits had nothing but praise for its

ride and handling, superb for a large saloon, but some dared to suggest that it could have been quicker off-the-line, while others raised eyebrows at the lack of rear seat legroom in such a huge car. Aston tried to answer these criticism with a still-born twin turbo version, while Tickford did a trio of stretched Lagondas with twin colour TVs. Never the car for the shy shrinking violet, the Lagonda then began its sad decent into the role of tacky oil-sheikh special painted white and fitted with body kits.

Towns tried to redeem his rapidly aging super saloon with a more rounded offering in 1987, but Aston messed-up his specifications and the car looked, if anything, worse.

It was too late. The dream car made flesh that had raised so many pulses back in 1976 died quietly in 1990 with 645 cars sold. There is talk of a successor but new owners Ford may decide that Aston should stick to what they do best – building Aston Martins.

■ FAR LEFT *Englishman William Towns styled the car.*

■ NEAR LEFT *Razor-edged design aged rather quickly.*

LAMBORGHINI

■ LAMBORGHINI 350GT

Launched in March 1964, the 350GT was the first Lamborghini production car.

Its Touring body was all new and prettier than the earlier 350GTV prototype, its alloy panels stretched over a steel frame on the usual Superleggera principle. At its heart was a four-cam 60-degree V-twelve engine, its crank machined from a solid billet. Detuned to 270bhp for the 350GT, the production engine had side-draught carburettors for a low bonnet line. Suspending the meaty round-tube chassis was a pukka coil spring and tubular wishbone suspension, with assisted Girling discs from the UK.

■ ABOVE *The classic 4-cam Lamborghini V-twelve engine which gave 280bhp.*

LAMBORGHINI 350GT (1964–68)	
Engine	V-twelve
Capacity	3464cc
Power	280bhp @ 6500rpm
Transmission	5-speed manual
Top speed	152mph (244kph)
No. built	143

■ ABOVE *The interiors were functional but luxurious. The five-speed gearbox was of Lamborghini's own manufacture and had synchromesh on reverse.*

ZF supplied the steering box and the five-speed transmission, and at the rear was a Salisbury differential. This advanced specification was schemed by rising star engineers Giampaolo Dallara and Giotto Bizzarini, laying the ground for the Lamborghinis yet to come.

Shatteringly fast, superbly smooth and very flexible, all this fine-handling 160mph (257kph) car lacked was matinée idol looks. Eschewing the classic, sinewy muscle tone of Pininfarina, Touring of Milan sketched a dramatic coupé for Lamborghini – memorably rounded, obviously fast,

■ ABOVE *For the rich family man there was always the 400GT two-plus-two with two small extra seats in the back. Note the quad lamps.*

definitely pleasing from some angles but, somehow, not quite right.

The initial alloy-bodied 350GT was the lightest and fastest of these early front-engined cars. Later 400GT and GT two-plus-twos were steel-bodied (the bootlid and bonnet were still alloy), with more torque and bhp in order to counteract the added weight, now a corpulent 2862lb (1298kg).

A four-litre engine became optional in 1965, but only 23 were built before the introduction of the steel-bodied 400GT two-plus-two in 1967.

LAMBORGHINI

■ RIGHT *The Miura was good for at least 170mph (273kph), but early cars suffered from front-end lift at high speed.*

■ LAMBORGHINI MIURA

Was there ever a more dramatic road car than the Lamborghini Miura? Pioneering the mid-engined configuration on a road car, it lifted this still-young company from promising newcomer to serious contender, eclipsing Ferrari in some people's eyes as a maker of advanced supercars: it would be a further seven years before Enzo produced a 12-cylinder mid-engined road car, the Boxer.

LAMBORGHINI MIURA (1966-72)	
Engine	V-twelve
Capacity	3929cc
Power	350-385bhp
Transmission	5-speed manual
Top speed	170mph (273kph)
No. built	762

■ LEFT *The Miura's beautiful shape was by the young Marcello Gandini of Bertone.*

■ ABOVE *It is hard to believe that this design came out in 1966: orders came flooding in when Lamborghini showed the prototype – and that was only a chassis.*

Though Ferruccio Lamborghini wouldn't let his young design team build a racer, he was happy to give the go-ahead for a super-sportscar, borrowing mid-engined principles from the latest crop of Formula 1 cars and sports racers, the 250LM and GT40. When the Miura was finished, Ferruccio thought it was too wild to sell to the public, seeing it more as an image-boosting show car that would help to sell his more conventional front-engined machines. The Miura – named after a Spanish fighting bull – turned out to be one of the company's best-selling and most profitable models.

Taking a sideways glance at the Ford GT40 chassis, designer Giampaolo Dallara schemed a unitary steel hull, but, unlike the Ford, comfortably big enough for two very rich occupants. To keep the length down, the four-litre, 350bhp V-twelve engine was mounted transversely behind the cockpit. To get the drive to the rear wheels, Lamborghini designed a special transaxle, mounted at the rear of the engine in unit with the light alloy crankcase, in a concept not unlike the BMC Mini but revolutionary on a car with such high performance. Suspending the whole chassis on coil

■ ABOVE *The interior was as futuristic as the body but could get very hot and noisy when the car was being driven hard.*

■ LEFT *With the nose and tail sections raised, the monocoque central hull is clearly evident.*

■ ABOVE *Eyelashes around the pop-up headlights were a Miura trade mark.*

springs and wishbones, he displayed the ensemble, still without a body, at the 1965 Turin show. Orders soon started rolling in and with a stack of deposits Ferruccio felt able to commission Bertone to clothe the naked car.

Nuccio Bertone put his best man on the job – Marcello Gandini. Just 25 at the time, he designed a bold, sensual car that, 30 years on, has lost none of its head-turning appeal. 'Eyelashes' around the flip-up lights and louvered engine cover were memorable styling signatures for what was easily the best-looking Lamborghini made. It was a year after its 1966 Geneva show introduction that the car, designated P400, went into full production, beset by assembly-line hiccups. It was worth the wait, however, for the car hit the headlines with a

170mph (273kph) top speed. Sheer performance was only half the story: the balance, traction and cornering power conferred by the mid-engined location put the Miura in another dimension. For advanced students with the requisite buying power it was dream come true, and anyone who complained about the glorious noise, heavy gear change, and the misery of driving it in traffic could go out and buy a more compromised automotive trinket.

Not that Lamborghini didn't fine-tune the somewhat raw original P400. The S of 1969 had a stiffer shell, wider tyres, improved suspension, vented disc brakes and a bit more power, plus little luxury touches like power windows and the option of air-conditioning. Best of the breed was the 1971 SV, with 385 bhp and completely redesigned front and rear suspension to eliminate aerodynamic lift which some owners had complained they suffered from at high speeds. A new sump cured engine-damaging oil surge during sustained hard cornering. The SV lasted just a year, bowing out in late 1972 as the LP400 Countach came on stream.

■ ABOVE *The Miura S of 1969 had a stiffer shell, wider tyres, vented disc brakes and improved suspension.*

■ RIGHT *The SV was the best of the lot, producing 385bhp and with the tendency towards high-speed lift finally cured.*

LAMBORGHINI

■ LAMBORGHINI ESPADA

While some lesser Italian supercars pretended to be four-seaters, only Lamborghini's Espada offered genuine comfort and space for its rear occupants.

Thus unique as a V-twelve express, this dramatically-styled car was certainly the fastest four-seater in the world when it was introduced in 1968. Top speed was an impressive 150mph (241kph), rising to 155 (249) on later versions; power crept from 325 to 350bhp on the 1970 Series 2, then 365bhp for the 1972 Series 3.

Inspired by the Marzal show car, Bertone designed a big waist-high coupé with a sweeping window line and a sharply cut-off tail. The glazed rear panel above the tail lights was unique

■ ABOVE *The first of the Espadas was seen in 1968. It was the world's fastest four-seater at 150mph, Lamborghini's answer to the Rolls-Royce.*

■ LEFT *You either love or hate Bertone's unmistakable shape, but you can't ignore it. It is blade-like and aggressive – and very big.*

■ ABOVE *Rear shot shows glazed rear panel to aid reversing. This early car has knock-on alloy wheels with spinners.*

■ BELOW *The original dashboard is bold and stylish. There really is room inside the Espada for four adults.*

and improved rear vision.

Up front under a huge alloy bonnet with NACA ducts was Lamborghini's classic quad-cam four-litre V-twelve, driving through a purpose-built five-speed gearbox. Wishbone suspension all round gave the big four-seater a superbly supple ride, but not at the expense of its handling, whose stability and lack of roll was in a different league to most big four-seaters. Early cars did without power steering, while on later versions there was the option of an automatic gearbox, not much fancied today.

The Espada ran from 1968 to 1978 and remains one of the best-selling Lambos ever. It is something of a supercar bargain today.

■ ABOVE *With the five-speed manual box and the most powerful 365bhp model, produced from 1973, top speed crept up to 155mph (248kph).*

■ BELOW *The wide track, fat tyres and suspension made for powerful cornering. Power steering and automatic transmission were available on later versions.*

LAMBORGHINI ESPADA (1968-78)	
Engine	V-twelve
Capacity	3929cc
Power	325-365bhp
Transmission	5-speed manual 3-speed auto
Top speed	150-155mph (241-249kph)
No. built	1,217

LANCIA

■ LEFT *The 3rd Series Aurelia, lighter and fatter in the background, and the 6th Series, more luxurious and refined.*

■ LEFT *The 6th Series B20 can be identified by its quarter-lights in the doors. 6th Series Aurelias had 112bhp and good torque from the 2.5-litre V-six.*

■ LANCIA AURELIA B20 GT

Honed through six series of careful development, with little thought to cost or compromise, the Lancia Aurelia B20 was a classic from birth. Discerning drivers respected its pace and handling – Formula 1 aces Fangio and Hawthorn both loved their B20s – while styling connoisseurs fêted Pininfarina's trend-setting coupé envelope for its elegant simplicity. Even in 1958, at the end of its eight-year cycle, a B20 was still one of the quickest, and most stylish, methods of arriving at your destination.

Schemed by Vittorio Jano, the Aurelia B10 saloon was at the frontier of motorcar design in 1950, and even when the final 6th series B20 coupés were rolling out of the Pininfarina works in 1958, few, if any, cars had caught up with it.

Early two-litre Aurelia coupés (1st and 2nd Series) are much coveted by the cognoscenti, while the 5th and 6th Series B20 coupés have a softer, more touring character than the earlier cars. You can spot a 6th Series coupé by its front-opening quarter-lights in the doors and chrome gutter and bonnet strips. The monocoque shell was assembled from hand-beaten steel panels, welded together, Lancia supplying a rolling platform to Pininfarina.

At the B20's heart was a V-six engine,

the first in series production, its capacity increased to 2451cc for the 3rd Series coupé of 1953. By the time the 6th Series cars were announced in 1957, it was producing a modest 112bhp: 5th and 6th Series Aurelias were actually detuned for increased torque by way of a softer cam. Its alloy block was short and stiff and well mounted on rubber to absorb some of the unavoidable roughness – inherent – in some parts of the rev range in a V-six design. It made do with a single camshaft in the valley of the V, operating light alloy pushrods. In-line valves worked in a modern

hemispherical combustion chamber. A double-choke Weber 40 sat in the centre of the V.

All Aurelias used a new rear-mounted, alloy-cased gearbox housing clutch, gears, final drive and the mountings for the inboard drum brakes. It even had its own oil pump and used massive aluminium pot joints mounted outside the wheel hub to reduce angular movement and wear. The 5th and 6th Series cars had a strengthened first gear and clutch but retained the fashionable column gear change: a Nardi floor-shift was a contemporary conversion. The 6th

■ LEFT *The classic shape of the Aurelia evolved from the Cisitalia: it was the world's first Gran Turismo car.*

■ OPPOSITE *The rear suspension of the Aurelia used semi-trailing arms on early cars, and a DeDion axle from the 4th Series on.*

■ RIGHT *Vignale built this coupé on the platform chassis supplied to coachbuilders.*

■ BELOW *The Aurelia was just as beautiful from the back, with its smooth, sweeping roof line.*

■ BELOW *Vignale was one of many coachbuilders who tried to improve on the Pininfarina design. None could match the elegance of the original.*

Series pulled 22mph (35kph) per 100rpm in its non-overdriven top ratio. From the 4th Series onwards, the Lancia semi-trailing arm suspension was discarded for a DeDion system that gave slightly more predictable wet-weather handling. Classic sliding pillar suspension remained at the front, its "I" beam axle strengthened on these later cars in an attempt to banish brake judder and steering shimmy.

Such was the popularity of the B20 that production carried on into the Flaminia era, the last 6th Series being built in the summer of 1958.

LANCIA AURELIA B20 GT 6 SERIES (1950-58)	
Engine	V-six
Capacity	2451cc
Power	112bhp
Transmission	4-speed manual
Top speed	112mph (180kph)
No. built	All models: 3,871

LANCIA

■ LANCIA FULVIA 1.6 HF

Shrouded in mystique and mythology, the 1.6 HF was a prince among Lancia Fulvias. It had a magnificent rally pedigree (with two world championship wins), 115mph (184kph) ability and an exotic and muscular specification.

Under the bonnet was a gem of a narrow-angle 1585cc V-four only used on early HFs. Carburettors were twin Weber 42s which made a throaty 115bhp, peaking at 6200rpm, though a handful of specially-tuned factory cars had 132bhp. The bespoke "piggy-back" five-speed gearbox – using the four-speed casing extended to house an extra set of gears – drove the front wheels, and like all Fulvias the HF had excellent handling. It did without a servo for its Dunlop disc brakes.

Outwardly the wheel arches probably gave it away first; black glassfibre fillets covered wider tyres on deep-rimmed Campagnolo alloys. The back sat quite high, the nose low, sniffing the road, and from the front there was a definite touch

■ LEFT *The 3rd Series Fulvia in its UK market version with higher-mounted headlamps.*

■ ABOVE *The 2nd Series 1.6 HF with flared arches, alloy wheels and high-backed seats.*

■ LEFT *The Zagato was a rare, special-bodied version with good aerodynamics. This is the desirable 1600 version.*

■ ABOVE *The Fulvia as it first appeared in 1965, with steel disc hubcaps and big lights.*

of grip-enhancing negative camber. Other HF giveaways were the lack of bright trim around the windscreen rubber, the subtle badges, alloy opening panels and, most significantly, massive 7-in (17.8-cm) driving lamps. HF points inside are more numerous. Seats are lightweight skeletal buckets, with a skimpy padded bench behind, rather than the standard coupé's proper moulded affair. Later "*lusso*" 1600HFs were softer, more luxurious cars, still fast but much less specialized.

Just 1280 1.6 HF Fulvias were built in 1968 and 1969 to homologate the car for international rallying. A batch of 30 came to the UK in right-hand-drive form with more trim for British customers who didn't want Plexiglas and vulnerable bumperless bodywork.

The HF was the spiritual progenitor of today's pocket-rocket homologation specials such as the M3 and Integrale "Evo".

When the final chapter on the motorcar in the 20th century is written, the jewel-like 1.6 Fulvia will probably go down as one of the great driving machines.

■ BELOW *With its very free-revving 1.3-litre engine, even the standard Fulvia was quick. It was practical, too.*

LANCIA FULVIA 1.6 HF (1968-69)	
Engine	V-four
Capacity	1588cc
Power	115-132bhp
Transmission	5-speed
Top speed	115mph (185kph)
No. built	1,280

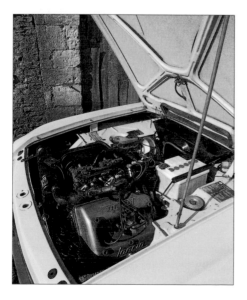

■ LEFT *The V-four engine was a jewel which – in its most powerful guise – sent up to 132bhp to the front wheels through a four- or five-speed gearbox.*

■ RIGHT *The unmistakable tail-end of the Fulvia. You can see simple but effective beam-axle and leaf springs underneath.*

LANCIA

■ LEFT *The road-going Stratos was good for 142mph (227kph) with the Ferrari Dino engine.*

■ LANCIA STRATOS

The sensational wedge-shaped Lancia Stratos was conceived because Lancia needed a new rally weapon for the 1970s. The Fulvia HF, by the late 60s/early 70s, was looking and feeling old and couldn't put enough power through its front wheels for predictable handling. The 170bhp Renault Alpines – despite delicate gearboxes – were embarrassing the once-proud Lancia coupé. What Lancia's competitions boss Cesare Fiorio knew he needed was a specially tailored rally car homologated for Group 4: powerful, light, mid-engined and strong enough to compete on rough events like the Safari with suspension that could be adjusted to suite the conditions.

He saw his salvation in an unlikely place: the Bertone stand of the 1970 Turin motor show. Here sat an incredibly low wedge of a car called Stratos (short for stratosphere). It was designed by the young Marcello Gandini, best known

■ BELOW LEFT *The engine sat behind the passengers' heads, the lights were flip-up, and the short wheelbase meant hair-trigger handling.*

LANCIA STRATOS (1973-75)	
Engine	DOHC V-six
Capacity	2418cc
Power	190bhp @ 7000rpm
Transmission	5-speed
Top speed	142mph (228kph)
No. built	492

■ LEFT *Nothing looked quite like the Stratos, designed by Marcello Gandini of Bertone. It has inspired at least one kit-car replica.*

■ BELOW RIGHT *The Stratos was conceived as a rally car. The road car was incidental, existing only to homologate the car for competition.*

then for his Lamborghini Miura. Mid-engined and light, it used a Lancia engine, the V-four 1600HF from the Fulvia: Fiorio saw at once that the screen-cum-door layout and the extremely laid-back driving position could never be practical on a rally car,

but the car ran under its own power and *concept* was there.

With the blessing of Lancia's new managing director Ugo Gobbato, Bertone – and Gandini – were commissioned in 1971 to build a more conventional device, still mid-engined

and sitting on the same wheelbase but built around a new drive train, the Ferrari Dino 2.4 V-six and its five-speed transaxle. There was talk of a cheaper alternative Fiat 132 drive train, and Lancia even threatened to use the Maserati Bora 4.7-litre V-eight when the

■ LEFT *Although Stratos production finished in 1975, new cars were still available in 1980.*

■ BELOW *Some say 1,000 Stratos road cars were built, but 500 seems more likely. All were Dino-powered, although a cheaper Fiat-engined car had been proposed.*

request for 500 Dino engines met with some political resistance within Maranello. In fact – apart from a single four-cylinder prototype – the Stratos only ever used this four-cam iron block unit, mounted on a beefy box section with beams welded to the firewall of the steel driving compartment/monocoque. Front suspension was coils, wishbones and an anti-roll bar, while at the rear a stronger system of Beta-style struts with lower wishbones replaced a double wishbone and coil-spring set-up that had proved fallible during testing.

A prototype, looking more or less like the eventual production car, was shown at Turin in 1971 on the Bertone stand: testing continued in 1972 and 1973 until production finally began tentatively late in 1973. They needed to build 400 cars to homologate the Stratos for Group 4 international rallying. Some say Bertone built 1,000 cars, others say under 500, and the latter figure seems to be the most widely accepted. The car was finally passed for homologation on 1 October 1974.

Bertone built the monocoque and glassfibre nose/tail sections in Turin with final assembly (trimming, painting, testing etc.) at Lancia's Chivasso factory. Production was pushed quickly during the summer to get the car homologated and officially ended in 1975.

■ LEFT *The Stratos in the famous works livery with Alitalia sponsorship.*

■ BELOW *The Stratos was the ultimate expression of the wedge. Its wheelbase was no longer than a Mini's.*

LINCOLN

■ LINCOLN CONTINENTAL

Collectors now recognize the 1961 Lincoln Continental – the "clap door" – as one of America's most influential motorcars. At a time when fins and chrome were still popular on most domestic cars, Lincoln – an up-market division of Ford – launched a car with clean, unadorned lines, very much American in scale but almost European in feel. The rear-hinged rear door gave it the clap-door nickname and chrome was applied sparingly to its crisp-edged flanks. It became the "in" car with the rich and famous in America and was even the White House vehicle of choice: it was in a stretched, Presidential clap-door that President John F Kennedy was

LINCOLN CONTINENTAL (1961-79)	
Engine	V-eight
Capacity	7045/7565cc
Power	300-365bhp
Transmission	3-speed auto
Top speed	125mph (201kph)
No. built	342,781

■ ABOVE *The Continental of the mid-1950s was the most luxurious car in the American industry: Lincoln lost money on every one they built.*

■ ABOVE *The original Continental was an instant classic, inspired by Henry Ford's son Edsel.*

■ RIGHT *The presidential stretched Lincoln Continental, with bullet-proof windows and metal-work.*

■ BELOW *The MKII Continental was virtually hand built and featured every extra you could think of.*

■ RIGHT *The MKII Continental of 1956 had very clean lines for the period and was colossally expensive.*

■ ABOVE *The 1961 Continental won much praise for its styling.*

assassinated in Dallas, Texas in 1963.

Lincoln knew they were on to a winner and changed the Continental only subtly in a long nine-year production run: some new chrome here, a new grille there (and almost every year a longer wheelbase) but essentially the same clean shape all the way through. There was a power-top four-door convertible version alongside the saloon from the start and a hardtop coupé from 1966. The Continental always had the biggest V-eight engine – 7.0-litre at first, 7.5-litre later – automatic transmission and every conceivable labour-saving device as befitted a car comparable with the most luxurious in the world: power seats, air conditioning,

power steering, electric windows and much more. Packing up to 365bhp, the 5215lb (2366kg) Continental was a fast car, capable of up to 125mph (201kph) but like all large American saloons was an unruly handful on anything but a straight, smooth road. Not that such things mattered to the middle-aged Americans who bought the Continental: it had a boot big enough for the golf clubs, lots of snob appeal and it never broke down.

It was the last good-looking Lincoln for a long time. The MkIII Continental – a two-door personal luxury car with a strong whiff of the pimp-mobile about it – ushered in a new era of chintzy styling. But it was nice while it lasted.

■ NEAR RIGHT *Lincoln emphasized the elegance and good taste of their flagship, not to mention its White House connections.*

■ FAR RIGHT *The Continental had cleaner styling and smaller fins – though the car remained huge.*

LOTUS

■ LOTUS 7

Although the first production Lotus was the Six of 1953, sold as a kit and intended for use in club racing, it was the now-legendary Seven of 1957 that put the fledgling company on the road to success. A skimpy and extremely basic two-seater, the new car had a cleverly designed multitubular space-frame chassis with a stressed aluminium body making no concessions to access for the driver and passenger: there were no doors, just cutaway sides, and if the hood was up it was nearly impossible to

■ ABOVE *The Seven was a Spartan sportscar ideal for club racing. It was light and fast.*

■ BELOW *A super-Seven like this is stunningly quick owing to its excellent power-to-weight ratio. The style has changed little over the years.*

■ ABOVE *This is a very early Seven and could be had with a Ford side-valve or Coventry Climax engine. The body was made from stressed aluminium.*

■ RIGHT *Only 15 Sevens were fitted with the desirable Lotus twin-cam engine, as used in the Elan.*

get in. Minimal mud-guards covered the front wheels and the headlights were free-standing.

There was coil-sprung independent front suspension and a well-located live rear axle with radius arms and coil spring/damper units, which produced superb handling. Straight-line performance depended on the engine fitted by the owner: most went the Ford route with a side-valve 100E unit; a few used the Coventry Climax FWA engine and some late S1s had the BMC A Series unit. The space frame was

■ RIGHT *The early car again, with its wire wheels and polished aluminium body. The Seven was Colin Chapman's first true production model.*

■ BELOW *The S4 of the 1970s was an attempt to cash in on the Midget/Spitfire market.*

LOTUS SEVEN AND SUPER SEVEN (1957-70)

Engine	4-cylinder
Capacity	997-1599cc
Power	37-115bhp
Transmission	4-speed
Top speed	80-108mph (128-173kph)
No. built	242/1,350/350

■ BELOW *The dashboard had the bare minimum of instruments, and the hood was functional rather than attractive.*

simplified on the S2 of 1962, which could also be recognized by its flared clam-shell wings.

The Super Seven, available from 1961, came with a series of progressively more powerful engines: a Cosworth-tuned 1340cc Ford Classic unit and, later, a bigger 1498 Cortina GT or Cosworth 1599cc engine. Disc brakes appeared on the front for the first time. The S3 car used a 1600 Cortina engine, although 15 had a Lotus twin-cam engine of the type fitted to the Elan. Attempting to bring the concept up to date – and take some of the

Midget/Spitfire market – the Seven S4 of 1970 had a chunkier-looking glassfibre body bonded on to a modified chassis with Europa Type front suspension and a Watts linkage at the rear.

It was softer and more civilized than the earlier cars and hard-bitten Seven enthusiasts didn't take to it, yet it sold respectably – more than 900 cars in three years.

With the arrival of value added tax (VAT) in 1973, Lotus decided to bail out of the kit-car market altogether and sold the design rights to Catherham Cars who build the car in S3 form to this day.

■ LEFT *As with most Lotus parts, the instruments and switch gear could be found on lesser production saloons.*

■ ABOVE *The cycle wings offered minimal protection from road spray. Doors were detachable to give more elbow room.*

LOTUS

■ LOTUS ELITE

If the Seven was a spartan club racer, then the Elite was the first proper Lotus road car, a sophisticated little GT blessed with superb handling and memorable looks. Launched in 1959 (prototypes had been seen as early as 1957), it was the first car to have a glassfibre monocoque made up of floor, body and a structural centre section with the outer opening panels bolted into place afterwards. Power for this lightweight structure came from an

LOTUS ELITE (1959-63)	
Engine	4-cylinder
Capacity	1216cc
Power	71-105bhp
Transmission	4/5-speed
Top speed	110-130mph (177-209kph)
No. built	998

■ LEFT *Thanks to lightweight construction and clever suspension, the Elite had superb handling: few cars could out-corner it.*

overhead-cam 1216cc Coventry Climax engine, first with 71bhp in single-carburettor form, later with 83bhp and twin carbs giving 118mph (189kph) potential. The high top speed was attributable to the low drag shape by stylist Peter Kirwan Taylor, with its amazing 0.29(cd). A creditable 35mpg was well within reach.

What made the Elite really special was its nimble handling. With coil-spring damper units at the front and modified MacPherson struts (Chapman struts) at the rear, it cornered like a go-kart, yet not at the expense of ride

■ LEFT *The Elite was launched in 1959, but the first prototypes had been seen as early as 1957. The body is a glassfibre monocoque – there is no separate chassis.*

■ RIGHT *From the rear you can see how the Elite inspired the Elan, its much more successful younger sister. Because of the shape of the door glasses the windows wouldn't wind down very far.*

comfort. It had rack-and-pinion steering and high-specification disc brakes on all four wheels.

The model was much praised but had its problems. The monocoque shell promoted lots of drumming and vibration, and the cabin was very poorly ventilated – the profile of the door glass meant it was impossible to wind the windows down! Quality was never top-drawer stuff and the price was high – more than a Jaguar XK150. From 1960

there was revised rear suspension and improved interior trim.

The SE model had 85bhp and a close-ratio five-speed ZF gearbox rather than the standard BMC-derived unit. The 95, 100 and 105bhp versions were offered

before Lotus eventually pulled the plug on their prodigy in 1963.

By then Lotus needed all the production capacity they had for the Elan, which was much easier to produce and equally talented.

■ LEFT *Because of its low-drag shape the Elite had a high top speed – up to 130mph (209kph) with the most powerful engine option.*

■ ABOVE *The simple dashboard echoes the profile of the car. Interior comfort wasn't a strength of the Elite.*

■ RIGHT *Superb handling and a good power-to-weight ratio made the Elite a popular racing car.*

■ LEFT *The Elan took over from the troublesome Elite in 1962. This is the big valve sprint of the early 70s.*

LOTUS

■ LOTUS ELAN

First seen in 1962, the Elan put Lotus of Hethel, Norfolk on the map as a make of world-class road cars. Central to design was a steel back-bone chassis, fork-shaped with wishbones and coils at the front, Chapman struts and lower wishbones at the back with centre-lock steel wheels. All gave the car tremendous agility and excellent ride. The steering rack came from Triumph. Girling disc brakes were used all round.

The Elan's 105bhp engine had twin chain-driven cams. The block and bottom end came straight from Ford, pre-Heron head iron lump bored out to 1558cc. The four-speed gearbox was from Ford, too.

This powerful, light car, innately balanced and voraciously quick, set the standard for the perfect B-roads dicer. Current for 10 years, it spawned a coupé and a bigger two-plus-two sister. Quality and reliability improved all the while.

The 1971 Sprint was the final flowering of the 1962 Elan with a Tony Rudd-developed big-valve engine giving 25 per cent more power – 126bhp at 6500rpm. Acceleration, always rapid, was now explosive: to put things in perspective, the big-valve Sprint could

■ BELOW *Only when you put somebody in the driving seat do you get an idea of the diminutive size of the Elan.*

■ ABOVE *The twin-cam engine was based on the Ford Cortina iron block. It gave the lightweight Elan superb acceleration and proved reliable in service.*

LOTUS ELAN (1962-73)	
Engine	In-line four
Capacity	1588cc
Power	105-126bhp
Transmission	4/5-speed manual
Top speed	115-118mph (185-189kph)
No. built	12, 220

■ FAR LEFT *The Elan coupé proved a popular option from the mid-60s onwards.*

■ LEFT *Like all Lotuses, the Elan had a glassfibre body. It wouldn't rust but was subject to crazing and cracking.*

■ RIGHT *Three ages of Elan: early car, SE and Sprint. Note knock-on wheels with spinners and rude exposed door handles. Bonnets come away completely for good engine access.*

get to 60 as quickly as a Lamborghini Islero and, in top gear, had the edge on the likes of the 246 Dino and Porsche 911E at up to 80mph (128kph). It was a more oil-tight and quieter engine, claimed Lotus, with a less raucous exhaust note than earlier cars. Big-valve Sprints reverted to Weber carbs, and a few had the five-speed Austin Maxi-derived gearbox from the Plus 2.

Elan production ended in 1973 as Lotus tried to move away from its kit-car image – the car had been available in weekend do-it-yourself form from the start – and moved towards more up-market machines like the Elite and the Esprit. Today the spirit of the Elan has been revived in the Elise.

OTHER MAKES

■ LAGONDA

Bought by David Brown in 1947 and now part of Aston Martin, Lagonda was founded in 1906 by an American, Wilbur Gunn, at Staines, Middlesex (from 1974 Surrey). The firm made both light cars and more powerful tourers before 1939, the late 30s models being honed by WO Bentley, notably the V-twelve. The David Brown takeover enabled Bentley's last design to enter production, as the 2.6-litre. Lagondas were made – with one break – until 1965 (the DB4/5-based Rapide), then there was another gap until 1974–75. Latterly, the most famous Lagonda-badged car has been the wedge-shaped V-eight, first seen in 1976, but there have been no Lagondas since 1990.

■ LANCHESTER

The Lanchester of 1895 was remarkable in that it was designed as a motor car from the ground up rather than as a horseless carriage. The Lanchester brothers' innovatory spirit can be seen in all their pre-1930 products. A pioneer British motoring concern, Lanchester faded after acquisition by BSA in 1931 – the armaments and motorcycle firm also controlled Daimler. By 1956, the make had been quietly phased out of production as fellow-marque Daimler teetered towards extinction.

■ LEA-FRANCIS

In the late-1920s the British firm Lea-Francis made fine small sporting cars, but in 1935 the cash ran out and reorganization was needed before another sporting range emerged in 1938. Updated versions of the pre-war cars were made after the Second World War but were always expensive, with limited appeal, and by 1952 the firm was in trouble. They made their last car, the Lynx, in 1960.

■ LLOYD

Production of the Lloyd car, brainchild of British motor trader Roland Lloyd, started in Grimsby, Lincolnshire (Humberside) in 1936 with the rear-engined 350 model. The car which followed, the 650, built from 1946, was far more advanced and lasted until 1950. Sales were poor because of price.

■ LMB

Leslie Bellamy made his name as the creator of the LMB split-beam ifs conversion. Associated with Nordec in the 1950s, he became a key figure in providing tuning gear for Britain's "perpendicular" Fords. The short-lived LMB Debonair was the logical conclusion to these endeavours, intended for assembly by both LMB and EB.

MASERATI

■ MASERATI GHIBLI

Maserati conceived the 1967 Ghibli as
its ultimate late 60s road car. It might
not have been as technically advanced
as its rivals from Ferrari (the 275
GTB/4) and Lamborghini (the 350GT)
but it was at least as beautiful, with a
lean, low shape by the talented young
designer Giorgetto Giugiaro, then
working for Ghia. Even today it is one of
the designs of which he is most proud,
and some say it is a better-looking car
than the Daytona.

The performance left nothing to be
desired, even though Maserati made no
attempt to keep weight down with this
luxurious, steel-bodied car. With the
earlier type of 4.7 V-eight engine – a
four-cam design closely related to a type
that originated in a 300S racer in the
1950s – the Ghibli was a 150mph
(241kph) car.

With the later 4.9-litre SS engine. the

■ ABOVE *The Ghibli
was Maserati's
answer to the
Ferrari 275 GTB
and Lamborghini
350GT. It was
more beautiful
than either, if not
quite as
sophisticated.*

■ LEFT *The blade-
like lines were
penned by
Guigario, then
working for Ghia.
A Spider version
was also available.*

■ LEFT *The
Maserati V-eight
engine started life
in the beautiful
450S racer of
1957 and was still
in production in
the 90s.*

■ RIGHT *Unlike some rivals, the Ghibli's body was constructed in steel, so the car was no lightweight. Top speed was in the region of 165mph (265kph) with the biggest engine and manual box.*

■ BELOW *Installed in the Ghibli, the V-eight gave 330-335bhp with enormous torque.*

■ BELOW *Although the shape suggests a rear tail-gate, the Ghibli had a conventional bootlid. The car was a two-seater.*

■ RIGHT *The rare Ghibli Spider, built to compete with the Daytona Spider on the American market. It is the most valuable Ghibli model today.*

MASERATI GHIBLI (1967-73)	
Engine	V-eight
Capacity	4719/4930cc
Power	330-335bhp
Transmission	5-speed manual 3-speed auto
Top speed	165mph (265kph)
No. built	1274

top speed went up to 165 (265), though it only produced 5bhp more. Smooth and tractable, these engines majored on torque rather than ultimate power, with a fairly modest rev limit. The auto box option obviously cut performance considerably, but most Ghiblis had the five-speed ZF manual.

Maserati made the traditional suspension work beautifully. Cornering was flat, heavy steering precise,

lightening nicely at speed. The leaf-sprung live rear axle gave the game away, however, with a jiggly ride. The brakes, big four-wheel discs, were well up to the job of stopping the portly Ghibli.

To increase its appeal – especially on the American market – a Spider version of the Ghibli was launched in 1969 and is now one of the most collectable post-war Maserati road cars.

Those who required four seats could

buy the Indy from 1969, a car technically almost identical to the Ghibli but with a less pleasing body by Vignale.

Ghibli production faded away in 1973 as the Citroën-influenced Bora and Khamsin began to come on stream as Maserati's flagship supercars. By the standards of low-volume supercars, the Ghibli was successful, with 1,149 cars built plus a further 125 Spiders.

MASERATI

■ MASERATI KHAMSIN

The Maserati Khamsin was a front-engined supercar dating from the 1972 Paris show, although production didn't begin until 1974. Named after an Egyptian wind, it was crafted in steel by Bertone and angular and dart-like in

■ BELOW *The car's low build made retractable headlights obligatory.*

■ ABOVE *The top speed of the Khamsin was 153mph (245kph) with the manual gearbox.*

■ ABOVE *The interior was as well-stocked with dials as an airliner's flight-deck.*

MASERATI KHAMSIN	
Engine	V-eight
Capacity	4930cc
Power	320bhp at 5500rpm
Transmission	5-speed manual 3-speed auto
Top speed	153mph (246kph)
No. built	421

shape, with a swoopy wedge profile and an abruptly sawn-off tail. A feature was its glazed rear panel, with the tail-lights held in suspension by the glass.

Inside, the chunky dash, with its awful nylon-covered top, lacked both the symmetry and restraint of more tasteful 60s Maseratis, but air conditioning was standard and there was an adjustable steering column and hydraulic up-down seat movement.

All Khamsins came with the classic Maserati four-cam V-eight engine, mounted well back against the bulkhead so that, with the 20-gallon (91-litre) fuel tank filled, weight distribution was an ideal 50/50. The pedigree of this all-alloy powerhouse was impeccable. It was launched in the 450s in 1956 and its first road car application was in the flagship 5000GT in 1959. Thereafter, Maserati juggled with bore and stroke ratios depending on the application. There were 4.2 and 4.7 V-eights but the Khamsin came only as a dry-sumped

4.9, red-lined at 5500rpm to make a full-bodied 320bhp. Torque, though, was its forte: a colossal 354lb/ft (481.4Nm) at 4000rpm. Needless to say, the Khamsin had massive low-speed lugging ability, so thickly spread is this torque across the 800-5500rpm power band.

Conceived as a successor to the Indy and Ghibli, the Khamsin differed from its 60s front-engined predecessors in having proper double-wishbone rear suspension rather than an outdated, if well located, live axle. Further, it used Citroën hydraulics for steering, brakes, clutch and the pop-up headlights and driver's seat adjustment. It was the last Maserati to feel the technical influence of French control: by the time Khamsin production was getting into its stride in 1975, Citroën had pulled out.

As the last great, front-engined car to carry the Trident – a proper supercar rather than a jumped-up executive saloon – the Khamsin holds a special place in the history of the marque.

■ RIGHT *The Bora was Maserati's first mid-engined road car, although it still used the old four-cam V-eight. The style was by Italdesign.*

■ MASERATI BORA AND MERAK

With Lamborghini setting the technical pace with the mid-engined Miura, critics knew it was only a matter of time before Ferrari and Maserati would have their own mid-engined flagship supercars. In fact it wasn't until 1973 that Ferrari's Berlinetta Boxer became commercially available, just beaten by the Maserati Bora of 1971.

As on the Ghibli, the styling was by Giugiaro, who by this time had left Ghia and was running his own studio, Ital Design. His shape, first mooted in 1969, was elegant and clean-limbed but lacking perhaps the sheer animal beauty

of the Ghibli and the Lamborghini Miura. That the Bora was fast almost goes without saying: the 12-year-old 4.7-litre V-eight engine, punching out 310bhp, could push the slippery Bora up to 175mph (281kph) with 80 (128) coming up in second gear. What's more, the Bora was a refined car: audible conversation with a passenger was possible up to 150mph (241kph), then

MASERATI BORA (1971-80)	
Engine	V-eight
Capacity	4719/49430
Power	310-320bhp
Transmission	5-speed manual
Top speed	160mph (257kph)
No. built	571

unheard-of in a mid-engined. With Citroën now at the helm, it came as no surprise that a few complex hydraulics entered with super-sharp brakes and powered adjustment for the pedals, seats and steering-column rake. Handling was the last word in stability, a major advance on the front-engined Ghibli.

The Bora was joined in 1972 by a little brother, the Merak. At first glance, this new entry-level Maserati looked identical to the Bora, with the same front end panels, but from the B pillar back used awkward single-buttress sections sweeping down from the roof. The engine was the three-litre V-six from the Citroën SM. It was much shorter than the V-eight and allowed two rear seats to be incorporated. It handled well but lacked ultimate punch, a criticism answered by the 1975 SS version in which power was increased from 190 to 220bhp. For Italy there was a two-litre tax-break special Merak.

The Bora changed little in its nine-year history, gaining only the larger 4.9-litre engine in 1976 before bowing out in 1980. The Merak followed in 1981.

■ ABOVE *The Bora's cabin was civilized and remarkably quiet at speed.*

■ RIGHT *From the front the Bora and Merak were almost impossible to tell apart, but the smaller-engined Merak had extra rear seats and different three-quarter treatment.*

■ ABOVE *The Maserati badge dates back to the birth of the company in 1926.*

■ LEFT *The Bora was capable of 160mph (257kph) but was never as popular as contemporary Ferraris.*

MAZDA

■ MAZDA COSMO

With the futuristic-looking 1967 Cosmo
110S, Mazda just pipped NSU to the
post as a producer of twin-rotary
wankel-powered production cars. Like
the Ro80, it was designed from the
ground up for the new engine, taking
advantage of its compact dimensions
and good power-to-weight ratio.
Capacity was equivalent to about two

MAZDA COSMO (1966-72)	
Engine	Twin-rotary wankel
Capacity	2000cc (nominal)
Power	110-128bhp
Transmission	4/5-speed manual
Top speed	116-125mph
	(186-201kph)
No. built	1,176

■ FAR LEFT *Rear
lights split by
bumpers were
among Cosmo's
styling features.*

■ ABOVE LEFT *The
Cosmo was
Mazda's first foray
into the world of
exciting, high-
performance cars.*

■ BELOW LEFT *The
Cosmo name lives
on today on top-
line cars but is
almost unknown
outside Japan.*

litres with an output of 110bhp at
7000rpm. Rather than using peripheral
ports for maximum power, Mazda had
its inlet ports in the casing in the name
of increased low-down torque, idling

smoothness and fuel consumption at low
speeds.
     In most other respects, the 110S was
a conventional, stylish luxury sports
coupé pitched against the likes of the

■ LEFT *With the
Cosmo, Mazda just
pipped NSU to the
post as makers of
the first rotary-
powered
production car.
Even so it was
something of a
test-bed and only
1176 were built.*

■ BELOW *The rotary engine built under licence to Dr Felix Wankel. It had fewer teething troubles than the NSU unit.*

Porsche 911 and the Jaguar E-Type. Top speed was 116mph (186kph) with 0-60 (96) in about 10 seconds, revving to 7000rpm in the usual smooth, vibration-free wankel fashion. With a DeDion axle at the rear and wishbones at the front, it had excellent handling with a rather hard ride and a good brake set-up with discs at the front and drums at the back. The Cosmo changed little in its six years of production, gaining a

closer-ratio five-speed gearbox, a longer wheelbase and a little more power – 128bhp – on the 1968 "B" model.

The Cosmo name lived on in a series of rather more conventional-looking saloon-based coupés and survives to this day on Mazda's high-tech luxury flagship. Mazda is the only company that still markets rotary engines in production cars most famously in its best-selling RX7 sportscar.

■ ABOVE *The Cosmo was designed to compete with the Porsche 911 and Jaguar E-Type and featured a Dedion rear axle. More powerful later models could reach 125mph (201kph).*

OTHER MAKES

■ MARAUDER

The 100mph (160kph) Marauder was the brainchild of Rover engineers George Mackie, Peter Wilks and Spen King, who set up their own firm to produce it. Bodies were made by Richard Mead and Abbey Panels. Just 15 of the P4-based cars were produced before rising costs sidelined the project.

■ MARCOS

Marcos has been making cars in Britain since 1959, when Jem Marsh and Frank Costin used a composite chassis and a lower body made of marine ply for their first car. The classic Dennis Adams-designed 1800 made the company's reputation, but the four-seater Mantis model of 1970 was badly timed and the company ceased production the following year. Manufacture restarted in the 1980s.

■ ABOVE *Today's Cosmo is a very high-tech luxury flagship packed with sophisticated electronics.*

■ RIGHT *By the mid-1980s, the Cosmo had begun to look very ordinary, as the coupe version of 1975 shows.*

MERCEDES-BENZ

■ BELOW *The 300SL roadster was announced in 1957 and had better handling than the gullwing.*

■ MERCEDES-BENZ 300SL

The Mercedes-Benz 300SL was one of the most sensational sports cars of the 1950s. It was easily one of the fastest, with a top speed of 130-155mph (209-249kph), depending on axle ratio. Only a handful of Ferrari and Maserati road cars could approach this performance at the time – and, strictly speaking, they were not fully fledged production cars like the SL ("super light").

The original Gullwing coupé, with its unique roof-hinged doors, was launched in February 1954, though the Le Mans-winning prototypes had already been given a sneak preview in 1952. The body, built in steel with alloy panels, was supported by a complex space frame of tubes not seen before or since on a road car, the deep sills necessitating the use of Gullwing doors. With its blistered wheel arches and smoothly-curved rump, it was one of the most instantly recognizable shapes on the road.

Under the bonnet was an advanced, fuel-injected overhead-cam three-litre engine canted over to keep the bonnet

■ LEFT *The convertible model was designed to appeal to the Americans and was easier to service.*

■ ABOVE *The cutaway shows canted-over straight-six engine and coil-spring suspension.*

■ RIGHT *Mr and Mrs Tony Hancock with their new 300SL convertible. These cars were popular with celebrities.*

■ LEFT *Gullwing doors on the original coupé meant that the car could have deep, strong sills, but they were difficult to open in an accident if the car rolled on to its roof.*

■ BELOW *Le Mans-winning 300SLRs gave a sneak preview of the 300SL.*

■ ABOVE *1,858 roadsters were built before the new 230SL took over in 1963.*

■ ABOVE *The interiors were beautifully finished but a bit fussy – note the white steering-wheel.*

■ ABOVE *300SLs could do anything between 130mph (209kph) and 150 (241), depending on the axle ratio.*

line low. Derived from the straight-six used in big 300 saloons, it pioneered the use of fuel injection on road-going cars, delivering a reliable 240bhp at 6100rpm. A price tag in Britain approaching about twice the price of the contemporary Jaguar XK140 – made the 300SL the preserve of the very rich and it was also a favourite with celebrities.

The 300SL had its problems, however. Suspect swing-axle rear suspension needed an expert to tame it if the SL were to be driven to the limit of its capabilities, although in the right hands it was supremely capable, as its fine record in racing and rallying testifies. The body was prone to leaks and the space-frame construction was difficult to

repair, making the car unpopular with dealers.

Thus, the Gullwing coupé was replaced, after 1,400 units had been made, by the 1957 roadster, a successful attempt to make the 300SL easier to live with. Low-pivot swing axles, with a horizontal compensating spring, made roadholding far more predictable. The light-alloy three-litre engine was tuned to give 10bhp extra (now 250 at 6000rpm) and marginally more torque for flexibility. It was also easier to build, slimmer sills allowing conventional doors. Beautifully made in the Mercedes-Benz tradition, the roadster had a top which folded neatly away under an elegant steel lid behind the sports bucket seats. The roadster proved

even more popular than the Gullwing, 1,858 examples finding rich new owners by the time production ended to make way for the far less specialized 230SL, in 1963.

MERCEDES-BENZ 300SL (1954-63)	
Engine	SOHC in-line six
Capacity	2996cc
Power	240bhp
Transmission	4-speed manual
Top speed	130-150mph (209-241kph)
No. built	1,400 Gullwings/ 1,858 roadsters

MERCEDES-BENZ

■ MERCEDES-BENZ 230/250/280SL

The 230, 250 and 280SL Mercedes sports cars are as sought-after today as they were in their 1960s heyday. They offer a mix of chic styling, solid German build quality and engineering and spirited driving qualities that few could equal. Always a firm favourite with women drivers, the cars offered handling and performance that also won approval from Stirling Moss, one-time works driver for Mercedes in Grand Prix and sports-car racing, who owned a 250SL. A well-sorted SL can inspire an enthusiastic driver with its fine handling, roadholding, braking and a surprisingly sporty automatic transmission.

Many see the SL as too sumptuous, spacious and sybaritic to be a true sports

car, yet it proved itself in Europe's toughest rally, the Marathon de la Route, over a Spa-Sophia-Liège route, won in 1963 by a 230SL driven by Eugen Böringer. The SL designation – first used on the much more powerful 300SL of the 1950s – stood for "super light", although the cars were heavyweights ranging from 2855lb (1295kg) for the 230SL to 3120lb (1415kg) for the 280SL. The only concessions to weight saving were

MERCEDES-BENZ 230/250/280SL (1963-71)	
Engine	Straight six
Capacity	2306/2496/2778cc
Power	150-170bhp
Transmission	4/5-speed manual 4-speed auto
Top speed	120-127mph (193-204kph)
No. built	19,831/5,186/23,885

■ ABOVE *The 250SL had a slightly bigger six-cylinder engine and disc brakes all round.*

■ LEFT *The 190SL was a forerunner of the 230SL, a cheap alternative to the 300 and with drastically less performance from its 190 saloon engine.*

■ LEFT *The simple lines of the 230SL have weathered the years well.*

■ RIGHT *The 280SL was the last of the Pagoda-roofed cars and probably the best. Many were automatic yet performance was still strong – over 120mph (193kph).*

the doors, bonnet, bootlid and hood stowage panel, made of aluminium.

The first 230SLs – with removable "Pagoda" steel roof panel – were built in March 1963. They featured a 150bhp four-bearing straight-six engine (with Bosch injection pioneered by Mercedes on its W196 Grand Prix cars of 1954 and 1955), front disc brakes and optional power steering. Sales neared

■ FAR LEFT *The SL for the 1970s was the V-eight engined 350SL, hugely popular during a near 20-year life span.*

■ NEAR LEFT *Its wide track and fat tyres gave the SL impressive grip and handling.*

■ ABOVE *All these SLs had a fuel-injected straight-six engine renowned for its reliability.*

20,000 in 1967 when the 230 made way for the 250SL. Power stayed at 150bhp but the engine was sweeter and had more torque, while the 250 had discs all round and power steering as standard. Best of the bunch was the 280SL, built from November 1967 to March 1971. With a 170bhp seven-bearing engine

this version goes well with automatic transmissions, though there were four-speed manual options and a rare five-speeder. The only external recognition point was one-piece wheel trims. Some later cars had optional alloy wheels. Production totalled 23,885, making the 280SL the most popular model.

■ LEFT *The 230SL was launched in 1963. Its styling hardly changed in nearly a decade of production.*

MERCEDES-BENZ

■ **RIGHT** *From the front you can tell a 3.5-litre convertible by its stacked headlights. The bodyshape dates from the early 60s.*

■ MERCEDES-BENZ 280SE 3.5 COUPÉ

Elegant Mercedes-Benz W111 coupés and convertibles were based on new mid-range W111 saloons, though styling – by Paul Braqc who later penned the 230SL – was bereft of the saloon's clumsy fins. He drew a tight, handsome, Detroit-influenced pillarless hardtop for the coupé, with fashionable wraparound front and rear screens, squared-off rear haunches and stacked lights at the front, glass-bubble covers echoing the design of the top-of-the-range Fintail saloons. Doors were long and heavy. The rounded profile of the flanks – with a crease to break up the flat expanse of steel – suggested weight and solidity.

For 1962, the 220 was joined by the air-suspended, fully disc-braked power-steered 300SE coupé using the big alloy 160bhp three-litre straight six first seen in the Fintail saloons a year earlier. It was all change again for 1965 when the 250 replaced the 220 range. From this point, the two-door cars took technical lead from the new W108 S-Class saloons that replaced the upper-range Fintails that year. With higher final drive gearing and bigger, 14-in (35.6-cm), wheels, the 250 coupé was almost as quick as the 300. It shared the bigger car's disc

■ *ABOVE This is an earlier six-cylinder convertible 220 with single vertical lights each side.*

■ *ABOVE The handsome coupé had distinctive American-influenced pillarless styling and vestigial tail fins. The 3.5 badge on the back lets you know it's a V-eight.*

brakes. Thus, it seemed perfectly rational to Benz-watchers when Stuttgart rationalized the coupé range with a single 280SE model in 1967, the smooth, flexible 2778cc unit pumping 160 real horsepower in fuel-injected form.

The final and best W111 coupé derivative was the 1969 V-eight, confusingly badged 280SE 3.5. Conceived to appease American buyers

weaned on lazy, high-torque V-eights, this single-cam per bank electronically-injected engine gave a full-blooded 200bhp at 5800rpm in "dirty" European tune, good for 125mph (201kph) with 60 (96) in under 10 seconds.

Still top of the Mercedes range – if you discount the 600 Limousine – the W111 two-door stayed in production until 1971, when it was replaced by the 350SLC.

MERCEDES-BENZ 280 SE 3.5 COUPÉ (1969–71)	
Engine	SOHC injected 90-degree V-eight
Capacity	3499cc
Power	200bhp @ 5400rpm
Transmission	5-speed manual 4-speed auto
Top speed	125mph (201kph)
No. built	4,502

■ **LEFT** *Apart from the 600, the 3.5 coupé and convertible were the flagships of the Mercedes range – and very expensive.*

■ RIGHT *The 600 was designed to take on the best cars in the world. Apart from its width it looks, at a glance, very similar to other models.*

■ BELOW *The stretched six-door model was much loved by tycoons and pop stars: this one belonged to John Lennon.*

■ MERCEDES-BENZ 600

With the 1961 600, Mercedes set out to build the world's ultimate saloon – a Rolls-Royce beater – with no regard to cost or compromise. Millionaires could choose the standard 126in (320cm) wheelbase, 18ft (5.5m) four-door 600. Heads of state had the Pullman, its wheelbase stretched to 153in (389cm) and available with an optional six doors,

MERCEDES-BENZ 600 (1963–81)	
Engine	V-eight
Capacity	6332cc
Power	250bhp
Transmission	4-speed auto
Top speed	123mph (197kph)
No. built	2,190 saloon/487 Pullman

■ LEFT *The 600 in its normal wheelbase form was the ultimate in saloon car luxury with its V-eight engine, air suspension and electric adjustment for everything.*

extra occasional seats and a glass division between front and rear compartments. Both used a 6.3-litre fuel-injected V-eight engine producing 300bhp, driving through an obligatory four-speed automatic transmission. Independent suspension used air bags on all four wheels, powered by an under-bonnet pump, for a firm, comfortable ride. Seat adjustment, steering assistance and door locks were linked to

a central hydraulic system.

Despite its enormous weight – 5000lb (2268kg) for the saloon, 5850lb (2654kg) for the eight-seat Pullman – the 600 was no sluggardly barge: it would top 120mph (193kph), storming to 60 (96) in not much more than 10 seconds – though the penalty was fuel consumption in low teens. Handling, too, was surprisingly nimble, with good power steering, plenty of grip and

brakes – big four-wheel discs – that were beyond reproach. There were plenty of sports cars, never mind luxury saloons, that couldn't live with a well-driven Mercedes 600. Hugely expensive and hand built in tiny numbers, the 600 stayed on the Mercedes price lists until 1981 and had no effective replacement. The technology found its way on to lesser Mercedes, most famously the 300SEL 6.3 saloon of 1968.

■ RIGHT *The massive six-door car had extra occasional seats and a glass division. It would do 120mph (193kph).*

MG

■ MG TC/TD/TF

To get back into production quickly after the Second World War, MG of Abingdon, Oxfordshire had no option but to warm up its pre-war model, the TB. Thus the TC of 1945 had the same big 19in (48cm) wheels, fold-flat screen, crude semi-elliptic suspension and slab-tank body with ash framing. The body was wider now to give more elbow room for its passengers, while synchromesh on second, third and top gear made it more pleasant to drive. Hydraulic brakes were

■ ABOVE *The TD of 1949 was the first MG sportscar to have the independent suspension system from the YA saloon.*

MG TC/TD/TF (1945-55)	
Engine	In-line four
Capacity	1250/1466cc
Power	54-63bhp
Transmission	4-speed manual
Top speed	78-86mph (125-138kph)
No. built	10,000 TC/ 29,664 TD/9,800 TF

another welcome improvement.

Traditionalists loved it: it was nippy – 78mph (125kph) flat-out – and fun to drive. Nobody seemed to mind the heavy steering and rock-hard suspension. US servicemen stationed in the UK loved them so much they took them home and gave Americans a taste they never lost for European sports cars. Soon the TC was spearheading an export drive to the USA – and that's where most of the 10,000-car production run ended-up.

Charming as it was, the outdated TC couldn't go on for ever, so for 1949 MG introduced the TD: same chassis, same 1250cc four-cylinder engine but with

■ ABOVE *The TC has been a successful club racer. The normal screen is replaced by aero screens on this car; the roll-bar is a modern addition.*

■ RIGHT *A standard TC had a 1250cc engine and differed from the pre-war TC in its use of a wider body, synchromesh gearbox and hydraulic brakes.*

■ RIGHT *The TF was announced in 1953 with a more modern, sloping grille, and fuel tank. Inside there was a restyled dashboard and better seats.*

■ BELOW *The trade mark MG grille looked much as it did before the war.*

■ ABOVE *MkII TDs had a higher compression engine; 29,664 of them were built.*

■ LEFT *The TF was a holding operation until the MGA appeared. Later cars had a 1500cc engine.*

the new independent front suspension and the rack-and-pinion steering of the YA. Bumpers front and rear and smaller-disc wheel didn't do much for the looks, but the TD was roomier and slightly faster, especially in higher compression MkII form from 1952. The TD was a big seller, racking up 29,664 units in its four-year production run.

The final flowering of the traditional MG was the TF of 1953. By moulding the headlamps into the front wings, which sloped the grille and fuel tank,

Abingdon had gently modernized the shape. Inside, there were individual front seats and a restyled dashboard. Early cars had the 1250cc engine, but from 1954 a 1500cc unit giving 63bhp restored some of the performance.

The TF looked what it was — warmed-up leftovers — and was really a holding operation while Abingdon prepared its first modern post-war model, the MGA of 1955. Ironically, the TF is the most sought-after of the three "square-rigger" post-war MGs.

OTHER MAKES

■ MESSERSCHMITT

This West German aircraft manufacturer took over production of this design in 1953, continuing until 1962 before selling the project back to Fritz Fend, the maker of invalid carriages who had originally designed the car. The TG500 (Tiger) model was the most interesting, with a top speed of 75mph (120kph) on 20bhp and four wheels.

■ METROPOLITAN

Made by BMC and variously known as an Austin, Nash or Hudson, the little Pininfarina-designed coupé and convertible Metropolitan was conceived by Nash president Bill Mason as a small car for the American market. It was never a huge success, but at one time was the best-selling US import after the Volkswagen Beetle.

MG

■ LEFT *The A was the first modern MG in years. It had very pretty styling and a stiff box-section chassis, the last used on an MG.*

■ MGA

The A was the first modern post-war MG. As the first new MG produced after the merger of Nuffield and Austin, it was also the first to use the corporate mechanical parts: much of the drive train was derived from the Austin A50 saloon. Its pretty pinched-waist body was derived from a special TD raced at Le Mans and was based on an enormously strong box-section chassis. Some said it was too strong and unnecessarily heavy, but it was certainly rigid.

There was nothing groundbreaking about the suspension, with its front wishbones and leaf-spring rear beam axle, yet the handling of the A was more than a match for its contemporary Triumph and Austin Healey rivals. Bolt-on steel wheels were the standard offering, with centre-lock wires as an option. On 1489cc and 72bhp from its B Series engine, it wasn't wildly quick, but 95mph (152kph) was respectable, as was the potential 30mpg.

It was joined by a handsome coupé version in 1956 and in 1958 by the exciting twin-cam with its Harry Weslake-designed twin overhead-camshaft 1588cc engine. With 108bhp, top speed went up to 110mph (177kph). It was a highly desirable property but the engine – based on a modified B series block – had a poor reliability record,

MGA (1955-62)	
Engine	In-line four
Capacity	1489/1588/1622cc
Power	72-108bhp
Transmission	4-speed
Top speed	95-110mph (152-177kph)
No. built	101,081

■ LEFT *The MGA twin-cam was an exotic development using a new double overhead camshaft version of the B Series engine. It was powerful but troublesome. Dunlop centre-lock disc wheels are a twin-cam signature.*

■ RIGHT *The 1600 MGA had front disc brakes and could do a genuine 100mph (160kph). With its recessed front grille, this is a MkII.*

■ BELOW *The coupé version had well-balanced styling but was not as popular.*

■ BELOW *The simple dash featured basic instrumentation and a large steering-wheel.*

with a reputation for burning pistons. It was available in coupé and roadster form and could be recognized by its handsome Dunlop centre-lock lightweight steel wheels. Dunlop disc brakes on all wheels were standard. High prices and its dodgy reputation kept sales low. BMC killed this most exotic of MGs in 1960.

By that time the standard MGA had become the 1600, with 80bhp, disc front brakes and genuine 100mph (160kph) ability. The only outward difference, aside from badging, was the separate rear indicators. Optional was the DeLuxe, with the standard pushrod engine but the disc brakes and centre-lock wheels of the slow-selling twin-cam.

The final MkII 1600 of 1961 had a slightly bigger bore 1622cc engine, pushing the power output to 86bhp. You can identify a MkII by its recessed front grille and horizontal rear lights. Production finished in 1962, giving way to the unitary MGB, certainly a more modern MG than the A but not such a pretty one.

■ LEFT *To use up the remaining twin-cam parts, MG built the 1600 deluxe with the same disc brakes and centre-lock wheels.*

■ ABOVE *The B Series was an uninspiring engine but was reliable, cheap to build and simple to work on.*

■ LEFT *Today, enthusiasts have the twin-cam's engine problems licked.*

MG

MGB

The MGB is still one of the most numerically successful sports cars ever built, with more than half a million made between 1962 and its demise in 1980. At the height of its popularity Abingdon was making more than 50,000 a year.

The main difference between the MGB and its forebear the A was in construction: gone was the rugged and heavy separate chassis, replaced by a

■ LEFT *From the rear in particular, the B lacked the character of the more curvaceous MGA.*

■ BELOW LEFT *From 1962 to 1967, the MGB roadster looked like this with a chrome grille.*

■ BELOW RIGHT *The interiors were traditional but comfortable. Early cars had a large, sprung wheel.*

lighter unit construction shell. The car appeared originally as an open roadster with a three-bearing version of the venerable B Series 1798 four-cylinder engine. Torque was its main strong point – 110lb/ft (149.6Nm) at 3000rpm – but on twin SU carburettors its 95bhp at 5400rpm was creditable, if unsensational. Suspension, steering and rear axle came straight from the BMC parts bin to keep costs down, so there were few technical highlights, but the B was a genuine 100mph (160kph) car with safe, if uninspired, handling.

It was joined in 1965 by the Pininfarina-inspired BGT with its tailgate rear doors and occasional rear seat – strictly for children. It was 160lb (72.7kg) heavier than the roadster but

had the five-bearing engine and quieter rear axle from the start. MkII models from 1967 had the improved rear axle across the board as well as an all-synchromesh gearbox and the option of automatic transmission. Fashion dictated some minor styling tweeks in 1969 in the form of a recessed matt black grille and trendy Rostyle wheels. The interior suffered some minor styling tweeks around this time too, with more modern seats and steering wheel. For the American market this was when, in terms of power output, the rot began to set in, with lower compression ratios to satisfy local emission regulations.

There was much worse to come, however: in 1974, MG announced the black bumper cars with grotesque plastic

bumpers and increased ride height to keep the aging model legal in North America, where most production still went. Performance was in decline – the GT wouldn't even manage 100mph (160kph) – and the handling was ruined by its new, taller stance, but the car

MGB (1962-80)	
Engine	4-cylinder
Capacity	1798cc
Power	95bhp
Transmission	4-speed with overdrive
Top speed	106mph (170kph)
No. built	387,259 125,621 GTs

■ RIGHT *The hood folded well out of sight but was difficult to erect compared with foreign convertibles like the Fiat and Alfa Spider.*

■ BELOW *The B would do around 100mph (160kph) and could be had with overdrive or – later on – an automatic option.*

continued to sell because it was one of few open cars available. The B survived until 1980 with few changes, and it seemed likely that it would be the last proper MG sports car when British Leyland announced its decision to abandon the Abingdon factory.

There were two rather more exciting versions of this evergreen sports car. The MGC of 1967 was a three-litre version of the B designed to take the place of the "Big" Healey 3000 models. Bigger 15-in (38-cm) wheels and a bonnet bulge differentiated the C from the B and, underneath, there was torsion-bar front suspension rather than wishbones. With a 145bhp six-cylinder engine, the C was certainly fast, but nose-heavy weight distribution spoiled the handling. Just

under 9000 roadsters and GTs were sold in less than two years.

Four years later, British Leyland answered calls for a more powerful version of the car with the GT V-eight. With its smooth, quiet and very torquey Rover 3.5 V-eight this was a much better prospect, but yet again success eluded this 125mph (201kph) machine. It didn't look different enough from the stock four-cylinder car, and the critics panned its lack of suspension refinement, the wind noise and its relatively high price. Few wanted the V-eight in its day – only 2,591 were sold between 1973 and 1976 – but today it is a sought-after and entertaining classic, easily the best B of the lot.

■ ABOVE *The MGC was a six-cylinder version of the B. Its three-litre engine gave it 120mph (193kph) capability, but too much weight over the front wheels spoiled the handling.*

■ BELOW *An early three-bearing MGB on rare disc wheels. The styling was influenced by Pininfarina.*

MINI

■ MINI

The BMC Mini, launched in 1959, is Britain's most influential car ever. It defined a new genre. Other cars used front-wheel drive and transverse engines before but none in such a small space. Packaging was its greatest strength – interior space was staggering. Every square inch was used: there were big door-bins, tiny 10-in (25-cm) wheels that didn't intrude on passenger space and a bootlid you could fold down to use as a luggage platform.

Designer Alec Issigonis sketched his ideas on the back of envelopes, envisaging the most compact possible "cube" in which four passengers would sit, headed by a space-saving front-wheel-drive system. The gearbox was mounted *under* the engine instead of behind it, saving more inches. Another major innovation was a new rubber-cone suspension system designed by Dr Alex Moulton. Inspired by the Suez Crisis of 1956, the Mini amazingly took BMC just two years to develop and put into production. Launch was set for 26 August 1959.

There were four initial versions: the Austin Mini Seven and Morris Mini-

■ LEFT *The Mini Cooper was the precursor to today's hot hatchbacks.*

■ ABOVE *You can spot an early Mini by its outside door hinges, but the shape remains basically unchanged to this day.*

■ ABOVE *One of the famous works rally Minis still in action today.*

Minor, both available in basic or de luxe trim. Costs were pared down by fitting sliding windows, cable-pull door releases and those trademark externally welded body seams.

On the road, it handled better than any rival (and most sports cars) and

boasted "penny-a-mile" running costs. Nippy, easy to park, it quickly became fashionable to own and the word Mini passed into everyday English language. Subframes allowed a huge variety of Mini derivatives: van, pick-up, estate, long-boot Riley Elf and Wolsley Hornet,

■ ABOVE *Initially the cars were sold as the Austin Seven and the Morris Mini-Minor but in the late 1960s the Mini became a marque.*

■ RIGHT *The quaint Countryman version used non-structural timbers, in contrast to the Morris Minor.*

■ LEFT *BMC fielded the Cooper S with much success, winning the Monte Carlo Rally three times.*

■ LEFT *Today Rover has reinvented the Cooper as a trendy town car, but the original went out of production in 1971, in favour of the 1275GT.*

the Mini Moke workhorse-turned-leisure-vehicle and, recently, the Mini Cabriolet.

What sealed the Mini's reputation among enthusiasts, however, was the legendary Mini-Cooper, launched in 1961. Grand Prix-winning constructor John Cooper persuaded BMC to extract the most out of the Mini's innate handling prowess by stroking the 848cc Mini engine up to 997cc (later 998cc) and increasing power from 34bhp to 55bhp. Now 87mph (139kph) was possible, fast enough to justify fitting tiny front disc brakes. Later, there was an "S"

■ LEFT *An unmistakable shape, the superbly packaged Mini was voted "car of the century" by motoring pundits.*

MINI (1959–)	
Engine	4-cylinder
Capacity	848-1275cc
Power	33-76bhp
Transmission	4-speed manual 4-speed auto
Top speed	74-96mph (119-154kph)
No. built	More than 5,300,000

model with 70bhp on tap (later 1275cc versions were boosted to 76), capable of almost 100mph (160kph). BMC fielded works Mini-Coopers with incredible success. "Normal" Coopers won the Tulip Rally in 1962-63. The "S" was all-conquering in British saloon car racing and the Monte Carlo Rally, which it won in 1964, 1965 and 1967. Sadly, the Cooper was dropped in 1971 in British Leyland's rationalization.

The Mini has seen many technical changes: hydrolastic liquid suspension

from 1964; winding windows from 1969; the option of square-nosed Clubman and 1275 GT versions from 1969; bigger 12-in (30.5-cm) wheels from 1984 and standard 1275cc engines from 1992. Nearly 40 years on, the Mini has as passionate a following as ever and was recently voted "Car of the Century" by motoring pundits. It provides cheap transport and is a technical triumph, a dominant rally car, a packaging masterpiece and, as Britain's best-selling car ever, a runaway sales success.

■ ABOVE *Radford and Wood and Pickett offered luxury Minis trimmed to Rolls-Royce standards in the 1960s and 70s. Peter Sellers owned a Radford Mini.*

MORGAN

■ MORGAN 4/4

Morgan made its name with three-wheeled tricycles. It didn't make its first four-wheeled sports car until 1936. That, the original 4/4, disappeared in favour of the more powerful Vanguard-engined Plus Four in 1950. However, by the mid-50s Morgan perceived a need for a more basic car priced below the Plus Four. Thus the Series II 4/4 was reborn after five years.

Like all Morgans, it used a simple ladder-frame chassis, sliding-pillar front suspension and ash framing for the traditional-looking steel or light alloy bodies with the new-style cowled waterfall grille seen on the Plus Four from 1954. Up to 1960, power came from the Ford side-valve Anglia 100E engines. From 1960, in SIII form, there were 997cc overhead-valve engines from the 105E Anglia and four speeds at last.

Series IV cars from 1961 to 1963

were given a bigger 1340cc engine, pushing the top speed above 70mph (112kph) and now there were front disc brakes for the first time. In 1963, it was given the latest Cortina engines in

standard 1498cc and GT form. In 1968, it had the crossflow Kent engine, usually in 95bhp competition form, which was standardized anyway from 1971. From 1969, a four-seater body – with an ugly

■ ABOVE *The shape of the Morgan has hardly changed since the early 1950s. Only the disc wheels date this car.*

■ ABOVE *The car that started it all, the Morgan three-wheeler.*

■ LEFT *The body is aluminium fashioned over a traditional ash frame.*

■ ABOVE *Today Morgans are still built slowly by hand in the Malvern factory. There is a long waiting list.*

■ ABOVE *The period styling of the Morgan is its main attraction, but it also drives like a car from the 1930s, with a hard ride and very few creature comforts – but that's how the buyers like it.*

pram-like hood – was offered.

Since the early 80s, various power plants have been available, including the Fiat 1600 twin-cam and 1600 CVH Ford Escort engine. A five-speed gearbox was offered from 1982. The car continues to this day with the Rover twin-cam engine.

With its rock-hard ride, flexing body and anachronistic looks, the Morgan 4/4 has a unique post-vintage thoroughbred appeal. Hand built very slowly in Morgan's Malvern factory in Hereford and Worcester County, the 4/4 is still hugely popular – if you want one, you'll have to join a five-year waiting list.

MORGAN 4/4 (1955–)	
Engine	4-cylinder
Capacity	1172-1599cc (Ford engines)
Power	36-96bhp
Transmission	3/4/5-speed
Top speed	75-110mph (120–177kph)
No. built	6,803 up to 1991

■ LEFT *Minimal instruments and a big, sprung steering-wheel give the Morgan a traditional feel inside, too.*

OTHER MAKES

■ MINIJEM

Closely derived from the 1964 DART prototype of Dizzy Addicott, the Jem was thus a sister-car to the Mini-Marcos, which was also spawned by the DART. It was made at four locations over the years, its principal homes being Penn, in Buckinghamshire, and Cricklade, in Wiltshire.

■ MONTEVERDI

These Swiss-built, American-engined supercars were designed by Peter Monteverdi, who built his first car in 1951 at the age of 17. In 1956 he took over his father's repair shop in Basle (Basel), and orientated it towards specialist sports cars, becoming the world's youngest Ferrari importer. The first of the big V-eight cars was the "High Speed" of 1967. Vehicle manufacture continued until 1982. It included luxury saloons and off-roaders based on Mercedes saloons and American models.

MORGAN

■ MORGAN PLUS 8

When supplies of the 2138cc Triumph four-cylinder engine dried up in the late 60s, Morgan were left without a high-performance engine for their flagship Plus 4 model. Help was on the horizon, however, in the form of Rover's all-alloy 3.5-litre V-eight derived from a discarded Buick design of the early 60s and recently introduced in the big P5B saloon and coupé. Light, compact and powerful (165bhp), it was ideal for the job and transformed the Morgan into a real road-burner: top speed leapt to more than 120mph (193kph) with stunning rapid acceleration matched by very few road cars. Renamed the Plus 8, it looked at first glance identical to its predecessor but in fact had a slightly longer wheelbase and wheel track and subtly different body contours. The most obvious change was the light alloy wheels but, underneath, the sliding pillar front suspension and leaf-sprung live rear axle remained – along with the rock-hard vintage-style ride.

It was an immediate success, with more than 4,000 built to date, though

■ ABOVE *You can spot a Plus 8 by its light alloy wheels, though the wheelbase was longer and the track wider than the 4/4.*

■ LEFT *The Rover V-eight engine gave the Plus 8 electrifying performance.*

■ ABOVE *The body of the Plus 8, like all Morgans, was fashioned in alloy over a timber frame.*

■ RIGHT *Announced in 1968, the Plus 8 is still in production today.*

■ BELOW *The four-seater Plus 4 Morgan was practical but suffered from an unattractive hood.*

■ RIGHT *The body of the Plus 8 was wider than lesser Morgans. By the late 70s there was a five-speed gearbox from the Rover SD1 saloons.*

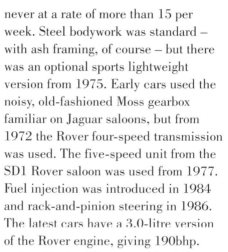

never at a rate of more than 15 per week. Steel bodywork was standard – with ash framing, of course – but there was an optional sports lightweight version from 1975. Early cars used the noisy, old-fashioned Moss gearbox familiar on Jaguar saloons, but from 1972 the Rover four-speed transmission was used. The five-speed unit from the SD1 Rover saloon was used from 1977. Fuel injection was introduced in 1984 and rack-and-pinion steering in 1986. The latest cars have a 3.0-litre version of the Rover engine, giving 190bhp.

As with the 4/4, demand for this anachronistic car remains healthy, with a waiting list of several years.

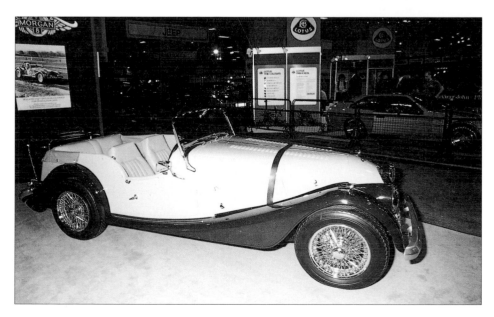

■ ABOVE *More than 4,000 Plus 8s have been built since production started in 1968.*

■ LEFT *Production of the four-cylinder models continues alongside the Plus 8.*

MORGAN PLUS 8 (1968-)	
Engine	V-eight
Capacity	3528cc
Power	160-190bhp
Transmission	4-5 speed
Top speed	125mph (201kph)
No. built	4,000 plus

MORRIS

■ MORRIS MINOR

The much-loved Morris Minor was the outstanding economy car of its day and became one of the best-selling and longest lived too – production ran from 1948 to 1971.

Its rack-and-pinion steering and torsion-bar independent suspension gave superb handling. Modern unitary construction and smooth styling made the Minor seem ultramodern after the warmed-up pre-war cars British motorists were used to. Designer Alec Issigonis had wanted a flat-four engine for the car but had to make do with the existing Series E flat-head in-line unit,

smooth but under-powered. These, known as the MM Series cars, had low-mounted headlights until 1950. The two-door and open tourer were joined by the four-door at about the same time, but the most important change came in 1952 when the overhead-valve Austin engine was fitted, first fruit of the BMC merger. The classic half-timbered Traveller was announced in 1953.

■ ABOVE *The early Minors had a split two-piece front screen.*

MORRIS MINOR (1948-71)	
Engine	In-line four
Capacity	918/803/943/1098cc
Power	27-48bhp
Transmission	4-speed manual
Top speed	60-78mph (96-125kph)
No. built	1,583,619

■ ABOVE *The classic Minor convertible, or tourer, was announced alongside the saloon in 1948. It is now the most sought-after of them all.*

■ RIGHT *A later Minor 1000 tourer. By 1959, production of the Minor had turned a million cars. The last cars had a bigger 1098cc engine.*

■ ABOVE *Overhead-valve A Series engines from the Austin A35 much improved the Minor's performance. The last cars could achieve 70mph (112kph).*

■ ABOVE *The four-door Minor 1000. All Minors had excellent handling thanks to rack-and-pinion steering and well thought-out suspension.*

The next landmark was the introduction of the 948cc engine in 1956 when the cars were badged Minor 1000. Combined with the higher final drive, this put the top speed up to a respectable 70mph (112kph). You could recognize the Minor 1000 by its larger rear window (on the saloons) and one-piece front screen. There were wider opening doors from 1959. Flashing indicators replaced semaphores in 1961. When production turned 1 million in

1959, BMC produced 350 commemorative Minor 1,000,000s with lilac paint and white seats. The last major update was introduction of the 48bhp 1098cc engine in 1962. The open tourers and four-door saloons died out in the late 60s, but the two-door – and the Traveller – continued until 1971. Simple, enjoyable and easy to drive, Minors survive in large numbers and remain one of the most affordable true classics you can buy.

OTHER MAKES

■ MORRIS

William Morris introduced his "Bullnose" Morris Oxford in 1913. His aggressive price-cutting enabled the Morris car to be made in such quantity and at such a price that by the end of the 1920s the company held 51 per cent of the market. The best-selling Eight was the mainstay of the 30s, replaced in 1948 by the Minor. In 1952 came the merger with Austin to the British Motor Corporation (BMC). From then, the marque began to lose its identity, culminating in the demise of the name in 1983.

■ MOSKVICH

Moskvich – "Son of Moscow" – was at first a pre-war Opel Kadett, built from 1947 with appropriated German tooling. Home-grown products took over in 1956. The model most sold in Britain was the 412 Series, universally panned for its handling and terrible brakes, although its performance was good for the low price.

■ LEFT *The Traveller with its half-timbered rear end was a much-loved variant. Along with the two-door, it was the last Minor to be dropped in 1971.*

N S U

■ NSU Ro80

The German company NSU established its reputation in the post-Second World War years building well-engineered rear-engined economy cars. The Ro80, its first and only big luxury car, startled the motoring world. Here was the world's first purpose-built twin-rotor wankel-engined saloon. Not only was the Ro80 fast – top speed 112mph (180kph) – and supersmooth, but it was beautiful, too, with a futuristic and slippery five-seater body that pointed the way to styling in the 1980s.

Front-wheel drive, superb power

■ LEFT *The Ro80 looked amazingly futuristic in 1967 with its rising waistline, high tail and big glass area. Many considered it the world's finest saloon.*

■ ABOVE *NSU's gamble with the Ro80 didn't pay off, and VW ended up buying the company in 1969.*

■ ABOVE *The shape was highly aerodynamic, making for relaxed and quiet high-speed cruising.*

■ ABOVE *In their advertising, NSU tried to convince buyers that they had the car's problems licked.*

steering and four-wheel disc brakes gave it excellent handling; long-travel strut suspension gave it a comfortable, absorbent ride. To mask the wankel's poor low-down torque and over-run snatch, NSU specified a three-speed

NSU Ro80 (1967-77)	
Engine	2-rotor wankel
Capacity	1990cc (nominal)
Power	113bhp
Transmission	3-speed semi-automatic
Top speed	112mph (180kph)
No. built	37,204

■ LEFT *An early Ro80 on steel wheels. With its three-speed semi-automatic transmission, the car could achieve 112mph (179kph), but fuel consumption was heavy.*

■ OPPOSITE *The shape of today's Audis and VWs owes much to the bold originality of the Ro80.*

■ LEFT *Later cars like this had revised tail lights. Otherwise the style changed hardly at all in the 10-year production run.*

■ BELOW *The engine was a two-rotor unit giving 113bhp: it was nominally rated at just under two litres.*

semi-automatic transmission: there was no clutch pedal but an electric switch in the gearknob that operated a vacuum system when a gear was selected. NSU called them "performance ranges", with second gear taking the car from a standstill to 80mph (128kph).

The car, a minor masterpiece, had a fatal flaw: its engine. Inadequately developed, it suffered from acute wear of its rotor-tip seals, and after 15,000 miles (24,150km) (or less) owners

noticed lack of power and higher fuel use. Engines became difficult to start and smoked like chimneys. NSU were generous with warranty claims. Many cars had as many as nine new engines! Owners, legend has it, didn't wave when they saw another Ro80 but displayed fingers to denote how many new engines they had had . . .

The costs sent NSU into the arms of Volkswagen in 1969. As word spread about the wankel engine's problems,

sales plummeted. Production, at a lower level, lasted until 1977 when the NSU name died along with this beautiful, innovative saloon. Values of second-hand cars also plummeted in the 70s and 80s, and many owners fitted Ford V-four engines to keep the cars going. Twenty years after the Ro80's demise, collectors are rediscovering it now that engine problems are solved (many have fitted the Mazda RX7 unit). For the brave, a good one is still a superb car.

OTHER MAKES

■ NOBEL

This was a licence-built version of the fellow-German Fuldamobil, which was also manufactured (apparently) in South Africa, Chile, the Netherlands, Greece, Sweden and India. In Britain, it was assembled by Ulster shipbuilders Harland & Wolfe, with a chassis made by aviation firm Shorts and a group body by the Bristol Aircraft Company; it was briefly marketed by the fading Lea-Francis concern.

OLDSMOBILE

■ BELOW *The clean-cut styling of the massive Toronado gave no hint of the new technology underneath – front-wheel drive.*

■ OLDSMOBILE TORONADO

The Oldsmobile Toronado of 1965 brought front-wheel-drive (FWD) technology to the mass American market for the first time, not in a compact runabout but a huge, stylish supercoupé. In Europe, the likes of Issigonis said big engines and front drive would never mix, but Oldsmobile didn't listen: the Toronado was always going to be a big one.

Under the flamboyant sheet metal, the Toronado was a clever concoction of conventional Detroit practice – drum brakes all round, beefy perimeter-frame chassis – but plenty of trick stuff, at

least by American standards. The seven-litre "Rocket" engine was mounted in-line with the torque converter on the back but, cunningly, the usual three-speed Hydra-Matic gearbox (running the opposite way to normal) was nestling under the left-hand cylinder bank. They were connected by a multiple-link Morse chain – lots of work went into making this quiet – and the power fed into a spiral bevel diff.

The resultant power-pack was mounted on a rubber-insulated sub-frame which allowed a complete

■ ABOVE LEFT *Headlights live under electrically operated flaps. The style is commendably fuss-free.*

■ ABOVE *The Toronado's shape was free of excessive glitz, although the dimensions were very Detroit.*

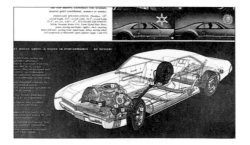

■ ABOVE *The cutaway shows the perimeter frame chassis and front-drive power-pack. But the brakes were not up to the job.*

OLDSMOBILE TORONADO (1965-70)	
Engine	V-eight
Capacity	7446cc
Power	385 @ 4600rpm
Transmission	3-speed auto
Top speed	130mph (209kph)
No. built	143,134

■ RIGHT *The two-tone Toronado could do 135mph (217kph) and had better handling than the average American car – but few buyers noticed the difference.*

flat-floor. Torsion-bar suspension was used up front, attached to the subframe, while a dead axle, single-leaf springs and twin vertical and horizontal dampers were used at the rear to limit hop under hard braking. Firestone developed special tyres for the Toronado with stiffer sidewall construction and more grip to take advantage of the front-wheel drive, although in service they gained a reputation for savage wear rates. Wheels were slotted to cool the finned brake drums.

After being exhaustively tested – General Motors didn't want any reliability problems prejudicing buyers against FWD – the Toronado was finally launched in the autumn of 1965 to rave reviews. Not only did its bold styling set it apart from the big-coupé herd; its handling really was more capable on the road: 60 per cent of the weight overhanging the front driving wheels meant lots of traction and fine stability yet less of the plough-on than you'd find in the comparable Buick Riviera. The Toronado could pull you out of trouble, not push you into it. Only the too-small drum brakes were criticized in this

two-ton (2032kg), 135mph (217kph) car.

American buyers had a year-long honeymoon period with the Toronado (buying 40,000 in 1966) but from 1967 they tended to prefer the Riviera, which looked – and was – more conventional, as well as being cheaper. The purity of the original car was lost on most Americans, who couldn't tell if it was front driven or not – and didn't care. It was given a completely new and awful bodyshell from 1971 and from then on looked like every other slobwagon on the freeway.

Today, a good example of the original Toronado would make an entertaining and intriguing addition to any collection of milestone cars – if you have the room.

OTHER MAKES

■ OGLE

David Ogle's first design in 1959 was based on a Riley 1.5, with the neat SX1000 coupé following in 1963. However, Ogle's death in an SX1000 and the British firm's loss-making production saw car manufacture cease the following year. The firm did make some one-off designs afterwards and is most famous for its Reliant Scimitar.

■ OPEL

Opel produced its first car in 1898 and by 1928 was the largest car maker in Germany. In the late 1920s, the firm was reorganized as a joint-stock company, with majority shareholding going to General Motors. During the 1930s, Opel ranked first among European car producers. After the Second World War its products tended to be very Americanized, but by the mid-60s it was producing clean European designs like the Rekord, the Commodore and the little 1900GT. Opel is today the driving force behind GM's potent presence in Europe.

■ LEFT *Inevitably, the stylist began to fiddle with the clean shape. From the late 1960s, the shape got progressively boring.*

PANHARD

■ PANHARD 24CT

Founded in 1889, the French firm of
Panhard was one of the pioneers of
motoring, but by the 1950s its star had
begun to fade as sales went into decline
in the face of more conventional
opposition from Peugeot, Citroën and
Renault. This is not to say, however, that
the company didn't make some
impressive machines: the Dyna was one
of the best and fastest economy cars of
its era, giving 75mph (120kph) on two
cylinders and 745cc, while the PL17
that followed was a futuristic family six-
seater, still with a mere 845 air-cooled
flat-twin engine yet capable of 90mph
(145kph) in Tigre form.

■ ABOVE *The last Panhard was the stylish
24 Series coupé, still with the small 650cc
air-cooled flat-twin engine.*

PANHARD 24 CT (1963-67)	
Engine	Flat-twin
Capacity	845cc
Power	60bhp
Transmission	4-speed manual
Top speed	100mph (160kph)
No. built	23,245 all models

■ ABOVE *The PL17
was one of the
best, and fastest,
economy cars of its
era.*

■ RIGHT *In Tigre
form the PL17
could achieve
90mph (145kph)
on a mere 845cc.*

Even more desirable was the
glamorous little 24 Series, introduced in
1963 and the last Panhard of all. Here
was a modern-looking two-plus-two
coupé with a stylish, slippery shape
distinguished by large window areas and
cowled-in lights behind glass. It used
the same drive train as the PL17 with
front-wheel drive, four speeds and two
engine options, the most powerful being
the Tigre unit giving 60bhp with a twin-
choke carb (24CT). Top speed, even
with just 845cc, was an amazing
100mph (160kph), still with potential if

■ LEFT *The original post-war Panhard was the Dyna, its design attributable to Gregoire.*

driven normally. The flat twin, related to the original Grégoire design of the 1940s, couldn't disguise its poor, low-speed torque and roughness, but it smoothed out beautifully at higher speeds where the CT excelled. The 24CT had the lower-powered 50bhp unit. The range was broadened by the 24B, BT and BA with a longer wheelbase and full four-seater body. All cars had a four-speed floor gear-change and, from 1965, four-wheel disc brakes.

By then, Citroën had taken over the ailing Panhard and were struggling to make the expensive-to-build 24 Series profitable. Sales were slow. and Citroën gave up the unequal struggle in 1967, killing the marque and using the Paris factory to increase their own production capacity.

■ ABOVE *The 24 Series handled well but would lift a wheel, as here, if pressed hard.*

■ LEFT *The Dyna was the French equivalent of the Morris Minor, but rather more advanced with its front-wheel-drive chassis.*

■ BELOW *Front-wheel drive made them competitive rally cars too. This is a PL17 on the 1956 Monte Carlo Rally.*

■ ABOVE *With special lightweight bodywork, the Panhards were successful in their class in competition. This is a Monopole Panhard at Montlhery.*

PEGASO

■ PEGASO Z102 AND Z103

The Spanish company Pegaso's main
commercial concern has always been
trucks and motor coaches, but for a brief
period in the 50s it was also noted for its
cars, perhaps the most glamorous and
certainly among the fastest of their day.
They combined racing-car design and
engineering with exotic Italian styling,
but only 100 cars were produced – some
say only 84.

■ BELOW *Apart
from the bodywork,
everything for the
Pegaso was
produced in-house
at the Barcelona
factory.*

■ LEFT *The original Z102 prototype, had
slightly dumpy styling and in steel, rather
than aluminium.*

First of the line was the Z102 of 1951.
Cast in the mould of the Aston DB2 and
Lancia Aurelia, here was a super sports
car with a specification that was pure
copybook stuff: four-cam V-eight engine,
dry-sump lubrication, five-speed gearbox
mounted in unit with diff, all mounted in
a state-of-the-art pressed platform
chassis. Everything was produced in
house at the Barcelona factory, including
the rather dumpy – and overweight –
coupé and convertible prototype steel
bodies. Production Z102s had 2.8-litre

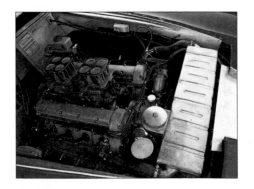

■ ABOVE *The four-cam engine had dry-sump
lubrication and produced 175-360bhp.*

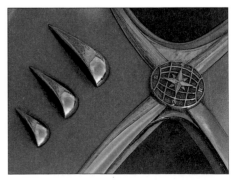

■ ABOVE *The four points of the compass
badge showed ambitions for worldwide
sales – in fact only eight were exported.*

■ LEFT *The fastest of the Pegasos were good for 160mph (257kph). Surprisingly, they had little success in racing.*

■ ABOVE *The best-looking of the bodies used on the Pegasos was the Touring Spider, but only one was built.*

■ RIGHT *That dumpy prototype with the original 2.8-litre engine.*

■ ABOVE *The Pegaso badge: the company was better known for its trucks and motor coaches.*

engines and a much lighter and more elegant Touring body, crafted in alloy. This would become the definitive Pegaso style, although there was one beautiful Touring Spider. The French company Saoutchik also did a few coupés, without much success.

Pegaso constantly meddled with the specification of the car: the 2.8-litre engine came with single and multi-choke carburettors (giving between 175 and 190bhp), and later there was a 3.2-litre option with twin four-barrel carbs and 230bhp. A supercharged version of the 2.8 gave up to 280bhp, and there was even a 3.2-litre version with 360bhp.

The performance was fantastic, with up to 160mph (257kph) in its most powerful form and an amazing noise generated by its gear-driven camshafts. They were heavy, brutish cars to drive, and despite their good handling and power they never found much competition success.

The cars were always built on a cost-no-object basis, and the Z103 was a last-ditch effort to make them more commercially successful, using simpler single overhead-camshaft V-eight engines with 3.9, 4.5 and 4.9-litre capacities.

Pegaso built its last sports cars in 1958. They never made any money for

the company but at least they proved they could do it and compete with the best in the world.

PEGASO Z102 AND Z103 (1951-58)	
Engine	V-eight
Capacity	2816/3178/3988/4450cc
Power	175-360bhp
Transmission	5-speed manual
Top speed	120-160mph (193-257kph)
No. built	About 100

■ FAR LEFT *The gearbox was mounted in unit with the diff at the back for good handling.*

■ LEFT *This is the Pegaso racer, in Spanish racing colours.*

PORSCHE

■ **ABOVE LEFT** *The 356 defined the classic Porsche look. This is a "C" model, available with the 75bhp engine or as the 95bhp "super".*

■ PORSCHE 356

Ferdinand Porsche set up his design consultancy in 1931 but the first car to bear his name – the 356 – was not built until 1946. A dumpy-looking little rear-engined sports car, the 356 was closely related to the VW Beetle – another famous Porsche design – with an air-cooled flat-four pushrod engine and the same kind of trailing-link front suspension with high-pivot swing axles at the rear. There were coupé, cabriolet and shallow-screened sportster versions, the latter now much sought-after (and replicated by kit-car builders).

Early cars, built in Austria up to 1950, had split windscreens and 1100cc versions of the aircooled flat four producing just 40bhp. There were further 1287, 1290 and 1488cc versions producing up to 70bhp. The original

■ **LEFT** *The 356A was an improved version of the original 1946 car, announced in 1955.*

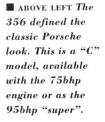

■ **LEFT** *An air-cooled flat-four engine was the trademark of the 356, mounted in the rear.*

PORSCHE 356 (1949-65)	
Engine	Flat four
Capacity	1086-1966cc
Power	40-155bhp
Transmission	4-speed
Top speed	87-130mph (139-209kph)
No. built	82,363

rounded roly-poly styling was changed on the 1955 356A to a crisper shape with a curved one-piece screen, improved front suspension and steering and a bigger 1600 engine.

From here on the story gets complex: the 356B of 1959 had a higher nose and came in two new styles – the speedster-based Roadsters and a notchback coupé by Karmann. Top of the standard range was the 110mph (177kph) Super 90, but even the standard 60bhp car could

achieve 100mph (160kph). The last-of-the-line, the 356C, had ZF steering and four-wheel disc brakes. The names were changed, too: the Super became the 1600C, the Super 75 the 1600S and the Super 90 the 1600SC, with an extra 5bhp.

For advanced students there were the Carrera versions of the 356 from 1955. Engines were still flat fours but totally different in detail: the crank was a roller bearing type and instead of pushrods

■ **ABOVE** *The interiors of all models were stark and functional but entirely comfortable.*

■ BELOW *Cabriolet versions,
much sought-after today, could
be had with a factory hardtop.*

■ RIGHT *Versions with a special
four-cam with dry-sump lubrication
and up to 125mph in two-litre
form were also available.*

there were four overhead camshafts with
twin-plug per-cylinder ignition. With
lighter bodywork, the first 100bhp cars
were good for 120mph (193kph) and
1.6-litre models from 1958 an amazing
130mph (209kph). The Carrera 2, based
on the B/C series, appeared in spring
1960 with a new two-litre version of the
complex four-cam flat four which
produced up to 155bhp in GT form.

The 356 improved dramatically over
the years, growing more and more
specialized and increasingly distant
from its VW Beetle roots. Compact,
beautifully built and in some cases very
fast, it was the car with which Porsche
built its reputation in the 50s, and its
passing was much mourned when the
911 Series took over completely in
1965.

This left a gap in the range for a
cheaper Porsche, filled by the 912
which used the pushrod 356 engine in a
911 shell.

■ BELOW *The C was the last of the line,
with more power and four-wheel disc
brakes.*

■ ABOVE *The flat-four engine lived at the
back and had a distinctive throbby beat.*

PORSCHE

■ PORSCHE 911

A triumph of development over design, the Porsche 911, launched in 1964, is still going strong. There have been countless variations, but first-generation pre-1974 cars are seen as the most classic. Built before impact bumpers, they have cleaner looks and are purer in conception. Conceived by "Ferry" Porsche (son of the company's founder) and styled by Butzi Porsche, the 911 has been honed year-by-year to iron out detail weaknesses and to conquer handling deficiencies inherent in having its air-cooled flat-six engine located behind the rear wheels. Fast and agile, the 911 is one of the most practical supercars, with rear seats and a formidable reputation for reliability.

All models had four-wheel disc brakes and five-speed gearboxes on manual cars. Front suspension was by wishbones and torsion bars, the rear tied down by trailing arms and torsion bars. Superbly communicative steering and faithful, pin-sharp handling endeared the car to many, though it has never shaken off the suspicion of unruly lift-off oversteer in extreme situations, promoted by the high inertia of the rear engine position.

The first cars used a 1991cc version of the SOHC flat-six engine producing 130bhp. The Targa with removable roof panel was announced in September

■ ABOVE *The first Porsche cars were built in Austria, but the 911s have always been built in Stuttgart, Germany.*

■ ABOVE *The ultimate early type 911 is the 2.7RS Carrera with its lighter shell and stiffer suspension.*

1966. Top of the range was the 160bhp 911S, with forged pistons and larger valves, which could do 140mph (225kph). The brakes were now vented but as always unservoed, for better feel. 1966 saw the début of the classic five-spoke alloy wheels, hallmark of the early 911.

In 1967 the 911L replaced the standard 911 (130bhp, similar trim to 911S) and there was a new base-level 911T with 110bhp. The semi-automatic "Sportsmatic", three speed and no clutch pedal, is little fancied today.

1968 saw introduction of the B-Series models with a 2.2in (5.6cm) increase in wheelbase – for better weight distribution and handling. Meanwhile,

PORSCHE 911 (1964-73)	
Engine	Aircooled flat six
Capacity	1991-2993cc
Power	130-230bhp
Transmission	5-speed manual
Top speed	130-155mph (209-249kph)
No. built	89,256

■ OPPOSITE *The enduring shape of the 911 is much the same today. This is a 911 2.4S from the early 1970s.*

■ ABOVE LEFT *Today's 911, available with two- and four-wheel drive and as popular as ever.*

■ LEFT *In the 1960s and 70s the 911 had considerable rallying success thanks to its power and traction.*

the new 911E model replaced the 911L, and there was now Bosch mechanical fuel injection for between 140bhp (E) and 170bhp (S), although the 110bhp 911T kept its Weber carbs.

The 1969 C-Series models had 2195cc engines for more bottom-end torque. The flat six had larger valves, magnesium crankcase and lower compression; power outputs ranged from 125bhp for the T to 155bhp for the E and 180bhp for the S, which had standard alloy wheels and a rear anti-roll bar. Faster 2.4 cars came in from September 1971, ranging from 130 to 190bhp.

The ultimate early 911 was the Carrera 2.7RS with a lighter shell and stiffer suspension. Launched in Sport, Touring or Racing form, it was built for just one year (1972–73) as a homologation car for Group 4 racing. A bore increase gave 2687cc and 210bhp thanks to flatter forged pistons and Nikasil cylinders. Only 500 were required for homologation, but the car proved so popular that Porsche built more than 1500. These ultimately early 911s, capable of 150mph (241kph), were characterized by a ducktail spoiler, flared rear arches and bold Carrera side decals.

■ ABOVE *The last 59 Carrera RS lightweights had a three-litre engine, giving 230bhp.*

■ OPPOSITE *Early cars had 130bhp, still good enough for a top speed of 130mph (209kph).*

OTHER MAKES

■ PARAMOUNT
The Ford-based sporty tourer Paramount was first shown to the British press in 1950. By 1951, making was taken over by the Meynell Motor Co, before being done by Camden Motors who formed Paramount Cars (Leighton Buzzard) Ltd. The car's price was too high and by 1956, with just a handful built, Paramount was finished.

■ PEEL/VIKING
The 50cc Peel P50 of 1962–66 and the "astrodome" Peel Trident 100cc bubble-car were austere runabouts. The firm then developed the Trident Mini but after two were built the project was taken over by Bill Last, later to make the Trident. He renamed the car the Viking Minisport.

■ PEERLESS/WARWICK
The Peerless was created by British special-builder and engine-tuner Bernie Rodger. Two alloy-bodied prototypes were built in 1957. Manufacture started in Slough,

Berkshire in 1958, with backing from hotelier Jim Burns and John Gordon. After the demise of Peerless Cars, Bernard Rodger Developments was set up in Horton, Buckinghamshire, to continue Peerless production. Gordon stayed at the retail outlet of Peerless Motors and worked on the Gordon GT, which became the Gordon Keeble.o

■ PIPER
Originally, Piper offered sports-racing and Formula 3 cars. A separate enterprise developed the dramatic GTT with its space-frame, square-tube chassis and Ford engines. Plans for V-eight-powered road and competition cars were shelved but GTT/P2 production continued until 1974.

■ POWERDRIVE
Another of the late-1950s crop of British economy cars, the Powerdrive had a 322cc motorcycle engine and gearbox and a three-seater roadster body with twin-tube frame. It survived until 1958. Low road tax, insurance and fuel consumption were the attractions. It is *not* related to the similar Coronet three-wheeler.

RELIANT

■ LEFT *Tom Karen of Ogle gave the Scimitar its distinctive shape, based on the original Scimitar Coupé.*

■ RELIANT SCIMITAR GTE

Today's sporting Estates come from BMW and Volvo, but it was Reliant of Tamworth – a marque synonymous with the three-wheeler – that originated the genre in 1968. Its trend-setting Scimitar GTE inspired imitators worldwide.

The Scimitar GTE (Grand Touring Estate), based on Reliant's existing Ford three-litre V-six engined Scimitar coupé, had a trendy rising waistline and a wedge-like profile which skilfully hid the 36 cu ft of load space, accessible through a stylish one-piece glass hatch supported on spring struts. The full four-seat GTE was the first car to have rear seats that folded *separately*, an arrangement copied by almost all hatchbacks. Styled by Tom Karen of Ogle (responsible for the Scimitar coupé and Robin three-wheeler), like every other Reliant the GTEs body was moulded in rust-resistant glassfibre while retaining a steel box-frame chassis for strength and rigidity. Ford's big pushrod three-litre V-six engine in such a light car meant the Scimitar was fast – it could do 120mph (193kph) – and reliable. Frugal overdrive cars did 27mpg. The Scimitar was soon the darling of the English country-house set, an image boosted when Princess Anne received a GTE as a

Christmas gift in 1970.

In 1975, Reliant introduced wide-bodied SE6 cars. These softer, more comfortable Scimitars – built to enter the executive market – never recaptured the elegance of the 1968 original. Cheaper mass-market imitators were eating into the market the GTE once had to itself. By the early 80s, Reliant were losing heart, ravaged by recession and unable to find investment to bring the GTE up to date. The last car was built in 1986.

■ ABOVE *The Scimitar GTC was a convertible version of the late 70s, designed to rekindle some showroom interest in the Scimitar.*

■ LEFT *The most desirable of the Scimitars was the narrow-bodied SE5A, here on alloy wheels.*

SCIMITAR GTE (1968–86)	
Engine	Ford V-six
Capacity	2994-2792cc
Power	135bhp @ 5500rpm
Transmission	4-speed manual
Top speed	121mph (195kph) (SE5a)
No. built	15,273

RENAULT

■ LEFT *With its 16 of 1964, Renault invented the five-door hatchback. Every major manufacturer has since copied it.*

■ RENAULT 16

Today, the front-wheel-drive hatchback is the mainstay of the family-car market in Europe, but when Renault introduced its 16 in December 1964, the concept of a five-door saloon was very new. With its rear hatchback door and fold-down rear seats, the 16 was unparalleled when introduced, even if you didn't appreciate the slightly awkward styling.

Front-wheel drive gave it excellent roadholding while long-travel, all-independent suspension ensured a soft, absorbent ride on even the roughest of French roads. Disc front brakes were also to its credit, and even on a modest 1470cc the original 55bhp 16 could touch 90mph (145kph). It was an instant hit and had a long production life, finally giving way to the Renault 20 in 1979.

The 16TS of 1968 was a higher-performance 1565cc, 88bhp version of the car giving 100mph (160kph), though the ultimate 16 was the TX of 1973 with power increased to 93bhp. Five speeds made it an ideal motorway cruiser, while electric front windows were a rare luxury on a family car in the mid-70s. You could spot a TX by its four-headlamp nose and sports wheels.

Enthusiasts are now beginning to rediscover the excellent qualities of this ground-breaking saloon, which is now a rare sight.

■ BELOW LEFT *The 16 was no beauty, but its looks were honest and distinctive. Later TX models had four square lights.*

■ BELOW RIGHT *With its long wheelbase and high roof-line the 16 was a generous five-seater with comfortable long-travel suspension.*

RENAULT 16 (1964–79)	
Engine	In-line four
Capacity	1470/1565/1647cc
Power	55-93bhp
Transmission	4/5-speed manual 3-speed auto
Top speed	90-105mph (145–169kph)
No. built	1,846,000

■ ABOVE *In 1964-65 the rear hatch was the ultimate in family car practicality, but today we wouldn't accept the high loading sill.*

OTHER MAKES

■ RELIANT

A development of the Raleigh Safety Seven three-wheeler, the first Reliant three-wheeler car was a girder-forked and handlebar-steered van. It gained an Austin Seven engine in 1938, and the following year Reliant took over production of the Austin engine. In 1953 came the Regal, Reliant's first production passenger car. Ten years later, Reliant introduced its own all-alloy engine – by which stage it had moved into four-wheeler production with the Sabre. It made its name, and began a new genre of sporting estates, with the Scimitar GTE of 1968.

RILEY

■ RILEY RM SERIES

By the time the RM series appeared in 1945, the great days of Riley had passed. Founded in 1898, the Company made its reputation in the 1920s and 1930s with a series of well-built saloons and thoroughbred small sports cars. It forged a fine racing record too, but, by the late 1930s, finances were looking shaky and the Nuffield organization took the helm in 1938.

Even so, the immediate post-war cars managed to retain their individuality: RMA and RMB models had a classic high-cam four-cylinder engine, torsion-bar independent front suspension and elegant fabric-topped, timber-framed, steel-bodywork bodies. The 1½-litre RMB could manage 75mph (120kph) the 90bhp – later 100bhp – 2½-litre RMB a highly respectable 95mph (152kph) with long-geared cruising at about 85mph (136kph).

With the longest stroke of any post-war British production car, the RMBs were extremely torquey, too. They handled well, though heavy steering at low speeds was a constant source of criticism.

For enthusiasts, the ultimate RM variant will always be the RMC, an open, three-seater roadster with sweeping, rakish lines. This was built to capture American sales (hence the column gearchange). A fold-flat screen

■ ABOVE *The cars were built with either a 1.5 or 2.5-litre high-camshaft four-cylinder engine, the latter giving a top speed of 95mph (152kph).*

■ RIGHT *Built for the American market, 507 RMCs were sold, along with a further 502 four-seater drophead RMDs.*

■ OPPOSITE *The most desirable of the RM Rileys was the three-seater roadster with its cut-away doors.*

■ BELOW *The rare drophead version, now highly prized by collectors.*

and lowered bonnet line were other recognition points. 507 were built, plus a further 502 four-seater drophead RMDs which had more conventional lines.

Last of the RM line were the 1952 RME (1496cc) and RMF (2443cc) with full hydraulic brakes, a hypoid back axle and bigger rear windows. For the run-out 1954 model year the styling of the RME underwent subtle changes: no running boards, streamlined headlight

■ OPPOSITE *The saloon RMA and RMB were very elegant cars with their distinctive fabric roof covering.*

RILEY RM SERIES (1945–1954)	
Engine	In-line four
Capacity	1496/2443cc
Power	54-100bhp
Transmission	4-speed manual
Top speed	75-100mph (120-160kph)
No. built	RMA 10,504/RMB 6,900/ RMC 507/RMD 502/ RME 3,446/RMF 1,050

■ RIGHT *Handling of all the RMs was good, particularly the 1.5-litre with its lighter steering.*

pods and rear wheel spats.

By that time the flagship RMF had been replaced by the unfortunate Gerald Palmer-designed Pathfinder, which had nothing but the traditional four-cylinder Riley engine to recommend it.

After the death of the RME in 1955, there were no more thoroughbred Rileys; instead the famous jewel badge was progressively debased on a succession of badge-engineered BMC saloons until the end of the 60s.

■ ABOVE *The RM Series Rileys were built until 1955. They were replaced by the much less satisfactory – but much more modern-looking – Pathfinder.*

OTHER MAKES

■ ROCHDALE

The first complete car produced by the British firm Rochdale was the 1960 grp-monocoque Olympic, but they had been producing glassfibre bodies for the specials market since 1952. The MkVI was followed by the F-type, C-type, ST, GT and Riviera bodyshells. Volume production of the 100mph (160kph) Olympic had ceased by the mid-60s, but the last Olympic shell was sold in the early-70s.

■ RODLEY

The Leeds, Yorkshire-built Japanese-engined Rodley was another short-lived baby car from the 1950s, although it did look more serious than some of its contemporaries. Production was supposed to reach 50–60 a week, but few were made in the car's short production life of just over a year. The firm disappeared in 1955.

ROLLS-ROYCE

■ ROLLS-ROYCE SILVER CLOUD

The Rolls-Royce Silver Cloud and the virtually identical Bentley S-Type were revealed in 1955. Beautifully proportioned, exquisitely constructed and near-silent in operation, they were everything the traditional Rolls buyer could have hoped for.

This was Crewe's second "standard steel" car after the post-war Dawn and R-Type, with an off-the-peg factory body rather than a made-to-measure hand-crafted aluminium item in the pre-war tradition. Mulliner Park Ward, James Young and others all built exquisite special bodies on this chassis, and there was a long-wheelbase version of the standard body with an extra four inches (10cm) of rear leg room and a division. The traditional Rolls and Bentley radiator grilles were retained – these and a few badges and items of insignia were

■ FAR LEFT *Mulliner's famous Continental style was carried over from the R-Type but was phased out in favour of more modern coach-built styles.*

■ NEAR LEFT *The Flying Spur Bentley had a lightweight aluminium body on the Continental chassis. This is an S3 V-eight.*

the only differences between the two otherwise identical cars. They rode on a substantial, and resolutely separate, traditional box-section chassis with independent front suspension and rear damper rates that could be altered from the driving seat to suit whatever type of road you were thinking of taking your Bentley or Rolls down. The interior was nothing if not luxurious, with superbly crafted leather seats and a magnificent walnut dashboard.

The engine in the Cloud and S1 was basically the same 4.9-litre power unit carried over from the previous R-Type (and Silver Dawn), except that it had a new aluminium cylinder head and twin SU carburettors. Transmission at the start offered a choice of either four-speed synchromeshed manual or four-speed Hydramatic automatic, manufactured under licence by Rolls from General Motors in the USA. In fact, after just 18 months, the manual option was dropped,

and Rolls never encouraged owners to order it anyway. While the engine was incredibly refined, it wasn't really that powerful – the maximum speed was 106mph (170kph). It was Rolls-Royce's policy never to reveal specific power outputs but the estimated 178bhp had 40cwt (2032kg) to pull along.

The S-Type, known retrospectively as the S1, and the Silver Cloud 1, were built until 1959, with 3,072 Bentleys being made against 2,238 Rolls-Royces.

■ BELOW *The cut-away shows the Cloud's old-fashioned separate chassis, big drum brakes and aluminium V-eight engine.*

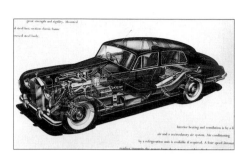

■ LEFT *The Cloud as it appeared in 1955 with single headlights and a six-cylinder engine. The V-eight Cloud II looked identical.*

ROLLS-ROYCE SILVER CLOUD AND BENTLEY S-SERIES (1959–65)

Engine	Straight six and V-eight
Capacity	4887/6230cc
Power	N/A
Transmission	4-speed manual 4-speed auto
Top speed	106-116mph (170-186kph)
No. built	Cloud 1/S1 3,107/2,231 Cloud 2/S2 2,417/1,932 Cloud 3/S3 2,044/1,318 Plus 671 Clouds I/II/III

■ ABOVE *The Bentley version was technically identical – only the grille and badges were changed.*

■ ABOVE *Park Ward's famous Chinese Eye Continental, here in convertible form – the ultimate in open car luxury.*

Bentley/Rolls fans today are split on whether the S1 Series are better than the later V-eight-powered SII and SIII cars, the latter having a lower bonnet line and quad headlamps reckoned by some to spoil the cars' looks. The V-eights are far more powerful – good for nearly 120mph (193kph) with a likely 200bhp and far more torque on tap – but not as refined and quiet. American-inspired (some say by the Chrysler hemi), this alloy engine was the unit Rolls had wanted for the car all along. It's just that it took, in typical Crewe style, an awfully long time to make perfect. Rolls engineers started work on the unit in the very early 1950s, intending that it would be one of the world's best. It survives in vastly updated form in today's Rolls and Bentley cars.

To own and drive a Bentley is a satisfying and ethereal experience as long as you don't want blistering performance and can afford the expensive maintenance. These days, it's cheaper to buy but costly to restore.

■ NEAR RIGHT *For lightness, the body of the Continental models was finished in aluminium; the factory saloon came in steel only.*

■ FAR RIGHT *The HJ Mulliner convertible, heavier but just as beautiful as the Continental versions.*

ROLLS-ROYCE

■ BELOW *The Shadow was also produced as a Bentley T1. Again, only the grille and the badges were different.*

■ OPPOSITE *The Shadow II of 1977 with its rubber-faced bumpers, air dam and smaller radiator grille.*

■ ROLLS-ROYCE SILVER SHADOW

If the boxy shape of the 1965 Silver Shadow was something of a shock for Rolls-Royce traditionalists after the flowing lines of the Cloud, there were much more revolutionary changes under the skin: all-independent self-levelling suspension, disc brakes and a monocoque structure came as a powerful retort to critics who accused Crewe of falling behind the times. In one fell swoop Rolls-Royce had entered the modern era.

Built by Pressed Steel at Oxford, the main bodyshell was steel while doors, bonnet and bootlid were aluminium. The all-round independent suspension by coil springs with wishbones at the front and single trailing arms at the back had hydraulic height control at

both ends, a system supplied by Citroën. At last disc brakes all round replaced the big drums used on the Cloud.

The 6.2-litre V-eight engine and GM Hydramatic four-speed automatic gearbox – made under licence by Rolls – were standard and carried over almost unchanged from the outgoing Silver Cloud. With a 115mph (185kph) top speed, a 0-60mph (96kph) time of 10.9 seconds and a standing quarter-mile covered in 17.6 seconds, the Shadow

■ ABOVE *The long-wheelbase Shadow II – badged Silver Wraith – with its trademark Everflex roof.*

■ LEFT *The Silver Shadow was announced in 1965, the first modern Rolls-Royce for many years.*

■ RIGHT *The alloy Rolls-Royce V-eight is whisper quiet and super-smooth but not particularly powerful by big luxury car standards. This one is a Camargue.*

■ ABOVE *The Camargue was the Rolls-Royce flagship from 1975 until the mid 80s. It was one of the most expensive cars in the world.*

■ BELOW *The styling was less happy from the rear, even if it did echo the lovely Fiat 130 coupé.*

was a fast car. Fuel consumption was good by Rolls standards, indulgent by everyone else's: between 12 and 15mpg on a run. There was, as usual, a Bentley version of the new car, called the T-Series or, retrospectively, the T1. The differences, however, were limited to a 'B'-winged radiator grille, badges and small items of trim. With the advent of the monocoque range, Bentley sales fell dramatically – only eight per cent of the Shadow I/I1 cars were Bentleys, compared with 40 per cent of the previous Cloud/S-Series cars.

Changes came slowly until the engine was enlarged to 6.75 litres in 1970: three-speed torque converter transmission replaced the four-speed fluid flywheel transmission in 1968; 1969 saw a long-wheelbase version of both cars, while air conditioning and a safer American-style dashboard came as standard. The Shadow II models of the mid 70s had rack steering to tighten up

ROLLS-ROYCE SILVER SHADOW (1965–80)	
Engine	V-eight
Capacity	6230/6750cc
Power	N/A
Transmission	4/3-speed
Top speed	117mph (187kph)
No. built	20,000 plus

■ ABOVE *The square-cut nose of the Camargue was never quite as Pininfarina intended.*

the soggy handling, rubber bumpers and an air-dam, plus Crewe's impressive split-level air-conditioning system.

Because there was no separate chassis, coach-built versions weren't possible. However, Rolls's subsidiary, Mulliner Park Ward, announced the Silver Shadow coupé in 1966 and a year later a convertible. Both were built at MPW's north London factory and adopted "Coke bottle" shapes for waistlines to look more handmade. Both were renamed Corniche in 1971. There were even a few two-door Shadow saloons, specially made by coachbuilder James Young.

Rolls-Royce Silver Shadow and Bentley T-Series cars were made in much larger numbers than any previous models: by the time they were replaced by the Shadow II/T2 cars in 1977, 20,000 of all types had been built. Today's Silver Spirit uses much of the technology pioneered on the Shadow.

ROVER

■ BELOW *The 3.5-litre Rover in saloon and coupé form (nearest camera) was one of Britain's best-loved luxury cars, built from 1967 to 1973.*

■ ROVER P5

There was nothing to replace the Rover P5 as a ministerial barge when production stopped in 1973. No other British car being built in the 1970s had the same air of solid worth and self-effacing dignity. They were still doing sterling service when Margaret Thatcher arrived in Downing Street in 1979 to begin her 11-year tenure. The elderly saloon was held in such esteem that a batch of the last cars were kept in storage and used for high-ranking cabinet duties well into the 80s. For years they were a regular feature for news bulletins, sweeping into Parliament and Buckingham Palace or pulling up outside No. 10. Harold Wilson had a

■ ABOVE *The P5B had a new Buick-derived aluminium V-eight engine. Rostyles wheels mark the car out as a V-eight model.*

■ LEFT *The P5 was previously offered with a less powerful three-litre straight-six engine. This is a MkIII coupé.*

ROVER P5 3½-LITRE (1967–73)	
Engine	V-eight
Capacity	3528cc
Power	185bhp
Transmission	3-speed auto
Top speed	110mph (177kph)
No. built	20,000

■ LEFT *The 3.5-litre V-eight could do 110mph (177kph) with acceleration that surprised some sportscar drivers.*

■ LEFT *For many years the 3.5-litre saloon was favoured transport for British government ministers: Harold Wilson had a special pipe rack fitted to his. A batch was set aside at the end of the production run for Goverment use, and the cars could still be seen in the 1980s.*

special ash-tray fitted to his to cater for his pipe. Even the Queen had a 3½-litre saloon: rumour has it that it was her favourite car and that she could often be seen driving it around Windsor.

Dispensing at last with the separate chassis of the P4, the three-litre of 1958, or P5 (post-war design number 5), was a Rolls-Royce for the middle classes. With modern but dignified styling by David Bache and a traditional interior with African cherry wood on the dash, thick Wilton carpet under foot and leather almost everywhere else, this was

an Edwardian drawing-room on wheels, perfect for the power brokers of the 60s.

At first, nobody really minded that the three-litre, joined by a hunch-roofed coupé version in 1962, was a bit slow, its soothing refinement being all that was asked of it by most owners. By the mid 60s, however, mere gravitas was not enough. Even on the gravel drives of leafy suburbia, the corpulent three-litre's lack of urge – it struggled to reach 100mph (160kph) as an automatic – was becoming embarrassing. Enter the Buick V-eight engine, a left-over from

General Motors's brief flirtation with "compacts" in the early 60s and acquired by Rover as an end-of-line bargain in 1966. Packing 184bhp (the last three-litres gave 134), it was a perfect fit under the P5's bonnet. It gave this stately boardroom barouche – renamed the 3½-litre in 1967 – speed and a new lease of life.

Suddenly the P5 was the car it always should have been. With a reasonable price tag Rover could barely keep pace with demand, which remained strong until its death in 1973.

■ NEAR RIGHT *A neat toolkit was fitted in a slide-out tray in the centre of the dash.*

■ FAR RIGHT *The "Office", with its huge wheel and neatly grouped instrumentation. Power steering was standard on the V-eight.*

ROVER

■ ROVER P6

The Rover 2000 – P6 – was the first young man's Rover. Bristling with new technology, it was ideal for the new breed of thrusting executives who wanted big-car ambience with sportscar manners in something a little more compact. Here was a 100mph (160kph) saloon, ripe for the dawn of Britain's motorway age, that didn't appeal exclusively – as did most prestige cars (and every previous Rover) – to grey-templed men in Homburg hats.

It was an immediate hit, lavishly well-reviewed around the world: *Car and Driver* magazine said it was "the best sedan ever presented in the pages of this magazine", while American safety campaigner Ralph Nader paid the 2000 the ultimate compliment when he cited it as a prime example of "how all cars should be built". It inspired many inferior imitators in the genre it created, and sold, by Rover standards, in huge numbers – not only to young executives but to all the old-style Rover customers too: doctors, bank managers, lawyers and every other shade and shape of

■ LEFT *In the early 1960s the 2000 set new standards of safety and driver appeal in the two-litre executive class.*

■ BELOW *The ultimate P6 was the 3500S with its V-eight engine and manual gearbox.*

■ LEFT *The 2000 TC had twin carbs, Rover's answer to the standard 2000's lack of urge.*

■ ABOVE *The 2000 was a firm favourite with young executives as well as bank managers and doctors. Wire wheels are a rarely seen option.*

middle-class professional bought the 2000 in their thousands, just as, today, they buy BMWs.

For the first time, Rover were selling safety with the 2000, long before it was fashionable. With its muscular "base unit" cage (a steel skeleton to which all the unstressed outer panels were attached), four-wheel disc brakes and well-padded interior, this was a great car in which to have an accident. Best of all, in the 2000 you stood a good chance of avoiding an accident in the first place. The DeDion suspension at the back followed race-car practice, so the 2000 didn't just ride softly but had prodigious grip, more than enough to keep the new overhead-camshaft four-cylinder engine in check. It easily equalled the superb 3.5-litre V-eight transplant thanks to which the P6 turned into a real Jag-eater in 1968 (and was much favoured by the police as a Jag-catcher).

If the P6 2000 didn't go like any past Rover, then it certainly didn't look like one either: David Bache's shape did full justice to the modern mechanisms underneath. This was a crisp, restrained

car, modern without being gimmicky, which resisted all later attempts to tart it up. The Rover 2000 was one of the great saloons of the 60s, a car as mouldbreaking in its class as the Mini.

ROVER P6 (1963–77)	
Engine	4-cylinder
Capacity	1978cc
Power	90-124bhp
Transmission	3-speed manual
	3-speed auto
Top speed	104mph (167kph)
No. built	329,000

■ ABOVE *The shape of the 2000 was by Rover's David Bache; its crisp, restrained lines were influenced by the Citroen DS – look at the rear of the roof-line.*

■ BELOW *Rare options on this TC are the wooden steering-wheel and extra round gauges.*

■ ABOVE *The 3500S was easy to spot thanks to its sports-wheel covers. All were Series 2 models with plastic grilles.*

■ RIGHT *The only way of spotting a TC was by its badges.*

SAAB

■ SAAB 96

Saab – Svenska Aeroplan AB – built its last 96 in 1980, but the roots of this tough, rally-winning saloon can be traced back to 1945 and the 92. A teardrop-shaped aerodynamic saloon with a two-cylinder two-stroke engine driving the front wheels (through a three-speed box with freewheel), the 92 model was current from 1950 to 1956 as Saab began to diversify from its aircraft-making interests. The 93 which followed it had a three-cylinder two-stroke engine, providing up to 55bhp in twin-carb GT form and improved coil-spring suspension with a conventional dead-beam axle at the rear to cure the once wayward handling.

The definitive Saab 96 was launched in 1960. The most noticeable feature on the outside was its larger wrap-around rear window, while under the bonnet was a bigger 841cc two-stroke giving 38bhp

SAAB 96 (1960–80)	
Engine	2-stroke 3-cylinders/ V-four
Capacity	841/1698cc
Power	38-65bhp
Transmission	3/4-speed
Top speed	79-95mph (127-152kph)
No. built	547,221

■ ABOVE *Front-wheel drive gave the 96 sure-footed handling and the free-wheel saved on fuel costs.*

■ ABOVE *The definitive 96 was launched in 1960 with its wrap-around rear window.*

■ ABOVE *The solid, low-slung shape of the 95 estate has been likened to that of a brick-built bungalow.*

■ ABOVE *The interior of the desirable Sport with its extra dials and stylish wooden steering-wheel.*

in standard form. For enthusiasts, there were the 65bhp Sport and Monte Carlo models with triple carburettors and front disc brakes. Other goodies included a four-speed gearbox and full pressure lubrication, eliminating the need for the usual petrol/oil mix in the fuel. Top speed was a very creditable 90mph

(152kph), and it was in this form that the car proved such a rally winner in the hands of Erik Carlson.

For those with more utilitarian needs there was the 95 Estate, introduced before the 96 and always using the four-speed gearbox. Saab stuck with the two-stroke until 1968, but by then the V-four

engine, bought from Ford of Germany, was selling strongly. It gave Sport and Monte Carlo performance but with much better economy.

Good handling and solid build quality were the most endearing qualities of this tough little classic, of which many examples survive to this day.

■ OPPOSITE *The shape of the 96 can be traced back to 1945 and the original 92. It lasted until the mid-1970s.*

■ BELOW *The badge shows Saab's heritage as a plane maker.*

■ BELOW *The two-stroke engine was replaced by a Ford V-four in the mid 1960s.*

■ BELOW *The 96 was a famous rally winner, most notably in the hands of Eric Carlson.*

OTHER MAKES

■ SIATA

Siata of Italy had been modifying cars, mainly Fiats, since 1926 and made its first production vehicle, the Amica, in 1949. Most Siatas were Fiat-derived, including some handsome V-eight-engined Vignale-bodied coupés, and the firm lasted until 1970, pooling resources with Abarth from 1959 to 1961. Its last model was the Fiat 850-based Spring of 1968–75.

■ SIMCA

Simca was founded in France in 1934 by HT Pigozzi to make Fiat cars under licence. The first uniquely Simca model, the Aronde, appeared in 1951, and such was its success that the firm started its policy of acquiring other makes, taking over Unic in 1951, Ford France in 1954 and Talbot in 1958. In 1958, Chrysler bought a minority stake in Simca. By 1963 this was a controlling interest, preceding the change of name in 1970 to Chrysler France SA. The last Simca cars, Horizon and Alpine, were built in 1981.

■ SINGER

Singer made its first car in 1905, and by the late 1920s it was Britain's third largest car maker. The first of a long line of OHC engines was launched in 1926, and the Le Mans Nine and 1.5-litre were credible sportscars in the 30s. A dull post-war range, the SM1500, sealed the firm's fate and in 1956 the ailing concern was taken over by Rootes. Henceforth, Singers were to be badge-engineered Hillmans and the last Singer-badged car was built in 1970.

■ SKODA

The first of the Czech-made Skoda cars were seen in 1925. Early products were conventional but the mid 1930s saw a range of more advanced offerings. Following the Second World War, after which the firm became state-owned, products were essentially evolutions of pre-war designs, until the arrival of the rear-engined Renault-inspired 1000 series in 1964. Once the butt of endless jokes, Skoda is now part of the Volkswagen group.

■ STANDARD

By 1906, three years after its formation, Standard was marketing Britain's first inexpensive six-cylinder car. A small car, the Nine, helped to circumvent increasing financial problems in 1928. After the Second World War, the firm acquired Triumph and two years later introduced the famous Vanguard, spearheading the export drive. This was the sole Standard model until the 1953 launch of the Eight. Leyland took over the Standard Triumph in 1961, and the Standard name was quietly dropped from passenger cars in 1963.

■ STEYR-PUCH

Before 1939, the Austrian firm Steyr made some interesting cars, some designed by Ferdinand Porsche. From 1949 onwards, there were no home grown models, only licence-assembled Fiats. Latterly the high-performance 650TRII was based on the 500. Steyr now produces four-wheel-drive (4WD) vehicles and systems and collaborates with Chrysler, VW-Audi and Mercedes-Benz.

SUNBEAM

■ SUNBEAM TIGER

The sunbeam Tiger, introduced in 1964, was in essence nothing more than a V-eight-engined version of the four-cylinder Alpine whose pretty, open body dated from 1959. As with the AC Cobra, the initial engineering was carried out

■ ABOVE *Brochure artwork shows the rare MkII Tiger with its bigger 4.7-litre engine.*

■ BELOW *The 4.7-litre MkII had 200bhp, up from the 164bhp of the 4.2. The roll-bar is non-standard.*

■ TOP LEFT *The Sunbeam Tiger is often modified by its owners.*

■ BOTTOM *An egg-crate grille was another MkII recognition point. When Chrysler bought Rootes, the car was killed because it used a rival Ford engine – and no Chrysler V-eight would fit.*

■ BELOW *The body shell of the Tiger was a direct carry-over from the Alpine. The cars were assembled by Jensen.*

by American Caroll Shelby, but all subsequent work was done by the parent company Rootes. Out came the four-cylinder 1592cc engine and in went a Ford V-eight of 4.2 litres along with a new "top loader" four-speed gearbox and beefed-up final drive.

This much bigger engine required extensive re-engineering under the bonnet and a stiffened-up shell. Rather than clog up the higher-volume Alpine

production lines with the new car, Rootes subcontracted the job to Jensen. Located just up the road in West Bromwich, in the West Midlands, Jensen were famous for their own big V-eight GT – the CV8 – and were already producing the big Healey models for BMC.

With a leap from 97 to 164bhp, the Tiger was a very different kind of car from the modest little Alpine, though they

SUNBEAM TIGER (1964–68)	
Engine	V-eight
Capacity	4260-4727cc
Power	164-200bhp
Transmission	4-speed manual
Top speed	120-125mph (193-201kph)
No. built	6,495 MKI/571 MkII

■ LEFT *The powerful Tiger with its relatively light bodywork was a natural in racing and rallying, though it was never fully developed.*

looked identical apart from discreet badging. Top speed was 117mph (187kph), with 0-60 (96) in 9.5 seconds, the enormous torque rendering the gearbox almost superfluous. The Tiger was no car for the novice, however: the rack-and-pinion steering – somewhat hastily contrived – wasn't of the highest quality, and the Hillman-derived suspension was never really adequate for the power now on tap, even with the Panhard rod and optional limited-slip diff. Still, it was good value and sold well in America. It wasn't offered in Britain until 1965.

Its life was cut short when Chrysler took a controlling interest in Rootes: the new regime didn't like the idea of a car using an engine from its Detroit arch-rival. Thus, the axe came down on the Tiger, but not before Rootes had produced 571 MkII models in 1967-68 with a bigger 4.7-litre engine from the Mustang. This version had wider gear ratios and was easily identified by its body stripes and egg-crate grille.

Today these exciting cars are much sought after as a cheaper alternative to the AC Cobra.

■ ABOVE *Just 571 MkII Tigers were built. Body side stripes were another recognition point.*

■ LEFT *The big V-eight was a tight fit under the Tiger's bonnet – overheating was a problem.*

OTHER MAKES

■ SUNBEAM-TALBOT

Sunbeam-Talbot was a marque invented in 1938 by the Rootes brothers. The cars were derived from contemporary Hillmans and Humbers, but in most instances carried individual coachwork. The "90" models of the 50s were surprisingly good sports saloons. In 1954 the Talbot suffix was dropped.

■ SUNBEAM

The first British manufacturer to win a Grand Prix, Sunbeam made its first car in 1899. In 1920 it became part of the Sunbeam-Talbot-Darracq combine, and after the collapse of STD it was bought by Rootes in 1935. The name was dormant from that point until 1953, when the sports version of the Sunbeam-Talbot 90 was re-launched as the Sunbeam Alpine. The Alpine and Rapier of the 60s were good sellers, but the name faded away in 1976 with the Hunter-based Rapier fastback.

■ SWALLOW

Originally part of Jaguar, the Swallow Coachbuilding Co (1935) became part of the giant Tube Investments organization during the Second World War. Its sportscar, the Doretti, was destined mainly for the American market. It used Swallow's spare capacity but was dropped because parent company TI (Tube Investments) decided they could not go on supplying sportscar manufacturers producing a rival product.

TATRA

■ TATRA 603

First sight of the 603, Tatra's bold rear-engined V-eight saloon, came in 1957. There had been no Tatra passenger cars since the demise of the flat-four Tatraplan in 1954, but the new 603 kept the tradition of an air-cooled V-eight rear mounted in a six-seater saloon, the last in a line of streamlined Tatras that started with Ledwinka's Jaray-styled T77 in the 1930s.

The 603 took its name from its hemi-head V-eight, a 2.5-litre unit with pushrods and twin Jikov down-draught carbs (Weber copies) first seen in a single-seater Tatra racer in 1950. Twin belt-driven scavenge-blowers did the cooling, with vents let into the rear wings plus a thermostatically-opening grille in the bumper. Alloy build meant low weight (373lb/169kg), but with a low 6.5:1 compression ratio it packed just 100bhp, denying the 3240lb (1470kg) car sparkling acceleration. On the other hand, top speed was 100mph (160kph), testimony to the car's slippery shape: the floorpan was virtually flat with no exhaust or propshaft to impede clean air flow.

■ ABOVE *The Tatra 603 as it looked from the mid 1960s onwards, though many earlier cars were modified.*

■ LEFT *The 2.5-litre V-eight engine was air-cooled and gave 105bhp in its latest form. Twin blowers can be seen in the lower part of the picture.*

TATRA 603 (1955–75)	
Engine	Aircooled V-eight
Capacity	2472cc
Power	95-105bhp
Transmission	4-speed manual
Top speed	100mph (160kph)
No. built	22,422

■ LEFT *The unmistakable front end of the 603. Luggage lives in the front with the fuel tank.*

■ ABOVE *The rear view shows the split rear window and remnants of the dorsal fin seen on earlier Tatra models.*

■ BELOW *Late 603s like this had disc brakes all round, and all were good motorway cruisers with a high top gear.*

Drive went through a four-speed transaxle with column shift, and early 603s used big hydraulic drums with advanced twin circuits. Dunlop discs, built under patent, didn't arrive until the mid-60s. At the back, trailing arms with coil springs were no surprise, but for the front of the 603 a new suspension system was schemed, a form of MacPherson strut with trailing swinging arms to save space in the big front luggage compartment.

In looks, the 603 couldn't have been anything but a Tatra, somewhere between Jaray's classic brave-new-world modernism and fashionable Detroit

■ ABOVE *Although little known in the West, the Tatra marque is one of the oldest in the world. New Tatras are still available.*

kitsch. At the front, three lights peered from behind a one-piece glass panel, giving the 603 the look of a bullet-nosed diesel express train. At the back, the roof line swept down sharply into the engine cover, the panoramic back window split by the remnants of an embryonic dorsal fin that was left off at the last minute.

Through the 60s, Tatra made gradual changes. They toned down styling with a new split, four-light nose. The 603-2 of 1967 had a wider grille with lights spaced farther apart in a glassfibre panel. Accidents or factory refits meant

that many earlier 603s gained this later front-end look. Miniature chrome fins evolved on the rear wings, the over-riders were tamed and the car lost its bonnet vent. The roof line became slightly more bulbous too, and front-door windows on these later cars had quarter-light vents. The 603H engine of 1969 gave 105bhp and used electronic ignition, still a rarity on western cars. Initially fitted only at the front, by this time servo discs were used all round. Production ended in 1975 as the 603 began to give way to the four-cam, Vignale-styled 613.

■ ABOVE *Cooling air is sucked in through a hole under the bumper.*

■ RIGHT *The 603 was a full six-seater, favoured transport of government officials.*

TOYOTA

■ TOYOTA 2000GT

Toyota launched its beautiful 2000GT as an image-building loss leader. Its birth was convoluted. It was Nissan, not Toyota, who in 1963 had originally commissioned the styling from Graf Goertz, the New York-based industrial designer, best known for his 503 and 507 BMWs. Yamaha built a running prototype, but Nissan backed out at the last minute, leaving Yamaha free to sell the design package to Toyota. Because production levels were always going to be low, Toyota farmed out the work to Yamaha and the first prototype was presented at the Tokyo show in 1965. The production car stood just 45in (114cm) high on tall, slim 165/15 shod centre-lock alloys. The sweep of its roof and its rounded rear haunches were undeniably influenced by the E-Type, but there was much that was bold and original about this now 30-year-old design with its upswept slash-like side windows, slim pillars and plunging, sensual bonnet line.

Under its seductively curvaceous shell, the 2000GT's hardware lived up to the looks. There were twin-cams (a free-breathing and sophisticated hemi-head design with straight-through ports

■ RIGHT *The beautiful shape of the 2000GT was by Goertz, also responsible for the BMW 507 and, later, the Datsun 240Z.*

■ ABOVE *When it was introduced in the USA in 1967, the 2000GT was priced well above the Porsche 911 and Jaguar E-Type.*

■ ABOVE *Production stopped in 1970, just as Datsun were introducing the 240Z.*

and big valves), a brace of double-throat Mikuni/Solex carburettors and a purposeful six-branch exhaust manifold, one outlet for each cylinder. The gearbox had five speeds, there were four-wheel disc brakes, and the Lotus-like back bone chassis used wishbones all round.

Back in 1965, this was copybook stuff: rare in high-calibre European machinery, unheard of on a Japanese car. There were three optional final drives, but with the 4.375 ratio a 2000GT should be good for 130-135mph (209-217kph), which means

■ OPPOSITE *The 2000GT was probably the first truly desirable car to be built by Toyota: only 337 were built.*

■ RIGHT *There was certainly a touch of E-Type about the 2000GT, but it had a dynamic elegance all of its own.*

TOYOTA 2000GT (1967–70)	
Engine	Straight six
Capacity	1988cc
Power	150bhp @ 6000rpm
Transmission	5-speed manual
Top speed	135mph (217kph)
No. built	337

100mph (160kph) in third and 115 (185) in fourth. The high second will run the 2805lb (1272kg) 2000GT to 70mph (112kph) in 12.7 seconds.

You couldn't actually buy a 2000GT until May 1967. Changes were few in a protracted five-year cycle although, towards the end of its life, Toyota built nine simplified single-camshaft cars with air conditioning and the option of automatic transmission to stir up interest in North America. Despite an ecstatic *Road and Track* test report on the twin-cam version, only 63 American buyers could be persuaded to part with $6,800 for a 2000GT, a price well above that of more prestigious Porsche and Jaguar competition. Even at that price, Toyota probably lost money on every one: you only have to look at the specification – and the complex curvatures in the body and glass – to see why. Production ceased in October 1970, just as Datsun were coming on stream with the 240Z. With only 337 produced, the 2000GT is one of the most collectable post-war Japanese classics.

■ ABOVE *The 2000GT had a six-cylinder engine with twin overhead camshafts and a five-speed gearbox.*

■ TOP RIGHT *Driving lights at the front were supplemented by retractable headlights.*

■ BOTTOM RIGHT *The 135mph (217kph) performance was stunning for a two-litre car, but the complex curvature of the body made it expensive to produce.*

TRIUMPH

■ TRIUMPH 1800/2000 ROADSTER

A torquey tourer rather than a true sportscar, the Triumph roadster with its "dickey-seat" fold out was one of the most memorable British cars of the immediate post-war years.

Standard's British boss Sir John Black bought Triumph in 1944 to take on Jaguar, using the Triumph name as an upper-crust sister marque to Triumph and trading on the make's pre-war prestige. Jaguar's boss William Lyons had built his business with the help of Standard, which had provided engines, gearboxes and chassis for his stylish SS – later Jaguar – saloons and sportscars, yet he had brushed aside Black's proposal of a takeover. Enter the roadster, a new breed of Triumph using existing Standard mechanics and calling on engineering skills developed during the

■ RIGHT *With just 60bhp the Roadster was grossly overweight, but its looks have a certain appeal today – as does the car's rarity.*

■ ABOVE *The rakish looks of the Triumph Roadster were designed to tempt buyers away from Jaguar: few were convinced.*

TRIUMPH ROADSTER (1946–49)	
Engine	In-line four
Capacity	1776/2088cc
Power	65-68bhp
Transmission	3-speed manual
Top speed	75mph (120kph)
No. built	2,501/2,000

company's wartime experience in aircraft manufacturing. Out of the parts bin came the 1776cc Standard 14 engine and matching gearbox. In fact, the power unit selected was the overhead-valve variant created by Harry Weslake to the order of William Lyons and since 1937 made by Standard exclusively for the SS-Jaguar

1½-litre. Black had wanted a straight six originally but in a moment of weakness had sold the tooling for Standard's own six-cylinder engine to Jaguar. The transverse-leaf independent front suspension of the Flying Standard Series was used with a Standard Fourteen back axle.

The underslung chassis of the new Triumph was a completely new design, a simple ladder frame made of the 3½in readily available, round-section tubing. In a similar vein, bodying the car in aluminium, over a timber frame, got around the steel shortages of the immediate post-war years. For the

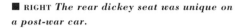

■ BELOW *The two-litre engine from the Vanguard was introduced in 1948, but the top speed was still just 75mph (120kph).*

■ RIGHT *The rear dickey seat was unique on a post-war car.*

■ BELOW *Cabin was functional but hardly sporting in flavour, with seats offering little support. It was a three-seater.*

■ LEFT *Produced between 1946 and 1949, only 4,500 Roadsters were built. The bulbous shape tried to evoke the pre-war Jaguar SS100.*

■ BELOW *With the hood up the cabin looks cramped. Doors are rear-hinged. The long bonnet promises an exciting power unit.*

Roadster's styling, Black wanted something in the style of the SS-100 with big headlamps and flowing wings. He wanted a dickey-seat too, a hangover from the pre-war Triumph Dolomite Roadster coupé. Styled by Frank Callaby, it had a long bonnet with full-bodied front wings, a hunched rear and a cramped-looking passenger compartment.

At the time of its 1946 introduction, the cheap-to-build 1800 was a unique concept, with its bench front seat and its two jump-seats in the capacious boot. It offered a three-plus-two configuration that made it a more versatile package than any other post-war open car.

In 1948, after 2,501 Roadsters had been made, the car received a new wet-liner Vanguard engine along with the Vanguard three-speed gearbox. In this form, a further 2,000 examples were made before production ceased in October 1949.

The bigger-engined car was 0.7cwt (36kg) lighter and with 3bhp more it was better accelerating – 0-60mph (96kph) in 27.9 seconds, against 34.4 seconds for the 1800 model.

TRIUMPH

■ BELOW *The TR2 was Triumph's bid for the American sportscar market. On 90bhp it would do over 100mph (160kph).*

■ TRIUMPH TR2/3/3A

To challenge MG in the all-important post-war North American export market, Standard/Triumph boss Sir John Black knew he needed a more credible sportscar than the quaint, under-powered 2000 Roadster. With his bid to take over Morgan rejected, he initiated a prototype of an affordable Triumph sportscar.

A Standard Vanguard 2-litre engine was installed in a shortened Standard 8 chassis and clothed by a two-seater roadster body. Called the TS20, it was revealed to muted applause at the 1952 London Motor Show. The runtish looks were not liked, but Black gave the concept of a cheap and cheerful sportscar the go-ahead.

The TR2 revealed a year later overcame the TR1's problems: it featured a simple ladder-type chassis and a longer body with a much bigger boot. A 90bhp 1991cc version of the Vanguard engine with twin carbs was mated to a four-speed gearbox, while suspension was coil spring and wishbone at the front and a live rear axle on semi-elliptic springs.

It could reach 60mph (96kph) in

under 12 seconds, return fuel consumption of 25mpg in daily use, yet still do 100mph (160kph) – or 108 (173) with optional overdrive. This simple, enjoyable small sportscar was lapped up by American buyers and the TR2 quickly became the company's top dollar earner.

The TR2 sired the similar 1955 TR3. It had a bit more power and a new front grille, and a factory hard top was offered as part of an optional GT package. In

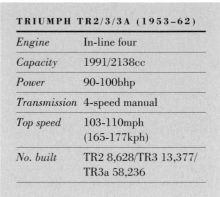

TRIUMPH TR2/3/3A (1953–62)	
Engine	In-line four
Capacity	1991/2138cc
Power	90-100bhp
Transmission	4-speed manual
Top speed	103-110mph (165-177kph)
No. built	TR2 8,628/TR3 13,377/ TR3a 58,236

■ RIGHT *The TR3A had a new full-width front grille, a 100bhp engine and exterior door handles.*

■ LEFT *The hole-in-the-wall grille is a trademark of the TR3, produced from 1955. The earlier car had a recessed grille.*

■ LEFT *Cut-away doors and a pinched waist are hallmarks of the TR2 and 3. Wire wheels and overdrive were optional.*

■ BELOW *The basic shape of the TR2 was first seen on the unlovely TR1 at the 1952 Motor Show. The look was much improved on the production cars.*

■ ABOVE *The functional interior featured a big steering-wheel, bucket seats and plain, but comprehensive, instrumentation.*

■ ABOVE *Though somewhat crude, the TR2 and 3 had a reputation for toughness.*

■ ABOVE *Smiths dials gave temperature and oil pressure information. Engines were comparatively low-revving but had good pulling power.*

1956, it became the first mass-produced car with front disc brakes. Triple overdrive and a token rear seat became available at the same time. The 1957 TR3a was the last of the cutaway-door TRs with a full-width grille, door handles and a 2138cc engine. The TR3b was a version with full synchromesh gearbox of the later TR4, produced for the American market only.

Although the TR4 that came next had smoother Italian styling, mechanically it followed the same rugged principles. Indeed, the basic TR chassis survived, albeit with independent suspension, until the TR6 came to an end in 1976.

■ LEFT *Late TR3s had the biggest 2138cc engine and the full synchromesh gearbox later found on the TR4.*

TRIUMPH

■ ABOVE *The TR4 and 5 were designed by Michelotti of Italy. This is a six-cylinder TR5 with fuel injection.*

■ TRIUMPH TR4/5/6

Launched in 1962, the Triumph TR4 was the first "pretty" TR sportscar, with a roomier Michelotti body and a smattering of creature comforts. Under the skin, though, it retained all the solid, proven qualities of the 2 and 3. It had a big-banger 2.2-litre wet-liner four, giving 100bhp (and ample torque), and the reassurance of a simple, solid rear axle for predictable handling, improved on the 102mph (163kph) TR4 by wider wheel tracks and rack-and-pinion steering. An all-synchromesh gearbox was another innovation.

Inside the car, the cockpit was roomier and occupants enjoyed face-level ventilation. The TR4 featured an early form of the Targa roof, later adopted by Porsche on the 911, with a removable panel (Surrey top in Triumph parlance), and had wind-up side windows. The TR4 answered criticisms of poor roadholding and a rough ride on the early TR4 with a new independent rear suspension system, a semi-trailing link system first seen on the Triumph 2000 saloon.

Calls for more and smoother power were answered in 1967 by the TR5 with a 2498cc six-cylinder engine. Boasting the notoriously troublesome mechanical

TRIUMPH TR4/56 (1962–76)	
Engine	Straight six
Capacity	2498cc
Power	150bhp
Transmission	4-speed, optional overdrive
Top speed	119mph (191kph)
No. built	91,850

■ ABOVE *The TR6 was mechanically almost identical to the TR5 but restyled by Karmann.*

Lucas fuel-injection system, this 150bhp car was capable of 120mph (193kph). It was a short-lived variant, supplanted 15 months later by the TR6. Mechanically, little was changed, but the TR6 had a crisper, more modern body courtesy of Karmann of Germany. The TR line had traditionally enjoyed a strong following

in the USA and so it was with the TR6 which continued in that market until 1976 in detuned carburettor form.

By that time the controversial wedge-like TR7 was getting into its stride. Never as well loved by enthusiasts as its rugged forefathers, it was the last and numerically most successful, TR of all.

■ FAR LEFT *On 150bhp the TR5 was good for nearly 120mph (193kph). The six-cylinder engine was also found in the 2.5 PI.*

■ NEAR LEFT *The TR6 was the last of the traditional TRs, with a separate chassis and a straight-six engine.*

■ RIGHT *To overcome engine problems, many owners substituted the Rover 3.5-litre V-eight for the Stag's 3.0-litre unit with its inherent snags.*

TRIUMPH STAG

British Leyland had a world-beater in the Triumph Stag – making its poor execution, dodgy reputation and untimely demise more tragic. First seen in 1970, this four-seater convertible looked good with top up or down, the strength-giving roll bar skilfully blended into the profile by Michelotti to become part of the character of the styling, rather than detracting from it.

The Stag's brand-new 2998cc V-eight engine produce 145bhp, which in manual overdrive guise made this 2810lb (1275kg) luxury four-seater good for 116mph (186kph) with 60 (96) coming up in 9.3 seconds. Automatics were good for about 110 (177) and fuel use in both versions was about 20mpg. With struts up front and semi-trailing arms behind, the Stag had neat, conventional handling but always lacked the well-bred poise of its German contemporary, the Mercedes SL.

It lacked the German's reliability, too. Overheating was the initial snag, usually triggered by a blocked radiator which was sensitive to silting (in the service schedule Triumph omitted to mention

TRIUMPH STAG (1970–77)	
Engine	V-eight
Capacity	2998cc
Power	145bhp @ 5500rpm
Transmission	4-speed manual overdrive 3-speed auto
Top speed	116mph (186kph)
No. built	25,939

the need for a yearly coolant flush and new antifreeze). A blown head gasket usually followed and, at the same time, the thinned-out, overheated oil that resulted from a boil-up did little to protect crank bearings. A worn timing chain on a neglected engine also gave trouble: left too long, the chain would wreck the valve gear. Initial sales were healthy but, as word got around about the engine, it bombed. The V-eight was not used in any other car. The last Stags, MkIIs with detail changes, were built in 1977.

These days, specialists seem to have the Stag's engine problems licked. Now with uprated radiators, hardened cranks and regular 3000-mile (4800-km) oil changes, the engines can have a long life. It is tragic that Triumph got the engine so wrong first time around, because the rest of the car is quite well sorted.

The Stag was a great idea. Indeed, it still is, if the car's continuing popularity, almost 20 years after its death, is anything to go by.

■ ABOVE *The one-off prototype Stag three-door coupé of the mid 1970s.*

■ RIGHT *MkII Stags had body stripes, chrome sill covers and optional alloy wheels. The roll bar gave effective protection in an accident and helped the rigidity of the body.*

■ ABOVE *Though it had a family resemblance to the 2000/2500 saloons, the Stag shared no body panels with them.*

TVR

■ TVR GRANTURA & VIXEN

The first TVR Grantura sportscars were built in Blackpool in 1958, using VW suspension on a tubular backbone chassis, clothed in a pretty glassfibre body and powered by a choice of Ford, BMC and Coventry Climax engines. By 1962 the MkIII Grantura had evolved, a crossover model mixing quaint early styling elements with the increased chassis sophistication of the later cars.

There was no longer a choice of engines – it came with MGA power, take it or leave it – and best of all it had a new chassis, eschewing the ultra stiff-riding VW trailing-link design for a proper factory-fabricated double-wishbone and coil-spring suspension. Although still built from 16-gauge steel tube, the frame – with a slightly longer wheelbase – was more rigid, good enough to live on into the early 1970s until introduction of the "M" series. The cast-alloy front suspension uprights are unique to TVR, and although the diff internals are MG, they sit in TVR's own cast-alloy housing.

The look was familiar: the stub-tailed coupé shape dated from the first 1958 Grantura and had a Perspex wrap-around rear window, Ford Consul front screen, blistered wheel arches and low, almost Porsche-like bonnet, a one-piece

■ LEFT *Early TVRs came with a variety of engines, from small Coventry Climax units to monster 4.7-litre Ford V-eights. The bodies were always glassfibre, while the shape, based on a rugged tubular backbone chassis, dates back to 1958.*

■ LEFT *TVRs came ready built or in kit form for the do-it-yourself enthusiast. The rear window is perspex, the front screen from the Ford Consul.*

moulding hinged at the front.

With such a relatively light engine, mounted well back, the Grantura felt delicate and well balanced on the road. The Spitfire-sourced rack was light and accurate, and the braking progressive and powerful with Girling discs at the

front but no servo assistance.

By 1967, the Grantura had become the Vixen, via the 1800S and 1800S Mk IV. The former introduced the squared-off 'manx' tail with the bigger rear window and MKI Cortina rear lights: the latter merely heralded detail refinements

■ ABOVE *The wide transmission tunnel was a hallmark of early TVRs, along with a slightly home-made look to the fixtures and fittings.*

■ ABOVE *The early manx-tailed Grantura: the basic shape – with changes – lived on until the 1970s.*

■ ABOVE *The bonnet has a hint of Porsche 356 about it and forms almost the entire front of the car, giving good access to the engine bay.*

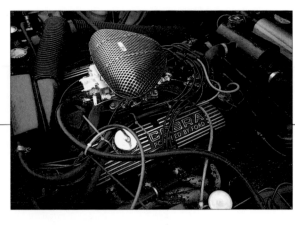

■ FAR LEFT *Even with the smaller engines, the top speed of the early cars was over 100mph (160kph).*

■ LEFT *The Ford 4.7 V-eight made the TVR into a very desirable car.*

to the suspension and interior. The sausage-bonnet Vixen was essentially a Ford Cortina GT-engined version of the 1800S, using a lighter 88bhp crossflow unit with matching all-synchromesh Ford gearbox.

The Vixen S2 replaced it after just 12 months, using the longer-wheelbase chassis developed for the Tuscan V-eight SE. That meant larger doors, wraparound MkII Cortina lights, a new bonnet bulge and lots of detail changes. Also, it was the first TVR in which the body was bolted, rather than bonded to the chassis. You could still buy it as a kit, though the new Lilley management didn't encourage do it yourself builders, and by the turn of the decade, new purchase-tax rules wiped out the kit market anyway.

Despite a high price, the Vixen made a credible MGB GT alternative in its day and sales figures proved it: 746 were produced before the 1600M took over as the small-engined car in the TVR range in 1973.

TVR VIXEN S1 (1968–69)	
Engine	4-cylinder
Capacity	1599cc
Power	88bhp
Transmission	4-speed manual
Top speed	106mph (170kph)
No. built	117

OTHER MAKES

■ TALBOT-LAGO

After the 1920 formation of the Anglo-French company Sunbeam-Talbot-Darracq, Darracq cars became known as Talbots in Europe and Darracqs in England to avoid confusion with the British Talbot firm. Major Anthony Lago took over Darracq's Suresnes works in suburban Paris after the 1935 STD collapse and set to making a new line of six-cylinder cars. After 1945, car sales were hit by high taxation, shaky finances and a misguided model policy, although the flagship Grand Sport was the ultimate touring car of its day. The company was absorbed by Simca in 1959.

■ TRABANT

The now famous Trabant was a product of the IFA grouping, a nationalized consortium of all car plants in the German Democratic Republic (DDR). It was a smaller sister to the 686cc Zwickau P70 of 1955-59, which was a development of the preceding IFA F8 – a DDR version of the pre-war twin-cylinder DKW Meisterklasse. It features a separate chassis, rot-free glassfibre bodywork and smoky two-stroke engines, though later cars had VW Polo power.

■ TRIDENT

The sleek Fiore-style Trident has a troubled history. Unveiled at the 1965 Geneva Show as a TVR, the body moulds were bought by TVR Dealer Bill Last when TVR hit financial trouble. He set up his own manufacturing operation in Suffolk and the firm produced cars in Woodbridge and then in Ipswich. Trident folded in 1974, but the car made a brief reappearance in 1976 before the firm folded finally in 1977.

■ TURNER

Jack Turner built small glassfibre-bodied, tubular-framed sportscars with various proprietory engines ranging from the 803 A30 engine to the Climax unit used from 1959 with up to 90bhp. Fast and agile, they were among the best British cars of their type. However, they could never compete with the mass-produced Soprite/Midget and the company went into voluntary liquidation in 1966.

■ UNIPOWER

The mid-engined Unipower was conceived by BMC works driver Andrew Hedges and racing driver/power-boat racer Tim Powell. A small, high-quality GT coupé capable of up to 120mph (193kph) with the biggest Mini-Cooper power-pack, it was built at Perivale, Middlesex, from 1966 to 1968 by Universal Power Drives, makers of fork-lift trucks and forestry tractors. A new company, Unipower Cars Ltd, took over but folded in 1970.

VAUXHALL

■ VAUXHALL CRESTA

Few cars are more evocative of late-50s Britain and its popular obsession with all things American than the Vauxhall PA Cresta. This was Vauxhall's answer to the Ford Zodiac, obviously inspired by the products of Vauxhall's American parent, General Motors of Detroit. Small fins sprouted from rear wings. Front and rear screens had a heavy "dog-leg" wraparound. Optional whitewall tyres and two-tone paint only emphasized the heavy American influence.

Launched in 1957, the PA Cresta (and its cheaper, less well-equipped sister the Velox) leaned heavily on the E

VAUXHALL CRESTA PA (1957–62)	
Engine	Straight six
Capacity	2262/2651cc
Power	78-95bhp
Transmission	3-speed, overdrive and auto
Top speed	90-97mph (145-156kph)
No. built	81,841/91,923

■ ABOVE *The post-war Cresta line-up: from left to right, the PC model of 1965, the PA and the PB.*

■ BELOW *Some brave drivers campaigned the Cresta in rallying: this model is an Army team car.*

■ ABOVE *The styling of the PA was very transatlantic, with fashionable rear fins, wrap-around screens and two-tone paintwork.*

■ BELOW *This is a pre-1959 PA with the distinctive three-piece rear window and egg-crate grille.*

■ ABOVE *Inside the car, bench seats, white steering-wheel and column gearchange added to the American flavour.*

■ ABOVE *Rust ravaged many PA Crestas, so fine survivors like this one are rare.*

■ LEFT *PA engines were straight sixes with up to 95bhp for a top speed of over 90mph.*

Series mechanically, though they were physically bigger cars. The smooth, understressed 2262cc pushrod six remained, now producing 75bhp for a top speed of more than 90mph (145kph). The three-speed, column-shift box was all synchromesh now, but the PA retained the leaf-spring rear axle and soft wishbone and coil-spring suspension of its predecessor.

For 1959 the wrap-around rear screen became one-piece and there was a new grille, along with the option of an estate car model, built by Friary (the Queen had one for many years). The best of the bunch was the 1960 model with a bigger

2.6-litre, 96bhp engine. Other recognition points were bigger wheels and fins. Two-pedal "Hydramatic" control or dual overdrive for the manual box broadened the car's appeal. Servo-assisted front disc brakes were another welcome improvement.

Sales remained strong right up to the model's death in 1962. By then, fins were somewhat *passé* and Vauxhall had a cleaner looking Velox and Cresta on the stocks, the PB. The Cresta name finally died with the PC model, discontinued in 1972, but the PA remains the best-loved and most collectable of this breed of big Vauxhalls.

■ LEFT *In 1962 the PA Cresta was replaced by the PB, with a bigger engine and cleaner, more modern styling. This is the 3.3-litre PB, one of the fastest accelerating family saloons of its day.*

OTHER MAKES

■ VANDEN PLAS

Guillaume Van den Plas, originally a Brussels wheelwright, entered the coach-building market in 1884. In 1913, a British licensee was appointed, and in 1923 this offshoot, always known as Vanden Plas, moved to Kingsbury, in north-east London. Many high-class British cars such as Alvis and Bentley received Vanden Plas bodies. In 1946, Austin took over the firm and from 1960 it became a BMC marque in its own right, producing up-market versions of the 1100, the three-litre and finally the Allegro. It was famous for its large formal limousines, too, such as the big Austin Princess-based four-litre and the Daimler DS420. The works closed in 1979.

■ VOLGA

The post-Second World War Volga M21/22 was a product of the USSR's giant Gorky auto works. It was a big tough saloon (or estate) with a conservative technical specification, poor performance and dated styling; one of the few highlights was a vast tool kit. In Russia, it served as a taxi and transport for middle-ranking officials.

VW

■ VW BEETLE

The Volkswagen Beetle, born out of Adolf Hitler's desire to provide low-cost motoring for the masses, needs little introduction. Its rounded shape and air-cooled throb are familiar around the world. Although the last German-built cars came out of the Wolfsburg factory, Lower Saxony, in 1978, the model is still in production in South America. Total sales stand at 21 million (it overtook the Model T's 15 million in the early 70s), a figure unlikely to be beaten.

Ferdinand Porsche designed the original rear-engined, air-cooled design, although very few were actually built before 1939. Production started again in

■ LEFT *The most familiar car of all, the Beetle, dates from well before the war. It soon gained a reputation for reliability and good quality.*

■ BELOW *The Beetle's shape and engineering were conceived by Dr Ferdinand Porsche.*

■ ABOVE *The split-screen models are the most collectable of the lot. Early cars had non-synchromesh transmissions and feeble 50mph (80kph) performance.*

VW BEETLE (1945–77)	
Engine	Flat four
Capacity	1131–1584cc
Power	25–50bhp
Transmission	4-speed
Top speed	50–84mph (80–135kph)
No. built	21,000,000

1945 with a very basically specified 1100cc model with a non-synchromesh gearbox, cable brakes and very little brightwork. In America, the model started a small-car revolution as millions of drivers, looking for a cheap second car, fell in love with the Beetle's good engineering, practicality and economy.

The size of the flat-four pushrod engine grew from 1131 to 1200cc in the 50s, and the range expanded with the pretty Karmann Ghia sports models and a cabriolet with its pram-like hood.

Calls for a faster, more modern-driving Beetle were answered in the mid 60s with the 1300 and 1500 models, which gained an all-synchromesh box and could be had with disc brakes and even a semi-automatic transmission. Ultimately, however, VW's reliance on one basic model had a serious effect on sales in the later part of the decade. Buyers began to tire of the noisy, slow Beetle. The 1961 1500 amounted to nothing more than a dressed-up version of the original car, and even the big four-door 411 with its fuel injection didn't

■ LEFT *The 1300 and 1500-engined cars of the mid-1960s answered calls for more performance.*

fool many buyers: under the skin it was still pure Beetle.

Salvation for VW arrived in the form of the water-cooled, front-engined Golf in 1974, a benchmark for front-wheel-drive hatchbacks two decades ago, though the Wolfsburg-made Beetles

continued until 1977.

Today, the Beetle is a cult machine and the older cars, particularly the "split window" model from the early 50s, command high prices, while the 60s and 70s models are still plentiful and cheap.

■ ABOVE *The Beetle has long been a cult favourite with customizers all over the world.*

■ BELOW *The car's good traction makes the Beetle an ideal choice as a beach buggy.*

■ ABOVE *The Karmann Ghia was a luxurious sporty version of the Beetle: sadly VW never gave it extra performance.*

■ RIGHT *One of the most sought-after Beetles is the convertible, also by Karmann.*

■ ABOVE *The flat-four aluminium engine was noisy but ultra-reliable and was responsive to tuning.*

VOLVO

■ LEFT *An early P1800 – with cow-horn bumpers – in the foreground, an 1800ES in the background. Mechanically the cars were identical to contemporary Volvo saloons.*

■ VOLVO P1800

The initial production of Volvo's stylish Ghia-designed P1800 coupé was somewhat convoluted. The steel bodies were tooled-up for and built in Britain by Pressed Steel in Scotland and then sent to Jensen of West Bromwich who, with chassis parts supplied from Sweden, assembled the complete cars.

Although not a sportscar in the true sense of the word, the high-waisted P1800 was a good, long-legged cruiser, and with its overdrive gearbox had a respectable top speed of more than 100mph (160kph). The 107bhp engine was the familiar twin-carb in-line four unit (B18) with a four-speed transmission sending the drive to a coil-spring live rear axle. Servo-assisted front disc brakes were standard, enhancing handling qualities which were safe but uninspiring. All the

P1800's mechanics were shared with the contemporary "Amazon" 120 Series saloons. Handsome and practical, the P1800 quickly gained popularity despite a high price tag, and its profile was further raised by its weekly appearances in the television series *The Saint*, driven by the show's star Roger Moore (who also owned one in real life).

Volvo were never very happy with the quality of the Jensen-built cars, and in 1964 they shifted production over to

VOLVO P1800, 1800S, 1800E & 1800ES (1960–73)	
Engine	4-cylinder
Capacity	1778/1986cc
Power	90–125bhp
Transmission	4-speed manual 3-speed auto
Top speed	102–115mph (163–185kph)
No. built	P1800 6,000/ 1800S 23,993/ 1800E 9,414/ 1800ES 8,078

Sweden. With more power and detail trim differences (the cow-horn bumpers of the Jensen-built cars were replaced by conventional items), the car became known as the 1800S. The engine became a full two-litre with 115bhp in 1968 and from 1969 gained fuel injection, upping the power output to 125bhp. There was an automatic option on this version and an "E" can be spotted by its alloy wheels.

The final flowering of the design was the 1800ES, Volvo's answer to the Reliant Scimitar GTE. With its extended roof line and rear hatchback, it was a useful small-load carrier with a good turn of speed – 115mph (185kph). However, by the early 70s Volvo were beginning to lose interest in their aging sportscar and stopped production.

■ ABOVE *The ES was Volvo's answer to the Scimitar GTE but proved short-lived. Top speed with injection was 115mph.*

■ ABOVE *The ES had leather seats and was a comfortable long-distance express, especially with overdrive.*

■ ABOVE *Both versions had ample luggage capacity, useful in their role as long-legged GT cars.*

■ ABOVE *The famous profile of the P1800 was from Ghia of Italy and dated from the 1950s. Early cars were built in Britain.*

WOLSELEY

■ LEFT *The 6/80 was a prestige car in its day, with a surprising turn of speed from its six-cylinder engine.*

■ WOLSELEY 6/80

Born into a grim post-Second World War world starved of new cars, the six-cylinder Wolseley 6/80 – and its four-cylinder sister the 4/50 – headed the Nuffield range for 1948.

Based on the M/0 Series Morris saloons, the basic monocoque hull looked like an overgrown Morris Minor (basically what it was), but in 6/80 form it shared the 13in (33cm) longer wheelbase of the Morris Six. A bold grille and twin spotlights gave it a more

■ ABOVE *The interiors were luxurious: drivers needed the big wheel to get to grips with the handling.*

■ BELOW *The shape owed a lot to the Morris Minor and shared panels with the Morris MO Series.*

WOLSELEY 6/80 (1948–54)	
Engine	In-line six
Capacity	2215cc
Power	72bhp
Transmission	4-speed manual
Top speed	85mph
No. built	24,886

■ ABOVE *A sight to fill the hearts of criminals with fear in the 1950s. The Wolseley badge lights up.*

up-market image. The 6/80 shared its straight-six overhead-cam engine with the Morris Six, at 72bhp a heady six horsepower stronger than the Morris.

Its best feature was its interior, with leather seats, wooden dashboard and the rare luxury of a heater as standard equipment. Less impressive was the steering, a Bishop cam system which was both vague and heavy and no doubt somewhat off-putting in a car that was actually quite powerful for its day: the 6/80 could pull 85mph (137kph) easily.

It was the performance of the big Wolseley that attracted police forces all over Britain in the late 40s and early 50s – even today the model is synonymous with 50s law enforcement. If you watch late-night TV, the cars are hard to miss, with bumper-mounted bells ringing and a tense driver battling with the car's wayward handling.

By the end of the decade, the 6/80 was struggling to keep pace with the new breed of Jaguar-driving criminals, though remarkably, with production having ended in 1954, the last cars were still in use in 1961.

OTHER MAKES

■ WARTBURG

Like the Trabant, the Wartburg was a product of the nationalized East German combine IFA. An evolution of the preceding IFA F9, which was a DDR-built version of a 1940 DWK prototype, it was manufactured at the former BMW plant in Eisenach, Thuringia. The 312 and later 353 Knight were front-wheel-drive two-stroke saloons sold in the West at low prices, but the cars found few friends: handling was poor and the economy unremarkable at 25mpg.

■ ZAPOROZHETS

Clearly inspired by Western designs, this Soviet minicar, made in the Ukraine, was first seen in 1960 and survived three decades with only one restyle. It retained its rear-engine configuration to the end and had an unusual air-cooled V-four engine. A prototype front-wheel-drive replacement was shown in 1987 but the NSU-like ZAZ 966 was still listed in 1990.

A–Z of Classic Cars from 1976–present

This section brings future classics to life from 1976 to the present day, and identifies the cars that have had the impact necessary to qualify them as genuine classics. Every car included is great in some way. Perhaps, like the Peugeot 205GTI, it was viewed as the best car in its class. Perhaps, like the Renault Espace or Audi Quattro, it changed motoring life and the way we look at cars. You won't find just sportscars or super-luxury coupés in this section, for many affordable "cars for the common people" are every bit as classic as the great Ferraris and Porsches of their era.

ALFA ROMEO

■ ALFA ROMEO GT/GTV

This smart sports coupé was launched in 1974 as the Alfetta GT. It was based on a shortened version of the Alfetta saloon floorpan, so it shared its racing-inspired rear-mounted gearbox. Perhaps the car's best feature was its superbly clean

■ RIGHT *The 1980 GTV6 brought fuel-injected power to the Alfa, and there was also a major face-lift.*

ALFA ROMEO GT/GTV (1974–86)	
Engine	4/V-six-cylinder
Capacity	1570–2934cc
Power	109–186bhp
Transmission	5-speed
Top speed	111–140mph (179–225kph)
No. built	136,275

■ LEFT *All Alfa GT/GTV models handled superbly, and the best of the bunch was this late-model GTV6.*

■ ABOVE *For a coupé, the GTV was very practical, with four full seats and a proper opening tailgate.*

■ ABOVE *The 2.5-litre V-six engine in the GTV6 delivered 160bhp – enough for a top speed of 127mph (204 kph).*

styling by Giugiaro. This was also a very practical car thanks to its hatchback rear opening.

The interior was very distinctive: only the rev counter (tachometer) was sited in front of the driver. All the other gauges were stacked in a central

binnacle. There was more room for people than in most coupés in the GT class.

Initially, there was only one engine, the Alfetta 1.8, but by 1976, 1.6 and 2.0-litre units were added, the latter called GTV. There was even a very potent turbocharged model, but this was

sold in tiny numbers (around 20). In 1980, the 2.0 GTV became the only model sold and got a face-lift, featuring larger bumpers and a more conventional instrument layout.

The best GTV of all was undoubtedly the GTV6 of 1980. Into the familiar body Alfa Romeo fitted a fuel-injected 2.5-litre V-six engine. Performance was now extremely high, and suspension changes and a limited slip differential made it handle superbly. Yet this was not the quickest GTV of all: that honour goes to the GTV 3.0 produced in Alfa Romeo's South African factory. Like other GTV models, this boasted considerable success on the race-track, as well as being a very satisfying car to drive on the road. Today, it is the most desirable of the classic GTV family.

■ BELOW *The 164 was responsible for reviving Alfa Romeo's reputation for making desirable large saloon (sedan) cars.*

■ ALFA ROMEO 164

Traditionally, Alfa Romeo produced rear-wheel-drive sporting cars and was generally most successful with its smaller saloons and coupés. Its track record with larger cars was not very good, the 1970 Montreal and 1979 Alfa 6 being complex, poor-selling, problem-ridden machines.

That all changed with the 164, the first Alfa to emerge following Fiat's 1986

take-over of the group. Not only was the 164 quite the most handsome saloon (sedan) car of its day – thanks to Pininfarina's master hand – but it had sharp front-wheel-drive handling and, most importantly of all, it was built up to a quality that rivalled Germany's best. The interiors looked as if they had been designed by an architect.

The floorpan was shared with three other cars: the Fiat Croma, Lancia Thema and Saab 9000. However, Alfa installed its own range of engines, which was always the marque's best feature. The range started with a two-litre Twin Spark (two spark plugs per cylinder) and culminated in a three-litre V-six. All engines were capable of reaching 125mph (201kph). The ultimate Q4 model had four-wheel drive, six speeds and a 230bhp Cloverleaf engine.

If there was one criticism of the 164, it was a tendency to suffer from torque-steer, which means pulling right or left

under acceleration. Alfa Romeo addressed the worst of the problem early on and also developed a Super version with longer body-coloured bumpers and chrome strips.

The 164 undoubtedly led a renaissance at Alfa Romeo, and re-establishing confidence in the marque. It left production in 1997 after a distinguished career.

■ FAR LEFT *Pininfarina's styling was widely admired for its crispness and distinctively Alfa Romeo character.*

■ LEFT *Pininfarina's extraordinary sculpted dash was a work of art, but the profusion of switches was criticized as confusing.*

ALFA ROMEO 164 (1987–97)	
Engine	4/V-six-cylinder
Capacity	1962–2959cc
Power	114–230bhp
Transmission	5/6-speed manual
Top speed	125–152mph (201–245kph)
No. built	248,278 (to end 1994)

■ BELOW *Technically, the 164 borrowed its floorpan from Fiat/Lancia, but added its own engine range and sports-tuned suspension.*

ALFA ROMEO

■ OPPOSITE *It was difficult to describe the SZ's stocky shape as beautiful. The Italian press affectionately called it "Il Mostro" – the monster.*

■ ALFA ROMEO SZ/RZ

Italians coined a new phrase to describe the amazing Alfa Romeo SZ: "Il Mostro", or The Monster, and it is easy to see why. In no way could the bodywork be described as handsome, but if you were looking to make a visual impact then this Alfa supercar was king. Although Alfa Romeo announced the birth of this amazing new model under its internal type designation of ES30, production cars were known as SZ.

The design house responsible for the SZ was Zagato, which has always had a strong association with Alfa Romeo. Zagato also produced the SZ for Alfa at its Milanese factory. The time it took for Zagato to develop and produce the SZ was a remarkably short two years. To

■ ABOVE *The striking SZ made its debut at the 1989 Geneva Motor Show where it created many headlines.*

■ LEFT *Even more desirable among Alfisti was the convertible RZ model, only 241 of which were made.*

make the bodies, Zagato elected to use plastic composites (a mixture of thermosetting resins and glassfibre), mounted on a steel chassis. The result may have looked spectacularly ugly but it was surprisingly aerodynamic: its Cd (co-efficient of drag) figure of 0.30 was superior to that of many other cars.

Underneath that extraordinary coupé bodyshell was basically the mechanical package from the racing version of the Alfa Romeo 75, including its layout of longitudinal engine, rear transaxle and rear-wheel drive. The familiar Alfa

3.0-litre V-six engine was given even more power thanks to integrated fuel injection/ignition systems, new camshafts and modified manifolding. Maximum power was now up to 207bhp.

Since the SZ weighed only 2822lb (1280kg), performance was deeply impressive: a top speed of over 152mph (245kph) and 0–62mph (0–100kph) in only seven seconds was quoted. The SZ was quite capable of handling all this

■ RIGHT *Underneath the exterior lay what was basically a racing car. This made the SZ feel very much like a circuit racer on the road.*

power thanks to its sophisticated suspension and asymmetric Pirelli P-Zero tyres. One interesting feature was hydraulic adjustment for the rear suspension, which was occasionally needed to overcome ramps and other obstructions because ground clearance was just 2.4in (6cm).

Inside, the Alfa 75 driver would have felt immediately at home, since the instruments and much of the switchgear came from this humble saloon (sedan). Luxury was not overlooked, though, as standard equipment included leather seats and electric windows.

At the end of 1992, the SZ was joined by an open-topped model called the RZ. This was more than just a roofless version of the SZ, as it incorporated a number of detail changes like a shorter front spoiler, thinner body panels, lower windscreen and reshaped sills. The chassis was considerably stiffened to compensate for the loss of the roof, and in consequence its weight went up by 220lb (100kg).

■ ABOVE *The three-litre V-six engine under the bonnet (hood) was familiar, but it was tweaked to give 207bhp – enough for a 150mph (241kph) top speed.*

■ ABOVE *Milan-based coachbuilder Zagato was responsible for the design and construction of the SZ.*

■ TOP *Perhaps the most flattering view is from the bird's eye.*

■ ABOVE *Luxurious leather seating contrasted with humble switchgear from the Alfa 75.*

ALFA ROMEO SZ/RZ (1989–94)	
Engine	V-six-cylinder
Capacity	2959cc
Power	207bhp @ 6200rpm
Transmission	5-speed
Top speed	152mph (245kph)
No. built	1,035/241

As planned, Zagato built just over 1000 examples of this exceptional sportscar, despite the fact that Alfa Romeo had received 1600 orders for the model, almost before it had even been seen by the public. An additional 241 copies of the RZ drop-top model were made in 1992–3. That means the SZ and RZ will always be among the rarest and most sought-after Alfa Romeos of all.

ALFA ROMEO

■ ALFA ROMEO SPIDER/GTV

The name Spider in Alfa Romeo's vocabulary dates right back to 1955, and the most famous incarnation of the model – the one driven by Dustin Hoffman in the film *The Graduate* – lasted 18 years in production. At the Paris Salon in September 1994, Alfa Romeo not only used the name for its exciting new roadster, it also revived another famous name from its past for a sister coupé model – GTV.

■ ABOVE *The classic Alfa Romeo Spider dynasty began back in 1966 and ended with this model, the Series 4, in 1994.*

The most striking feature of this new sportscar couple was the styling. The elegant and dramatic wedge shape recalled the 1991 Proteo show car and, if anything, the production cars' styling was even more adventurous than the

■ BELOW *If the Spider's handling was affected by its non-rigid bodyshell, the GTV was the opposite: taut, sure-footed and rewarding.*

show car's. A collaboration between Alfa Romeo's own Styling Centre and Pininfarina, the body made full play of the famous Alfa triangular grille. Other features included a plastic clam-shell bonnet (hood) with cut-outs for the high-intensity headlamps, an uncompromising rising belt-line indentation, tapering rear flanks and air intakes at the front, which were strongly reminiscent of past Alfas.

However, Alfa Romeo departed from its sportscar traditions by opting for front-wheel drive. If anyone was in doubt about how well the new car would handle with this set-up, a simple test drive dispelled all such concern. A unique multi-link rear suspension system allowed for a degree of rear-wheel steering, and in terms of steering response and grip around corners, the new Alfa could hardly be surpassed. There was a big difference between the ultimate abilities of the fixed-top GTV and the open Spider, though: the loss of rigidity in the body structure of the Spider let it down compared to the super-sharp GTV.

The GTV also differed from the Spider in another important respect: it had two seats in the rear, although they were so tiny that only very small children could ever be comfortable.

Performance was a definite strong suit. In Italy, there was a choice of three engines: a brand new 150bhp 2-litre 16V Twin Spark engine with variable valve timing, a 200bhp 2-litre V-six Turbo unit (GTV only) and a 192bhp 3-litre V-six. In Britain, only the Twin Spark engine was offered. All engines

■ ABOVE *Alfa's sportscar twins took a healthy share of the market, and have already become living classics.*

provided acceleration to match the sharp styling.

The cockpit was a triumph of clean design and classic feel: shrouded circular dials, sculpted steering wheel, pleasing upholstery and a profusion of Alfa Romeo badges. The driving position was unusually good for an Italian car, too.

For their price, there was little to touch Alfa's new sportscar twins in the desirability stakes. Perhaps it was the ineffable magic of the badge, or the strikingly bold shape, or the class-leading levels of handling and response. Whatever the appeal, the Spider and GTV have already passed into the realm of instant classics.

■ BELOW *The Spider was an exciting car to drive, even if some testers criticized the lack of rigidity in the bodyshell.*

ALFA ROMEO SPIDER/GTV (1994–)	
Engine	4/V-six-cylinder
Capacity	1970–2959cc
Power	150–200bhp
Transmission	5-speed
Top speed	130–146mph (209–235kph)
No. built	Still in production

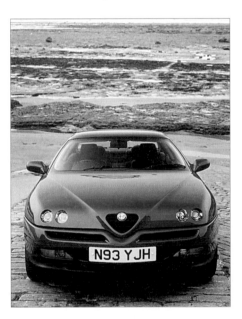

■ RIGHT *The front end of both cars was a triumph of styling: an adventurous clamshell bonnet with cut-outs for the high-intensity projector headlamps.*

■ ABOVE *The name GTV (last used in 1987) was revived for the fixed-head two-plus-two sister of the Spider, which was perhaps even more striking in its presence.*

ASTON MARTIN

■ ASTON MARTIN DB7

Aston Martin is part of a rich tradition of British coachbuilt sportscars. Its place is unique as a purveyor of brutally powerful, finely handcrafted, traditionally finished grand tourers. The "DB" dynasty of cars stretches back to 1947, the letters DB harking back to Sir David Brown, who owned Aston Martin from 1947 to 1972, and who helped design the DB7.

Ford became the new owner of Aston Martin in 1987. As well as giving the company the backing of a large

■ RIGHT *There is no doubt that the two Aston Martin DB7 models made an extremely strong pairing: elegant, powerful, luxurious, meticulously crafted and rich in character.*

■ BELOW *The most handsome car in the world? With the DB7, British designer Ian Callum created one of the great Aston Martin shapes.*

■ LEFT *The sumptuous interior reflected Aston's very British heritage and its tradition of hand-built quality: Connolly leather, tasteful British burr walnut, yet with plenty of modern electronics.*

organization, it instituted a new model programme, reviving the DB name on a new car that was designed to slot in below the existing Virage range. To develop this important newcomer, it turned to Tom Walkinshaw's TWR organization to do its best on the ageing platform of the Jaguar XJS.

The DB7 was the supremely elegant result. In style it was a classic, two-plus-two, front-engined, rear-wheel-drive car with superbly integrated, flowing lines designed by Ian Callum. Some were tempted to call it the most beautiful car in the world.

It was powered by a new 3.2-litre six-cylinder engine, which looked back to the past to boost its horse power: an Eaton supercharger helped it develop a

ASTON MARTIN DB7 (1994–)	
Engine	6-cylinder
Capacity	3239cc
Power	335bhp @ 5750rpm
Transmission	5-speed manual 4-speed auto
Top speed	155mph (249kph)
No. built	Still in production

■ RIGHT *The DB7 Volante immediately made an impact in sales terms, especially in America, boosting Aston Martin's production levels to an unprecedented high.*

massive 335bhp, enough to take the DB7 to a top speed of 155mph (249kph), with acceleration to match. Technically, the DB7 was very sophisticated, having sequential fuel injection, four-piston brakes and specially designed tyres.

This was a superb car to drive, sharp enough to cut it as a sportscar yet refined enough to make a convincing grand tourer. The chassis was pure magic.

Inside, rich Connolly leather upholstery was standard, as was traditional British burr walnut for the dashboard and centre console. Standard equipment included electric front-seat controls, air-conditioning, electric roof and Alpine sound system. There may not have been much room in the rear seats but at least they were there, and they could always double up as extra luggage space.

If the coupé looked seductive, the Volante convertible was the ultimate temptress in markets such as the US where up to 80 per cent of Aston Martin sales were of this model.

This was certainly not a cheap car, especially in Volante convertible form, and some people questioned whether it

was worth paying the extra for the DB7 when the Jaguar XK8, launched shortly after, looked and behaved so similarly and cost so much less. The Aston Martin was very much more exclusive, however, since a maximum of 700 per year could be built at the factory, and the badge carries a special set of qualities.

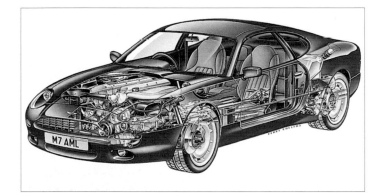

■ ABOVE *It may have had a mere six-cylinder engine, but supercharging and sophisticated fuel injection gave it 335bhp. The rest of the package was equally well engineered.*

■ ABOVE *Everyone who drove a DB7 was deeply impressed by its chassis, which provided keen handling, entertaining controllability and an accomplished ride.*

■ LEFT *A new Volante full convertible was presented ready for a 1996 launch. The hood (top) stacked under a tonneau cover in the British fashion.*

ASTON MARTIN

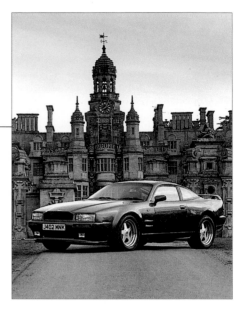

■ ASTON MARTIN VIRAGE

By 1988, Aston Martin had been relying on its mighty V-eight model for no less than 20 years, and it desperately needed a new car to tempt supercar owners. To design its car, it took the unusual step of asking several independent British car stylists to offer proposals, including Richard Oakes and Aston Martin veteran William Towns. The winner was John Heffernan's elegantly understated design, realized in aluminium by Aston Martin's skilled craftsmen.

The new Virage was unveiled at the 1988 Birmingham Motor Show and was greeted as the latest in a line of great British sportscars from the Newport Pagnell firm. It might have cost a six-figure sum, but its sumptuous specification, tremendous performance and hand-crafted quality were certainly appreciated by devotees.

■ ABOVE *Vast swathes of leather completely cloaked the cockpit; what it missed was covered with deep-pile carpets or polished wood.*

■ ABOVE *Even more muscle-bound was the later Vantage version, its twin supercharged engine boasting an incredible 557bhp.*

■ LEFT *For such an imposing, heavy and dimensionally grand car, the Virage managed to retain a certain elegance.*

■ ABOVE *When its V-eight engine kicked in, the Virage really flew. Its most impressive characteristic was almost limitless quantities of torque.*

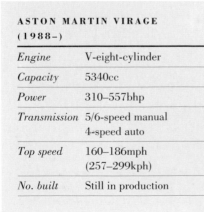

ASTON MARTIN VIRAGE (1988–)	
Engine	V-eight-cylinder
Capacity	5340cc
Power	310–557bhp
Transmission	5/6-speed manual 4-speed auto
Top speed	160–186mph (257–299kph)
No. built	Still in production

In true Aston Martin tradition, each engine was hand-built and the name of the builder was placed on a plaque on the engine block. The familiar 5.3-litre V-eight engine was given a four-valves-per-cylinder head, developed by the American tuning company Callaway Engineering. Now power was up to 310bhp, and even more impressive was the torque figure of 340lb ft (461Nm (Newton metre)).

That all spiralled up to new heights with the pumped-up Vantage model of 1992. Twin superchargers raised the power figure to 557bhp and torque to just about the highest figure of any road car: no less than 550lb ft (745Nm) at 4000rpm. It was quicker than just about anything else on the road.

The most popular Virage model of all was the Volante, the convertible member of the family. Further choices were Shooting Brake (estate/station wagon) and Lagonda (four-door saloon/sedan) versions, a special 500bhp 6.3-litre engine and a version simply called V8 Coupé with Vantage-style wide bodywork and "only" 350bhp.

■ RIGHT *A mere 50 coupés was the plan, but a further run of convertibles brought the total of Aston Zagatos up to 89.*

■ ASTON MARTIN ZAGATO

All Aston Martins are rare but the 1986 Zagato was guaranteed to be one of the rarest of all. When Aston Martin released pictures and announced that it would be building only 50 cars at £70,000 ($117,810) apiece, buyers came

■ RIGHT *Aston Martin revived an old relationship with coachbuilder Zagato to create the fastest, most exciting production Aston yet in 1986.*

■ FAR RIGHT *There was only space for two passengers but they were treated to an Italian-styled cockpit trimmed to the highest standards.*

ASTON MARTIN ZAGATO (1986–90)	
Engine	V-eight-cylinder
Capacity	5340cc
Power	310–432bhp
Transmission	5-speed
Top speed	157–190mph (253–306kph)
No. built	89

rushing and all were pre-sold before any had been made. Speculators forced the price up as high as £500,000 ($841,500).

So what was all the fuss about? Italian coachbuilder Zagato had an illustrious history with Aston Martin stretching back to 1958, and this was to be a modern equivalent of the immortal DB4 Zagato. In addition to being a special-bodied Aston, it would be the company's

quickest ever car. An already mightily powerful Vantage V-eight engine was tuned even further to give over 430bhp, and Aston Martin quoted a top speed of 190mph or 306kph.

This was essentially a special-bodied, lightweight, short-wheelbase Aston Vantage with two seats and an Italian-designed interior. Zagato not only designed but also built the car. There was some concern that the finished article did not look much like the drawings that had convinced buyers to hand over deposits, but there was no doubting the brutal nature of the drive. Acceleration was explosive at 0–60mph (0–96kph) in under five seconds and handling was certainly more incisive than other Astons.

It was decided that the exclusivity of the coupé would not be harmed by adding a limited run of 25 Volante convertibles to the roster, and the

prototype drop-top was shown at Geneva in 1987. In fact 52 coupés and 37 Volantes were made in total, the last one being produced in 1990. Controversial it may have been, but it was also the ultimate in Aston exclusivity.

■ ABOVE *The performance was brutal. A top speed of 190mph (306kph) was claimed, and you could do 0–60mph (0–96kph) in under five seconds.*

AUDI

■ AUDI QUATTRO

The idea of four-wheel drive as an aid to fast road driving rather than pure off-roading may not have been new (Jensen introduced the FF supercar in 1966), but Audi certainly pioneered the art-form in the real world. The 1980 Quattro was the first mass-produced performance car to feature permanent four-wheel drive.

■ FAR LEFT *The Quattro Sport was a strict two-seater with a 300bhp engine – expensive and a very rare sight.*

■ LEFT *Safe and forgiving, the Audi Quattro became the handling benchmark of the 1980s.*

■ LEFT *Not only was the Quattro grippy, it was very quick too, thanks to its five-cylinder turbo engine. This is a 1988 20V version with 220bhp.*

The four-wheel-drive system rewrote everyone's definition of handling limits. It certainly made it probably the safest car to be driving in wet or icy conditions. Reports in some journals even seemed to suggest that the Quattro was invincible around corners whatever the road conditions; in fact of course every car has its limits, and the Quattro's were simply much higher than other cars', but unfortunately dozens of owners found this out the hard way by asking too much of the car, and ending up in a ditch.

The body was based around the recently launched coupé, with suitably bulging wings and a deeper front spoiler. Audi was not above adding gimmicks to the package, notably a dubious digital talking dash.

Power was also very high thanks to a turbocharged 2.1-litre five-cylinder engine. There was mighty turbo lag (the time it took for the turbocharger to cut

AUDI QUATTRO (1980–91)	
Engine	5-cylinder
Capacity	2144–2226cc
Power	200–220bhp
Transmission	5-speed
Top speed	135–142mph (217–228kph)
No. built	11,452

in), but when it did, the Quattro simply flew: 0–60mph (0–96kph) in 6.3 seconds was stunningly fast for 1980. Braking was criticized for having too much front bias, but Audi soon corrected this with standard anti-lock brakes.

This was not a cheap car by any standards: it cost more than a Jaguar XJS or Mercedes-Benz SL, but then it did offer a completely new class of driving experience.

■ OPPOSITE *The Quattro Sport was homologated for rallying and continued Audi's dominance in the sport for many years.*

■ BELOW *It was on slippery surfaces like snow-bound mountains that the Quattro really shone, gripping the road where others wandered.*

The Quattro permanent (full-time) four-wheel-drive system also turned the rally world upside-down. Audi swept the board with its newcomer, and very soon everyone recognized that they weren't going to win anything unless they, too, adopted an all-wheels-driven strategy.

Later models got a bigger engine and more power, and the ultimate Quattro was the short-wheelbase Sport model launched in 1983. This limited-production homologation (production-recognized) special had a 300bhp 20V engine and was capable of 155mph (249kph). At three times the price of a standard Quattro, it was strictly for rich would-be rallying stars.

When Audi announced that Quattro would soon be axed, there was an outcry from enthusiasts and the production run

■ ABOVE *The road-car interior was extremely well designed, if a little sombre.*

was extended, the model finally bowing out in 1991, after 11 years of service. For many people, this superb Audi was deserving of the title "car of the decade".

OTHER MAKES

■ AC

Thames Ditton-based AC started life in 1911 as Autocarriers and, post-war, AC progressed through ever-more powerful sportscars, culminating in the legendary V-eight-powered, Shelby-developed Cobra and the Frua-styled 428. By 1973, AC needed a new model and the ME3000, with its mid-mounted Ford V-six, was shown in 1973 but not actually produced until 1979, and then in tiny quantities. The project went to Scotland in 1984, and was modified to become the Ecosse, but ended in bankruptcy. Bryan Angliss's Autokraft revived the Cobra and in 1986 showed a new Ace model (scrapped by new owners Ford in 1987). Ford sold out again to Autokraft in 1992, and an all-new Ace model was produced. Today, AC produces the Ace and a new version of the Cobra called Superblower.

■ ABOVE *Because of its superior traction the Quattro was a runaway success in rallying, where it dispensed with the rough stuff and scored dozens of victories.*

■ AUTOBIANCHI

Part of the Fiat empire since 1955, by the 1970s Autobianchi was firmly established as the "character" wing of the small-car department with models like the 500 Giardinera and Fiat 127-based A112. In the 1980s, Autobianchi was allied to the Lancia brand, producing the Y10. When the Y10 was replaced in 1996, subsequent products were badged as Lancias, and the Autobianchi name sadly died.

■ AVANTI

Raymond Loewy's swoopy Avanti was produced by Studebaker for just two years (1963–4), but a private consortium took it over and continued to make it right up until the present day. The styling was very un-Detroit, the bodywork glassfibre, the interior very luxurious and the price exorbitant. Avantis have a small but fanatically loyal band of followers.

BENTLEY

■ BENTLEY CONTINENTAL/AZURE

In the 1950s, the name Continental represented the very pinnacle of superior transportation: with such a badge on your Bentley, you were assured of absolute opulence combined with effortless touring power, and everyone else could be assured that you were driving quite the most expensive car money could buy.

That was Bentley's golden age, at least in post-war terms. After the great Continentals were retired by the parent company, Rolls-Royce, Bentleys became merely badge-engineered versions of Rolls-Royce products. By the 1970s, Bentley represented a mere 5 per cent of

all Rolls-Royce group sales. A great name was being squandered.

Luckily, the management at Crewe realized this fact and began a steady renaissance of Bentley. First came the Mulsanne Turbo, basically a much more powerful version of the Rolls-Royce Silver Spirit, which also benefited from being less ostentatious.

■ ABOVE *The addition of a T to the Continental name meant a complete transformation: fat wheels, short wheelbase, 400bhp engine – an upper-class hot rod.*

BENTLEY CONTINENTAL/AZURE (1991–)	
Engine	V-eight-cylinder
Capacity	6750cc
Power	385–400bhp
Transmission	4-speed auto
Top speed	155mph (249kph)
No. built	Still in production

■ ABOVE *A fabulously evocative interior with milled aluminium made the Continental T feel very special. Note the red starter button in the centre console.*

■ BELOW *All the Bentley trademarks were present: an imposing gait, sporting demeanour and a large grille surmounted by a simple winged "B" badge.*

The sporting heritage of the Bentley badge deserved more, however, and in 1991 it got it. The Continental name was revived for a model that had no Rolls-Royce equivalent: here was a true-blood Bentley that lived up to the provenance of its name.

The new car was actually christened the Continental R, the R nominally referring to Roadholding. This was a handsome and imposing two-door coupé, some 17ft 6in (5.34 metres) long, 6ft 2in (1.88 metres) wide and 2.5 tonnes (2.46 tons) heavy. The extravagance of such an ample car was

■ OPPOSITE *Without a roof the Continental transmuted into the Azure. Pininfarina engineered the superb electric folding roof.*

■ RIGHT *Perhaps the R's handling was still a little barge-like compared with some rivals, but it was far better than previous Bentleys.*

flaunted at its Geneva Motor Show launch, as the show car was painted the brightest shade of red obtainable.

To pull all that bulk, Rolls-Royce engineers stayed with its familiar 6.75-litre V-eight and truck-derived Garrett turbocharging, in this form good for about 385bhp and a huge 553lb ft (750Nm) of torque. Transmitting this tidal wave of power through a GM four-speed automatic gearbox, the R was indecently fast: 0–60mph (0–96kph) in 6.1 seconds and a top speed of 155mph (249kph), or enough to despatch a well-driven Porsche.

Rolls-Royce called the new Continental "the finest sporting coupé in the world", and with some justification: despite its proportions, it handled respectably, rode very comfortably, cosseted the driver and passengers in the utmost luxury and sustained the most unerring ambience of serenity and superiority.

At £160,000 ($269,000) this was also, in 1991, the most expensive British car ever made, yet it sold better than any other model in the Bentley range. Bentley even saw fit to induce yet more from its superlative creation. First came the Continental S, with over 400bhp at its command. Then followed the Azure, the convertible version of the Continental, which was for some time the only car in which to be seen on the Côte d'Azur, justifying setting its owner back a cool £215,000 ($362,000).

The mighty Continental T is the most radical member of the Bentley family. Its wheelbase was shortened, its wheel-arches were flared, and its wheels were massive five-spoke alloys. The interior was laced with milled aluminium. Delightfully, you had to press a big red button to start the engine, which now had no less than 590lb ft (800Nm) of torque to dig into, making it surely the world's most upper-class hot rod.

■ ABOVE *Nothing less than the renaissance of the Bentley marque was how many described the impact of the Continental R, the first specific new Bentley for three decades.*

■ ABOVE RIGHT *Costing a cool £215,000 ($362,000), the Azure was for the seriously wealthy only. The south of France was its natural habitat.*

■ RIGHT *The R had huge pace thanks to its turbocharged 6.75-litre V-eight engine. Naturally, the ride quality was superlative.*

BITTER

■ BITTER

German-born Erich Bitter was a race driver and car-accessories tycoon. He was smitten by two Opel CD prototypes presented in 1969 and 1970 and was so disappointed that Opel did not go into production that he managed to persuade the General Motors-owned company to hand the project over to him. Opel even helped him develop the car into production-ready form.

Since Bitter did not have the resources to set up his own factory, production began in 1971 at coachbuilders Baur of Stuttgart. An Opel Diplomat saloon (sedan) chassis was shortened and its suspension retuned for the lighter car, but otherwise the mechanicals were left untouched, including GM's 5.4-litre V-eight engine.

This was a very handsome car, and definitely in the same league as Italian exotics. It could be ordered in any of 45 different colours, had a luxurious cabin trimmed by Baur and an Opel-sourced dashboard. It was certainly not a cheap car, costing almost as much as a Rolls-Royce, but its quality and dashing looks

persuaded many customers to flock to the hitherto unknown marque. Production got underway at the rate of about one car per week.

The big American-designed V-eight engine provided refined, torquey performance, making it ideally suited to a grand touring role, rather than an overtly sporting one. Handling was sharp but not in the same league as greats like Ferrari and Porsche.

Just as handsome as the CD was Bitter's next car, the SC. This was first shown in 1979 but took another two years to enter production. Again this used Opel parts – the newly launched Senator – and the coupé body was styled by Bitter himself. The 3.0-litre fuel-injected six-cylinder engine was more in keeping with the times than the the old GM V-eight, and the later Bitter-modified 3.9-litre version was even more suitable, having an extra 30bhp at

■ ABOVE *The proud badge of the Bitter CD, neat and effective like the car itself.*

■ RIGHT *The CD's styling was widely admired for its simplicity and good proportions. The elegance factor drew buyers by the dozen. Bitter's cabin used an Opel dashboard but was sumptuously trimmed by specialists Baur of Stuttgart.*

BITTER CD (1971–79)	
Engine	V-eight-cylinder
Capacity	5354cc
Power	230bhp @ 4700rpm
Transmission	3-speed auto
Top speed	129mph (208kph)
No. built	390

■ OPPOSITE *Perhaps even more handsome than the CD was the 1981 SC. Its three-box design was sharp and Italianate, often being compared with the Ferrari 400.*

210bhp. There was even the option of four-wheel drive, but only two cars were so equipped because of the expense.

Attractive cabriolet and long-wheelbase four-door versions were added in 1985, but this course proved far too ambitious: by then the company had overstretched itself and unfortunately production ended the following year; some 450 examples of the SC had been made.

■ BELOW LEFT *With a 6-cylinder fuel-injected engine, the SC was impressively rapid, but its best role was long-distance cruising.*

■ ABOVE *Although it used simple Opel mechanicals, the CD was a real driver's car: fast, assured and a comfortable cruiser.*

Bitter went on to develop other projects but so far these have remained in prototype form. The first was a convertible called the Rallye, based on the Opel Manta, but the impending demise of the Manta led to an evolution called the Type III. In production form, this would have had Opel Senator underpinnings, but sadly plans to market the car were dropped in 1992 amid continuing financial problems. Some years later, Bitter resurfaced with an imposing and elegant new four-door saloon (sedan) car, again based around Opel components, but its production fate remains in the balance.

■ ABOVE *Erich Bitter was the man behind the German-made Bitter CD. He cleverly persuaded Opel to release one of its prototypes for him to modify and manufacture.*

■ BELOW *The Bitter interior cleverly made use of Opel's parts bin in its own setting.*

■ RIGHT *Bitter faded from the scene in 1986, but it continued to exist, promoting new concept cars like the Type III. Isuzu was at one stage going to market this car but sadly that never happened.*

BMW

■ BMW M1

The motivation for the BMW M1, still BMW's one and only mid-engined supercar, came from racing and a new set of regulations. In the Group 5 Silhouette formula of 1976, BMW's aging CSL was losing out to Porsche's 935. To regain lost face, BMW needed a mid-engined chassis worthy of its magnificent twin-cam 3.5-litre straight-six engine: 400 examples would have to be built over a two-year period to qualify for the formula.

The M1 was conceived by BMW's Motorsport division. It was to be the first road-car application for BMW's superb M88 twin-cam straight-six engine. In Turbo Group 5 form it would give up to 700bhp, but for the road, BMW deemed

277bhp enough. Only the cast-iron bottom end came off the regular BMW production line; the M88 had a unique 24-valve twin-cam head with chain drive, a pukka forged-steel crank, race-style dry sump and longer connecting rods. It breathed through Kugelfischer-Bosch indirect injection.

The engine sat in-line and well down in the chassis behind the cockpit. Suspension was by unequal-length wishbones and coils, with huge vented disc brakes and rack-and-pinion

steering. There was a five-speed ZF transaxle to put the enormous power down on the road.

Initially, BMW turned to Lamborghini to sort out the details of the tubular steel chassis, build prototypes and assemble the 400 road cars required for homologation at the rate of two a week. Giugiaro's Ital Design was contracted to shape the body, taking inspiration from Paul Bracq's 1972 BMW Turbo show car. Prototypes were seen being tested

■ ABOVE *Thanks to its racing-derived 3.5-litre engine, the M1 was extremely rapid: a top speed of 161mph (259kph) was recorded by one magazine.*

■ RIGHT *BMW's M1 was its only true supercar, conceived as a machine that would be practical and reliable yet racing-car quick.*

■ LEFT *There was no doubt that the M1 was an expensive supercar, but it was also one of the most exclusive ever made.*

■ BELOW *Clever aerodynamics played a large part in the success of the M1's shape. The black ducts are for engine cooling.*

around Sant'Agata in 1977, but by then Lamborghini was in deep financial trouble – and the M1 looked like a possible casualty. Lamborghini's government funding ran out, and delays caused BMW to snatch its M1 project back in April 1978, by which time seven prototypes had been built. It decided to transfer production to Baur, in Stuttgart.

Formally launched late in 1978, the M1 immediately fell foul of new Group 5 regulations that were its *raison d'être*. The revised rules said that 400 cars had to have been already sold to the public before a racing version could be used properly. By the time homologation was completed in 1981, the Group 5 M1 was already out of date, overweight and outclassed by a younger opposition.

If the M1 racer was never much more than a promising also-ran, the road car was always top-drawer material, not only fast (M1s were independently clocked at 161mph, or 259kph) but comfortable, refined, surprisingly frugal and beautifully built.

Handling was impeccable, and no mid-engined upper-echelon supercar rode so well or cruised so quietly. Disparate and convoluted as its cross-Europe design and manufacture had been, the values and quality behind this unfulfilled racer were always pure Munich. It bridged the gap between yesterday's dinosaur heavyweights and today's versatile supercars and is rightly regarded as one of the all-time classic supercars.

BMW M1 (1978–81)	
Engine	6-cylinder
Capacity	3453cc
Power	277bhp @ 6500rpm
Transmission	5-speed manual
Top speed	161mph (259kph)
No. built	450

■ ABOVE *The BMW "kidney" grille looked very purposeful on the aerodynamic nose of the M1. Pop-up headlamps improved airflow in the crucial nose section.*

■ ABOVE *Giugiaro designed the very simple and handsome shape, and it was built half in Italy and half in Germany in a very convoluted production-process.*

BMW

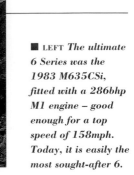

■ BMW 6 SERIES

BMW has a strong reputation for producing powerful sporting coupés, its tradition stretching back to the earliest days. In the early 1970s, the BMW coupé ideal reached its zenith, the celebrated CSL becoming invincible on the track and accomplished on the road.

■ LEFT *The ultimate 6 Series was the 1983 M635CSi, fitted with a 286bhp M1 engine – good enough for a top speed of 158mph. Today, it is easily the most sought-after 6.*

■ ABOVE *Handsome, well-engineered, powerful and classy – the 6 Series was BMW's coupé for the 1980s.*

■ ABOVE *In typical BMW fashion, the dashboard was designed to curve around the driver. The cockpit was very spacious.*

BMW 6 SERIES (1976–89)	
Engine	6-cylinder
Capacity	2788–3453cc
Power	184–286bhp
Transmission	5-speed
Top speed	122–158mph (196–254kph)
No. built	80,361

By 1975, BMW needed to develop a successor, and the car earmarked to do this was the 630CS/633CSi, launched in March 1976. Compared to the old CS series, the 6 Series was larger, more cosseting and more expensive – a grand tourer, which was extremely good at its job of whisking along the autobahns, but not a true sporting car. The 1979 628CSi, with its even smaller engine, did little to enhance the image.

BMW attempted to remedy a lack of sporting feel by fitting its venerable 3453cc engine into the 6 Series in July 1978, creating the 635CSi. This engine was architecturally the same as that fitted to the M1, though it developed less power (218bhp). A far more sporting feel than the 633s was engendered by uprated dampers, springs and anti-roll bars and ventilated disc brakes.

It was really only a matter of time before BMW bit the bullet and fitted the full-house 24-valve M1 engine to create the M635CSi (M6 in the US). It shared the M1 specification very closely; with its light-alloy 24-valve head, twin overhead camshafts and central spark plugs, but owing to new induction and twin-pipe exhaust systems and the use of Bosch Motronic II digital engine electronics, it developed 9bhp more than the M1 engine. The new M635CSi was a real road burner.

The more powerful 6 Series BMWs were extremely good cars, notable for their fine handling, luxury, refinement and quality. The successor, the 8 Series, was in many ways less appealing.

■ RIGHT *Later 6 Series models got more power, sophisticated electronics and heightened levels of luxury.*

■ FAR RIGHT *While it was refined and rapid, the 6 Series was less sporting than the earlier CS series it replaced. It was really better suited to motorway driving.*

■ LEFT *BMW Technik was responsible for the short, neat shape of the Z1. A mere 8,093 examples were built.*

■ BMW Z1

The Z1 was a curiously un-BMW-like product, but enthusiasts everywhere were thankful that the company had the courage to put it into production. BMW was used to making drivers' cars, for sure, but its tendency was always toward the conservative. The Z1 was radical and highly specialized.

The project began life as a development mule for a new type of suspension for the BMW 3 Series. BMW Technik – the company's technical wing, mainly responsible for research and development – designed a body for it that was meant to show BMW was ahead of the game. It was displayed at the 1986 Paris Salon as a pure concept car, but the public response was so overwhelming that BMW boss Eberhard von Kuenheim gave the go-ahead for a production run.

After a series of modifications, the production Z1 was ready in 1988. Its basis was a steel monocoque chassis fitted with a composite thermoplastic body. Immense strength was engineered in by keeping very high sills, which raised a question about the doors; BMW solved this little conundrum by designing doors that dropped away into the sills, operated by electric motors –

■ ABOVE *The Z1 project began life as this development mule for new suspension systems, but the public reaction to its looks persuaded BMW to enter production.*

■ ABOVE *When the electric motors retracted the doors into the sills, getting in was an awkward exercise if the hood (top) was raised.*

great for fine-weather motoring. Aerodynamics were a strong point, and one novelty was a rear silencer (muffler), which also acted as an aerofoil.

The Z-axle rear suspension was the prototype of that for the forthcoming

BMW Z1 (1988–91)	
Engine	6-cylinder
Capacity	2494cc
Power	170bhp @ 5800rpm
Transmission	5-speed
Top speed	140mph (225kph)
No. built	8,093

3 Series, and gave great handling. The chassis could have handled more power than BMW gave it (the standard 325i engine was installed) but there was no questioning the fun factor. Equipment was deliberately sparse but the price tag was distinctly up-market: the Z1 cost the same as a BMW 735i, and was only ever a very limited-production prospect.

■ LEFT *The main party trick was doors that slid down into the high sills, bringing a new dimension to the term open-air motoring.*

BMW

■ **BMW M3**

In the 1970s and 1980s, BMW was the most successful Touring Car racing constructor, a remarkable feat since none of its cars was a "homologation special" – they were merely modified versions of prosaic road cars. That all changed with the M3, a legendary road car which also swept the board in racing.

According to BMW's advertising, "M is the most powerful letter in the world."

■ LEFT *The magic initials M3 stood for everything the driving enthusiast lusted after: high performance, brilliant controllability and lots of character.*

■ LEFT *The new-shape 3 Series was also made into an M3 version with even more power from a six-cylinder engine, and it had far fewer rough edges.*

BMW M3 (1986–91)	
Engine	4-cylinder
Capacity	2302cc
Power	195–220bhp
Transmission	5-speed
Top speed	146–152mph (235–245kph)
No. built	17,969

M stood for Motorsport, a special division within BMW, which was responsible for racing and the development of advanced road-car projects. The M3 was actually based on the current BMW 3 Series, but Motorsport altered almost every component on the car.

■ ABOVE *The interior of the Sport Evolution model was covered in leather and race-style suede and had very special seats. This was the ultimate M3 model.*

The bodywork became aggressive, with its flared arches and spoilers, and four individual bucket seats in the interior. Under the body, the suspension and braking were beefed up and the gearbox had a race-style dog-leg first gear.

Most importantly of all, the M3 got a very special engine: a large-capacity four-cylinder unit fitted with a 16-valve head modelled after the M1. With 200bhp available, it made the M3 outrageously quick. More than this, it was endlessly entertaining to pilot along twisty rounds, almost without vices. Very quickly the M3 became a legend.

Limited-edition Evolution models were even better, with enhanced aerodynamics and, in ultimate Sport III guise, a bigger 238bhp, 2.5-litre engine. The most expensive M3 of all was the Cabriolet, individually hand-built by Motorsport staff.

When the old-shape 3 Series was retired in favour of the smart new shape car, there was of course an M3 version, but it was ruthlessly efficient rather than exciting. Many enthusiasts remember the first-generation M3 with greater affection, particularly its fabulously controllable handling and raw character.

■ ABOVE *The heart of the M3 was its four-cylinder engine with a head derived from the M1. Even in its least powerful incarnation, it still had 195bhp on tap.*

■ LEFT *That BMW could successfully tackle the small sportscar market was proved with the Z3. This is the 1.9-litre model with a 140bhp engine.*

■ BMW Z3

Not to be left out of the fashionable and burgeoning junior roadster market, BMW launched its Z3 range towards the end of 1995. The plan was certainly ambitious: to engineer a car from scratch and build it in a brand-new factory in Spartanburg, South Carolina, USA. Yet, it definitely paid off: even before the car's official launch in October 1995, posters advertising the new James Bond film, *Golden Eye*, showed exactly what the secret agent's new transport was – a Z3! Within 18 months, over 40,000 had been sold worldwide.

The new BMW roadster handled beautifully and made significant use of existing bottom-of-the-range BMW components, thus keeping the price of

the "poverty" variant down to below £20,000 ($35,000). Where BMW's previous sportscar model (the 1980s Z1) had seemed crisp and forward-looking, many were underwhelmed by the Z3 shape, a not altogether happy mix of current BMW styling cues and half-hearted retro touches, such as the wing vents inspired by the classic 507 of the mid-50s. However, most buyers loved its sassy, overstyled shape.

The Z3 was stronger in many respects than competitors like the MGF and Mazda MX-5 Miata: it had a very solid shell, excellent build quality and great presence. Frugal but uninspired four-cylinder 1.8 and 1.9-litre engines were quickly joined by a powerful 2.8-litre six-cylinder and, in the spectacular M Roadster, the M3's 321bhp engine. This last was a real bargain supercar with beefed-up styling and a special interior.

■ ABOVE *With a 2.8-litre engine, the Z3 became much more of an out-and-out sportscar. Note the wider alloy wheels for extra grip.*

BMW Z3 (1995–)	
Engine	4/6-cylinder
Capacity	1796–3201cc
Power	116–321bhp
Transmission	5-speed manual
	4-speed auto
Top speed	115–155mph
	(185–249kph)
No. built	Still in production

■ ABOVE *The BMW roadster was built at a completely new factory in America, which could hardly keep up with demand.*

■ RIGHT *The Z3 was a real driver's car, as James Bond found out when he drove one in the film* Golden Eye. *The rear-wheel-drive chassis was impeccable.*

BRISTOL

■ BRISTOL 412 TO BLENHEIM

Bristol enthusiasts wept bitter tears when the 407 – Bristol's first Chrysler V-eight-powered model – hit the road in 1961. Out came the thoroughbred all-alloy straight-six engine – lovingly crafted by Bristol themselves – and in went an iron V-eight, shipped over in a wooden packing case from Canada (to evade import duty) and hitched up to an automatic transmission. To add insult to injury, it even had push-button controls.

It was the only way out for Bristol: the sweet little six, a mere 2.2 litres and 110bhp, was struggling with the weight of the opulent 406, and since Bristol could not afford to fund their own new 3.5-litre straight six, Detroit power was the only way to go.

It was the right decision. Bristol rode out every storm by keeping small, and

■ LEFT *In the early 1970s, Bristol's offering was the 411, a hand-built grand tourer, which essentially dated back to the 1950s.*

selling alloy-bodied, separate-chassised cars to a discreet and discerning few. The shape changed over the years, but the proportions – tall, slim and long – remained consistent right up to the latest Blenheim, still available today.

By 1975, the 411 was the latest incarnation of the Bristol ideal.

Radically different was the curious Zagato-styled 412 of 1975, a convertible coupé with big double roll-over bar. However, it still rode the classic 9ft 6in (2.89 metres) wheelbase chassis – which could be traced back to BMW's pre-war 327 coupé – and still had the 6.6-litre Chrysler V-eight engine.

BRISTOL 412 TO BLENHEIM (1975–)	
Engine	V-eight-cylinder
Capacity	5211–5665cc
Power	Not disclosed
Transmission	3/4-speed automatic
Top speed	120–140mph (193–225kph)
No. built	Not disclosed

■ LEFT *Zagato was responsible for the controversial styling of the 412, launched in 1975. This was a targa-topped convertible four-seater.*

■ OPPOSITE *All Bristols featured this hinging side panel, inspired by aerodynamics. On the other side was a panel for the spare wheel.*

■ BELOW *Many famous celebrities were attracted to the understated character of the Bristol, which was very much a car for the wealthy.*

In 1976, the 412 became a convertible saloon (sedan) with a standard hardtop, while the S2 of 1977 had a smaller 5.9-litre engine. The rapid 140mph (225kph) Beaufighter of 1980 had an American Rotomaster turbocharger, beefed-up gearbox and a restyled front-end, and remained in production until 1992.

The curious 603E and 603S of 1976–82 featured new styling on familiar hardware. They replaced the long-running 411, whose alloy body was basically that of the 406 of 1958. The short-lived E was a 5.2-litre "economy" model, while the S had the usual 5.9-litre engine. Both had cruise control, air-conditioning and the latest Torque-Flite automatic gearbox with long-striding "lock-up" top (a locking torque converter) and self-levelling suspension.

The Brigand and Britannia replaced the 603 in 1982. The Brigand was turbocharged and could sprint to 60mph (96kph) from rest in under six seconds and reach a 150mph (241kph) top speed. The cars ran on alloy wheels and featured new front and rear styling.

The Blenheim of 1993 had yet another new front- and rear-end restyle, but the basic shape was the familiar 603/Britannia body. Bristol claimed that only the roof and doors were retained, but much of the interior looked familiar from previous Bristols, notably the handsome binnacle and round white-on-black instruments.

The Blenheim was fitted with the latest fully managed and injected 5.9-litre Chrysler engine and four-speed automatic gearbox. There was no turbocharger this time, but economy was much better, and certainly the Blenheim made a consummate long-distance express for the wealthy enthusiast who wanted to be a little bit different – owners included Liam Gallagher, lead singer of the UK rock band Oasis, and Virgin business entrepreneur Sir Richard Branson.

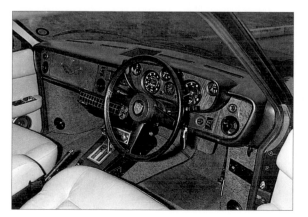

■ LEFT *Traditional British luxury in the cockpit of this Britannia: leather, wood and Wilton carpeting.*

BUGATTI

■ BUGATTI EB110

Following the Second World War, Ettore Bugatti's fabulously engineered, but vastly expensive creations were at odds with the times, and production never really restarted. There were many attempts to revive the name but none was very convincing – until a man called Romano Artioli stepped into the arena. This canny Italian magnate managed to rekindle the Bugatti magic in spectacular fashion, but ultimately the dream proved overambitious and ended in bankruptcy.

The plan was grand: a state-of-the-art factory was built in northern Italy, industry greats were hired (including Paolo Stanzani as technical director and Marcello Gandini as designer – both of them effectively fired later on), and a brand-new V-twelve engine was created from scratch.

The new Bugatti EB110 was to be a superlative mid-engined supercar, the sort of car that Ettore would have been making if he were still alive. The EB110 name was chosen as a composite of Ettore Bugatti's initials and the fact that the car was to be launched on the 110th anniversary of his birth.

The aluminium-bodied Bugatti's styling (created by an Italian architect) was dramatic but controversial: the lines were hardly harmonious and the traditional Bugatti horseshoe grille looked almost farcically small on the car's nose. Inside, meanwhile, the level of finish was superb and equipment levels were generous, but space was severely limited.

Mechanically, the Bugatti was highly advanced. Its centrepiece was a

■ ABOVE *The new EB110 was launched at an incredibly lavish party in Paris. It attracted a huge amount of publicity.*

■ LEFT *The avant-garde new Bugatti factory in Italy was highly regarded.*

■ LEFT *This is the prototype workshop. Clearly visible is one of the amazing V-twelve engines, which were hand-built by Bugatti. Each unit developed at least 553bhp.*

■ ABOVE *Reviving the fabled Bugatti badge was always going to be a hard task. "EB" stands for Ettore Bugatti, the marque's founder.*

■ RIGHT *If the standard car seemed a bit dull to you, you could order this Supersport version with less weight, a rear spoiler, bigger wheels and no less than 611bhp and 221mph (356kph).*

V-twelve engine fitted with no less than four turbochargers and 60 valves, developing 553bhp. There was a six-speed gearbox mated to a four-wheel-drive system and suspension, which delivered handling akin to a grown-up Lancia Integrale. Bugatti claimed a top speed of 212mph (341kph) and stated that this was the fastest road car in the world; Jaguar with its XJ220 and McLaren with the F1 might have questioned this, but no one was in any doubt that the Bugatti was an extraordinarily fast and very capable machine.

By the time the EB110 was launched (at a lavish party in Paris in 1991), the

supercar sales boom of the 1980s was already well and truly over. The list price was a walloping £285,000 ($486,000) and, if that all seemed a bit pale, Bugatti also developed a lightweight

SS model with a 611bhp engine and up to 221mph (356kph) – total cost was an extra £50,000 ($93,000).

In the end, Artioli simply became too ambitious. First he bought up Lotus from General Motors in 1993, then he commissioned Ital Design to build a new four-door super saloon (sedan) called the EB112, but Ital Design stopped work on the project, claiming lack of payment. By 1995, Bugatti was bankrupt and its showcase factory lay tragically deserted. Unfortunately, it is not known exactly how many cars were built; Artioli claimed 154, including the one built for the German racing driver Michael Schumacher.

■ LEFT *Bugatti commissioned a second model, called the EB112, from Ital Design. This would have been an opulent limousine but production was prevented by Bugatti's liquidation.*

■ LEFT *The new Bugatti EB110 was in all respects an amazing car. Strikingly styled, enormously powerful and superb to drive, it fittingly revived the Bugatti name.*

BUGATTI EB110 (1991–95)	
Engine	V-twelve-cylinder
Capacity	3500cc
Power	553–611bhp
Transmission	6-speed
Top speed	212–221mph (341–356kph)
No. built	Not known

CATERHAM

■ CATERHAM 7

The basic design of the Caterham 7 can lay a strong claim to be the oldest still in production. Its origins stretch back to the 1957 Lotus 7, a car that engineering genius Colin Chapman said he "knocked up in a weekend". Lotus made the car for 15 years, while Graham Nearn's Caterham Cars sold them, often when everyone else had given up on it.

When Lotus decided to end production of the 7, Graham Nearn's special relationship with Colin Chapman enabled him to acquire the rights to make the car in 1973. Initially, Caterham Cars struggled to make the plastic-bodied Series 4 Lotus 7. Soon, however, it turned to the simpler and ultimately more purist aluminium-bodied Series 3.

In many ways, the 7's appeal lies precisely in what it does not have. There are no gadgets, no complicated electronics, no expensive compound-curved body panels. The 7 is fixed on one goal: providing the maximum driver enjoyment with the minimum of material. This was the very essence of Colin Chapman's committed crusade for light weight.

In construction, the 7 had a tubular steel chassis clothed in aluminium panels; only the nose cone and wings were made of glassfibre. The rear axle came from either Ford or Morris, and later Caterham devised its own de Dion rear-end.

For its engines, Caterham initially continued using Lotus's brilliant 126bhp, 1558cc Twin Cam, but eventually stocks ran out and it switched to Ford engines in a variety of states of tune: GT (84bhp), Sprint (110bhp) and Supersprint (135bhp). If you wanted more power you could go for a Cosworth BDA engine with up to 170bhp and, later, a Vauxhall 2.0-litre unit with 175bhp. From 1991, Caterham switched

■ RIGHT *7s were typically very stark affairs, but this cockpit shows that luxury need not be abandoned, with leather trim and a plethora of gauges.*

■ FAR RIGHT *Caterhams were usually powered by Ford-derived engines, but 1991 saw a switch to Rover power, of which this is an example.*

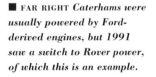

■ LEFT *There is no other car so focused as the Caterham 7. Developed from Colin Chapman's Lotus 7, it embodies speed, passion and sharp senses.*

to Rover K-series engines: 1.4 (103bhp), 1.4 Supersport (128bhp), 1.6 (115bhp) and 1.6 Supersport (138bhp).

The ultimate 7 was, however, the JPE (which stood for Jonathan Palmer Evolution, after the Formula 1 driver who helped develop it). With its 250bhp race-spec engine, lack of windscreen, carbon-fibre wings, extreme light weight and phenomenal braking, this was a very fast car: it did 0–60mph (0–96kph) in under 3.5 seconds and could beat a Ferrari F40 to 100mph (161kph).

■ RIGHT *The sensation of piloting the 7 is unique. A simple journey to the shops feels like driving a lap around a racing circuit.*

■ OPPOSITE *The image of the Super 7 was immortalized in the 1960s TV series The Prisoner, starring Patrick McGoohan. Caterham launched a special edition that encapsulated the spirit of "I am not a number, I am a free man!"*

Caterhams of whatever type offered more fun for your money than any other car. Most were bought in near-complete kit form with some components needing to be installed by the customer, which kept costs down and got round the need to Type Approve (legalize) the design. Most production was exported – Caterham received the Queen's Award for Export in 1993. Even today, over 40 years since the 7 appeared, the Caterham remains the absolute benchmark as far as handling and pure fun for the driver is concerned.

■ LEFT *Caterham promoted several one-make racing series involving 7s. This is action from the fastest class of all, the Vauxhall-powered Class A.*

CATERHAM 7 (1973–)	
Engine	4-cylinder
Capacity	1298–1998cc
Power	72–250bhp
Transmission	4/5/6-speed
Top speed	100–150mph (161–241kph)
No. built	Still in production

■ LEFT *The ultimate road-going 7 was the JPE, which stood for Jonathan Palmer Evolution, for the F1 driver helped develop this 250bhp thundering chariot. It once held the world record for the fastest-accelerating car.*

CATERHAM

■ CATERHAM 21

One guiding principle lay behind Caterham's custody of the 7 legend: you could do anything underneath the car to improve it, but the shape must remain untouched. With the 21, that philosophy was turned upside-down: here was a new model with a chassis based very closely on that of the 7 but with a totally new body. The 21 name indicated the

■ LEFT *For over 20 years the 7 never changed shape; then Caterham launched the 21, a bold new sportscar with a completely enveloping body.*

■ LEFT *This prototype was aluminium-bodied, an option that remained on the price lists after launch. The styling was by Iain Robertson.*

CATERHAM 21 (1996–)	
Engine	4-cylinder
Capacity	1588cc
Power	115–138bhp
Transmission	5/6-speed
Top speed	118–131mph (190–211kph)
No. built	Still in production

way Caterham was thinking: this was its vision of a car for the 21st century.

The plan to create an all-new Caterham began as an intention to make a mid-engined monocoque sportscar, but that would have been too ambitious. Instead, it was decided to create a new enveloping body over a modified 7 chassis. Journalist and designer Iain Robertson was called in to do the styling. For inspiration he turned to the classic racing Lotus XI, and his proposal looked exactly right: curvaceous, taut, recognizably British.

The interior architecture was adventurous and appealing, featuring an elegantly symmetrical design. The narrow cockpit was inherited from the 7, but the wide sills improved elbow room and leg room significantly. A narrow centre console housed switches and minor dials, the speedo and rev counter (tachometer) being sited directly in front of the driver.

Engineering the 21 posed a whole new set of problems for Caterham: never before had it been forced to deal with hinging doors and boot (trunk) lids, curved glass, sophisticated hoods or trimming the boot. It was getting all

these details right that delayed the start of production for two years after the car's first showing in 1994.

The official launch at the October 1994 Birmingham Motor Show was spectacular: no one was expecting the car to be shown in gleamingly

■ RIGHT *In general, production cars had glassfibre bodywork and a painted finish. Demand for the new 21 was high, but production was limited to 200 per year.*

■ ABOVE *On the road, the 21 was every bit as thrilling as the 7, but was far more practical, thanks to a locking boot, weather gear and doors.*

■ ABOVE *The lithe, taut shape drew from past Lotus models for its inspiration, but was undeniably modern as well.*

■ LEFT *The cockpit was a triumph of ergonomic design and beautiful shapes. Note the vertical central instrument cluster and very narrow seats.*

silver-polished aluminium. This would be an expensive option on the production 21, and most customers opted for the more viable choice of glassfibre. Prices were naturally higher than the 7, but the 21 was excellent value compared with rivals such as the Lotus Elise and Renault Sport Spider.

The valuable aluminium prototype was loaned to the press for early analysis, and testers were uniformly enthusiastic. This prototype was fitted with a Vauxhall JPE engine and six-speed gearbox – a unique specification, since all production 21s would have Rover K-series 1.6-litre engines or a very special version of the 1.8-litre MGF engine called the VHP (Very High Performance). Thanks to superior aerodynamics, the 293lb (648kg) 21 boasted a much higher top speed and far greater practicality than the 7, while inheriting all of the 7's handling finesse.

With an anticipated production volume of just 200 cars per year, the 21 will always be a rare beast, and its single-minded pursuit of driving pleasure will endear it to future generations of sportscar drivers.

■ ABOVE *The new badge reflected the company's assertion that this was a Caterham for the 21st century.*

■ LEFT *The first car was fitted with an extremely powerful Vauxhall JPE engine and was staggeringly fast. Production cars had Rover engines.*

CHEVROLET

■ CHEVROLET CORVETTE

America's greatest sportscar – and for many years its only sportscar – is the Chevrolet Corvette. The name was born as long ago as 1953 when Detroit launched its plastic-bodied answer to the flood of European imports. A whole dynasty of 'Vettes followed on, up to the Stingray of the 1970s, which was as American as they come.

Then General Motors upped the stakes with a totally new generation Corvette launched in early 1983 as a 1984 model. Here was a thoroughly modern-looking sportscar that was still recognizably a 'Vette. The coupé shape was cleaner both aesthetically and aerodynamically and featured a hatchback and a removable roof panel.

The choice of glassfibre for the body remained, but the chassis was all new and the overhauled suspension used lightweight aluminium and even a plastic transverse spring.

The engine remained the faithful small-block Chevy V-eight, rated at 205bhp. It initially drove through a four-

speed automatic transmission, but soon a four-speed manual was offered with no less than three overdrive ratios. Performance was a strong suit: 0–60mph (0–96kph) in 6.6 seconds was incredibly fast in anyone's book, and the roadholding was excellent.

A he-man clutch, tough steering and heavy brakes justified its reputation as a "muscle car". If there were criticisms to be made, they were minor: an awkward-to-view digital dash, harsh ride, irksome entry and snappy wet-weather handling.

Innovations in coming seasons included, from 1986, a new convertible and, from 1989, a six-speed gearbox and a three-position Selective Ride Control with adjustable shock damping.

■ LEFT *The ZR1 streaked away when the accelerator was depressed, and in addition to its dazzling acceleration was quite capable of reaching a top speed of 180mph (290kph).*

■ ABOVE *All Corvette interiors were luxuriously appointed and extremely well-equipped in the best American traditions.*

■ RIGHT *The Corvette as launched for the 1984 model year was available in one body style: a hatchback coupé with a removable roof panel.*

CHEVROLET CORVETTE (1984–96)	
Engine	V-eight-cylinder
Capacity	5727–5733cc
Power	205–411bhp
Transmission	4/6-speed manual 4-speed auto
Top speed	142–180mph (228–290kph)
No. built	Approx. 320,000

■ RIGHT *The new 1984 Corvette had quite a heritage to live up to: its eponymous brethren stretched all the way back to 1953. No one was in any doubt that the new 'Vette justified its billing.*

While the standard backbone chassis looked as if it came from Lotus, the ZR1 – then the ultimate Corvette of all – did actually owe much of its prowess to the English engineering firm (bought by GM in 1986). The 1990-model-year ZR1 was the new "King of the Hill", boasting a new, technically advanced LT5 375bhp engine that transformed the 'Vette into a crushing supercar: it could do 180mph (290kph) and reach 60mph (96kph) from rest in 4.5 seconds. Small wonder that this was the most expensive car in GM's history, retailing at £35,000 ($59,000). The ZR1's power went even higher in 1993, stretching to 411bhp. Ultimately, the King dropped off the price lists in 1996.

Meanwhile, the standard Corvette range continued, also with more power (305bhp). This generation of Corvettes was replaced by an all-new one in January 1997. The Corvette may never have been a huge seller or a big dollar-earner, but that wasn't the point: it was America's sportscar statement, and a remarkably good one. It's a fitting tribute that, thanks to over 40 years of continuous production, more Corvettes have been made than any other sportscar in the world.

■ LEFT *As America's only sportscar, the Corvette was quick in a straight line and much better around corners than virtually any other American car.*

■ BELOW *The heart of the new ZR1 was its quad-cam 32-valve LT5 V-eight engine, which developed a storming 375bhp.*

■ LEFT *Technically, the Corvette reiterated all the famous themes: a glassfibre body, powerful V-eight engine and muscle-car running gear. The chassis and suspension were all new, however.*

CHEVROLET

■ CHEVROLET CAMARO

The unprecedented success of Ford's Mustang sent rivals General Motors into a scurry of activity. However, in the two years it took to bring its answer to production, the great heyday of the "personal coupé" had already passed.

Its answer was the Chevrolet Camaro, and even General Motors could not have been disappointed when it sold 220,000 units in its first year. It was based on the uninspiring Chevrolet Nova body/chassis and mechanical package, but its strong suit was undoubtedly its classic "Coke bottle" styling by Bill Mitchell.

Both six-cylinder and V-eight engines were offered in various states of tune,

■ ABOVE *The fourth-generation Camaro arrived in 1993 as a smooth-looking coupé only; the convertible version did not appear until the following year.*

■ LEFT *The familiar Chevy "small block" V-eight engine powered most Camaros. This is the Z28 version with additional power, although in the 1970s emissions laws strangled power outputs across the board.*

■ ABOVE *One of the best of the "Coke bottle" first-generation Camaros was the Z28 edition, with its uprated engine, transmission, brakes and duck-tail rear spoiler.*

the most extreme being the SS (Super Sport) – of which 96,275 were built – and the RS (Rallye Sport) – 143,592 built. These have since become the most prized of all Camaros. As well as the more common coupé, Chevrolet also offered convertibles.

When it came to replacing the Camaro in 1970, General Motors took its

■ ABOVE *An all-new body shape arrived in 1970 and was essentially "right", lasting a full 11 years in production with no major changes.*

■ LEFT *The Camaro story kicked off in 1966, when General Motors came up with a car to rival the runaway success of the Ford Mustang.*

■ LEFT *The third-generation Camaro kept up the tradition for a very American four-seater coupé. These are IROC-Z and Z28 editions from 1985.*

time and created a bespoke model (dedicated chassis) with monocoque construction instead of a separate frame. While the Mustang became bloated, then emasculated, the Camaro felt balanced in style and leaner, too. While the styling may have been less subtle than the first series (especially from the mid-1970s when the nose was reshaped to satisfy safety laws), the interior may have been cramped and there was no convertible option, it nevertheless struck a chord with the American buying public.

The 1970s Camaro was a big dollar earner for GM, selling almost two million examples. Overall it was nowhere near as powerful as the original series Camaro – even in Z28 form, the most desirable of 1970s Camaros. There was also a Pontiac clone called the Firebird with different engines and alternative front end styling.

■ FAR LEFT *As the years progressed, the Camaro kept up with the times. This 1991 RS model has a sculpted body, side skirts and modern sports wheels.*

■ LEFT *The Camaro badge always meant something special to American buyers.*

CHEVROLET CAMARO (1970–81)	
Engine	4/6/V-six-/V-eight-cylinder
Capacity	2475–6573cc
Power	90–360bhp
Transmission	3/4-speed auto 4/5-speed manual
Top speed	96–125mph (154–201kph)
No. built	1,811,973

■ RIGHT *The ultimate Camaro in its third generation was the Z28 edition, with a healthy increase in power.*

CITROËN

■ CITROËN CX

For most people the name Citroën
conjures up images of cars that are
quirky, eccentric, idiosyncratic – in
short, weird. More than any other model,
the CX is the one which firmly reinforces
these beliefs.

However, the CX is also one of the
most misunderstood and underrated cars
of all time. On the one hand, it is
remembered as one of the all-time greats
of motoring history; on the other, it has
been dismissed as an unreliable, rust-
infested, needlessly complex nightmare.

The CX was undoubtedly the last
great Citroën, the last car Citroën got to
design entirely in-house, before Peugeot
bought the company in 1974 and began
shaking its rod. Historically, it was the
replacement for the brilliant DS, in
production since 1955 and in dire need
of a modern successor.

What arrived shortly after was more
than just modern: it was positively
futuristic. Its GS- and SM-inspired
shape was not only one of the most
aerodynamic ever seen on a motor car, it
was also beautiful. Like the DS before it,

■ ABOVE *The cockpit looked like a mix
between French art and Star Trek. Note the
single-spoke steering wheel, rotating yellow
dials and spherical ash-tray.*

■ ABOVE *This is a 1985 GTI Turbo with a
168bhp engine providing near-sportscar levels
of performance. The CX was also extremely
impressive around corners.*

it bristled with advanced features. The
brilliant self-levelling hydropneumatic
suspension was there, tied in with the
braking and power-steering functions.
On all but the earliest CXs, the steering
also came with Vari-Power, Citroën's
patented weighted power assistance,
which altered the weighting of the
steering according to your speed.

Europe was impressed enough to
award the CX the Car of the Year trophy.
Its handling was assured, its ride
magical, its cruising ability ultra-
relaxed, its character unique. The
interior looked as if it had been sculpted
by an artist rather than designed for

CITROEN CX (1974–91)	
Engine	4-cylinder
Capacity	1985–2500cc
Power	66–168bhp
Transmission	4/5-speed manual C-Matic semi-auto 3-speed auto
Top speed	91–137mph (146–220kph)
No. built	1,042,300

■ LEFT *The extraordinary shape of the CX,
launched in 1974, was unique and way ahead
of its time.*

■ ABOVE *The carrying capacity of the estate (station wagon) was enormous: it was Europe's most capacious car for the whole of its production life. Antique dealers loved them.*

■ RIGHT *Prestige was the name given to the long-wheelbase luxury model that whisked French presidents around Paris.*

mass consumption, and the instruments, sited in a space-age binnacle, revolved themselves around stationary needles. Compared to the competition, the CX cleaned up – or should have done.

Where Citroën got it so badly wrong was in the build quality. In particular, there was a terminal rust problem every bit as bad as Alfa Romeo's during the 1970s, and it was this, more than anything, which crippled the CX. By the time Citroën had sorted the problem out – which took fully seven years – the CX already had a very bad name, made worse by the public's and the trade's suspicion of the eccentric hydraulic system.

History may well be kinder to the CX. In GTI Turbo form, it was stunningly quick and handled like a hot hatch. In long-wheelbase, luxury Prestige form it was the choice of French presidents. In eight-seater estate (station wagon) form, it was the most capacious European car around. Its replacement, the XM, looked just as individualistic as the CX, but it lost many of the features that made the CX unique.

■ ABOVE *From the rear the CX looked highly unconventional, with its concave rear window and rear wheels set closer together than the front pair.*

OTHER MAKES

■ CADILLAC

General Motors' premium brand is almost the American Rolls-Royce, with more glitz than any other marque. In the 1970s, it was producing huge, bloated cruisers like the Fleetwood and Eldorado. A significant move toward smaller cars was the 1976 Seville, famous for its 1980 "trunkback" restyle. The 1982 Cimarron (a jazzed-up Chevrolet) was a dead end, as was the Pininfarina-created Allante convertible. Cadillac's main business has always been selling luxury cars to the US establishment, a task which it continues to date, although Seville and recent Opel Calibra-based Catera have been respectable performance saloons (sedans).

■ CHRYSLER

The 1970s was a decade of crisis for America's Number Three car-maker. Ex-Ford man Lee Iacocca reversed the company's fortunes with government help. Chrysler was one of the first to down-size with its 1981 K-series (LeBaron, New Yorker and Laser). The most interesting models

in its line-up were the Laser and LeBaron coupés, plus the TC by Maserati, a high-spec soft-top with a Maserati-tweaked engine, which bombed spectacularly. After flirting with Maserati, Chrysler bought Lamborghini, but this relationship did not last long. Chrysler also invented the "people carrier" (minivan) phenomenon with the 1983 Voyager. Chrysler has pioneered many trends, including "cab-forward" design and the launch of the Viper and Prowler.

■ CLAN

The Clan Motor Company was formed by a group of former-Lotus men in Washington, County Durham. The 1971 Clan Crusader was a quirky little two-seater coupé of glassfibre monocoque construction with a Sunbeam Imp Sport engine. The car passed crash tests and a big factory was set up to produce large numbers of cars, but the economic crisis dragged the firm down in 1973. There was an attempt to revive a modified Clan in Northern Ireland in 1982, and the same operation produced the Alfasud-engined Clan Clover of 1986, but by 1987 it had ended in bankruptcy.

DE LOREAN

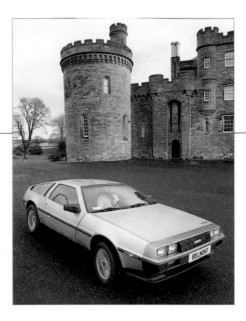

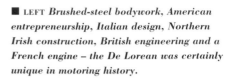

■ LEFT *Brushed-steel bodywork, American entrepreneurship, Italian design, Northern Irish construction, British engineering and a French engine – the De Lorean was certainly unique in motoring history.*

■ DE LOREAN

The John Z. De Lorean story is quite an epic. An ex-General Motors high flyer, De Lorean touted his idea for a dramatic but high-volume sportscar around several countries, in the search for financial support. The British government took the bait, offering grants and loans totalling more than £80 million ($134 million) if De Lorean would set up shop in economically disadvantaged Northern Ireland, and he accepted.

The ingredients of the De Lorean

■ BELOW *The use of gullwing doors was chosen for dramatic impact. In practice, the doors caused countless expensive production headaches.*

■ ABOVE *The V-six Peugeot/Renault engine sat in the tail under a large cover. Lotus designers helped sort out the handling challenges of such a layout.*

DMC-12 should have led to success: a chassis engineered by Lotus, a body styled by Giugiaro and a V-six engine from the Peugeot/Renault factory. Nor, given that it was only for the US market, was there anything wrong with its projected price of £15,000 (US $25,000).

But somehow the reality was different. De Lorean elected to use brushed stainless steel for the bodywork, which looked novel in the showroom but attracted dirt and scratches like chalk in the real world. The gullwing doors were another novelty, but they often leaked and, it was rumoured, could trap the car's occupants in a crash. Furthermore,

DE LOREAN (1980–82)	
Engine	V-six-cylinder
Capacity	2849cc
Power	145bhp @ 5500rpm
Transmission	5-speed
Top speed	130mph (209kph)
No. built	8,583

the quality of the early cars, built by an inexperienced workforce, was such that a second factory had to be opened in Los Angeles to rebuild them. Despite the effort of Lotus, the rear-mounted engine

■ ABOVE *After only a brief two-year existence, the De Lorean fluttered out amid financial crisis and scandal.*

layout never delivered anything better than indifferent handling. De Lorean announced massive production targets, but only 8,583 cars were built between the car's launch in 1980 and the collapse of the DeLorean Motor Company in 1982.

Thereafter it was controversy all the way: financial irregularities came to light and John De Lorean was arrested, but cleared, on drug-trafficking charges. The De Lorean is now something of a cult car with its own following of devotees.

DE TOMASO

■ DE TOMASO PANTERA

Elvis Presley shot his Pantera when it wouldn't start, and that is undoubtedly how many other owners felt about this enigmatic but slightly dodgy supercar.

Alejandro De Tomaso, an Argentinian tycoon who settled in Italy, built his first car, the Cortina-engined Vallelunga, in 1963. It flopped, and while his second effort, the Mangusta, was fast and beautiful, it quickly got a reputation for evil handling.

With the 1970 Pantera, De Tomaso was determined to get it right – and start making some money, too. He struck a deal with Ford of North America whereby they got his Ghia coachbuilding firm (hence the Ghia badge on today's Escorts and Fiestas) in return for selling his new car – powered by a 5.8-litre Ford V-eight engine – through their dealers in the US. It proved a sharp move as 4000 Panteras were unloaded on unsuspecting Americans before Ford shut the door on imports in 1974, beleaguered by complaints about build quality, rust and overheating.

The Pantera was fast in a straight line, topping 160mph (257kph), and with that mid-mounted engine the handling was copy-book stuff. It was practical, too: smash an engine in a Pantera and there

was no need to take out a second mortgage to replace it because it was just a big, dumb Ford V-eight as found in millions of lumbering American saloons (sedans).

The model lasted into the mid-90s, its image progressively cheapened by boy-racerish spoilers and stickers and ever-fatter tyres. De Tomaso, however, had rather lost interest in the car that bore his name in the 1970s when he acquired several new business toys to play with, including Maserati and Innocenti.

■ ABOVE *In GTS form its massive spoiler, fattened wheel arches and prominent decals were so loud they were almost deafening.*

DE TOMASO PANTERA (1970–95)	
Engine	V-eight-cylinder
Capacity	4942–5763cc
Power	247–350bhp
Transmission	5-speed manual, 3-speed automatic
Top speed	150–160mph (241–257kph)
No. built	10,000

■ BELOW *Later Panteras became more rounded in profile, although no more subtle in style. The model stayed in production for an amazing 25 years.*

■ ABOVE *Classic 1970s themes in the interior: lots of chrome-ringed gauges, black-stitched trim and sports-style seats.*

■ LEFT *The relatively obscure Italian De Tomaso name won widespread fame with the Pantera, which was distributed in America by Ford.*

DODGE

■ DODGE VIPER

For decades, America's sportscar tradition hung on one sole car, the Chevrolet Corvette. By the end of the 1980s, however, Chrysler had come through its troubled times and was healthy enough to produce a new American sportscar legend.

When it was first shown at the 1989 Detroit Show, the Dodge Viper RT/10 stunned the crowds. The phrase "AC Cobra for the '90s" was bandied about at the show, and the impression was reinforced by the involvement of Carroll Shelby, the legendary creator of the Cobra, as a consultant. Chrysler

executives displayed it as a concept car, and such was the public reaction that Team Viper was formed to turn dream into production reality, a process that took only 30 months.

The Viper was an amazing machine in all respects. Its plastic bodywork was pure machismo, a bristling contortion of muscular curves and suggestive ducting. There was no roof – except for a tent-like piece of vinyl and side curtains, which were supplied for use in the event of a shower. Just in case you got caught out, the interior was trimmed in waterproof materials. There were no exterior door handles, and the Flash Gordon three-spoke rear wheels were no less than 13-in (33-cm) wide.

The concept car had a truck-derived V-ten engine fitted and, in production form, Lamborghini made some changes, such as switching the block to aluminium rather than iron and giving it a bright-red head. But it remained

■ ABOVE *Viper was a fitting name for a car that recalled the glory years of the Shelby AC Cobra. Indeed, Carroll Shelby was even involved in the Viper's creation.*

■ ABOVE *With its 8-litre V-ten engine, the Dodge Viper was a monster performer. It needed all of its 13-in (33-cm) wide wheels to rein in its 400bhp.*

distinctly low-tech: two valves per cylinder, hydraulic lifters, long pushrods. 400bhp may have been mightily impressive but the truck-like torque curve, peaking at 450lb ft (610Nm), was awe-inspiring. It didn't seem to matter that the engine note was rather subdued.

Acceleration was ballistic: 0–60mph (0–96kph) in 4.5 seconds.

DODGE VIPER (1992–)	
Engine	V-ten-cylinder
Capacity	7990cc
Power	400–455bhp
Transmission	6-speed
Top speed	165–180mph (265–290kph)
No. built	Still in production

■ LEFT *Viper owners usually drove their cars open-topped, but a special "double bubble" hardtop was developed in case you had to go out in rain.*

■ OPPOSITE *The GTS was a hard-top-coupé version of the Viper with a much bigger boot (trunk), almost completely revised bodywork and much greater luxury inside.*

■ BELOW *America took the Viper to its heart. It was an obvious choice as Pace Car for the famous Indianapolis 500 race.*

The Viper was one of the first cars to be fitted with a six-speed gearbox, but that was more to help fuel economy than to encourage stick-shifting: you could exceed 100mph (161kph) in sixth without going over 2000rpm, and still be turning just 3250rpm when you reached 165mph (265kph).

Perhaps the best thing about the Viper was its price: at £30,000 ($50,000) this was a supercar that many could afford, even though its impracticalities made it strictly a fair-weather fun car.

If you wanted more practicality, then Dodge offered just that with the Viper GTS coupé, shown in 1993 but not produced until 1996. This was more than a roof-up roadster, though: just about everything on it was changed. If you opened up the hatchback you had enough room for golf clubs, and you could even power-wind the glass windows: now the Viper had luxury and practicality as well as drop-dead good looks and gargantuan power.

OTHER MAKES

■ DAEWOO

Formed in 1967, Korean-based Daewoo has already become one of the world's great industrial giants. Cars form only a strand of its empire and began as licence-built products of General Motors, such as the Opel Rekord. By the 1980s, it was starting to modify GM's designs for the home market and then began an impressive export operation. The first car engineered by Daewoo was the 1997 Lanos, partly designed by newly acquired operations in Britain and Germany.

■ DAF

For many years the Dutch motor industry was DAF. In 1975, it was bought by Volvo and its existing range of small cars was rebadged Volvo, while a new model in the pipeline emerged as the Volvo 343. DAF's main contribution to the motoring world was its continuously variable transmission by rubber bands. DAF still exists as the factory where the Volvo S40 and Mitsubishi Carisma are made.

■ DAIHATSU

One of Japan's second grade of car-makers, Daihatsu has always specialized in small cars. It had the distinction of being the first Japanese marque to be exported to Europe (in 1965). In the 1980s, it became the leading maker of micro-class cars, and its Mira model was the best-selling car in Japan.

■ DAIMLER

Daimler, one of Britain's pioneering car names, was best known for its limousines (favoured by royalty) and for its sporting saloons (sedans). However this proud company came under Jaguar's control in 1960. Daimler's impressive V-eight engine continued in production until 1969, but by 1964 Daimlers had become essentially badge-engineered Jaguars with fluted grilles and occasionally more luxurious trim, which remains the position today, although Jaguar preserves its identity. The last model unique to Daimler was the darling of mayors across Britain, the DS420 limousine, which survived until 1992.

■ BELOW *The Viper's brawny shape began life as a show car, but public adulation brought it to production. Its burgeoning curves, massive wheels and side-exit exhausts were throwbacks to the muscle-car era.*

FERRARI

■ FERRARI BERLINETTA BOXER

The immortal Boxer was Ferrari's first attempt at a flagship mid-engined model, though its history can be traced back to the 250LM Road Berlinetta, a road version of the 250LM racer, while some see the weird three-seater, centrally steered 365P show car of 1966 as its true spiritual father.

It was not until 1968, with the beautiful P6 show car, that Ferrari's favoured couturier Pininfarina really began to think aloud – and clearly – about the swoopy wedge profile of Maranello's supercar for the 70s, built to challenge the Lamborghini Miura and take over from the front-engined Daytona. Pininfarina's stylists started with a "big Dino" look, then flirted with the radical wedge influence of the 512 Modulo and futuristic 512S Berlinetta. Eventually, they settled on the elegant simplicity of the final production car, announced, prematurely, at Turin in 1971: production did not actually begin until 1973.

Under the big alloy engine cover was a new aluminium 4.4-litre four-cam

■ ABOVE *Ferrari owners are fanatical about their cars, and the Boxer inspired a new kind of loyalty. For many, this was the best car in the world.*

flat-twelve engine, descended from the 1500c 512 Formula 1 car of 1960. Breathing through four triple-choke (throat) Weber carburettors, it was for many the best engine in production, combining searing punch with pin-sharp throttle response and spine-tingling sound effects. Top speed was quoted as 188mph (302kph) – though no independent source confirmed it – 0–60mph (0–96kph) came up in 5.2 seconds.

To save space, the five-speed transaxle was tucked up under the engine, alongside the sump, all hung in an exotic multi-tube frame with a central

FERRARI BERLINETTA BOXER (1973–84)	
Engine	12-cylinder
Capacity	4390–4823cc
Power	340–360bhp
Transmission	5-speed manual
Top speed	175–188mph (282–302kph)
No. built	2,323

■ LEFT *Later cars had a 5-litre twelve-cylinder engine, which was more tractable in everyday use.*

■ OPPOSITE *As Ferrari's first-ever mid-engined flagship, the Berlinetta Boxer was always going to be a classic, and its Pininfarina-styled shape is one of the all-time greats.*

■ LEFT *With radical bodywork modifications, the 512 BB made a fearsome circuit racing machine.*

■ RIGHT *The Boxer's dart-like profile was extremely aerodynamic and unfussy. Note the long black cooling ducts over the mid-mounted engine.*

■ RIGHT *Subtle flowing lines combined with great presence. The rear end was surprisingly compact because the gearbox was mounted underneath the "flat 12" Boxer engine.*

the rear brakes, differently vented engine lid and four tail lights, not six.

The final incarnation of the Boxer was the 512i BB with Bosch K-Jetronic injection, which hacked an alarming 20bhp off the quoted power output but improved tractability and emissions. Production ended in 1984, making way for the controversially styled Testarossa. Ferrari built 2323 Boxers: 387 of the 365 model, 929 of the 512 and 1007 of the 512i.

steel monocoque around the passenger cell. Though the low-slung flat "boxer" configuration had the advantage of a low centre of gravity and better aerodynamics, the 365GT 4BB had a definite rear weight bias, with 56 per cent of its total weight over the rear wheels. At the limit, the handling could be a little ragged, and the Boxer certainly never had the cornering finesse of its arch rival, the Lamborghini Countach. The interior was finished in high-quality leather, and most cars came with air conditioning.

The five-litre 512 BB took over in 1976: its bigger bore engine, now with dry-sump lubrication, produced no extra power but 10 per cent more torque. A 512 could be spotted by its front spoiler, wider rear tyres, side air vents to cool

■ ABOVE *In its day, this was probably the fastest production car in the world. It was also*

fabulously sharp to drive, boasting instant throttle responses and tenacious handling.

FERRARI

FERRARI 308GTB/328GTB

With the authority of a "proper" Ferrari badge – the previous 246 Dino had been marketed as a Fiat – the 308GTB was announced at the Paris show in 1975, supplementing the Bertone-styled four-seater 308GT4. It also marked a return to Pininfarina as Ferrari's favoured stylist with a classically aggressive coupé that displayed little in the way of unnecessary ornament. That it changed so little in 13 years of production says much for its elegant purity. A strict two-seater, the 308GTB reverted to the 92in wheelbase of the V-six Dino, but

■ LEFT *Few cars of the 1970s had as much poise and balance as the GTB around corners. The mid-engined layout and V-eight engine combined to make this one of the best drivers' cars of all time.*

borrowed the tubular-steel chassis and uncompromised double wishbone suspension of the GT4. The large vented and servo-assisted (power) disc brakes made light work of the 1270kg (2800lb)

GTB, but with 3.5 turns lock-to-lock, the rack-and-pinion steering was not startlingly fast.

Mechanically, the car was almost identical to the GT4, producing 255bhp from a dry-sump version of the strident four-cam V-eight with twin distributors, an oil cooler and transistorized ignition. Rational toothed-belt drive for the camshafts hinted at the influence of Fiat, who were paying the bills. The engine was mounted transversely amidships ahead of the rear wheels, with the five-speed transaxle and limited slip diff tucked in behind it. Running a modest 8.8:1 compression ratio, the five-bearing unit took in fuel and air through four Weber carburettors.

■ ABOVE *The circular tail lamps were a real Ferrari/Pininfarina hallmark, distinguishing the already elegant shape.*

■ RIGHT *As a replacement for the classic Dino, the 308GTB was a brilliant effort. It had all the hallmarks of a classic Ferrari, and yet was the marque's entry-level model.*

■ ABOVE *Ferrari were not averse to making the driving environment luxurious as well as sporty, as the beautifully trimmed leather and electric switchgear show.*

■ LEFT *Pininfarina's devastatingly simple, uncluttered bodywork brought the 308GTB instant recognition as one of the design greats.*

■ BELOW *With the name GTS, the targa-topped "spider" version was extremely popular in hotter climates. Not recommended in the snow, though.*

The first cars had glassfibre bodywork, but after 18 months this was abandoned for more traditional steel body construction – adding 250lb (113kg) and the promise of rust problems for future owners. The Americans in particular lapped up the 308, particularly the targa-topped GTS model, which consistently outstripped sales of the closed car by a huge margin.

A significant change was Bosch Digiplex fuel injection (first seen on Ferrari's Mondial), which brought cleaner running but milder performance, as pcak power tumbled to just 214bhp for the 1981 GTBi. Within 18 months, the Quattrovalvole (four-valve) model raised power to a healthy 240bhp with an accompanying increase in torque. With subtly bespoilered front and rear to prolong its shelf life, the QV's performance returned to its earlier pre-injection levels.

The final incarnation of this body shape was the 1985 328, bored and stroked to give 3185cc and 270bhp for a top speed of 160mph (257kph). Ferrari claimed that build quality was better and the handling sharper.

Some Ferrari experts tend to think of the 308GTB/GTS as the Ferrari for the common man, which comparatively it is: almost 20,000 were built between 1975 and 1989, of which 1637 came to Britain, making it one of the most successful Ferraris ever in that market. Its exceptional qualities confer it genuine classic status.

■ RIGHT *In ultimate 328 guise, the "baby" Ferrari was even quicker, boasting 270bhp from a 3.2-litre engine.*

■ BELOW *V-eight power for the 308 meant four camshafts, transistorized ignition, a dry sump and 255bhp. Later units gained fuel injection.*

FERRARI 308/328 GTB/GTS (1975–89)	
Engine	V-eight-cylinder
Capacity	2926–3185cc
Power	214–270bhp
Transmission	5-speed manual
Top speed	140–160mph (225–257kph)
No. built	19,555

FERRARI

■ FERRARI TESTAROSSA

There is something magical about the word *Testarossa*, a name that Ferrari has used since the 1950s. All it means is "redhead", and it refers to the colour of the cylinder head on the engine, but the name has acquired a mythical status by association.

The 1984 Testarossa was the successor to the great Berlinetta Boxer, and duplicated much of its specification on the same chassis, but the new car was much more than a rebodied Boxer. The famous 5.0-litre flat-twelve engine was given completely revised cylinder heads with four valves per cylinder (and naturally painted red!), with the result that power rose to 390bhp and flexibility was enhanced. Ferrari also used high-tech nickel-alloy to prevent heat damage to the valves.

■ LEFT *From the rear, the tremendous width was emphasized. It gave the car fantastic presence but made manoeuvring a rather fraught experience.*

■ BELOW LEFT *The 12-cylinder engine's red-painted cylinder head gave the Testarossa its name (Italian for "redhead"), and it was the automotive equivalent of war-paint applied before going into battle.*

■ BELOW RIGHT *Thanks to its side-mounted radiators, the straked cooling side ducts became a distinctive hallmark of the model.*

While the Boxer always had front-mounted radiators, the Testarossa switched to rear-mounted cooling, just ahead of the rear wheels. This dictated a new styling trait in the form of extremely wide rear wings punctured by dramatic horizontal strakes, which began in the doors. Pininfarina was responsible for the shape of the body. It was undeniably spectacular from any angle – especially the low, wide rear – but some questioned its audacity after the classically understated Boxer.

To save weight, the bodywork was all aluminium (except the roof and doors) and Pininfarina's wind tunnel confirmed the slipperiness and inherent down-force of the shape. The trade-off of having such a wide body (it was 78in (198cm) across) was that manoeuvring the car proved difficult, and visibility was very poor. This more than anything affected just how fast you could safely pilot the Testarossa.

In other respects Ferrari's new mid-engined top-of-the-range supercar was everything it should be. The engine sounded superb, the cabin was comfortable, the controls were light and – most importantly of all – this was an

■ OPPOSITE *The Testarossa recalled the glory years of Ferrari's Formula 1 effort. The 1984 Testarossa also recalled F1 themes with its mid-engined layout and squat stance.*

■ RIGHT *The final incarnation of the Testarossa series was the F512M of 1994-96. The most notable visible change was the cowled headlamps, but extra power also boosted the top speed to over 200mph (322kph).*

extremely fast car to drive. It could do the 0–60mph (0–96kph) sprint in 5.5 seconds and would keep on going to 180mph (290kph). Responses were always delicate, and the handling was rewarding.

In January 1992, the Testarossa was renamed 512 TR and revised extensively, the aim being to reclaim from Lamborghini's Diablo its title as the fastest car around. The TR name echoed the fact that this was essentially still a Testarossa, and only the new 348-style nose and larger wheels were very different.

Much more happened under the skin: more power (428bhp), lower ride height, better gearbox and improved suspension. The cabin was heavily revised, too. In short, the 512 TR was the best – and fastest – supercar in production.

The final evolution of the redhead was the F512M of 1994. This reflected Ferrari's preferred F prefix, while the M stood for "Modificata". Power went up by another 13bhp, so that its top speed now approached 200mph (322kph) and 0–60mph (0–96kph) came up in under five seconds. Other changes included cowled headlamps, bonnet (hood) ducts, new turbine wheels, restyled interior and classic round tail lights.

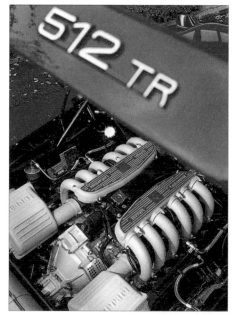

FERRARI TESTAROSSA (1984–96)	
Engine	12-cylinder
Capacity	4943cc
Power	390–441bhp
Transmission	5-speed manual
Top speed	180–200mph (290–322kph)
No. built	n/a

■ LEFT *In 1992 the Testarossa was renamed 512 TR after a minor restyle and a boost in power, from 390bhp to 428bhp, making it the fastest car in production.*

■ BELOW *Pininfarina's lines were widely admired – and copied – in the 1980s.*

FERRARI

■ FERRARI F40

In the 1980s, Ferrari extended the
boundaries of road-car performance with
cars such as the Testarossa and the
limited-production 288 GTO. Even
considering these and other supercars,
nothing came close to matching the F40,
one of the greatest Ferraris of all time.

Enzo Ferrari proposed celebrating 40
years of his marque with a very special
project that would combine race and
road car traits in one machine. The
Ferrari board agreed, and the F40, with
bodywork by Pininfarina, was brought to
production in just 12 months, helped by

the fact that it was based on the platform
of the 1984–87 288 GTO.

The underlying goal during the F40's
development was weight reduction. To
this end, the body made innovative use
of composite materials, which were
claimed to be 20 per cent lighter than
conventional metals. This priority also

meant the interior was utterly devoid of
carpets and door trim. Ferrari certainly
succeeded in its goal, since the F40
weighed in at just 2425lb (1099kg).

For power, Ferrari developed the 288
GTO V-eight to become a 3.0-litre twin-
turbocharged beast. With sequential
ignition and injection, silver/cadmium
conrod bushes and nicasil-coated liners,
the engine was capable of 478bhp –
and up to 200bhp more if you wanted
to go racing.

The performance figures spoke for
themselves: a top speed of 201mph
(323kph), 0–60mph (0–96kph) in 3.9
seconds and 0–124mph (0–200kph) in
12 seconds flat. This was far and away
the quickest machine on the road when
production began in 1988, almost a year
after its debut. It was also the fastest
road car Ferrari had ever built.

In character, the F40 was demanding
to drive but not overly difficult, while it
was hugely tractable yet superbly
balanced in handling terms. The fact

■ ABOVE *The F40
really looked like a
racing car from the
rear, and indeed
many owners used
their F40 in
competition. The
shape of the rear
wing was widely
copied by other
designers.*

FERRARI F40 (1988–92)	
Engine	V-eight-cylinder
Capacity	2936cc
Power	478bhp @ 7000rpm
Transmission	5-speed manual
Top speed	201mph (323kph)
No. built	1,311

■ LEFT *Features such as three-piece wheels,
racing brakes, removable rear bodywork and
soft fuel tanks (cells) hinted at racing origins.*

■ OPPOSITE *The inspiration for the F40 was a celebration of the 40th anniversary of Ferrari, and it was undoubtedly the best, and most audacious, car Enzo Ferrari had ever produced.*

■ ABOVE *The magic F40 sigil (seal) said it all. This ultra-rare Ferrari is bound to go down in history as one of the all-time greats.*

■ LEFT *With so much power going to the rear wheels – even with their massively wide tyres – burn-outs like this were almost inevitable at racing circuits.*

that the cockpit was sparsely trimmed was a positive point, and the sight of raw carbon fibre and exposed tubing was a delight, not a penance. It meant that being in an F40 was an extremely noisy experience but given the sound – as close to a racing engine as you could get – that was also part of what made the F40 experience so unique.

Considering its intended role as a dual-purpose road/race car, the F40 came with numerous competition features such as Group C brakes, three-piece wheels and bag fuel tanks (cells) ahead of the rear wheels.

It was very focused and technically advanced, but not the technological *tour de force* that the Porsche 959 was. Rather it was a car for the dedicated enthusiast, everything being directed towards making it faster and more precise. The fact that many owners successfully took their £163,000 ($275,000) F40 racing proved the point.

■ RIGHT *It may only have had three litres, but the V-eight engine was twin turbo-charged and provided with very special innards. The result was a 478bhp power output in standard road-going tune.*

■ ABOVE *The ultra-lightweight F40 was numbingly fast, and very close to a true racing car in feel and in the demands made on the driver. With a top speed of 201mph (323 kph), it was also the fastest Ferrari yet made.*

FERRARI

■ FERRARI F50

When the time came for Ferrari engineers to build a new flagship in the mid-1990s, the brief was simple and uncompromising: take our 1990 Formula 1 racer (the 641/2) and transform it into a street-legal 200mph (322kph) road car. Enter, in March 1995, the F50, the spiritual successor to the F40 and certainly the most potent road car yet made by Ferrari.

Clothed in a flat-bottomed Pininfarina body that recalled Ferrari's sports racers of the early 70s, it was easily the wildest road car Ferrari had ever built. With such headline-making performance figures, pundits made immediate comparisons with McLaren's stunning F1. It was understandable but in reality these were two very different cars: where the F1's designers pursued refinement and build quality as well as ultimate performance, the F50 – a shade slower than the bigger-engined and lighter McLaren – was more of a raw sportscar created to give its owner Formula 1 sensations on the road.

The F50 nevertheless proved a surprisingly easy car to drive with a superb six-speed gearbox, reasonable ride (despite the rock-hard computerized damping and massive 335/30 ZR 18 tyres) and a user-friendly engine. Then there was the small matter of price: at £330,000 ($555,000) the

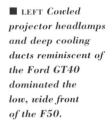

■ LEFT *Cowled projector headlamps and deep cooling ducts reminiscent of the Ford GT40 dominated the low, wide front of the F50.*

■ LEFT *It may not have had the stripped-out racer feel of the F40, but the F50's very simple cockpit was based on an ethos of comfort and light weight, as evidenced by the leather-covered carbon-fibre seats.*

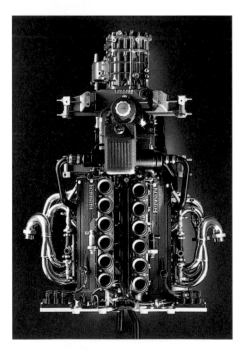

■ ABOVE *The V-twelve engine was essentially a Ferrari Formula 1 unit from 1990. Producing 521bhp, it was the closest a road-car driver could get to the sound and feel of an F1 car.*

■ LEFT *Pininfarina's stylists pulled another design classic. Despite the tight parameters supplied by Ferrari, the shape felt just right.*

■ LEFT *Few people imagined that Ferrari would trump its F40, but it did so with the superlative F50 in 1995. It was more dramatic, faster and more exclusive than the F40.*

■ ABOVE *The liquid-crystal instrument display was inspired by Formula 1 experience. There was even a "black box" flight recorder on board.*

■ LEFT *Everything was derived from racing, including the brakes, titanium uprights, ball joints and inboard pushrod/rocker-arm suspension.*

F50 was hardly cheap but still about half the cost of the British McLaren.

Boasting 521bhp from its Formula 1-derived five-valves-per-cylinder V-twelve engine, the F50 could do 64mph (103kph) in first, 112mph (180kph) in second, 124mph (194kph) in third, 138mph (222kph) in fourth, 160mph (275kph) in fifth and 202mph (325kph) in sixth. The handling was more forgiving than the F40 despite the extra speed, with superb non-assisted steering giving little kick-back but masterly precision.

With the iron crank-cased engine mounted rigidly to the chassis – and the rear wishbones attached to the gearbox – the noise was incredible, both in volume and quality, but nobody was complaining about that. In fact, chain rather than gear drive for the quad overhead camshafts meant less noise than the Formula 1 unit, while producing a smooth

idle and lower peak revs: 8500rpm instead of 14,000. Titanium connecting rods gave the unit high-rev strength.

Like the F1 car it was derived from, the F50 used proper inboard coil springs operated by pushrods and rocker arms, although, to make room for two people's feet, the front-end spring/damper units were transverse

rather than longitudinal. With titanium uprights and magnesium wheels, not to mention all-metal ball joints, it was no wonder the F50 steered with such precision. The F50 was to be much rarer than Ferrari's previous flagship hypercar, the F40: the company decreed that only 349 would be built, compared with 1311 F40s.

FERRARI F50 (1995–97)

Engine	V-twelve-cylinder
Capacity	4968cc
Power	521bhp @ 8500rpm
Transmission	6-speed manual
Top speed	202mph (325kph)
No. built	349

■ RIGHT *An extremely neat hardtop could be fitted in poor weather, although the noise with the top on was simply deafening.*

FERRARI

■ FERRARI 348/F355

When it came to replacing the noble and long-running 328, Ferrari was forced by tougher crash regulations to expand the size of its new entry-level car, called the 348tb. It also decided to fit the familiar V-eight engine longitudinally rather than transversely as before; the overall length was greater but the engine could now be sited a full 5in (12.7cm) lower down in the chassis.

The lower centre of gravity and stiffer chassis transformed the mid-engined Ferrari's handling from merely superb to deeply impressive. On-the-limit manoeuvres could be accomplished without fear of sudden tail-end break-away, yet it was at all times thrillingly rewarding to drive.

The engine was expanded to 3.4 litres and almost 300bhp, allowing for the expected levels of Ferrari forward thrust. Although the engine pointed front-to-rear, the gearbox was mounted transversely – hence the "t" in the name. Naturally, Pininfarina was called

■ ABOVE *Understated simplicity was the theme of the styling, from the mono-colour circular tail lamps to the lack of spoilers.*

■ ABOVE *A typically functional yet elegant and comfortable interior from Ferrari. Note the hallmark metal gear-lever gate.*

■ LEFT *With the 348, Ferrari created a genuine masterpiece, especially in dynamic terms. Its low centre of gravity and ultra-rigid chassis produced a handling gem.*

upon to shape the 348 and it did another superb job. Testarossa-style side strakes endowed the otherwise subtle bodywork with a distinctly Ferrari character. A more spacious interior made life much easier, too. As well as the fixed-head tb, there was also a ts model with a removable targa roof and a full Spider

soft-top. In 1994, the 348 was updated to become the F355. At the heart of the newcomer was an expanded quad-cam five-valves-per-cylinder 3.5-litre V-eight. With up to 381bhp on tap, this supremely characterful power-plant delivered even more blistering performance: 183mph (0–294kph) top speed and 0–60mph (0–96kph) in 4.8 seconds. In-gear acceleration was optimized by a six-speed gearbox.

FERRARI 348/F355 (1989–)	
Engine	V-eight-cylinder
Capacity	3405–3495cc
Power	296–381bhp
Transmission	5/6-speed manual
Top speed	171–183mph (275–294kph)
No. built	Still in production

■ LEFT *The full range of 348 models encompassed the tb (coupé), ts (targa) and Spider (full convertible). This series was the most popular Ferrari had yet made.*

FERRARI 550 MARANELLO

Maranello is the northern Italian home of Ferrari, and it is fitting that at least one model should bear its name. Ferrari chose it in 1996 for its first new front-engined two-seater since the 365 GTB/4 Daytona, which was launched 28 years previously in 1968.

What could have caused such an about-face following its predecessor, the mid-engined F512M? The answer is that a front-engined car broadened Ferrari's range and made it very much more practical than the old F512M.

In terms of ancestry, the 550 was most closely related to the 456GT, a four-seater Ferrari Grand Tourer launched in 1992. It shared its basic V-twelve engine and suspension layout. Apart from the very special F50, the Maranello slotted in as the company's quickest car, claimed to reach 199mph (320kph) and to do the 0–60mph (0–96kph) sprint in 4.3 seconds.

It was a lot more refined than previous Ferraris, but that was again a reflection of the times. On Ferrari's fabled Fiorano test track, the new 550 proved to be 3.2 seconds a lap quicker

■ LEFT *550 Maranello was the evocative name, steeped in Ferrari lore, that was given to the replacement for the F512M. It marked the birth of a new ethos at Ferrari.*

than the model it replaced. Perhaps the 550's greatest strength was that it felt so capable and refined: the world's fastest grand tourer, perhaps.

Some observers felt Pininfarina's styling lacked any real finesse. Good points were the elegant glass house, the subtle hump in the rear wings, the classic circular tail lamps; the real disappointments were the fussy

FERRARI 550 MARANELLO (1996–)	
Engine	V-twelve-cylinder
Capacity	5474cc
Power	484bhp @ 7000rpm
Transmission	6-speed manual
Top speed	199mph (320kph)
No. built	Still in production

■ ABOVE *Perhaps this was not one of the great Ferrari shapes, but the 550 found instant acceptance as a very rapid, more user-friendly Ferrari.*

front-end, the un-Ferrari-like shape and unhappy kicked-up tail.

At £145,000 ($244,000) the 550 cost over 50 per cent more than the dynamically more enthralling F355. In truth, the new Ferrari had a different sort of appeal: this was a tool as much for arriving at a destination feeling relaxed as for the sheer experience of driving.

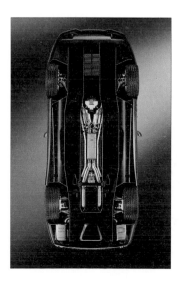

■ FAR LEFT *Where the 550 differed radically from previous range-topping Ferraris was in its front-mounted engine. Note the superbly profiled aerodynamics of the undertray.*

■ LEFT *The 550 lapped Ferrari's Fiorano test track over three seconds faster than the F512M, thanks to a 484bhp V-twelve engine that was capable of powering it to a top speed of nearly 200mph (322 kph).*

FIAT

■ FIAT X1/9

The Fiat X1/9 is historic for this single fact: it brought mid-engined handling sophistication, previously reserved for exotica like Lamborghini and Ferrari, to a mass audience. Launched to rapturous praise from the world's motoring press in 1972, it was, like its predecessor, the Fiat 850 Spider, destined to sell in large numbers, especially in North America.

Bertone's razor-edged styling incorporated a nifty removable targa roof panel, stored in the front boot (trunk) when not in use. Pop-up headlights were also a novelty for the time.

Initially fitted with a 1290cc four-cylinder 85bhp single overhead-camshaft engine and four-speed gearbox from the Fiat 128 Rallye, the X1/9 was adequately brisk, with a top speed of 110mph (177kph) and a 0–60mph (0–96kph) time of around 13 seconds,

■ ABOVE *Extremely compact, the Fiat X1/9 brought the delights of mid-engine motoring to a wide public. Previously the layout had been the almost exclusive province of expensive exotics.*

FIAT X1/9 (1972–89)	
Engine	4-cylinder
Capacity	1290–1499cc
Power	75–85bhp
Transmission	4/5-speed manual
Top speed	100–110mph (161–177kph)
No. built	180,000

■ LEFT *Pop-up headlamps were a distinctive feature. This is a later-model X1/9 produced by the coachbuilder Bertone (which originally designed the car).*

■ FAR LEFT *Removing the standard targa roof panel produced a virtual convertible - great for sunny days, but practical as well.*

■ LEFT *If you thought, because the engine was in the middle, that you had luggage space in the front, you had to think again, as this picture shows.*

■ RIGHT *Despite its small-capacity engine, the X1/9 was a creditable performer for its day. 100mph (161kph) was available in all versions.*

but this was frankly a waste of its potential grip and razor-sharp handling. Even so, novices and seasoned drivers alike took it to their hearts because it was so easy to drive. The steering was light, precise and full of feel, and the balance of the car was neutral.

Even driven at its limit an X1/9 never snapped, but telegraphed its warnings miles ahead of an impending loss of adhesion. As a bonus, strut suspension gave a relatively comfortable, civilized ride. Fiat boss Agnelli even abandoned his limo so he could drive himself to work every day in an X1/9.

Extra performance was achieved in 1978 by using the 1500cc engine from the Ritmo/Strada hatchback. The revvy 1.5 unit would whistle round to nearly 7000rpm and turn in 30mpg economy. A good 1500 would touch 110mph (177kph), break 60mph (96kph) in

under 10 seconds and cruise at 100mph (161kph), but by then many ordinary high-performance hatchbacks could out-run it. You got five speeds with the 1500, but big impact bumpers had by then spoiled the once-crisp looks.

In 1982, production was taken over by Bertone, which continued to manufacture and market the car as the Bertone X1/9 until its demise in 1989. Late cars had desirable touches like leather seats, alloy wheels and electric windows. By then the car was notorious for appalling corrosion, and many of the early examples have long since disappeared from the road.

It wasn't until the mid-80s that it had a serious competitor in the shape of Toyota's MR2. There is no doubt that the little Fiat is the father of today's popular mid-engined sportscars. Fiat did not produce its own spiritual successor until the front-wheel-drive Barchetta of 1995.

■ RIGHT *Beautifully balanced handling was the main attraction of X1/9 ownership. The chassis was much more communicative than that of almost any other car of its price.*

■ FAR LEFT *A strict two-seater, the X1/9's cabin was cosy rather than spacious. The architecture was distinctly Italian.*

■ LEFT *The X1/9 left production in 1989 with no mid-engined successor. The plain fact was that developments in the front-engined layout had made it a more feasible proposition.*

FIAT

■ FIAT BARCHETTA

Barchetta is an Italian word meaning "little boat", and has come to describe a whole class of open-topped Italian sportscars. Fiat's version was undoubtedly one of the high points of the genre and applied Italian flair to the challenge laid down by the Mazda MX-5.

In style, the Barchetta was both retrospective and modern. The door handles, which popped out of the bodywork at the press of a button, harked back to a classic era, but the purposely curvaceous body accent line and aerodynamic accoutrements

■ LEFT *Sportscar drivers felt immediately at home in the cockpit, which was relatively sparsely equipped but suitably angled towards the enthusiast's needs.*

■ ABOVE *On the road the Barchetta was a delight, combining zippy acceleration with tenacious cornering, light steering and a free-revving engine.*

FIAT BARCHETTA (1995–)	
Engine	4-cylinder
Capacity	1747cc
Power	130bhp @ 6300rpm
Transmission	5-speed
Top speed	124mph (200kph)
No. built	Still in production

■ BELOW *The truncated tail with its oblong lamps contrasted with the long nose. The "humped" profile was emphasized by body side accents.*

reminded the casual onlooker that this was a contemporary sportscar.

It may have been based on the floorpan of the humble front-wheel-drive Fiat Punto, but the Barchetta packed a strong punch under its bonnet in the form of a new 1.75-litre fuel-injected 16V twin-cam engine. As the whole car weighed only just over one tonne (ton), performance was enjoyable and the engine would happily spin away up to 7000rpm. That spirited pace was matched by grippy cornering ability and super-sharp steering.

Inside there was a minor feast of detail, from the angled centre console and the smoothly sculpted doors to the intriguing eyeball vents. There might not have been much room for luggage, but this was a sportscar so that was to be expected.

Good value was another Barchetta strong point, and it sold particularly well in Italy. British customers had to make do with left-hand drive but even so were appreciative of the diminutive Fiat sportscar. After all, the Barchetta had all the makings of a genuine classic.

■ RIGHT *Bold slashes in the body sides, bisected door mirrors, a clamshell bonnet and a strongly wedged profile – this could only be Pininfarina's extraordinary design for the Fiat Coupé.*

■ FIAT COUPÉ

Pininfarina was extremely adventurous with its brief to design a new coupé for Fiat, which arrived in 1993. No one could ever mistake the Coupé for anything else, and even if its appeal was not universal, it had all the character you could ever wish for.

From the bold rising slashes in the flanks to the elegantly curved roof, and from the curious "double bubble" headlamp covers to the evocative circular tail lamps, the Coupé made a very strong statement.

Although in feel it seemed like a miniature Ferrari or Maserati, the new Coupé was actually based on the platform of the ageing Fiat Tipo. Considering this basis, Fiat engineers worked miracles to create such a fine-handling sports coupé as this. Limited slip differential kept the front wheels

from spinning when the accelerator was pressed to the floor, while tyre grip remained superb even at very high cornering forces.

At first, there was a choice of two 2.0-litre engines: a 142bhp 16V unit or a 195bhp Turbo. Both were quick but the Turbo was exceptional, having a 0–60mph (0–96kph) time of just over seven seconds. In 1995, the engine range was renewed, starting with the 131bhp Barchetta 1.8 and ending up with a pair of brand-new five-cylinder 2.0 units; the most powerful had a

turbocharger and no less than 220bhp – and was almost indecently quick.

Accommodation was surprisingly spacious for four people, although that meant boot (trunk) space was rather restricted. The adventurous themes of the bodywork were extended into the cabin, such as an effective swage of painted metal running right across the dashboard and doors.

■ BELOW *Few cars in any class handled as well as the Fiat Coupé, which boasted fine grip, sharp responses and entertaining handling for the driver.*

■ RIGHT *With its bold body-coloured finish through the middle of the dash, the Coupé felt very special. The driving position was excellent.*

FIAT COUPÉ (1993–)	
Engine	4/5-cylinder
Capacity	1747–1998cc
Power	131–220bhp
Transmission	5-speed
Top speed	127–155mph (204–249kph)
No. built	Still in production

■ RIGHT *From the rear, the styling was every bit as adventurous as from other angles. The circular rear lights recalled Farina designs for countless Ferraris.*

FORD

■ FORD SIERRA RS COSWORTH

The "Cossie" Sierra has passed into the annals of motoring history as the car that brought rally-style levels of power and grip to a broad public. Its phenomenal performance became a legend, all the more so because it was such exceptional value.

When, in 1986, Cosworth installed its new two-litre twin overhead-camshaft turbo engine into the Sierra bodyshell,

FORD SIERRA RS COSWORTH (1986–92)	
Engine	4-cylinder
Capacity	1993cc
Power	204–224bhp
Transmission	5-speed manual
Top speed	143–149mph (230–240kph)
No. built	26,771

■ ABOVE *Piloting the powerful RS500 was a very special experience, all the more so because a mere 500 examples were built in total.*

■ LEFT *The true "popular" Cosworth was the four-door Sapphire, built from 1988. A modest body kit package and sober clothing belied the car's tremendous ability.*

the inherently fine handling of Ford's rear-wheel-drive hatchback was matched by the power to exploit it. Its 204bhp was generous to say the least and the performance figures proved it: a top speed of 145mph (233kph) and 0–60mph (0–96kph) in 6.2 seconds. What was more, the engine could be easily tuned to stratospheric heights.

Ford's humble sales-rep special could now out-perform some Ferraris, yet it cost only £16,000 ($27,000) – about the same as a BMW 325i or Toyota Supra. The badge on the back – RS Cosworth – came to signify a performance icon.

In truth, the Cosworth may have looked superficially like a body-kitted Sierra but there was little resemblance under the skin. Ford's Special Vehicle Engineering department intended this to be a convincing Group A race and rally car (which it was), and decided to beef up the whole car. There was a close-ratio five-speed gearbox, limited slip differential, power steering, anti-lock braking, thick anti-roll bars, stiff suspension, wide alloy wheels and tyres, and huge disc brakes with four-piston calipers.

The bodywork incoporated no less than 92 modifications, from the widened wheel arches to the dramatic whale-tail spoiler. The aim was to increase

■ RIGHT *The massive rear aerofoil brought instant fame and recognition to the RS Cosworth. The intention was to increase downforce over the rear-end.*

■ LEFT *A genuine performance legend was created when Ford put its RS badge together with the Cosworth tuning company. It was scintillatingly quick, yet reasonably priced.*

downforce, which it did, but aerodynamics suffered, with the Cd falling to 0.34 and criticism coming from certain quarters about stability in cross-winds. Aesthetically, it was hardly subtle either. These drawbacks hardly mattered, however, to the drivers who revelled in the Cosworth's neck-snapping acceleration and finely balanced handling.

Because it was intended as a homologation special for racing, only 6021 Cosworth hatchbacks were made, plus an additonal 500 evolution RS500 models with 224bhp and an even larger rear spoiler. Their successor was the Sapphire Cosworth, a four-door model with much more restrained styling but all the driving ability of the earlier car. Added bonuses included greater practicality and more generous equipment levels.

The theme was extended in 1990 with the 4x4 version, developed to give the Sierra a better chance in rallying. The 4x4 gained an extra 16bhp, thanks to a new 16-valve cylinder head. That meant even more performance as well as sure-

footed handling, which left virtually every other car on the road for dead.

Having been in its lifetime the number one target for thieves and joy-riders in Britain, and hcncc almost impossible to insure, the "Cossie" has since assumed the mantle of a respected and affordable classic.

■ RIGHT *Able to reach 60mph (96 kph) from rest in a little over six seconds, this Ford, despite its humble origins, could outpace many so-called supercars.*

■ LEFT *Cosworth's 16-valve turbocharged engine produced 204bhp in its original form. Ford lost no opportunities in exploiting the Cosworth connection to the full.*

FORD

■ FORD RS200

In the 1980s, a new breed of supercar hit the streets. Manufacturers wanting to muscle in on the prestigious Group B rally scene were forced by the regulations to build a minimum of 200 cars for homologation purposes, which usually meant having to sell some as road-going cars. Many of these beasts, while brutally effective on forest roads, were hopelessly impractical if you had to drive anywhere on public roads.

Ford's Group B effort, the RS200, was certainly effective, but in road form it was also one of the most practical and comfortable of all, having such luxuries as a fully-trimmed cockpit and even provision for a radio. In racing terms, the RS200 never achieved its full potential because, after just one season (1986), the sport's governing body cancelled the Group B category. It was left to private entrants to pick up honours such as the European Rallycross Championship.

The RS200 was conceived as early as 1983 as a bespoke (dedicated) rally machine. Ghia styled the monocoque bodyshell, which was made of glassfibre and Kevlar over an aluminium honeycomb floor with steel front- and rear-box sections. It looked a good deal prettier than any other Group B car around. It was short and stubby yet had an undeniable presence, mainly thanks to its large tail spoiler and roof-mounted spoiler/air dam. The windscreen derived from the standard production Ford Sierra.

Cosworth provided the engine, a turbocharged, slightly enlarged BDT development of the BDA unit fitted to the Escort RS1700T. It developed 250bhp in road-going form and could be tuned as high as 450bhp – or even higher – for competition use.

The four-wheel-drive transmission was unusual in that the magnesium-

■ ABOVE *To make the most of the mid-engined layout, there was an unusual four-wheel-drive system developed by FF.*

■ LEFT *The RS200 arrived too late to have much impact on the doomed Group B rally scene, but it was a devastatingly effective rally machine.*

FORD RS200 (1984–86)	
Engine	4-cylinder
Capacity	1803cc
Power	250bhp
Transmission	5-speed
Top speed	140mph (225kph)
No. built	200

■ OPPOSITE *Ford's modestly-named RS200 was a full-blown bespoke (dedicated) rally car also sold for road use. Ghia styled the bodywork and Ford's rally department did the rest.*

■ RIGHT *The rally impetus is obvious in this picture of the hinging front and rear ends, the idea being to allow instant easy access to all the mechanical components.*

cased Hewland transaxle was mounted well away from the engine, immediately behind the front differential and effectively between the passengers' legs. This was, incidentally, Ford's first-ever four-wheel-drive road car.

Because of the car's light weight (just 2315lb (1050kg)), it performed superbly. It could reach 60mph (96kph) in only six seconds, and top speed was quoted as 140mph (225kph), limited by a disappointing Cd figure of 0.40.

The RS200 was launched at the 1984 Turin Motor Show, but preproduction delays meant that the car did not get its homologation papers until early 1986, by which time the required 200 units had already been built. The demise of Group B meant RS200 production would never resume, although much development was later given to it to keep it competitive in racing well into the 1990s.

■ LEFT *Considering it was a rally car, the cockpit was surprisingly civilized, with its proper trimming, leather steering wheel and provision for a hi-fi system.*

■ LEFT *The mid-mounted engine was developed by Cosworth. Its capacity was only 1.8 litres, but its highly developed innards and turbocharging took standard power to 250bhp.*

■ ABOVE *The RS200 was effectively rendered obsolete by the demise of the Group B rally class, adjudged to be too fast and dangerous.*

HONDA

■ HONDA NSX

With all its reputation for mastery in engine and suspension technology, culminating in a successful Formula 1 racing programme, it is perhaps surprising that Honda did not attempt to produce a supercar before the NSX. When it did give the go ahead for this risky project, the end result was typically clean, business-like and incredibly effective: in essence, the NSX was the most user-friendly of an inherently impractical breed.

Here was a car that bristled with exciting yet pertinent features. Honda recognized the need for light weight, so specified an all-aluminium monocoque body and forged alloy suspension components, which were tested by racer Ayrton Senna. The abilities of the NSX can be judged by the fact that Senna owned several over the years, as did McLaren F1 engineer Gordon Murray.

It was simply the best supercar to drive and own, equally capable of idling around town as doing an impression of a Le Mans racer.

The 3.0-litre engine, which was mounted centrally, was a tour de force: four camshafts, 24 valves, variable valve

■ LEFT *In America the NSX was marketed under the Acura brand name. Elsewhere it was sold alongside humble Civics as a Honda.*

■ BELOW *Later versions of the NSX were faster, lighter and more powerful, and came with the option of a removable targa top.*

■ LEFT *Honda showed the prototype of its new NSX sportscar in 1989, and the world was prepared to make the acquaintance of one of the finest cars ever made.*

HONDA NSX (1990–)	
Engine	V-six-cylinder
Capacity	2977–3179cc
Power	270–294bhp
Transmission	5/6-speed manual, 4-speed automatic
Top speed	161–171mph (259–275kph)
No. built	Still in production

■ OPPOSITE *The NSX was designed to compete with Europe's best, such as Porsche and Ferrari. In absolute terms it was easily their equal, perhaps only lacking an indefinable excitement factor.*

■ LEFT *In typical Honda fashion, the NSX's lines were simple and unadorned. This was a devastatingly efficient machine in all respects.*

■ ABOVE *In motion, the 3.2-litre engine had a sound and a performance that denoted engineering purity. Road testers were struck by the sheer ability and range of its dynamics.*

timing and induction, titanium connecting rods, separate coils for each spark plug and an ability to rev to 8300rpm. Its power delivery was smooth, the throttle response was electric, and the noise it emitted ranged from a sweet purr to the scream of a thoroughbred racer. In short, the NSX engine was one of the all-time great power plants.

Its 270bhp was hugely impressive for a 3.0-litre engine. Even though by supercar standards its acceleration was not class-beating, 0–60mph (0–96kph) in 5.8 seconds could hardly be described as sluggish.

In handling terms, the NSX was both forgiving and communicative, aided by superb traction control and accurate steering. This was one of the true masters of the art of cornering.

The NSX was the most expensive car Japan had ever made, but its price still undercut rivals like the Ferrari 348. With almost no faults, it was unquestionably the most mature exponent of the supercar breed.

Later years saw it improve still further, and in 1997 it got the biggest revamp of its life, with a bigger 3.2-litre engine, six-speed gearbox, variable-weight power steering and bigger brakes. It remains one of the most respected cars in the world.

OTHER MAKES

■ HOLDEN

Holden is the Australian outpost of the global General Motors empire. Occasionally it produced or imported European and American GM products (and even badged many models produced by Japanese companies), but more usually it developed cars specially suited to the Australian market. Its main model lines included the Monara, Commodore, Torana and Statesman, which were great cruising machines halfway between European and American idioms.

■ HYUNDAI

The biggest car-maker in Korea has always been Hyundai, and its current size is all the more impressive considering it only began making cars in 1967, producing a version of the Ford Cortina. Its first all-new car was the 1975 Pony designed by Giugiaro. Gradually, its allegiance to Ford switched to Mitsubishi, and it made several licence-built models in Korea. Its position in the West grew yearly stronger with burgeoning exports of conventional but cheap family cars.

■ INNOCENTI

Innocenti began life as the holder of licences to make BMC products in Italy, and it produced the Austin A40, Mini, 1100 and Allegro. In 1976, ownership passed from British Leyland to De Tomaso, which produced over 200,000 Bertone-styled small cars based on the Mini platform. Subsequently, it turned to Daihatsu for its engines. Fiat acquired the marque in the 1980s and kept the name for imported versions of the Fiat Uno, Yugo and Daihatsu Hijet. The marque survived until 1997.

■ ISUZU

In Britain, the Japanese Isuzu name is best known for its four-wheel-drive vehicles, and in America it is remembered for the Gemini (a version of the Opel Kadett world car). Isuzu is basically General Motors' foothold in Japan, but has also made some interesting models. The Bertone-styled 117 coupé of 1968–81 was a design classic, and its 1980s Giugiaro-designed Piazza coupé Impulse was a best-seller. More recently Isuzu has concentrated on licence-built Hondas and sport-utility vehicles.

JAGUAR

■ BELOW *The mid-1970s was an awkward time to launch a luxury sportscar to succeed the immortal E-Type, and the XJS was always more of a grand touring car.*

■ JAGUAR XJS

Jaguar had charmed the world with its glorious E-Type in 1961, but by 1975 this was looking decidedly outdated and needed a successor. That car was the XJS, a car which had all the ingredients in place to make it perhaps the greatest car in the world: a fabulous V-twelve engine, world-beating suspension and all the prestige of the Jaguar badge.

Somehow the XJS lost the magic that made the E-Type so great. The styling rubbed everyone up the wrong way: traditionalists bemoaned its slab flanks, trapezoidal headlamps and black rubber bumpers and asked what had happened

■ ABOVE *The styling attracted some controversy, particularly the treatment of the flying buttress rear pillars. The XJS was accused of a "design-by-committee" birth.*

to Jaguar's traditional grille, its chrome and its walnut veneer dashboard. Sportscar drivers questioned its curious flying buttress styling and cramped interior. The truth is that, unlike the E-Type, which was designed by one talented professional, the XJS was styled by committee and ended up being a compromise.

Jaguar chose to base the XJS on a shortened version of the XJ12 saloon (sedan) platform, so that it kept its drive train, suspension and brakes intact. The standard transmission was a Borg Warner three-speed automatic, and

■ ABOVE *The last XJS models benefited from a major revamp in terms of styling, interior treatment and new 4-litre six-cylinder and 6-litre V-twelve engines.*

■ RIGHT *Front-seat passengers were cosseted in impressive chairs, although those in the rear were severely limited for space.*

■ RIGHT *Every XJS model drove impressively. Some magazines were tempted to call it the best grand touring car available by virtue of its impeccable ride and excellent driving characteristics.*

■ ABOVE *The fuel-injected V-twelve engine was a tight fit under the low bonnet-line (hood line), but the rewards were immeasurable since this was one of the finest engines produced.*

JAGUAR XJS (1975–96)	
Engine	6/V-twelve-cylinder
Capacity	3590–5994cc
Power	223–333bhp
Transmission	3/4-speed automatic 4/5-speed manual
Top speed	141–158mph (227–254kph)
No. built	112,000

although a manual gearbox was offered only 352 customers opted for it. Performance was superb for a grand touring four-seater, with a top speed of 150mph (241kph) and bustling acceleration.

The interior was based around the XJ saloon parts bin but featured a curious instrument binnacle with inset main dials and revolving minor gauges on the dash. There was plenty of space in the front seats, but the rear pair was really suitable only for children.

The 5.3-litre V-twelve engine was given better fuel economy and more power in 1981 and re-christened XJS HE (High Efficiency). Now the XJS started to get some of the chrome and wood that had been missing. The range was expanded in 1983 by the addition of a six-cylinder 3.6-litre XJS and a brand-new Cabriolet model, which had rigid

targa roof panels and a folding rear section and was a strict two-seater. This drop-top model lasted until 1988, when it was replaced by a new top-of-the-range full Convertible V-twelve model with an electric folding roof. A TWR-developed 333bhp XJR-S version arrived at the same time.

For 1991, the XJS got a £50 million ($84 million) investment and a new lease of life. The bodyshell was heavily reworked, especially at the rear-end, and the interior was thoroughly revamped. Another major change was the adoption of the new AJ6 four-litre engine. Within three years this was uprated to AJ16 specification and got an extra 15bhp, while the venerable old V-twelve engine expanded to six litres.

The XJS survived until September 1996, making it the longest-lived Jaguar ever at over 21 years. One measure of its excellence is that its replacement, the XK8, was based on the XJS floorpan.

■ ABOVE *The first XJS models had no wood and little leather, but later examples redressed the imbalance.*

■ LEFT *The convertible XJS, which arrived quite late in the model's production career, was an extremely popular choice and highly rewarding to own.*

JAGUAR

JAGUAR XK8

After years of rumours about a true E-Type replacement called the F-Type, Jaguar finally presented its crucial new sportscar, the XK8, at the 1996 Geneva Motor Show.

Officially, this was the replacement for the XJS, but it had so much more appeal that it was really viewed as the spiritual successor to the E-Type. Its svelte lines were created at Jaguar's design headquarters in Whitley, West Midlands, and it was engineered using the XJS floorpan as its starting-point. The XK8 delivered a distinct blend of style, luxury, craftsmanship and performance in a car that was uniquely British in flavour.

Central to the new design was the all-aluminium AJV-eight engine, the very first V-eight engine ever produced by Jaguar, after an investment of £200 million ($337 million). The 32-valve quad-cam engine delivered power, smoothness and refinement and had such advanced features as variable cam phasing, platinum-tipped spark plugs, split-block cooling and catalysts that began operating only 30 seconds after start-up. The ZF transmission was also new, Jaguar's first five-speed automatic. Other technical advances were electronic variable ratio power-steering, new

■ ABOVE *Jaguar rightly played on the heritage of its E-Type sportscar, for the XK8 was its spiritual successor. Unlike the XJS, it was a genuine sportscar, as well as a comfortable grand tourer.*

JAGUAR XK8 (1996–)	
Engine	V-eight-cylinder
Capacity	3996cc
Power	290 bhp
Transmission	5-speed auto
Top speed	154mph (248kph)
No. built	Still in production

■ LEFT *Underneath the bonnet of the latest sleek cat lay Jaguar's first-ever V-eight engine, the AJ-V8, which was a technical tour de force.*

■ ABOVE *Rich traditions of leather and wood were kept up, and the game was moved on by the installation of state-of-the-art high-tech electronics.*

■ LEFT *The fabulous XK8 was the successor to the long-running XJS and was a quantum leap beyond it, even though its floorpan was merely an XJS derivation.*

■ LEFT *The design of the XK8 was completed entirely in-house, and revived the glory days of Jaguar's founder William Lyons.*

■ BELOW *The XK8's striking similarity to the Aston Martin DB7 was not lost on many observers. The XK8 was, however, considerably cheaper to buy.*

computer-active double-wishbone front suspension, XJR-derived rear suspension and multiplexed (integrated) electronics.

The result of all this technology was a car which performed superbly. Indeed, it went as fast as the Aston Martin DB7 (a car designed by the same team), and many hailed the far cheaper XK8 as a better car all round. Refined yet explosively fast, smooth yet sporting in character, the XK8 was a brilliant grand tourer and sportscar.

Launched just after the coupé at the New York Motor Show was a convertible with an electric top, which raised in just 20 seconds. Unlike some competitors, the soft top stacked up behind the seats in order not to compromise boot (trunk) space. With the top raised the XK8 felt just as refined as the coupé. The cabin oozed classic-leather ambience and was available in two styles: fashionable art-style "Sport" and full "Classic" treatment with walnut trim and colour-coordinated carpets. All models had air-conditioning, electric seats and cruise control, while audiophiles could specify a Harman Kardon hi-fi.

The XK8 maintained Jaguar's reputation for best-in-class ride and handling. A good example of Jaguar's attention to detail was the fact that each aircraft-spec aluminium front-suspension cross-beam was X-ray inspected prior to installation.

■ LEFT *The addition of a convertible model boosted the XK8's appeal. The soft top could be raised electronically in only 20 seconds.*

■ BELOW *Jaguar's noble sports-roadster heritage stretches back to the SS100 of the 1930s, and the XK8 justifiably took its place alongside the greats.*

J A G U A R

■ JAGUAR XJ220

There are very few production cars that can claim to be have been born out of a spare-time project, but the Jaguar XJ220 is the most famous of all. Jaguar's chief engineer, Jim Randle, dreamt up the idea of creating the ultimate supercar one Christmas and fired up enough enthusiasm with colleagues to start a "Saturday club" to work on the project.

At first not even the Jaguar board knew about the secret tinkering going at its Engineering Department at Whitley in the West Midlands of Britain. When it did find out, the enthusiasm bubbled over, and the new XJ220 was wheeled out at the 1988 Birmingham Motor Show as an official Jaguar concept car. The prototype XJ220 was an immense beast, mainly because it had to be accommodated around TWR racing components and Jaguar's massive V-twelve engine mounted in a central position. Still, Keith Helfet's aluminium bodywork design was a sublime piece of sculpture.

■ LEFT *The V-six engine had twin turbochargers and racing-car-type materials and construction. Its output was a remarkable 500bhp.*

The response at the 1988 show was rapturous, and the affluence of the times persuaded Jaguar to embark on a production run. Because of production practicalities the design was substantially modified. It was decided that the V-twelve engine was too bulky and so a race-derived 3.5-litre V-six engine was installed instead. Its state-of-the-art specification included four camshafts, twin injectors, twin turbochargers, four valves per cylinder and dry sump lubrication, and it was capable of pumping out 500bhp.

JAGUAR XJ220 (1991–94)	
Engine	V-six-cylinder
Capacity	3498cc
Power	500bhp @ 6500rpm
Transmission	5-speed
Top speed	220mph (352kph)
No. built	350

■ LEFT *After it was presented as a prototype in 1988, the public clamour surrounding the fastest Jaguar ever made persuaded the company to enter production with the XJ220.*

■ OPPOSITE *The imposing authority of the XJ220 was confirmed by anyone who drove it. Here was a car which had phenomenal dynamic ability, helped by aircraft-inspired engineering.*

■ ABOVE *The best place to enjoy the full performance of the XJ220 – 220mph (352kph) – was undoubtedly a race-track,*

for the immense girth and negligible visibility made it difficult to exploit its potential on real-world roads.

The smaller engine meant that overall length could be trimmed down by a sizeable 10in (25cm), but there was no escaping the massive girth of this sportscar: at 6ft 6in (nearly two metres) wide, this was the broadest British car ever made.

The specification sheet of the XJ220 read like a sportscar-driver's dream. Its bodywork was an aerospace-type bonded-aluminium honeycomb with Group C racing inspired aerodynamics, the five-speed transaxle was mated to a racing AP clutch, there were centre-lock (knock-off) alloy wheels, massive brakes with four- piston calipers and racing-derived wishbone/inboard suspension.

Jaguar's performance claims were equally exciting. Its top speed of 220mph (352kph) and 0–60mph (0–96kph) time of 3.5 seconds made it easily the fastest road car on earth at the time. In-gear acceleration was

absolutely brutal. To match that explosive power, the racing suspension made the XJ220 probably the best-handling supercar ever.

A joint Jaguar–TWR venture called JaguarSport set up a brand new production facility in Bloxham, Oxfordshire, to make a strictly limited

run of 350 cars, each priced at £403,000 ($678,000). At first, the order book was over-subscribed by speculators but, when it became obvious that the market for supercars had collapsed, legal proceedings ensued as buyers tried to pull out – an ignominious end to an amazing story.

■ RIGHT *The impeccable detailing reflected the XJ220's hand-built nature and extraordinary price.*

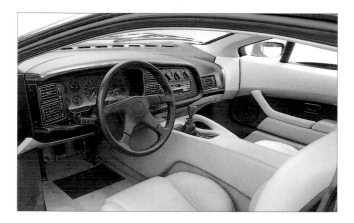

■ LEFT *For all its exotic specification, the interior was a thoroughly comfortable place to be. There was room for luxury even at stratospheric speeds.*

■ ABOVE *In high-speed tests the XJ220 proved capable of speeds approaching 220mph (352kph), and of reaching 60mph (96kph) from rest in just 3.5 seconds.*

JEEP

■ JEEP

The great American legend that is the Jeep has its origins in desperate times. In June 1940, the US Quartermaster Corps published requirements for a compact 4x4 quarter-ton truck. It asked potential contractors that a fully functioning prototype should be ready within one month. Of 135 firms polled to do this near-impossible job, only two took up the challenge: Willys–Overland

■ LEFT *Where the legend started: the Second World War Willys Jeep was conceived in double-quick time, and it got on with its job. It inspired a whole dynasty of civilian jeeps.*

aluminium pistons, producing only 49bhp but a massive 105lb ft (142Nm) of torque at just 2000rpm. Drivers had three gears to choose from, plus a two-speed transfer box and switchable freewheel for the front axle.

It was basic in the extreme, but the hastily conceived design was inherently right: no major changes were made despite the arduous tests of war use. Over 600,000 of these machines were churned out until the end of production in 1945, after which the French firm Hotchkiss made Jeeps into the 1960s.

After the war, Willys plugged on with the Jeep in civilian CJ-2A form, with the advertising line, "The sun never sets on

(which asked for an extra 45 days to prepare a car) and a small Detroit engineering firm called Bantam, which got the contract.

Production started at Ford, Willys and Bantam factories. The basic chassis was a box-section twin-rail frame with cross-members, fitted with low-carbon steel bodywork, ultra-simple for ease of manufacture. To enable Jeeps to be stacked on top of each other, the windscreen was removable.

Suspended by leaf springs (and dampers – shocks – only at the rear), the Jeep was powered by Willys's "Go-Devil" 2.2-litre four-cylinder unit with

■ ABOVE *The whole jeep story can be traced through these cars, from the Second World War fighter through the CJ models at the rear, and up to date with the Wrangler editions of the 1980s and 1990s.*

■ RIGHT *This 1990 Wrangler Laredo proves the durability of the Jeep phenomenon. The famous hallmarks of square-cut wings, simple flat surfaces and grille all remain.*

■ LEFT *Modern Jeep Wranglers in their element, crossing the most inhospitable terrain. Jeeps gradually became more lifestyle vehicles than working cars.*

■ BELOW LEFT *A whole new strain of Jeeps was launched with the Cherokee, a multi-purpose 4x4 four-door. This is one of the compact modern versions, dating from 1984.*

■ BELOW RIGHT *Although this is merely a concept exercise called the Jeep Freedom, it shows there is a spiritual connection between the Cherokee and original-type Jeeps.*

the Willys-built Jeep". Farmers loved them, and Jeeps provided cheap, practical transportation in austere times.

The 1946 Station Wagon was America's first steel-bodied estate. The body was recognizably Jeep, but it was on a longer wheelbase, had a six-cylinder engine option and only two-wheel drive. It had non-structural wood applied to its sides and split rear doors. Even more "civvy" was the Brooks

Stevens-styled Jeepster with its bright colour schemes, whitewall tyres, luxurious fittings and detachable hood. The Jeepster name was revived briefly in 1967.

The Jeep CJ evolved slowly, the CJ5 and long-wheelbase CJ6 versions lasting from 1952 into the 1970s, by which time AMC had become the parent company. An important variant was the 1972 CJ5 Renegade, a sporty Jeep with a V-eight

engine, which pointed the way ahead in terms of style development.

Gradually, the range expanded to include the Commando pickup, the four-door Wagoneer and, from 1974, Cherokee sport-utilities. While the CJ soldiered on around the world, in America the Cherokee and larger Cerand Cherokee assumed greater significance, as well as "retro" reworkings of the original idea, sold under the name Wrangler.

JEEP WRANGLER (1986–)	
Engine	4/6-cylinder
Capacity	2464–4235cc
Power	112–184bhp
Transmission	5-speed manual 3/4-speed auto
Top speed	84–108mph (130–174kph)
No. built	Still in production

■ RIGHT *Largest of the jeep family is the Grand Cherokee with its large-capacity V-eight engine and very comfortable interior.*

LAMBORGHINI

■ BELOW *Bertone's stunning original Countach design left every other exotic car for dead. Ultimately, it was the most beautiful Countach of all, completely unadorned by superfluous decoration.*

■ **LAMBORGHINI COUNTACH**

To top the amazing mid-engined Miura, unquestionably the most exotic car of the 1960s, Lamborghini had to come up with something decisively more dramatic. In that at least the amazing Countach succeeded superbly.

The original bright-yellow Bertone-styled prototype of 1971 was dramatic yet remarkably pure and unadorned compared with the more familiar models of the late 1970s and 80s. Where the Miura had been sensual and muscular, the Countach was futuristic, razor-edged,

■ RIGHT *Banana-shaped leather seats looked more enticing than they really were. Luxury was not squandered in the Countach cabin.*

wedgey, breathing aggression from every pore. Wild as it looked, the Countach was a much better developed car than the flawed Miura, even though it was no easier to live with, owing to the problems with the show-off lift-up doors.

It was a sensation to drive, of course: as well as being more forgiving in its handling – the gearbox was now mounted in-line, ahead of the engine between the seats – it was even faster than the Miura: good for 186mph (299kph), claimed Lamborghini, if you could find a stretch of road long enough. Most road testers managed about 160mph (257kph).

The word "*countach*" is a Piedmontese expletive meaning wow – or something stronger depending on how it was pronounced. The first Countach went to

■ ABOVE *Opening the doors was as dramatic an experience as seeing the car for the first time. This is an LP500 model from 1982.*

■ LEFT *The trapezoidal tail lamps were an unmistakable Countach hallmark, punctuating one of the longest rear decks of any production car.*

LAMBORGHINI COUNTACH (1974–91)	
Engine	V-twelve-cylinder
Capacity	3929–5167cc
Power	375–455bhp
Transmission	5-speed manual
Top speed	186–200mph (299–322kph)
No. built	609

■ RIGHT *Fast, winding roads were the Countach's element, where it was almost indecently fast. Owners were always attracted as much by its brash character as by its raw ability.*

its owner in 1974 amid a blaze of publicity. However, the clean lines of the original became progressively more tasteless as the years went by, especially once the LP500 five-litre model appeared in 1982: its spoilers did nothing for stability, while big ugly wheel-arches housed improbably fat tyres, matched by even bigger NACA ducts to get air into the enlarged engine.

It also became apparent that build quality was merely adequate and the car began to put on as much flab as muscle. Yet its unremittingly powerful character overcame such quibbles and kept the

■ BELOW *Lamborghini's raging bull emblem was sustained by the success of the long-running Countach.*

■ ABOVE *The very last Countach QV models got yet another restyle and a four-valves-per-cylinder head. The model was retired finally in 1991.*

■ LEFT *The powerhouse in the middle of the Countach was a fabulously expressive V-twelve engine, claimed to return 200mph (322kph) performance.*

troubled Lamborghini – long since out of its founder's control – afloat through the dark abyss of the 70s and 80s when lesser models like the Urraco and Jalpa failed to find buyers. Having said that, the Countach never enjoyed the commercial success of Ferrari's much less radical Boxer and Testarossa.

The ultimate QV model – indicating Quattro Valvole (or four valves per cylinder) – bowed out in 1991. By then, its top speed was quoted as 200mph (322kph). In later years, the Countach had become a kind of parody of itself – a car for anybody with too much money and not enough taste – but at least it was recognizable.

■ ABOVE *No one was in any doubt that the Countach was a very quick machine, but in the latter half of its life Lamborghini felt* *obliged to add aerodynamic aids such as giant rear spoilers. In practice they had little effect beyond visual stimulation.*

LAMBORGHINI

■ LAMBORGHINI LM002

When you look at the back catalogue of Lamborghini cars, you will find only high-performance supercars: names like Miura, Countach, Espada, Diablo. There is one name that sticks out in this sleek, knee-high company: what on earth is an LM?

To realize why Lamborghini produced the equivalent of Mad Max, you have to understand why most European farmers are also familiar with the Lamborghini name: its other main business is making agricultural tractors. The LM002 was the perfect, if audacious, synthesis of these two sides of Lamborghini's business – a four-wheel-drive monster with a V-twelve Countach engine!

Its story actually begins with a request to produce a military vehicle for the US, in conjunction with Chrysler. This resulted in the Cheetah of 1977, a massive doorless all-terrain buggy with a mid-mounted Chrysler V-eight engine.

■ ABOVE *Dauntingly large wheels and tyres were specially designed to withstand large, sharp rocks.*

■ ABOVE *Straddling an immense central tunnel, four passengers could be seated in air-conditioned, leather-lined comfort. There was space for four or more on the pick-up rear-bed.*

■ ABOVE *The V-twelve engine from the Countach was stuffed under the bonnet to make a thundering beast in every sense. It had to be mounted rather high up.*

The tail-heavy weight distribution under which this layout suffered led the American government elsewhere (the US-built Hummvee, or Hummer, got the deal in the end).

Lamborghini pressed ahead with its own interpretation of the ultimate off-roader. Its production LM002 was shown for the first time in autumn 1985 with a Lamborghini Countach V-twelve engine up front. Everything about it was bigger and better than any other car.

The LM was immense. At over 16ft (495cm) long, it was about the same length as a Jaguar XJ, and it was over 6ft 6in (200cm) wide, 73in (185cm) high and weighed nearly 3 tonnes (2.95 tons). It could seat four people inside, two on each side of the largest central tunnel ever seen in a car, and four-to-six more passengers could perch in the pick-up rear. The enormous 345 x 17 tyres were specially made by Pirelli.

That giant Countach engine meant the LM was the fastest off-roader in the world: it could lug the LM up to a top speed of 126mph (201kph), while its 0–60mph (0–96kph) time of 8.5 seconds

■ RIGHT *The audacity which produced the LM002 can only be gawped at. This leviathan was conceived as an all-terrain army vehicle but found favour with anyone with enough money and a desperate need to cross deserts at terminal velocities.*

could embarrass quite a few sportscars. The trade-off was fuel consumption in the region of 7mpg (11.2kpg) – you really needed the 70-gallon (318 litre) fuel tank. Off-road ability was deeply impressive thanks to the all-independent suspension and massive ground clearance.

If you were used to the utility treatment in your off-roader, the LM packed a few surprises. Here was a tough brute with all the fancy trimmings of a limousine: leather upholstery, air-conditioning, lots of electric gadgets, a wood dashboard and deep-pile carpeting.

The LM's natural habitat was the Middle East, where the military and the oil barons lapped it up, and that's just as well because the LM cost even more than the Countach and you really needed your own oil well to run one.

■ LEFT *The world's biggest bonnet (hood) bulges were required to clear the most powerful engine ever fitted to a standard 4x4 vehicle.*

LAMBORGHINI LM002 (1985–93)	
Engine	V-twelve-cylinder
Capacity	5167cc
Power	450bhp @ 6800rpm
Transmission	5-speed, drive to all four wheels
Top speed	126mph (203kph)
No. built	n/a

■ LEFT *On the road the LM002 turned into a GTI, capable of 126mph (203kph) and 0–60mph (0–96kph) in 8.5 seconds. The pay-off was the greediest fuel consumption figures ever recorded for a production car.*

LAMBORGHINI

■ LAMBORGHINI DIABLO

"*Diablo*" means devil in Spanish, a curious choice for the Italian successor to the legendary Countach. The Diablo was the first fruit of Lamborghini's brief spell under Chrysler's wing, and cost £50 million ($84 million) to develop.

Following the Countach was never going to be easy, but the Diablo succeeded. Above all it looked absolutely startling thanks to the gifted penwork of Marcello Gandini. The dramatic scissor-type doors were retained for the new car and incorporated a deeply swooping waistline. The tail seemed to stretch back for ever, its long centre cut-out full of louvres, its air dams looking purposeful, its profile widening all the way. The nose could hardly have been lower or more stubbed. Construction was of aluminium and composite-plastic body panels over a chassis reinforced with carbonfibre.

Mechanically, the Diablo looked back to the Countach for its inspiration. Its V-twelve engine was a development of the Countach's, expanded, catalyzed and given sequential fuel injection. The result was 492bhp and 428ft

■ ABOVE *Even faster than the Countach it replaced, the Diablo – or "devil" – was a true giant of the supercar world.*

LAMBORGHINI DIABLO (1990–)	
Engine	V-twelve-cylinder
Capacity	5729cc
Power	492–525bhp
Transmission	5-speed
Top speed	186–210mph (299–338kph)
No. built	Still in production

(1404cm) of torque, plus one of the most fulfilling soundtracks of any engine. There was also a new five-speed gearbox geared so that 100mph (161kph) could be reached in second gear.

Lamborghini claimed that the Diablo's top speed of 202mph (325kph) could beat arch-rival Ferrari's F40. It was certainly very quick, as tests of the even more powerful, lightweight limited-edition 525bhp SE30 would show: 0–60mph (0–96kph) in 4.2 seconds was exceptionally rapid. Only its bulk and the heaviness of its steering knocked the edge off this good machine.

■ LEFT *An improbably long tail housed the engine, while the scissor-type doors were a continuation of the theme first seen in the Countach.*

■ ABOVE *The exceptionally neat-looking V-twelve engine developed no less than 492bhp in its original – and least powerful – guise.*

■ ABOVE *In Lamborghini's vocabulary, SV meant Sport Veloce. In other words, it signified light weight, massive (510bhp) power and special gearing tuned for maximum acceleration.*

■ LEFT *A Ferrari-style exposed gear-lever gate fronts an impressive array of standard controls. The air-conditioning system was complex enough to fill the front compartment.*

■ ABOVE *On its way to a 202mph (325 kph) top speed the Diablo would leave behind it a plume of smoke from the quad-exit exhausts – and a terrifying noise.*

Most of the Countach weaknesses – cramped interior, poor visibility, difficult access – were resolved in the Diablo. Luggage space was still at a premium, but the cabin looked and felt classy, boasted a great driving position and featured a control to adjust the suspension settings from the driver's seat. Lamborghini was confident that it could sell 500 cars a year, far more than the Countach had ever achieved.

New for 1991 was the VT (Viscous Transmission) model with full four-wheel drive, although the front wheels only ever got a maximum of 29 per cent of the overall power, and then only after the rear end began to lose traction. Four-wheel drive made the already fine handling even more assured, and the standard adoption of power steering made life behind the wheel much easier, although the penalty was the higher overall weight of the car.

Other variations followed in 1996. The Roadster was just what it said it was: a Diablo with a removable roof, intended to do battle with the similarly configured Ferrari F50. The SV (for Sport Veloce) was the most focused of all the Diablos: a 510bhp engine, lighter weight, lower gearing and even more startling acceleration (although the top speed dropped to "only" 186mph (299kph) owing to the new gearing). There was little doubt that this was the best of the exclusive Diablo family.

■ LEFT *The Roadster version had a hardtop which could be removed completely or pushed back and fixed above the engine bay.*

LANCIA

■ LANCIA GAMMA

When Fiat took control of Lancia and its huge debts in 1969, many pundits guessed that there would be no more true Lancias – technically advanced cars with sporting character. They were wrong. The Pininfarina-styled Gamma saloon (sedan) and coupé announced at Geneva in 1976 boasted all the idiosyncrasies with associated Lancia.

■ LEFT *The 1976 Gamma was Lancia's stab at the executive car market. The big four-door model was always a rare sight, as it seemed to be bought almost exclusively by Italian embassies.*

■ ABOVE *For an interior conceived in the mid-1970s, this was unusually attractive and stylish.*

■ ABOVE *It was perhaps a strange choice to fit a four-cylinder engine in a luxury car, one of the biggest "fours" then in production.*

It was a shame that the Gamma was so underdeveloped because it was a great driving machine, with superb balance and the best power steering around. The saloon was handsome in its own way, but the coupé was a classic of elegant, perfectly proportioned styling.

Series 2 models gained fuel injection, a four-speed auto option and other detail modifications to make the engine more reliable, but it all came too late and in 1984 Gamma production ended. Had the model survived it would probably have been given effective 16-valve technology and there were even turbocharged 180bhp "Federalized" Gammas running as prototypes.

Pininfarina built a Spider version of the coupé in 1978, then a four-door, three-box Scala in 1980, and finally the Olgiata of 1982, a handsome estate (station wagon) version, but sadly all three remained prototypes.

Not the least of these quirks was the adoption of a big 2.5-litre flat-four engine in an executive class more used to six cylinders at the very least. Although the engine was torquey and smooth at high revs, it proved a difficult choice for buyers to accept, not only

because it was rather throbby and unrefined at tick-over but because it rapidly acquired a reputation for serious reliability problems: overheating was common, and the cam belt could strip its teeth if the steering was put on full lock from cold.

■ LEFT *Very communicative steering and balanced handling made the Gamma a real driver's car. Performance was respectable.*

LANCIA GAMMA (1977–84)	
Engine	4-cylinder
Capacity	2500cc
Power	140bhp
Transmission	5-speed manual 4-speed auto
Top speed	120mph (193kph)
No. built	22,085

■ ABOVE *The first-series Montecarlo was criticized for its braking performance and wet-weather roadholding, and was actually withdrawn from production for two years.*

■ LANCIA MONTECARLO

This interesting mid-engined sportscar began life in the Fiat empire as a future sister model for the little X1/9. Indeed, the project was referred to under the name X1/20, but a shuffle of priorities then switched the new model under Lancia's wing.

The Montecarlo was launched at the 1975 Geneva Motor Show in both fixed coupé and targa-topped "Spider" versions. Its clean lines, featuring prominent black bumpers, a forward-thrusting snout and rear flying buttresses, created a stir with fans.

Much of the car was plundered from the parts bin of the Lancia Beta range,

■ ABOVE *The cockpit was strictly for two passengers, but boasted Italian design flair and a removable targa roof panel.*

■ ABOVE *The Montecarlo brochure celebrated Lancia's racing achievements with its mid-engined sportscar.*

■ LEFT *Pininfarina created the pretty shape of the Montecarlo around mid-engine ideals. Note the rear flying buttresses.*

including its 2.0-litre engine and many detail items. That kept costs down, and enabled Lancia to sell a car that many likened to a miniature Ferrari for a bargain price.

The story was not all roses, however. The engine was not really powerful enough for a true sportscar, the roadholding was positively dangerous in wet conditions, and severe front-wheel lock-up under braking forced Lancia to suspend production in 1978 pending an 18-month-long return to the proverbial drawing board.

When the Montecarlo reappeared in 1980, Lancia had addressed the problems: the front brake problem was cured by removing the servo assistance and the tail-happy nature was tamed by revised suspension. Also new were the grille, bigger wheels and a six-year anti-corrosion warranty.

In America, the Montecarlo was sold as the Scorpion with a dreadfully underpowered 80bhp 1.8-litre engine. When production ended in 1984 there was no direct replacement, and this was effectively the last real Lancia sportscar.

LANCIA MONTECARLO (1978–84)	
Engine	4-cylinder
Capacity	1995cc
Power	120bhp
Transmission	5-speed
Top speed	118mph (190kph)
No. built	7595

■ RIGHT *Lancia's Montecarlo was the up-market sister of the Fiat X1/9, larger and more powerful, but no less attractive and very good value.*

LANCIA

■ LANCIA DELTA INTEGRALE

In Italian, *"Integrale"* means full, complete, whole, and that fittingly describes the abilities of Lancia's impressive Delta Integrale. Although it was conceived as a car to homologate for rallying, it was quickly recognized as one of the all-time great road cars.

Lancia was a consistently strong rallying contender – one has only to remember the Stratos and 037 – and it had built the mid-engined four-wheel-drive Delta S4 Group 4 car in 1984. However, after such Group B monsters were banned following major crashes and deaths (prompting the nickname "Killer B's"), all attention switched to the milder Group A category for 1987.

Lancia produced the Delta HF 4x4 all-wheel-drive car as a prelude to the full Integrale model, which was launched in October 1987, with its distinctive wide wheel-arches and fat tyres. The Integrale promptly swept the board in rallying events, taking 14

■ LEFT *The magical "HF Integrale" badge came to mean everything that was desirable in performance-car terms.*

■ ABOVE *Across country there was hardly a car that could match the Integrale's pace and roadholding.*

LANCIA DELTA INTEGRALE (1988–94)	
Engine	4-cylinder
Capacity	1995cc
Power	185–215bhp
Transmission	5-speed manual
Top speed	130–137mph (209–220kph)
No. built	Approx 25,000

■ LEFT *It was across rough terrain that the Integrale shone. In World Championship rallies, it was dominant for many years.*

World Championship rallies in 18 months and powering Miki Biasion to two world titles.

Road-car drivers quickly realized what a fabulous machine it was. The sophisticated four-wheel-drive system glued the car to the tarmac, while the 185bhp two-litre turbo engine sprinted the car across country faster than just about anything on the road. This was the fastest, safest point-to-point car in the world – and it was a practical five-door hatchback into the bargain. It felt special inside too: there were Recaro seats, electric front windows and unique instrumentation.

The Integrale just got better with age. In 1989, the old eight-valve cylinder head was upgraded to a new 16-valve head, which pushed power up to 200bhp. The main reason was to homologate the head for rallying, and it took only a few months to sell 5000 cars. The 16V cars won 13 World Championship rallies, and Kankkunen drove one to the 1991 title.

In 1991, a further evolution HF Integrale boasted even more power (210bhp – and later 215bhp – thanks to a larger exhaust), even wider wheel-arch flares to cover extended front and rear tracks, restyled grille, air intakes, bonnet, wings, bumpers and skirts, and a dramatic new adjustable tailgate spoiler. Officially, this edition was called just HF Integrale (no "Delta" in the name). It took until early 1992 to sell the requisite 5000 copies, and yet again Lancia took the 1992 Championship for Makes, in its last year as an official works team – not bad for a car that had its roots in the 1970s.

Today the Integrale has a hallowed status among keen drivers. Although it left production in 1994, examples are avidly sought after because there really is nothing like it still in production.

■ BELOW *Cornering at improbable speeds was the Integrale's true forte, and it could show its heels to just about everything else on the road.*

■ ABOVE *Lancia's Delta Integrale did not take long to make a huge impact on the motoring world. Its devastatingly effective brew of all-wheel drive and performance led to it becoming a legend in its own lifetime.*

LEXUS

■ LEXUS SC

In 1989, Toyota set out to beat Europe's finest marques at their own game. It wanted to steal a march on Mercedes-Benz, BMW and Jaguar by producing the world's best luxury saloon (sedan) – even though it had no experience in this market area. It invented a new brand, Lexus, sent its designers to California to discover what customers really wanted, and came up with the LS400 saloon, a car which signally succeeded in providing a genuine alternative to Europe's classic brands.

Lexus did not stop at the LS saloon, which was supremely competent but ultra-conservative in character. In 1991, it added a bit of spice into its new brand with a coupé version, known in the USA as the Lexus SC and in Japan as the

■ ABOVE *In export markets, the svelte Toyota-built coupé was badged as a Lexus SC. This is a top-of-the-range SC400 model.*

■ RIGHT *Overall the Lexus offered fine value, superlative build quality, attractive styling and crushing ability.*

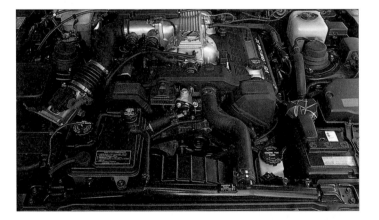

■ LEFT *Highly sophisticated electronics dominated the engine bay of the SC. Several engines were built, from 2.5 litres to 4 litres.*

■ BELOW *Based on the successful Lexus LS400 four-door saloon (sedan), the coupé version added stylé and a sporting slant. Japanese versions were called Toyota Soarer.*

LEXUS SC (1991–)	
Engine	6-cylinder
Capacity	2491–3969cc
Power	225–280bhp
Transmission	5-speed manual 4-speed automatic
Top speed	146–155mph (235–250kph)
No. built	Still in production

■ RIGHT *The Toyota Soarer took off not only in Japan but also in America, where it stole sales from the prestige coupés of Mercedes-Benz and BMW.*

Toyota Soarer (it was never officially marketed in Europe).

The most striking aspect of the SC was the clean, restrained yet dramatic shape, created in Toyota's California studio. Although it was based on the floorpan of the Lexus saloon, the profile was fresh and boasted many beautiful touches, such as spotlamps shrouded by the subtlest of bulges running the whole length of the bonnet (hood).

In Japan, the catchphrase for the Soarer was "for mind cruising" – which conveyed the new model's primary objective: to transport its occupants over long distances in relaxation and comfort. It also happened to be sizzlingly quick.

The new SC range spanned three engine sizes, from a 225bhp 3.0-litre straight six up to the 4.0-litre V-eight used in the Lexus saloon; not sold in the US, the most powerful member of the family was the 2.5-litre Twin Turbo in-line-six engine, developing 20bhp more than the 4.0-litre V-eight, at 280bhp. The 4.0-litre engine scored 0–60mph (0–96kph) in 6.9 seconds with an automatic gearbox, while the five-speed manual Twin Turbo was nearer six seconds dead.

There was also a choice of three suspension systems. The first was conventional springing. The second was Piezo TEMS, an electronic air-suspension

■ RIGHT *With full active-ride suspension, the Lexus was a forgiving and accomplished cornerer. Its ride was also superior to that of almost any coupé in its class.*

system, which obviated the need for conventional shock absorbers. Controlled by a microchip in the central electronic management computer, it adjusted each wheel's suspension according to the load on it at any given time. Top models got full Active Suspension.

Toyota's engineers went to great lengths to make driving the Soarer an

easy experience. Progressive power steering, which stiffened up as speed increased, limited slip differential and a powerful ABS system eradicated the worries of piloting such a potent machine. Seating was comfortable and the cabin was full of gadgets: satellite navigation, an all-electronic dash with touch-sensitive controls and a television.

■ LEFT *An all-digital dashboard was perhaps a little gimmicky but it fitted the high-tech nature of the Lexus perfectly.*

LOTUS

■ LOTUS ESPRIT

Colin Chapman, the founder of Lotus, always said that he built the cars he wanted to own, which explained why, as he grew older, his designs matured into ever more sophisticated realms. By the early 1970s, the days of stark Lotus 7s sold in kit form were gone and a new era was dawning.

Chapman was extremely impressed by a mid-engined prototype, which Giorgetto Giugiaro had created for Lotus in 1972. This was the car that, with remarkably little modification, became the new Lotus Esprit, first shown in October 1975.

In construction, the Esprit was classically Lotus, having a steel-backbone chassis, all-independent suspension and a glassfibre body. As launched it had Lotus's brilliant 2.0-litre 16-valve four-cylinder engine mounted amidships. This not only

■ LEFT *Giugiaro's prototype Esprit dates from 1972 and was remarkably similar to the finished production version of the car.*

■ ABOVE *Clean lines, a mid-mounted engine and Lotus's fabled handling prowess made the Esprit a desirable, if flawed, sportscar.*

■ ABOVE *The interior architecture of the Esprit cabin was interesting, the sloping dashboard being a key feature.*

■ LEFT *Lotus boosted the power of its four-cylinder engine by turbocharging it. Up to 264bhp was a remarkable output for a 2.2-litre engine.*

provided convincing performance for its day, but produced probably the best-handling Lotus yet. The five-speed gearbox was taken directly from the Citroën SM.

As it transpired, Giugiaro's clean-cut and simple shape would stand the test of time with honours. The interesting interior architecture was perhaps less

appealing over the longer term but, for its day, the Esprit was a state-of-the-art mid-engined sportscar.

Lotus kept abreast of the opposition's advances with constant developments. An S2 version with an integrated front spoiler appeared in 1978, and the S2.2 with an expanded 2.2-litre engine in 1980, the same year the spectacular

Esprit Turbo was launched. The 2.2-litre Turbo engine developed 210bhp, enough to force a much stiffer chassis with larger wheels and brakes and revised suspension, creating a peerless car in handling terms. The S3 of 1981 incorporated most of the Turbo chassis refinements and added a wraparound front bumper.

■ LEFT *All Esprit models were fast, and no car handled as well as an Esprit. This is a Series 3 model at full chat.*

■ LEFT *The Esprit proved to be a very long-lasting model for the Norfolk company.*

■ ABOVE *In its ultimate guise, the Esprit gained a V-eight engine and a phenomenal power-to-weight ratio.*

In this form the Esprit continued until 1987, when Lotus's in-house designer, Peter Stevens, effected a brilliant restyle of the bodywork, creating smoothed-off and more aerodynamic lines. At the same time, the chassis was stiffened and the gearbox switched to Renault's GTA. The popular Turbo survived in even more powerful guise, boasting up to 264bhp.

There was another restyle in 1993, when the nose and rear wing were reshaped, the interior was improved and power steering standardized. Two new models were launched: the S4S and the Sport 300 with its 302bhp engine (still from just 2.2 litres and four cylinders).

By 1996, the Esprit was 21 years old and still going strong, but it desperately needed some extra urge to compete with the best from Ferrari. Lotus developed a brand-new V-eight engine for the purpose, twin-turbocharged to produce a massive 349bhp. Fitted with a six-speed gearbox, the new Esprit V8 was a formidable performer, and looked set to continue to uphold the Lotus tradition for many years yet.

■ LEFT *In 1987, the Esprit got a major redesign by Peter Stevens, rounding off its edges and adding some length.*

■ BELOW *Despite its increasing age, the Esprit remained a competitive and very British sportscar.*

LOTUS ESPRIT (1975–)	
Engine	4/V-eight-cylinder
Capacity	1973–3179cc
Power	160–349bhp
Transmission	5/6-speed
Top speed	130–170mph (209–274kph)
No. built	9,150 (to end of 1996)

LOTUS

■ **LEFT** *The Elan powered its way into the sports history books with its amazing handling ability, which was all the more remarkable since this was Lotus's first-ever front-wheel-drive car.*

■ LOTUS ELAN

In the 1960s, the Elan name meant just one thing: the best-handling, most fun-to-drive small sportscar you could buy. When Lotus decided, in 1989, to revive the name on its first all-new car in 14 years, it was fully aware of the legacy it had to live up to. Thankfully, in all major areas, it succeeded in creating a worthy successor.

In conception, the new Elan was unlike anything Lotus had tried before, and for one reason: it had front-wheel drive. If traditional Lotus enthusiasts were nervous about this development, they had no need, for the Elan was probably the most competent handling car available. In some eyes it was too efficient, simply gripping the road tighter the more you asked of it and lacking the involvement of other Lotus cars.

Peter Stevens designed the stubby bodywork and ex-Formula 1 driver John Miles developed the interactive suspension. Lotus went to Isuzu in Japan for its engine – a 1.6-litre twin-cam unit in normally aspirated or turbocharged SE forms.

The Elan sold for a very reasonable price, too reasonable as it turned out, as Lotus lost money on each one sold. Yet sales were disappointing, mainly because a worldwide economic recession was beginning to bite and the near-simultaneous release of Mazda's Miata, which offered comparable performance at half the cost. Amid financial problems, Lotus was forced to abandon production after just two years.

A saviour appeared in the form of Bugatti, which bought Lotus from its parent company General Motors and in 1994, using existing components, embarked on a limited run of 800 additional S2 Elans. These featured some 100 changes, including better suspension, larger wheels, new seats and a better hood. Later, the Elan project was revived by Kia in Korea.

ABOVE *All black and red: the cockpit was completely geared towards making the driving experience as visceral as possible.*

LOTUS ELAN (1989–94)	
Engine	4-cylinder
Capacity	1588cc
Power	130–165bhp
Transmission	5-speed
Top speed	122–137mph (196–220kph)
No. built	4,655

■ **LEFT** *Peter Stevens created another masterpiece of design, no mean feat considering the very short wheelbase he had to work with.*

■ **ABOVE** *The stubby two-seater had an effective folding top to make it a practical year-round car.*

■ RIGHT *The first new Lotus for a decade was always going to be greeted with intense interest, and the Elise marked a true revolution in sportscar design with its extruded-aluminium chassis.*

■ LOTUS ELISE

Light weight was always Colin Chapman's very first priority when designing a new Lotus. After his death in 1982, Lotus engineers adhered to this principle, and in the Elise, which epitomised it, they produced a spiritual successor to the immortal Lotus 7.

The heart of the Elise, and the reason why it was so light, was its perfectly functional chassis. Breaking with Lotus tradition, it was a monocoque design formed from pieces of lightweight aluminium, literally stretched into shape and glued together. Even the brakes were aluminium composite. This was the secret of its lightness.

The suspension was so good it needed no anti-roll bars, and testers were unanimous in their praise: this was simply the finest handling car ever made.

While the 1989 Elan was front-engined and front-wheel drive, the Elise was mid-engined and rear-wheel drive, and all the more enjoyable for this change. The chosen engine was Rover's all-aluminium 1.8-litre K-series (as fitted to the MGF), complete with its gearbox. This provided all the performance it needed: after all the Elise was only about half the weight of a small family hatchback.

The best thing about it, though, was its price: at under £20,000 ($33,000) in the UK it was a bargain.

■ ABOVE *Leaving the aluminium chassis exposed in the cockpit was an inspired move, utterly in keeping with its role as a super-lightweight, no-frills sportscar.*

■ ABOVE *Thanks to extreme light weight, the Elise was a good performer despite its mild 120bhp engine: 0-60mph (0–96 kph) in 5.5 seconds was extraordinarily quick.*

LOTUS ELISE (1996–)

Engine	4-cylinder
Capacity	1795cc
Power	120bhp @ 5500rpm
Transmission	5-speed
Top speed	124mph (200kph)
No. built	Still in production

OTHER MAKES

■ LAND-ROVER

After the Second World War, Britain needed a jeep-style all-rounder and the Willys Jeep was used as a template to create the Land-Rover in 1948. It quickly became an international legend, very tough and unassailable off-road. The same basic design remains in production today as the Defender, although Land-Rover branched out in 1970 with the sophisticated Range Rover, in the 1980s with the Discovery all-rounder, and in the 1990s with the smaller Freelander series.

■ LIGIER

French millionaire racing driver and ex-rugby international Guy Ligier decided to build his own sportscar in 1970. The JS designation was in memory of his friend, Jo Schlesser, killed racing in 1969. A pressed-steel platform was fitted with a glassfibre coupé body. As presented at the 1970 Paris Salon, it had a mid-mounted Ford Capri engine, but production cars had Citroën SM V-six engines. Ligier went on to make very successful Formula 1 racing cars and a range of top-selling microcars.

■ LINCOLN

Ford of America's premium brand is Lincoln, purveyors of limousines and the darling of American presidents. Its mainstay, the Continental, was by the 1970s obscenely bloated. Long after every other American marque had down-sized, Lincoln continued to offer "full-size" cars. By 1977, even Lincoln was offering an alternative with the luxury, compact Versailles, which did not do well. More successful were its big coupés such as the Mark VII and LSC, but overall Lincoln never matched the success of its main GM rival Cadillac.

MARCOS

■ MARCOS

The name Marcos was a composite of two illustrious characters in the world of specialist motoring, Jem Marsh and Frank Costin. The first model they created was an all-wooden sportscar, which was brilliant on the track (Jackie Stewart started off in one) but was so hideous that it acquired the nickname "ugly duckling".

Out of this unusual birth came the definitive Marcos in 1963, whose basic shape remains in production today. The

■ ABOVE *In the 1980s, Marcos's founder Jem Marsh began altering the basic coupé concept by, for example, introducing this convertible version.*

■ ABOVE *Enthusiasts respect the Marcos badge as one of the great British sportscar companies, with an impressive competition record and successful road-car range.*

■ ABOVE *It is an impressive fact that Marcos began producing this GT car in 1964, and it continues to be a popular new sportscar in its fourth decade.*

■ ABOVE *Aerodynamic and lightweight, all Marcos models were fast and furious, especially with the modifed Rover V-eight engines the company fitted from the mid-1980s.*

Adams brothers, Dennis and Peter, designed the new Marcos and, at its debut at the 1964 Racing Car Show, it stole the honours. A futuristic glassfibre body sat on the familiar Marcos wooden chassis.

The original intention had been to create an "all-new" car with its own tailor-made suspension, but financial constraints led to Triumph wishbones being used on the front, although a novel de Dion rear end with Triumph arms was

fitted. Even this, however, was later changed to a Ford live-axle set-up. Marcos cars used Ford, Volvo and Triumph engines.

Marcos's "pot-boiler" in the 1960s was the Mini-Marcos, a quite ugly little buzz-box whose main distinction lay in its being the only British car to finish the 1966 Le Mans 24-Hour Race. Powered by a Mini engine, it was cheap but crude and was still available new as late as 1994.

MARCOS GT (1964–)	
Engine	4/6/V-eight-cylinder
Capacity	1498–4999cc
Power	82–352bhp
Transmission	4/5-speed manual
Top speed	110–171mph (177–275kph)
No. built	Approx. 1,500 to date

■ RIGHT *There was no other car with a shape like that of the Marcos, which was at once muscular, individual and futuristic.*

■ ABOVE *Despite its extremely low profile, there was enough room to make the driver feel very comfortable. The seats were fixed and the pedals could move to fit the driver.*

Marcos underwent a temporary demise as a producer of cars in 1971. Marsh continued to provide servicing and parts for Marcos cars for ten more years, and then boldly relaunched the two-seater in 1981 with a variety of Ford engines. In a world starved of sportscars, the Marcos met with immediate success, especially when Marsh installed a Rover V-eight engine to create the Mantula in 1983. Even more attractive was the drop-top Spyder model of 1985. All Marcos models shared the same basic shape as the classic Adams-penned

1800 of 1963, though the profile evolved with wider wheel arches, spoilers and fatter wheels and tyres.

In 1992, a new chapter was written with the arrival of the fully built Mantara, a totally new car with different front suspension and a more radical interpretation of the classic body shape. The Mantara had the option of a Rover 4.5-litre engine, giving a top speed of 160mph (257kph) and a 0–60mph (0–96kph) time under five seconds.

Even more spectacular was the 1994 LM series, the letters of its name hinting

at Marcos's re-entry into the Le Mans racing arena. Two versions were offered, the LM500 with a 4.0-litre V-eight engine and the LM600 with a 5.0-litre engine and 320bhp, enough to reach a cool 169mph (272kph).

In 1996, Marcos turned to Ford of America for the Mantis which had a quoted top speed of over 170mph (274kph) and a 0–60mph (0–96kph) time of 4.1 seconds. Ford's quad-cam V-eight engine, with its 352bhp of power, was described as "adequate for a car that weighs 1050kg (2316lb)"!

■ ABOVE *As the years progressed, Marcos cars developed wild arches and aerodynamic aids. This is a 1993 Mantara.*

■ RIGHT *In 1996, Marcos switched from Rover to a Ford V-eight engine in its Mantis. With a top speed of 171mph (275kph), this was now a true supercar.*

MASERATI

■ MASERATI BITURBO

By the 1980s, the once-great name of Maserati was fading fast. Citroën had taken an interest in 1968 but sold out to De Tomaso in 1975, after which Maserati's model development stagnated and production dwindled. When a bold new model was launched in 1981, the intention was to boost Maserati production. The Biturbo certainly did that, but at the cost of permanently denting Maserati's reputation.

While the car had its faults, the main problem was that it didn't look or feel like a real Maserati. In style it was

a dead-ringer for the BMW 3 Series; but for its trident grille it looked utterly anonymous.

If the Biturbo had one strength, it was the performance delivered from the

twin-turbocharged multivalve V-six engine. Producing 180bhp initially, it was a very quick car if one had the patience to wait for the turbo-lag to disappear after the throttle was floored. The original 2.0-litre engine (really confected to exploit Italian tax rules) was expanded to 2.5 litres in 1983, and up to 2.8 litres in 1987, by which time power output had reached 224bhp.

Its price and badge made a quick killing for owners De Tomaso. In America especially, the Biturbo sold in very large numbers in the booming 80s. This was a quick route into sharp-suited Italian haute couture, especially in ostentatious open-top Spyder form.

Its oft-quoted shortcomings included evil handling, especially in the wet, cramped rear-seat accommodation and an interior of dubious taste, crowned as it was by a huge clock and acres of lush wood. Owners also found themselves stranded by unreliable engines and

■ ABOVE *The appeal of the Biturbo range was extended with the launch of a 425 four-door-saloon (sedan) version in 1983.*

■ LEFT *The maze of plumbing betrays the technology that gave the Biturbo its name: two turbochargers. They boosted out 180bhp but suffered from turbo lag.*

MASERATI BITURBO (1981–91)	
Engine	V-six cylinder
Capacity	1996–2790cc
Power	180–241bhp
Transmission	5-speed manual
Top speed	132–143mph (212–240kph)
No. built	Approx. 40,000

■ OPPOSITE *The world was plainly ready for a compact sports saloon with a Maserati badge, as the popularity of the Biturbo proved throughout the 1980s.*

■ BELOW *Later Biturbo models were badged 222, 224 (illustrated here) and 228. These were even more powerful than the early cars.*

■ ABOVE *Perhaps the most desirable of the Biturbo models was the fully convertible Spyder. It offered the same huge performance, open-topped fun and seating for four adults.*

distinctly cheesed off all round by rather poor craftsmanship.

Perhaps the redeeming feature of the Biturbo was that it put Maserati back on the map. It sold well enough to re-establish a fading name, and it did give rise to a bewildering profusion of follow-up models. These included a four-door version variously called the 420/425/430, a Spyder convertible, and the second-generation 2.22 and 2.24 (which lost the Biturbo label). Vastly superior were the stunningly fast Karif, Shamal and Ghibli of the 1990s, whose heritage was clearly traceable back to the first Biturbo but otherwise had almost nothing in common with it.

When Ferrari assumed overall control of Maserati in 1997, quality took a quantum leap in the right direction and the bad old days were forgotten. The Biturbo can be seen as the model that delivered Maserati safely into its new owner's hands.

■ ABOVE *Sumptuous leather and rich wood was a Maserati hallmark, and made the cabin feel very special. The dash was dominated by Maserati's trademark oval clock.*

■ RIGHT *The smart Italian clothing stood the Biturbo in good stead for many years, although some Maserati aficionados bemoaned a certain flash-in-the-pan flavour.*

MAZDA

■ MAZDA RX-7

Mazda will go down in history as the staunch defender of Wankel's rotary engine, and as the company which finally sorted its problems out. Long after pioneer NSU had bitten the dust, Mazda pursued the rotary ideal with a whole string of models, including saloons (sedans), coupés and sportscars.

Mazda had the courage to realize the inherent strengths of the rotary engine. The design was very compact and lightweight, it could run to extremely

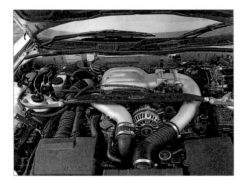

■ ABOVE *The heart of the RX-7 was its rotary engine. Long after other manufacturers had abandoned it as a poor idea, Mazda proved it was possible to make it a success.*

■ BELOW *The second-generation RX-7 was softer, more practical, less characterful and more comfortable, but still had rotary power.*

■ ABOVE *Mazda's RX-7 sportscar was highly respected in enthusiast circles. Its smart shape, speed, technology and character were sharply focused.*

■ LEFT *Although the raw performance of the first-generation RX-7 may not have been high-ranking, its cornering ability certainly was.*

high revs and was smoother than any other four-stroke engine. Its biggest fault was a propensity for drinking fuel.

The other original major concern was reliability. The engine depended on the integrity of the tips of the rotating triangle, which span around inside the combustion chamber. These tended to wear quickly and cause running difficulties. Modern technology finally addressed this problem (Mazda certainly had it cured during the life cycle of its RX-7) but by then the make's poor reputation was firmly established.

In later years, Mazda reserved the rotary engine for its range-topping coupés and sportscars. The RX-7 was an undoubted classic. For its day (it was launched in 1978), it was a unique blend of style and talent.

The centre of the magical RX-7 equation was the engine. Charismatic, sweet-running and powerful, there was nothing else like it. It may not have been overly fast, with a top speed of 120mph (193kph) and 0–60mph (0–96kph) in 8.6 seconds, but it was entertaining – except for a tendency to back-fire. When taken around bends there was little to fault the RX-7's

enthusiasm, and in character it was pure sportscar. If you wanted more performance you could take your RX-7 to a specialist like TWR, which offered a potent turbocharged conversion – and many customers did.

The RX-7's shark-nose coupé style was distinctive and, with the pop-up headlamps down, extremely clean.

Although it had a pair of rear seats, they were so small that this was essentially a two-seater. The first cars were quite starkly equipped, but gradually refinements like electric windows and a spoiler were introduced.

The second-generation RX-7 of 1986 was larger, heavier and softer, far less of a sportscar and more of a boulevard cruiser (especially in soft-top form, a body style never offered on the first RX-7). By 1992, the third-generation RX-7 had catapulted Mazda back into the sportscar league with a twin-turbo engine, an advanced and extremely attractive body structure and bristling performance.

Neither really duplicated the original purity of the first RX-7, which ranks as one of the most successful sportscars ever, with almost half a million of the first generation sold.

■ ABOVE *Japan had learned from Europe's best, and the latest RX-7's interior oozed class and purpose.*

■ BELOW *In 1992, the RX-7 evolved into a real supercar, with high performance now top of the agenda. 237bhp was very healthy for a car of its price.*

■ ABOVE *The more cosseting interior of the 1986-92 RX-7 reflected its move up-market.*

MAZDA RX-7 (1978–86)	
Engine	Twin-rotor Wankel
Capacity	2 × 573cc
Power	105–135bhp
Transmission	5-speed manual 3-speed auto
Top speed	113–125mph (182–201kph)
No. built	474,565

Mazda

MAZDA MX-5

In the 1980s, sportscars went completely out of fashion, not just passé but completely dead. All the great open sportscars were stamped on: MG, Triumph TR, Fiat Spider; only the Alfa Spider could be said to have kept the spark alight, and then only just. Against this background, Mazda made a courageous decision: it would single-handedly engineer the rebirth of the sportscar.

That 1989 decision was bold but it paid off handsomely. Other manufacturers may have decided that sportscars were no longer profitable, but the consumer had different ideas. The

■ ABOVE *Simple in style, the MX-5 exploited the rear-wheel-drive two-seater-roadster style abandoned by virtually every other major manufacturer.*

■ LEFT *The 1.8-litre engine was modest, perhaps, but just right for a car that was designed as an accessible small sportscar.*

■ LEFT *At speed the MX-5 impressed all who drove it. It was snappy, sharp around corners, responsive, yet refined.*

■ ABOVE *There were no frills in the instrument layout and choice of materials. The inspiration came from classic sportscars such as the MGB.*

world still wanted to drive sportscars, and Mazda got the confection absolutely right in its MX-5.

Here was a cheap two-seater open-topped car with a front-mounted engine and rear-wheel drive. To many onlookers this sounded rather like an MGB, an impression reinforced by the compact, curvaceous shape. Where the MX-5 excelled – and dispelled any criticism of plagiarism – was in its handling. Unlike the antiquated manners of the MGB, the

MX-5 was superbly modern: just the right degree of handling aplomb was engineered in for safety and fun.

This was a classic design in which everything was somehow right, from the evocative rear lights and front pop-ups to the simplicity of the specification and the enjoyment factor. Underneath it was brilliantly engineered, with engine, gearbox and final drive carried on a separate subframe, and double-wishbone suspension for crisp handling.

The interior was kept sparse in the best sporting traditions: little in the way of electronic gizmos and a great sense of quality and simplicity. The only criticisms were over-light power-steering and a lack of performance from the 1.6-litre engine.

In Japan, the car was launched as the Eunos Roadster, in Europe it was the Mazda MX-5 and in America it was the Miata. In each market, the model became a legend. Thanks to its very

■ LEFT *The world welcomed the Mazda MX-5 with open arms. Here was a car designed for pure enjoyment to a fabulous classic formula.*

reasonable price, it was accessible to many drivers and it sold in vast numbers. Admittedly, it had little competition, but there is no denying its essential brilliance. In any case, in many markets the MX-5 sold best in its later years when there was plenty of competition from the likes of the MGF, Fiat Barchetta and BMW Z3. The plain fact was that the little Mazda paved the way for everyone else: it really brought about the renaissance of the sportscar.

Very little changed during its career. The addition of safety features such as side-impact bars and airbags increased its weight, so the MX-5 got a 1.8-litre fuel-injected engine in 1993; a 1.6-litre model was kept going as a bargain entry-level model.

It took until 1997 for a replacement for the MX-5 to arrive, and it precisely duplicated the format of this ultra-successful car. By then the MX-5 had become the world's favourite sportscar, with a production tally over 400,000.

■ ABOVE *Two comfortable seats, an open roof and an open road – one very simple formula for success.*

■ LEFT *A big splash is the only way to describe the MX-5's impact. Within a few years, numerous manufacturers had launched their own junior sportscars on the back of the MX-5's success.*

MAZDA MX-5 (1989–97)	
Engine	4-cylinder
Capacity	1597–1840cc
Power	90–131bhp
Transmission	5-speed manual 4-speed auto
Top speed	108–122mph (174–196kph)
No. built	Over 400,000

■ BELOW *The McLaren F1 laid the strongest claim to be the world's ultimate car. Its provenance from a World Championship Formula 1 team was decisive.*

McLaren

■ McLaren F1

It's not every designer or engineer who has the chance to build the ultimate car, with absolutely no expense spared. Perhaps Bugatti did it with the extravagant Royale in the 1930s, but few in the industry could argue that Gordon Murray's McLaren F1 was anything but the ultimate road-going car.

A former chief Formula 1 designer at Brabham, then at Woking-based McLaren, Murray had a burning but unfulfilled passion to build a machine that qualified as the fastest, most involving road car yet made – and, of

course, the most expensive. Yet it would also have to be a car you could happily drive into town.

Ideas at McLaren began crystallizing during 1988, and in March 1989 Murray announced his plans to the public. Murray was in charge of design and development, while Lotus stylist Peter Stevens would pen the car's shape, and BMW's Motorsport division had agreed to design an all-new V-twelve engine from scratch. Everything revolved around Murray's ideal precepts, such as the innovative three-seater cabin with

■ ABOVE *The purchase of an F1 was reserved for the privileged few, since its price (£635,000 ($1,070,000)) was vastly higher than that of any other car ever made.*

■ ABOVE *Surrounding the specially designed BMW V-twelve 6.0-litre engine was a hand-finished film of pure gold, chosen for its heat-dissipating qualities.*

MCLAREN F1 (1993–97)	
Engine	V-twelve-cylinder
Capacity	6064cc
Power	609-627bhp @ 7400rpm
Transmission	6-speed
Top speed	231mph (372kph)
No. built	100

■ LEFT *The stunningly simple yet aggressive shape was designed by Peter Stevens. The bodywork was realized in exotic carbonfibre.*

■ **LEFT** *In dynamic terms the F1 had no peers: it was faster, more responsive, more refined and more rewarding in every way than any other car in the world.*

■ **ABOVE** *Project creator Gordon Murray insisted that there should be three seats, the central one occupied by the driver. The "arrowhead" formation proved practical.*

the driver sitting in the middle ahead of the two passengers.

Another crucial factor was the target weight: an unbelievable 2205lb (1000kg) (Ferrari's F40 weighed 2720lb (1235kg) and Jaguar's XJ220 weighed 3240lb (1470kg)). Every detail was under scrutiny to see if it could be made lighter.

With no less than 627bhp on tap from the 6064cc BMW V-twelve engine, the truly explosive performance which Murray had been aiming for became a reality. Ex-Formula 1 driver Jonathan Palmer flew to the Nardo test track in Italy in August 1993 and, in the searing heat, he drove the F1 at an incredible 231mph (372kph). Tests betrayed more amazing figures: 0–60mph (0–96kph) in 3.2 seconds, 0–100mph (0–161kph) in 6.3 seconds and 30–70mph

■ **ABOVE** *Every component on the F1 was designed especially for its role, from the wheels and tyres to the hi-fi system. Everything was engineered down to a weight.*

(48–113kph) in just over 2 seconds. Such incredible performance made the F1 almost invincible on the track: an F1 GTR came first in virtually every GT Endurance race it entered, and the F1 was triumphant at Le Mans in 1995.

Then there was the cost: no less than £635,000 ($1,070,000), reflecting the huge development budget, ultra-high

technology and the fact that, initially, each one took 6,000 man-hours to build. Then there were all the little touches that made the F1 so special, like the gold-insulated engine bay, the unbelievably complex sound system, total leeway for individual colour choice and tailored luggage. If you had car problems, McLaren would jet out a mechanic on the next available flight.

The first customer car was finished on Christmas Eve 1993, and the last one of a total of exactly 100 cars – far short of the initial target of 300 – was completed in 1997. There could hardly be a more exclusive car than this.

■ **ABOVE** *The high-tech gauges said it all: with a dial going up to 240mph (386kph) .*

■ **RIGHT** *The F1 LM was a limited-edition model painted in the racer and race-car constructor Bruce McLaren's racing orange and fitted with a rear spoiler, special wheels and modified bodywork.*

MERCEDES

■ MERCEDES-BENZ SL

SL has traditionally denoted Mercedes-Benz's sporting models, and the two letters were always taken to mean Sport and Leicht (lightweight). The first SL was the 1954 300SL Gullwing coupé, and the most popular were the "pagoda roof" models produced between 1963 and 1971.

When it came to replacing these classic SLs, Mercedes-Benz took an important step into its own future in 1972. Gone were the stacked headlamps of all

MERCEDES-BENZ SL (1989–)	
Engine	6/V-eight-/V-twelve-cylinder
Capacity	2799–5987cc
Power	190–389bhp
Transmission	5-speed manual 4/5-speed auto
Top speed	138–155mph (222–249kph)
No. built	Still in production

■ LEFT *In one of its ultimate W107 series guises, the 500SL seen here, the drop-top Merc had a fabulous 241bhp 5.0-litre V-eight engine*

previous Mercedes models, replaced by strong horizontal rectangular units (US models received a pair of round lamps) and wrap-around indicators, anticipating future themes on its saloons (sedans).

Viewed objectively, the so-called

■ RIGHT *With a lengthened wheelbase and a fixed roof, the SL transformed into the Grand Touring SLC four-seater, a strong contender in its day for the accolade of best car in the world.*

W107 SL was an absolute classic, which lasted in production for almost 20 years. It was quite a different car, expanded in every way over the "pagoda roof" SL and considerably improved in safety matters.

The new SL was initially powered by

Mercedes-Benz's 3.5-litre V-eight, or its even more powerful 4.5-litre V-eight. Modernized suspension featured a semi-trailing-arm rear-end, and there was standard power-steering, and a popular optional automatic gearbox. From 1974, the entry-level 280SL was launched in Continental Europe (but not in the UK or the US), sporting the twin-cam six-cylinder engine from the 280E.

The SL Series was revamped in 1980 as a new range of engines slotted in. The full list during the 1980s was: 280SL, 300SL, 380SL, 420SL, 500SL and 560SL. A second SL sub-species was the longer-wheelbase fixed-head SLC series produced from 1972, which were proper four-seaters and probably the best grand tourers made in the 1970s.

By the late 1980s, the SL had lost its sporting edge, and Mercedes-Benz aimed to address that problem with a brand-new SL series in 1989. The result was one of the best cars Mercedes-Benz ever produced. It looked wonderfully balanced, drove like a sportscar or a tourer, depending on your mood, and had all the qualities one would expect of a top-flight model from Stuttgart.

It was launched with a choice of two engines: the 300SL six-cylinder (offered in 190bhp standard and 231bhp twin-cam forms), and the deeply impressive 500SL V-eight. Naturally, there was a power-operated soft-top and a wind deflector to keep your hair style in order, and one extraordinary novelty was a hidden roll-over bar, which popped up when the car reached a certain angle,

■ ABOVE *The SL heritage stretches right back, through these five generations, to the celebrated 300SL of the 1950s.*

■ LEFT *In addition to a very effective electric folding roof, an important safety measure was a roll-over bar, which automatically popped up in case of an accident.*

■ BELOW *With an optional hardtop fitted, the SL became an attractive and snug coupé.*

telling an on-board computer that a serious accident was imminent. Another interesting option on the V-eight was its speed-sensitive suspension.

Mercedes-Benz's most expensive car arrived in 1992 in the V-twelve-powered 600SL. With its 48-valve 389bhp engine and automatic damping it was crushingly quick, yet still superbly refined. The ultimate version was the six-litre V-eight AMG-tweaked SL60 with body kit, 381bhp and huge 18in (45.7cm) wheels.

■ ABOVE LEFT *When it came to replacing the SL in 1989, Mercedes produced its best incarnation yet. Low-slung and elegant, it epitomized the luxury roadster form.*

■ RIGHT *Mercedes interiors are nearly always sober affairs, with solidity and logic given higher priority than design flair.*

MERCEDES

■ MERCEDES-BENZ SLK

In the parlance of Mercedes-Benz, "K" signals *"Kompakt"*, and indeed the SLK was a smaller breed of bargain-priced Mercedes SL sportscar, and the first junior Mercedes sportscar since the 190SL of the late 1950s. It was a perfect foil to the new Porsche Boxster and BMW Z3 roadster, selling to a new kind of customer for Mercedes: a telling statistic is that over half of those who ordered an SLK had never had a Mercedes before.

■ ABOVE *A brilliantly effective solid roof folded at the touch of a button under the boot (trunk) lid. The lid would then open the opposite way to permit luggage storage.*

■ BELOW *In its most sporting guise, the 230 Kompressor pictured here, the SLK was a very rapid sportscar, up to 143mph (230kph) being possible.*

■ ABOVE *Mercedes-Benz could hardly have produced a more desirable junior sportscar than the SLK, its first attempt at this growing market. With the top raised, it looked and felt like a proper coupé.*

To cut costs, the engine and driveline components were shared with the C Class saloons (sedans), the brakes came from the E Class, and seats were bought in from Recaro. The headlights were unique but moulded in plastic. Expensive magnesium structural components were used, but they saved space and enhanced safety.

The car's party trick was an exotic electric roof. In 25 seconds, the SLK's solid Vario roof arched into the air, folded itself in two and carefully stowed itself away in the boot (trunk) before a metal cover snapped shut. The sequence even wound the windows down for you. It worked just as well in reverse, transforming the SLK back into a draught-free coupé, and you didn't even have to clip the roof on to the windscreen edge. Mercedes promised that the electric motors and hydraulic rams were good for at least 20,000 repeat performances.

Inside, the car's cabin was highly styled with embracing bucket seats, and carbonfibre-look cladding on the dashboard and white back-lit dials sunk into chrome-edged portholes.

■ RIGHT *The entry-level model pictured here was the non-supercharged 200. Note the bonnet (hood) hump lines, reminiscent of the classic SL of the 1950s.*

This was a rear-drive car but, with anti-lock brakes and traction control, only the reckless could provoke the back of the SLK out of line. Its ride and roadholding balance were superbly fluid, and, as with all Mercedes automatics, you could flick the shift down for a faster getaway or change-down for a corner. With the 193bhp supercharged four-cylinder engine, the car's top speed was more than 140mph (225kph), with 0–60mph (0–96kph) in 7 seconds, while there was a cheaper non-supercharged model, too.

The SLK proved amazingly popular, with orders backed up until the end of the century: it seemed that Mercedes's biggest problem with the SLK was building enough of them.

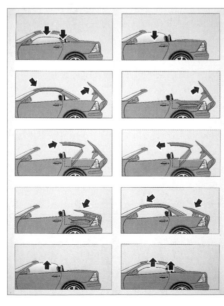

■ ABOVE *Detail of the ingenious electric hood (top) operation.*

■ ABOVE LEFT *The word Kompressor on the cylinder-head cover indicates the presence of a supercharger in the 2.3-litre engine, good enough for 193bhp.*

■ ABOVE RIGHT *Especially classy was the interior treatment, with carbonfibre-style overlay, white dials apparently hewn out of the dash and a classic Mercedes steering wheel.*

MERCEDES-BENZ SLK (1996–)	
Engine	4-cylinder
Capacity	1998–2295cc
Power	136–193bhp
Transmission	5-speed manual or auto
Top speed	126–143mph (203–230kph)
No. built	Still in production

MG

■ MG RV8

MG is without doubt one of the great sportscar names. Sadly, however, that name was squandered by British Leyland, its parent company in the 1970s, and its once-great sportscar line was left to wither on the vine until the compromised, outdated MGB shuddered out of existence in 1980.

Although the MG badge survived on performance versions of some Austin cars, this seemed to be the end for the MG sportscar. MG enthusiasts never forgot the "B", however, and a huge industry quickly grew up around

■ LEFT *Thirty years after the MGB's birth, Rover revived its seminal sportscar and gave it a thorough revamp and a V-eight engine to create the MG RV8.*

■ BELOW *The gadget-laden RV8 interior, rife with gauges, was a much more cosseting location than the stark old MGB.*

■ LEFT *No MGB-manufactured roadster had ever had a V-eight engine. The 1990s version was engineered to accept Rover's 3.9-litre Range Rover unit which developed 190bhp.*

■ ABOVE *After more than a decade in a wilderness devoid of sports models, the MG badge was revived to the cheers of enthusiasts.*

restoring this enduring classic. Even Austin-Rover got involved in 1989 when its Heritage division went into production with brand-new replacement MGB bodyshells.

The Rover Group realized that the MG badge still had tremendous potential, and it set about a relaunch of the brand. Its main aim was to produce an all-new mid-engined car (which became the MGF), but almost as an appetizer it decided to produce a radically updated MGB for the 30th

anniversary of its birth. Not only would it look different, it would have an engine that the drop-top "B" had never had – the venerable Rover V-eight – and would come with the name MG RV8.

The idea came about because its Heritage division had the capacity to make a respectable number of bodyshells (about 15 per week). Although the new design was much modified, many of the original pressings were unaltered, so it made sense logistically to do this.

■ BELOW *Always exclusive, the MG RV8 found many homes in export markets such as Japan.*

■ RIGHT *Typically British in every way, the interior reeked of walnut capping, rich leather and chrome detailing.*

Rover stylists set about beefing up the old "B". The bonnet (hood), boot lid (trunk) and doors were kept the same but the rest of the bodywork was retouched, notably having wider wheel-arches, new bumpers, faired-in headlamps and skirts. Its more purposeful look was boosted by very smart spoked alloy wheels and wide tyres.

The basics of the mechanical package remained rather antique, including a live rear axle suspended on leaf springs. Rover's team tried to improve handling by widening the track and fitting Koni dampers, but there was no escaping the age of the design.

The best news was the installation of Rover's aluminium 3.9-litre V-eight engine, not only decently powerful but boasting a huge spread of torque. A claimed 0–60mph (0–96kph) figure of six seconds was backed up by a top speed of 135mph (217kph).

The interior was classically British: walnut veneer for the dashboard and door cappings, chromed door handles, lots of leather trim and a plethora of small gauges. The lack of such modern-day gadgets as electric windows and mirrors and power-steering merely

seemed to add to the olde worlde aura.

Its launch price of just over £25,000 ($42,000) looked good, and immediately there was a long queue of customers. Admittedly, since the RV8 was hardly at the cutting edge of sportscar technology, the main appeal was nostalgia and the fact that production would be very limited, but the RV8 was always in demand right up until its demise in 1996.

MG RV8 (1992–96)	
Engine	V-eight-cylinder
Capacity	3946cc
Power	190bhp @ 4750rpm
Transmission	5-speed
Top speed	135mph (217kph)
No. built	n/a

■ BELOW *It may have shown its age in action, but there was no denying that the RV8 had strong performance and great presence.*

MG

◼ MGF

Those who thought that the MG sportscar was dead eventually got the news they had been hoping for: the MG RV8 retro sportscar would be a precursor to an all-new, thoroughly modern MG. This would be a car as the MGB would have evolved, not a throwback to an antique age. For sure, all the qualities which made an MG special would be carefully dialled into the design equation, but this was meant to be a cutting-edge, affordable sportscar for the 1990s.

When it was launched at the 1995 Geneva Motor Show, the new MGF did not disappoint the crowds. Parent company Rover decided to opt for a centrally mounted engine because it gave the best handling potential, and in

that respect the MGF was triumphant. Every tester returned with stories of tenacious grip, fluid cornering and an impressively stiff bodyshell.

The shape was tailored to appeal. Unambiguously modern, it took the theme of the MG grille and extrapolated a smooth, purposeful profile. Some thought it perhaps too anodyne, too close to the Japanese school of design, but no one questioned its effectiveness.

Inside, the traditional MG cues were

more abundant but still not over-embellished. Even the moulded MG badges were restrained. The general feel was very classy, with white dials, leather steering wheel and attractive trim.

For its power, the MGF drew on the acclaimed K-series engine in 1.8-litre form. Two versions were offered: the 120bhp 1.8i and the powerful 145bhp 1.8i VVC, which could reach 60mph (96kph) from rest in just seven seconds thanks to its Variable Valve Control

◼ LEFT *In 1997, a heavily modified MGF called the EXF was driven at the Bonneville salt flats in America to a top speed of 217mph (349kph) – the fastest MG ever.*

◼ ABOVE *With the VVC engine, the MGF was capable of 0–60mph (0–96kph) in seven seconds and a top speed of 130mph (209kph).*

MGF (1995–)	
Engine	4-cylinder
Capacity	1795cc
Power	120–145bhp
Transmission	5-speed manual
Top speed	120–130mph (193–209kph)
No. built	Still in production

◼ LEFT *Sportscar enthusiasts around the world applauded the official rebirth of the MG sportscar when the MGF was launched.*

■ OPPOSITE *In 1.8i VVC form, the MGF was equipped with special five-spoke alloy wheels, power-steering, ABS and – most importantly – a more powerful 145bhp engine. An optional hardtop was available.*

■ BELOW *The cockpit of the MGF was very sporting (white gauges, sports steering wheel, attractive upholstery) and was applauded for not overdoing the number of MG badges.*

engine mapping. The VVC also added standard power-steering, anti-lock brakes and unique alloy wheels.

A waiting-list immediately sprang up for the MG in Europe and Japan, with most buyers wanting the VVC version. The average age of an MGF buyer was over 50, but this came down as the model grew in acceptance.

■ ABOVE *The MGF may have looked back to the MGB for its grille, but there the similarity ended. The mid-engined layout was thoroughly modern and delivered one of the best driving experiences around.*

OTHER MAKES

■ MATRA

With a background in aerospace and weapons, Marcel Chassagny's Mécanique Aviation Traction (or Matra) also became a car-maker when, in 1964, it took over René Bonnet's sportscar operation. The bizarre 530 followed the Djet in 1967 and, in 1970, Chrysler-Simca took the firm over. The 1973 three-seats-abreast Bagheera used a Simca engine. After the post-Peugeot take-over, another name change in 1979 to Talbot-Matra coincided with the launch of the Murena coupé and Rancho estate. Renault acquired Matra in the 1980s and inherited an MPV (minivan) prototype that Matra had developed (the Espace, which Matra manufactured).

■ MERCURY

Mercury was born in 1939 as a species of Ford that slotted in below Lincoln. Its 1970s offerings mirrored Ford's, the highlights being the Cougar and Marquis coupés and the Capri (initially a German Ford import, later a clone of the Mustang II). In the 1980s, Mercury's success was bolstered by solid mid-range virtues and the occasional character car like the Capri convertible.

■ MINI

Alec Issigonis's masterstroke Mini started off life in 1959 with Austin and Morris badging. After ten years in production, the Mini was launched as a marque in its own right under British Leyland. The legendary Mini-Cooper was launched in 1961 and production ended in 1971. Mini became Britain's best-selling marque in the 1970s (over five million made). Packaging included larger wheels in 1984, a Cooper relaunch in 1990, 1275cc engine only from 1992 and fuel injection from 1996. The Mini brand was relaunched in 1996 as a prelude to an all-new, 21st-century Mini.

■ MITSUBISHI

Japan's Number Three marque has always been very conservative and sold better in the domestic market than abroad (where it was called Colt for many years). The most interesting Mitsubishis were the 1970–6 Galant GTO coupé (a Japanese Mustang), the 1976–85 Sapporo, the 1982–90 Starion and the Car of the Year award-winning 1994 FTO coupé. Mitsubishi also pioneered direct petrol injection technology and established a European co-venture with Volvo in Holland.

■ MORGAN

Morgan is a unique company. It alone continues to make a car that looks and behaves exactly the same as it did 50 years ago: separate chassis, sliding pillar suspension, ash frame and hand-made bodywork. H.F.S. Morgan started production of three-wheelers in 1910 at Malvern, England, and this was continued by his son Peter and grandson Charles. Four-wheelers were made from 1936. The best Morgan was the Rover V-eight-engined Plus 8, made from 1968. Morgan has always thrived: there is a long waiting-list for all of the 450 cars it can produce per year – still in the factory where the cars have been made for over 75 years.

■ MORRIS

In 1912, William Morris (later Lord Nuffield), started building cars in Cowley, Oxford, and Morris Motors became one of the Britain's biggest companies. It grew up to become the Nuffield empire, incorporating names such as MG, Riley and Wolseley. In 1952, the group united with Austin to form the British Motor Corporation, then Europe's biggest car concern. By the 1970s, Morris was earmarked as the conventionally engineered badge. The last Morris was the lack-lustre Ital, which died in 1984.

NISSAN

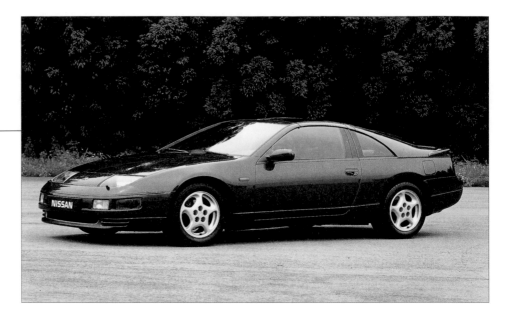

■ NISSAN 300ZX

Nissan's Z series sportscars date back to the classic Goertz-styled 240Z coupé, one of the world's most successful sportscars. By the 1980s, however, the original ideals of light weight, sharp styling and quick responses had been lost in the bloated, suburban ZX of 1984–9, which was obviously meant for posing rather than driving.

That whole dead end was smashed through with the stunning new 300ZX of 1990. *Autocar* magazine called it "Japan's first-ever supercar" after it recorded a top speed of 155mph (250kph) and a 0–60mph (0–96kph) time of just 5.6 seconds. That was

■ ABOVE *The cabin could have been mistaken for that of a prestige European sportscar. The two-plus-two seating arrangement was, however, rather cramped.*

courtesy of a 300bhp twin-turbocharged three-litre engine with variable-valve timing sited up front and driving the rear wheels.

Even more impressive was the suspension, a complex multi-link set-up with HICAS four-wheel steering which automatically adapted itself to the driver's style. This enhanced turn-in, improved grip and stability and helped provide magnificently neutral cornering, although caution was required in very wet weather.

The interior looked and felt better than most Japanese cars, although it was rather cramped. Lift the T-bar roof off, however, and you had a feeling of open-air motoring.

Like the styling, the character of the 300ZX was up front, and customers appreciated its fine value for money and

■ ABOVE *Japan's first supercar was an accurate assessment of Nissan's bold new 300ZX of 1989.*

rewarding attributes. In America a convertible version won even more friends, but in Britain the 300ZX was suddenly dropped in 1994 after falling foul of emissions legislation. Elsewhere it continued for another two years.

NISSAN 300ZX (1989–1996)	
Engine	V-six-cylinder
Capacity	2560cc
Power	300bhp @ 6400rpm
Transmission	5-speed manual 4-speed auto
Top speed	155mph (250kph)
No. built	Not known

■ FAR LEFT *An attractive fully convertible 300ZX was sold in certain markets such as the USA. This model was selected as the PPG circuit Pace Car in America.*

■ LEFT *The twin-turbocharged 3.0 litre V-six engine developed 300bhp. This was a very sophisticated unit boasting variable valve timing.*

■ RIGHT *The normal Skyline was a saloon (sedan) car from the middle of Nissan's range, but the GT-R with its spoilers and skirts was a technological firecracker of a fast car.*

■ NISSAN SKYLINE GT-R

Skyline is a badge which Nissan has used since 1955, more recently denoting its more sporty upper-medium saloon (sedan) range. Everything changed in the 1989 eighth-generation Skyline, however, for a brand-new model joined the line-up: the legendary GT-R.

With its deep front air dam, wide wheel-arches and tall rear spoiler, this two-door saloon (sedan) looked as if it would go fast. The 2.6-litre twin turbo six-cylinder engine made sure that it did, all 280bhp of it ensuring sizzling performance, such as 0–60mph (0–96kph) in five seconds and a top speed of 153mph (246kph).

That was just the start of the GT-R's wizardry. It also boasted four-wheel drive with sensors on each wheel to control the split of torque front-to-rear, plus active suspension and four-wheel steering, which adjusted the angle of the

NISSAN SKYLINE GT-R (1989–)

Engine	6-cylinder
Capacity	2569cc
Power	280bhp @ 6800rpm
Transmission	5-speed manual
Top speed	153mph (246kph)
No. built	Still in production

rear wheels according to the pressure being exerted on them. The result was that the GT-R pulled through corners amazingly quickly and safely while the excitement of piloting it was undiminished. It's little wonder that a GT-R recorded the fastest time ever for any road-going car around the legendary Nürburgring circuit in Germany.

In 1994, the next generation GT-R arrived, looking smoother and more rounded but with no loss of character. Initially sold only in Japan and Australia, it became a UK market debutante in 1997 with a price tag of £50,000 ($84,000).

■ LEFT *If 280bhp was too little for you, the GT-R provided the ideal basis for extreme tuning for road and track. Power outputs were known to go as high as 1200bhp.*

■ LEFT *A GT-R famously recorded the fastest time ever for a production car around the Nürburgring in Germany: it was the only such car to go round in under eight minutes.*

OTHER MAKES

■ OLDSMOBILE

Born in 1897, Oldsmobile is America's oldest name-plate and part of the General Motors combine. By 1975 it was a middle-class luxury leader with a conservative slant, although models like the Starfire coupé and front-wheel-drive Toronado were more adventurous. Gradually, most of Oldsmobile's own model range declined into badge engineering, but unique cars such as the Cutlass and Aurora kept the flame burning.

■ OPEL

Opel has been General Motors' German wing since 1929. It relied on volume sales of medium-class cars like the Olympia, Rekord and Kapitän before moving into the small car arena with the 1962 Kadett. In the 1970s, Opel's strength lay in producing good-looking cars such as the Manta, GT and Commodore, while the 1973 Kadett was a true world car. British Vauxhall and German Opel products converged so that, by the 1980s, the differences were in the grilles and wheel-trims only.

PANTHER

■ PANTHER

Panther is one of the most unusual companies in motoring history. In the 1970s, it became one of the most spectacularly successful British specialist manufacturers with a startlingly wide range of products.

Founded by Robert Jankel in 1972, Panther Westwinds started life with pastiches of bygone classics. The J72 was the first, a copy of the pre-war SS100 using Jaguar engines. The hand-built J72 sold to the rich and famous, including the film star Liz Taylor, for it certainly wasn't cheap, retailing at almost twice the price of an E-Type Jaguar.

Its next car was the 1974 De Ville, a creation of unrestrained opulence, with vaguely Bugatti Royale lines and superb craftsmanship. Mechanically, the De Ville was all Jaguar XJ12, including its suspension. In 1976, came the two-door De Ville Convertible, famous for being the most expensive car on British price lists – and the motorcar star of the film *101 Dalmatians*.

The concept behind Panther's 1975 Rio was quite sound: to create a small, economical car with the finish and luxury of a Rolls-Royce. In the troubled fuel crisis days of 1975, it looked

■ ABOVE *This is the interior of the J72, a feast of walnut and leather in the best neo-classic traditions.*

promising but suffered from comparisons with the car on which it was based, the Triumph Dolomite, which cost a third of the price. In commercial terms, the Rio was a complete flop and perhaps deserved a better fate.

■ ABOVE *Panther Westwinds made its living producing hand-built pastiches of a bygone era of motoring. The Kallista vaguely recalled the 1930s.*

■ ABOVE *Acres of chrome dazzled for effect on the nose of the De Ville. The hand-crafted coachbuilder's art was fostered at Panther.*

Not so the Lima, Panther's "car for the masses", which sold very well. The recipe was simple: a 1930s-style two-seater open glassfibre body on a strengthened Vauxhall Magnum floorpan, including the Magnum's engine, gearbox, suspension, steering and brakes.

Its successor was the 1982 Kallista. This used all-Ford components, including Cortina double-wishbone front suspension and a Capri live rear axle, and the revised bodywork was aluminium. It was not particularly quick, but was more roomy, more refined and better-handling than the Lima. It sold very healthily.

Apart from the incredible six-wheeled

■ LEFT *Panther's most extravagant car was the De Ville, a huge Bugatti-inspired device using Jaguar parts. In the film 101 Dalmatians it was the ideal choice for Cruella de Ville.*

mid-engined Panther 6, Panther's last model was the 1990 Solo, a monocoque aluminium-and-carbon-fibre 2+2 supercar fitted with Ford's Sierra Cosworth 2.0-litre turbo engine and Ferguson four-wheel drive, making it the world's first mid-engined four-wheel-drive production car. Some described it as the best-handling road car of all time, but its disappointing performance, harsh ride and questionable build quality were unforgivable in a £40,000 ($67,000) sportscar. Even at that price, it was uneconomic to make. After one of the shortest production runs ever, the Solo was axed with just 12 cars sold.

In 1987 Panther had been acquired by the Korean firm SsangYong, which wound production down and used Panther expertise to design new SsangYong products. In retrospect, Panthers are often regarded as vulgar and unseemly jewellery, but they were all hand-built to the highest quality.

■ ABOVE LEFT *Most road testers were agreed that the Solo was an exquisite car to drive: very fast and extremely good around corners.*

■ ABOVE *The small Kallista was Panther's car for the common man, and easily its best-selling model. It used Ford engines.*

■ LEFT *Mid-engined finesse from the 1990 Solo, a striking coupé with such advanced features as four-wheel drive, aluminium and carbonfibre bodywork and Cosworth turbo power.*

■ RIGHT *The Solo was a sad exit for Panther, who lost money on every example built. It remains extremely rare, since only 12 were sold.*

■ LEFT *Six wheels on my wagon. Only Panther could have come up with such an outlandish creation. Its mid-mounted turbocharged Cadillac V-eight was claimed to push this leviathan to 200mph (322kph).*

PANTHER LIMA (1976–82)	
Engine	4-cylinder
Capacity	2279cc
Power	108bhp @ 5000rpm
Transmission	4-speed manual 3-speed auto
Top speed	105mph (169kph)
No. built	918

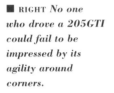

PEUGEOT

■ PEUGEOT 205GTI

The Volkswagen Golf may have started the hot-hatch craze in the 1970s, but it was Peugeot that made the best of the breed in the 80s. Its 205GTI became a performance car legend, for it stood head-and-shoulders above the competition, right up until its death.

It started from a wonderful basis: the Pininfarina-designed 205 was a very competent little hatchback. Its combination of a pleasing shape, supple ride and outstanding handling made it one of the most popular cars of its time – and it was still in production after 14 years. However, it cried out to have more power, and so the GTI was born in 1984.

Crisp, agile and offering more grip around corners than anyone had a right to expect from a car costing so little, the 205GTI was an instant hit.

Perhaps the power output of the first 1.6-litre engine was too low: 105bhp was less than rivals such as the Opel Astra GT/E and VW Golf GTI. Peugeot offered a Sport kit to boost power by 20bhp, but plainly the standard GTI needed to keep pace, and within two years Peugeot had upped the output of the 1.6-litre engine to 115bhp, and at the same time an even more powerful 130bhp 1.9-litre model was added. This larger engined version with its bigger alloy wheels proved to be the definitive GTI.

Inside, rally-style seats hugged the passengers and a tasteful arrangement of black, red and grey upholstery was standard. Instrumentation was complete and equipment generous. There wasn't much to criticize. The hard suspension gave an uncomfortable ride but this improved with successive tweaks. Build quality was a consistent problem, too, but probably the worst foible was on-the-limit handling. Although it took a lot to get a 205GTI out of shape around corners, when you did (by lifting off the throttle in mid-corner for instance), it was all rather a handful.

Another GTI variant was the 1986 CTI, the convertible version, which was partly built by Pininfarina. Most were made with 1.6-litre 115bhp engines, but eventually Peugeot succumbed and fitted the 130bhp 1.9 unit for another cracking car.

■ RIGHT *No one who drove a 205GTI could fail to be impressed by its agility around corners.*

■ BELOW *The 205GTI sired the very special Turbo 16 mid-engined road/rally car. It arrived shortly before the Group B rally class was axed.*

■ OPPOSITE *Compact, nimble, very grippy and entertainingly fast, the Peugeot 205GTI redefined the parameters of the hot hatch in the 1980s.*

■ LEFT *With the arrival of the 1.9-litre 205GTI (identifiable by its larger alloy wheels and 1.9 badging), power rose to 130bhp and the 205GTI stepped up another rung in the performance league.*

When the 205GTI retired in 1994, there was no direct successor. The 306 was a much larger car, which, initially at least, had none of the GTI's performance and agility. Eventually, hot versions of the 306 and smaller 106 came along to fill the gap: the 306 S16 and GTi-6 were stormingly powerful hot hatches in the best traditions, while the 106GTI was possibly the most entertaining performance hatchback being made when it arrived in 1997.

By this stage, however, the heyday of the GTI had already passed. And in the 1980s, when it really was all the rage, the little Peugeot 205GTI was undoubtedly king of the breed.

■ LEFT *Like the hatchback, Pininfarina designed the attractive CTI convertible, but here it also helped to manufacture it.*

■ BELOW *Top down, the CTI could be happily described as a 1980s equivalent of a sports roadster.*

PEUGEOT 205GTI (1984–94)	
Engine	4-cylinder
Capacity	1580–1905cc
Power	105–130bhp
Transmission	5-speed manual
Top speed	115–123mph (185–198kph)
No. built	Over 4 million 205s

■ RIGHT *Simple yet stylish, the GTI's interior was a feast of sporty details. The red/black/grey colour scheme was effective.*

PLYMOUTH

■ PLYMOUTH PROWLER

Having paved the way with the extraordinary Viper, Chrysler's management (headed by Bob Lutz) felt bullish enough to take its dream-car-to-production route one step further. The Plymouth Prowler was a rare example of a genuine show car reaching the public.

It all started with Tom Gale, the head of Chrysler's design team, who had always harboured a passion for hot rods.

■ LEFT *This is the sort of car you'd want to step aside for if you saw it bearing down on you.*

the Prowler on the market. Its rod style was neat, melding classic themes such as separate fenders, jut-forward chin and a lack of spurious adornments with modern materials and a technological spin around the edges. Underpinning it all were massive 20in (50cm) rear wheels and fat 295-section rubber, alongside which the still-large 17in (43cm) front wheels looked dwarfed. There was no room for two spare wheels, so the rear ones had a run-flat capability. The sophisticated suspension was elegantly exposed to view. Cockpit space was generous, although the boot (trunk) was completely taken up by the folding roof when it was down.

He penned a modern interpretation of the classic "bucket-rod" theme and put it on Chrysler's stand at the 1993 Detroit Auto Show. The reaction to it was so positive that Chrysler's board ordered a feasibility study and gave it the green light for production with a budget of $75 million – peanuts in Detroit terms.

Chrysler's theory was that hot rods were ingrained in the American subconscious and lots of people actually wanted to own one but never had the time or inclination to build their own. Step in the Plymouth Prowler, ready-made in Detroit for such an audience.

There was nothing else remotely like

■ ABOVE *Chrysler's Plymouth division went out on a limb to produce its Prowler, born of designer Tom Gale's passion for hot rods.*

■ RIGHT *The cabin was a mix of modern and classic hot-rod themes. Note the bold scalloped instruments.*

■ LEFT *The styling themes were all pure American hot rod, with a dash of modern spice to give it a marketing shine. Only 3,000 were to be made in the first year.*

■ ABOVE *Hot-rod fans might have been disappointed by the fitment of a V-six engine rather than a V-eight, but in truth it was quick enough for most tastes.*

In construction the Prowler was formed of steel and aluminium panels over a steel frame. Despite its radical looks, it complied with US safety laws, which necessitated such features as big front and rear bumpers and a high-level stop light.

Hot-rod fans were mildly miffed when, instead of a true blue American V-eight engine, Chrysler decided to fit its Vision 3.5-litre V-six instead. Still, with its 218bhp it was more than fast enough to satisfy most tastes: since it weighed only 1315kg (2900lb), 0–60mph (0–96kph) came in an

impressive 7.7 seconds, and top speed – limited by poor aerodynamics – was 125mph (200kph).

Chrysler showed the series-form Prowler at the 1996 Detroit show, and production was due to begin for the 1998 model year. All 3000 of the first year's production were to be painted the same colour – purple! If nothing else, the Prowler raised dowdy Plymouth's profile. By tapping into a national passion for hot-rodding, Plymouth had cleverly earned itself a whole set of values that no amount of advertising could ever have created.

PLYMOUTH PROWLER (1997–)	
Engine	V-six-cylinder
Capacity	3523cc
Power	218bhp @ 5850rpm
Transmission	4-speed automatic
Top speed	125mph (200kph)
No. built	Still in production

■ ABOVE *The chiselled jaw and narrow grille were genuine hot-rod throwbacks, although the "dodgem" bumpers were a concession to current safety laws.*

■ LEFT *If you went out on the prowl, the original Plymouth show car featured this natty trailer for your effects.*

PONTIAC

■ PONTIAC FIREBIRD

The first-generation Pontiac Firebird
was sired by Chevrolet's Camaro,
arriving some six months after it, and
differing only in terms of trim, engine
choices and the traditional Pontiac split-
grille treatment of its nasal styling. It was
restyled below the waist for 1969 and
given a dose of safety equipment, while
convertible versions were also listed.

The most classic of the early Firebirds
was the 1969 Trans Am. It took its name
from the Trans-American road-race
series organized by the Sports Car Club
of America, and began a whole dynasty
of Firebirds with this name. Its special
white-and-blue stripes paintwork, rear
spoiler, beefed-up chassis and
335–345bhp Ram Air power made it
distinctive and much better on the
tarmac than standard Firebirds.

An all-new Firebird arrived as a mid-
1970 model with a distinctive style that
lasted through 1981, minor restyles
occurring for 1974, 1977 and 1979.
Again there was a high-performance

■ LEFT *This is where
the Firebird story
first began: a sister
model to the
Chevrolet Camaro
with a traditional
Pontiac split-
grille nose.*

Trans Am model, which was a highly
marginal seller to start with (only 2116
sales in 1971), but became the most
popular Firebird of all by the end of the
decade (more than 93,000 were sold in
1978). There were also standard, luxury
Esprit and Formula models.

The Firebird almost died in 1972
when General Motors began asking
serious questions about the future of the
performance-car market. Luckily it was
decided to keep it going and the

PONTIAC FIREBIRD (1971–81)	
Engine	6-/V-six/V-eight-cylinder
Capacity	3785–7456cc
Power	105–345bhp
Transmission	4-speed auto 5-speed manual
Top speed	96–125mph (154–201kph)
No. built	1,061,719

■ LEFT *There was no mistaking
the snout of the second-
generation Firebird. This is a
1972 Trans Am, the high-
performance model of the range.*

■ ABOVE *The 1974 Firebird was
restyled with Federal laws in
mind. The car pictured is a Trans
Am 455 Super Duty.*

■ ABOVE *Towards the end of its life, the second-generation Firebird sprouted decoration (as this 1980 Trans Am shows) but lost power.*

■ ABOVE *The third-generation Firebird series arrived in 1982. This is a line-up from 1987, when the 5.7 litre V-eight reappeared.*

■ LEFT *The Trans Am name-plate continued to denote the top-of-the-range performance version.*

Firebird did extremely well for GM.

Power dropped steadily through the 1970s due to increasingly strict US government emission controls. Still, the Firebird never succumbed to pressure to lose its optional V-eight power, and a turbocharged 301 cubic inch (4936 cubic centimetre) version added a bit of spice for the 1980 model year.

For the third-generation, 1982 Firebird, again the basic bodywork was shared with Chevrolet's Camaro, but Pontiac stylists designed a distinctive chiselled, cowled-headlamp nose for the 'Bird. Base, S/E and Trans Am models were listed, while a return to the big 350 cubic inch (5740 cubic centimetre) V-eight arrived for 1987, also powering a top-level model called the GTA with

its distinctive spoiler and skirts. With 245bhp in its most powerful guise, the Firebird could manage 0–60mph (0–96kph) in just 5.4 seconds.

Falling sales and a lack-lustre image in the face of ever-improving imported competition characterized the final years of this long-running design. It was not

finally replaced until 1993, when the latest Firebird was unveiled (again closely based on the new Chevy Camaro but featuring a sharp, eagle-like nose, which varied slightly according to model). Initially available only as a coupé, an attractive-looking full convertible was added in 1994.

■ ABOVE *Quintessentially American, the Firebird (seen here in Trans Am guise) offered coupé style and V-eight power for a bargain price.*

■ ABOVE *This is a 1991 Firebird GTA. Two years later the series was replaced by a new fourth-generation Firebird.*

PORSCHE

■ PORSCHE 911

Today's Porsche 911 shares only a few nuts and bolts with the original edition of 1963, yet few modern classics have such a strong hereditary line and identity. The original Porsche 911 was to have been called the 901 until Peugeot reminded Porsche that it had the copyright on all model numbers with "01" in them, and so the magical formula was born.

Styled by Ferry Porsche's eldest son Butzi, it is still recognizable today, although spoilers and fat arches altered its elegant profile throughout the 1970s. The development potential of the flat-six engine, with one of the most distinctive growling engine notes on the road, seems

■ LEFT *When Porsche launched a convertible version of the 911, it became instantly popular. This is a Carrera Cabriolet.*

■ BELOW *Porsche brought turbocharging into the modern age. Its 911 Turbo was a hugely powerful supercar, easily the fastest-accelerating production car of its day.*

limitless: it grew from just 2.0 litres to 3.6 litres in the latest versions, while power leapt fom 125bhp to 408bhp in the latest Turbo – leaving aside the 450bhp of the 911-based 959.

For drivers, the best of the "classic" 911 bunch was the 2.7 RS Carrera of the 1970s, a lightweight homologation special with stiffer suspension and a hallmark duck-tail spoiler. There have been some surprisingly mild variants, too, such as the Sportomatic with its semi-auto clutchless gear-shift and the 912, a budget model using the four-cylinder engine of the old 356.

Tail-happy handling has always been part of the 911's mystique, but much of that was cured early on when the wheelbase was lengthened. For modern 911 owners, talk of "lift-off (trailing-throttle) oversteer" is largely bar-room bravado. In any case, for those who harboured serious doubts about the handling, in the 1990s Porsche offered a four-wheel-drive model called the Carrera 4. More to the point was the car's superb steering and progressive,

powerful brakes, which gave the driver such vivid road-feel.

Those who get hooked on the 911 rarely go back to other cars. The legends about build quality and reliability are all true, and longevity is another strong suit since all 911s have been built out of non-rusting galvanized steel since the mid-70s. The 911 image has changed over the years though: for the buyer of the 60s and 70s, the 911 was the choice of the seasoned connoisseur; by the mid-80s it had become a yuppie icon, a rolling symbol of fast, flash cash. For some, including Porsche, this image has lingered a little too long.

The Porsche 911 is an abiding legend

■ ABOVE *The characteristic whale-tail rear spoiler of the Turbo found its way on to most versions of the 911 during the 1980s.*

■ RIGHT *Oversteer was always part of the 911 mystique, although the limits of its roadholding were always very high up the scale.*

that has defied all attempts at replacing it. By rights it should have been killed off by the 928 in the mid-70s but somehow sales never slackened off: the worthy but uncharismatic 928 had none of the 911's enduring appeal and Porsche has no plans to do away with its classic rear-engined coupé. After all, it has been the company's meal ticket through some tough times. In 1997 the 911 was replaced by an all-new flat-six-engined coupé with water-cooling. The name? 911. . .

PORSCHE 911 (1963–)	
Engine	6-cylinder
Capacity	1991–3600cc
Power	125–408bhp
Transmission	4/5/6-speed manual semi-auto
Top speed	130–183mph (209–294kph)
No. built	Approx. 430,000 (to date)

■ LEFT *Porsche introduced a four-wheel-drive system in the Carrera 4 in 1989 for sure-footed handling. Note how far behind the rear axle the six-cylinder engine is.*

■ ABOVE *The 911 evolved through several incarnations. This is a Carrera RS model, a stripped-out version with a 260bhp version of the classic flat-six engine.*

PORSCHE

■ PORSCHE 928

The whole of Porsche's glowing reputation was based on a format that it had used since 1948, namely a rear-mounted engine. The 924 of 1975 was its first-ever front-engined car but, since this was an Audi cast-off, it is fair to say that the 928 was the first car conceived by the Porsche team to have a front engine.

The 928 was always intended as a range-topping supercar, but secretly Porsche hoped it would prove to be a natural successor to the rear-engined 911. In the end, of course, it never did displace its more sporting sibling, and the 911 remained the seminal Porsche. In truth, the 928's main success was in attracting a new class of buyer to the Porsche brand, someone who might otherwise have elected to buy a Mercedes SLC or Jaguar XJS, for this was more of a grand tourer than an outright sportscar.

Porsche built an all-new 4.5-litre V-eight for the 928, which was fabulously

■ ABOVE *The flop-forward headlamps and highly rounded styling of the 928 met with some controversy.*

■ ABOVE *The wrap-around facia gave the impression of completely cosseting the driver. The standard of finish and level of luxury were of a very high order.*

■ ABOVE *Porsche originally harboured ideas that the 928 might one day replace the long-lived 911, but instead it slotted in as a top-of-range grand tourer.*

PORSCHE 928 (1977–95)	
Engine	V-eight-cylinder
Capacity	4474–5399cc
Power	240–350bhp
Transmission	5-speed manual 4-speed automatic
Top speed	143–171mph (230–275kph)
No. built	Approx. 35,000

■ LEFT *The GTS was a run-out (final) version, and the pinnacle of a long line of 928s.*

smooth and flexible but ultimately not as quick as the 911. There was a choice of rear-mounted manual transmission or, more commonly, Mercedes-built automatic. An attempt to give it some more power was made with the later 4.7-litre 928S (which had an extra 60bhp at 300bhp).

In character, the 928 was ruthlessly efficient rather than exciting, a trait that its clean but uninvolving styling seemed to exacerbate. It was also very comfortable, at least for the two front passengers; rear seat space was available, but very limited. Lavish equipment levels matched its "soft" image. Handling could not be faulted, and it was as forgiving as the 911 was tricky at its limit.

■ ABOVE *The front-mounted V-eight engine gave the 928 a very different character from more traditional Porsche models: powerful yet unruffled and refined.*

■ BELOW *In its ultimate guise, Porsche tried to give the 928 more sporting appeal, with fatter wheels, lower suspension and lower-profile tyres.*

■ ABOVE *With its 5.4-litre 350bhp engine, the GTS was the fastest and most rewarding of all 928 models, but always a real rarity.*

Power jumped again in 1986 with the launch of the S4. Its 5.0-litre power-plant now had a twin-cam head, 32 valves and a maximum output of 320bhp: the 928 was finally coming of age. The S4 restyle altered the nose and tail sections.

The best versions of all were saved for last, however. To counter criticisms that

this was not as sporting as some rivals, Porsche offered a GT version with an extra 10bhp, electronic limited slip differential and sports suspension (which improved handling but made the ride harder). The package became even sharper with the 1992 GTS, now sporting a 5.4-litre 350bhp engine, wider wheels and a more vigorous feel.

After a production run of 18 years, the 928 was retired in 1995. The model was not as successful as Porsche had initially hoped, but it had provided a useful lesson: traditional Porsche people stuck with what they knew and liked – the 911 – and the Stuttgart firm meddled with this fact of life at its peril. It has never looked back.

PORSCHE

■ PORSCHE 924/944

The Porsche 924 was conceived in the early 1970s as a joint project with Volkswagen/Audi, to be designed by Porsche but produced and marketed by Volkswagen using as many stock VW parts as possible. The engine was the fuel-injected 2.0-litre unit from the Audi 100 – also found in the VW LT van – and, while the rear transaxle was new, the gears inside were Audi, too.

It was only when the fuel crisis began to bite hard, and sales of the ugly-

■ BELOW *In Carrera form (a 1980 limited edition), the 924 was very powerful and boasted a dramatic body kit that presaged the 944.*

■ ABOVE *In profile, the 944 was very similar to the 924, but its flared wheel-arches were an instant give-away that this had pukka Porsche power.*

duckling VW-Porsche 914 began to flag, that Porsche realized it was faced with the prospect of having no cheap sports-car to sell in the second half of the 70s. With the 911's future also uncertain, Porsche decided to take over the project as a pure Porsche model, with production subcontracted to VW.

Launched in 1975, the 924 was an instant success. However, this was no 911: the van-derived engine could be raucous when pressed, even if it endowed the 924 with brisk acceleration and a 125mph (201kph) top speed in its long-legged fifth gear. More impressive was the handling, the perfect 50/50 weight distribution giving the 924 a well-balanced poise that allowed even novices to drive quickly and safely, with

PORSCHE 924/944 (1975–93)	
Engine	4-cylinder
Capacity	1984–2990cc
Power	125–211bhp
Transmission	4/5-speed manual 3-speed auto
Top speed	125–160mph (201–257kph)
No. built	122,304/163,820

■ RIGHT *Many people were surprised to find Porsche producing a front-engined four-cylinder car, and indeed the 924 began life as an Audi project.*

■ RIGHT *This is a full line-up of 944 models at Porsche's Stuttgart facility.*

precise, informative and light steering – not unlike a 911's – allied to slight roll angles. The gearbox was pleasant to use and a few 924s were even built with automatic transmission.

The 924 Turbo of 1978 hardened the model's performance image in the late 70s. Its 170bhp came courtesy of a KKK turbocharger. Top speed surged from 125mph (201kph) to 141mph (227kph), and acceleration was almost in the supercar class with 0–60mph (0–96kph) in 6.9 seconds. Stiffer suspension and better brakes meant the handling was even more polished. Cooling slots in the nose and discreet spoilers singled this model out from the the ordinary 924.

In the 1980s, the 944, with a proper Porsche 2.5-litre four-cylinder engine – effectively half a 928 V-eight – finally shook off associations with the VW LT van, although the 924 itself lingered on until 1985. In fact, the 944 was a very different car with big wheel-arches, fatter wheels and tyres and a lower stance. It got twin cams in 1986, and was joined by a Turbo version in 1986, that was good for nearly 160mph (257kph). The last-of-the-line three-litre models came in both closed and convertible forms. Even then the model did not die: the 1993 Porsche 968, which lasted until 1995, was a radically evolved version of the 944.

■ LEFT *The 944 was undoubtedly one of the best-handling cars made in the 1980s, thanks to its wide stance and competent chassis engineering.*

■ LEFT *Even the basic 944S was a quick car, but in Turbo form the 944 was good for 160mph (257kph).*

■ BELOW *In many ways, the 944 Cabriolet was the most attractive 944 variant. Its hood (top) was simple and effective.*

■ RIGHT *The final evolution of the 924/944 series was the 968 of 1993–5, sold in coupé and convertible styles.*

PORSCHE

■ PORSCHE 959

Porsche built the 959 with the intention that it should become a formidable Group B racing car, and it was shown at the 1983 Frankfurt Motor Show as the "Gruppe B". But when Group B cars were banned from racing in 1986, Porsche switched the emphasis of its design programme to create the ultimate road car.

It started by drastically reshaping the basic 911 body, using high-tech plastics and aluminium doors and front lid. The suspension was all new and multi-adjustable, while a clever system monitored tyre pressures on the move.

Then there was the engine, a monstrous twin turbocharged version of the familiar flat six. With only 2.85 litres, it developed 450bhp and could accelerate the 1450kg (3200lb) 959 from rest to 60mph (96kph) in an unbelievable 3.6 seconds, or 0–100mph (0–161kph) in a stunning 8.2 seconds.

The *pièce de résistance* was undoubtedly the transmission. Not only was four-wheel drive permanent, and not only did it have six speeds, but there

was also a choice of four computer-controlled traction settings to suit different conditions: thick snow/mud, ice, wet and dry. Even so, the rear-engined 959 was challenging to drive.

Only existing Porsche owners could buy the £155,000 ($261,000) car, and very quickly a "grey market" sprang up, boosting used prices to ridiculous levels. Since less than 300 were ever made, demand would always outstrip supply, and remaining examples are blue-chip classics of the first order.

■ ABOVE *The idea for the 959 was born as early as 1983 when this so-called Gruppe B prototype was displayed at the Frankfurt Motor Show.*

■ LEFT *The 959 sat low and squat on multi-adjustable suspension. It also had permanent (full-time) four-wheel drive, six speeds and selectable traction control.*

PORSCHE 959 (1987–88)	
Engine	6-cylinder
Capacity	2850cc
Power	450bhp @ 6500rpm
Transmission	6-speed manual
Top speed	197mph (315kph)
No. built	283

■ BELOW *Wild in every way, the 959 was loosely based on the 911, but its bodywork was drastically altered, featuring both plastic and aluminium body panels.*

■ ABOVE *Tremendous urge was tempered by phenomenal grip. Even so, driving a 959 was never a relaxing experience, thanks to the explosive power of 450 horses sitting in the tail.*

■ LEFT *From within the engagingly styled interior, the electric soft-top could be folded down in just 20 seconds.*

■ PORSCHE BOXSTER

After the death of Porsche's front-engined models (the 968 and 928), the Stuttgart firm was left with just one model once again, the venerable rear-engined 911. Having passed through such a painful period of front-engined cars, Porsche elected to take a new direction with its first all-new model in 18 years: the Boxster.

What distinguished the new Boxster was its engine position – in the middle of the car, driving the rear wheels. Porsche claimed that "the mid-engine provides ideal driving dynamics", and the world was forced to agree.

The new Boxster was fabulously entertaining to drive, balanced, responsive and surprisingly forgiving. Powered by a brand new 204bhp 2.5-litre six-cylinder "boxer" engine, in the best Porsche tradition, the Boxster was

as fast as it was smooth. Porsche claimed a top speed of 149mph (240kph) and a 0–62mph (0–100kph) time of 6.9 seconds, or slightly less if you ordered the attractive option of the Tiptronic S gearbox, which allowed gear-changes to be made from paddle controls on the steering wheel.

The four-piston mono-block brake caliper system was for the first time fitted to a road-going Porsche, and was claimed to have 100 per cent fade-free characteristics. It enabled the Boxster to pull up short from 62mph (100kph) in just 2.7 seconds.

Perhaps the Boxster's greatest allure

lay in its purposeful styling. Boasting the lowest drag coefficient of any car in its class (0.31), it was elegant, smooth and timeless. The striking headlamps were shrouded by durable plastic covers.

An enticing cockpit boasted instruments grouped in an arc, slightly overlapping each other. The electric soft-top could be lowered in just 12 seconds and stowed underneath a metal cover.

The Boxster undoubtedly represented a serious part of Porsche's future. Priced very competitively to do battle with the Mercedes-Benz SLK and BMW Z3, it also attracted a whole new generation of drivers to the Porsche marque.

■ ABOVE *Beautifully balanced in action thanks to its mid-engined layout, the Boxster was reasonably fast and boasted race-car braking ability.*

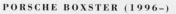

■ LEFT *The name Boxster was a joining of two Porsche classics, the "boxer" engine layout and the Speedster body style.*

■ BELOW *There was little room for doubt that Porsche created one of the most desirable of all sportscars in the Boxster, and yet this was its entry-level model.*

PORSCHE BOXSTER (1996–)	
Engine	6-cylinder
Capacity	2480cc
Power	204bhp @ 6000rpm
Transmission	5-speed manual
Top speed	149mph (240kph)
No. built	Still in production

RENAULT

■ RENAULT 5 TURBO

The idea of a car created specially to compete in rallies was Renault's. The 5 Turbo, introduced in 1978, spawned a string of copycat homologation specials like the Lancia S4 and Ford RS200, all sold for road use as well, because the rules stated that a minimum number had to be built. As a pioneer, the Renault was also the only rally car which made complete sense as a road car.

In fact, an impressive tally of nearly 5,000 Renault 5 Turbos were built because of customer demand. It's easy to appreciate why. The 5 Turbo had a centrally mounted turbo intercooled engine, which offered scorching acceleration, massive grip and endless handling entertainment.

Very little of the shopping (standard) Renault 5 (Le Car in the US) remained. Renault's Alpine factory bolted on

■ ABOVE *In the massively flared arches sat very wide alloy wheels and tyres, which boasted huge grip.*

RENAULT 5 TURBO (1978–86)	
Engine	4-cylinder
Capacity	1397cc
Power	160bhp @ 6000rpm
Transmission	5-speed manual
Top speed	125mph (201kph)
No. built	4,997

■ ABOVE *The mid-engine looks tiny – in fact, it was only 1.4 litres – but it kicked out 160bhp for some screaming acceleration.*

wildly flared wheel-arches, gaping cooling vents and big spoilers, and the doors, roof and tailgate of the first cars were in aluminium. The interior was a typically French mix of bold primary colours and avant-garde design.

Mechanically, the story was even more divergent. Racing suspension, big brakes and hugely fat tyres

■ ABOVE *Unlike the Gallic artscape of the Turbo 1, the Turbo 2's interior was based on that of the standard Renault 5 (Le Car).*

complemented the heavily heat-shielded engine (which sat just inches from your ears, inside the cockpit).

From 1983, there was a Turbo 2 version with minor trim changes, a recognizably Renault 5-derived interior and a heavier all-steel body; in contrast to the first edition (of which 1,830 were built), some 3,167 Turbo 2s were sold.

■ LEFT *Although its name and some body panels were derived from the Renault 5 shopping car, the 5 Turbo was a real mid-engined beast.*

■ RIGHT *The 1984–91 GTA was the latest in a long line of Renault-based sportscars from Alpine, which was France's equivalent of Porsche.*

■ RENAULT ALPINE GTA/A610

Launched in 1984, the Renault Alpine GTA was the last of a famous line of rear-engined French sportscars using Renault V-six power in a steel back-bone chassis. Gunning for the Porsche 911 market, it offered superb driver involvement and high levels of grip (despite the tail-happy layout) but never managed to tempt many buyers away from Porsche.

They were certainly quick cars, particularly in Turbo form, topping 150mph (241kph) and turning in 0–60mph (0–96kph) times in the six-second bracket. Drivers loved the GTA for its feel and responsiveness, yet it was a comfortable, quiet long-distance machine. Despite its exotic looks, it was surprisingly practical, with usable rear seats and rust-free plastic bodywork. The Douvrin V-six engine – straight out of the big Renault 25 – offered no reliability problems either, and the overall quality of the cars was acceptable, if not in the 911's league.

In 1991, the GTA evolved to become the A610 with a few styling tweaks that somehow robbed the crisp-edged shape of character but gave it broader showroom appeal: pop-headlights are the quickest way of identifying the new model. The power of the Turbo model was hiked up to 250bhp thanks to a

■ ABOVE *The unusually styled interior raided the Renault parts bin for its switchgear.*

larger 3.0-litre engine, and top speed rose to 165mph (265kph) with no turbo-lag. The double-wishbone suspension was tweaked to cure any hint of the twitchyness suffered by the older model. With the inclusion of power-steering, parking the A610 wasn't such a muscle-building exercise either.

The GTA and A610 Alpines were hailed as classics while still in production, but always lived in the shade of the Porsche 911. Production ended in 1995, with no successor.

RENAULT ALPINE GTA/A610 (1984–95)	
Engine	V-six-cylinder
Capacity	2458–2975cc
Power	160–250bhp
Transmission	5-speed manual
Top speed	146–165mph (235–265kph)
No. built	17,450

■ ABOVE *An expanded 3.0-litre V-six engine sat in the tail. It had 250bhp on tap.*

■ LEFT *In Turbo form the GTA was exceptionally fast. The rear-sited V-six engine inevitably caused tail-happy manners, but the GTA was grippy nonetheless.*

■ RIGHT *The A610 Turbo stepped up a rung: a 160mph (257kph) top speed and improved handling made it a Porsche rival.*

RENAULT

■ RENAULT ESPACE

Other car manufacturers can lay claim to having invented the people carrier, otherwise known as the Multi Purpose Vehicle (MPV), but Renault was the first to produce an MPV specifically created from the ground up as such and make it popular. It revolutionized the car market and the repercussions of its success are still being felt, with every major manufacturer producing a rival.

The origins of the Espace actually began with the French sportscar constructor and aerospace leader Matra. In the late 1970s, it was allied to Simca-Talbot and produced a proposal based on the Horizon for a radical "one-box" people carrier. But Matra was sold on to Renault and with it went the MPV project. Renault immediately recognized

■ ABOVE *With a restyle in 1991, the Espace moved on to ever-greater success.*

■ ABOVE *Tremendous adaptability was the Espace's strength: the front seats could swivel around, and you could fold down a central seat to make a picnic table.*

its potential and brought its new Espace to production in 1984, the same year as Chrysler Corporation's minivans.

The first and most striking feature was the shape, an exceptionally neat and integrated design with a long, steeply raked windscreen. In construction it was equally different: a steel-skeleton frame clothed with plastic panels.

The single most significant factor in the Espace equation was its interior. The fact that it was spacious, airy and cleanly designed was secondary to its tremendous adaptability. There were three rows of seats for up to seven passengers in all, and each of these seats could be removed to increase luggage space. The front seats could

swivel round to face the others, and the central one could fold to make a table. Picnic-goers and mobile office workers were happy and Renault never looked back, dominating the European MPV market with successive Espace cars.

■ ABOVE *Up to seven seats could be fitted in the Espace, and then removed individually at will to turn it into a load-lugger.*

RENAULT ESPACE (1984–91)	
Engine	4-cylinder
Capacity	1995cc
Power	103–120bhp
Transmission	5-speed
Top speed	106–111mph (171–179kph)
No. built	147,960

■ LEFT *Renault inherited the innovative Espace project from Matra, and made it Europe's first – and the world's most convincing – MPV or people carrier.*

■ RIGHT *The van-like driving position was criticized but it gave wonderful visibility.*

■ RENAULT TWINGO

One of the first things that Renault's new design chief Patrick Le Quément did when he joined the firm was to let it be known that Renault would be taking the lead in design terms, producing the best innovative new cars. The Twingo was the perfect expression of this ideal.

Le Quément skilfully extended the idea of the "one-box" design pioneered by Renault's Espace to the smallest car in the range. The line from the front bumper to the top of the windscreen was one elegant curve, broken only by the characterful hooded headlamps and bonnet (hood) cooling vents.

The hatchback Twingo may have looked cute from the outside but its cabin was its best feature. The digital instruments were sited in a pod in the centre of the dash, and all the switchgear was in contrasting colours and a tactile material. There was a huge amount of space, made all the more practical by the four individually reclining and sliding seats. Optional extras included a full sliding sunroof and air-conditioning.

Considering the avant-garde look of the Twingo, it was mildly disappointing to find old-world mechanicals underneath, taken directly from the antiquated Renault 5. The engine was harsh and the

■ LEFT *The Espace-style "monobox" design was applied to a miniature city car to create the brilliant Twingo.*

■ ABOVE *Little eyebrows over the headlamps and interesting air vents in the bonnet (hood) added character to the design.*

■ ABOVE *The Twingo was the ideal city car: very compact, nimble and economical.*

road behaviour nothing special. It took until 1996 for Renault to fit a modern engine in the form of a brand-new 1149cc unit with more power and extra zing. An automatic version dubbed Easy was launched at the same time.

The Twingo rose to become the best-selling car in France as buyers rushed to share in its chic, and a whole culture seemed to spring up around it. The millionth example was built in 1997.

RENAULT TWINGO (1992–)	
Engine	4-cylinder
Capacity	1149–1239cc
Power	54–58bhp
Transmission	5-speed manual 3-speed automatic
Top speed	93mph (150kph)
No. built	Still in production

■ RIGHT *Très jolie – the Twingo endeared itself to French buyers, who elevated it to the Number One best-seller in 1995.*

■ FAR RIGHT *Interior packaging was impressive, and the rear seats could slide fore-and-aft individually. Note the centrally mounted digital dash.*

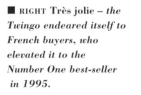

RENAULT

■ RENAULT SPORT SPIDER

So-called niche cars began to assume tremendous importance in the 1990s. Sales of mainstream models went down while low-production models sold proportionately more. Usually, niche cars were merely cleverly positioned conventional designs, but that is not a description you could apply to Renault's amazing Sport Spider.

The recipe was exciting, and wildly out of the ordinary for a major company like Renault. Here was a car built for one purpose only: pure driving enjoyment. The brief called for a lightweight, mid-engined sports two-seater, which was so pure in its ethos that it made do without a roof.

Indeed, the first Sport Spider made do without even a windscreen. The design team, led by the brilliant Patrick Le Quément, sculpted a radical shape, which incorporated a solid wind deflector where a windscreen might have been. Later on, a version was offered with a windscreen and wiper in

■ ABOVE *Renault was amazingly ambitious and adventurous with its Sport Spider: mid-engined, roofless and even devoid of a windscreen!*

■ BELOW *The styling was by Patrick Le Quément's innovative team at Renault. Although a return to the theme of the Lotus 7, it was unashamedly modern in appearance.*

■ ABOVE *A deliberately sparse cabin reflected the lightweight, bare-boned nature of this stripped-out road racer. Note the exposed aluminium basis (framework).*

place, but you still got no side windows or roof. That didn't seem to matter, because owners got the chance to drive and enjoy a car which had the look and feel of an advanced concept car.

The Sport Spider was equally radical in construction. The chassis was made of lightweight aluminium, which was also extremely rigid. The suspension was by race-inspired, rose (spherical)-jointed double wishbones, and the huge vented disc brakes came from the A610 supercar.

For its power, Renault opted to fit the sizzling 150bhp two-litre engine of the Clio Williams. That was sufficient to take it to 62mph (100kph) from rest in just 6.9 seconds.

■ RIGHT *The Sport Spider was also meant for racing, and Renault organized a one-make series, which supported British Touring Car races in 1996.*

Overall the Sport Spider was incredibly quick, both in a straight line and through corners. At 1740lb (790kg), it may not have been as light as a Lotus Elise, but it was certainly no heavyweight. It cornered with almost no roll.

The umbrella organization that created this unique car, Renault Sport, also ran a racing series exclusively for the Sport Spider. Race cars got more power (175bhp), so the action was fast, furious and incredibly exciting, and attracted many talented drivers and large viewing audiences.

This was perhaps the main point of the project. Renault knew the Sport Spider was not going to be a strong seller. It cost much more than rivals like the Lotus Elise and Caterham 21, and it was obviously too impractical to be used on a daily basis. Production volumes (at Renault's Alpine works in Dieppe) were tiny but the publicity gained for Renault's radical design work was huge – and its courage in putting such a machine into production at all was widely applauded.

■ ABOVE *In practice, most Sport Spider customers opted for the version with the full windscreen.*

RENAULT SPORT SPIDER (1995–)	
Engine	4-cylinder
Capacity	1998cc
Power	150bhp
Transmission	5-speed manual
Top speed	134mph (216kph)
No. built	Still in production

■ RIGHT *This image suggests that the Sport Spider was somehow acceptable in rain. True, you had a windscreen wiper on this version, but no roof or side windows.*

ROLLS-ROYCE

■ ROLLS-ROYCE CAMARGUE

The Pininfarina-styled Rolls-Royce Camargue, Crewe's flamboyant 1970s super-coupé, was a car for kings, princes, diplomats and superstars, a hedonistic two-door with no true rival. There was little to match it for size in the coupé stakes, and nothing approaching its price: the Camargue was the most expensive car on the market at its launch in 1975, 50 per cent dearer than a Corniche convertible.

Pininfarina was the natural choice for styling this new flagship, having done one-off designs on various Bentleys and Rolls-Royces in the 50s. Sergio Pininfarina even moderated his usual fee, but the styling got a luke-warm reception from some quarters. Farina did the interior, too, and designed a new dashboard using standard Silver Shadow instruments but with square black plates similar to an aircraft cockpit.

Launched in Sicily in 1975, the 120mph (193kph) Camargue was the first Rolls-Royce to have curved window glass and the first ever designed to metric dimensions. Mechanically, the car used a slightly more powerful 6.75-litre alloy Rolls pushrod V-eight engine and the usual independent suspension and complex hydraulic systems for the four-wheel disc brakes and self-levelling suspension.

■ BELOW *The Camargue was one of Rolls-Royce's most exclusive models. Over an 11-year period, only just over 500 were made.*

■ ABOVE *If you wanted the most expensive car in the world in 1975, the Rolls-Royce Camargue was your choice: a two-door coupé from the "best car company in the world".*

The star technical attraction of the £29,000 ($48,850) Camargue was its superb split-level air-conditioning system, which cost as much as a Mini and had the cooling capacity of 30 domestic refrigerators.

Each Camargue took six months to make, at a rate never higher than one per week. Unsurprisingly, the Camargue's best market was the USA (280 cars); 75 went to Saudi Arabia, while in Europe the car's best market was its native Britain with 136 sold.

■ ABOVE *Pininfarina also styled the interior, which was a palace of leather and wood, topped off by the most sophisticated air-conditioning system yet seen in a car.*

■ ABOVE *The clean and simple styling was done by Pininfarina, and was good enough to hide the model's considerable bulk.*

■ ABOVE *Fit and finish were superlative, while the detailing was quintessentially British, with hand-stitching and chrome handles.*

ROLLS-ROYCE CAMARGUE (1975–86)	
Engine	V-eight-cylinder
Capacity	6750cc
Power	Not quoted
Top speed	120mph (193kph)
No. built	534

ROVER

■ LEFT *Rover's David Bache admitted to using Ferrari's Daytona as inspiration. For a luxury saloon (sedan), the SD1 looked extremely sporty.*

■ ROVER SD1

With the P6 saloon (sedan) car range Rover had scored an undoubted winner, as European journalists recognized when they awarded it the very first Car of the Year award. Its successor, the so-called SD1, won it again in 1977.

For a Rover, the new SD1 3500 was pretty radical. Gone were all traces of chrome and all wood dashboards, which were seemingly permanent fixtures on Rover's past. Gone was the traditional, sober saloon layout in favour of a hatchback. And the interior (with its separate "box of instruments") was anything but conservative.

The architect of the SD1 shape was Rover's David Bache, and he had the probity to acknowledge the Ferrari Daytona as a direct influence: the

prominent mid-riff indentation and narrow headlamps were unmistakable. As a result, the 3500 looked distinctly sleek for 1976.

As launched, the 3500 had Rover's familiar V-eight engine. In other respects it was a mixture of old and new: the live rear axle and drum brakes were hardly ground-breaking, but the MacPherson strut front suspension sharpened up the handling considerably. Less powerful 2000, 2300 and

2600 six-cylinder versions followed.

The best model of all was the 1982 Vitesse with its 190bhp fuel-injection engine, lowered suspension, spoked alloy wheels and tailgate spoiler. Although it was rare (less than 4,000 were built), the Vitesse added a true performance edge to the SD1 range, which was replaced in 1986.

■ ABOVE *The most powerful SD1 model of all was the Vitesse, with its 190bhp fuel-injected V-eight, lowered suspension and tailgate spoiler.*

■ ABOVE *Rover departed from its traditions with the interior. Most notable was the separate binnacle housing all the instruments.*

■ ABOVE *The range of SD1 engines started with a 2.0-litre four-cylinder unit and went up to the popular 3.5-litre V-eight.*

■ LEFT *The ultra-quick Vitesse was a fitting end to an innovative chapter in Rover's long history.*

ROVER SD1 3500 (1976–86)	
Engine	V-eight-cylinder
Capacity	3528cc
Power	155–190bhp
Transmission	5-speed manual 3-speed automatic
Top speed	125–135mph (201–217kph)
No. built	113,966

S A A B

■ SAAB 99 TURBO

Sweden's aerospace leaders are very well known for their motor cars, and the string of models Saab has produced for over 50 years have always been unconventional, highly distinctive and instantly recognizable. The 99 Turbo was a model that launched Saab into a new era.

Saab's traditional front-wheel-drive layout remained, but the engine was new, jointly developed by Triumph and Saab. When it came to extracting more performance from this engine, Saab adopted turbocharging technology. Turbos were still a novelty in 1977, and Saab made the turbocharger an art-form of its very own. Long after other makers had abandoned this route, Saab plugged away with it as a performance and emissions device.

As a result of turbocharging, the standard fuel-injected 2.0-litre engine's power was boosted from 118bhp to 145bhp, very high for an engine of this size in 1977. New heights of performance were achieved – 0–60mph (0–96kph) in nine seconds, 125mph (201kph) top speed – though Saab never did iron out drastic turbo lag (the time it took for the turbo to cut in once the throttle had been pressed), nor a tendency to ferocious take-offs.

■ ABOVE *Fitting a 145bhp turbocharged engine into the unassuming 99 bodyshell created one of the performance icons of the 1970s.*

Saab pioneered the birth of the popular turbo car with the 99, and it became something of a cult car. Its ruthless turbo speed was quickly duplicated by others such as Audi and many Japanese makers, but none made the formula quite as attractive as Saab.

■ LEFT *Under the forward-hinging bonnet (hood) was Saab turbocharger technology. The Swedish company made the turbo a real speciality.*

SAAB 99 TURBO (1977–80)	
Engine	4-cylinder
Capacity	1985cc
Power	145bhp
Transmission	4-speed manual
Top speed	125mph (201kph)
No. built	10,607

■ ABOVE *The 99 Turbo was angled toward safety: hence the impact (energy-absorbing) bumpers and headlamp wipers.*

■ RIGHT *No one could describe the 99 as a handsome car, but it was utterly unique.*

SUZUKI

■ SUZUKI SC100 WHIZZKID

When your traffic jams are in danger of becoming full-scale preserves, you are forced to do something drastic. The traffic jams of Tokyo and Osaka are the worst in the world, and the Japanese government's solution was to offer tax and parking breaks for owners of very small cars, called K-class cars.

Suzuki was the first company to offer a "K" car (in 1955), and its offerings have always been among the best. One interesting departure was the Cervo of 1972. This was a rare attempt to introduce some zing into the species. It was a two-plus-two coupé based on the rear-engined Suzuki Fronte saloon, measuring just 126in (320cm) long. It used a tiny 539cc two-stroke engine developing 28bhp. Its top speed of 65mph (105kph) was hardly thrilling, but then this was always intended to be a city car first and foremost.

For export Suzuki transformed the Cervo to become the rumbustious SC100 GX, which was known in Britain by its nickname, Whizzkid. The old two-pot engine was replaced by a 970cc four-cylinder Alto engine developing 47bhp, still sited in the tail. Now the little coupé really flew: its top speed jumped

■ LEFT *Whizzkid seemed just the right name for Suzuki's tiny sporting projectile. It was an official nickname in Britain.*

■ ABOVE *The SC100's minute size can be gauged from this shot of one next to a Princess limousine. It was just 10ft 6in (320cm) long.*

■ ABOVE *It was the SC100's narrowness that was surprising to western drivers, but it was designed to conform to Japan's city laws.*

to 85mph (137kph), and there was sparkling acceleration and brilliant fuel economy to match.

It sold for a bargain price, too, and at this level no European maker had ever offered the SC100's lavish list of equipment: rev counter, reclining front seats, cigar lighter, front disc brakes and all-round independent suspension. Suzuki's British importers sold all the cars they could from 1979 to 1982, and now it has minor classic status.

SUZUKI SC100 WHIZZKID (1979–82)	
Engine	4-cylinder
Capacity	970cc
Power	47bhp @ 5000rpm
Transmission	4-speed
Top speed	85mph (137kph)
No. built	894,000 (7,539 UK Whizzkids)

■ FAR LEFT *In action the Whizzkid was a real joy. Its 1.0-litre engine gave it nippy acceleration, but it was dodging through heavy traffic that was most fun.*

■ LEFT *The engine was sited in the tail, making passenger accommodation tight. Giugiaro was responsible for the styling.*

SUZUKI

■ **LEFT** *It only had three cylinders and 658cc at its disposal, but a turbocharger assured that the Cappuccino was nippy and great fun to drive.*

■ SUZUKI CAPPUCCINO

If Cappuccino means a hot frothy coffee brew that gives you a lift when you need it, then Suzuki's car truly lived up to the name. The little Cappuccino sportscar began life as a show car in 1989, intended to show what could be done within Japan's "K" class mini-car regulations.

The reaction was so good that Suzuki went into production in early 1992 at the very limited rate of 200 per month. It was a car dedicated to the eccentric Japanese market, but there were still some exports to certain markets such as the UK.

The Cappuccino may have been a tiny car – just 130ins (330cm) long and 55ins (140cm) wide – but it was big on character. The rounded curves were reminiscent of the Austin-Healey Frogeye Sprite. The tail was cut off so

■ **ABOVE** *The little Suzuki sportscar was designed around Japanese city car rules – just 130in (330cm) long and 55in (140cm) wide.*

SUZUKI CAPPUCCINO (1992–)	
Engine	3-cylinder
Capacity	658cc
Power	64bhp @ 6500rpm
Transmission	5-speed
Top speed	87mph (140kph)
No. built	Still in production

that you could almost stretch out a hand from the cockpit and touch the rear bumper.

The Cappuccino's *pièce de résistance* was its ingenious three-piece folding hardtop roof, which could be put into no less than five positions: fully enclosed; with one targa panel removed, both removed for "T"-bar motoring; all roof panels out but the rear-window section in place, or with the rear part folded down

OTHER MAKES

■ SEAT

Spain's only home-grown marque started life as a branch of the Fiat empire in 1953, though it made several models unique to its own market. The most interesting of these was the Sport coupé of 1975–80, a small Fiat 128 3p rival. In the 1980s, Seat shed its Fiat chains and was bought by VW, which developed the marque as its sporty, Latin brand.

■ SKODA

The Czech-made Skoda marque can be traced back to the last century and has an illustrious history. By the 1970s, however, it had become a bit of a joke with its poorly made, wayward-handling rear-engined cars. The 1970–81 S110R coupé was the only vaguely "classic" model, although *Autocar* called the later 136 Rapid a "mini-Porsche". After a take-over by VW, quality and design improved.

for the complete open-air treatment.

Considering its 658cc three-cylinder engine, this was a surprisingly rapid little machine: if you removed the 87mph (140kph) top-speed limiter, it was capable of reaching 110mph (177kph) and sprinting from 0–60mph (0–96kph) in about nine seconds. It also handled incredibly well, sounded great and was amazing fun, all for a price that embarrassed any other sportscar.

■ STUTZ

An American industrialist bought the famous pre-war Stutz name in 1969 and launched a Virgil Exner-styled coupé to revive the long-lost marque. It was based on a Pontiac Grand Prix and was partly made in Italy. The tastefulness of the design might have been questionable but the model hit a chord in Hollywood and Arab markets. Various body styles were offered, including convertibles, saloons (sedans) and a mammoth Royale limousine.

■ SUBARU

Hill farmers loved the Subaru because it combined saloon (sedan) car urbanity with unstoppable four-wheel-drive transmission. Subaru built on this all-wheel-drive reputation with a range of interesting cars, culminating in the curious XT sports coupé, the Legacy saloon and the stunningly fast, rally-winning Impreza Turbo. Quality was always high on the agenda.

TALBOT-SUNBEAM LOTUS

■ TALBOT SUNBEAM LOTUS

"Put a Chrysler Sunbeam in your life" went the glib ad campaign for the new supermini from Chrysler in 1977. Within two years the group had been sold to Peugeot, which renamed all Chrysler models as Talbots, including the Sunbeam.

This thoroughly unexceptional hatchback was based on the Hillman Avenger, but that did engender one strong advantage: unlike most superminis, this model had rear-wheel drive and therefore exploitable handling. In short, it was ripe for a pump up in volume.

So the Sunbeam Lotus was born. Lotus had a history of engineering exciting road cars for mainstream makers (witness the Ford Lotus Cortina), and it did a wonderful job on the Sunbeam. Into the engine bay went Lotus's 2.2-litre twin-cam engine, whose 150bhp made this one of the fastest of the brat pack of rally-orientated specials around at the time: 121mph (195kph) top speed and a 0–60mph (0–96kph) time of 7.4 seconds.

Lotus also specified a five-speed ZF gearbox with first gear canted over to the

left in true racing style. The suspension was lowered and stiffened and brand new wide alloy wheels were created. The live axle and rear drum brakes may not have been very sophisticated but the set-up was certainly effective, as Henri Toivonen found out when he won the World Rally Championship in a Sunbeam Lotus.

The Sunbeam Lotus felt special, too, with its black (later also blue) paint, silver side stripes and prominent Lotus badging. Its career was cut short in 1981 when the plug was pulled on the whole Sunbeam range.

■ LEFT *While the Talbot Sunbeam was an instantly forgettable hatchback, the Sunbeam Lotus was a memorable performance car.*

■ BELOW *The Lotus 2.2-litre twin-cam engine was a comfortable fit. Its 150bhp power output made the Sunbeam the quickest hot hatch around.*

■ LEFT *In overall terms, the Sunbeam Lotus was highly effective and, because only 2,308 were made, it is now very collectable.*

TALBOT SUNBEAM LOTUS (1979–81)	
Engine	4-cylinder
Capacity	2174cc
Power	150bhp
Transmission	5-speed manual
Top speed	121mph (195kph)
No. built	2,308

■ RIGHT *Although it was based closely on the standard Sunbeam, the interior had a special rally-style feel to it.*

TOYOTA

■ TOYOTA CELICA

In Toyota's sprawling range of models, the Celica stands out as a model that has consistently had integrity, style and a certain panache. In the Toyota scheme of things, it has always slotted in as the four-seater coupé model and for the first generations it was based on the Carina saloon (sedan) floorpan.

The first Celica appeared in 1970 with exactly the right balance of Coke-bottle styling and good proportions. For the first three years, the shape was always a notchback, but from 1973 an attractive new Liftback rear-end was also offered.

Various engines were used, the most popular being the 1600 and 2000,

■ ABOVE *In Liftback style, the Toyota Celica looked stylish, and it is a rare popular Japanese car with true classic credentials.*

■ ABOVE *Engines offered in the first-generation Celica range from a 1600 OHV up to a 2000 OHC, which developed 130bhp.*

TOYOTA CELICA (1970–77)	
Engine	4-cylinder
Capacity	1407–2289cc
Power	86–130bhp
Transmission	5-speed manual 3-speed auto
Top speed	102–112mph (164–180kph)
No. built	1,500,000

which were available in overhead-valve, overhead-cam and twin-cam forms. The best models were the GT versions with their extra power and sports equipment.

Toyota made sure, in true Japanese style, that every Celica was lavishly equipped. Even the most basic model had five gauges, a cigar lighter and stereo – real luxuries in those days.

The first-generation Celica was

replaced in 1977 by another stylish model, and then again in 1981. In 1985, the fourth-generation Celica became very much more stylish, with its smooth shape, pop-up headlamps and airy cabin, while a convertible version was new to the range. The 1989 edition sold as well as ever, and the Celica – now in its sixth generation – is a much-valued name in the Toyota portfolio.

■ ABOVE *The fifth-generation Celica was controversial in appearance but continued to forge ahead in the sales charts.*

■ RIGHT *This is a fourth-generation Celica, the first to be offered in a convertible body style.*

■ TOYOTA MR2

Twelve years after the launch of the mid-engined Fiat X1/9, Toyota came up with the first credible rival, the MR2, in 1984. Many expensive and exotic cars used the layout, but on affordable sportscars it had previously been the exclusive province of Fiat and, perhaps, the Pontiac Fiero in America.

MR2 stood for Midships Recreational 2-seater. By plundering the corporate parts bin Toyota created a good-value, sure-fire winner. It had a smooth, responsive twin-cam engine matched to immaculate mid-engined poise, a combination nobody could touch in the affordable sportscar arena. If traditionalists were suspicious of the

slightly bland angular styling – not to mention Toyota's questionable pedigree as a maker of exciting cars – then one drive around the block in the 120mph (193kph), 30mpg (48kpg) MR2 would almost certainly win them over.

Without doubt this was a very special car, justifying its reputation as a "mini-Ferrari". To keep its appeal broad Toyota made sure the MR2 rode like a saloon (sedan), was acceptably quiet and had a saloon-car driving position, not a low-slung sporty one that might have been off-putting. About the only black mark was the lack of cockpit space.

From 1986 there was a T-bar version with a removable roof section. In Japan, there was an even more exciting 145bhp supercharged model, but that was not imported to Europe because it would only run on unleaded fuel. It was sold in North America however, and there was a rather dull single-cam model for the home market.

The original MR2 has inspired two more generations of mid-engined Toyotas – and indeed Britain's mid-engined MGF – and looks set to become a sportscar classic of the next century.

■ LEFT *Nothing less than a miniature Ferrari was how many press writers were unashamed to describe Toyota's brilliant MR2 sportscar.*

■ LEFT *The MR2 badge came to mean everything enjoyable in handling terms.*

■ ABOVE *Thanks to its mid-mounted engine, the MR2 had not only sporting performance but also balance and poise.*

■ ABOVE *The standard 1.6-litre engine developed 130bhp and was sited, crucially, amidships.*

■ ABOVE *A new-generation MR2 replaced the squarish first series in 1989, expanded both in size and appeal.*

TOYOTA MR2 (1984–89)	
Engine	4-cylinder
Capacity	1587cc
Power	130bhp @ 6600rpm
Transmission	5-speed manual
Top speed	120mph (193kph)
No. built	166,104

TRIUMPH

■ TRIUMPH DOLOMITE SPRINT

The Triumph brand could be described as the BMW of the British car industry, since its strength lay in creating high-quality saloons (sedans) and sportscars with appeal for the enthusiastic driver. No other car summed this up so well as the Dolomite Sprint.

It was the engine that set the Sprint apart from most other British saloons of the 1970s; 16-valve technology was unusual in 1973, and Triumph's overhead-cam unit pioneered 16V technology two decades before it became *de rigueur*. The engine was simple, retaining a single chain-driven camshaft – and the design was so clever that it won a Design Council Award in 1974.

Certainly the engine was punchy and effective: 0–60mph (0–96kph) in under nine seconds was blistering for a saloon car in 1973, and embarrassed many so-called sportscars such as the MGB. The parent company, British Leyland, was keen to promote its sporting image and entered it for many races; a Sprint won the British Saloon Car Championships of

■ ABOVE *Triumph was a name associated with high-quality sporting saloons (sedans), and its Dolomite Sprint was the best of them all.*

■ LEFT *The 16-valve head on top of the 2.0-litre engine was ahead of its time in 1973, allowing 127bhp.*

TRIUMPH DOLOMITE SPRINT (1973–80)	
Engine	4-cylinder
Capacity	1998cc
Power	127bhp @ 5700rpm
Transmission	4-speed manual 3-speed auto
Top speed	115mph (186kph)
No. built	22,941

■ LEFT *The Dolomite Sprint lasted until 1980, and there was no direct replacement for its combination of rear-drive handling, keen performance and classic style.*

■ RIGHT *Italian stylist Michelotti was responsible for the stylish shape, even though it looked a little outdated by the mid-1970s.*

1975 and 1978, and many rallying successes were also scored.

The four-speed gearbox was derived from the TR6 and could be had with optional overdrive (standard from 1975). Alternatively, you could choose an automatic (which was very rare, with only 1,634 built). Other significant changes over the standard-issue Toledo/Dolomite were larger brakes,

■ RIGHT *In handling terms the Sprint was very sharp around corners, yet it was equally at home cruising down the motorway.*

■ ABOVE *Conservative in style, the interior was a rather messy array of classic dials in a wood facia.*

twin headlamps, a vinyl roof, front spoiler and alloy wheels (the first time any British production car had boasted these as standard).

The Dolomite Sprint had a rounded character. It was rapid and urgent when pressed, yet refined and relaxed when cruising in overdrive top. The handling was sharp at all times, mild understeer transferring into power oversteer if you provoked the car around bends.

The character of the interior was typically British: a full-width wood dashboard, hard-wearing trim and a profusion of traditional gauges.

Overheating, head gasket problems and poor-quality control marred an otherwise brilliant car. Also, it was poorly timed, being launched just as the Arab–Israeli conflict forced petrol shortages in Britain, and thirsty cars like the Dolomite Sprint fell out of favour.

An interesting Dolly Sprint variant was the 1975 Panther Rio built by a British specialist. This was a real mini-Rolls-Royce with hand-beaten replacement panels and a leather-and-walnut luxury interior. However, at three times the price of the Dolomite Sprint, only a handful were ever made.

■ RIGHT *Thanks to its advanced engine, the Sprint was a real performer; a 115mph (186kph) top speed was very healthy for a small saloon.*

When the Dolomite left production in 1980, that was sadly the end of the line for old-style Triumphs, and on the death of the model the Canley and Speke plants that had made it were closed. The following year the Honda-based Acclaim scotched any remaining pride in the marque, and it died three years later.

TRIUMPH

■ TRIUMPH TR7/TR8

The long line of TR-badged Triumph sports cars stretches back to the TR2 of the early 1950s and boasts some of the most charismatic sporting machines among its family. For many the ultimate TR7 was the runt of the litter, a quirky, unappealing product of the depressing British Leyland years of the 70s.

Certainly the TR7 was controversially styled: its lines were penned by Harris Mann (who also has the Austin Allegro to his credit). Build quality was never up to much: they tended to break down and catch fire, and the fixed-head model in particular had very little appeal. Yet there is much to be said in favour of the maligned TR7. It sold in greater quantity than any other TR model, and in due course it became a rather attractive sportscar, at least in convertible form.

The original plan had been to make a drop-top TR7, but concerns about American legislation possibly banning open cars led Triumph to launch the new sportscar in fixed-head form only in 1975. For lovers of the machismo of Triumph TR straight-six power disappointment lurked, for British Leyland opted to fit a mere four-cylinder

■ LEFT *TR8 models were quite rare and much sought-after by aficionados.*

■ ABOVE *The TR7 enjoyed some success in rallying. With a V-eight engine in place, it was undoubtedly the quickest rally car around.*

■ RIGHT *With age the TR7 matured into a much better car. Sadly, the 16-valve Dolomite Sprint engine never made it into a production TR7.*

engine (the 105bhp Dolomite 1850 unit), driving through a Morris Marina four-speed gearbox. It was frankly not a sporting package at all.

Despite this, export sales went pretty well, especially in America (British sales did not begin until May 1976). Some of the criticisms were addressed with the adoption of a Rover SD1 five-speed gearbox in 1976 and lowered suspension the following year. But it was not until the drop-top model was added in 1979 that the TR7 turned the corner and became a real sportscar.

Still there was not enough power for many tastes. Triumph fitted its fine twin-cam Dolomite Sprint engine to its rally cars, but road cars were denied this option. Instead a stunning Rover V-eight-powered version was offered for export

■ LEFT *The TR8 is regarded as the poor relation of Triumph sportscars and is often derided. It did, however, become a true sportscar, and its day as a classic will surely dawn soon.*

■ BELOW *With a Rover V-eight engine fitted, the TR7 became the TR8 and made some inroads into the American market.*

■ ABOVE *The interior was a typical 1970s concoction of black plastic. The drop-top looked particularly neat when folded.*

TRIUMPH TR7/TR8 (1975–81)	
Engine	4/V-eight-cylinder
Capacity	1998/3528cc
Power	105/137bhp
Transmission	4/5-speed manual 3-speed auto
Top speed	110–120mph (177–193kph)
No. built	112,368

only, dubbed the TR8. This model was actually quite rare (only 2,497 were made) and soon private owners were doing their own V-eight installations on TR7s, a fad that assumed epidemic proportions since the performance was so much better: 137bhp in "soft" tune meant 120mph (193kph) instead of 110mph (177kph) and 0–60mph (0–96kph) in 8.4 seconds. These figures could be greatly enhanced by tuning the V-eight engine to even higher levels.

Production finally ended in 1981, and few enthusiasts mourned the death of the TR7; far more sad for them was that this event marked the demise of the great Triumph sportscar. The TR7 was a car that never fulfilled its potential but which has recently started to gain a following. Its distinctive style and bargain prices make it a surprisingly attractive sportscar and a sure-fire candidate for future classic status.

TVR

■ TVR 3000S

TVR is one of those very British specialist car-makers, producing highly individual sportscars against all odds of success. The company's convoluted history goes back as far as 1947, and by the late 1970s it was firmly established as an iconic sportscar-maker.

The 3000S was the ultimate expression of a line of TVR sportscars stretching back to the 1957 Grantura. The TVR formula was very traditional: a separate chassis, glassfibre body, Ford V-six engine and luxuriously trimmed cabin. However, the idea of a convertible was new to TVR, and the 1978 "S" was its very first drop-top.

Based closely on a one-off produced for TVR boss Martin Lilley, the 3000S shared most of its specification with the fixed-head TVR 3000M Taimar, including the chassis and mechanicals. The bodywork was much lower, the doors were new and the tail was revised to incorporate a boot (trunk) lid. The lower scuttle line (hood line) also forced the instruments to be repositioned, with the rev counter (tachometer) now facing the passenger! Another traditional-style feature was removable soft side screens.

■ BELOW *After more than 20 years, TVR's first convertible model was the 3000S, based on the 3000M seen in the background.*

TVR 3000S (1978–79)	
Engine	V-six-cylinder
Capacity	2994cc
Power	142–265bhp
Transmission	4-speed
Top speed	133–150mph (214–241kph)
No. built	258

■ ABOVE *Proving that the formula of a good-value, open-topped two-seater sportscar never died, TVR made a relaunched S model from 1986 until the mid-1990s.*

The 3000S lasted for just one year, when a brand-new model range took over. In that time, a mere 258 cars were made, including 13 turbocharged cars. The 3000S Turbo is the most classic of all the earlier TVRs, having incredible performance and rarity on its side. The S was so sorely missed that in 1986 TVR relaunched it in revised form.

■ ABOVE *In character and form, the 3000S recalled the great days of British rag-top roadsters like the Austin-Healey 3000.*

■ ABOVE *In action, the TVR was keen thanks to its Ford-derived V-six engine. With an optional turbocharger, it became a brutal machine.*

■ RIGHT *With the Cerbera, TVR took a bold new direction in 1994. Here was its first two-plus-two model for a decade, its first all-new engine ever, and its most sophisticated project ever.*

■ TVR CERBERA

The Cerbera, named after a creature from classical mythology, was first seen at the 1994 Birmingham Motor Show. The long, low two-plus-two coupé may have drawn on other TVR models for its styling inspiration, but the outcome was the best model TVR had ever produced.

TVR's dynamic approach to design meant that, from debut to production readiness, the Cerbera took little over two years. Especially challenging was the all-new AJP V-eight engine, the first engine designed and developed entirely by TVR. It was initially used in racing TVR Tuscans but was refined enough to pass tough emissions tests. Like all other power plants used in TVRs, the AJP sounded raw and urgent, yet was also remarkably smooth.

The 4.2-litre engine developed a monstrous 350bhp and could rev as high as 7000rpm. Unencumbered by aerodynamic weakness, the Cerbera was capable of staggering performance: 0–60mph (0–96kph) in 4.0 seconds and up to 185mph (298kph) top speed. An even more thunderous 4.5-litre GT version was shown in 1996 – it had no less than 440bhp.

The Cerbera's chassis was quite capable of dealing with all that power. Its handling was safe yet exploitable and fun, while the ride quality was firm yet comfortable.

Undoubtedly one of the car's best features was its interior. The cabin was a haven of curves, which were almost sci-fi in the way their loops swathed the passengers – all four of them, at a push. The leather-stitched console incorporated classy black-on-white dials, while the underslung cluster of dials below the steering wheel worked very well. The Cerbera has become a fitting top-of-the-range model in TVR's line-up.

■ LEFT *The muscular, almost hot-rod appearance was widely admired, and neat details like the hidden electric door "handles" made it unique.*

■ BELOW *Not only was the design work stunning, the new Cerbera was one of the fastest cars of its day: 185mph (298kph) from TVR's AJP V-eight engine.*

TVR CERBERA (1996–)	
Engine	V-eight-cylinder
Capacity	4185cc
Power	350bhp @ 6500rpm
Transmission	5-speed
Top speed	185mph (298kph)
No. built	Still in production

■ ABOVE *The interior was equally innovative. The sculpted dashboard looked fabulous and the siting of an instrument cluster under the steering column worked very well.*

TVR

■ TVR GRIFFITH

TVR progressed into the 1980s with a new chairman at the helm, businessman and true enthusiast of the marque Peter Wheeler, who succeeded in turning TVR's fortunes around in no uncertain terms. Wheeler quickly realized what his customers wanted and concentrated his efforts on making convertible two-seaters with glassfibre bodies and brawny Rover V-eight engines.

The angular Tasmin series of 1980–91 was successful, if not exactly pretty, but the car it led to was undeniably a masterstroke. The Griffith had its roots in the TVR Tuscan racer

■ ABOVE *Power slides were part and parcel of the Griffith package. With 280bhp on tap and no traction control system, care was always required.*

■ LEFT *The Griffith marked a radical break away from TVR's past into a bold and highly successful future. Mature styling and increasingly powerful V-eight engines headed the move.*

■ ABOVE *Few other cars could match the character of the Griffith's leather-and-wood sculpted interior.*

first seen in 1988, which used the familiar TVR tubular chassis, uprated suspension and a monster 400bhp V-eight engine. Tuscans were raced in one of the quickest and most exciting one-make series in the world but were never officially homologated for road use.

The spirit of the Tuscan resurfaced in the new Griffith, a pukka road-going car launched at the Birmingham Motor Show in 1990, but not actually available until late 1991. The Griffith name harked back to the magnificently hairy Ford V-eight powered TVRs of the mid-

1960s. The justification for exploiting that heritage was certainly there, since the first edition of the new Griffith sported a V-eight engine based on the unit still used in the Range Rover, and developing either 240bhp or 280bhp.

In looks, the Griffith was far removed from TVRs of old: instead of angular and slightly gawky lines there were swoopy curves everywhere, a profile unbroken by styling adornments and clever air ducting at the leading edges of the bonnet (hood) and doors. Other neat styling details included a lack of

■ LEFT *In a Griffith 500 you could screech away from rest to 60mph (96 kph) in just over four seconds. This was an old-school macho sportscar for the modern age.*

■ RIGHT *The powerful Griffith boasted one of the greatest exhaust notes in motoring.*

exterior door handles, evocative aluminium knobs in the cabin and a removable solid-centre roof section. Perhaps the most impressive aspect of the Griffith was that it was almost totally designed and produced in-house. Considering the brilliance of the end product, this was a remarkable achievement for such a small size company.

Testers were immediately impressed by the Griffith's character: an almost forgotten formula of raw V-eight power, rear-wheel drive and a rich, burbling exhaust note that was like no other car. Some even compared its overall impact to that of the E-Type Jaguar in 1961, since the TVR offered a similarly intoxicating brew of luscious curves, superior performance and exceptional value for money. No other sportscar offered so much for so little, and TVR grew in size and importance on the back of Griffith sales.

If the press was impressed with the Griffith, it was rapturous about the 1993 Griffith 500, whose engine grew in size to five litres and which developed no less than 345bhp. Now you could expect

a 0–60mph (0–96kph) time of a little over four seconds and mid-range punch and low-speed torque the like of which was simply not available elsewhere.

TVR followed up the Griffith with other models such as the cheaper Chimaera and even more potent Cerbera, but neither had the impact of the original, svelte Griffith, which remains one of the most popular models in the Blackpool manufacturer's repertoire.

TVR GRIFFITH (1990–)	
Engine	V-eight-cylinder
Capacity	3947–4997cc
Power	243–345bhp
Transmission	5-speed
Top speed	152–163mph (245–262kph)
No. built	Still in production

■ LEFT *The gauges had to be recalibrated in a Griffith to suit its phenomenal performance – up to 163mph (262kph) top speed. Cabin architecture was widely admired in TVRs.*

■ ABOVE *The innocuous-seeming "500" tag on the end of the Griffith name hinted at its new 5.0-litre V-eight engine and its 345bhp of raw power.*

VAUXHALL

■ VAUXHALL LOTUS CARLTON

In March 1989, news filtered through that Vauxhall was cooperating with Lotus in the development of a high-performance version of the Carlton saloon (sedan) (known as the Opel Omega outside Britain). When it became clear that General Motors was not going to follow the lead set by BMW and Mercedes-Benz in limiting top speed to 155mph (249kph), a minor media storm broke out. The new Lotus Carlton, said the press, was irresponsible: its top speed of 176mph (283kph) was more than anyone should ever be doing.

The controversy over the Lotus Carlton's speed was spurious. Any number of cars from Porsche, Ferrari or Aston Martin were capable of going much faster than this. The germ of the problem in the media's eyes was that the Carlton was a family car, capable of seating four adults in comfort. In practice, this was the Lotus Carlton's unique selling point, since no other supercar could transport so many so fast. In truth, it was all a storm in the proverbial teacup, since the volume of

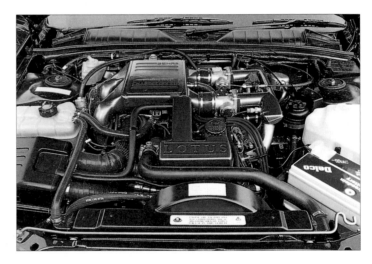

■ ABOVE *A four-seater saloon (sedan) with a Vauxhall badge that was capable of 176mph (283kph) – it could only be the Lotus Carlton.*

■ LEFT *The prominent Lotus badging betrayed the work done to this 3.6-litre six-cylinder engine, which developed 377bhp.*

VAUXHALL LOTUS CARLTON (1989–92)	
Engine	6-cylinder
Capacity	3615cc
Power	377bhp @ 5200rpm
Transmission	6-speed manual
Top speed	176mph (283kph)
No. built	440

■ LEFT *Apart from a body kit, rear spoiler and five-spoke alloy wheels, this could have been any member of the rather ordinary Carlton/Omega family.*

cars sold was tiny; General Motors wanted to sell 1,100, but, in fact, only 440 were built because of the effects of the recession on sales.

The heart of the new supersaloon was its Lotus-developed 3.6-litre six-cylinder 24-valve engine. With its twin turbochargers, catalysts and advanced electronic management, it had huge power and torque. This, together with a Corvette ZR-1 six-speed gearbox, gave performance that was simply sensational. The Carlton accelerated faster than a Ferrari Testarossa and could reach 160mph (256kph) in under a mile.

Not only did it go fast in a straight line, it cornered and stopped with great finesse – a car with the Lotus badge on it should behave in no other way. Self-levelling dampers controlled the suspension superbly, providing handling of an order that belied the car's bulk. *Autocar* magazine described the braking as "the best we've tried on a road car".

Far from being a nervous, temperamental sportscar, the Lotus Carlton was benign and extremely safe. It would happily idle around town and was forgiving if abused. You could also go

shopping, since the boot was huge – and the rear seats folded to increase capacity.

Passengers were supremely cosseted. You got leather seats, a leather steering wheel, polished wood and pleated cloth trim, plus head restraints all round, six-speaker CD hi-fi, air-conditioning, electric windows and a sunroof. The

Lotus Carlton looked the part too. Its body kit comprised a deep front spoiler, wheel-arch extensions, aerodynamic side skirts, a new rear bumper and a boot spoiler; and there was just one colour, Imperial Green. The price was certainly high at £48,000 ($80,840) but entirely justified by the car's rarity and specification.

■ LEFT *As well as being exceedingly quick, the Lotus Carlton was fun around corners and extremely safe into the bargain.*

■ LEFT *Apart from the Lotus badging, 180mph (290kph) speedometer and extra electrical equipment, this could have been an ordinary saloon (sedan) car dashboard.*

■ ABOVE *This was a very comfortably trimmed car, with standard leather, polished wood and a host of equipment.*

■ RIGHT *In the tail-pipes of the Lotus Carlton was a whiff of the political controversy that surrounded its high top speed.*

VOLKSWAGEN

■ VOLKSWAGEN GOLF GTI

Based on the best supermini the mid-1970s had to offer, the VW Golf GTI was the father of the modern hot-hatch brat-pack, setting the standards for two generations to come. When the first Golf GTI appeared in 1975, who could have guessed that production figures would pass 1.35 million by the time the car reached its 20th birthday? Certainly not Volkswagen itself, which only envisaged a short run of 5,000 units for the sporty hatchback in those gloomy years following the fuel crisis.

The first prototypes were fitted with the 80bhp carburettor engine from the Audi 80 GT, but by the time the car appeared at the 1975 Frankfurt Motor Show it was sporting fuel injection for an output of 110bhp. The first model had a four-speed gearbox driving through the front wheels.

Outwardly there was very little to mark the GTI out from the standard Golf: discreet badging, side stripes, a chin

■ RIGHT *GTI became the term used to describe the hot-hatch generation, which was kicked off by this car, the Volkswagen Golf GTI, in 1975.*

■ BELOW *At first, the Golf GTI was considered a low-volume production special, but as the years progressed drivers recognized its greatness and bought it in huge volumes.*

■ ABOVE *Apart from the subtlest of spoilers and very minor trim differences, the GTI looked like a standard hatchback – the ultimate in understatement.*

spoiler and plastic wheel-arch lips. The car was an instant hit, mixing punchy performance and tenacious knock-about handling from the firmed-up strut suspension with the practicality of a well-built three-door hatchback body of well proven durability. Production figures leapt from just over 10,000 in 1976 to 31,000 in 1977 and an amazing 42,000 in 1978.

The first right-hand-drive cars were not launched until July 1979, and that year multi-spoke BBS alloy wheels and a five-speed gearbox became part of the specification. There was a popular cabriolet version of the GTI, but the handling suffered from the extra weight involved in the strengthening of the Golf shell. The drop-top MkI body shape lasted right up until 1992.

■ LEFT *Available only as a three-door hatchback, the GTI was every bit as useful as a shopping car as for hacking around country roads.*

■ BELOW *The Mk1 convertible body style lasted right up until 1993.*

The best of the MkI GTIs was the 1800 model, replacing the 1600 in 1982. Power went up only marginally, but there was 8lb ft (10.8Nm) of extra torque, produced 1500rpm lower down. You could spot an 1800 by its new wider alloys, twin headlights and steel sunroof.

The GTI has lived through two generations since the demise of the MkI in 1985. The shape has been gradually rounded-off and the power – and luxury – increased. The 16-valvers of the mid-1980s packed 139bhp and came complete with electric windows, sunroof, central locking and driver's seat height adjustment. The facelifted 1990-model-year cars had deeper spoilers and power steering. The most coveted of all the MkIIs is the Rallye, a 5,000-off limited edition four-wheel-drive Golf using VW's Syncro system allied to a 1756cc supercharged engine. Built as a homologation special for rallying, the Rallye spawned the front-drive but supercharged G60. This was built on normal GTI production lines – unlike the Rallye, which was produced in Belgium.

The concept continued in the MkIII Golf, either as a 155bhp 2.0-litre or the blockbuster 140mph (225kph) VR6 complete with super-sweet 2.8-litre V-six power – and that is a guaranteed future classic.

VW GOLF GTI MK1 (1975–85)	
Engine	4-cylinder
Capacity	1588–1781cc
Power	110–112bhp
Transmission	4/5-speed manual
Top speed	115mph (185kph)
No. built	350,000

■ LEFT *As a convertible, the GTI caught the mood of the 1980s, even if ultimately it was not as sharp-handling or rigid as the saloon.*

■ ABOVE *As a lightweight car with a powerful 1.6 or 1.8-litre engine, the GTI was a stormer, and its leech-like behaviour around twisty bends won it many friends.*

VOLKSWAGEN

■ VOLKSWAGEN SCIROCCO/CORRADO

Having relied on the rear-engined Beetle and various derivatives for four decades, Volkswagen underwent a complete revolution in the 1970s. It followed the lead taken by its sister company Audi in adopting front engines and front-wheel drive, completely renewing its model range and revitalizing its prospects.

The first of the new generation was the 1973 Passat, the most significant was the 1974 Golf, but the best was the Scirocco, launched two months before the Golf. The Scirocco was developed alongside the Golf and shared many common elements: platform, power trains, suspension and so on. Yet the Scirocco had style, and it also had clarity of purpose as an enjoyable coupé.

Italy's Giugiaro did a superb design job according to the folded-paper school of design. The shape was crisp, taut and light, and the rising glass line was utterly distinctive. For Volkswagen, the Scirocco was a specialist car, so it asked Stuttgart-based firm Karmann to build it. There was a large range of models, starting with

■ RIGHT *The first-generation Scirocco was like a sharp-suited coupé version of the Golf, and in GTI form became a performance icon.*

■ RIGHT *The second-generation Scirocco was styled in-house by VW and perhaps lost some of the Giugiaro charm of the first series.*

lowly 1100 and 1300 versions (though these were not widely exported). Far more satisfying were the larger-engined 1500 and 1600, but the best of all were the models powered by the 110bhp Golf GTI engine. These were variously badged GLI, GTI and Storm and became minor icons of performance motoring, not surprisingly with a top speed of

114mph (183kph) and a 0–60mph (0–96kph) time of 8.9 seconds. The Scirocco was an even better handling car than the Golf.

Automatic transmission was optional on all but the base models and the GTI engined versions. Four-speed manual was standard, although the very last 110bhp models got five speeds as

■ LEFT *All Scirocco models offered keen driving manners with a healthy dose of both style and practicality.*

■ ABOVE *The 1985 16V version of the Scirocco was quite a stormer, having 139bhp at its disposal.*

■ RIGHT *The GTX was a 111bhp mid-range model with a sporting close-ratio five-speed gearbox.*

standard. In 1981 an all-new Scirocco was launched, although to many it was a retrograde step. It had a blander profile, disappointing ride and handling.

Officially the 1989 Corrado was not a replacement for the Scirocco, which was perhaps auspicious because it was a far better car in all respects. The shape returned to the sharp, compact purposefulness of the original Scirocco, but it was underneath where the most impressive work had been done.

Put simply, the Corrado had one of the best front-wheel-drive chassis ever made. Neither the standard 136bhp 1.8-litre engine nor the supercharged 160bhp G60 engine did it justice; drivers had to wait until the 1992 VR6, with its blistering 190bhp 2.8-litre V-six engine, to exploit the chassis to the full: it was fluid, composed, controlled and extremely quick. By the time Corrado production finished in 1995, VW had made half a million.

■ ABOVE *The Corrado was altogether a step up: every department had been improved.*

■ RIGHT *Fast, responsive, well-built and very good value, the Scirocco was a bestseller throughout the 1970s and 80s.*

VOLKSWAGEN SCIROCCO MK1 (1974–80)	
Engine	4-cylinder
Capacity	1093–1588cc
Power	50–110bhp
Transmission	4/5-speed manual 3-speed auto
Top speed	89–114mph (143–183kph)
No. built	504,200

■ ABOVE *With one of the best front-wheel-drive chassis ever, the Corrado was capable of stunning speeds around corners and, with the right engine, in a straight line, too.*

VOLVO

■ VOLVO C70

Volvo design chief Paul Horbury said that he knew he had succeeded with the new C70 when he parked an example outside a prominent Californian hotel, and the valet attendants left it there for show rather than parking it in the parking lot underground.

Volvo's image in the 1970s and 80s was one of staid dreariness. The C70 was symptomatic of the company's turn-around. For its first sports coupé since the '60s it formed a co-venture with UK-based TWR (which engineered the chassis) and the result was the most desirable Volvo ever.

■ ABOVE *With the C70, Sweden's leading car-maker entered new territory, doing battle with Mercedes and BMW coupés.*

VOLVO C70 (1996–)	
Engine	5-cylinder
Capacity	2319–2435cc
Power	193–240bhp
Transmission	5-speed manual 4-speed auto
Top speed	137–146mph (220–235kph)
No. built	Still in production

■ ABOVE *The extremely handsome design of the C70 was penned by Volvo's British-born design chief Paul Horbury.*

■ RIGHT *In full convertible form, the C70 was yet another new departure for Volvo: never before had it offered a series (production) drop-top model.*

■ RIGHT *The C70 was as effective in action as it was great to look at. Its turbocharged five-cylinder engine and chassis dynamics engineered by TWR guaranteed it fine manners.*

The C70 borrowed much of its technology from the 850R saloon (sedan), including its 240bhp turbocharged five-cylinder engine driving the front wheels. Since it was lighter and more aerodynamic, the C70 posted even better performance figures than the 850R: 146mph (235kph) top speed and 0–60mph (0–96kph) in 6.7 seconds.

The cabin reflected functional Scandinavian themes, with a huge choice of colour schemes and tasteful, luxurious decoration. The ten-speaker

■ ABOVE *Volvo's new executive-class coupé looked like a convincing alternative to the best coupés in its class.*

■ ABOVE *Described as "typically Swedish", the C70 interior was a paragon of tasteful luxury. Full four-seater convertibles have always been rarities.*

hi-fi was among the best available anywhere in the world. Even more attractive than the coupé was the full convertible version announced shortly afterwards at the 1997 Geneva Motor Show.

The C70 secured a starring role in the Hollywood film *The Saint* starring Val Kilmer. Through the TWR connection, two of the first "customers" for the new Volvo were Formula 1 racers Damon Hill and Pedro Diniz, who both received a C70 as personal transport.

■ RIGHT *Even with its hood (top) raised, the C70 managed to look aristocratic and stylish.*

A-Z of Dream Cars

The pure dream car was born in 1939, when General Motors presented the Y-Job. This was not a car designed for general consumption, but one created by a styling department as an "ideas" car, a sleek, chrome-adorned sculpture designed to inflate passions and inspire imaginations.

The true golden age of dream cars was the 1950s, when the fantastic was normal and bizarre shapes and schemes were required. The aftermath of flying cars, nuclear-powered cars and gyroscopically controlled two-wheeled cars left America having had too much, and so the European design houses became the home of dream cars in the 1960s and 1970s. Here we bring dream cars right into the present day and beyond as we marvel at the creative genius behind some of the greatest cars ever designed.

ALFA ROMEO

Traditionally, Alfa Romeo has aligned itself to the major Italian carrozzieri (design houses) when it comes to design work. It has favoured Bertone, Pininfarina and Zagato, but many other independents have been drawn to the magic that is Alfa Romeo, and Alfa itself has occasionally produced a few of its own dreams in the metal.

Flying saucers and BAT-mobiles

After the Second World War, Alfa Romeo encouraged experimental bodies on its chassis. The Disco Volante ("flying saucer") race cars were a collaboration with Touring, for example, but of all Alfa Romeo's dream cars, the most spectacular were undoubtedly the incredible BAT series – BAT standing for Berlina Aerodinamica Tecnica. All were designed by Franco Scaglione of Bertone. The first in the series of three was the so-called BAT 5, which in 1953 was as way-out as they come. The aim was to create the most aerodynamic shape possible on an Alfa Romeo 1900 chassis, and with a claimed Cd figure of 0.23, it certainly was. The faired-in wings, sideways-popping headlamps and

hawk-like nose were striking enough, but it was the rear-end that got all the attention. Two huge, inward-curving wings rose fantastically around a long central rear "tunnel".

Things got even more outrageous with the BAT 7 prototype of 1954. The rear wings began at the windscreen pillars and became so curved-in that they almost touched each other over the razor-sharp central fin. Huge slots in the

fins equalized side pressure, and an even more aerodynamic Cd figure was claimed. By the time the third and final BAT 9 arrived in 1955, the rear wings had been clipped back to vaguely modest proportions, and there were now side fins from door to tail. After three successive years of making Turin Show crowds swoon, the BAT series was retired. All these cars have since been restored to a glorious condition.

■ LEFT *Ital Design was responsible for the 1969 Iguana prototype, based on the near-racing-specification 33. It was at one point scheduled for a production run but this didn't materialize.*

■ ABOVE *The 1971 Caimano was designed by Giugiaro and featured very angular lines, a flop-forward canopy, pop-up headlamps and an air brake. It was based on the Alfasud.*

■ LEFT *Proteo was the name of this Alfa Romeo Centro Stile prototype. It clearly prefigured the general profile of the later GTV production car.*

■ BELOW *Walter de Silva's masterful hand created the stunning Nuvola, an exercise in a classically inspired sports coupé.*

■ ABOVE *A long bonnet (hood), short tail and classically curved cabin excited public passions.*

■ ABOVE *Ital Design was again responsible for this Alfa Romeo design study called the Scighera. It was intended as an exotic road or racing car.*

Iguana, Spider, Proteo and Nuvola

Ital Design developed another spectacular Alfa concept car, the Iguana prototype of 1969. This was intended to enter production in a small series but it never did. Based on the 33 Stradale mid-engined chassis, it was notable for its brushed-steel body (ten years before the De Lorean) and sharp nose treatment.

■ ABOVE *Simple, stylish and sporty: the Nuvola's wood-and-chrome interior looked both backwards and forwards in time.*

To many eyes the 1994 Spider and GTV production models looked like show cars. To prepare the public for the radical shape of these newcomers, Alfa Romeo designed the Proteo prototype in 1991. This had the rising belt-line and bonnet (hood) cut-outs for the headlamps, which made the Spider/GTV so distinctive, but was based on the 164 and featured four-wheel drive, four-wheel steering and removable glass roof panels.

Alfa Romeo's design boss Walter de Silva was responsible for the striking Nuvola concept car shown at the 1996 Paris Salon. For its inspiration, this handsome car looked back to the great days, not only in its proportion and detailing but also in that it had a separate chassis, in theory allowing any body shape to be designed around it.

Alfa's own shape was extremely elegant: a long, classic bonnet, low, tapering rear, recessed lights and lots of chrome. Despite the retro flavour, it was also ultra-modern: 300bhp aluminium V-six engine, four-wheel drive, six speeds and glorious 18in (45.7cm) alloy wheels. Sadly, despite the precedent set by the Proteo, the Nuvola looked unlikely to become a production model.

AUDI

The Audi name is one of the oldest in the German motor industry, but its post-war career did not begin until Volkswagen bought the Auto Union combine, and the Audi name was revived in 1965. Audi has always been associated with front-wheel drive (and later four-wheel drive) quality saloons (sedans) and coupés.

The brand had just the right qualities for extending the Volkswagen-Audi Group's interests in bold new directions: sportscars, supercars and dream cars, but it was only with the Quattro that Audi finally became a truly aspirational marque.

Quattro Spyder, Avus Quattro

Without a doubt, the Quattro Spyder was the star of the 1991 Frankfurt Motor Show. It also signalled the way ahead for Audi in its exclusive use of aluminium in the bodyshell: this lightweight route would ultimately be used for the A8.

■ BELOW *Undeniably Germanic in form and function, the TT coupé recalled in spirit its ancestors of the 1930s, the great Auto Union racers.*

■ ABOVE *Emphasized by its unpainted finish, the aluminium structure of the Avus was ultra-smooth and lightweight, so that this 6.0-litre V-twelve car was capable of 211mph (339kph).*

■ ABOVE *The Quattro Spyder was a four-wheel-drive mid-engined supercar. Its major significance was the use of aluminium in the bodyshell and a roof-line that inspired a generation of VW/Audi products.*

Equally arresting was the dramatic shape (penned by Erwin Hammel) – all the more so for its bright orange colour scheme. Fitted with a mid-mounted 2.8-litre V-six engine and four-wheel drive, it was claimed to do 155mph (249kph) and reach 60mph (96kph) from rest in less than six seconds.

A mere two months later, at the Tokyo show, Audi upstaged every other concept car with its Avus Quattro, very similar in shape to the previous Spyder but finished in glorious polished aluminium. The quicksilver showstopper recalled the racing heritage of the great Auto Union record-breakers of the 1930s. The specification was breathtaking: a 6.0-litre 60V 12-cylinder engine arranged in three banks of four cylinders and developing 509bhp, four-wheel drive and six speeds. Audi claimed an amazing top speed of 211mph (339kph) and 0-60mph (0–96kph) in just three seconds.

TT and TTS Roadster

The name chosen for Audi's next-generation 1990s sportscars recalled the world's oldest motor race held on public roads, the Isle of Man TT. Destined to become a production model, the TT was first shown as a concept car at the 1995 Frankfurt Motor Show.

■ LEFT *Polished aluminium detailing reflected the use of aluminium in the doors, bonnet (hood), boot (trunk) and engine. Circular dials and red leather trim completed a classy cabin.*

■ BELOW *At the 1995 Tokyo Motor Show Audi presented the TTS roadster, probably even more desirable than the TT coupé. Note the hood (top), held taught like a parachute.*

■ RIGHT *Strong, simple lines epitomized Audi's philosophy of design, while its high performance potential was realized by a turbocharged 210bhp engine.*

A group of young Audi designers created the TT as a car they desired to own, but was accessible to a wide public. Hence, existing Audi technology was used wherever possible: the five-cylinder turbo engine from the A4, and Audi's four-wheel-drive system was used. The 150bhp engine was claimed to produce a very fast top speed of 140mph (225kph).

In style the TT was described as "Germanic" and a vision of the Audi brand. The curves recalled Bauhaus design and pre-war Auto Union racing cars. The show cars' silver paint emphasized the Teutonic element and also betrayed the choice of aluminium for the engine, doors, bonnet and boot (hood and trunk).

The two-plus-two interior was functional and sporting. Traditional sportscar themes were pursued, such as circular dials, leather upholstery, aluminium grab handles supporting the centre console, even exposed rivets securing many metal items. Following quickly on the heels of the TT hatchback coupé show car, at the 1995 Tokyo Motor Show Audi presented the TTS roadster. The most obvious changes were the open top, only two seats, larger wheels and thong-laced leather seats. Under the bonnet, the engine was a more powerful "concept" evolution of the A4 1.8-litre turbo engine, developing no less than 210bhp – good for 149mph (240kph) and 0–60mph 0-96kph) in six seconds.

The most exciting part of the TT/TTS twins story was that Audi planned to put the models into production before the end of the century at a plant in Hungary. This meant that they would be ready to compete with such rivals as the Porsche Boxster and Mercedes-Benz SLK.

■ RIGHT *Both the TTS and its fixed-head TT brother were scheduled to go into production by the end of the century.*

BERTONE

Alongside Pininfarina, Bertone is the greatest design house in the world. Its history stretches back to 1912, when Giovanni Bertone founded a *carrozzeria* in Turin. Bertone's great days began in the 1950s, and it became the first port of call for numerous manufacturers seeking the right design for their new products.

Nuccio and his wicked children

Giovanni's son Giuseppe "Nuccio" Bertone steered the company through its greatest era, boasting a propensity for spotting brilliant young talent: such great names as Giugiaro, Gandini, Michelotti and Scaglione all served their apprenticeships at Bertone. No one doubts the brilliance of Bertone's production designs such as the Alfa Romeo Giulietta Sprint and Giulia GT or the Lancia Stratos, nor its capacity for manufacturing for Alfa, Fiat, Volvo and others. Bertone also badged several models under its own name, such as the Fiat-engined 850 Coupé, Ritmo Cabriolet and Freelimber off-roader.

The most striking category of Bertone designs were undoubtedly his show cars,

■ ABOVE *Nuccio Bertone was unquestionably one of the most profoundly influential figures in the car world, with a brilliant eye for design talent and an unending capacity to surprise. He died in 1997.*

which he called his "children", and especially those "wicked children", which were controversial or inspired comment. Bertone was rarely interested in practical innovations in his show cars: these were pure dream machines.

Marzal and Carabo

Bertone produced many special bodies in the 1950s on the chassis of Alfa Romeo, Jaguar, Aston Martin and Maserati, but he did not really get into his stride as a producer of dream cars until the late 1960s. One of the most striking of all was the 1967 Lamborghini Marzal, a very novel concept car, which directly inspired the later Espada series production car. Bertone's scheme for a four-seater Lamborghini called for enormous gullwing doors with surfaces almost entirely of glass. This solved the problem of entry to the rear seats and drew attention to the idea. So did the all-silver upholstery!

■ RIGHT *The Marzal was an adventurous step forward in four-seater supercar design. It directly inspired the production of the Lamborghini Espada, although not with the Marzal's glass gullwing doors.*

■ LEFT *The Stratos HF prototype of 1970 was just 33in (84cm) high. The windscreen opened for the passengers to enter, and the steering wheel folded away for easier access.*

■ OPPOSITE *With the Lamborghini Bravo, Bertone experimented with the use of glass as an integrated part of the design.*

■ ABOVE *The Villager was a typical product of the early 1970s fad for beach/ leisure vehicles.*

■ RIGHT *Bertone designed the X1/9 for Fiat, and his own Dallara radical show-car interpretation was intended for racing in the Group 5 class.*

A year later, the Carabo marked another mould-breaking shape: something between a wedge and an arrow. The visual equivalent of a Doppler effect was created by the fluorescent red nose and green tail. The upward-hinging doors anticipated Bertone's Countach by four years, and gave the car its name – Carabo is a contraction of the Italian for "beetle".

Stratos, Bravo and Sibilo

With the 1970 Lancia Stratos show car, Bertone teetered on the edge separating car design from pure sculpture. This amazing machine was designed with a completely free hand and was a car of extremes. It was so low that the driver had to flip up the windscreen and walk in over the front end. To see out, you looked through small windows placed directly behind the front wheels – there was no rear visibility at all. To access the mid-mounted engine, a triangular shape panel hinged upwards like a piano.

The 1974 Lamborghini Bravo (based on the Urraco) integrated elements like the lights, air intakes and rear quarter-lights into the design of the car itself. Another feature was the dark glass, which appeared to form a seamless pane. This theme would be refined with the 1978 Sibilo, an exercise based on the Lancia Stratos. Here the distinction between the metal and glass surfaces was blurred, creating the impression that the body was hewn from a single piece. Inside, the Sibilo's steering wheel was a single solid piece, and the dashboard featured digital instruments set very far back directly in the driver's line of sight.

BERTONE

■ ABOVE *Bertone built his Navajo show car on an Alfa Romeo T33 racing chassis, complete with a flat-12 engine. The use of front and rear wings aided downforce.*

■ RIGHT *Along with many others, Bertone must have been disappointed by the styling of Jaguar's XJS. This is his re-interpretation, called the Ascot.*

Rainbow and Athon

Many observers felt that Bertone's Ferrari Dino 308 GT4 was a disappointingly boxy production design. Perhaps to address such criticism, Bertone produced the Rainbow in 1976, based on the mid-engined 308. The name came about because the solid roof could pivot to the vertical and drop down behind the seats, so making the car perfect for rain or sun. The angular

lines were uncompromising: there were literally no curves to be seen other than the wheels and exhaust pipes. This model had the distinction of being advertised in the exclusive American Neiman Marcus store catalogue in 1979 but, with a price tag of $200,000, it scared any customers off.

Extending Bertone's reputation for creating pure dream cars, the 1980 Athon was an uncompromising roadster

based on the Lamborghini Urraco. It typified Bertone's penchant for bold, squarish shapes joining together to form a whole, themes that would be extended by such cars as the Alfa 6-based Delfino and Citroën BX Group B-based Zabrus.

Bertone's Corvette-based Ramarro won many awards and one designer described it as "representing Bertone's soul". Its hard, geometric shape was emphasized by a completely blacked-out

■ ABOVE *The name Rainbow was chosen for this Ferrari-based car because of its potential for use in rain or sun. This show car was unusual in that it was actually offered for sale to special order.*

■ RIGHT *Bertone began taking new dream-car directions with the 1983 Delfino, a three-box coupé based on the Alfa 6.*

■ BELOW *The 1986 Zabrus predicted future shapes like the Alfa Romeo 145. Its basis was the fearsome Group B rally Citroën BX.*

■ ABOVE *Using Chevrolet's Corvette as a basis, the Ramarro was long, low, cleanly finished and sleek.*

■ RIGHT *Bertone's interiors were typically highly sculpted, simple and clean. This is the Athon's exotic cockpit.*

■ BELOW *The 1980 Athon, based on a Lamborghini Urraco, was a widely admired roadster show car.*

glass top, but not everyone thought the shape had the timeless quality of previous Bertone efforts.

The 1988 Genesis was a people carrier with a difference: it had a 455bhp Lamborghini V-twelve engine mounted between the front passengers. There was space for five people, the rear three sitting in "arrow" formation. Its style and layout were controversial, and the point of having a V-twelve engine was undermined by a long-legged three-speed automatic gearbox.

BERTONE

■ ABOVE *Marking a return to the impact of the great show cars of the 1970s, the Nivola used a Corvette ZR1 engine.*

■ RIGHT *"People carriers" were never so radical as Bertone's startling Genesis. The gullwing doors suited its mechanical basis – the Lamborghini Countach V-twelve!*

Nivola, Rush and Blitz

For the Nivola of 1990 (its name recalled the great Italian race driver Tazio Nuvolari), Bertone turned to the Chevrolet Corvette ZR1 for its motive power – and, like all Bertone's show cars, it was a full runner. The bright-yellow concept car featured a targa roof, which stowed above the engine, and hydropneumatic suspension. Most bizarrely of all, it had massaging vibrators in the backs of the seats, claimed to relieve the stress of long

journeys! Perhaps they were needed, for the Nivola measured an expansive 78in (1.98m) wide.

At the 1992 Turin show, Bertone presented two concept ideas. One was part of Fiat's Cinquecento concept display, an outlandish two-seater 4x4 buggy called the Rush. The other was the Blitz electric sportscar. The Blitz was described as a car/bike cross-over.

The sportscar angle was not out of place in an electric car since power response is near-immediate in electric vehicles.

Karisma and Slalom

Despite its rather tacky name, the 1994 Karisma was a fine-looking car based on a Porsche 911 platform. It revived the gullwing four-seater theme pioneered by the 1967 Marzal, and deliberate

■ RIGHT *The exposed front wings and near-tandem seating position echoed Bertone's intent that the Blitz should be a motorcycle/car cross-over.*

■ RIGHT *With its big gullwing doors and four-seat interior, the Porsche-based Karisma was a spiritual successor to the Marzal, seen in the background.*

reference was made to this early Bertone design. The leather-trimmed interior had full seating for four adults, and the gullwing doors were claimed to "allow dignified entry".

A startling shade of orange – said to be inspired by Bertone's favourite champagne, Veuve Clicquot – at least made the 1996 Slalom stand out, not that it needed to with its sports-coupé shape and audaciously designed stacked front and clipped-in rear lights. Adjustable rear seats made the two-plus-two interior fairly practical. Based on the Opel/Vauxhall Calibra Turbo 4x4 floorpan, it was also surprisingly effective to drive.

Nuccio Bertone died in 1997, but left behind him a design and manufacturing empire with the highest reputation, 1500 staff and dozens of clients from around the world. Perhaps his most important characteristic was an ability to spot talent: Marcello Gandini and Giorgetto Giugiaro, the two greatest car designers of recent years, both served as apprentices under Bertone.

■ ABOVE *The orange paintwork of the Opel Calibra-based Slalom was said to be inspired by Nuccio Bertone's favourite champagne.*

■ ABOVE *Rush was the name of this fun-packed, little, two-seater sports off-roader, based on Fiat's tiny Cinquecento.*

■ ABOVE *The Lancia Kayak was undoubtedly more accomplished than Lancia's own later coupé effort, the Kappa.*

CHRYSLER

From Thunderbolt to Turboflite
After GM's Buick had produced the Y-Job, the world's first ever "dream car", in 1939, the first to follow up the idea was its rival Chrysler. Two years later its styling chief Alex Tremulis created the Thunderbolt, a bulbous retractable-top two-door with push-button controls.

After the war, Chrysler collaborated with the Italian design house Ghia to create such dream cars as the Plymouth XX-500 and Chrysler K-310 in 1951. A man called Virgil Exner emerged as the head of styling for Chrysler and directed a whole string of unusually smooth shapes by American standards, notably the Firearrow series of 1953–54, the 1954 De Soto Adventurer and the ill-fated 1956 Norseman, which sank the Andrea Doria.

The Ghia connection resulted in the striking 1956 Dart, an impressively clean, aerodynamic car (claimed to have one third the drag of conventional cars) with probably the tallest rear fins ever seen. The steel roof was designed to slide back into the rear compartment.

■ ABOVE *Under the tutelage of Virgil Exner, Chrysler produced some extraordinary show cars. This Plymouth Special was seen in the 1957 film, Bundle of Joy.*

■ BELOW *By 1965, the first American dream-car golden age was already over, as this tame Plymouth VIP shows. Its main feature was a cantilever roof and rear "office".*

■ LEFT *If you are wondering how you got into the outlandish 1961 Turboflite, when you opened the door, the whole roof and glass lifted up like a clamshell.*

By 1958, Exner's direction had lost its way a little, the Imperial d'Elégance being anything but elegant. The 1961 Dodge Flitewing advanced an interesting solution for a hardtop coupé: the windows opened outwards and upwards automatically on exit. The Turboflite went one better: the whole roof and glasshouse lifted up as one for entry.

Lamborghini revives the dream
Throughout the 1960s Chrysler experimented in the dead-end of turbines, handlebar steering and even

■ LEFT *A liaison with Lamborghini produced the 1987 Portofino, a dramatic mid-engined four-seater with Lamborghini V-eight power.*

■ LEFT *Plymouth's Speedster show car was only 10in (25.5cm) longer than a Mini. It had a mid-mounted 2.0-litre engine.*

■ ABOVE *One of Chrysler's most daring show cars was the Plymouth Slingshot, designed for optimum acceleration.*

vacuum-operated ashtrays. As the years progressed, the dream cars got more predictable; the 1965 Plymouth VIP was typically unadventurous, and Chrysler seemed to have a rude awakening from its dream state.

It took until the 1980s for Chrysler (along with other American manu-facturers) to rejoin the dream train and re-establish the American tradition for producing other-worldly machinery.

Perhaps it was Chrysler's purchase of Lamborghini in 1987 that set the ball rolling, although the rise of designer Tom Edle and president Bob Lutz had a huge influence. Certainly its immediate action to create a co-project, which would demonstrate the abilities of the new alliance, produced one of the great show cars of the 1980s. At the Frankfurt Motot Show in the autumn of 1987, the Portofino was displayed. Chrysler described it as the "ultimate mid-engined touring sedan", and most were

■ RIGHT *Extreme light weight and optimized aerodynamics were behind the Aviat, whose aerospace bias was notable.*

inclined to agree. Using a 250bhp Lamborghini Jalpa V-eight engine, this imposing machine featured seating for four, a clamshell bonnet and boot (hood and trunk), and four Countach-style doors, which opened upwards for entry.

The Plymouth Speedster of 1989 was remarkable for its size: at 130in (330cm) long, it was minuscule by American standards, but this marked an attempt to link motorcycle and sportscar themes for the youth market. The result

included a small air deflector, central pop-up headlamps and an interior trimmed in wetsuit rubber.

The wild styling of the 1991 Chrysler 300 show car picked up on Viper themes and catapulted them into the arena of a 17ft-long four-door sports saloon (sedan). Under the long bonnet sat the 8.0-litre V-ten Viper engine, and in front of it was an Allard-style grille. The rear doors were "suicide" (i.e. rear-hinged).

CHRYSLER

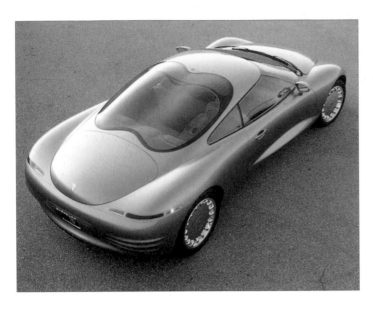

■ ABOVE *The name Back Pack suggests outdoor use, and that is precisely what this Plymouth concept car was designed to do.*

■ ABOVE *The double-curvature rear glass of the Thunderbolt was extremely effective. The cab-forward design permitted ample space for four passengers.*

■ RIGHT *Chrysler's portfolio of makes also includes Jeep. This Ecco concept car aimed to take the jeep idea into a more modern fun/sports role.*

Other 1991 show debuts were the Jeep Wagoneer 2000 (a huge estate car (station wagon) with massive 20in (50.8cm) wheels) and the Dodge Neon (a compact saloon (sedan) with sliding doors, fabric roof and a three-cylinder two-stroke engine).

Chrysler increasingly investigated "cab forward" design, and the most extreme expression to date was the 1992 Cirrus; it genuinely did point the way toward Chrysler's future saloon output, although the pillarless construction sadly did not.

From Expresso to Jazz
The 1994 Expresso was a curious taxi-styling exercise described as "Happy Face". Seen from the sides, the windows formed eyes and the bold side accent became a smiling mouth. Making sure you remained happy inside the car was a computer games console and an LCD entertainment module.

Also at the 1994 Detroit show was the Venom, a revival in spirit of the great muscle-car years of the 60s. Its matt-black bonnet (hood), chiselled nose and scooped body sides may have looked evocative but the reality underneath was less intoxicating: it was based around a Neon with a 3.5-litre V-six engine taken from the LH saloon.

Challenging GM's Ultralite in the aerodynamic, low-weight stakes was the

LEFT *Undeniably handsome, the Thunderbolt reflected a new design ethos at Chrysler, the so-called "cab-forward" approach.*

■ RIGHT *This is the 1995 Eagle Jazz show car, whose design traits such as large-diameter wheels and snubbed nose predicted future trends but could not revive the Eagle nameplate.*

Aviat. Looking remarkably similar to the Ultralite, it was claimed to weigh less than 2000lb (900kg) and have a Cd figure of 0.20, thanks to clever ducting at the front and almost jet-plane-style exits in the tail.

For 1995, Chrysler produced a stunning retro-coupé, which owed more than a nod to the 30s Bugatti that shared its name – Atlantic. It was a two-plus-two based around a Viper chassis and was styled by Tom Gale as an expression of the coupé art form. Power

came from two Neon engines joined together to make an eight-cylinder block, with an estimated power output of 325bhp.

Inside, the Atlantic bristled with cushioned leather, rosewood and classical, Swiss-watch-style dials.

When Chrysler's subdivision, Eagle, presented the Jazz at the 1995 Detroit show, pundits instantly recognized this as the future of the model's styling: a bold, snubbed nose, a very long wheelbase and a striking two-piece hatchback tail.

■ RIGHT *The ostentatious Atlantic was made into a proper running car, although, unlike the Viper on which it was based, it looked unlikely to reach production.*

■ ABOVE *For the Atlantic, two Chrysler Neon four-cylinder engines were joined together to make a single 325bhp V-eight with a glorious architectural feel.*

■ RIGHT *The Atlantic was an unashamed throw-back to the design world's glory years of the 1930s. It even shared its name with the car that inspired it, Bugatti's sublime Atlantic coupé.*

CHRYSLER

■ LEFT *The Chrysler LHX was a highly advanced-looking luxury saloon (sedan) concept. Its flowing lines were echoed in later production models, though the low roof-line proved impractical.*

■ BELOW *The more aggressively styled sister to the LHX was the Dodge Intrepid ESX. It had a diesel/electric hybrid engine.*

Pick-ups and concept cars

The Dakota Sidewinder, seen in 1996, reflected an American passion for pick-ups, taking it to the extreme. Chunky, open-topped with a narrow hot-rod-style windshield and a Viper GTS-R 600bhp engine under the bonnet (hood), this was bound to make an impression. The "gas" pedal was marked "Go" and the brake pedal "Whoa"! Perhaps even more outrageous was the Dodge T-Rex, a 6-wheeler based on the Ram pick-up and sporting a 500bhp V-ten engine.

At the opposite extreme. Chrysler presented a China Concept Car, created to satisfy a request from the Chinese

■ LEFT *The engaging little CCC was intended as a vehicle for China, although Chrysler hinted that its all-plastic body (surely inspired by the Citroën 2CV) could have a wider impact on production processes.*

authorities to tender for a new "people's car". The CCC seemed an up-date of the Citroën 2CV, even down to its Bauhaus glass treatment and full fabric roof. Sadly production looked unlikely.

Perhaps Chrysler's most important concept cars for many years appeared at the 1996 Detroit show: the stunningly sleek and sensual LHX and ESX. These were not guts-and-glory sportscars, merely four-door luxury saloons (sedans), but they succeeded in getting everyone excited. The ESX was the more aggressive, despite its diesel/electric hybrid power. The LHX was more traditional and flowing, with a huge

■ LEFT *Imposing in every way, the grand Phaeton measured over 21 ft (5.4m) long and had enormous 22in (55.8cm) aluminium wheels.*

■ BELOW *The Jeep Icon interior had an exposed, pared-down, almost industrial feel to it.*

■ RIGHT *The "dual-cowl-phaeton" style means separate front and rear compart-ments, even two windscreens. The opulence of the rear compartment was unstinted.*

cabin featuring rear-seat airbags and entertainment centre. Its fuss-free, almost pancake-flat shape drew admiring comment from all quarters and some themes appeared in the 1998 model year Concorde/Intrepid production cars.

From Copperhead to Phaeton

A return to sportscars marked the 1997 Detroit show, and the Dodge Copperhead was an exciting 2.7-litre V-six two-seater. It took its name from the Copperhead snake; the dashboard was said to mimic the shape of the snake's head.

Chrysler concepts did not stop there, as it also showed the Pronto small family car, Jeep Icon (the first monocoque Jeep, and very trendy-looking), the Dakar and

■ RIGHT *The Jeep Icon shown in 1997 boasted lightweight unit-body construction, while its youthful looks promised much for the future.*

– probably the most spectacular of all – the Phaeton. This leviathan measured 5.4 metres long and was powered by a 5.4-litre V-twelve engine. It was a modern homage to the great "dual-cowl-phaeton" style typified by the 1940 Newport parade car. The rear passengers had their own windshield, and even their own set of instruments. This was a car conceived to titillate the fancies of a mythical future generation of *concours*

d'élégance devotees, a sad evocation of champagne-glass applause being pushed by Chrysler in its literature.

If there was one thing Chrysler had proved, with its cab-forward revolution and projects like the Viper and Prowler, it was that dream cars need not be confined to an upper stratum strangled by *haute couture* but could genuinely percolate through to the real world, and reach a truly wide public.

CITROËN

Experiment is the very life-blood of Citroën, as innovations have made their way into its road cars years before other manufacturers come up with similar solutions. One has only to think of the great *Traction-avant* (front-drive) DS, GS, CX and SM to realize how advanced, how individual, was Citroën's technology.

Karin, Xenia and Eole

Falminio Bertoni was the leading light behind Citroën's glory years, but for its birth into the pure dream-car era it appointed a new design chief, Trevor Fiore. His first work was the Karin, presented at the 1980 Paris show. Its pyramid shape was utterly unique, and a reflection of a logical driving position with the driver seated in the middle. This was followed the next year by the Xenia, a rather more conventional hatchback, which nevertheless showed crisp, clean lines.

It was the arrival of American Art Blakeslee that shaped Citroën's real future. Steeped in Peugeot-Simca-

■ RIGHT *Activa 2 was a two-door development of the Activa theme, with a fully active suspension system, which made it into production in the Xantia road car.*

■ BELOW *In 1996, Citroën invited students to design a city car for the 21st century. Norwegian Per Ivar Selvaag's extraordinary proposal was adjudged to convey Citroën's cultural values in a radical package.*

Chrysler values, he began with the ECO 2000, an ultra-economical small car project, and built up to the Eole. Named after Aelos, Greek god of the wind, Citroën's 1985 exercise was a car designed to cheat the wind. Based on CX components, it was a full four-seater claimed to have a Cd figure of just 0.19, achieved by using flexible body panels, cooling flaps and suspension that lowered as speed increased.

Activa, Citéla and Xanae

The name Activa was used on Citroën's flat-riding Xantia production car, but it first appeared in 1988 on an advanced four-door prototype. This had four-wheel drive and four-wheel steering,

■ BELOW *Although it looked like a three-wheeler, Citroën's 1991 Citéla electric city car prototype in fact had a pair of narrow-set rear wheels.*

■ LEFT *Bertone was responsible for designing the Coupé de Plage, based on the Berlingo van. Its leisure accent is self-evident.*

"managed" suspension, highly advanced aerodynamics and a 220bhp V-six engine.

The 1990 Activa 2 was a two-door coupé development of the theme with full active suspension and advanced electronics. However, some industry observers reckoned it looked a little too much like Ford's production line Probe for comfort.

The Citéla of 1991 was an idea for a city electric vehicle, and it was an extremely compact car (just 116in (296cm) long). The rear wheels were set very close together, and the sodium cadmium battery was claimed to last 600,000 miles (966,000km).

Xanae was the name given to a very attractive family car concept vehicle presented at the 1994 Paris Salon. Predicting the way Renault would go with its Scenic, the Xanae was a one-box mini-MPV. It had one door on the left, and two pillarless doors on the right. The quite radical transparent roof was an unbroken continuation of the windscreen.

■ RIGHT *The concept of a compact "people carrier" was given a futuristic slant with the 1994 Xanae. The side doors hinged in opposite directions and the front seats swivelled.*

■ ABOVE *Airflow-style design features included the lights, wing mirrors and a glass roof, which was essentially part of the windscreen.*

DAEWOO

Korean firm Daewoo had a problem of image: it was never one of experimentation, more of solid marketing success based on hand-me-downs from other makers. It addressed this by hiring Ital Design to come up with a concept car for the 1995 Geneva Motor Show. The Bucrane was a comparatively low-key debut, but this was intentional.

■ ABOVE *Ital Design was hired to come up with the Bucrane to give Daewoo a new design credibility. It was a four-seater coupé with V-six power.*

The Bucrane was a two-box four-seater coupé based on the mechanicals of its top-line model, a licence-built version of the Honda Legend. This meant a front-mounted 240bhp V-six engine and automatic transmission.

The styling was soft and mildly retro, but devoid of any real beauty. Its main features were heavy side scallops as engine air outlets and thick rear pillars forming a rear roof spoiler. The glazed roof and sweeping expanses of glass (the rear one was described as "lentil-shaped") gave it an airy feel inside. The temptation to fit a large chrome-plated grille was easily succumbed to.

In retrospect Daewoo was probably happier with the end product than Ital Design, and it began a fruitful association between the two firms (the Italian *carrozzieri* styled the later Lanos and Leganza ranges). The Bucrane had also freed Daewoo from its image as a builder of outdated designs, and established it as an innovator.

■ ABOVE *The name "No.1" hints that this was Daewoo's first self-produced concept car, an open roadster presented at the Frankfurt show in 1995.*

■ BELOW *A "No.2" was a novel exercise in the small one-box family-car idiom. Notable was the very low glass waistline.*

From Mya to Joyster

Daewoo improved its design credentials by acquiring, in 1994, the IAD design offices in Worthing, Britain, and by founding a design centre in Bavaria. The first fruit of this new direction was the 1996 Mya concept car. Based on the floorpan of forthcoming Daewoo cars, it was partly realistic, partly dreamy. The gullwing doors, for instance, looked totally impractical for a four-seater car, but the soft, mature and sporty lines enhanced Daewoo's credibility.

■ ABOVE *The Mya's cabin reflected a youthful design input, featuring highly textured surfaces and stylized controls.*

■ RIGHT *The Korean giant Daewoo's ambitions were laid bare with the Shiraz, an impressive-looking concept car hinting at a possible future presence in the Mercedes/ Jaguar class.*

■ ABOVE *With the Mya, Daewoo entered a new era of maturity, helped by its acquisition of a British design office. This gullwing coupé was smart and soft-edged.*

Daewoo stepped up its concept-car visions in 1997 with the launch of a whole vault of dream cars. These included the mundane (such as the Lanos Cabriolet and the small-car pairing of the Matiz and Mantica), but also provided a glimpse of enticing future possibilities.

The Shiraz, for instance, was a new departure for Daewoo: a V8-engined limousine to rival Mercedes and Jaguar. Designed by stylists in Britain, the Shiraz looked surprisingly sophisticated, even elegant. The interior featured silver and wood veneers and paddle switches on the steering wheel to change gear.

■ RIGHT *The best of all Daewoo concepts was undoubtedly the Joyster, an extremely neat sports two-seater designed by Ital Design. Note the curious front-grille treatment.*

Rear-seat passengers were treated to tables, which folded out to reveal PC units and a printer/fax output.

Other new directions included the Tacuma, a medium-sized leisure-type people carrier, and the DEV 5, a small,

electrically powered car, which was capable of reaching 75mph (121kph). Most exciting of all Daewoo's dream cars must be the Joyster, a highly characterful and compact (13ft (4 metres) long) two-seater roadster designed by Ital Design. Its lines perhaps recalled the Ghia Focus (which is no bad thing), and it featured vertically stacked lights front and rear and a very distinctive front grille in which the traditional Daewoo fan was flanked by curious panels drilled with holes of differing sizes.

DAIHATSU

■ BELOW *A town car, a buggy or a sports/off-roader? Daihatsu let you decide with its Urbanbuggy of 1987.*

Considering its position at the lower end of the Japanese market, Daihatsu has an impressive record of dream and show cars to its credit. These cars go far beyond the self-defined limits of its road-car programme.

Weird dreams

Daihatsu never followed convention. This was proved over and over again by such weird, but fun, concepts as the 1987 Urbanbuggy (an MPV/off-road/buggy cross-over) and the 1985 Trek (a single-seater "box" with a canvas camping-tent top, telephone, TV, spade and winch). With the 1989 Sneaker, a curious little goblin of a car with seating for three, Daihatsu even cast a little bit of magic: the Sneaker lowered a fifth wheel from its rump and rotated itself into tight parking spots.

In 1991, a maturing face was in evidence with the highly appealing X-021, a smooth, retro-styled roadster in the Mazda MX-5 Miata vein. That meant

a front-mounted engine (a 1.6- litre 16V 140bhp "four"), rear-wheel drive and an open two-seater cockpit. It was novel in that it had an aluminium space frame, plastic bodywork and race-derived suspension – all expensive items, so it is not surprising that the very pretty X-021 did not make production.

Wacky concepts

Just as impressive was the 1993 Personal Coupé, which, although it was based on humble Charade front-wheel-drive mechanicals, looked neat and was a distinct prospect for production. The same could not be said of the Ultra Mini of the same year, whose main strength was managing to fit four seats into a 98 in- (250cm-) longcar. Its 660cc engine sat under the rear seats. Likewise the Multi Personal 4 was a light-hearted but ultimately daft sports-utility with an interior which it was claimed was fully washable. Yet another 1993 concept car was the Dash FX21, a very neat electric/petrol hybrid four-door saloon (sedan).

Daihatsu's crazy Midget III show car of 1995 almost reinvented the Citroën 2CV with its bug-eye headlamps, high roof-line, tiny (659cc) engine and overall charm. Based on a single-seater pick-up, it added rear bodywork and two

■ LEFT *The Midget was a production single-seater pick-up, and the Midget III added a pair of rear seats too.*

■ RIGHT *It was a shame that the handsome X-021 never passed the dream car stage. 140bhp and aluminium/plastic construction sounded enticing.*

rear seats to make a three-seater. Even more ridiculous was the Town Cube, literally a cube on wheels, designed as a joke around the maximum permitted size for Japan's legal class of micro-cars. For the 1997 show round, Daihatsu previewed its vision of a future compact car, the NCX. A capacious, five-seater interior resulted from a long-cabin, short-nose ethic, and the 1.0-litre three-cylinder engine was claimed to produce amazing fuel economy. It proved that, while Daihatsu specialized in small cars, its ideas were actually broad-ranging and consistently forward-looking and experimental.

■ ABOVE *The 1995 Town Cube was really an in-joke: a vehicle designed around the maximum size limits for microcars.*

■ LEFT *Smart, understated and appealing, the 1993 Personal Coupé was a novel idea for a 1.0-litre compact coupé.*

FORD

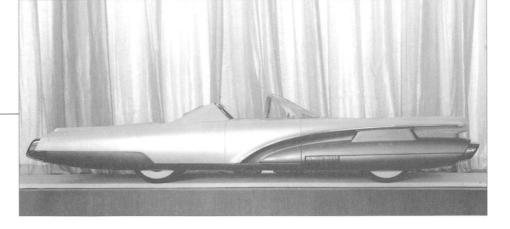

Perhaps it was Henry Ford's prosaic image as a provider of popular cars that delayed Ford's entry into the dream-car arena. Whatever the reason, Ford lagged behind Chrysler and General Motors in the razzmatazz world of futuristic ideas.

Ford's first dream car

Probably the first true Ford dream car was the X-100 of 1953, which anticipated the torpedo styling themes of later Fords like the 1961 Thunderbird. Another indication of Ford's new directions from the same year was the Mexico – only a scale model, but the result of wind-tunnel testing and an important pointer to future trends. Ford claimed 50 engineering firsts for this car, including a moisture-sensitive cell on the roof, which automatically closed the plastic sliding roof panel.

More extreme was the 1956 Mystere, at once the most amazing and most repulsive of dream cars. Its excessive chromework, double headlamps and heavy body accents appeared in production Fords in years to come, but mercifully the lifting bubble canopy,

swinging steering wheel and gas turbine power did not.

One of the most famous of all 1950s dream cars was the Lincoln Futura of 1955, if only because it was later modified to become the Batmobile in the popular TV series of the 60s. When the double-bubble canopy housed the caped crusaders, its kicked-up tail fins evoked just the right bat-like connotations.

Ford suffers hangover

Ford worked its way through many contorted schools of styling such as the Z-back roof (in the 1957 La Galaxie). It went on to become increasingly unhinged as it proposed a nuclear-powered dream car called the Nucleon in 1958, a gyroscopically controlled two-wheeled car called the Gyron in 1961, a three-wheeled flying car called

■ LEFT
Aerodynamics was one of the obsessions of the 1980s. The Probe IV may have been exceptionally wind-cheating but its wheel spats (skirts) and window cut-outs were utterly impractical in the real world.

■ ABOVE *It took until the 1980s for Ford to come back to the dream-car arena with an aerodynamic two-door concept car called the Probe.*

■ RIGHT *It wasn't realized at the time, but this odd-looking 1981 creation, the aerodynamic Probe III, was basically the forthcoming Ford Sierra. It prepared the public for a radical production shape.*

■ OPPOSITE *Details surrounding this 1956 ⅜ scale model, called X-1000, were extremely vague, like a poorly remembered dream. Ford said the engine could be front or rear mounted, and that the car might even fly!*

■ RIGHT *The name Splash for this 1988 concept car hinted at its capacity to get drenched without getting slushy carpets: the interior was waterproof!*

■ LEFT *The Probe V marked a return to the good old days of gimmickry. The sliding doors and engine cover prove as much.*

Probe and Splash

Future Ford Probe show cars were far more adventurous. The 1983 Probe IV was an amazingly aerodynamic yet practical hatchback. Its Cd figure of 0.15 was spectacular, achieved by wheels covered by urethane "membranes", meticulous airflow management and a spoiler at the base of the windscreen. The ultimate Probe V of a few years later extended the aerodynamic theme still further.

Uniting sportscar and pick-up truck themes was the purpose of the 1988 Splash. Looking like a space-age beach buggy, this striking two-seater had removable windows, roof and rear hatch. Its four-wheel drive, adjustable ride height and retractable mud flaps boosted its chunky off-road flavour, and the colourful weatherproof interior looked trendy enough for its intended youth market.

the Volante the same year and a vast six-wheeler called the Seattle-ite in 1962.

It should not be surprising that, after that lot, Ford's design team and the public had something of a dream-car hangover, and Dearborn's output of show specials petered out in the 1960s.

It took Ford's purchase of the Italian Ghia styling house to kick-start its dream-car programme again in the 1970s. Ghia's creations for Ford (such

as the Coins, Megastar and Action) are described in the pages devoted to Ghia. Ford's domestic US styling studios took longer to return to the dream-world.

Meanwhile, Ford's European subsidiary started a trend of creating show cars that anticipated future production models with the Probe III in 1981. It was all but identical to the Ford Sierra, only the aerodynamic appendages being really different.

■ LEFT *Lincoln's concept car for 1988 was the Machete, whose blade-edged shape perhaps presaged Ford's vaunted "edge-design" school. Note the narrow headlamps.*

■ ABOVE *Inside the Machete, ultra-simple curves combined with digital electronics.*

FORD

■ RIGHT *"Edge design" was a term Ford used to describe its new corporate design identity. It meant the use of hard-edged surfaces seemingly colliding with one another, and emerged with the GT90 of 1995.*

The Contour, shown at the 1991 Detroit Show, was revolutionary in so many respects. Its engine was the first straight-eight since Pontiac's in 1954 and was mounted transversely to save space. The shape of the car was dramatic with steeply raked screens and a long cabin dominating. It was mounted on an aluminium chassis entirely bonded together. The headlamps were 1in- (2.5cm-) high arc discharge rods and there were two floating rear spoilers.

■ LEFT *The GT90's triangular surfaces were most marked from the rear. The large black central triangle is the exhaust outlet.*

■ LEFT *Drawing its inspiration from the GT40 race car of the 1960s, the GT90 was a very low, rakish, mid-engined supercar.*

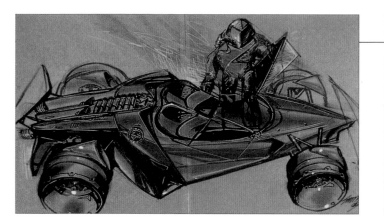

■ ABOVE *Ford's designers applied "edge design" to a road-going IndyCar-inspired concept car called the IndiGo.*

■ ABOVE *A black front spoiler and wings created a race-car feel on the outside, while the hi-tech construction and sequential six-speed gearbox did so under the skin.*

Edge design

To describe its fresh way of thinking in design terms, Ford coined the term "edge design". Before production cars like the Ka and Puma took to the streets, Ford displayed numerous concept cars at motor shows around the world, which dramatically demonstrated its new philosophy.

Edge design burst on to the scene with the revolutionary GT90 in 1995. The name hinted at the inspiration for the car, Ford's highly successful GT40 road/race car of the 1960s. In format, there were similarities: this was a very low, mid-engined two-seater with fantastic

performance potential, but in truth the cars were very divergent.

The GT90 resembled a Stealth bomber in the way that its triangular flat surfaces intersected one another. Under the skin, its technology was bang up-to-date racing-car: a honeycomb aluminium chassis, carbonfibre body and space-shuttle-type ceramic exhaust. Powered by a quad-turbo 720bhp V-twelve engine, it was intended to be launched in a limited series of 100 cars, but the plan never materialized. Much more significant was the GT90's effect on the future of Ford design.

IndiGo racer

It was not just the name of the IndiGo that was clever (playing on its association with IndyCar racing). This was no mere show car but a concept designed from the outset to be feasibly manufactured at some point. Even though most people who worked in the trade accepted that this was too radical to be offered for sale, it was a driveable car.

Ford said that the IndiGo "captures the essence of the race-track and transforms it into a realistic design for the street". The styling was strongly race car in feel, from the bespoilered, narrow nose to the blacked-out wings, while its construction (carbonfibre, aluminium and glassfibre) also mimicked competition use.

A 441bhp 6.0-litre V-twelve engine – formed by mating two V-six units together – was estimated to give a top speed of 170mph (273kph) and a 0–60mph (0-96kph) time of under four seconds. The six-speed sequential gearbox was derived from race cars, and changes were made by pressing buttons on the steering wheel. Even the instrument panel on the dashboard was Formula 1 inspired.

■ LEFT *In the centre of the car was a six-litre V-twelve engine with 441bhp at its disposal.*

FORD

Lincoln, meanwhile, forged ahead with its own L2K concept (in 1995), a possible future competition for the Mercedes-Benz SLK. Its blade-like shape (created by an affiliated design house called Concept Car Company) hid a 250bhp 3.4-litre V-eight engine. The following year came the Sentinel, a

■ ABOVE *Lincoln's L2K concept car was a V-eight front-engined roadster, pitching Lincoln into an area it had not explored before.*

■ LEFT *With a different set of wheels, the L2K was able to do the rounds of the show circuit with a dash of novelty.*

startling expression of Ford's edge design ethos: a high waistline, wonderfully sculpted lighting, ultra-clean, flat shapes and elegant proportions. It was a huge car, but felt right, and was even made into a runner on a lengthened Jaguar platform.

■ ABOVE *A very high waistline, clean shapes and good proportions made the Sentinel one of the most striking concept cars of 1995.*

■ LEFT *One of the most extreme expressions of "edge-design", if not the most elegant, was the Lincoln Sentinel.*

■ ABOVE *Computer animation and advanced voice-activated controls made the Synergy 2010's interior appear vastly different from today's cars.*

■ ABOVE *Synergy 2010 was an extremely bold styling statement, projecting ideas for a family car for the year 2010.*

The Synergy 2010 was Ford's idea of a family car for the year 2010, presented in 1996. As such, it featured two power sources – a 1.0-litre direct-injection engine feeding an electric motor – extremely lightweight materials (it weighed just one tonne (ton)), "air fences", which dictated the car's advanced, aerodynamic styling and voice-activated controls matched by computer-animated instruments. You could even call up the phone book by issuing a simple verbal command!

Just as the Ghia Saetta broke the path for the radical new Ka, so the 1996 Lynx dropped a few clues about the forthcoming Fiesta-based Puma coupé. One element that was lost in production was the odd twin roll-bar layout, which also formed the side window frames and guides for a fold-away roof.

Mercury's 1997 MC4 extended edge design to a mid-market four-seater. It looked good but still incorporated such dream themes as miniature "suicide" rear doors and a gullwing boot (trunk). More exciting still was the MC2 concept car shown at the 1997 Frankfurt Motor Show, in essence a new Ford Cougar. Here was the most successful and satisfying expression of edge design yet, a powerful combination of good proportions, aggressive angles and a lean profile.

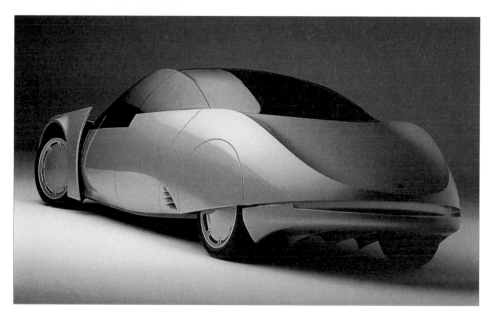

■ ABOVE *Extremely light weight and aerodynamic, the Synergy 2010 used a petrol/electric hybrid propulsion system.*

■ BELOW *Shown at the 1997 Frankfurt Motor Show, the Mercury MC2 was perhaps the most elegant "edge design" concept yet from Ford.*

GENERAL MOTORS

■ BELOW *The world's first-ever "dream car" was the Buick Y-Job of 1939: a styling exercise created purely for show.*

More than any other car-maker in the world, General Motors has embraced the dream-car theme with a vengeance. It was arguably the creator of the world's first dream car in the sense of a car created purely for advancing ideas rather than production realities: the Buick Y-Job of 1939 was a world pioneer. It had long, sleek lines, concealed headlamps and an electric top, which hid under a metal cover when lowered. The dream car had been born.

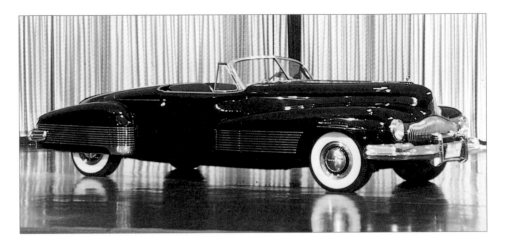

Harley Earl and Motorama

From then on, General Motors was the spiritual home of the dream car. The architect of this style revolution was Harley Earl, and it was his 1951 Buick Le Sabre that launched the jet-plane era

of car design in America. Not only did it look fantastic, it bristled with innovation: cast-magnesium panels, a hood (top) that raised itself automatically when a sensor detected rain and heated

seats. The Buick XP-300 of the same year was also ahead, with sleek styling, locking side-impact bars, hydraulic seats and a methanol-powered engine.

Throughout the 1950s, GM laid on the flash, brash razzmattazz in giant mobile shows called Motoramas. The centre-pieces of these showy extravaganzas were always the latest creations of stylists obsessed with futuristic visions of a brighter, faster, bigger age. In the peak Motorama year (1956), GM spent £6 million ($10 million) on the shows and attracted two million spectators.

By then Harley Earl was the General's styling supremo. It was he who introduced the very idea of "style" into everyday motoring and the yearly changes of model, which are pursued in America to this day. Earl liked to introduce "concepts" at Motoramas, which might one day reach production. Some did, like the Corvette and Cadillac Eldorado Brougham, but most were, of course, far too way-out.

Firebirds and the Bonneville Special

These were the crowd-pleasers. The public swooned at the sight of cars like the Buick Le Sabre and XP-300. Most drastic of all, the XP-21 Firebird of

■ LEFT *One of the stars of GM's Motorama road shows of the 1950s was the Pontiac Club de Mer. This blue-anodized aluminium roadster was just 38in (96.5cm) high.*

■ BELOW *The 1954 Buick Wildcat II had a glassfibre body. Note the "leaping-cat" bonnet mascot (hood ornament) and headlamps mounted by the windscreen.*

■ BELOW *Jet turbine styling and some genuine jet-fighter components gave the Pontiac Bonneville Special a science fiction spin.*

■ ABOVE *The 1956 Oldsmobile Golden Rocket featured roof sections that folded upwards when the door opened, while the seats swivelled and the steering wheel split in two to aid access.*

■ BELOW *Firebird II toned down the fighter plane extremes of the XP-21 in a body that could seat four people. Fins, turbines, a bubble roof and titanium bodywork kept the razzmatazz going.*

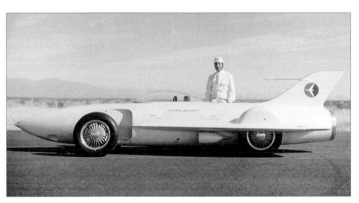

■ ABOVE *Nominally a feasibility study to ascertain the viability of gas turbine power, the XP-21 Firebird was essentially a shock publicity exercise.*

1954 was utterly sci-fi, its small jet-plane turbine propulsion being taken to extremes with a jet-fighter-style body: if you took away the wheels it really looked like a single-seater plane.

The Firebird evolved through two further generations. The Firebird II of 1956 had a central joystick and was claimed to have overcome the heat and noise-generation problems of a jet turbine engine. The more down-to-earth bodywork was in titanium, while passengers entered through a transparent canopy. The 1958 Firebird III returned to moon-rocket influences, sprouting aero-fins all over and boasting double bubble tops, a central lever for steering/braking/acceleration, cruise control, remote door-opening and "electroluminescent" instruments.

One of the best 50s dream cars was the 1954 Pontiac Bonneville Special. This was Earl's idea of a dreamy sportscar, full of glitz like fat chrome bonnet (hood) strips, chrome-mustachioed gaping grill, wrap-around screens, gullwing bubble-top and aircraft-style interior. It was the rear-end that was best, however: a Continental-style spare wheel cover with a turbine trim, flanked by jet-style tail lights.

■ LEFT *Sci-fi met hi-tech in the Firebird III. Beneath the huge fins lay pioneering electronic controls. There was even provision for the car to drive itself via cables mounted under GM test tracks.*

GENERAL MOTORS

General Motors' output was prolific. In just one year (1954) no less than 12 different dream cars were paraded in front of the public. This was the golden age of the dream car, and GM was its golden child. GM stuck to "style" and "innovation" less than the outlandish themes of other US names, and often its show car ideas would become production realities.

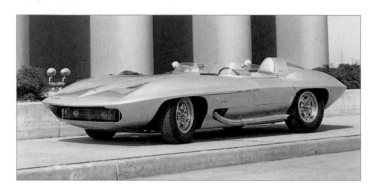

■ LEFT *GM styling supremo Bill Mitchell built the Sting Ray as early as 1959 as his own personal car. It inspired the later Corvette Sting Ray production car.*

■ BELOW *In 1962, the Mako Shark evolved from the Sting Ray. It was Corvette-based, and took shark-like styling themes to their conclusion.*

Rocket, Shark and Stingray Roadster
Highlights of the 1950s included the Buick Centurion, the remarkably clean Oldsmobile Golden Rocket, the 38in- (96.5cm-) high Pontiac Club de Mer, the

1957 Chevrolet Corvette SS (reminiscent of Jaguar's D-Type in many ways), and the jet-style Cadillac Cyclone.

General Motors lost none of its touch in the 1960s. Stylist Bill Mitchell drew inspiration from sharks in his 1962

Corvette Shark study: inlets for gills, exhaust pipes for fins, a pronounced snout and a graduated blue colour scheme. This followed the design of his own personal car, the Sting Ray Roadster, which also did the show rounds.

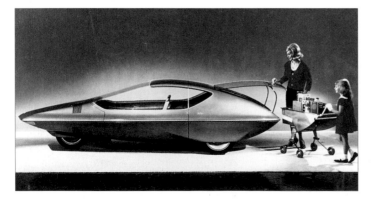

■ ABOVE *A paragon for suburban shopping bliss: the Runabout's front wheel could turn through 180 degrees to ease parking, while the tail contained two detachable shopping trolleys (carts)!*

■ ABOVE *To get into the 1967 Chevrolet Astro I, you popped a switch and the roof rose up, carrying the seats with it. It looked spectacular but was plainly a crazy idea.*

■ RIGHT *By the 1970s, the Golden Age of dream cars was over. In 1973, Bill Mitchell created this Pontiac Phantom show car as a swansong.*

Similar themes persisted in the 1963 Corvair Monza prototypes, transforming the beleaguered rear-engine Corvair into lithe sportscars, which undoubtedly influenced the next generation of sports shapes.

From Runabout to Aerotech

GM pursued other ideas too. Its Runabout was a vision of tomorrow's shopping car, a three-wheeler with two removable shopping trolleys (carts) built into the rear. The XP511 was a hybrid commuter trike with a huge clamshell canopy, and the Astro I incorporated a novel system of entry: the whole rear bodywork raised upwards, lifting the two seats with it.

Unlike the other US car manufacturers, GM never gave up its show car programme, pursuing dream themes into the 1970s with projects like the quad-rotor Chevrolet Aerovette and Pontiac Phantom.

The next major GM activity occurred from the mid-1980s on. GM concentrated on exceptionally exotic supercar projects like the Buick Wildcat of 1985, the Corvette Indy, the Pontiac Pursuit and, possibly the most extreme of all, the Oldsmobile Aerotech, with an amazing top speed in excess of 250mph (400kph).

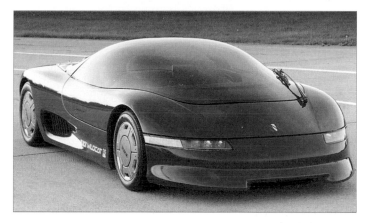

■ LEFT *General Motors returned to the dream-car arena with a bang in 1985: the Buick Wildcat revived a famous dream-car name and catapulted it into the present day.*

Cadillac pursued a theme of luxury express transport. Following the 1988 Voyage, the more accomplished Solitaire of the following year was "one of the world's most aerodynamic vehicles" with a Cd of 0.28, the result of such wind-cheating additions as wheel spats (skirts) and faired-in headlamps. It was powered by a 6.6-litre V-twelve engine developed by GM and Lotus and featured electronic articulated doors.

■ ABOVE *The 1986 Corvette Indy concept car judged the spirit of the times to perfection, as an all-out mid-engined supercar of prodigious performance.*

■ RIGHT *In 1986-87, the Oldsmobile Aerotech broke new world speed records: the short-tail car reached 257mph (414 kph), the long-tail an incredible 278mph (447 kph). And all from a 2.0-litre engine...*

GENERAL MOTORS

Stinger, Sunfire and Camaro

In 1989 came the Pontiac Stinger, an aggressively styled sports-utility vehicle. Adaptability was the name of the game here: all of its carbonfibre panels could be removed, as could the glass roof and the lower glass door panels (which could be replaced by a cool box and storage unit). Inside, four seats were adjustable six ways, while the rear passengers could elevate themselves by 15in (38cm) for a grandstand view over the roll-bar. Also

■ ABOVE *Impressive aerodynamism and a V-twelve experimental engine made the Cadillac Solitaire a limousine for dreamers. The Voyage is in the foreground.*

■ BELOW *Chevrolet's California Camaro was a vision of the future direction of GM's successful Camaro series.*

■ ABOVE *Pontiac's Sunfire was GM's expression of the cab-forward style espoused by Chrysler. The rear doors hinged from the back.*

supplied were a compass, phone, vacuum cleaner, stove, picnic table, umbrella and dustpan!

Pontiac's 1990 two-litre turbocharged Sunfire concept stole a page from Chrysler's cab-forward school of design in a two-plus-two coupé shape. One unusual feature was a set of "suicide" doors for the rear occupants, an idea dropped two decades earlier by every car-maker. The main point of interest, however, was the instrument binnacle: it was located in the centre of the steering wheel but was mounted to remain upright whichever way the steering wheel was turned.

The Camaro was always a badge that GM liked interpreting for the future. The California Camaro was typical: a far-sighted "running sketch in metal". A flamboyant use of glass, gullwing doors

■ LEFT *Impact was the name GM gave to its initial prototype for an electric sportscar. It actually entered production in little modified form as the EV1.*

■ BELOW *The Ultralite showed GM was thinking in many directions. Thanks to extreme light weight and smooth airflow, the Ultralite could reach 135mph (217kph) yet return up to 100mpg (160kpg).*

and a sharp-nosed treatment were notable features, while such fripperies as a vacuum cleaner in the console undermined its seriousness.

Experimental and Rageous

Chevrolet's CERV (Corporate Experimental Research Vehicle) projects stretched from the cigar-shaped 1960 single-seater to the 1990 CERV III, which built on the 1986 Corvette Indy. The CERV III was created with assistance from GM's newly acquired Lotus wing and used a heavily modified Corvette ZR1 engine producing no less than 650bhp, mounted centrally. Drive was to all four wheels through an automatic gearbox with six speeds, and the top speed was quoted as 186mph (299kph), with 0–60mph (0-96kph) coming up in 4.2 seconds. Active suspension, carbonfibre brakes and a Cd figure of just 0.274 were also

something GM wanted to shout about.

For the 1992 Ultralite, the claims were different: 100mpg (160kpg) economy and a top speed of 135mph (217kph). This was possible thanks to a carbonfibre body weighing just 420lb (190kg) and a Cd figure of 0.192. Yet it could still fit four adults.

The Sting Ray III (also 1992) pointed a little toward a new Corvette, with its longer wheelbase and shorter length.

Some regarded this concept car as superior to the C5 Corvette of 1997.

GM pioneered the productionization of a ground-up electric vehicle: the EV1 was launched in 1996. It all started life as the Impact concept car, an innovative and very sleek (Cd 0.19) coupé. Unlike any other electric car then developed, the Impact was a performance car, capable of accelerating to 0–60mph (0-96kph) from a standing start in under nine seconds. Its bonded aluminium spaceframe and composite body helped in keeping overall weight down.

With its Rageous concept car (1997), GM's Pontiac division created a Batman-style car described as a "sports coupé with the practicality of a sports-utility". Clearly an answer to Ford's edge-design thinking, it was a striking but not entirely happy mix of bold, folded edges and colliding shapes. Space inside was far better than in most sports coupés.

■ LEFT *General Motors built this Sunraycer solar-powered car to compete in long-distance sun-propelled competitions.*

GHIA

It is perhaps a sad reflection that to most people Ghia means a trim-level badge on their humdrum Ford. That all stems from Ghia's 1973 acquisition by Ford, but its history as one of the most illustrious Italian design houses stretches back to the early years of the 20th century. Ghia's main business was creating bespoke (dedicated) coachwork for high-quality Italian chassis, in which

■ ABOVE *Virgil Exner was responsible for the extraordinary Selene II. The driver sat alone in a central position, while the passengers faced backwards and had a TV screen to watch!*

■ ABOVE *The 1959 Selene was a sleek, nose-heavy "people carrier" styled by Tom Tjaarda. This forward-control style was advanced by several designers, but its dynamic shortcomings consigned it to an early grave.*

it was extremely successful. These were the original dream cars – one-offs built for wealthy clients, certainly not "show cars" in the accepted sense.

In 1950, Chrysler sent a Plymouth chassis to Turin, and Ghia rebodied it to become the XX-500. Although it looked ponderous, it sparked an association that led to Ghia building many of Chrysler's 50s dream cars. Ghia got into its stride with some stunning coachwork, and the 1953 Fiat 1100 Abarth and Fiat 8V were trend-setting.

Aerodynamics and style
Undoubtedly, the 1955 Ghia Streamline (or Gilda) was one of the most spectacular shapes of the 1950s. Created in a wind tunnel at Turin Polytechnic, this long, radically finned

device mutated through several generations, still being displayed at shows with great succes as late as 1960. Aerodynamics were a Ghia speciality, as proven by the Nibbio record breaker, which reached 100mph (161kph) on

350cc. Ghia also made the beach-car milieu its own with a string of wicker-seated Fiats called Jolly, and manufactured its own range of sportscars with the Dual-Ghia Firebomb, L6.4, 450/SS and 1500.

■ LEFT *At the 1961 Geneva Motor Show, Tom Tjaarda's IXG dragster was displayed. However, it was too streamlined to accept its intended Innocenti engine.*

■ OPPOSITE *The 1955 Turin show, where the world was enraptured by Ghia's incredible Streamline/Gilda, which boasted the largest tail fins of the era.*

■ RIGHT *The 1974 Coins was a vision of a future Ford Capri, although its bulbous styling (by Tom Tjaarda), three-abreast seating and single hatchback door for entry represented gimmickry, not advancement.*

A very talented man called Tom Tjaarda became one of Ghia's main stylists, and he made a big impression with the 1959 Selene, a sort of super-sleek forward-control "people carrier". Its follow-up, the Selene II of 1962, had a central driving seat and two rear seats facing backwards.

Then another brilliant stylist called Giorgetto Giugiaro joined Ghia from Bertone and designed many exceptional production cars. He also penned some attractive Ghia show cars, such as the Maserati Simun, the De Tomaso Pampero and the Oldsmobile Toronado Thor.

After its acquisition by Ford Ghia in 1973, Ghia was used as the European styling and prototype wing of Ford's global organization. Immediately, Ghia came up with a string of concept cars, inevitably based on Fords. Early examples were the Mustela (a Capri

alternative), the Tuareg (an off-road Fiesta) and the Microsport (a truncated Fiesta-based sports coupé).

Radical wedges

Its best designs in the 1970s were also its most radical. The 1974 Coins was a striking curved wedge with a single rear-sited door. The 1977 Megastar was a Granada-based saloon (sedan), though you

would never guess so from its amazing glass-house moulding (the front doors were 80 per cent glass). The Corrida was a chunky little safety-orientated sports coupé.

Probably the most striking Ghia show car of all was the 1978 Action, the most severe wedge shape ever seen. Designed by Filippo Sapino, it had a rear-mounted DFV Formula 1 V-eight engine and completely enclosed rear wheels.

■ LEFT *The Corrida was a pretty 1976 gullwing show car based on a Fiesta floorpan.*

■ BELOW *In 1977, Ghia showed the Megastar, a four-seater with a very swoopy glass waistline, based on Ford Granada parts.*

■ ABOVE *This car's name – Action – says it all. Styled by Filippo Sapino, its uncompromising wedge shape was highly dramatic for 1978, as was its Formula 1 power plant.*

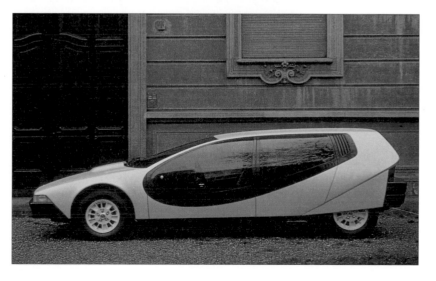

GHIA

■ LEFT *Based on the Ford Granada, the Altair was a very successful design exercise.*

■ ABOVE *One of Ghia's most attractive concept cars was the Escort XR3-based Brezza. Its engine was mid-mounted.*

In the 1980s, Ghia continued as a prestige *carrozzeria*. Its Granada Altair project was dignified in its simplicity, while the Avant Garde and, in particular, the Brezza (both Escort-based) were delightful compact coupés. Ghia also produced an attractive body for the mid-engined AC ME3000.

A host of microcars followed: the five-seater but small Pockar, the Shuttler, the three-wheeled Cockpit and the Trio. It was a shame to many that more was not made of the Barchetta, a Fiesta XR2-based roadster, which might have been a

■ RIGHT *Ghia even flirted with the idea of a tandem two-seater three-wheeler called the Cockpit. The whole glass roof lifted up for access.*

■ BELOW *The British sportscar firm AC had connections with Ford, and this handsome 1981 Ghia reworking of its ME3000 sports car was once destined for production.*

modern Ford-badged answer to the MG Midget. Less successful was the seven-seater APV, a car which the then UK Prime Minister, Margaret Thatcher, famously wanted to be redesigned.

Via, Zig/Zag and Connecta
Much comment was attracted by the 1988 Saguaro, which predicted the softer, rounder styles of the 1990s in a sporty, four-door package. The 1989 Geneva showing was the Via, a "Ford Sierra Cosworth for the next decade". Designed by a team of British stylists – brothers Ian and Moray Callum, David Wilkie and Sally Wilson – it was a very smart and sleek four-door saloon with an intended specification that included a turbo V-eight engine and six-speed

■ ABOVE *Perhaps the Barchetta represented a missed opportunity, for this could easily have been a compact Ford roadster ahead of its time.*

■ ABOVE *The Zig and Zag were a jocular pair of extremely compact youth-oriented show cars. Zig was the sportscar, Zag the van.*

gearbox. One of its highlights was a fibre-optics system for navigating in fog; another was a fully detachable photo-sensitive glass roof.

An interesting pair of leisure cars was created for the 1990 Geneva Motor Show, both based on a cut-down Fiesta platform. The Zig was the more engaging of the Zig/Zag pair (the Zag was a van). Designed by David Wilkie, the Zig had a very short bonnet (hood) flanked by pinhole headlamps and a perspex (clear plastic)-shrouded cockpit. The Sally Wilson-designed interior was strikingly finished with dashboard instruments painted blue, green and orange and a rear-view mirror that sprouted, tentacle-like, from the facia.

■ ABOVE *The 1989 Ghia Via was a high-performance four-door saloon (sedan) with V-eight power and super-sleek styling.*

■ ABOVE *Ghia went microcar-mad in the 1980s with a whole string of city car projects. This one is called the Trio, because three people could be seated in it.*

■ RIGHT *Saguaro was the name of this 1988 sporty four-door, which predated shapes like the Renault Mégane by a decade.*

GHIA

■ ABOVE *The extremely lightweight Connecta marked a new direction for Ghia – electric power.*

■ RIGHT *Ghia styled this Lagonda Vignale-badged show car for Aston Martin. It revived the Vignale name-plate – Ghia having taken over coachbuilders Vignale in 1969.*

Having an Escort van as a basis might not sound very exciting, but Ghia's 1992 Connecta was an important show car: it was Ford's first electric show car. The body-shell was in lightweight carbon-fibre and could seat six people (four forward-facing, two rearward) in a length of only 166in (421cm).

Focus and Lagoda Vignale

One of the most radical and adventurous dream cars ever was the Ghia Focus, presented at the 1992 Turin show. Based on a shortened Ford Escort Cosworth platform, it was naturally a very rapid sportscar. But it was Taru Lahti's styling that made the biggest impression. Novel features included whale-like front stabilizers, interesting headlamp architecture, distinctive air intakes,

■ ABOVE *The Alpe was Ghia's vision for a competitor in the burgeoning sports-utility market sector.*

alien-like grab handles down the body sides, scalloped rear fins, central rear-exit exhaust and amazing "bubble" rear lights. The cabin was equally avant garde, combining organic shapes and natural materials with an exposed, stark treatment and curious, off-centre detailing. The Focus might have made production as a Ford but was judged too radical and too expensive.

Of the Lagonda Vignale shown at the 1993 Geneva show, much was said and even more expected, for this might have made a future four-door Aston Martin (Ghia and Aston were now owned by Ford). Moray Callum designed the Lagonda Vignale, which was variously described as "trend-setting", "marvellous" and "the ugliest car around" – it all depended on your viewpoint. There was certainly nothing retiring about this substantial saloon (sedan), least of all the grille, the high waistline, huge wheels and drooping tail.

Ford's design dynamo

Ghia cemented its reputation as Ford's think-tank with two concept cars launched at the 1996 Turin show. One

■ ABOVE *One of the most radically styled of all Ghia show cars was the 1992 Focus, which stood a strong chance of entering production. Note the intriguing side "rails".*

■ RIGHT *Based on an Escort Cosworth floorpan, the Focus was extremely accomplished in action. Note the curious "bubble" rear lamps.*

was a clear signal of how the forthcoming Ford Ka would look: the radical Saetta's front end was shared with the Ka. In other respects, it was wildly different, Ford's prevailing edge-design mentality being taken to the limit. Dominated by a central roof rib, the silver-and-blue concept was bold in its geometric shapes, especially the rear lights. The other Turin debutant was the Alpe sports-utility, based on the Escort, with chunky, solid styling and a hint of off-road ability.

Today, Ghia's role is less as a creator of dream cars and more as a design dynamo in Ford's global empire, and a useful prototype-building facility in Italy's car design heartland. The Ghia badge persists on Ford products as an indicator of the highest level in its car ranges, but it is perhaps more fitting to remember the great legacy of the Ghia name by its impressive back catalogue of striking and innovative car designs. If only Ford had the courage to produce such brilliant creations as the Focus, the motoring world would be a better place.

■ LEFT *The gauges reflected the Focus's forward-thinking yet classically inspired form. Organic forms melded with stylized detailing.*

■ BELOW *The 1996 Saetta fitted in with Ford's "edge-design" mentality, and prepared the public in for the radical small Ka.*

HONDA

Traditionally, Honda always shied away from producing concept cars, presumably because it viewed its mainstream cars as advanced.

Biting the dream-car bullet

Finally in 1991, Honda bit the dream-car bullet when it displayed a pair of models at Frankfurt.

These were the FS-X saloon and EP-X coupé. The FS-X (Futuristic Sports Experimental) was a bold and sleek

■ LEFT *Honda's first-ever concept car was the FS-X, a sporting saloon (sedan) with advanced engineering and a sharply styled aluminium body.*

Electric and novel

For the 1993 Tokyo Show, Honda unveiled two further concepts. The first nailed its commitment to electric vehicles to the wall: the compact EVX predated the arrival of Honda's series production EV model, one of the first-ever ground-up electric cars. The second was the FSR, billed as "the ideal sedan for the 21st century". It was a technology car with such futurist goodies as active headlamps, radar braking, a message board for drivers following, reflective paint and a front-mounted camera for better visibility in adverse conditions. The wheel-arch

design clearly targeted at the Lexus and Infiniti luxury Japanese brands, which had had such success in America. Typically advanced in engineering terms, the FS-X sported a 3.5-litre VTEC V-six engine developing 280bhp, an all-aluminium body, four-wheel drive, liquid crystal sun visors and four airbags.

The little EP-X (Efficient Personal Experimental) was a curious, narrow tandem two-seater, also made entirely from aluminium. Powered by a 1.0-litre three-cylinder engine, it was claimed to be highly aerodynamic, efficient and safe if impractical.

■ ABOVE *Light weight, safety and aerodynamics were high on the agenda of the EP-X commuter vehicle.*

■ RIGHT *The EP-X was very compact, most notably in terms of width: the two passengers sat in tandem.*

■ LEFT *With its engine sitting inches to the right of the driver, the Side-by-Side sports racer was well named.*

treatment front and rear was novel, but the well-laid-out interior was more down-to-earth.

SSM stood for Sports Study Model, and this interesting 1995 show car was widely expected to enter production in modified form. It used NSX-style aluminium construction and ensured sharp handling through its front-engine/rear-drive layout: Honda claimed a perfect 50/50 weight distribution front-to-rear. One novel feature on the car was a central "spur", which separated the driver's and passenger's compartments and was claimed to improve rigidity significantly.

The SSM's power was supplied by a 2.0-litre five-cylinder VTEC engine, driving through a new electronic sequential-shift automatic gearbox derived from that in the NSX. The instrument pack was an LCD display with a card-style ignition system and push-button starter.

Another novelty in 1995 was the Side-by-Side, a racing single-seater with a 650cc V-twin motorcycle engine mounted alongside the driver. Weighing just 380kg (840lb), it was fast, superbly balanced and a possible production prospect.

■ ABOVE *Angular shapes realized in aluminium pointed the way ahead for Honda design. The passenger and driver were separated by a metal bar.*

■ ABOVE *SSM stood for Sports Study Model. Although it first appeared in 1995, its appearance at shows for a further two years fuelled speculation about possible production.*

■ RIGHT *Coupés have always been a strong suit at Honda, and this aggressively styled four-seater shadows the American-market Acura CL.*

IAD

■ BELOW *The spectacular Venus was a dramatically wedge-shaped piece of sculpture, yet was fully functional, based around a Lotus Elite engine.*

International Automotive Design was founded in Britain in the 1970s, but its real glory days did not arrive until the 1980s. Eventually, it opened offices in California, Detroit, Tokyo, Paris, Frankfurt and Turin and became one of those quiet operations behind numerous mainstream products.

From Alien to Venus

After a few innocuous design studies, IAD burst on to the world scene with "an attempt to 'out-Countach' the Countach", as the designer of the Alien described his work at the 1986 Turin show. As an exercise in attracting international attention to the young British design company, the Alien was incredibly successful – crowds surrounded the car all through the show. Eventually, IAD attracted many big names, including Fiat, Mazda and Volvo, who beat a path to its door for design work.

The Alien was a stunning, waspish supercar with a F16 fighter-style glass

canopy over the passengers. Its handlebar steering and centre console reinforced the jet-plane impression.

Further concepts followed thick and fast. The Impact and Interstate were outrageous developments of the off-

roader/leisure vehicle (sports-utility) genre. Then came the Venus, audaciously launched at the hallowed Tokyo Motor Show in 1989, and later made fully functional for a Turin debut the following year. The canary-yellow Venus (designed by Michael Ani) used a Lotus Elite drive-train in another wedge-shaped body, dominated by a table-like plateau to the rear and ingenious wheel covers. These almost completely shrouded the wheels, and had a bold yellow accent across one-quarter of the circumference. IAD was flooded with Japanese work following the Tokyo debut.

Another highly impressive exercise was the Royale, an imposing luxury express (grand tourer) with mature lines. The interior was perhaps its most striking feature, decked out with leather and high-tech equipment, including one of the most sophisticated hi-fi systems ever seen on a car.

■ LEFT *The Venus, launched at the 1989 Tokyo Motor Show, made a big impact for British-based International Automotive Design.*

■ RIGHT *IAD's Hunter was a go-anywhere vehicle with a complete lack of any glass or weather gear.*

Its 1992 Lancia Integrale-based Magia prototype was extremely well received but a hoped-for production run with Lancia never materialized.

Calling it a Daewoo

In addition to production cars, IAD had considerable input into other manufacturers' show cars; for example, it created the 1989 SRD-1 for Subaru, a mix of five-door estate (station wagon) and low-slung sportscar styles, which ITAL design's Giorgio Giugiaro described as "right for the future". Also, it came close to entering production with one of the world's first viable electric hybrid cars, the LA301, but this effort was ultimately doomed.

IAD was eventually overcome by financial problems. Half the organization was acquired by British design and engineering company Mayflower, while the original Worthing design office came under Dacwoo's control. IAD's talented design tradition therefore lives on in numerous Daewoo production and concept cars.

■ BELOW *With the Royale, IAD presented a mature-looking four-door executive-class saloon (sedan).*

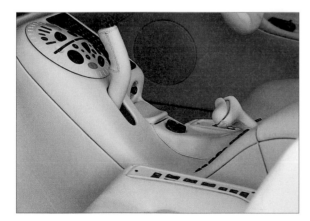

■ ABOVE *The intriguing white interior of the Royale featured advanced electronics, including an extremely powerful hi-fi system.*

■ RIGHT *Rear-seat passengers in the Royale were swathed in white leather and the latest in-car technology.*

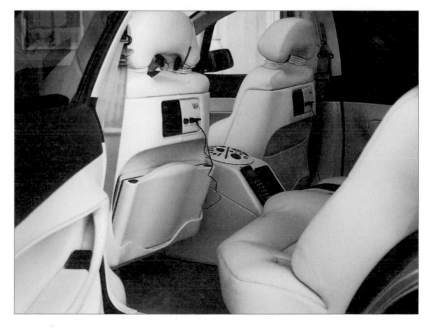

ISDERA

German stylist Eberhard Schulz made his name in the 1970s with b+b, the famous and well-respected tuning-and-styling operation that produced so many upgraded Porsches. The pinnacle of b+b's work was undoubtedly the 1978 CW311 prototype, whose inspiration (the Mercedes-Benz C111) was clear. Fitted with a mid-mounted AMG-tuned 6.3-litre V-eight engine, many industry experts reckoned it had enormous promise.

■ BELOW *The Spyder's cockpit was topped off by twin head fairings. Power came from a mid-mounted Mercedes-Benz engine from 2.3 to 3.0 litres capacity.*

■ ABOVE *Isdera's first project was the Spyder 033, which caused a stir with its decidedly Germanic styling and speedster-type roof arrangement.*

Teutonic Spyder

In fact this promise was so enticing that Schulz set up a separate company to market a range of similar products. That was in 1983, and the first car to be produced was the Isdera Spyder 033.

The 033 mid-engined sportscar was as close to a dream car for the road as you could get. Its styling themes were very Teutonic: silver paint, strong forms coalescing into a muscular whole and an almost industrial theme throughout. Evocative head fairings nuzzled up behind the two passengers, who were

■ ABOVE *In cabin architecture, Isdera was very German. Colour schemes like this were all the rage in the 1980s, though hardly the highest expression of good taste.*

■ LEFT *Isdera's second model – and its most popular – was the Imperator. It looked very much like a development of Mercedes/Benz's CW311 concept car.*

the 1993 Frankfurt Show, the 112i Commendatore. Its development period was quite lengthy but resulted in a car that followed Isdera traditions, in other words the sort of supercar that Mercedes-Benz might have been making, if it hadn't had to deal with environmental issues.

The Commendatore was a fearsome beast. The predictable Mercedes V-twelve engine sat in the centre of a much more curvaceous body, but was tuned up to 400bhp. This meant a claimed top speed of no less than 212mph (341kph) and the sort of reliability you would never expect from other super-powerful sportscars.

protected from the elements only by a small wind deflector (there was no weather gear). They got in by hinging the doors upwards; the doors also took the wind shields up with them.

The 033 was powered by a Mercedes-Benz 2.3-litre engine. From 1989, this was replaced by a 16-valve 2.5-litre unit (195bhp) or a 3.0-litre six-cylinder.

Ferocious Dreams

Isdera's second model was the enclosed Imperator 108i, which was clearly derived directly from the b+b CW311 prototype, even down to its periscope for a rear-view mirror. The 108i had full gullwing doors and larger overall dimensions, and was altogether in a different league in terms of performance thanks to the fitment of the 5.6-litre V-eight engine from the Mercedes-Benz 560SEC. If you wanted even more

power, you could opt for the ferocious AMG 32V 6.0-litre engine: its 390bhp would take you to 188mph (302kph).

Isderas were built in tiny numbers: by 1990, less than 20 Spyders and no more than two dozen Imperators had been made. Not greatly increasing these numbers was a new model presented at

■ LEFT *The wedge-shaped profile of the Imperator was born in the 1970s but remained in production into the 1990s.*

■ BELOW *With an optional AMG 6.0-litre engine, the Imperator could reach a top speed of 188mph (302kph).*

ISUZU

The name Isuzu is known in the West mainly through its successful off-road vehicles and, even in Japan, Isuzu is the smallest and least prestigious of the domestic brands. It is all the more amazing, then, that the company should have such a brilliantly rich stream of design talent at its beck and call, and that it has produced, over the years, a startling string of concept cars.

4200R – star of Tokyo

Although hints of Isuzu's dream-car specialization were already evident in the COA series during the 1980s, no Isuzu dream car better illustrates its talent than the 4200R, which was the star of the 1989 Tokyo Show. Through its General Motors connections, Isuzu had close contact with Lotus in Britain, and it was Lotus that, via Isuzu's Brussels-based design office, essentially created the 4200R.

Julian Thomson was the designer of one of the cleanest shapes of this period: well proportioned, elegant, unfussy and

■ ABOVE *Isuzu began to impress with its COA series. This is the COA/III of 1987, a sports coupé with off-road levels of ground clearance.*

■ LEFT *The 4200R had a huge impact for Isuzu. Designed and engineered by Lotus people, it stole the 1989 Tokyo Show.*

free of gimmicks. Ex-Lotus man Simon Cox was more adventurous with the textured gunmetal interior, a two-plus-two cabin entered by four cleverly designed doors, the rear pair hinging clear of the body and sliding backwards.

The intention was that under the skin would lie a Lotus-developed version of

Isuzu's 4.2-litre V-eight quad-cam engine, producing 350bhp. Other technical highlights were four-wheel drive, Lotus active ride, a head-up display and navigation system. Sadly, the 4200R never made production, despite some encouraging noises.

Also at the 1989 Tokyo Show were two home-grown concept cars, the Costa and Multi-Cross, both based around the MU (Frontera) 4x4 platform. The Multi-Cross was a simple, rugged enclosed car with interchangeable doors and bumpers, while the Costa had a nautical theme.

Como – the F1 pick-up

Nothing could have been as nautical as the 1991 Nagisa show car, for this was actually a boat! In fact it was an amphibian, capable of cruising in the sea as easily as transporting its two passengers through the Tokyo rush hour – a completely daft notion.

■ LEFT *Simon Cox created the startling Como, a car that combined supercar and pick-up styles over a Lotus V-twelve Formula 1 mechanical package.*

■ ABOVE *The Multi-Cross was a 1989 attempt at an off-roader with interchangeable panels, based on the Isuzu/Vauxhall Frontera.*

No such derision awaited the Como, even though the idea of a Formula 1-powered pick-up may have seemed odd. Styled by Simon Cox, it used a mid-mounted Lotus V-twelve F1 engine and had a very short nose, gullwing doors and a pick-up rear deck. At the same 1991 Tokyo show but from Isuzu's California studio came the Terraza, an urban car powered by a ceramic engine and featuring a fifth wheel at the back for parking manoeuvres.

Group B rally cars, rally-raiders and the Citroën 2CV were all cited as influences by the designer of Isuzu's 1993 VehiCross, Simon Cox. Although its styling looked almost like science fiction, it was extremely well designed and thought out. Its chunky shape impressed executives so much that a feasibility study was carried out, and the VehiCross became a production vehicle with amazingly little modification within three years (bypassing the similar-looking but larger 1995 Deseo show car). There was no such happy fate in store for a dreamy fellow off-roader created by Californian stylists, the Trooper-based XU-1.

■ ABOVE *The XU-1 was a great 1993 exercise combining the rugged form of Isuzu's specialist off-roaders with sportscar-type scissor doors.*

■ ABOVE *Is it a boat or a car? The Nagisa combined the two in one sublimely silly package.*

■ BELOW *Widely admired, the VehiCross was such a satisfying concept that Isuzu had the courage to re-engineer it for series production.*

ITAL DESIGN

Giorgetto Giugiaro's background in a family of artists helped him in his career as an "artist" of automotive forms. Even though his design career has encompassed such diverse areas as menswear, watches and pasta, his first passion has always been cars.

Giugiaro, the young art master
Aged just 17, Giugiaro joined Fiat's styling wing under Dante Giacosa and, two years later, accepted a job at Bertone and went on to become its youngest-ever head of styling.

In 1965, he left Bertone to head up Ghia and within three years had grown confident enough to set up his own consultancy with another ex-Fiat design and engineering expert, Aldo Mantovani. The office started in Turin but moved six years later to Moncalieri. Ital Design offered not only styling but also all the

services needed to bring a design to production, and soon manufacturers were flocking to his door.

As Ital Design, Giugiaro styled dozens of shapes for mass production, including the VW Golf, Maserati Bora, Lotus Esprit and BMW M1, all notable for an exceptional cleanliness of line. Ital Design has also produced some of the most admirable dream cars during its years, and has been highly influential in setting future trends.

Ital Design's very first project was the 1968 Manta, a dramatic coupé for the Italian specialist car-maker Bizzarrini. This was followed by sportscar designs

for Alfa Romeo (the 1969 Iguana and the 1971 Caimano), Abarth and Volkswagen (the VW-Porsche Tapiro and the Karmann Cheetah).

Boomerang and other prophecies
In 1972, the same year that Giugiaro designed the Esprit for Lotus, he also produced what many regard as his most extraordinary sportscar design, the Maserati Boomerang. This car, based on the Maserati Bora, pushed the frontiers of the accepted limits of car design. At only 42in (107cm) high, it was so low that the passengers were forced to become acrobats to get in, and the

■ LEFT *Geometric forms dominated the Boomerang and set Ital Design's agenda for two decades.*

■ RIGHT *Giugiaro cites the Tapiro as one of his most successful ever designs from a technical point of view.*

■ LEFT *The Lancia Megagamma of 1978 was a pioneer of the MPV form which grew up in the 1980s.*

■ ABOVE *Wind tunnel testing became one of the most important factors in the car design process. Here the Medusa is put through its paces.*

15-degree angle of the windscreen was the steepest rake you could achieve and still be able to see out. The wedge shape originated from a point in the nose, expanded to the base of the windscreen and extended to a geometric tail. Only the lower glass in the door opened.

As Ital Design extended its base of clients in the late 1970s, its concept cars became more prosaic, but the 1976 New York Taxi and the 1978 Lancia Megagamma were prophetic, proposing the idea of a compact, high-roof car with an adaptable interior layout – an MPV ahead of its time. In 1980, Giugiaro's Medusa showed a way forward in aerodynamics, proving it was possible to create a very clean four-door shape. This Lancia Montecarlo-based proposal boasted a Cd figure of just 0.263, then the most aerodynamic road car ever.

In 1984 Ital Design created the Etna for Lotus, which was at one stage earmarked for production. This was a supercar fitted with a stillborn Lotus four-litre V-eight 360bhp engine in the centre of the car. The contrast between its upper and lower halves was

emphasized by using thin, black-painted pillars, creating the impression of a transparent dome. The similar-looking Ford Maya from the same period was intended as a genuine production possibility and was full of practical features. It also had a removable targa top.

■ ABOVE *The Medusa proved that a long-wheelbase four-door design could be extraordinarily aerodynamic.*

■ RIGHT *The Etna was built for Lotus in 1984, and should have become that company's first-ever V-eight supercar, but it was not to be.*

■ ABOVE *With a front end almost indistinguishable from the Etna, the Ford-based Maya struggled to find its own identity.*

ITAL DESIGN

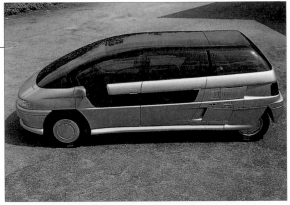

■ LEFT *Outlandishly different, the Machimoto combined the joys of the motorcycle and car worlds. All passengers sat astride seats arranged in rows.*

Giugiaro struck out on a startlingly original course with the 1986 Machimoto, a hybrid of motorcycle and car elements. Although it looked like a cabriolet and used VW Golf GTI mechanicals, passengers sat astride twin rows of seats, rather like a motorbike, but the layout allowed seating for up to nine people. It could be steered either by a conventional wheel, by handlebars or by vertical hand grips. Another novelty was the prominent design of the wheel spats (skirts).

A similar feel recurred in 1996 with

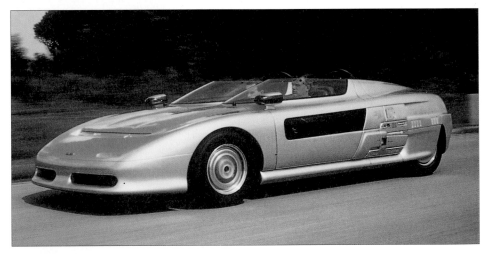

■ ABOVE *The Aztec was a typically adventurous idea for a four-wheel-drive two-seater sportscar.*

■ LEFT *No less than three similar concepts were all based on Audi components: from front to back, the Aztec, Aspid and Asgard.*

the Formula series. This was a concept for multi-adaptable bodies to be fixed over the same structure. Giugiaro initially showed two ideas: the Formula 4 with its demountable speedster body and aero screens, and the Hammer with its open sides, split windscreen and more conventional seating. Neither was especially handsome but they both provided yet more evidence of his original thinking.

Aztec, Aspid and Asgard

More creativity arrived in a trio of designs produced in 1988. Each of the Aztec/Aspid/Asgard triplets shared a

■ LEFT *A favourite theme of design houses is to propose their own interpretation of famous names, and this is Ital Design's Jaguar – the Kensington.*

■ ABOVE *More effort was expended on the Nazca than any other Ital Design concept car, but then this was a highly sophisticated BMW-engined supercar.*

common design theme and similar Audi mechanicals but had very different intentions. The most notable design element was the so-called "service centres" on either flank, which included sculptured gauges, read-outs for fluid levels and intricate compartments for tools and flashlights.

The Aztec was a four-wheel-drive two-seater with symmetrical but separate compartments accessed by doors, which hinged along a central point. The passenger's dashboard looked like the driver's, but the "steering wheel" was in fact a handle and the "instrument panel" was a screen to display car information on request.

The Aspid was identical to the Aztec up to the waistline and was a coupé version, which featured complex double-

■ ABOVE *The Nazca theme was later developed by Ital Design to become the Spider, with an open roof.*

■ BELOW *The Nazca M20 boasted conventional doors with gullwing window flaps. Some observers would have liked to see the Nazca enter production as a BMW.*

camber (dual-angle) glass, fold-up roof sections and conventionally hinged doors. The Asgard was a one-box eight-seater design, which broadened the extent of the extraordinary glass surfaces seen on its smaller coupé sister.

With the 1990 Kensington, Ital Design suggested a future shape for a Jaguar saloon, and used Jaguar's V-twelve engine. The Jaguar chassis was left untouched but a modern yet recognizably "Jaguar" body was created. Interestingly, the windscreen was sited so far forward that it needed to be removed to dismantle the engine.

Nazca, Columbus and Firepoint
The Nazca of 1991 was probably the most talked-about of all Giugiaro's concept cars, and there was speculation that it might enter production as a BMW. Everyone remembered the

ITAL DESIGN

Giugiaro-styled BMW M1 supercar and the Nazca seemed to be the natural successor. It had a mid-mounted BMW V-twelve engine and styling, which inspired dozens of magazines to run cover stories. Entry was by conventional doors and flip-up side windows. Despite the fact that the Nazca went through two further evolutions, including a Spider version, BMW was adamant that it would not build such a supercar.

BMW did donate another V-twelve engine for the stupendous Columbus of 1992, which celebrated the 500th anniversary of the discovery of America. This was a huge machine: 19ft 6in (6

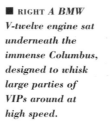

■ RIGHT *A BMW V-twelve engine sat underneath the immense Columbus, designed to whisk large parties of VIPs around at high speed.*

metres) long, 7ft (2.2 metres) wide and over 6ft 6in (2 metres) high. Its specification was equally grand: four-wheel drive, four-wheel steer, mid-mounted 300bhp engine and 20in (50.8cm) wheels. The interior was split into two compartments: the driver sat on a higher level with up to eight additional seats "below" in three rows.

In 1994, Fiat asked all the major Italian design houses to create a special body for the Punto (which was a Giugiaro design in the first place). Ital Design's interpretation was the Firepoint, a novel two-plus-two coupé with aircraft-inspired aerodynamics, such as the teardrop roof and reversed windscreen pillars. The side and rear windows could be removed, cleverly creating a roadster.

■ ABOVE *The electric-powered Biga was a minute little box capable of seating five people.*

■ BELOW *A V-ten engine sat amidships in the two-plus-two Cala prototype.*

■ ABOVE *Ital Design teamed up with Lamborghini to create the Cala, which was interestingly styled and could have become a production model.*

Cala and Legram

Lamborghini asked Ital Design to create a new two-plus-two targa sportscar that would slot in as an entry model below the Diablo, and so it created the Cala, which came tantalizingly close to production. The compact mid-engined two-seater used a brand new Lamborghini V-ten engine capable of phenomenal performance. Stylistically, its detail cues came from the Miura, though the overall shape was more of a wedge. Its advanced construction

consisted of an aluminium chassis clothed in carbonfibre body panels.

The 1996 Legram was an almost unrecognizable development of the Formula "infinity project" begun by the Formula 4. On the basic Formula platform went an elegant sporting four-seater body with an exceptional Cd figure of just 0.25. A transparent dome of glass stretched from the windscreen base to the rear window, broken only by aluminium cross-beams. Another outstanding feature was the treatment of the rear lights, which looked like horizontal slits.

Ital Design's back catalogue of dream cars is bewilderingly complete and belies the relative youth of the company. Equally impressive is the depth of its engineering expertise and the extent of its penetration into the design of production models. In all cases, Ital Design has been a trailblazer of ideas and an initiator of clean design principles and high-quality execution.

■ RIGHT *Firepoint was the name given to Ital Design's Fiat-sponsored proposal on the Punto.*

■ ABOVE *The idea behind the Formula project was to have bodywork that was easily interchangeable. This is the Formula 4 sportscar.*

■ ABOVE *The Legram proved that the Formula concept could produce a more serious outcome. Note the intriguing use of glass surfaces.*

■ RIGHT *By changing a few of the upper panels, you could create the Formula Hammer. Some thought that this design idea was seriously compromised.*

MAZDA

Of all the Japanese manufacturers, Mazda has historically been the most adventurous in its production programme. Witness such extremes as the Wankel-engined Cosmo, the lithe RX-7 and MX-5 sportscars and the amazing AZ1 micro-gullwing coupé.

Alongside Nissan and Toyota, Mazda was one of the first of the Japanese show car originators, with cars like the 1970 RX 500. An early impact was achieved in 1981 when its MX-81 show car made its debut. The interest was the stylist, Bertone.

Mazda charted its direction with dream cars like the MX-03 of 1985. With the interesting MX-04 (1987) Mazda showed its ingenuity: this was a four-wheel-drive chassis shown with interchangeable bodywork – Mazda suggested roadster, coupé and buggy styles.

One of the three versions of the micro AZ550 Sports prototypes shown at the 1989 Tokyo show led to a production vehicle, the AZ1, a sports projectile designed within Japan's micro-car laws (maximum length 126in (320cm), maximum engine capacity 550cc).

Type A had a strikingly simple shape dominated by its glassy gullwing doors. Type C did not actually conform to the

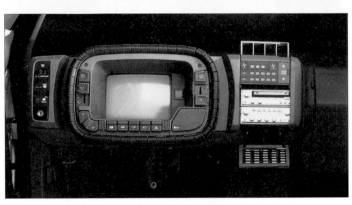

■ ABOVE LEFT *Mazda teamed up with Bertone to create its 1981 show car, the MX-81. Typically clean lines combined with a large glass surface area.*

■ LEFT *There was no steering wheel as such in the MX-81, merely an oblong "track" surrounding a TV display.*

■ ABOVE *Interchangeable bodywork provided the 1987 MX-04 with a choice of buggy or sports styles, the latter prefiguring the MX-5 production roadster.*

■ ABOVE *Mazda's cute and tiny AZ550 Sports Type A actually became a production model (the slightly modified AZ1).*

■ LEFT *The AZ Type B was a funny little creation designed with removable roof panels for open-topped motoring.*

■ RIGHT *Despite being only just over 10ft long, the Type C AZ550 looked like a proper Group C racing-car.*

legal micro size requirements, but it was an amazing concoction looking like a toy-sized Group C racer, complete with a slanted front profile, large radiator intake and rear spoiler. Type B was perhaps the runt of the litter with its awkward humped lines.

Japanese Jekyll and Hyde

The 1989 Mazda TD-R was the first car to combine two potentially burgeoning fields, melding the apparently incongruous worlds of sportscars and off-roaders. Its nod to the sportscar world was its mid-engined two-seater layout, turbocharged 1.8-litre engine and ventilated disc brakes. Its off-roading alter ego emerged in permanent (full-time) four-wheel drive, minimal front and rear overhangs and deep sills. Joining Jekyll and Hyde was a novel wishbone suspension system, which could adjust the TD-R's ground clearance between 5in and 9in (130mm to 230mm).

Mazda's 1991 HR-X did not win any awards for styling, but that was not its main *raison d'être*. The HR-X pioneered a hydrogen-powered variant of Mazda's twin-rotor Wankel engine, which could

■ LEFT *Mazda's M2 division created a variety of special bodies, such as this M2 1008 coupé conversion for the MX-5. The headlamps are fixed behind cowls.*

also power an on-board hybrid electric motor. The bulky hydrogen tank was sited under the floor, but whatever its advantages, hydrogen looked an unlikely future power source, especially in such an outlandish shape as the HR-X's.

Centre stage at the 1995 Tokyo show went to the RX-01 prototype, a vision of a future, lighter, cheaper RX-7 sportscar. The rotary engine was retained, without the sequential turbocharging of the

contemporary RX-7, but with dry-sump lubrication and improved breathing – still good for 220bhp. It weighed only 2425lb (1100kg) and had aluminium suspension based on the MX-5.

Mazda was also unique in having an operation called M2, a dedicated design company based at its own office block in Tokyo. It created all sorts of alternative bodywork and engine modifications on existing Mazda cars, notably the MX-5.

■ ABOVE *Rotary power remained a Mazda forte, and the 1995 RX-01 provided a lightweight sportscar vision of its possible future.*

■ RIGHT *The TD-R successfully combined elements of sportscar and buggy themes: mid engine, four-wheel drive and variable ground clearance.*

MERCEDES

The C111 was not one project but five. This supercar blueprint was first shown in 1969, and was outside Mercedes-Benz's normal frame of reference.

A laboratory on wheels

Mercedes-Benz described the C111 as a "laboratory on wheels", and some were actually used on the road. Some of the features included gullwing doors, leather-trimmed cockpits and even air-conditioning.

■ BELOW LEFT *Breaking diesel speed records at Nardo in 1978: the aerodynamic C111/112 achieved an average top speed of 200mph (322kph).*

■ BELOW RIGHT *Mercedes-Benz show cars often anticipated forthcoming production cars. The F-200, despite its scissor-type doors and joystick controls, prefigured the new S-Class.*

The first example had a glassfibre body over a steel chassis and was fitted with a mid-mounted triple-rotor Wankel engine with fuel injection. That expanded to four rotors in the second generation C111 of 1970 – said to be good for 370bhp and 180mph (290kph). In its third form, a 3.0-litre five-cylinder turbodiesel engine was fitted, and the C111 immediately took all existing world speed records in the diesel class.

Further evolutions, with quite different bodywork, took more records: over 200mph (322kph) with a diesel engine (and 12 hours at an average 195.3mph (316kph)) and still more records with a 500bhp 4.8-litre twin-turbo V-eight.

There was a follow-up to the C111, logically called the C112. It appeared at the 1991 Frankfurt Show as a mock-up, by which time Mercedes-Benz was convinced that the market for such a supercar was not right – probably correctly, given Jaguar's experiences with the XJ220. The C112 would have been a stunning 6.0-litre V-twelve-powered mid-engined supercar. Mercedes even took orders for it (700 were received), but it returned them all.

Mercedes thinks small

As Mercedes-Benz began to diversify, it launched various concept vehicles to

■ OPPOSITE *Perhaps the most famous of all Mercedes-Benz concept cars was the C111, which first appeared in 1969 with a triple-rotor Wankel engine.*

■ ABOVE *The AAV excited many show-goers because here, said Mercedes-Benz, was a clear indication of how the M-class (M320) off-roader would be.*

■ RIGHT *The stylish and highly textured interior of the AAV was typical of the boldness of concept cars.*

■ ABOVE *Presented at the 1997 Frankfurt show, the F-300 Life-Jet was an amazing three-wheeler designed to lean into corners to simulate the behaviour of motorbikes.*

■ OPPOSITE *What might have been: the C112 was going to be a production V12 supercar but instead it was shown simply as a dream car in 1991.*

■ ABOVE *As the climate for supercars became more favourable in the mid-1990s, Mercedes-Benz and AMG built this stunning CLK GTR as a homologation road/race special.*

prepare the public for future changes. One example was the 1991 F100 MPV show car, paving the way for Mercedes' forthcoming V-class MPV.

The next obvious prediction of future models was the Vision, shown in 1993. For Mercedes-Benz this was a very radical concept, its first-ever small car. For the rest of the world it was also radical, featuring a ground-breaking layout of an engine sited so that it would move underneath passengers' feet in a head-on collision – good for driver and front-seat passenger safety, said Mercedes. By 1997 it was ready to launch the A-class, whose profile differed little from the Vision.

The same thing happened with the SLK (shown in concept form in 1994 and later somewhat diluted, particularly in the design of the headlamps and twin head fairings), the F200 (previewing the 1998 model S-class coupé) and especially the AAV, Mercedes' prototype 4x4, which fired so many imaginations – the eventual M-class road car was very staid in comparison. Perhaps most radical of all the designs was the F-300 Life-Jet trike, which leant into corners via computer control. Young, fresh and innovative, this exciting concept car brought to Mercedes a new sense of fun and experimentation.

MITSUBISHI

Mitsubishi burst into the dream-car arena with its HSR series which originated in 1987. Active ride, four-wheel drive and four-wheel steering may not have been very original in the concept car world but the fact that 295bhp and 186mph (299kph) were available from a 2.0-litre turbo engine certainly was.

A show-stopping car
Show-goers were impressed by the HSR's dramatically skirted shape, sophisticated electronics and novel seating, which swung out with the doors.

■ ABOVE *Mitsubishi's reputation for high-technology solutions reached new heights with the 1995 HSR-V, whose aerodynamics were claimed to have been inspired by dolphins.*

The stunning 1989 HSR II follow-up was officially only ever meant as a rolling test bed for technology and ideas, but the amazing shape attracted virtually all the attention, an aim that Mitsubishi surely intended, since it featured widely in corporate advertising campaigns. Mitsubishi called this project a Control Configured Vehicle, in other words a machine stuffed with computers and electronic displays. At various points around the body were flaps and wings whose position was controlled by computer so that airflow was optimized in any given situation.

■ ABOVE
Biodynamic suspension and an elastic (flexible) tail spoiler were two very '90s features of the HSR-IV.

■ RIGHT *The HSR-III was strikingly styled and also technically advanced, with electronic suspension, four-wheel drive and four-wheel steer.*

■ ABOVE *This tiny bespectacled Lynx off-roader had an engine of just 660cc capacity.*

■ ABOVE *Some people likened the oddball mS 1000 saloon (sedan) to a modern-day duotone Morris Minor. Certainly it reflected a trend towards "retro" design.*

Less noticed but perhaps more significant at the 1989 Tokyo Show was the RVR leisure car. Its novel retractable windscreen and targa roof were striking, and the latter made it into production in the Japanese-market RVR (Space Runner), which arrived in 1991.

The HSR evolved into a third generation in 1991. More compact but equally striking in its powerfully styled presence, the HSR III boasted electronically controlled suspension and traction control and a new 177bhp twin-cam 1.6-litre V-six engine. More far-fetched was the fitment of twin levers on the steering wheel in place of controls for the automatic transmission.

Inspired by dolphins

More outlandish 1991 Tokyo debutants were the mS 1000 and mR 1000 pairing. Catching the tidal wave of Japanese interest in all things "retro", the mS 1000 was an utterly bizarre two-tone curve-haven with a tiny chrome grille. It had two doors on the left and only one on the right, while the stubby little boot (trunk) led Mitsubishi to call it a "2.5 box" car. The mR 1000 looked more feasible: a two-seater targa-roofed runabout (commuter car), spoiled by flying buttresses at the rear and ugly tail lamps.

■ RIGHT *At the 1995 Tokyo Show, the Gaus offered a modern solution to adaptable luxury multi-purpose transport. The gullwing doors were more fanciful.*

The proportions shrank even further in 1993 with the presentation of the tiny 101in- (257cm-) long, two-seater Mum, powered by a 500cc 30bhp engine, and the Lynx, an off-roader designed around Japan's micro-car regulations – meaning maximums of 660cc and a 130in (330cm) overall length.

By 1993 the HSR series was in generation IV, its styling ever more

avant-garde, notably its elastic (flexible) aerotail rear spoiler. More significant was its "biodynamic" suspension, which became a production reality in the Galant.

Even more bells and whistles sprouted from the HSR-V in 1995, from elastic stabilizers to a vibrating under-floor, which was "a revolutionary way of reducing drag inspired by the skin of dolphins".

■ LEFT *Even by Japanese standards of miniaturization, the Mum was truly Lilliputian. It had a 500cc engine.*

NISSAN

Like most Japanese car-makers, it took Nissan almost two decades to refine its dream-car programme into something that was relevant and palatable for a worldwide audience. Early efforts, such as the 1970 126X, were characterized by dubious extremes and a certain lack of sophistication. However, Nissan did have some interesting ideas, including inflatable passenger airbags as early as 1971.

The dream car that catapulted Nissan into a more serious arena was the MID-4, which was a major Nissan project. It was first seen in 1985 as a Ferrariesque pure show car, but had matured by 1987 to look like a credible exotic rival for Porsche.

It was engineered around a 330bhp longitudinal 3.0-litre V-six twin-turbo engine and boasted four-wheel drive and four-wheel steering. There were serious noises about this becoming a production prospect as a new Nissan supercar, probably with a V-twelve engine and two-wheel drive, ready to do battle with Ferrari et al. That plan was scotched as the times did not favour such "hypercar" projects, although the production 300ZX of 1989 was hailed as "the first Japanese supercar".

The elegant 1986 CUE-X and ARC-X of 1987 also marked a new maturity.

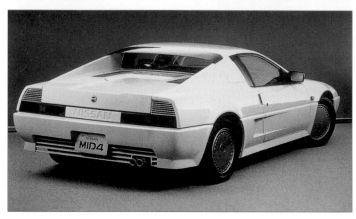

■ LEFT *With a 330bhp twin-turbocharged V-six engine mounted amidships, the MID-4 promised much, although its styling was perhaps a little bland.*

■ ABOVE *The cleanliness of line and sensibility of proportion won many admirers when Nissan displayed its CUE-X in 1986.*

■ LEFT *The ARC-X of 1987 was a sophisticated precursor to Nissan's luxury-car programme Infiniti.*

Here was a pair of super-sleek, beautifully proportioned four-door saloons, which were also highly aerodynamic. The ARC-X featured four-wheel drive, four-wheel steer and a staggering array of electronics.

Pike dreams

Perhaps Nissan's most celebrated dream cars were the so-called Pike series of boutique models. Nissan set up a sub-division to manufacture special models,

■ OPPOSITE *The MID-4 was one of the more significant Japanese dream cars of the 1980s, as at one stage it was slated to become a production rival for Porsche and Ferrari.*

■ ABOVE *The first of the so-called Pike series was the curious Be-1, a retro-styled small car, which was so well received that it went into limited production.*

■ ABOVE *If the Be-1 evoked the 1960s, the Pao plunged further back to a utilitarian post-war era of flat glass, exposed hinges and sober lines. Again it was sold in small series.*

or "niche" cars in marketing language. The first of these was the Be-1, shown at Tokyo in 1985 and so well received that it went into production 18 months later. Its Mini-style round headlamps and retro-styling cues overcame the fact that it was based on the dowdy one-litre Micra, and it was widely admired.

Then in 1987 came the Pao (a 1940s-style runabout) and the humorously named S-Cargo, a bizarre arch-shaped van, which achieved tremendous popularity. Another design from this series (but destined not to go into production) was the 1989 Chapeau, a curious glass-house car, which looked somewhat like a telephone kiosk (booth) on wheels.

Perhaps the most charming of all the Pike cars was the Figaro, initially shown as a concept car but actually put into production. This heralded a new era of "retro" design in the car world, for here was a 1940s-style chrome-and-round-headlamps little car. Some details were appealing, like the electric canvas roof and chromed CD player; others were more dubious, like the all-white interior and toggle switches, which looked like Victorian cutlery. Also, it may have had the appearance of a sportscar but its 1.2-litre Micra engine and automatic transmission did nothing to make it behave like one.

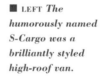

■ LEFT *The humorously named S-Cargo was a brilliantly styled high-roof van.*

■ RIGHT *With the Figaro, Nissan exploited nostalgic yearnings for a different age. Production was very limited, and the 20,000 run was vastly over-subscribed.*

NISSAN

■ RIGHT *The Duad's name hints at its stepped passenger arrangement, dictated by the engine's position alongside the driver.*

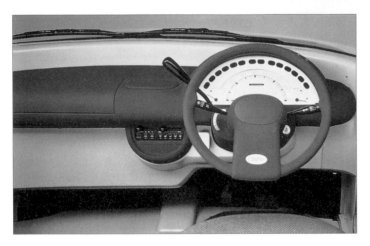

■ ABOVE *This bold, retro, ultra-simplistic fascia comes from a 1989 concept called the Chapeau. While the interior was admirable, the exterior looked preposterously like a telephone kiosk (booth).*

■ ABOVE *The Rasheen brought a unique boxy style to the sports utility market. When it was shown as a concept car, western tastes were not motivated, but in production the Rasheen became a hot seller in Japan.*

From Boga to Duad

Nissan lost the plot a little with the 1989 Boga, its idea of a new city car. The concept was clever, to fit a four-door shell with luxury car space into an overall length of a supermini (compact), but the 1.5-litre Boga's style missed the mark, and it perhaps got less attention than it deserved. Similar styling marred the 1991 Cocoon six-seater, whose party piece was a wake-me-up system: when it sensed that the driver was drowsy, it would spray a refreshing scent into the cockpit.

Nissan's 1989 UV-X was more down-to-earth, a neat one-box shape designed by Yoshio Maezawa, stylist of the 300ZX sportscar. Apart from being tipped to look like a future Bluebird (it didn't), its main feature was computer-controlled adjustable pedals and steering.

The 1991 TRI-X show coupé looked disappointingly back to the 1980s, and was clearly targeted at an American audience; this sort of thing reappeared in 1993 with the Marcello Gandini-styled AP-X. Much more engaging was its quirky Duad show car, which revived in spirit its 1987 Saurus. Intended as a modern interpretation of the immortal Lotus 7, it weighed merely 1035lb (470kg). Its quirkiness stemmed from the fact that the 1.0-litre engine was

■ LEFT *Although it looked perhaps like a dumpy VW Beetle, the FEV II had a more serious purpose, exploring city car possibilities.*

■ RIGHT *Nissan said of the AA-X that it combined practical and sportscar modes.*

mounted alongside the driver, forcing the passenger's seat to be sited 15in (38cm) further back. Nissan hoped to launch the Duad as another in its Pike boutique series, but this never happened.

From Rasheen to Trailrunner

A different fate awaited the Rasheen, shown at Tokyo in 1993. This extremely box-like concept, described as "a totally new type of four-wheel-drive wagon",

actually made it into production. Its compact dimensions, practical Sunny mechanicals and characterful style endeared it to Japanese drivers, and led to a crew-cab-type (four-door pick-up) show car called the XIX in 1995.

Combining two-seater drop-top excitement with four-seater practicality was how Nissan described its 1995 AA-X, but the awkwardly colliding shapes looked uncomfortable, even if the idea itself was sound: to combine sportscar and family-car modes.

Nissan followed a happier path with its 1997 4x4 concept vehicle, the Trailrunner. Sporty styling crossed the bridge between the coupé and off-road worlds, and a unique design feature was a prominently displayed sliding spare wheel in the tail. Its 190bhp 2.0-litre engine and sequential six-speed CVT gearbox also promised a sporty temperament.

■ ABOVE *Nissan's designers were called upon to complete the R390 GT1 project in a short space of time.*

■ BELOW *To homologate the R390 for Le Mans in 1997, a tiny batch of road-going cars was built for discerning customers.*

OGLE

David Ogle founded his own industrial design company in 1954 and decided to branch out into car design (and indeed manufacture) in 1960 with a four-seater GT coupé based on Riley 1.5 mechanicals, but only eight were made. More successful was the pretty SX1000 coupé of 1962–64, an extremely curvaceous glassfibre body based on Mini parts.

Ogle also designed the very handsome SX250 body on the chassis of the Daimler SP250. This was shown at the 1962 London Motor Show and impressed British specialist company Reliant so much that it was modified to become the

Reliant Scimitar coupé. Ogle then took the Scimitar and made a Triplex GTS estate (station wagon) special with a rear-end made of Triplex heat-absorbing glass. This car became the property of HRH Prince Philip for a time.

Tragically, in 1962 David Ogle died at the wheel of an SX1000, effectively ending the company's manufacturing life. Direction was taken over by Tom Karen, an innovative Czech-born designer. He was responsible for some effective designs, most significantly the Reliant Scimitar GTE sports estate.

The tangerine bug

The car of which Karen was most proud was the 1970 Bond Bug, a highly individual-looking three-wheeler based on a Reliant chassis. In many respects it was ground-breaking with its hinging canopy, its fixed, moulded-in seating, its use of aircraft-style black decals. Intended as a cheap fun car, it was available in only one colour – bright tangerine! Despite this, several thousand were sold.

Perhaps Ogle's most ambitious project was an Aston Martin DBS-based

sportscar created for the 1972 Montreal show. This sharply styled coupé featured much Triplex Sundym (tinted) glass, a green corduroy-and-leather interior with seating for three (the rear passenger sited diagonally behind) and brushed-steel highlight panels. Most remarkable of all was the rear-lamp panel, which had 22 circular lights. Many of these were sequential indicators, which flashed outwards in the direction you were turning; six others were for braking, the severity being indicated by the number of lamps lit.

Ogle went on to design a number of further one-offs such as the Princess 10-20 Glassback, the Mogul (which was a full-size version of a child's toy car Ogle had already designed), a modified Vauxhall Astra and various taxi projects.

Ogle Design's automotive work gradually dwindled away into occasional ventures such as the Project 2000 and a proposal for an updated three-wheeler to celebrate 21 years of the Bond Bug. Today, Ogle's car connections are at best tenuous as it concentrates on other industrial design work.

■ ABOVE *The Bond Bug was the most characterful of all Ogle Design's cars. A front-engined three-wheeler, it was available in only one colour – bright tangerine.*

■ BELOW *Ogle's Aston Martin DBS Special was state-of-the-art in 1972, featuring large Sundym (tinted) glass areas and brushed steel. Two examples were built.*

■ ABOVE *To get into the Bug, the roof canopy had to be lifted up, taking the sidescreens (windows) with it.*

■ RIGHT *The tail of the Ogle Aston housed no fewer than 22 lamps for braking, reversing and rear lighting.*

PEUGEOT

■ LEFT *Peugeot's best-known dream car is the Oxia, and not without reason. Its low, wide face was distinctively Peugeot.*

With Paul Bracq at the helm, Peugeot has had an illustrious design influence. Its true dream-car programme began with the Quasar at Paris in 1984. Based on the 205 Turbo 16 rally car, it was a formidable compact mid-engined sportscar with four-wheel drive and 200bhp. Its styling was light and forward-thrusting, its interior dramatically encased by a red roll cage.

The spectacular Oxia

Without a shadow of doubt, Peugeot's most important ever show car was the Oxia, first seen in 1988. Unlike many other dream cars, the Oxia was a fully-functioning prototype, quite capable of stunning levels of performance, as Peugeot proved during numerous well-documented test runs.

In its looks, too, the Oxia was absolutely spectacular. It was designed in-house by Gerard Welter and incorporated such Peugeot elements as low-cut headlamps, horizontal grille and rampant lion badge. The flamboyantly rakish and wide shape was realized in lightweight carbonfibre, and was topped off by an adjustable rear spoiler to help stability.

On a high-tech menu to set technophiles' palates slavering were a four-wheel steering system with variable weighting (variable assist), permanent (full-time) four-wheel drive (via a Ferguson viscous coupling), six-speed gearbox, anti-lock brakes, electronically controlled axle differentials and automatic

■ LEFT *With a turbocharged race-spec engine developing 680bhp, Peugeot was justified in claiming a top speed in excess of 200mph (322kph).*

■ BELOW *Based on the rallying Peugeot 205 T16, the mid-engined Quasar not only looked purposeful, it had the power and punch to carry out that purpose.*

■ ABOVE *The 1984 Quasar demonstrated that Peugeot's in-house design team had plenty to offer.*

tyre-pressure monitors. Inside, traditional leather blended with solar-powered air-conditioning, a personal computer, a sound system described as "intergalactic" and a navigation system.

The basic engine was Peugeot's familiar 2.85-litre V-six but monstrously modified to full race specification with twin turbochargers to develop no less than 680bhp. Peugeot claimed – with justification – that the Oxia was capable of a top speed of 205mph (330kph).

■ ABOVE *Opening the Proxima's roof canopy revealed an uncompromisingly scarlet cockpit.*

Ion, Asphalte and Touareg

At the 1994 Paris Salon, Peugeot presented the Ion, an urban study vehicle powered by electricity. Only 11ft (3.3 metres) long, its monobox style was compact and modern, yet could fit four adults. Perhaps the main novelty was the total absence of door handles; to get in, you pressed a sensitive area on the rear wing – with your hip if your arms were full – and so released the locks. The same system worked for the large rear hatch.

"Crazy" was how some professionals described the extraordinary 1996 Paris Salon debutante called the Asphalte. The front-end picked up Peugeot design themes – wide snout, narrow headlamps – but toward the back-end things got very strange. The rear track was extremely narrow, so that from the side it looked like a three-wheeler with a pinched-in tail. The ultra-smooth topless profile promised sizzling performance, but strangely Peugeot opted to install a mere 1.6-litre engine and an automatic gearbox.

The Touareg off-road buggy stood out because of its mighty, even frightening wheels, straight off a science-fiction film set. One interesting quirk was its choice of power: four electric motors, one for each of those Tonka-toy wheels.

■ ABOVE *All attention focuses on the moon buggy wheels and tyres with Peugeot's 1996 Touareg concept car.*

■ LEFT *Although it looks like a three-wheeler, the Asphalte in fact had a pair of rear wheels, which were very narrowly set.*

PININFARINA

At only 5ft (1.5 metres) tall, Battista Farina's nickname of Pinin – "kid" – is altogether fitting; so much so in fact that the name stuck and late in life he changed it officially. He founded a design centre of true genius, which his son Sergio continues to run from Turin, the capital of Italian and indeed world car design. He is among the great names of car design.

The pinnacle of car design

To cast back over the company's long list of production greats confirms the consistency of quality and proportion that distinguishes his work. From the

revolutionary 1945 Cisitalia (displayed in the New York Museum of Modern Art) to present-day Ferraris (which, since 1952, have almost exclusively carried the Pininfarina badge), the mark of genius is evident in the little blue 'f' badge with a crown on top. In between are dozens of designs for Alfa Romeo, Fiat, Peugeot, Honda, Rolls-Royce and many others.

■ ABOVE *Farina's fascination with aerodynamics was evident in the extraordinary PFX prototype of 1960. Its diamond-wheel footprint helped reduce frontal area and thus drag.*

■ BELOW *The 1968 Ferrari P6 Berlinetta Speciale looked beautiful from all angles and became the point of departure for the Berlinetta Boxer.*

■ ABOVE *Despite a fascination with flowing shapes, aggression had its place in Farina's school of thought, as the Can-Am-inspired 1968 Alfa Romeo P/33 shows.*

■ ABOVE *The 1969 special-bodied Alfa Romeo 33 was one of the great shapes of the 1960s, inspiring a generation of supercars.*

■ LEFT *Pure sculpture on wheels is the almost inevitable description for the extraordinary Modulo of 1970, based on a Ferrari 512S.*

Pininfarina's dream cars are united by one theme: a flowing shape and perfect proportions. While others explored geometric shapes, Farina was inspired by the way snow in the Italian mountains was shaped by the winds, and the wind-cheating shapes of all his cars owe something to this stimulus. Others claimed that Farina said his ground-breaking stimulus came from well-formed female shapes.

The art of aerodynamics

Pininfarina was one of the first companies to install a wind tunnel (in 1972). A direct result of testing in this environment was the PF-CNR family-size car, which achieved a world record Cd figure of 0.161 and had a curious banana-shaped form: Pininfarina proved it could be practical by creating a version with air intakes, lights and mirrors (though the Cd figure increased to 0.23).

Not that aerodynamics was a new art-form, as the 1960 PFX proved. This extraordinary befinned, egg-shaped car even used a diamond-shaped-wheel footprint in its search for wind-cheating efficiency. A seminal aerodynamic study was the 1967 Dino 206SP, based on a racing Ferrari. It featured adjustable front and rear spoilers and gullwing doors. In the 1960s, Pininfarina experimented with some wild shapes, yet none of them had the glitzy fripperies of American show cars. Farina's designs were always classically elegant. One of the most influential was undoubtedly the 206 Dino and later Ferrari 365 P Special Berlinetta, which led directly to the Dino production car.

■ ABOVE *The Modulo had enclosed wheels and a canopy, which slid and cantilevered forward, drawing attention to what was in fact a brilliantly simple shape.*

■ RIGHT *One of Pininfarina's most admired production designs was the Fiat 130 Coupé. Here is the Maremma, an estate (station wagon) development study.*

![car icon] # PININFARINA

Farina Ferraris and Alfas

Pininfarina was always Ferrari's favoured couturier, not surprisingly in the light of such brilliant dream-car designs as the 250/P5 Berlinetta and the superbly clean P6 Berlinetta. Possibly the zenith of this golden era of mid-

■ LEFT *A world record co-efficient of drag was recorded for this windtunnel-honed CNR – just 0.161.*

■ ABOVE *No doubt disappointed that Jaguar had failed to replace, in spirit, the great E-Type, Pininfarina produced this 1978 Jaguar proposal, based on the XJS.*

engined fantasy were the Ferrari 512 prototype and very similar-looking Alfa Romeo 33 prototype, whose exquisite sculpted sides, gullwing doors and ultra-low profile clearly inspired the Boxer and Countach of the following years to come.

Exploring the wedge school of design was the 1968 Alfa Romeo P/33 Roadster, based on the mid-engined racing 33. This was intended for impact, as evidenced by the row of six headlamps, front stabilizing fins, cut-down wind deflector (airdam) and prominent rear spoiler.

With the 1970 Modulo, based on the ultra-rare Ferrari 512S racer, the very extremes of sportscar design were explored to the absolute limit. Its very low bodywork formed an almost flat, almost symmetrical arc and was made by joining separate upper and

lower halves together. The prominent waistline strip – so low that it could almost be called an ankle-line – was allowed to run uninterrupted right around the car, including the wheels. These were covered with spats (skirts) which incorporated cut-outs in their tops. To allow entry, a one-piece canopy cantilevered forward.

Honda, Peugeot and Jaguar

Equally dramatic was the 1984 Studio HPX, a mid-engined supercar using a 2.0-litre Honda Formula 2 V-eight engine. Its striking shape was highly aerodynamic, partly owing to ground effect technology and the curious extended canopy (a Cd figure of 0.25 was claimed).

■ LEFT *Ferrari was always the keenest on Pininfarina's shapes, and the Turin design house pushed the boat even further with this supremely elegant Pinin prototype of 1980.*

■ ABOVE *Honda is another firm with a long association with Pininfarina. This Honda HPX had an extended glass canopy for optimized airflow.*

■ RIGHT *The 1985 Peugeot Griffe 4 was a good example of Pininfarina's restrained good taste, even in its show cars.*

Widely admired for its simplicity was the 1976 Peugette, an exercise in virtual symmetry of form. In fact the front and rear bodywork sections were completely interchangeable, and hinged up in identical fashion. The lights were housed in the bumpers, and the interior was marvellously unadorned. Its mechanical basis was the Peugeot 104.

The 1978 XJ Spider showed what the fabled Jaguar E-Type might have become. On the basis of a Jaguar V-twelve engine, a timelessly elegant body was created, picking up the E-Type themes of an oval front air intake and a profile, which bulged over the front and rear wheels. Jaguar's boss Sir John Egan fell in love with the XJ Spider and even developed its themes with the intention of launching an F-Type Jaguar. This was scotched, but it's enlightening to see how the current XK8 picks up many of the XJ Spider's details.

Perhaps even more elegant than the Jaguar study was Farina's Ferrari-based

study for a four-door car of two years later, called simply Pinin. In proportion it was supremely correct, and its sharp yet soft-edged style predicted the way many cars would be designed in the late 1980s. Ferrari never officially made a four-door car, and after seeing the Pinin many observers felt they ought to have done so.

■ ABOVE *The HPX was typically clean but atypically geometric in its wedge-shaped profile.*

Mythos, Chronos and Ethos

After doing several relatively "sensible" concept cars (such as the 1988 HIT based on Lancia Delta HF mechanicals), it was time in 1989 to try something more ambitious, and the Mythos was the result. The designers at Pininfarina based the car on the Ferrari Testarossa.

■ BELOW *Disguising the extreme girth of the Ferrari Testarossa was a challenge that the 1989 Mythos addressed.*

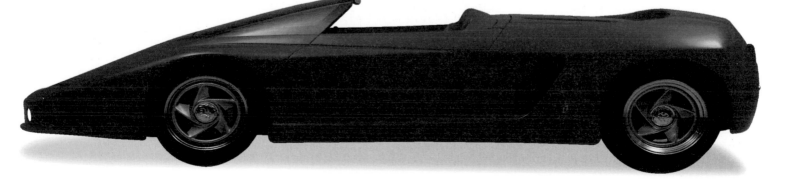

PININFARINA

■ RIGHT *Showing an originality of thought, the remarkable thing about the Ethos roadster was that at one stage Honda seemed likely to put it into production.*

■ ABOVE *To fit six people in the Ethos III, two rows of three seats had to be installed.*

The 1991 Chronos was a serious stab at a two-seater coupé based on Lotus Carlton/Omega running gear. Pininfarina wanted to persuade General Motors to go into production with the Chronos but ultimately did not succeed, probably because the shape was slightly disappointing for a Farina.

The same cannot be said of the 1992 Ethos, which also seemed capable of becoming a highly significant production car. It used an Australian-made Orbital 1.2-litre two-stroke engine mounted amidships and a sequential five-speed gearbox.

The Ethos body was penned by Stephane Schwarz, and was a steeply raked pure sportscar with deeply indented sides, virtually cycle-type rear wings, head fairings and a bold, stark interior with twin silver bars for a dashboard. At one stage, Honda looked likely to produce the Ethos, but the Orbital two-stroke engine unfortunately suffered many delays and the project faltered, despite the appearance of an Ethos II coupé.

The Ethos III of 1994 attempted to reinvent the city car. Into a body barely longer than a Fiat Cinquecento, Pininfarina managed to squeeze six seats – two rows of three with the middle seat offset. Crucial to the compact dimensions was the tiny 1.2-litre

■ ABOVE *The Ethos III was another extremely clever design. The body was smaller than virtually any car on the market, yet it could seat six people.*

■ BELOW *Argento Vivo is Italian for "quicksilver", and this Honda-based study was certainly mercurial in character. It combined "retro" and hi-tech themes.*

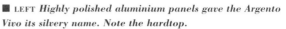

three-cylinder Orbital two-stroke engine. Lightweight aluminium kept the weight at 1720lb (780kg) and helped create 63mpg (100kpg) fuel economy.

■ RIGHT *As a fully functioning project using Honda Vigor and NSX components, the Argento Vivo might have made a practical production proposition, but Honda had irons in other fires.*

Honda and Fiat

A 16-year co-operation with Honda was finally cemented in 1995 with the Argento Vivo sportscar concept. This was a power-top roadster with striking polished aluminium boot and bonnet (trunk and hood), blue bodywork and wide use of plywood. It was notable for a folding transparent roof, which could also be left in a targa position. Unfortunately, Honda was already developing a similar car in the SSM, and the Argento Vivo remained a scintillating prototype.

For the 1996 Turin show, Fiat asked various stylists to come up with ideas on its Bravo/Brava. Pininfarina's concept was the Song, a compact MPV with a multi-adaptable interior and more than a hint of off-road influence in its roof rails, clipped overhangs and chunky wheels. At the same show was the Eta Beta, powered by a hybrid petrol/electric (gasoline/electric) system and featuring a tail section extendable by 8in (20cm) for extra carrying capacity.

In 1997 Pininfarina continued its rich tradition as the world's leading design house; its advanced Nautilus saloon (sedan) car concept for Peugeot proved that it was still very much on the leading edge of car design.

■ LEFT *The cleverest feature of the hybrid/electric Eta Beta was rear bodywork that could fold out to increase luggage capacity.*

■ BELOW *Farina's concept car for 1997 was the Nautilus, an extremely handsome four-door saloon (sedan) based on Peugeot components.*

RENAULT

The largest French car-maker founded its fortunes on comfortable, conventional and often rather boring family cars. It certainly did not go in for outlandish styling concepts and dream cars, preferring merely to hint at a little chic in its road-car offerings, which were deliberately designed for the masses.

That old attitude changed dramatically with the arrival of Patrick Le Quément as head of design in 1987. "We sell to people, not the masses" he said, and Renault's approach to its

■ ABOVE *Renault was one of the great show-car exponents. Here is an impressive selection of concept cars, starting with the 1990 Laguna (front right) and ending with the 1995 Initiale (second car in, top right)*

■ LEFT *The Zoom's headlight shows Renault's attention to stylized details.*

production car design was transformed with such innovative cars as the Twingo and Mégane Scenic.

Le Quément cleverly instituted a policy of producing show cars – and names – which clearly predicted future production Renaults, a trick he picked up during 17 years with Ford. In this way a lot of publicity was gained for Renault's show cars and the public was prepared for the revolutionary shapes and ideas of the next generation.

Le Quément banished the ghosts of such uninspiring experimental Renaults as the Vesta 1 and 2 (both super-economy cars) and the Eve Plus, an

■ ABOVE *Created by Renault-owned Matra, the tiny Zoom was a vision of a future electric city car.*

■ RIGHT *The Zoom's party piece was an ability to fold its rear under, shortening its overall length by 21.5in (55cm).*

■ LEFT *The moon-buggy Racoon was a go-anywhere vehicle in the widest sense: it could also take to the water!*

■ ABOVE *The Scenic concept car of 1991 (left) led directly to the production Mégane Scenic car (right).*

aerodynamic efficiency saloon (sedan). The first project he oversaw was the 1988 Mégane, an elegant three-box saloon with such essential 80s equipment as four-wheel steering, intelligent suspension and a turbocharged engine. It was highly aerodynamic, notching up the very impressive Cd figure of 0.21.

From Twingo to Zoom

A tremendous exponent of the one-box design embodied by Renault's Espace, Le Quément's team created the much-vaunted Twingo, having earlier shown a larger one-box design called the Scenic at the 1991 Frankfurt show. This evolved into the production Mégane Scenic of 1996, a car that can genuinely

be said to have revolutionized one segment of car design.

In 1990, Renault first used the name Laguna on an ultra-sporty open two-seater dream car. Underneath the swoopy shape lay a mid-mounted two-litre engine (210bhp), and the cockpit could be covered by a solid tonneau. The concept of a completely open mid-engined sportscar obviously struck a chord at Renault because, some five years later, the very similar Sport Spider actually entered production.

Renault's subsidiary, Matra, developed the 1992 Zoom prototype, a startling electric two-seater. Quite apart from its arresting egg-like appearance and scissor-type opening doors, the

Zoom could amaze onlookers by pulling its rear wheels in and under its body, shortening the overall length from 104.3in to 82.7in (265cm to 210cm) – handy for parking in that tight Paris spot.

From Racoon to Initiale

Renault described its adventurous 1993 Racoon concept car as "an amphibious go-anywhere vehicle". It had four-wheel drive, hydraulic jacks to elevate ground clearance, a watertight body and completely amphibious capability. Its mechanical specification was not retiring either: a twin-turbo 262bhp V-six engine and six-speed gearbox.

Equally striking was the Twingo-based Argos roadster of 1994. This show

■ RIGHT *Launched at the 1994 Geneva Motor Show, the Argos was a startlingly original design from design chief Patrick Le Quément. The "piano lid" is actually the hinging boot.*

■ FAR RIGHT *Argos details: retractable screen, doors and mirrors, exposed rivets and a single rear seat with hi-fi gear.*

RENAULT

car really gave rein to Le Quément's vision of breaking with the "organic" shapes of the early 1990s. The Argos was full of industrial, Bauhaus-style detailing and little technological tricks such as ignition-activated swivelling door mirrors, drop-down doors, a folding 1920s aeroplane-style windshield and a piano-like opening rear lid. Interior textures in shades of green, cork and silver made a visual feast.

If anyone thought one-box design was

■ ABOVE *The 1995 Initiale was a projected future Renault limousine of superb elegance and, thanks to a detuned Formula 1 engine, deeply impressive performance.*

■ LEFT *Hard edges and soft curves balanced the Initiale's presence superbly.*

■ ABOVE *Avant-garde detailing from the rear end of the Initiale.*

■ BELOW *The Modus and Ludo were Renault's 1994 vision of electric-powered city transport of the future.*

the only way to go, then Renault banished that idea with the Ludo concept car at the Paris Salon in 1994. The two-box Ludo had a very adaptable interior with foldable, removable seats and a huge interior volume; it anticipated similar treatment for the 1997 Renault Clio.

With the elegant Initiale (1995), Renault signalled a way ahead for luxury cars, and stole some of the thunder of Ford's edge-design programme. The Initiale was a super-saloon (high-performance sedan) powered by a detuned Formula 1 engine (claimed top speed was 190mph, or 306kph), yet had accommodation for four people. The tapered nose and tail recalled the style of the 40CV, Renault's prestige model in the 1920s.

Fiftie and Pangea

To celebrate 50 years of the highly successful Renault 4CV, Renault's design team produced the Fiftie for the

■ ABOVE *Novel interior treatment in the Fiftie included wickerwork (woven) trim and curious stacks at either end of the dashboard.*

■ RIGHT *Retro and resolutely modern influences met in the Fiftie concept car of 1996.*

Geneva show in 1996. This was a concept car out of the normal stream. Certain elements of the 4CV were recognizable – the curved roof-line, the raised bonnet (hood), the air intakes for a rear- mounted engine – but this was definitely not a retro design.

The fact was that the Fiftie had a Sport Spider chassis and was an ultra-modern two-seater. It marked the first fitment of Renault's new 1149cc engine (which would later power a revised Twingo), and was sporting in slant. The roof could be wound back and then folded down to make a virtual convertible, while the interior was a delightful blend of natural textures and curious "stacks" at either end of the dash. Particularly striking was the treatment of the lights, both front and rear, the tail-lamps "evoking waving flags," said Renault.

At the 1997 Geneva show, Renault displayed a concept van called the Pangea, which clearly predicted the shape of its forthcoming Kangoo utility/family car. In spirit, this was greeted as a revival of the long lost, greatly mourned Renault R4, as its boxy shape recalled the car that was France's best-selling machine of all time. Again this was no throwback, however, but was resolutely looking forward – like all of Renault's concept machines.

■ LEFT *The Fiftie's roof slid back and then down on to the rear deck. Note the rear lights – evocative of flags waving in the wind, said Renault.*

■ BELOW *The Pangea concept vehicle (complete with trailer) was exhibited as a high-tech remote office facility.*

RINSPEED

Based in Zurich, Switzerland, Rinspeed's main stock-in-trade has always been outrageously fast and furious conversions based on regular production performance cars. It started out turbocharging Volkswagen Golfs, then moved on to Porsches, with which it really made its name. One of its most celebrated conversions was a "droop-snoot" front-end on a 911, a style that Porsche itself later adopted for its own car designs.

Usually Rinspeed altered the aesthetics of its base cars, typically upgrading wheels and tyres, adding a body kit, installing pop-up or high-intensity headlamps, injecting leather and wood into the interior and stacking up a monster hi-fi system.

Eventually, it also turned to other, even more exotic projects. The Veleno was a mutated, 550bhp nitrous-oxide-injected Dodge Viper, for example, while Rinspeed also modified a Bugatti EB110 visually and mechanically.

Then, at successive Geneva Motor Shows, it surprised and occasionally

■ LEFT *Swiss specialist Rinspeed founded its fortunes on Porsche 911 conversions such as this Speedster-style car.*

shocked the world with its avant-garde dream cars. Unusually, these design extremes were actually offered for sale in series (regular production) at stupendously high prices, admittedly, at last offering some home-grown

competition for the king of automotive couture extraordinaire, Lausanne-based Franco Sbarro.

This achievement was realized by teaming up with American operations TLC and Panoz, which actually

■ LEFT *Called the Veleno, this heavily modified Dodge Viper looked different and – thanks to a nitrous oxide-charged 550bhp – felt quite different too.*

■ LEFT *The Roadster was a sportscar in the old-fashioned sense of the word. Note the strange "eyes-on-stalks" headlamp treatment.*

■ ABOVE *Fitted with a Ford Mustang V-eight engine, with up to 305bhp on offer, the Roadster was a very rapid machine.*

■ BELOW *The timelessly graceful lines of the 1930s were underscored by ultra-low-profile tyres and a supercharged 320bhp V-eight engine.*

■ ABOVE *The Yello Talbo was inspired by the classic 1930s Talbot-Lago but brought kicking and screaming into the '90s – hence the association with electro band Yello.*

manufactured the cars; Rinspeed was responsible for the outlandish additions to the coachwork.

Stars of the Geneva show

The first of the Geneva series was the 1995 Roadster, a sort of updated Lotus 7/AC Cobra cross-over with tiny doors, a narrow windscreen, separate wings and evocative roll-over hoops. It was the nose that grabbed all the attention: extraordinary "eyebrows" sprouted from either side of the jut-forward snout, housing compact, underslung double headlamps and indicator units sited on their tips. The impression was of the

face of some wild banshee, an effect augmented by the colour of the show car – bright orange!

Powering the Roadster was a five-litre Ford Mustang engine, available in two states of tune. The R version had 218bhp while the ferocious SC-R got 305bhp. Rinspeed claimed performance figures of 160mph (258kph) and 0–60mph (96kph) in 4.4 seconds for the faster SC-R version.

The following year (1996), Rinspeed presented the Yello Talbo, whose name derived from TLC's existing Talbo model in the USA and the urban/electro-pop music group Yello, which endorsed the

car. Inspired by a 1938 Talbot-Lago 150SS design by Figoni & Falaschi, the Yello Talbo resolutely brought the shape into the 1990s. Its supercharged V-eight engine developed 320bhp.

In 1997 came the strangest Rinspeed yet, the Mono Ego. Many questions were raised at its Geneva show debut. If this was a Yankee-style hot rod, why did it have a Hyundai engine (an "experimental V-eight") and Hyundai Coupé lights? Why one seat? Why was a famous French fashion designer involved? No satisfactory explanation was received, but that was in a way the point: a total defiance of logic.

■ RIGHT *An implausibly long bonnet (hood) covered an equally implausible engine – a V-eight from Korean company Hyundai.*

■ ABOVE *No one was quite sure what to make of the Mono Ego, a bizarre mix of haute couture fashion and American hot rod.*

SBARRO

Franco Sbarro is an Italian who emigrated to Switzerland in the 1950s and went on to become that country's most famous car-maker and one of the design world's most adventurous figures. His extraordinary work ranges through tiny electric cars, exquisite replicas of great classics, racing-cars, imaginative one-offs and innovative supercars.

He shot to fame in 1969 when he transformed a Lola T70 racing-car into the world's fastest road car, but his name

■ LEFT *Franco Sbarro's extraordinary dynasty kicked off with exquisite replicas such as this Bugatti Royale, which used two Rover V-eight engines joined together to make a V-sixteen.*

■ ABOVE *The Super Twelve may have looked like a hatchback with a simple paint job, but underneath it all lay two Kawasaki motorcycle engines making a 12-cylinder unit.*

became widely known through a string of replicas, including BMW 328, Bugatti Royale and Ferrari P4.

His "Super" series was particularly headline-grabbing. Its least spectacular members were the Super Eight, which looked like a VW Golf but had a Ferrari 308 chassis and engine, and a Porsche 928-engined Golf. The first of the series, the 1982 Super Twelve, was simply outrageous: an unassuming hatchback with two Kawasaki six-cylinder motorcycle engines joined together amidships for a single engine developing 240bhp.

Another project in a similar vein was the Robur, a very compact, 130in (330cm) long car with a 200bhp mid-mounted Audi turbo engine and a fifth wheel, which proved useful for pulling the rear-end into tight parking spots.

The Challenge came close to being a mass-production car by Sbarro's standards, since seven have been built to date. This uncompromising wedge-shaped car, first seen in 1985, looked like a slice of Gruyère cheese and was

■ ABOVE *Looking like a slice of Swiss Gruyère cheese, the Challenge was a very rapid sports coupé offered with Porsche or Mercedes engines.*

■ BELOW *The Challenge may not have been particularly handsome, but it was dramatic in every way.*

■ RIGHT *Sbarro's unconventional approach to improving engine access is plain for all to see in the Chrono.*

claimed to have a Cd figure of just 0.25. The doors folded forward for entry. Initially the Challenge was offered with a twin-turbo Mercedes V-eight engine, but later cars had Porsche engines mounted in the rear. All were capable of storming speeds – up to 180mph (290kph) was claimed.

"Throw out the hubs!"

Proving that extremes did not have to relate to speed alone, Sbarro's 1987 Monster G was a phenomenal all-wheel-drive concoction. It was not the four-wheel drive but the wheels themselves that impressed: they were taken from a Boeing jet! These made the Monster sit

some 7ft 5in (2.3 metres) tall, and the 350bhp Mercedes-Benz 6.9-litre V-eight was needed to get those wheels moving.

"Throw out the hubs!" exhorted Franco Sbarro at the 1989 Geneva show when he released on to the world a major innovation: the hubless wheel.

The concept of a wheel without a centre to it had a sound theoretical basis, as Gordon Murray confirmed. The idea was that the wheel rotated around bearings actually in the rim. Having the drive and braking applied directly to the rim meant greater rigidity, less weight, less

■ ABOVE *The Astro was relatively toned down by Sbarro's standards. It had a Ferrari engine and curious little projector headlamps under the windscreen.*

■ ABOVE *With its ex-Boeing aeroplane wheels, the Monster G was ideal for assaulting urban wastelands or indeed other forms of desert.*

■ LEFT *The hubless wheel was invented by Franco Sbarro. It actually worked, as this motorcycle proved.*

torque reaction, less axial and radial strain and perfectly vented braking. Sbarro had experimented with such wheels on a motorcycle a few years before; however, it was obvious that much more development was required, and this innovative scheme was left on the shelf.

Nevertheless, the Osmos show car, which incorporated the hubless wheel, was popular at motorshows. Cleanly styled, somewhat soberly perhaps for Sbarro, it boasted a 12-cylinder engine.

SBARRO

■ LEFT *Under the long bonnet of the concept Isatis lay a BMW 5.0-litre V-twelve engine.*

■ ABOVE *In characteristic red overalls, Franco Sbarro sits in one of his creations, the Urbi electric city car.*

Chrono, Isatis and Oxalys

The 1990 Chrono hinted at its purpose with Swiss watch badges dotted around the body. This was a car designed to go from 0–60mph (0-96kph) in the shortest possible time. Weighing just 1430lb (650kg), the same as a 2CV, yet powered by a 500bhp BMW M1 engine, it could do "the sprint" in 3.5 seconds. In a typical Sbarro touch, the whole car hinged in the middle for access to the engine.

For the 1991 Geneva show, Sbarro presented an interesting twin-chassis supercar. The V-twelve engine and gearbox, beam chassis and suspension were attached to the body by six hydraulic links. In theory, these allowed the body to be insulated from the chassis, which meant that a supremely comfortable ride was possible without sacrificing the firmness of the

suspension. The body could also be jacked up at will. Wild by anyone else's standards but shy by Sbarro's, the 1993 Isatis was based on the V12-powered BMW 750iL. The main interest lay inside, its steering wheel featuring a centre-mounted rev counter (tachometer) and speedo.

The next year came the Oxalys, an intriguing cocktail described as "designed by the young for the young". Underneath its smart exterior – designed by Espace Sbarro students – lay a 340bhp BMW M5 engine and Porsche 911 rear suspension and brakes. One novel feature of this

■ LEFT *Like virtually every Sbarro design, the 1995 Alcador was a fully functioning car capable of being driven in anger.*

■ ABOVE *With its muscular, sci-fi "shoulders" protecting the occupants, the Alcador had a 400bhp Ferrari V-twelve engine.*

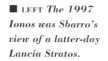

■ RIGHT *With the
1996 Issima Sbarro
turned his attention
to an Alfa Romeo
study. It was widely
admired by industry
professionals.*

"back-to-basics" roadster was a modern
version of a dickey (rumble) seat –
a convertible pair of rear seats.

Issima and Ionos

The main attraction of the 1996 Issima
lay under its long, Alfa-badged bonnet.
Nestling there were a pair of Alfa Romeo
3.0-litre six-cylinder engines joined to
make an in-line twelve with 500bhp on
tap. Its smart styling was admired by
Alfa's own styling boss, Walter de Silva.

According to Franco Sbarro's students,
who designed the 1997 Ionos, this was
how a latterday Lancia Stratos should
bc. Following Sbarro's joining of two
Alfa engines to make a straight eight,
the Ionos had two Lancia Kappa five-
cylinder units joined together to make
an upturned V-ten layout, with a Porsche
gearbox between the banks. Transmission
was Porsche four-wheel drive. The
"crash helmet" window profile was
reminiscent of the original Stratos.

Also at the 1997 show was a pair of
sportscars called the Formule Rhin and
Be Twin. They were conceived to teach
rich kids how to drive and were fitted
with two sets of controls. The 1320lb
(600kg) Formule Rhin had a ferocious
200bhp Peugeot 3.0-litre V-six engine
behind the seats, while the Be Twin, at
under 990lb (450kg), had a Lotus Elan-
style backbone chassis, stressed mid-
mounted engine (a 140bhp 1.6-litre unit
from the Citroën Saxo Cup racer), self-
ventilating disc brakes and double-
wishbone front suspension.

■ ABOVE *Yet another piece of radical engine
surgery saw two Alfa V-six engines being
joined together to create an Alfa V-twelve
in the Issima.*

■ LEFT *The Issima's interior was typically
clean, unfussy and devoid of ornament.*

■ LEFT *The 1997
Ionos was Sbarro's
view of a latter-day
Lancia Stratos.*

■ BELOW *Sbarro
founded a design
and engineering
school, and the
Oxalys was just one
of the projects
realized by his
students.*

TOYOTA

While most Japanese firms turned to European design houses for their innovative designs, Toyota struck its own course. The 1969 EX III was a case in point. Here was a sleek coupé, which advanced the dream-car ideal as much as the Europeans. Its sleek shape carried over to its ultra-smooth undertray (underbody), making it very aerodynamic.

■ ABOVE *Toyota's 1987 FXV-II prototype was typical of the characterless concepts produced by Japan in the 80s.*

■ ABOVE *It may not have been a great beauty to behold, but the 4500GT marked a brave tour de force for Toyota's design and engineering teams.*

Advanced technology, maturing design

Like most Japanese makers, Toyota's dream cars struggled to find an identity until the 1980s, when advanced technology and maturing design teams began to enhance the impact of its concept machines, such as the 1984 FX-1 with its electronic suspension, cantilevered doors and variable valve timing.

On Toyota's stand at the 1987 Tokyo show was a dream car that made it to production. The little gullwing AXV-II reappeared two years later as the Sera. It may only have been a Starlet underneath, but its character was made stimulating by its expansive glass bubble top – the glass in the doors curved round to form part of the roof.

One of the greatest technical *tours de force* of all time was the verdict on the 4500GT show car of 1989. Its Lexus-based V-eight engine had five valves per cylinder, the gearbox had six speeds, the suspension was variable and the run-flat tyres had pressure sensors on board.

■ ABOVE *Born out of the AXV-II prototype, the Sera was a rare example of a concept car making it into production.*

■ BELOW *The point of the AXV-IV was to reduce weight, and its advanced construction meant a total mass of just 990lb (450kg).*

■ ABOVE *With a Cd figure of just 0.20, the AXV-V had an aerodynamic profile equivalent to that of an aeroplane.*

■ RIGHT *With suspension that was adjustable on each side (and even a half-track option instead of wheels), the Moguls turned mountains into molehills.*

Novelties included LCD shutters for the vertically stacked headlamps and sun visor, ultra-sound wing mirrors to clear water droplets and a Noise Canceller, which emitted signals of opposite phase and amplitude to eliminate noise "booms". Although the 4500GT may not have looked very pretty, all five that Toyota built were fully sorted road-going machines.

Concepts of all sizes

The AXV III concept car was merely a taster for the forthcoming Carina, while the 1991 AXV-IV was far more interesting, mainly for its construction, in ultra-lightweight aluminium,

magnesium and carbonfibre; even the springs were plastic. Immensely strong yet incredibly light (just 990lb or 450kg), the little coupé-style commuter car was fitted with a 64bhp two-cylinder 800cc two-stroke engine.

Mega Cruiser is not a subtle name, but then this was not a subtle car. Presented at the 1993 Tokyo show, it was a monstrous off-roader, 16.4 feet (5 metres) long, with a 4.1-litre truck engine. Following a good reception, it actually made it into production as one of the world's widest cars – all 7ft 1in (2.17 metres) of it.

The AXV-V of 1993 combined aerodynamics with advanced direct-

injection engine technology. Toyota claimed a Cd figure of just 0.20 – equivalent to an aeroplane – which helped to give it remarkable fuel consumption. Other technological innovations included air suspension, an anti-collision automatic brake system, touch-shift transmission and LCD monitors.

In response to a new wave of roadsters from MG, Fiat and BMW, Toyota unveiled its MRJ prototype at the 1995 Tokyo show. Actually designed by Toyota's Brussels design office, it was the company's first-ever open mid-engined car. The roof was a so-called "aerocabin" hardtop, which retracted electronically at the flick of a button.

■ ABOVE *Over 7 ft wide (2.1 metre), the four-wheel-drive, four-wheel-steer Mega Cruiser was actually sold on the Japanese market as the most expensive car around (costing 20 million yen).*

■ ABOVE *The very pretty MRJ was a mid-engined styling exercise and Toyota's first-ever open mid-engined car. It paved the way for a future generation of convertible MR sportscars.*

V W

One of the most vaunted of all 80s concept cars was Volkswagen's Futura, created by Professor Ulrich Sieffert. A one-box Golf-sized car – years before the Mégane Scenic made the genre popular – it was full of ideas.

The car that parked by itself

The gullwing doors were purely for show effect, of course: the notion of two-piece doors, of which the upper half were gullwing and the lower half dropped into the sills, was hopelessly impractical.

■ RIGHT *If the gullwing doors of the Futura were perhaps gimmicky, even more so was its ability to park itself via electronic monitors.*

■ BELOW *The idea behind the Vario was that any body could be fitted on to a common platform. This is the Vario I open four-seat buggy.*

The mostly glass upper dome was equally striking.

More significantly, the direct-injection petrol (gasoline) engine was years ahead of its time. Aided by a G40 supercharger, the 1.7-litre engine was very economical and very clean.

The Futura's main party piece was its four-wheel steer system. Based on a Golf rear axle turned through 180 degrees, it provided plenty of fun when you wanted to park. Thanks to sensors fitted for restricted visibility and electronic throttle and transmission, the Futura could wriggle into a parking space all by itself, manoeuvring back and forth on its own.

Another novel city car proposal was the three-wheeled Scooter of 1986. Based on a Polo drivetrain, it was a lightweight, good-looking shuttle capable of 125mph (201kph). The two-seater interior included a dash-mounted briefcase!

At the 1991 Geneva show, VW presented another new concept called Vario. Two styles were displayed, to show how different the bodywork could

■ BELOW *The Vario II was an alternative bodywork proposal created by design students for VW.*

■ LEFT *VW explored new territory with the Chico, a city car capable of being propelled by a variety of power sources.*

■ ABOVE *A commuter car with three wheels? The Polo-engined Scooter actually made a lot of sense, and was quick into the bargain.*

■ LEFT *Nothing less than the rebirth of the Beetle was how Volkswagen presented the Concept 1, styled by VW's California studio.*

be on the same platform. VW actually planned to sell a platform (based on a lengthened Golf Synchro 4x4) on which specialists could create their own bespoke (dedicated) bodies. However, VW's own efforts – admittedly designed by VW students – were uninspiring, and, not surprisingly, little more was heard of this novel idea.

The Beetle reborn

It was a design nucleus in VW's studio in California which created the car that stole all the thunder at the 1994 Detroit show – nothing less than the rebirth of

the legendary Beetle. Called Concept 1, it took the rounded themes of the 60-year-old Beetle and brought them into contemporary fashion, with bold Bauhaus curves and giant wheels.

The technology under it was modern, too, deriving from the Polo, and that meant front-wheel drive (or even four-wheel drive) and a front-mounted engine. The reaction to the Concept 1 (and its convertible brother, which

appeared at Geneva three months later) was so overwhelmingly positive that VW took the bold decision to engineer a production version for 1998. The shape and dimensions were changed and the basis (mechanicals) switched to the Golf MkIV, but in spirit and broad brush strokes the new Beetle was essentially a concept car born in the flesh.

Following up that media event was always going to be difficult, and efforts like the Noah gullwing MPV study, while striking, have not had such an impact.

■ RIGHT *A handsome Cabriolet (convertible) version of the Concept 1 was displayed at Geneva in 1994 and looked equally likely to enter production.*

ZAGATO

Zagato belongs to a select band of Italian coachbuilder dynasties. It is one of the oldest of all, founded by Ugo Zagato in 1919 in Milan, and has an illustrious past. Its heyday undoubtedly came in the 1950s and 60s when it created superb coachbuilt bodies for Ferrari, Alfa Romeo, Fiat, Maserati, Aston Martin, Bristol and Lancia.

Brothers Elio and Gianni Zagato set up a new factory in 1962 and eventually expanded into other areas such as electric and armoured cars. A unique Zagato characteristic is the "double-bubble" roof, originally intended to clear the heads of passengers in its very low bodies, but this has since become an

■ LEFT *The Alfa Romeo-based Zeta 6 was a high point for Zagato: well proportioned, smooth and purposeful in appearance.*

■ ABOVE *The Zeta's cowled instruments were in deference to the traditional Alfa Romeo style.*

■ LEFT *The undoubted beauty of the Zeta 6 impressed Aston Martin enough to commission Zagato for one of its own projects.*

From Zeta 6 to Raptor

The 1983 Zeta 6 can be singled out as perhaps Zagato's best recent design. This two-plus-two coupé was based on the 2.5-litre Alfa Romeo GTV-six. Chief stylist Giuseppe Mittino extracted a classically graceful style from this project and gave it the Zagato trademark of a distinctive double-bubble roof. It was this car, seen by Aston Martin's director Victor Gauntlett at the 1983 Geneva Motor Show, which led directly to the Aston Martin Zagato project.

Zagato started to go off the boil in the late 1980s. First it presented a vision of a future Aston Martin Lagonda called the Rapide, which was so poor that Aston Martin boss Victor Gauntlett took the unusual step of distancing his company from anything to do with it. Then came the Stelvio AZ1 project for

unmistakable trademark. By the 1970s, Zagato's importance had faded somewhat but its fortunes revived with the 1986 Aston Martin Zagato project, the Alfa Romeo SZ, Lancia Hyena, Nissan Autech Stelvio and series production of the Maserati Biturbo.

Zagato's self-financed dream cars have been relatively rare and rather inconsistent in their level of satisfaction. Alongside such sublime pieces as the Zeta 6, there have been some real disasters like the Stelvio and Lagonda Rapide. Zagato was forced to reform for the 1990s as SZ Design with Andrea Zagato at the helm.

■ LEFT *Basing the extremely compact Hyena on Lancia Integrale components gave it performance credibility. This model was sold on a special-order basis.*

Autech, a subdivision of Nissan. Unveiled in 1989, it was a two-plus-two coupé seemingly designed from the wing mirrors out (the front wings bulged out to accommodate them). Incredibly, it actually reached series production for the Japanese market. Zagato followed this exercise up with the more acceptable Gavia, Bambu and Seta projects, plus a Testarossa-based supercar called the Z93.

Perhaps marking a rebirth of the Zagato (or SZ Design) name was its 1996 Geneva showing and possible production model, the Raptor – its name recalling one of the villains of Steven Spielberg's dinosaur epic, *Jurassic Park*. Its proportions were exactly right, its Lamborghini Diablo V-twelve engine and four-wheel-drive system suitably exotic and its flop-forward double-

bubble canopy scintillating enough to engage the imagination. It justifies a link with the early, classic Zagato designs that make this *carrozzeria* a legend in car design.

■ ABOVE *For a powerful supercar, the Raptor succeeded in looking light and purposeful.*

■ BELOW *The Raptor revived Zagato's tradition of a prominent double-bubble roof. The car was based on Lamborghini parts.*

■ ABOVE *Zagato was effectively reborn in the 1990s. Its most promising project was the Raptor, developed for the 1996 Geneva Motor Show.*

■ OPPOSITE *The Hyena's hunched haunches gave a hint of high performance.*

INDEX

The Publishers would like to thank the individual car manufacturers and *Classic and Sportscar* magazine; Haymarket Specialist Motoring; for supplying most of the pictures in the book.
Additional pictures supplied by: BFI Stills, Posters and Designs: pp 60MT; 61TL/MB.

Don Morley: pp 56; 73BL; 74TM/BM/BR; 75T; 78 all; 97BR; 98BL; 100BL; 134TR 146T/BL; 156T/ML/MR/BR; 157T/ML/B; 163BL; 178M; 188B; 196T/M/B; 197T/ML/ BL/BR; 198ML; 200T/M/B; 201ML/B; 202T; 203MR; 206BL/BR; 207T/MT; 208BR; 210BL; 211TL; 212BL/BR; 213TR; 218TR; 224ML/BR; 225T/M; 236T; 247TL/L/M; 250MTL; 254M; 255M.

John Colley: pp 20M; 186TL; 206MR; 222BL; 240BL; 250T; 257TL/TR/ML/MR/BL; 109BL.

National Motor Museum, Beaulieu, England: pp 3 (N Wright); 50; 88M; 88BL (N Wright); 100TR/M/BR; 104TR/M/BL; 105TR/MR/B; 106T (N Wright); 107TL/TR (N Georgano); 107MR; 110T; 124TR/M (N Wright); 125M/BR; 148T; 168BR; 174B; 184B; 214T; 216MR; 300TR; ML; 301BM; 360TR; 374BL; BR; 375 TL; 382TM/ BR; 384TM/M/RM/BL/BM; 390TR; 393TM; 401MR; 417TL; 448TR

Quadrant Picture Library: pp 193M; 214BR; 227T; 138TR/BL/BR; 216ML; 217B.

T=Top; M=Middle;
B=Bottom; R=Right; L=Left